CHEROKEE BY BLOOD

Records of Easter~~n~~ ~~Cherokee Ancestry~~
in the U.S. C~~ourt~~ ~~of~~ Claims
1906-1910

Volume 5
Applications 10171 to 13260

Compiled By

Jerry Wright Jordan

HERITAGE BOOKS, INC.

Published 1990 By

HERITAGE BOOKS, INC.
1540E Pointer Ridge Place, Bowie, Maryland 20716
(301)-390-7709

ISBN 1-55613-294-8

A Complete Catalog Listing Hundreds of Titles on
History, Genealogy & Americana
Free on Request

Dedicated to the memory of my father,

Clifford Lee Wright,

who kept our family's heritage alive.

PREFACE

The "Story-Teller" is an ancient respected role in cultures all over the world. Individuals committed to memory all the previous events and personages affecting their people's lives and then conveyed these "tales" to each succeeding generation. The purpose of this "story telling" was to instill an understanding of present circumstances and a pride in the heritage which had brought the people to a certain point in time.

Today's historians have taken on the role of the story teller, but they cover such a wide scope of time and people, their concentration is confined to a few major events and individuals, losing the personal touch history can provide.

Families, however, have kept the "Story Teller" role very much alive. In the first decade of this century 46,000 individual Americans repeated the "stories" passed down from generation to generation of their "Indian blood." These individuals were attempting to prove their descent from a member of the Eastern Cherokee Indian tribe in order to participate in a one million dollar fund appropriated by the United States Congress for descendants of this tribe. Mr. Guion Miller was appointed Special Commissioner to the United States Court of Claims to investigate and decide who was and was not eligible for this fund. Miller's report to Congress, reproduced in this and subsequent volumes, summarized his findings. Reading the various pages of testimony given by the applicants and witnesses on their behalf demonstrates the success of the family "Story Teller" in instilling a fierce pride in those who claimed to be...

CHEROKEE BY BLOOD!

COMPILER'S NOTES

The "Report of Guion Miller, Special Commissioner to the U.S. Court of Claims, 1906-1910" has been reproduced by the National Archives on 12 rolls of microfilm designated as M685.

The applicants were from across the country, from New York and New Jersey to Washington and California, and included known and accepted Cherokees, white and black families with strong family traditions of Indian ancestry and, interestingly, many Creeks from southern Alabama who had misunderstood who was eligible to participate in the fund.

Mr. Miller's "Report" was a summary of all the information gathered concerning the 46,000 applicants. The applications themselves have been filmed by the National Archives and are contained on 348 rolls of microfilm designated as M1104. The contents of two of the application files have been included in Volume 1 under the heading "EXAMPLE APPLICATIONS." From personal experience I urge readers to check the applications of all persons in Mr. Miller's Report indicated as being related. One applicant might not have remembered the maiden name of his or her grandmother, while a distant cousin may have known that plus additional family facts.

The films of Guion Miller's "Report" are available at the National Archives in Washington, D.C. and the Federal Records Center in Fort Worth, Texas, and possibly in other large libraries. However, the films are difficult to utilize, because in filming the records the first three to four digits of each application number have been cut off after the first 4,000 applications. This causes problems when dealing with numbers containing five digits. Many pages were duplicated in the filming, making it hard for a reader to count his or her way to a particular application number.

In transcribing these records, I have gone through each of the 12 rolls, gathering all information regarding a single application. My arrangement is as follows:

Applicant's name, residence, decision and reason; Miscellaneous Testimony and Exception Cases where applicable; Roll information for those admitted

There are many references throughout the applications to relationship to other applicants by means of application numbers. I have not transcribed the index to the applications, as all names will appear in my index.

All notes added by myself have been enclosed by square brackets []. Any text appearing in () are from the originals.

MISC. TEST.: The testimony of nearly 4500 people in 19 states was taken by Mr. Miller & his assistants. These testimonies give a great deal of information regarding family histories & migration. The assistants taking the testimony often inserted notes regarding early Cherokee rolls or testimony of other persons. Sometimes these insertions have been enclosed by () but many times they appear simply as part of the testimony. I have transcribed the testimonies in their entirety, without any changes of spelling or punctuation. Occasionally the testimony page number referred to in an application summary was transposed by the typist and I have been able to find the correct page in many cases and have added a note to that effect.

EXCEPTION CASES: Many applicants filed an exception case when their applications were rejected, seeking to give additional information in the hopes of having their names admitted. Additionally, clerical errors were sometimes discovered, in which case an exception was filed. Other individuals sometimes filed an exception case seeking to have an applicant disqualified. Applicants whose decisions were changed from "rejected" to "admitted" were then put on a supplemental roll, and those who were changed from "admitted" to "rejected" were stricken from the original roll.

ROLL INFORMATION: The "Roll" was similar to census reports listing a person's name, residence, age and relationship to the first person listed in a family. The roll contains the names of those individuals who had proven their descent and were admitted." THESE EXCEPTIONS MUST BE NOTED IN REGARD TO ROLL ENTRIES: Only those members of a family who were accepted descendants of Eastern Cherokees were included on this roll--all other members of a family were left off. When more than one member of a family was an "admitted" applicant, I have generally listed the roll information with the one who has the smallest number, and then referred the reader to the appropriate application number for the other family members. Many individuals died during the four years the information was being gathered, and unlike a census report, the deceased person's name, age and date of death were still included on the roll if he or she had been admitted.

The arrangement of the information included on the roll is as follows:

Page & Roll number
FCT & (Five Civilized Tribes – commonly referred to as "Dawes Commission number")
Name
Relation to 1st family member listed
Age in 1906
Application Number if different from 1st person listed

ABBREVIATIONS

Del.	Delaware
Can.	Canadian
Fl.	Flint
G. S.	Going Snake
Ill.	Illinois
Sal.	Saline
S. B.	Skin Bayou
Tah./Tahl.	Tahlequah
Dis.	Dispute District
Dist.	District

INTRODUCTION

On the 12 rolls of this microfilm publication are reproduced the report and related records of Special Commissioner Guion Miller. In 1906 Mr. Miller was appointed by the U. S. Court of Claims to determine who was eligible for funds under the treaties of 1835-36 and 1845 between the United States and the Eastern Cherokee. Mr. Miller submitted his report and roll on May 28, 1909, and submitted a supplementary report and roll on Jan 5, 1910.

An act of Congress approved Jul 1, 1902 (32 Stat. 726), gave the Court of Claims jurisdiction over any claim arising under treaty stipulations that the Cherokee tribe, or any band thereof, might have against the United States and over any claims that the United State might have against any Cherokee tribe or band. Suit for such a claim was to be instituted within 2 years after the act was approved. As a result, three suits were brought before the court concerning grievances arising out of the treaties. These suits were (1) *The Cherokee Nation v. The United States*, General-Jurisdiction Case No. Z3199; (2) *The Eastern and Emigrant Cherokees v. The United States*, General-Jurisdiction Case No. 23212; and (3) *The Eastern Cherokees v. The United States*, General Jurisdiction Case No. 23214.

On May 18, 1905, the court decided in favor of the Eastern Cherokees and instructed the Secretary of the Interior to ascertain and identify the persons entitled to participate in the distribution of more than $1 million appropriated by Congress on Jun 30, 1906, for use in payment of these claims. The task of compiling a roll of eligible persons was begun by Guion Miller, then special agent of the Interior Department. In a decree of Apr 29, 1907 the court vacated that part of its earlier decision that gave the Secretary of the Interior responsibility for determining the eligibility of claimants and appointed Mr. Miller as a special commissioner of the Court of Claims.

The decree also provided that the fund was to be distributed to all Eastern and Western Cherokee Indians who were alive on May 28, 1906, who could establish the fact that at the time of the treaties they were members of the Eastern Cherokee Tribe of Indians or were descendants of such persons, and that they had not been affiliated with any tribe of Indians other than the Eastern Cherokees or the Cherokee Nation. The decree further provided that claimants should already have applications on file with the Commissioner of Indian Affairs, or should file such applications with the special commissioner of the Court of Claims on or before Aug 31, 1907. According to the decree, applications for minors and persons of unsound mind were to be filed by their parents or persons having their care and custody, and applications for persons who had died after May 28, 1906, were to be filed by their children or legal representatives.

In his report of May 28, 1909, Guion Miller stated that 45847 separate applications had been filed, representing a total of about 90,000 individual claimants, of which 30254 were enrolled as entitled to share in the fund -- 3203 residing east and 27051 residing west of the Mississippi River. On Jun 10, 1909, the court confirmed and approved the roll of Eastern Cherokees who were entitled to share in the distribution of the fund as submitted by the special commissioner of the Court of Claims with his report of May 28, 1909, except "so much as shall be expected [excepted] to on or before Aug 30, 1909." After the exceptions had been filed and investigated, Mr. Miller submitted a supplemental report and roll to the court on Jan 5, 1910. In this report he stated that about 11750 exceptions had been made; that names of 610 persons of which 238 resided east and 372 resided west of the Mississippi, had been added to the roll; and that names of 44 persons, 5 residing east and 39 residing west of the river, had been stricken from the roll because clerical errors in enrollment had been discovered. Thus the final figure on the total number of persons entitled to share in the fund was 30,820 of which 3436 persons resided east and 27384 resided west of the Mississippi River. On Mar 15, 1910, the court finally decreed that the rolls be approved and that, after certain deductions for expenditures, payments were to be made equally among the Eastern Cherokees who were enrolled. The court also authorized the Secretary of the Treasury to issue a warrant in favor of each person.

In certifying the eligibility of the Cherokees, Mr. Miller used earlier census lists and rolls that had been made of the Cherokees by Hester, Chapman, Drennen, and others between

1835 and 1884. Copies of some of these rolls and the indexes to them are filed with the Guion Miller records and are filmed as a part of this publication. Other enrollment records used by Mr. Miller are among the classified files of the Bureau and are designated as "33931-11-053 Cherokee Nation."

The records reproduced in this microcopy are in the National Archives and are part of Record Group 75, Records of the Bureau of Indian Affairs, with the exception of the Supplemental Roll of Eastern Cherokee, Jan 5, 1910, and Supplement to the Siler Roll, Act of Congress, Jul 31, 1854, which are part of Record Group 123, Records of the United States Court of Claims. A Census Roll, 1835, of the Cherokee Indians East of the Mississippi and Index to the Roll, which have been reproduced on Microcopy T-496, are also part of Record Group 75. Other records relating to the enrollment, including applications submitted by claimants, are in Record Group 123.

CONTENTS OF MICROCOPY 685

[From M685 Roll #1]

IN THE COURT OF CLAIMS.

THE EASTERN CHEROKEE,   )
)
        vs.   )   No. 23214.
)
THE UNITED STATES   )

Report of Guion Miller, Special Commissioner.

In the matter of the enrollment of the Eastern Cherokee for participation in the fund arising from the judgment of the Court of Claims of May 28, 1906, and under the supplemental order of Apr 29, 1907, I have the honor to report that 45,857 separate applications have been filed, which represent a total of about 90, 000 individuals claimants. Of these I have enrolled 30,254 as entitled to share in the fund, 3203 of these residing east of the Mississippi river, and 27,051 residing west of the Mississippi. This roll I have made in two parts, as above indicated, so far as the alphabetical arrangement is concerned. The action taken upon each of these applications is set forth below.

In this report, references are made to the Eastern Cherokee roll of 1835 and to the rolls of 1851 made by Agent Alfred Chapman in the east, and by Agent John Drennen in the west. In the 1835 roll only the heads of families are designated, with the number of individuals in each family, without naming these individuals specifically. The Chapman roll is very complete and is arranged by number, each individual being named, and his age and relationship to other members of the family being distinctly set forth. References to this roll are therefore made by number. The Drennen roll is much less complete. It is divided into nine parts, representing eight districts as follows: Canadian, Delaware, Flint, Going Snake, Illinois, Saline, Skin Bayou and Tahlequah, together with a division known as the Disputed roll. In these rolls the family groups are indicated, but the relationship between the various members of the group is not stated, nor are the ages given. In my report references are made to these rolls by abbreviations, such as Del. for Delaware; G.S. for Going Snake, etc.

In 1851 an enrollment was made in the west of the Cherokees known as Old Settlers. Frequent references are made to this roll in the report, where it is usually indicated by the abbreviation O.S.

In addition to these regular rolls, under the Act of Con—

1

gress of 1854, a small additional roll was made by the Secretary of the Interior, of individual East Cherokees residing in the east, whose names were inadvertently omitted from the Chapman roll or 1851, or more strictly speaking, from the Siler Roll of 1851, upon which the Chapman pay roll was based. References in my report are made to this roll under the title of "Act of Congress roll", or abbreviated, A. of C. roll.

Also, in 1884 under the Act of Congress of 1882, a complete roll of the Eastern Cherokees residing east of the Mississippi river was made by Agent Joseph G. Hester, and frequent references in my report are made to this roll by way of confirmation.

Where the claimant has shown an ancestor enrolled upon either the Drennen or Chapman Rolls, or the Roll of 1835, his case has been marked for admission, unless he has become disqualified through affiliation with some other tribe. In a few cases where claimants have been unable to state the name of an ancestor found upon one of said rolls, testimony has been taken which has established the fact that such claimants are Eastern Cherokees by blood and their claims have been admitted. These cases are mostly among the full-blood Cherokees where the name under which their ancestor was enrolled in 1851 has been changed or forgotten by the present generation. In most of these instances, the claimants are now enrolled and allotted as Cherokees, and the fact of their Cherokee descent is in no way open to question, the only possible doubt being as to whether they might be included among the Old Settlers. In these cases, however, the names of the ancestors given have not been found upon the roll of the Old Settlers made in 1851, so the testimony of witnesses is accepted as establishing the fact of Eastern Cherokee descent.

In considering these applications they were first, as far as possible, arranged in family groups, and in the report the action taken is set forth at length in connection with the application in the group having the lowest number, and the action taken as to the other applications is indicated by reference to the number of the head of the group. In this way the action taken on each application is specifically indicated. There were quite a number of duplicate applications filed, which are shown in the report.

In 1835 the Eastern Cherokee domain comprised all or part of the following counties in the states of Georgia, Alabama, Tennessee, and North Carolina:

> Georgia,---Bartow, Catoosa, Chattooga, Cherokee, Cobb, Dade, Dawson, Fannin, Floyd, Forsyth, Gilmer, Gordon, Haralson, Lumpkin, Milton, Murray, Paulding, Pickens, Polk, Town, Union, Walker and Whitfield counties.

2

Alabama,---Blount, Calhoun, Cherokee, Cleburne, De Kalb, Etowah, Jackson and Marshall counties.

Tennessee,--Blount, Bradley, Hamilton, James, Marion, Meigs, Monroe and Polk counties.

North Carolina,--Cherokee, Clay, Graham, Mason and Swain counties.

In course of the investigation a large amount of testimony has been taken, either by me or my assistants. A copy of this testimony is filed, herewith, and references are made in my report to the same.

More than 4500 witnesses have been examined, in nineteen different states. This testimony is divided into four parts. One consisting of general testimony in regard to a large number of cases which is described as "Miscellaneous Testimony", and includes 4417 pages. The second relates exclusively to the claim of the "Sizemore family", and consists of 75 pages. The third is testimony taken in reference to the claims of certain Creek Indians, or persons located in southern Alabama and northwestern Florida, who, if Indians at all, are probably of Creek origin, and the testimony has been designated as "Creek Testimony", and consists of 12 pages. The Fourth relates to the claims of the "Poindexter family", and consists of 29 pages.

[From M685 Roll #2 - Applications]

3

THE EASTERN CHEROKEE,   )
)
        vs.   )   No. 23214.
)
THE UNITED STATES   )

ORDER.

Ordered this 10th day of June, 1909, that the report of Special Commissioner Guion Miller, bearing date the 28th day of May, 1909, together with the exhibits therewith, including the roll of the individual Eastern Cherokees reported by the said Special Commission as entitled to participate in the fund arising from Item 2 of the judgment filed in this cause, be received and filed in this cause.

2. It is further ordered that the said Special Commission cause the said roll of individual Eastern Cherokees found by him to be entitled to share in said fund, to be printed and distributed.

3. It is further ordered that the said roll of individual Eastern Cherokees entitled to share in the fund arising from the judgment in this cause, as reported by Special Commissioner Guion Miller on the 28th day of May, 1909, be and the same is hereby approved, ratified and confirmed, except as to so much of the same as shall be specially excepted to on or before the 30th day of August, 1909. All such exceptions shall be forwarded to the Clerk of the Court of Claims, Washington, D. C., and shall be in writing, and shall state fully the grounds upon which such exceptions are based, and shall be supported by an affidavit of a person having knowledge of the facts, and shall contain the name, age, and postoffice address of each individual claimed to have been omitted from said roll, or to have been improperly placed thereon. Said exceptions and affidavits shall be filed in duplicate in each case, but only the originals must be sworn to. In case an exception is filed on behalf of an individual whose name has been omitted from said roll the said exception shall set forth fully the English and Indian name of the ancestor through whom claim is made, who was living in 1835 or 1851, and shall give the age of said ancestor in 1835 or 1851. Such exceptions must further state the number of the claimant's application. All such exceptions shall be set down for hearing on the third Monday in October, 1909.

[From M685 Roll 6 - Roll of Eastern Cherokee & Exceptions]

4

am an emigrant Cherokee myself."
S. T. Davis, Porum, Okla., Mar 26 1909.
#4193 FCT COMM #16955 - Dave Barber - 37

LENA C. VOWELL and 1 child,   Porum, Okla
. First cousin of #4394. Claimant's maternal grand
nrolled in 1851 by Drennen Del. #431.
 #27889 FCT COMM #4296 - Lena C. Vowell   - 28
   27890   255m - Howell Carlile (son) - 2

JACOB W. WARWICK and 5 children,   Porum, Okla
. Brother of #11   and admitted for reasons   there set

 #28308 FCT COMM #15713 - Jacob M. Warwick - 44
   28309   15716 - William L. (son) - 19
   28310   15717 - Alice C. (dau) - 17
   28311   15718 - Francis M. (son) - 14
   28312   15719 - Le Roy (son)   - 6
   28313   - Lena (dau)   - 1/12

LI TAYLOR and 2 children,   Douglas, Ky
   Sizemore case.   See special report #417.

LIZA NELSON,   Sugar Grove, Va
   Sizemore case.   See special report #417.

. C. BALLOU and 6 children,   Sugar Grove, Va
   Sizemore case.   See special report #417.

ANE TAYLOR,   Douglas, Ky
   Sizemore case.   See special report #417.

AMES B. STAMPER,   Shelbina, Mo
   Sizemore case.   See special report #417.

ARTHA TAYLOR,   Holston, Ga
   Sizemore case.   See special report #417.

ALLIE DAVE BUDD,   Spavinaw, Okla
   Applicant's mother enrolled by Chapman 1851 #71.
ST. P. 3825.   14180-10207 - Lossie   Peter
hrough Martin Squirrel, Interpreter:
 about 40 years of age. My parents were living in the
Nation East in 51 but I don't know whether they were
gether or not. I came from North Carolina here with
North Carolina Cherokee that the Government sent out
380 or 1881. I was just a small girl then and don't
place we came from or what town. I remember going to
ad and getting on the train but don't know what the
s. My mother came out here with me but my father had
e then. My father's name was Andy or in Indian A-
 don't know who Andy's father was but his mother was

8

10171. CALINE HENSON,   Melvin, Okla
Admitted. Sister of #9795 and claims thru same source.
ROLL P74 #13930 FCT COMM #12185 - Richard Henson - 21
                               (App 28231)
        13931   17784 - Caline (wife) - 20
        13932   - Enoch (son)   - 1

10172. ANNIE CHICK-A-LEE-LAH,   Robbinsville, N C
Admitted. Claimant was enrolled by Chapman in 1851, together
with her father Too-wa-ya-lo Roll Nos. 1081 and 1079, respectively. [For Roll information See App 9908, Vol. 4]

10173. MARY CHICK-A-LEELAH,   Robbinsville, N C
Admitted. Sister of #8652 and admitted for same reasons.
ROLL P7 #479 - Stone Chickilula - 38 (App 26248)
        480 - Mary (wife)   - 37
        481 - Jacob (son)   - 15
        482 - Sowanu (dau)   - 9
        483 - Loosy (dau)   - 5

10174. SUSAN R. GOURD, Duplicate of #1982.

10175. ANNIE HOUSTON,   Tahlequah, Okla
Admitted. Niece of #627 and claims thru same source. [For
Roll information See App 8159, Vol. 4]

10176. ELINDER E. BENNETT and 3 children, Blue Ridge, Ga
Rejected. First cousin of #2877 (once removed). Claims thru
same source.

10177. ARCH BENNETT,   Fry, Ga
Rejected. Cousin of #2877 and claims thru same source.

10178. MONROE T. HEMBREE,   Blue Ridge, Ga
Rejected. Parents and grandparents do not appear to have been
enrolled in 1835 or 1851. Nothing to show association or recognition by the Cherokees at the time of the treaties of 1835
1836 or since. Claimant has failed to answer repeated letters
from the Commissioner asking for more specific information as
to ancestral connections with the Cherokee Indians.

10179. JANE A. PHILLIPS,   Vinita, Okla
Admitted. Son [sic] of #1073. Father of applicant enrolled
in 1851 in Tahl. #263. [NOTE: FCT COMM No. on roll was
crossed out an replaced by another number which is illegible]
ROLL P111 #21317 - Jane A. Phillips - 33

10180. NANCY E. DAVENPORT,   Blue Ridge, Ga
Rejected. First cousin once removed of #2877. Claims thru
same source.

5

10181. CAROLINE McKINLEY and 2 children,   Young Cane, Ga
Rejected. Aunt of #9876 and claims thru same source.

10182. ELIZABETH JONES and 5 children,   Baxter, Ga
Rejected. Aunt of #9876 and claims thru same source.

10183. J. MARTIN JONES and 1 child,   Baxter, Ga
Rejected. Cousin of #9876 and claims thru same source.

10184. DAVID DOWNING and 2 children,   Peggs, Okla
Admitted. Children included in #1225.   [For Roll information
See App 1225, Vol. 1]

10185. ANNIE M. BALLENTINE,   Tahlequah, Okla
Admitted. Sister to #10676.
ROLL P25 #4062 FCT COMM #5685 - Annie M. Balentine - 21

10186. WM. H. BALLENTINE,   Tahlequah, Okla
Admitted. Brother of #10676.
ROLL P25 #4067 FCT COMM # 5681 - William H. Balentine - 24
        4068   28175 - Ollie B. (wife)   - 21
                            (App 41008)

10187. LULA KEENER,   Hulbert, Okla
Admitted. Niece of #8800.
ROLL P84 #15935 FCT COMM #21273 - Lula Keener - 17

10188. MOLLIE C. MEIGS and 5 children,   Cookson, Okla
Admitted. Half sister of #2737 and claims thru same source.
ROLL P98 #18736 FCT COMM #16031 - Florein N. Meigs   - 39
                            (App 12411)
        18737   16032 - Mollie C. (wife)   - 39
        18738   16036 - Mary E. BROWN   - 15
                            (dau of w)
        18739   25308 - Josephine E. MEIGS - 7
                            (dau)
        18740   3398m - George McKee MEIGS - 4
                            (son)
        18741   16034 - Addie V. BROWN   - 19
                            (dau of w) (App 26029)
        18742   16035 - Bertha E. BROWN   - 17
                            (dau of w) App 26030)

10189. PEARLIE A. McKEE,   Park Hill, Okla
Admitted. Half sister of #2737 and claims thru same source.
ROLL P94 #17973 FCT COMM #16528 - Pearlie A. McKee - 21

10190. JOHN T. McKEE,   Parkhill, Okla
Admitted. Half brother of #2737 and claims thru same source.
ROLL P94 #17965 FCT COMM #16527 - John T. McKee - 23

10191. JOSEPH R. McKEE,
Admitted. Half brother of #2737; claim
[For Roll information See App 8667, Vol.

10192. GEORGE W. STARR and 2 children,
Admitted. Nephew of #920. Applicant's mot
Byers at Flint #387-1/2.
ROLL P132 #25445 FCT COMM #3267 - George
         25446   3268 - Floren
                            (App
         25447   3269 - David
         25448   3270 - Washin

10193. JOHN B. WEST,
Admitted. Cousin of #762 and claim
Grandparents enrolled.
ROLL P149 #28884 FCT COMM #28296 - John
          28885   1376m - Dora

10194. LUCY DAVIS and 1 child,
Admitted. Sister to #618.
ROLL P52 #9439 FCT COMM #12873 - Lucy D
         9440   4013m - Geo. A
[* applicant was listed on roll as wife
under Clerical Corrections is the entr
not the wife of Thompson Davis, Roll #

10195. RICHARD WEST and 1 child,
Admitted. Cousin of #762 and claims t
parents enrolled.
ROLL P149 #28900 FCT COMM #15743 - Ric
          28901   1350m - Luc

10196. JOHNSON MANNING,
Admitted. Half brother to #610.
ROLL P96 #18263 FCT COMM #16954 - Joh

10197. MAUD BARKER,
Admitted. Grandparents enrolled as
enrolled as Ah-yah-stah. See letter
ROLL P25 #4197 FCT COMM #16956 - Maud

10198. DANE BARBER,
Admitted. Evidence shows that appli
grant Cherokee and was considered
knew her. See Misc. Test. P. 4408 o
MISC. TEST. P. 4408. #10198 - S. T.
    "I am about 60 years old. I
known him a long time. I have al
mother was an emigrant Cherokee. M
mother was an emigrant Cherokee. H
Cherokee mixed. He is considered a

him.
SIGNE
ROLL

10199
Admitt
father
ROLL

10200.
Admitt
forth.
ROLL P

10201.
Rejecte

10202.
Rejecte

10203.
Rejecte

10204.
Rejecte

10205.
Rejecte

10206.
Rejecte

10207.
Admitted
MISC. T
Wolfe...
    "I a
Cherokee
living t
a band o
here in
know wha
the rail
station
died bef
nih-dih.

named Lossie, the Indian is Loh-sih. Losie was a colored woman. Andy's father was a full blood Cherokee I have been told.
My mother was a full blood Cherokee. Che-gay-you-ih. Her English name was Nancy. Her father's name was Dee-gah-se-na-gih.
Don't know of him having any English name. My mother's mother
was named Che-noo-yuh-duh-ih. Her English name was Sallie. My
mother and her parents all drew money in 51 somewhere in the
State of North Carolina but I don't know where. My mother had
one sister named Annie or A-nih. Another sister named Nah-nih.
Another sister named Ah-gah-te-yuh. She had a full brother
named Mi-he-gih or Mike. Another brother named Guh-naw-skee-
skih. I remember of Andy having one brother named Jo-wuh.
Don't remember of any other. My father died in North Carolina
and my mother died out here on Saline Creek, eight or ten
miles from here. I am positive that my parents were enrolled
in North Carolina in 51. Mollie Walker is no relation to me.
Tom Daniels is my sister Celia's son. Celia is still living
near Eucha and goes by the name of Celia Budd. Celia Budd and
Cyntha Blackbear are my half sisters on the mother's side.
Cyntha is now past 30 years of age. Celia and Cytha's fathers
came from North Carolina but I don't know anything about their
ancestors on that side. I am a Night Hawk. I and my people
have always lived with the Cherokees. I don't know whether my
grandmother Lossie was a slave or not. I and my sisters shared
in the Strip payment."
SIGNED: Lossie Peter Wolfe, Locust Grove, Okla., Oct 13 1908.

MISC. TEST. P. 4300. #10207 - Dave Budder...through Tom
Roach, Interpreter:
"I am about 41 years old; Celia Dave Budder or Buder is my
wife; My wife was born back in Old Nation; my wife's father
was Dee-squal-da-gee and her mother was Che-ka-you-ih. The
parents of Che-ka-you-ih were Chee-noo-yuh-da-gih; that was
the name of her mother; I do not know the name of her father;
I do not know the names of any of the brothers and sisters of
Che-ka-you-ih; I do not know who were the parents of Dee-
squal-da-gee. My wife came out to the Indian Territory about
1878 and 1879. I think she was enrolled on the roll of 1880
out in Indian Territory; Her mother died in the Indian Territory. Both the parents of my wife were full-blood Cherokees.
Lossie Wolfe's father was a full blood Negro. My wife has always been with the Cherokees in Indian Territory and drew in
all the payments of money made to the Cherokees. I do not know
where my wife lived in the east before she came out here; My
wife never had but one child by George Daniels; If there is
one who has filed application by the name of Tom I think that
he must be the one that I have included in my application
#9131, under the name of Jeff. Jeff's Indian name Oo-lo-gi-
lah; My wife is a full-blood Cherokee. I do not know the names
of any of the brothers and sisters of Dee-squal-da-gee."
SIGNED: Dave Budder, Eucha, Okla., Mar 20 1909.
[For Roll information See App 9131, Vol. 4]

10208. CYNTHA S. BLACKBEAR,   Locust Grove, Okla
Admitted. Sister of #4855; claims thru same source. [For
Roll information See App 10211]

10209. MARGARET CHAIR and 3 children,   Tahlequah, Okla
Admitted. Half sister of #1991 and claims thru same source.
[For Roll information See App 6806, Vol. 3]

10210. JOHANNA PARRIS, Duplicate of #5766.

10211. SCALE BLACK BEAR and 1 child,   Locust Grove, Okla
Admitted. Applicant's mother Un-nah-ye enrolled by Drennen in
1851, Del. 699 and grandparents La-se and A-ge enrolled at the
same time and place.
ROLL P30 #5170 FCT COMM #18594 - Scale Blackbear   - 28
        5171   30511 - Cynthia S. (wife) - 21
                               (App 10208)
        5172   4848m - Love (dau)   - 3

10212. LOSSIE PETERS, Gdn.   Spavinaw, Okla
Admitted. In application of mother #14180.

10213. POLLY BROOKS and 1 child,   McGrady, N C
Rejected. Sizemore case. See special report #417.

10214. SALLY STAMPER and 6 children,   McGrady, N C
Rejected. Sizemore case. See special report #417.

10215. LOUSANNA BROWN,   McGrady, N C
Rejected. Sizemore case. See special report #417.

10216. MOLLIE WALKER and 1 child,   Spavinaw, Okla
Admitted. The paternal grandmother, paternal aunt and uncle
were enrolled in 250 Del. Dis. in 1851 under the names of
Che-ne-lern-ka, Na-chel and James. F. A. B. See Misc. Test.
P. 4341 and 4342.
MISC. TEST. P. 4341.   #10216 - Mollie Walker - Jim Ellick...
thru Tom Roach, Interpreter:
"I am about 60 years old; I know Mollie Walker and I also
knew her parents; Both of the parents of Mollie Walker were
full-bloods and Emigrant Cherokees; The parents of Mollie
Walker were Jo-wuh-sin-nih and An-nih; the father of Jo-wuh-
sin-nih was Oo-gaw-law-gah or Leaf; Oo-gaw-law-gah was living
in Delaware District in 1851; He was living with a woman by
the name of Che-nee-lah-gih; They were living together at that
time of the enrollment of 1851; Chee-nee-lah-gih was the grand
mother of Mollie Walker; Chee-nee-lah-gih had two children in
1851, La-chil-le or Rachel and a son Jim-mih or James. (See
Del 250) Dave Leaf who lives at Chloeta, and Jo-wuh-sin-nih
were full brothers. Mollie Walker, #10216 is a first cousin
on the father's side of Quaity Falling, #17279. Mollie Walker
lived with one or two men and I think her child is by a man by

10

the name of Wolf."
SIGNED: Jim Ellick, Spavinaw, Okla., Mar 16 1909.

MISC. TEST. P. 4342.   #17279 - Quaity Falling...thru Tom
Roach, Interpreter:
    "My name is Quaity Falling. I am about 30 years old; Both
of my parents were emigrant Cherokees. My father is still
living. His name is Dave Leaf. He lives at Chloeta, Okla.
My father was born after 1851; my father's parents were Oo-
gah-law-guh or Leaf; and Chee-nee-luh-kih; I think that Chee-
nee-luh-kih had two children living in 1851; their names were
James and Rachel or La-chil-le. I do not know whether they
had one by the name of Wa-ke or not. (See Del. 250) I am
told by Jim Ellick that Oo-gah-law-gah lived near Ge-sah-he in
1851. (See 737 Del and 735 Del.) The mother of Che-ne-lern-
ka was Tah-ne-la. Tah-ne-la had other children by the name of
Coo-tau-keas-ke and Te-yau-teas-ke (See Del. 248) I am a Night
Hawk. I have been married about ten or twelve years; (See
Daws Commission #32633 ? [sic]) My husband is a Cherokee."
SIGNED: Quaity, Falling, Spavinaw, Okla., Mar 15 1909.
[For Roll information See App 3693, Vol. 2]

10217. MARY M. ENGLAND,   Locust Grove, Okla
Admitted. Half-aunt of #8118. Claimant's father enrolled in
1851 by Drennen, G. S. #275. [For Roll information See App
2934, Vol. 2]

10218. SEQUOYAH COCHRAN,   Melvin, Okla
Admitted. First cousin of #5549 and claims thru same source.
ROLL P45 #8017 FCT COMM #14988 - Sequoyah Cochrah - 34
        8018   21394 - Maggie (wife)   - 25
                             (App 24082)

10219. AH-LEE KINGFISHER and 2 children, Gideon, Okla
Admitted. First cousin of #5549 and claims thru same source.
[For Roll information See App 10266]

10220. JEW-LE-OR-WAH or CHULIO, included in App #10366*.
[* Should be "App 10266". For Roll information See App 10266]

10221. SAM BLACKFA and 6 children,   Oaks, Okla
Admitted. Mother of applicant enrolled in 1851 in Saline 184.
ROLL P31 #5220 FCT COMM #20574 - Sam Blackfox   - 41
        5221   20575 - Lucy (wife)   - 41
                             (App 11234)
        5222   20576 - Joe (son)   - 19
        5223   20577 - Susie (dau)   - 17
        5224   20578 - Sallie (dau)   - 15
        5225   20579 - Jonathan A. (son) - 13
        5226   20580 - Charlotte (dau)   - 11
        5227   30620 - Steve (son)   - 9

11

10222. E. G. MILLS,   Crumpler, W Va
Rejected. Sizemore case. See special report #417.

10223. H. G. WALKER and 4 children,   Crumpler, W Va
Rejected. Sizemore case. See special report #417.

10224. N. N. C. WALKER and 5 children,   Crumpler, W Va
Rejected. Sizemore case. See special report #417.

10225. ROSA TILLER,   Kimball, W Va
Rejected. Sizemore case. See special report #417.

10226. SARAH A. J. MILLS,   Crumpler, W Va
Rejected. Sizemore case. See special report #417.

10227. STELLA A. O'BRIAN and 3 children,   Lambert, W Va
Rejected. Sizemore case. See special report #417.

10228. L. M. C. WALKER and 4 children,   Crumpler, W Va
Rejected. Sizemore case. See special report #417.

10229. N. E. C. FARLEY and 6 children,   Crumpler, W Va
Rejected. Sizemore case. See special report #417.

10230. EDWARD A. COOK and 2 children,   Graham, Va
Rejected. Sizemore case. See special report #417.

10231. MARTHA YOUNG and 4 children,   Crumpler, W Va
Rejected. Sizemore case. See special report #417.

10232. NUMA MILLS,   Crumpler, W Va
Rejected. Sizemore case. See special report #417.

10233. MYRTIE BURNETT and 5 children,   Crumpler, W Va
Rejected. Sizemore case. See special report #417.

10234. VIOLA J. MILLS and 5 children,   Pinoals, W Va
Rejected. Sizemore case. See special report #417.

10235. N. C. C. WALKER,   Crumpler, W Va
Rejected. Sizemore case. See special report #417.

10236. HULDA MILLS and 6 children,   Crumpler, W Va
Rejected. Sizemore case. See special report #417.

10237. MARY F. CURTIS and 3 children,   Smithfield, Tex
Rejected. Sister of 5739.

10238. JENNIE KINGHORN,   Albany, Okla
Admitted. Applicant enrolled as Jane Hilderbrand, Tahl. #292.
Sister of #1913.
ROLL P86 #16368 – Jennie Kinghorn – 55

10239. CLARINDA MULKEY, Stilesboro, Ga
Rejected. Claims Cherokee descent thru her father, W. L.
Ingram but whose name does not appear on the rolls of 1851.
There is nothing to show Cherokee association, recognition or
affiliation upon the part of W. L. Ingram or of his parents.
Claimant notified to appear at Jasper, Ga., on July 9th, for
examination, but failed to appear.

10240. NANCY M. TIPPIN, Greeley, Kans
Rejected. Aunt of Wm. Oscar Boyd No. 8383 and claims thru the
same source.

10241. S. D. PAYNE, Medlin, N C
Rejected. Poindexter case. See Special report #664.

10242. IVEY A. GARRETT and 5 children, Hiawassee, Ga
Rejected. Kaziah Van case. See special report #276.

10243. ALLEN L. WARREN, Elma, Washington
Rejected. Cousin of #551 and claims thru same ancestors.

10244. GEORGE W. WARREN, Elma, Washington
Rejected. Cousin of #551 and claims thru same ancestors.

10245. ANNIE E. LAMBERT and 5 children, Macon, Ga
Rejected. It does not appear that ancestors were ever en-
rolled, or were parties to the treaties of 1835-36 and 1846.
They show no real connection with the Eastern Cherokees.
Misc. Test. P. 1372 and 1373.
MISC. TEST. P. 1372. No. 10245 - Annie E. Lambert:
    "My name is Annie E. Lambert and I reside at Aquone, N. C.
I was born in Macon Co., N. C. in 1857. I claim relationship
to the Cherokee Indians through my mother, Mary Ann Barnes,
whose maiden name was Mary Ann Ponder, and she was an eighth
Cherokee Indian, and she claimed through her mother, Sally
Martin, who was a quarter Cherokee Indian, and she claims
through her father, John Martin, who was a half Cherokee Indian. My mother was born in Greenville, S. C. about 1820.
Her mother was born also in South Carolina. I do not know
where my great great grandfather was born. My mother has
always told me that John Martin was enrolled as an Indian in
1835. My mother never visited the Indians, nor do I remember
them visiting her. My mother often told me that some of our
connections on the Martin side went West with the Indians and
some stayed in the East. I had several brothers and sisters,
but do not know if they are now living. Their names are
Jerry, John, James, Joseph and Louis, and Harriet. My mother
had several brothers and sisters, namely, Andrew, Jackson,
Malachi and Meredy and Harriet. These latter were all named
Ponder. All I know about my great great grandfather, John
Martin, is that my mother told me he was a Cherokee Indian and
we were descended from him. This is all I know about the

13

matter." SIGNED: Annie E. "X" Lambert, M. L. Daley, Test.,
Franklin, N. C., Jul 10 1908.
MISC. TEST. P. 1373. No. 10245 - David Lunsford:
    "My name is David Lunsford and I reside at Kyle, N. C. I
am seventy-four years of age. I am appearing as a witness in
this case for Annie E. Lambert; I have known her since she was
a child. I have known her mother ever since 1871. Her mother
always told me that she had Cherokee Indian blood and that she
was descended from John Martin. She has told me that John
Martin was enrolled as an Indian and was recognized as a member of the Cherokee tribe. Her mother and my wife have sat for
hours at a time and talked of John Martin, who Mrs. Ponders
always claimed as her great-grandfather. I have been present
at such times and heard the conversation. They were always
recognized as white with Indian blood. Her brother Meredy
Ponders, resembled the Indian more than she. This is all I
know about the matter." SIGNED: David "X" Lunsford, M. L.
Daley, Test., Franklin, N. C. Jul 10 1908.

10246. LYDA ROSE,   Brier, W Va
Rejected. Sizemore case. See special report #417.

10247. ELI ROSE,   Brier, W Va
Rejected. Sizemore case. See special report #417.

10248. ELIJAH SMITH,   Brier, W Va
Rejected. Sizemore case. See special report #417.

10249. JAMES T. McCRACKEN,   Nowata, Okla
        by J. K. Lowry, Gdn.
Admitted. Nephew of Vinita Crutchfield #977 and admitted for
same reasons.
ROLL P93 #17745 FCT COMM #30278 - James T. McCracken - 13
                                  by J. K. Lowery, Gdn.

10250. SARAH A. HILL and 6 children,   Sulphur, Okla
Rejected. It does not appear that any ancestor was ever enrolled or that any ancestor was a party to the treaties of
1835-6 and 1846. Shows no real connection with the Eastern
Cherokees.
EXCEPTION CASE.   10250. Mattie Bacon & 3 children, App
#10850, Bowie, Tex. Rejected. Total number of exceptions
filed in this group -- 7. Original recommendation renewed.

10251. ELIZABETH NEIGHBORS,   Temple, Ga
Rejected. Aunt of #2780. Claims thru same source.

10252. JAMES KING,   Dragger, Okla
Admitted. Cousin of #443 and claims thru same source.
ROLL P86 #16309 FCT COMM #29681 - James King - 25
        22905   - Susie (wife) - 19
                                 (App 26080)

14

10252. JAMES KING (Cont)
     22906   - West (son)   - 3
     22907   - Maggie (dau) - 1/12

10253. POLLY BOOTS and 3 children,   Hulbert, Okla
Admitted. Applicant claims thru father and mother, Tah-ne-no-
lo-lee and Tee-sy enrolled Tahlequah 329. Sister A-nee and
brother Chu-yu-nuh-tah also enrolled 329 Tahl.
ROLL P32 #5523 FCT COMM #21253 - Polly Boots   - 54
      5523   - Jim SMITH (son) - 15
      5524   21256 - Dick CAREY (son) - 14
      5525   21257 - Jim BEAN (son)   - 12

10254. ELZINA ROSS,   Locust Grove, Okla
Rejected. White woman and claims only thru her husband Oliver
P. Ross who was enrolled in Saline Dist. #448 and 447.

10255. WILLIAM MURPHY,   Locust Grove, Okla
Admitted. Nephew of #2497. Applicant's grandfather, Sar-tah-
te-he is enrolled by Drennen in Tahl. #414. Applicant's father
was born after 1851. [NOTE: App# is listed "10225" on roll]
ROLL P103 #19750 FCT COMM #20912 - William Murphy - 24

10256. LUCINDA HENSLEY and 1 child,   Flag Pond, Tenn
Rejected. Kesiah Vann case. See special report #276.

10257. CHARLES V. CARSELOWEY and 1 child, O'kee, Okla
Admitted. Brother of #7707.   Claims thru father enrolled as
Jas. Daniel by Chapman #36.
ROLL P39 #6888 FCT COMM #13588 - Charles V. Carselowey - 26
      6889   9606 - Mary D. (wife)   - 24
                   (App 25183)
      6890   - Charles M. (son)   - 1/12

10258. SEQUICHIE SQUIRREL,   Cookson, Okla
Admitted. Applicant was enrolled by Chapman as #242. Father
of #4855; claims thru same source. Misc. Test. P. 3327 and
3523. [For testimony See App 4855, Vol. 3]
ROLL P131 #25322 FCT COMM #20593 - Sequiche Squirrel - 66

10259. RUTH A. HOLDER,   Memphis, Tenn
Rejected. It does not appear that any ancestor was ever en-
rolled or that any ancestor was party to the treaties of 1835-
1836 or '46. Shows no connection whatever with the Eastern
Cherokees.
EXCEPTION CASE.   10259. Ruth A. Holder, Chattanooga, Tenn.
Rejected. Total number of exceptions filed in this group --
4. Original recommendation renewed.

10260. JOHN R. DORRIS,   Galena, Kans
Rejected. Applicant's ancestors were not parties to treaties
of 1835-6 or '46; never enrolled with the Cherokees. Misc.

15

Test. P. 2100.
MISC. TEST. P. 2100. No. 10260 - John R. Dorris:
"I am 54 years of age; was born in Fulton Co., Ky. I
claim Cherokee Indian blood through my grandmother on my mother's side. My mother was born in Hamilton County, Tenn. I
have never received any Indian money from the government. My
mother died when I was young in Missouri. I do not know if
she ever received any Indian money from the government. I have
seen my grandmother who was the Indian. Her name was Blythe.
She was living in Arkansas when I saw her. She moved to
Arkansas about 1813. I tried to get an allotment before the
Dawes Commission but never got anything from them."
SIGNED: John R. Dorris, Columbus, Kans., Aug 21 1908.

10261. JAMES L. HELTON,   Temple, Ga
Rejected. Uncle of #2780. Claims thru same source.

10262. MAGGIE LANGLEY,   Nowata, Okla
          by J. K. Lowry, Gdn.
Admitted. Cousin of #805 and claims thru same source. Father
"Noah Langley, 1905 Chapman.
ROLL P88 #16687 FCT COMM #28798 - Maggie Langley - 18
                                  by J. K. Lowry, Gdn.

10263. KETCHER WHIRLWIND and 2 children,   Spavinaw, Okla
Admitted. Applicant's father was enrolled by Drennen in Del.
Dis. #176.
ROLL P149 #28969 FCT COMM #18647 - Ketcher Whirlwind - 45
          28970   18649 - Mollie (dau)   - 17
          28971   18650 - Lizie (dau)   - 13

10264. FRANK SMITH, et al   Webbers Falls, Okla
          Famous Smith, Gdn.
Admitted. Minor brothers and sisters of #9402.
ROLL P128 #24776 FCT COMM #17036 - Frank Smith   - 20
          24777   17037 - Dave (bro)   - 17
          24778   17038 - Cherokee (sis) - 15
                                  by Fanous Smith, Gdn.

10265. FAMOUS SMITH,   Webbers Falls, Okla
Admitted. Father of #9402.
ROLL P128 #24771 FCT COMM #17033 - Famous Smith - 53

10266. WEST KINGFISHER and 1 child,   Gideon, Okla
Admitted. Half brother of #8272 on mother's side.
ROLL P85 #16363 FCT COMM # 6287 - West Kingfisher - 54
          16364   18807 - Ah-lee (wife)   - 27
                              (App 10219)
          16365   6290 - Oo-lo-gu-la (son) - 16
                              (or Chulio) (App 10220)
          16366   18808 - Charley WILLIAMS - 13
                              (son of w)

16

10266. WEST KINGFISHER (Cont)
      16367 FCT COMM #18809 - Betsy WILLIAMS   - 6
                    (dau of w)

10267. ZACHARIAH T. LANGLEY,   Chelsea, Okla
Admitted. Claimant enrolled by Chapman in 1851, C. 1909.
Parents enrolled by Chapman 1902-1903. Maternal grandmother
enrolled by Chapman 2010. Claimant's father is a white man.
See App. #805, et al.
ROLL P88 #16733 FCT COMM #967 - Zachariah T. Langley - 57
       16734   969 - Charley O. (son)   - 19

10268. JOHN J. JEFFERSON and 6 children, Mineral Bluff, Ga
Rejected. Nephew of James Cordell, app 7588 and claims thru
same source.

10269. PETER SMITH,   Rose, Okla
Admitted. Half brother of #641 and claims thru same source.
[For Roll information See App 5771, Vol. 3]

10270. ANNIE PHEASANT,   Rose, Okla
Admitted. Half sister of #641 and claims thru same source.
[For Roll information See App 8961, Vol. 4]

10271. WILLIAM SMITH and 3 children,   Oakes, Okla
Admitted. Half brother of #641 and claims thru same source.
ROLL P129 #25022 FCT COMM #20385 - William Smith - 55
       25023   20387 - Stan (son)   - 17
                     (App 13237)
       25024   20388 - Dave (son)   - 15
                     (App 13233)
       25025   20386 - Eli (son)   - 20
                     (App 13254)

10272. RACHEL HIDER,   Stilwell, Okla
Admitted with application #22525. [Notation on Roll "Hider,
Rachel. See Roll No. 29725"]
ROLL P153 #29723 FCT COMM # 1453 - Lincoln Wolfe - 30 [or 39]
                     (App 11162)
       29724   27108 - Lizzie (wife) - 30 [or 39]
                     (App 22525)
       29725   27109 - Rachel HIDER - 9
                     (dau of w)
       29726   27110 - George HORN - 6
                     (son of w)
       29727   2558m*- Ophelia WOLFE - 2
                     (dau)
       29728   2559m*- Lincoln WOLFE - 1
                     (son)
[* blurred]

10273. MARY SANDERS,   Wauhillau, Okla
Admitted. Niece of #1437 and claims thru same source. Appli-
cant's father O-sey enrolled by Drennen Flint #575.
ROLL P123 #23627 FCT COMM #19599 - Mary Sanders - 30

10274. WILLIAM SANDERS,   Wauhillau, Okla
Admitted. Nephew of #1437 and claims thru same source. Ap-
plicant's father enrolled as O-sey by Drennen Fl. #575.
ROLL P123 #23697 FCT COMM #19673 - William Sanders - 35

10275. DAVID L. BURNETT,   Mena, Ark
Rejected. It does not appear that any ancestor was ever enrolled or that any ancestor was a party to the treaty of 1835-
1836 or '46. Applicant states in letter that he thinks his
ancestors were "Old Settlers". He can give very little information. See letter herein.

10276. WILLIAM W. BURNETT,   Mena, Ark*
Rejected. Brother of #10275. [* "Duqueen, Ar" handwritten
below residence]

10277. RUBEN H. BURNETT and 4 children,   Mena, Ark
Rejected. Brother of #10275.

10278. MINERVA WOOLEY and 1 child,   Muldrow, Okla
Admitted. Applicant's father, grandmother and grandfather
were enrolled by Drennen in G. S. #548. Misc. Test. P. 3023.
MISC. TEST. P. 3023. Mother - Witness in re App. No. 16787-
10278 - Minerva Wooley - Nellie Holt - Interpreter used:
"My name is Nellie Holt. My age is 51 years. I live in
Sequoyah County. Was born and raised in the Territory. I am
the mother of Minerva Wooley. Minerva Wooley was enrolled by
the Dawes Commission, Cherokee Roll No. 27288. She got the
strip money. She gets her Indian blood from her father. She
was born and raised in this county. I am an Old Settler. My
husband was Bill Holt. He is not living. He died in 1890.
He was born out here. I think he was enrolled. He would be
about 60 years old if living. He lived in Sequoyah District.
One brother was Mose Holt, another named Dan Holt; I think
they were younger than him. He had a sister Lizzie Holt; a
sister living by the name of Sarah Holt. William Holt's father was called Tuxie Holt. Tuxie means something like Terrapin, or Tarpin. Lizzie was the oldest. Wm. Holt got his
blood from both parents. (G. S. 548.) They lived on Bigby's
Creek, Sequoyah District. Tuxie Holt's father was William
Holt and his mother Jennie Holt. Tuxie Holt's wife was Sarah
Fivekiller, and she was a sister to Rachel Fivekiller and
Jennie Fivekiller and Polly Fivekiller. Jack Fivekiller was
their brother. Tuxie Holt came from the East I think, but do
not know exactly which State he came from, but he came when
the Cherokees came out. He was Emigrant, and settled in Flint
District. They never lived in Going Snake that I know of, but

18

they moved around a good deal. They were always Cherokees.
Jennie and Rachel lived in Flint District. Polly also lived
in Flint District."
SIGNED: Nellie Holt, Sallisaw, Okla., Sep 18 1908.
ROLL P154 #29939 FCT COMM #27288 - Minerva Wooley - 20
            29940   3054m - Joseph E. (son) - 2

10279. MARY KING and 1 child,   Muldrow, Okla
Admitted. Sister to #10278.
ROLL P85 #16304 FCT COMM #11836 - George King - 26 (App 21831)
           16305   30276 - Mary (wife)   - 32
           16306   30277 - Emma HOLT (dau of w) - 11

10280. WILLIAM HOLT,   Muldrow, Okla
Admitted. Brother of #10278.
ROLL P77 #14541 FCT COMM #27287 - William Holt - 23

10281. SAMUEL J. JONES and 3 children,   McCoy's, Tenn
Rejected. Applicant's ancestors not on roll. Does not establish genuine connection with the Eastern Cherokee tribe.
Misc. Test. P. 1317.
MISC. TEST. P. 1317. No. 10281 - Samuel J. Jones:
    "I am 32 years of age; was born in Fannin county, Ga., and
have lived in this neighborhood all my life. I claim Cherokee
Indian blood through my mother. She never received any Indian
money from the government that I know of. My grandparents
never received any Indian money that I know of. I remember my
grandmother. She was the Indian. She lived in Fannin county,
Ga., but not with the Indians. I do not remember if she spoke
the Indian language. My mother never lived with the Indians
and did not speak the Indian language. I have heard of my
Indian blood ever since I can recollect. My uncle told me."
SIGNED: Samuel J. Jones, Ducktown, Tenn., Jul 10 1908.

10282. LIZZIE WASHINGTON,   Oktaha, Okla*
Admitted. Applicant's father was enrolled by Drennen in Saline Dis. #202. (Wat-te) Misc. Test. P. 3033. [* "Cookson,
Okla" on roll]
MISC. TEST. P. 3033.   Appl. #10282 - Lizzie Washington...
through Thomas P. Roach, Interpreter:
    "My name is Lizzie Washington. I live at Oktaha, Okla. My
father and mother were both Immigrant Cherokees. My father was
born in Illinois District. His name was Ce-gil Watt. His English name was Seigel Watt. I don't know whether my father had
any brothers or sisters. I was enrolled by the Dawes Commission. My number is 21152. My father's name was Seigel Wattie.
In 1851 my father was living north western part of Cherokee
Nation. My mother's name was before she was married Sallie
Tommie. Her father's name was Uhola, or Yo-ho-la. She had a
sister Annie. A brother by the name of Johnson Yo-ho-la. I
don't think my grandmother on my mother's side was living in
1851. My father had a brother and sister. Brother's name Tsoo-

waloo-ke. He was the oldest. My parents were born out here.
See Saline 202. My grandparents on my father's side were not
living in 1851."
SIGNED: Lizzie Washington, Muskogee, Okla., Sep 21 1908.
ROLL P146 #28341 FCT COMM #21151 - George Washington - 59
(App 11195)
```
        28342       21152 - Lizzie (wife)     - 50
        28343       21154 - Red (son)         - 17
        28344       21155 - Blue (son)        - 13
        28345       21156 - Leach (son)       - 11
        28346       21157 - Neque (dau)       - 10
```
[NOTE: Lizzie is listed again at roll No 28355 by herself and
age listed as 30]

10283. JAMES B. MARKHAM,   Locust Grove, Okla
          by Ewing Markham, Gdn. and brother, maternal
Admitted. Father, Jas. Marcrum 461 Saline. Applicant's grand
mother, Nancy Alberty, was enrolled by Drennen, Sal. Dis. 480.
ROLL P96 #18316 FCT COMM #28302 - James B. Markham - 17
                              by Ewing Markham, Gdn.

[NOTE: App 3753, Vol. 2, a rejected case with an exception,
included the name of Louisa Harrison and showed her application number to be 10283, as it appeared on the exception -
that was incorrect and her application number should be 10823]

10284. ALBERT M. PARKS,   Vinita, Okla
Admitted. Sister to #10283.
ROLL P108 #20728 FCT COMM #8616 - Samuel F. Parks   - 35
                         (App 24974)
          20729   8617 - Alberta M. (wife) - 26

10285. CHARLOTTE MARKHAM,   Vinita, Okla
          by L. S. Parks, Gdn.
Admitted. Sister to #10283. Father, Jas. Marcrum, 461 Sal.
ROLL P96 #18312 FCT COMM #8618 - Charlotte Markham - 15
                              by L. S. Parks, Gdn.

10286. ANNIE WOODALL (Now Aimes) and 3 children, Winer, Okla
Admitted. Daughter of #909 and claims thru same source.
[* Only 2 children on roll]
ROLL P153 #29801 FCT COMM #27577 - Anna Woodall - 24
          29802   27579 - Thomas J. GRAY (son) - 6
          29803   2908m - Myrtle AIMES (dau)   - 1

10287. MARTHA A. GREEN and 3 children,   Blue Ridge, Ga
Rejected. First cousin once removed of #2877 and claims thru
same source.

10288. JAMES V. KINCAID,   Blue Ridge, Ga
Rejected. 1st cousin once removed to #2877 and claims thru
same source.

20

10289. ISABELLE MELTON and 3 children,   Vinita, Okla
Rejected. Claims thru same source as #119 and rejected for
same reason.

10290. CORA E. BAYNE,   Francis, Okla
Rejected. It does not appear that applicant's ancestors were
parties to treaties of 1835-36 or 46, nor enrolled with Cher-
okees. Misc. Test. P. 2163.
MISC. TEST. P. 2163. No. 10290-10291 - James Robert Rushing:
    "My name is James Robert Rushing; my post-office is
Francis, Pontotoc Co., Okla.; I was born in Anderson Co.,
Texas in the year 1863; I claim relationship to the Cherokee
Indians through my mother, whose maiden name was Cornelia
Mitchell, who was a quarter Cherokee; My mother was born in
North Carolina in 1820; my mother's people moved from North
Carolina to Alabama, but I do not know the year; my mother's
people moved from Alabama to Texas about the year 1850; all my
mother's people lived either in Alabama, North Carolina or
Texas; none of them ever moved to the Indian Territory that I
know of. I file herewith affidavit signed by F. M. Rushing
and Mrs. S. A. Thomas."
SIGNED: J. R. Rushing, Ada, Okla., Aug 22 1908.
EXCEPTION CASE. Rejected. Total number of exceptions filed
in this group -- 1. Original recommendation renewed.

10291. JAMES R. RUSHING,   Francis, Okla
Rejected. Uncle of #10290.

10292. KATIE WARD,   Francis, Okla
Rejected. Cousin of #10290.

10293. MARY PRICE and 8 children,   Graysville, Tenn
Rejected. Ancestors never enrolled. Does not show any defi-
nite connection with the Cherokee tribe. Regarded as a white
in the community where she resides.
MISC. TEST. P. 438. No 10293 - Mary Price:
    "My name is Mary Price; I was born in Sequachie Co., Tenn.
in 1849. I am fifty-nine years old; I claim my Indian blood
through my mother and father both; my father's name was Norman
Mansfield; my father was born in Sequachie Co., Tenn. in 1813;
I also claim Indian blood through my mother; my mother was
born in Sequachie Co., Tenn. in 1820; my mother's maiden name
was Jane Hainey; my father claimed his Indian blood through
his father; my grandfather's name was William Mansfield; I
think my grandfather was born in N. C., I do not know what
county; my mother got her Indian blood through her father; my
mother's father's name was William Hainey; my grandfather on
my mother's side died when my mother was about eight years
old; I was never enrolled and none of my ancestors through
whom I claim were ever enrolled that I know of. I never had an
opportunity of being enrolled; none of the ancestors through
whom I claim were ever held as slaves; my father and mother

21

were always regarded as white people; my father and mother never lived with the Indians as a member of a tribe; I was always regarded as a white woman in the community in which I live; I first learned of my Indian blood at school; my father and mother never said very much to me about it; I have been told that I was three quarters Cherokee by the Indians; I have always been recognized as being part Cherokee; none of my ancestors went West with the Indians when they left this part of the country. My mother told me that my grandfather, William Mansfield, was a full blooded Indian and that he lived the life of an Indian, making baskets and hunting and fishing. My father, Norman Mansfield, was a minister of the gospel and preached to white people. (He was generally called the Indian minister)."
SIGNED: Mary "X" Price, Dayton, Tenn., Jun 24 1908.
EXCEPTION CASE. Rejected. Total number of exceptions filed in this group -- 7. Original recommendation renewed.

10294. ASA GOINS and 4 children, Graysville, Tenn
Rejected. Neither applicant nor ancestors ever enrolled; does not establish fact of descent from a person who was a party to the treaties of 1835-6 and '46. See report and decision in case filed herewith. See #996.

ASA GOINS, et al
Group #10294

Applicants in group #10294, Asa Goins, et al, claim thru John or James or Jimmie Goins and his children, Sanford, Thomas, Martin, Nathan, Jack, and Sandell Still, nee Goin, wife of George Still.

Neither the old ancestor, John, (or James or Jimme), nor any of his children, were ever enrolled with the Eastern Cherokees with the exception of Sandell Still. She was considered by Siler and Chapman and rejected by both, on the roll of the former at pages 78 and 79, her name with those of her children appears, with the remarks on the case as follows:

No. 25

Sarah Fields, widow of Geo. Fields, Lives in Hamilton Co, Tenn
   Valentine Fields, daughter
   Mary Fields,   "
   Rhoda "   "
   Tcippa "   "
   Chrissanna Fields,   "
   Riley Fields,   son
   Martin "   "
   Allen Still   "
   William Still   "

No. 26

John Still an orphan lives in Hamilton County, Tenn

22

No. 27

Mary Evans, formerly wife of Geo. Still
Thomas Still, son, lives in Hamilton Co., Tenn

No. 28

Margaret Still, lives in Hamilton Co., Tenn
Franklin Still, son, lives in Hamilton Co., Tenn
Houston Still, son
Joseph Still, son

"These families of John Fields, Sarah Fields, Margaret Still, Mary Evans, with the orphan boy, John Still, could produce no proof to show their Indian blood. I came to the conclusion that they were mixed with some other race. Afterwards Dr. J. S. Yarnell informed me that they are Cherokees. He gives no account of the history of the family except Sarah Fields is widow of George Fields and that Mary Evans was the wife of George Still, Dr. Yarnell is highly recommended.

"Her case was subsequently reconsidered by the Secretary of the Interior and she was enrolled by Act of Congress and paid under appropriation of July, 1854 (See Act of Congress Roll). Testimony therein and consideration of the case was set out in the statement of an examination of the report and accompanying papers submitted by A. Chapman on page 21 as follows:

Still,	Sandell,		50	years, Bledsoe Co., Tenn
	Vilinta,	d.	21	"
	Rhoda,	"	18	"
	Isippi	"	16	"
	Cuzzana	"	14	"
	Riley	s.	12	"
	Martin	"	11	"
	Allen	"	7	"
	Andrew	"	5	"
	Nancy	d	2	", Born since Siler's Roll

REMARKS

"This person was rejected by Siler in 1851 — Mr. Chapman says because he did not fully understand the case regarding her to be a Catawba and of course not entitled. Her claim is based on the Cherokee blood or rights of her deceased husband.

"George Field's name is familiar to the Department as connected with the affairs of the Cherokees. It is suggested that the claim be admitted."

EVIDENCE

"James T. Gardenhire is personally acquainted with Mrs. Sandal ["Samuel" crossed out] Fields and all of her family.

23

The list of eleven children and two grandchildren, etc., is
true; was well acquainted with Geo. Fields, her first husband,
before and after their marriage – knows that he was a Cherokee
and a full member of the Nation – he enrolled and went to Arkansas – received 1/2 of his removal and subsequent subsis-
tence money – came back for his family and died in 1841 or '42
in Tennessee – believes he was regularly married to his wife
before Treaty of 1835 – certainly he lived with her as a husband and was so considered. Mrs. F. afterwards married George
Still, a Cherokee Indian since dead, by whom she had Allen,
Andrew and Nancy.
    "Wm. H. Roberson is personally acquainted with Mrs Samuel
Fields or Still – not with the younger members of the family.
She was the regular wife of Geo. Fields – knew him to be a
member of the Nation.
    "Mr. Gardenhire also certifies that he is personally cog-
nizant of John Field's marriage with Nancy Goin and of the
existence of their child, Lydia Jane living with the mother
who is separated from her husband. Also of the marriage of
Mary Fields with Nathan Goin and of the existence of their
child Robert."
    From the above it appears that the Goins family afore
mentioned, if Indians, were Catawbas and Sandell Still, nee
Goins, was enrolled on the Act of Congress Roll only because
she married a Cherokee prior to 1835."
    Her claim is based on the Cherokee blood or rights of her
deceased husband." See above.
    In consideration of the premises the applications of all
persons claiming thru John, James or Jim Goins and his children afore mentioned are hereby rejected with the exception of
applicants claiming thru Sandell Goins Still and her husbands,
George Still and George Fields. The claims of such applicants, however, have been withdrawn from the group. (See Group
#10794).
EXCEPTION CASE. Rejected. Total number of exceptions filed
in this group — 30. Original recommendation renewed.

10295. JOHN GOINS and 4 children,   Graysville, Tenn
Rejected. Uncle of #6290 and claims thru same source.

10296. CATHERIN ELLIS and 4 children.   Children of #8861 and
included in that application. [NOTE: Given name should be
Charlotte – For Roll information See App 8861, Vol. 4]

10297. TAYLOR PRINCE,   Vain, Okla
Rejected. Applicant is dead. Information contained in application insufficient upon which to adjudicate claim. Does not
establish connection with emigrant Cherokee. Failed to answer
letters of inquiry from this office.

10298. HOLLEY B. DUKES*,   Choteau, Okla
Admitted. Nephew of #3165 and claims thru same source.

24

[* "Tucker" crossed out]
ROLL P56 #10247 FCT COMM #23080 - Hooley B. Dukes - 14
                                by Richard Dukes, Gdn.

10299. JACK R. GOURD,   Melvin, Okla
Admitted. Father of #5397 and claims thru same source.
ROLL P115 #22128 FCT COMM #21380 - Jack Rattlinggourd - 54
         21129   21381 - Nellie (wife)   - 59
                                 (App 10470)

10300. HENRY D. STARR,   Braggs, Okla
Admitted. First cousin of #4196 and claims thru same source.
Father of applicant enrolled in 1851 under name of Henry
Gearin in Ill. dist. #3.
ROLL P132 #25450 FCT COMM #5827 - Henry D. Starr - 26

10301. WILLIAM GRINNETT,   Cookson, Okla
Admitted. Applicant's father was enrolled by Drennen in Flint
Dis. #125. Misc. Test. P. 3538.
MISC. TEST. P. 3538. No. 10301 - Wm. Grinnett...through S. E.
Parris, Interpreter:
   "My mother was an Old Settler; my father an Immigrant. I
was told my father drew Immigrant money in 1851. I had an
aunt Rachel, an uncle William, an aunt Betsy. I never got any
Old Settler money."
SIGNED: Wm. Grinnett, Tahlequah, Okla., Oct 5 1908.
ROLL P68 #12684 - William Grinnett - 47
         12685 - John (son)   - 14 (App 12407)

10302. SOPHIA J. BROCKS and 3 children, Webbers Falls, Okla
Admitted. Sister of #2797 [? 2nd digit typed over]
ROLL P34 #5839 FCT COMM # 4275 - Sophia J. Brooks   - 41
         5840   4276 - Joseph A. SCALES, Jr. - 12
                                (son)
         5841   4277 - Frank V. SCALES (son) - 10
         5842   3876m - Eunice G. BROOKS (dau) - 3

10303. CHARLES BOLYN,   Cookson, Okla
        or Bowling or Bowlin
Admitted. Brother of #3697.
ROLL P32 #5461 FCT COMM #20171 - Charles Bolyn - 40
         5462   20172 - Sarah (wife) - 37
                                (APP 11700)
**   5463   20173 - Sallie (dau) - 16 **
         5464   10274 - John (son)   - 14
         5465   10275 - Lydia (dau)   - 13
         5466   10276 - Martha (dau) - 6
[** Entire entry crossed out - no explanation]

10304. RACHEL FEELING,   Tahlequah, Okla
Admitted. Applicant is a sister of Henry Dreadfulwater #2748.

25

ROLL P59 #10983 FCT COMM #25966 – Moses Feeling – 30
                                    (App 11689)
              10984   25997 – Rachel (wife) – 50

10305. THOMAS LEACH and 3 children,   Cookson, Okla
Admitted. Applicant's father enrolled by Drennen 1852, Flint.
581. Misc. Test. P. 3373.
MISC. TEST. P. 3373. No. 10305 – Thompson Leach...through S.
E. Parris, Interpreter:
    "I am forty odd years old; my mother and father both drew
Imigrant money. They lived in Flint District. My mother had
two children older than I but they had a different father. I
do not know if my mother and father were living together at
the time of the payment. I never got any Old Settler money.
I am a Cherokee alottee and my number is 20182."
SIGNED: Thompson Leach, Tahlequah, Okla., Oct 1 1908.
ROLL P88 #16818 FCT COMM #20182 – Thompson Leach – 40
              16819   20183 – Wakee (wife)   – 31
                                    (App 10322)
              16820   20184 – Henry (son)   – 17
              16821   20185 – Thomas (son)   – 15
              16822   20186 – Wat (son)   – 13

10306. LUCY BENDABOUT,   Cookson, Okla
Admitted. Sister of #697 enrolled in Flint 604 by Drennen in
1851. [For Roll information See App 10326]

10307. EMILY WICKET,   Cookson, Okla
Admitted. Grandparents enrolled as John King Fisher and Nee-
goo-dah-ye, Del. #526.
ROLL P150 #29121 FCT COMM #10871 – Emily Wicket – 35

10308. LINNEY WOLF, Melvin, Okla
Rejected. Cannot identify applicant with Emigrant rolls with
information furnished. Applicant failed to meet field parties
when notified to do so. Rejected for lack of further information.

10309. JOHN BIGFEATHER,   Melvin, Okla
Admitted. See App #9796. Children in this application listed
on 2nd card of #9796. [For Roll information See App 9234,
Vol. 4]

10310. LULA McKARTY,   Tahlequah, Okla
Admitted. Applicant's father and grandmother enrolled by
Drennen 1851 Tahl. #5.
ROLL P94 #17959 FCT COMM #32577 – Lula McKarty – 21

10311. ANNIE CRITENDAN,   Tahlequah, Okla
Admitted. Daughter of #5672 and claims thru same source.
ROLL P49 #8858 FCT COMM #30597 – Annie Crittendon – 23

10312. WILLIS McPHERSON,   Braggs, Okla
Admitted. Half brother of #5805 and claims thru same source.
ROLL P95 #18141 FCT COMM #25254* - Willis McPherson - 24
[* FCT # blurred]

10313. WOSTER BOLING,   Manard, Okla
           (Deceased June, 1908.)
Admitted. This applicant's father, George Boling and grand
father Johnson Boling are enrolled by Drennen from Dis. Dist.
under nos. 64 and 65 respectively. Misc. Test. P. 3370.
MISC. TEST. P. 3370. No. 10315--10313 - Ida B. Brown:
    "I am 38 years of age. My father, George Boling, was a
full blood. My father had a sister younger than he named
Jennie. My grandfather's name was Johnson Boling. I am a
Cherokee alottee. I have never gotten any Old Settler money.
My father was an Immigrant. Caty Boling was my father's first
wife and Charles Boling was my brother."
SIGNED: Ida B. Brown, Tahlequah, Okla., Oct 1 1908.
ROLL P32 #5460 FCT COMM #5841 - Worcester Boling - 35

10314. CHARLES BOLING,   Manard, Okla
Admitted. Brother of Woster Boling, App #10313 and is admit-
ted for same reasons.
ROLL P32 #5458 FCT COMM #15346 - Chas. Boling - 32

10315. IDA B. BROWN and 6 children,   Hulbert, Okla
Admitted. Sister of Woster Boling, App #10313 and is admitted
for same reasons. [NOTE: last child on roll by herself and
listed as App 10315. Her FCT Number is in sequence with Ida B.
Brown and her other children]
ROLL P34 #5898 FCT COMM #14530 - Ida B. Brown - 38
         5899   14532 - Roscoe (son) - 11
         5900   14533 - Geneva (dau) - 7
         5901   14534 - Charley (son) - 5
         5902   829 - Fannie (dau) - 3
         5903   - John (son)   - 1/6
   P41 7214   14531 - Florence CHANEY - 15*
                   by Alfred H. Chaney, Gdn. [Eureka Ok]

10316. MOLLIE E. ADAIR,   Tahlequah, Okla
Admitted. 1st cousin of #3461. Claimant's father enrolled by
Drennen G. S. #448. [For Roll information See App 7000, Vol 3]

10317. ELIZABETH TOTHEROW and 5 children, Topton, N C
Rejected. It does not appear that any ancestor was ever enrolled or that any ancestor was party to the treaties of 1835-
1836 and '46. Shows no connection with the Eastern Cherokees.
EXCEPTION CASE. Rejected. Total number of exceptions filed
in this group -- 5. Original recommendation renewed.

10318. MARTHA J. HOLLOWAY,   Topton, N C
Rejected. 1st cousin of #10317.

10319. JOHN POSTELL and 2 children,   Topton, N C
Rejected. Father of #10317.

10320. PEGGY TEEHEE, minor included on mother's application
#1001. [For Roll information See App 1001, Vol. 1]

10321. EMALINE GRIFFIN,   Carter, Ga
Rejected. Ancestors not on roll, probably ancestors were
slaves.
MISC. TEST. P. 1484. No 10321 - Emeline Griffin:
     "My name is Emaline Griffin; I was born in Cherokee Co.,
Ga. 1838; I claim my Indian blood through my mother; I also
claim my Indian blood through my father; I was a slave; I do
not remember anything about my father; I do not exactly where
[sic] my mother was born but I think it was in Ga.; I do not
know through whom my father claims his Indian blood, but my
mother claimed through both of her parents; I never saw any of
my ancestors on my mother's side; I have heard that my father
was not a slave; my mother was a slave of white people; I have
heard that my father was driven off with the Indians and went
with them to the West."
SIGNED: Emaline Griffin, Springplace, Ga., Jul 11 1908.
EXCEPTION CASE.   10321.   Emaline   Griffin, Carter, Ga.
Rejected. Total number of exceptions filed in this group --
2. Original recommendation renewed.

10322. WAKEE LEACH,   Cookson, Okla
Admitted. The applicant's grandfather Tom and grandmother
Nelly and also his father Wyley Bolyn are enrolled by Drennen
from Fl. District under group #580. Misc. Test. P. 3360.
MISC. TEST. P. 3360. Appl. #10322 - Wakee Leach:
     "My name is Wakee Leach. I live at Cookson, Okla. I am
enrolled by the Dawes Commission. My number is 20183. I
don't know whether my father was an Immigrant or not. I could
not say whether he was living in 1851 or not. His name was
Wyley Bollin. My grandfather's name on my father's side was
Tom. My father's Indian name was Kah-ti-sah-ti, which means
Wiley Tom. His mother's name was Nelly and father Tom. He
had a brother by the name of A-to-hee. See Flint 580."
SIGNED: Wakee Leach, Tahlequah, Okla., Oct 1 1908.
[For Roll information See App 10305]

10323. STEPHEN SITTINGDOWN and 6 children, Sallisaw, Okla
Admitted. Claimant is recognized as being of Emigrant Cherokee descent and is enrolled by the Dawes Commission under
#26362. See testimony of Nancy Seabolt Misc. Test. P. 3495,
and of claimant, Misc. Test. P. 3935* [* "3835" crossed out]
MISC. TEST. P. 3495. #16380 with #16379 - Nancy Seabolt...in
behalf of Allie Pritchett:
     "That I am 82 years of age. I don't think either of ap-
plicant's parents were old enough to have been on the 1851
roll. None of Allie's people were Old Settlers; they were

28

emigrants. Allie's grandfather on her father's side was Ste-
wih or Steve Sittingdown. Steve Buzzard is the same as Steve
Sittingdown. Ste-wih Su-lih was another name for him. Steve
had a sister named Sin-nih. Don't know of him having any
brothers. Don't know the name of his wife. Lee-stih was the
name of applicant's grandmother on the mother's side. That's
the only name I have ever heard of her having. Su-lih was the
name of applicant's grandfather on her mother's side. Su-lih
in English means Buzzard. My mother's father never had any
brothers. Don't know whether he had any sisters or not The
roll number of applicant by Dawes Commission is 18312."
SIGNED: Nancy Seabolt, Sallisaw, Okla., Sep 19 1908.
MISC. TEST. P. 3935. No. 10323 - Steven Sittingdown:
     "My name is Steven Sittingdown; my post-office is McKay,
Okla.; I am about thirty-five years old; my father's name was
Blue Sittingdown and sometimes called Blue Buzzard; I am a
half-brother of Allie Pritchett, Appl. No. 16380; my mother
was about forty when she died; This is all I know."
SIGNED: Steven "X" Sittingdown, Sallisaw, Okla., Mar 11 1909.
ROLL P127 #24518 FCT COMM #26362 - Stephen Sittingdown - 33
          24519   26363 - James (son)   - 13
          24520   26364 - Thadius (son)   - 11
          24521   26365 - Minnie (dau)   - 10
          24522   26366 - Agnes (dau)   - 8
          24523   26367 - Edgar (son)   - 5
          24524   4784m - Emma (dau)   - 3

10324. IRENA E. WELCH and 5 children,   Tecunnseh, Okla
Rejected. Daughter of #9192.

10325. BARNEY F. BALLARD and 5 children,   Gravette, Ark
Admitted. Applicant is a nephew of #1056.
ROLL P25 #4084 FCT COMM # 7335 - Barney F. Ballard - 44
          4085   7536 - Edna Pearl (dau)   - 15
          4086   7337 - Nellie G. (dau)   - 13
          4087   7338 - Eva M. (dau)   - 10
          4088   18314 - Percy Paul (son)   - 5
          4089   1795m - Freeman S. (son)   - 1

10326. MOSES BENDABOUT,   Cookson, Okla
Admitted. Father of 7674. Enrolled as Oo-wo-kah-sa-ie, Fl. 591
ROLL P29 #4811 FCT COMM #25839 - Moses Bendabout - 77
          4812   25840 - Lucy (wife)   - 57
                             (App 10306)

10327. THOMAS A. BEANE and 1 child,   Tahlequah, Okla
Admitted. 1st cousin of #537 and claims thru the same source.
Father of applicant, Anderson Bean, enrolled in Tah. Dist. 594
ROLL P27 #4540 FCT COMM #29905 - Thomas A. Bean - 24
          4541   14784 - Sarah E (wife)   - 26
                             (App 43092)
          4542   3732m - Gladys D. (dau)   - 4

29

10328. FANNIE L. BALLINGER and 1 child,   Tahlequah, Okla
Admitted. 1st cousin of #537 and claims thru same ancestors.
Father of applicant Anderson Bean, enrolled in Fl. Dist. #594.
ROLL P25 #4164 FCT COMM #14145 - Fannie R. Ballinger - 28
        4165   3189m - Maiva O. (dau)   - 1

10329. HIMON ENGLAND,   Locust Grove, Okla
Admitted. Son of #515 and claims thru same ancestors. [For
Roll information See App 4300, Vol. 3]

10330. MADIE ENGLAND,   Locust Grove, Okla
Admitted. Minor daughter of #515 and claims thru same ances-
tors and enrolled as such on her card. [For Roll information
See App 515, Vol. 1]

10331. ANNIE ENGLAND,   Locust Grove, Okla
Admitted. Daughter of #515 and claims thru same ancestors.
ROLL P58 #10660 FCT COMM #17920 - Annie England - 24

10332. ELLA LITTLEDAVE,   Locust Grove, Okla
Admitted. Niece of #8359 and claims thru same source. Grand
father enrolled. [For Roll information See App 3701, Vol. 2]

10333. MARY CUNNINGHAM and 5 children,   Spavinaw, Okla
Admitted. Mother of applicant, Rebecca Christy, enrolled in
1851 in Saline Dis. #163. Father of applicant, Ephriam Vann,
enrolled in 1851 in Saline District #27. Dawes Commission
#10103. Misc. Test. P. 3600.
MISC. TEST. P. 3600. Appl. #10333 - Mary Cunningham:
    "My name is Mary Cunningham. I live at Spavinaw, Okla. I
am enrolled by the Dawes Commission. My number is #10103. My
father was an Immigrant Cherokee. He got money in 1852. His
name was Eph Vann. He lived in Saline District. My father
had a good many brothers. I only know the names of a few of
them: Alexander, Josiah, sisters, Sallie and Nellie. They all
lived in Saline Dist. I don't know whether they were married
in 1852 or not. My grandfather's name was Arch Vann. My father had a sister named Katy, a brother named William. See
Saline 280.
    "My mother was an Immigrant Cherokee. My mother's maiden
name was Quakey Cristy. Becky was her English name. She also
lived in Saline Dist. She only had one brother, Tucksee. She
was older than Tucksee. My grandfather's name was Johnson
Christy. My grandfather was living in 1852. My mother was
married in 1852. I don't know whether my father and mother
were living together in 1852 or not. See Rebecca Christy.
Saline 163. and see Ephriam Vann. Saline 27."
SIGNED: Mary Cunningham, Pryor Creek, Okla., Oct 9 1908.
ROLL P50 #9043 FCT COMM #10103 - Mary Cunningham - 49
        9044   10105 - James M. (son)   - 17
        9045   10106 - Lizzie P. (dau) - 15
        9046   10107 - Charles F. (son) - 13

10333.   MARY CUNNINGHAM (Cont)
         9047 FCT COMM #10109 - Maggie (dau)   - 8
         9048   10108 - Lee Vann (son)   - 11

10334.   LARKEN SEVENSTAR,   Ochlelata, Okla
Admitted. Brother of #6050 and claims thru same ancestors.
ROLL P125 #24183 FCT COMM #18360 - Larken Sevenstar - 26

10335.   MAUD E. THARP and 2 children,   Ramona, Okla
Admitted. Sister of #9316.
ROLL P138 #26647 FCT COMM #12555 - Maud E. Tharp   - 34
          26648   12556 - Emma B. BUSSEY (dau) - 12
          26649   12557 - Jesse B. BROWN (son) - 9

10336.   MARTHA A. MERONEY,   Murphy, N C
Admitted. Aunt of 33734. Is enrolled in 1851 by Chapman #1284
ROLL P13 #1692 - Martha A. Meroney - 70

10337.   MANDA ANDERSON,   Springfield, N C
Rejected. Sizemore case. See special report #417.

10338. HENRY SHERRILL GIRD & 3 children, Governors Island, N C
Rejected. Betsy Walker case.   See special report #45 [sic -
should be 500]

10339. WM. A. STEPHENS,   Blansville, Ga
Rejected. Cousin of #4748 and claims thru same source.

10340. MILLY ANN HASH,   Major, Va
Rejected. Sizemore case. See special report #417.

10341.   CHEROKEE HILDEBRAND (6) children,   Pawhuska, Okla
         by Father
Admitted. 1st cousin to #4246. Osages. [sic]   Not included
by D C. Applicant's mother "Celia Jane" enrolled 280 Tahlequah. [NOTE: Confusing summary - "children" was written in
pencil - no children on roll with applicant and that might be
what "Osages" refers to]
ROLL P75 #14132 FCT COMM #10320 - Cherokee Hilderbrand - 34

10342. LEWIS* H. SMITH,   Robbinsville, N C
Admitted. Applicant enrolled by Chapman 1851 #1371. Uncle of
#613. [* "Lems" crossed out - For Roll information See App
3951, Vol. 2]

10343. JACOB JACKSON,   Robbinsville, N C
Admitted. Applicant is a minor 13 years old and has already
been enrolled with his father. See application of #6205.
Notice. [For Roll information See App 6025, Vol. 3]

10344.   JOHN L. ROBERSON and 3 children,   Little Creek, N C
Rejected. Kaziah Vann case. See special report #276.

10345. JEFFERSON TRENT,   Pawhuska, Okla
Admitted. Nephew to Jack Quinton (16904) and claims thru same
source.
ROLL P141 #27258 FCT COMM #12908 - Jefferson Trent - 20

10346. LORELLA SMITH and 3 children,   Brentwood, Tenn
Admitted. Sister of #12; claims thru same source.
ROLL P17 #2429 - Lorella Smith   - 53
          2430 - Addie Lela (dau) - 18
          2431 - Wallace J. (son) - 16
          2432 - Clea N. (dau)   - 13

10347. MINOR L. TIDWELL and 2 children,   Welch, Okla
Rejected. Claims thru John Tidwell. See #16.

10348. W. T. BURRELL and 1 child,   Enuna, Ga
Rejected. Son of Jesse Burrell, Jr., App #6917 and claims
thru same source.

10349. CHARLEY M. ADAMS and 6 children,   Melton, Okla
Rejected. Claims thru same source as #9629.

10350. ELEANOR ROBERSON and 2 children,   Adairsville, Ga
Admitted. Aunt of #1861. Enrolled as Eleanor Payne, in 1851
by Chapman #1355.
ROLL P16 #2166 - Eleanor Roberson - 56
          2167 - Sarah (dau)   - 19
          2168 - Ginty (son)   - 2

10351. NED COCHRAN,   Greenbrier, Okla
Admitted. Cousin of #4291; claims thru same source. [For
Roll information See App 873, Vol. 1]

10352. FANNIE G. STARR,   Porum, Okla
Admitted. Sister of #9906. Applicant's father enrolled at
Flint #570.
ROLL P132 #25439 FCT COMM #4249?* - Fannie G. Starr - 51
           25440   4253 - Margaret (dau) - 11
                               (App 16769)
           25441   4252 - Cherokee (dau) - 12
[* FCT # as written]

10353. JOHN R. HALL,   Chetopa, Kans
Admitted. Brother of #8035.
ROLL P69 #12993 FCT COMM #29476 - John R. Hall - 21

10354. WILLIAM T. BROWN and 2 children,   Resaca, Ga
Rejected. It does not appear that applicant or ancestors were
ever enrolled with the Cherokees or parties to the treaties of
1835-6 or '46. Misc. Test. P. 1298.
MISC. TEST. P. 1298. No. 10354 - William T. Brown:
    "My name is William T. Brown; I was born in Bradley Co.,

32

Tenn. 1868; I claim Indian blood through both my father and mother; my mother's maiden name was --?-- Springfield; [given name blurred] My father was born in S. C., I do not know what district; 1834; my mother was born in Murray Co., Ga. 1837; my father got his Indian blood through his mother, whose maiden name was Mary Ann Hester Hubbard; I do not know when my grand mother was born; my grandmother was born in S. C.; I do know what district.

"My mother got her Indian blood through her mother, whose maiden name was Mary Willbanks; Mary Willbanks was born in Murray Co., Ga.; I never say my mother's mother; I do not know when she was born; my grandmother on my father's side was living in Roseclair, Harden Co., Ill. at the time of her death; I do not know when my grandmother died; she died since the war; I am unable to trace my ancestry father back than my grandparents; in 1835 my father and his mother were living in S. C.; in 1851 they were living in Murray Co., Ga.; in 1835 my mother and her ancestors were living in Murray Co., Ga.; none of my ancestors through whom I claim were ever enrolled; none of my ancestors through whom I claim were ever held as slaves; my father claimed to be a quarter Cherokee and my mother also claimed to be a quarter Cherokee; both I and the the ancestors through whom I claim were always regarded as white people with Cherokee Indian blood."
SIGNED: William T. "X" Brown, Calhoun, Tenn., Jul 9 1908.
EXCEPTION CASE. Rejected. Total number of exceptions filed in this group -- 2. Original recommendation renewed.

10355. EUGENE W. LOUTHER and 3 children, Keefton, Okla
Admitted. 1st cousin once removed to #3080. Mother of applicant enrolled in 1851 under name of Jane McCoy in Disputed District #97. See letter herewith.
ROLL P91 #17308 FCT COMM #26274 - Eugene W. Louther - 36
            17309   26275 - Jennie Lee (dau) - 8
            17310   26277 - Willie E. (son) - 4
            17311   69m - Clifford (son) - 2

10356. MATHISON ROGERS and 7 children, Blue Mountains, Ark
Rejected. Claims thru same source as #9629.

10357. JUG ROGERS and 2 children, Blue Mountains, Ark
Rejected. Claims thru same source as #9629.

10358. EDLEY A. ROGERS, Riley, Ark
Rejected. Claims thru same source as #9629.

10359. WILLIAM S. CROW and 5 children, Oakman, Okla
Rejected. Claims thru same source as #9629.

10360. SIMON W. ADAMS and 3 children, Milton, Okla
Rejected. Claims thru same source as #9629.

10361. LOLA A. LIPE,   Milcruk, Okla
Rejected. Claims thru same source as #9629.

10362. ROBT. S. WILLIAMS,   Vanceburg, Ky
Rejected. It does not appear that applicant or anceswtors
were ever enrolled with the Cherokees or parties to the treaties of 1835-6 or '46.
EXCEPTION CASE. Rejected. Total number of exceptions filed
in this group -- 1. Original recommendation renewed.

10363. CYNTHIA HENDRICKS,   Ochelata, Okla
Admitted. Applicant's father Lit-tah-we enrolled by Drennen
1852 Flint. Misc. Test. P. 2405.
MISC. TEST. P. 2405.   No 10363 - Cynthia Hendricks...through
C. R. Hendricks, Interpreter:
    "My mother was an Old Settler. My father Si-gui-ya was
not an Old Settler. I have drawn Old Settler money. My father was enrolled in 1851. Polly Downing, name of applicant's
mother appears on Old Settler roll, Group 41, page 41. I was
only two years of age when my father went away to the war. I
do not know any name other than the one given above. He was
enrolled in 1851 in the Flint or Sequoyah District, Cherokee
Nation."
SIGNED: Cynthia, Hendricks, Bartlesville, Okla., Aug 28 1908.
ROLL P73 #13663 FCT COMM #22127 - David Hendricks - 55
                            (App 11166)
          13664   18438 - Cynthia (wife) - 48
          13665   22128 - Mike (son)   - 19
[NOTE: Applicant's App # omitted from roll]

10364. JAMES A. WATTS,   Rome, Ga
Rejected. Nephew of #7624.

10365. REBECCA NELSON and 3 children,   Topton, N C
Rejected. Sister of #10317.

10366. JOSEPH H. POSTELL,   Topton, N C
Rejected. Uncle of #10317.

10367. CHARLES POSTELL,   Topton, N C
Rejected. Brother of #10317.

10368. WM. C. POSTELL and 4 children,   Topton, N C
Rejected. Uncle of #10317.

10369. WILLER E. MARTIN,   Greenbrier, Okla
Admitted. Nephew of #873 and claims thru same source.
ROLL P97 #18508 FCT COMM #23477 - Willie V. Martin - 14

10370. JESSE TEE-HEE and minor children,   Choteau, Okla
Duplicate. Inc. in 1001 mother.

10371. CHARLEY TEE-HEE and minor children, Choteau, Okla
Inc. in #1001 mother. Duplicate

10372. NANCY M. REEVES,   Adair, Okla
Admitted. Sister to #5594.
ROLL P116 #22331 FCT COMM #13360 - Nancy M. Reeves - 56

10373. ELI MILLER,   Norwood, Mo
Rejected. The grandfather of the applicant was an Old Settler. None of his ancestors were on Emigrant Rolls. Ancestors thru whom claims Cher. blood were not parties to the
treaties of 1835-6 or '46. Misc. Test. P. 2120.
MISC. TEST. P. 2120. No 10373 - Eli Miller:
    "My name is Eli Miller; I was born in Goingsnake District,
Ind. Terr., 1840; I claim my Indian blood through my mother; I
make no claim of Indian blood through my father; I think my
mother was born in Georgia; I do not know the county; my mother got her Indian blood through her father; I think my mother
was born about 1814; I do not know when or where my grandfather through whom I claim was born; I do not know exactly when
my grandfather and mother came from the East to the Ind. Terr;
my grandfather and mother through whom I claim lived with the
Cherokee Indians; I do not know where they lived with the Indians before the Indians came West; I think that my mother and
grandfather lived with the Indians in Goingsnake District after the Indians came West; I do not know where my mother and
grandfather were living in 1835; in 1851 I was living in Ozark
Co.,Mo.; in 1851 my mother was dead; I do not know whether my
grandfather was living at that time or not; I think my grand
father and mother were enrolled; I was never enrolled that I
know of; I do not know where my ancestors were enrolled; I
guess they were enrolled before I was born; I think she was
enrolled under the name of Polly Miller, maiden name Polly
Love; neither I nor any of the ancestors through whom I claim
ever receieved any money or land that I know of; my mother was
a half Cherokee; my mother had a brother, whose name was Arch
Love, who went to the Ind. Terr. at the time my mother went
there; my cousin, Wedge Shirley, was enrolled in the Ind. Terr
and drew Indian money; I have also a cousin by the name of Ed.
Walkingstick, who was enrolled; I think my grandfather shared
in the Old Settler payment."
SIGNED: Eli Miller, Springfield, Mo., Aug 21 1908.
EXCEPTION CASE. Rejected. Total number of exceptions filed
in this group -- 10. Original recommendation renewed.

10374. WILLIAM C. McCRARY and 2 children, Denver, Colo
Admitted. Nephew of #735. Father of applicant enrolled by
Drennen in Delaware Dist. 25.
ROLL P93 #17755 FCT COMM #8800 - William C. McCrary - 30
            17756   8801 - Willie A. (son)   - 10
            17757   8802 - David E. (son)   - 8

10375. MAUD WATTS   Westville, Okla
Admitted. Daughter of #15955. 1st cousin of 12632, once re-
moved and claims thru same source. [For Roll information See
App 5854, Vol. 3]

10376. CHRISTIAN TEHEE, by Lizzie Tehee, Gdn., Rose, Okla
Admitted. Claims thru father enrolled as Jim Tehee #485 Fl.
ROLL P137 #26564 FCT COMM #6526 - Christian Tehee - 11
                                  by Lizzie Tehee, Gdn.

10377. MOODY M. TEHEE, by Lizzie Tehee, Gdn., Rose, Okla
Admitted. Sister of #10376 and claims thru same source.
ROLL P137 #26586 FCT COMM #6525 - Moody M. Tehee - 15
                                  by Lizzie Tehee, Gdn.

10378. TOM HYDER and 4 children,   Maysville, Ark
Admitted. Half brother of #8360 on the father's side. Father
of applicant enrolled in 263 Del. as Tuck-cab-too-nah-e in
1851. See Misc. Test. P. 4316. [For Testimony See App 8360]
ROLL P80 #15061 FCT COMM #28450 - Tom Hyder   - 28
         15062   28452 - Daniel (son) - 6
         15063   2726m - Lewis (son) - 4
         15064   2727m - Jesse (son) - 2
         15065   - Grace (dau) - 1/6

10379. JACK ROUND,   Maysville, Ark
Admitted. Claimant is a nephew on the mother's side of #6685.
Claimant's parents and three brothers and sisters enrolled by
Drennen Sal. 260. See Misc. Test. 3860. [For Testimony See
App 6685, Vol 3. For Roll information See App 5973, Vol. 3]

10380. YOUNGBEAVER HOGSHOOTER and 2 children, Maysville, Okla
Admitted. Brother of #5944 and claims thru same source. One
child, Joe Hogshooter, not allowed for reason that said child
was born after May 28, '06, namely, Sept. 4, 1907. [For Roll
information See App 1908, Vol. 2]

10381. ANNIE DEER IN WATER,   Welling, Okla
Admitted. 1/2 sister of #3285 and claims thru same source.
[For Roll information See App 8945, Vol. 4]

10382. SALLIE HAIR,   Proctor, Okla
Admitted. Sister of #10310.
MISC. TEST. P. 4093. #10382-10310 - Henry Walkabout...through
Tom Roach, Interpreter...in behalf of Sallie Hair:
    "I am 58 years old; I know Sallie Hair and both her par-
ents. The father of Sallie Hair was John Tobacco or Chah-nih
Oo-skee-le-aduh or John Frizzlyhead. He was living in 1851 and
drew money at that time. He lived in Illinois District. His
father and mother were separated in 1851. His mother lived in
Tahlequah District and his father lived in Illinois. I do not
know with whom the father of Sallie Hair was living whether

36

his father or mother. His mother's name was Dahne. Sallie Hair
has a half uncle on her fathers side by the name of Alec Deer-
in-the water, P. O. Welling, Okla. The father of Sallie Hair
and Alec Deer-in-the-water were half brothers on the mothers
side. The wife of Alec Deer-in-the-water is Annie. (Look up
this application and group if possible.) The mother of Sallie
is Wa-ke. The father of Wa-ke or Peggy is Ga-noo-gih. The
mother of Sallie Hair has a sister living now whose name is
Quaity Smith, husband George Smith, P. O. Tahlequah, Okla. The
mother of Wa-ke was Chow-wah-you-gah. I do not know whether
Chow-wah-you-gah was an Old Settler or not. I know two of the
brothers and sisters of Wa-ke were Quaity and Mandy or Ya-kin-
ne, now Mandy Hair, husband, dead, P. O. Proctor, Okla. (See
application of Mandy Hair) Lydia Mellowbug is a half sister of
Sallie Hair on the mother's side. They had the same mother.
(See Application #16929) I do not know any of the parties mentioned in Tahl. 5 nor in Tahlequah 341. I do not know with
whom either John or Wa-ke was living in 1851. I know that John
Tobacco, the father of Sallie Hair was not an Old Settler. My
mother's name was An-ne-wa-ke and she was a sister of the Paternal grandfather of Sallie Hair. My Indian name was Caw-ca-
lee-sky (See Tahl. 52) I am pretty sure that the mother of
Sallie Hair was an Emigrant Cherokee. I am sure that she never
drew any Old Settler money. Sallie Hair is a full-blood Cherokee and has drawn in all payments made to the Cherokees except the Old Settler payment. I do not know the ancestors of
Lula McCarty on the mother's side."
SIGNED: Henry "X" Walkabout, Tahlequah, Okla., Mar 29 1909.

MISC. TEST. P. 4279. No 10382-21791 - Henry Dreadfulwater:
"My name is Henry Dreadfulwater; my post-office is Gideon,
Okla.; my present wife, Annis is a white woman; my second wife
was named Peggy and we had one child, living named John Dreadfulwater - some call him John Henry - he must be over twenty
years old; my son John lives at Welling, Okla.; before marriage Peggy's name was Ca-noo-gi; I do not know who Ca-noo-
gi's father and mother were."
SIGNED: Henry Dreadfulwater, Tahlequah, Okla., Mar 29 1909.
[For Roll information See App 5622, Vol. 3]

10383. JAMES HAIR, Duplicate of #5622.

10384. THOMAS W. COWAND,   Warner, Okla
       by Thomas J. Cowand, Gdn. and father
Admitted. Grand nephew of #277 and claims thru same source.
ROLL P47 #8600 FCT COMM #23068 - Thomas W. Cowand - 13
                        by Thomas J. Cowand, Gdn.

10385. ELIZA BECK and 5 children,   Fawn, Okla
Admitted. 1st cousin of #6307 and claims thru same source.
ROLL P28 #4655 FCT COMM #17330 - Eliza Beck   - 32
         4656   17331 - Claud (son)   - 14

10385. ELIZA BECK (Cont)
     4657 FCT COMM #17332 – Lynda (son) – 8
     4658   17333 – Nannie (dau) – 6
     4659   17334 – Homer (son) – 4
     4660   3345m – Jos. R. (son) – 2

10386. THOMAS RATTLINGGOURD and 4 children, Moody, Okla
Admitted. Brother to 1865. [For Roll information See App
3144, Vol. 2]

10387. NANCY LEAF,   Westville, Okla
Admitted. Applicant's father and mother enrolled as Night
Killer and Susan in Flint #17. [Notation on Roll "Leaf,
Nancy. See Roll No. 16950"]
ROLL P89 #16949 FCT COMM #20032 – Tom Lee   – 54
                     (APP 16376)
       16950   20033 – Nancy (wife) – 50

10388. KATIE DEER-IN-WATER,   Braggs, Okla
Admitted. Applicant's mother enrolled by Drennen as Too-chah
in Ill. Dis. Group #124. Applicant's grandparents enrolled in
same group. Misc. Test. P. 3368.
MISC. TEST. P. 3368. No 10368 – Kate Deer-in-water...through
S. E. Parris, Interpreter:
    "I am about 39 years of age. My mother and father were
both full blood Cherokees. I drew strip money. I am a Cherokee
alottee and my number is 21143. My mother and father did not
draw Immigrant money ten years before the war. Father was living but was born too late for the payment. My mother lived in
Illinois District at the time of the payment. Her name was
Too-kah. She had a brother named Johnson Waters. They both
drew Immigrant money. My grandmother's name was Nancy. She
also had a brother named Lightning Bug. My father's name was
George Waters. My uncle is here with me now. His number is
10933."
SIGNED: Katie Deer-win-water, Tahlequah, Okla., Oct 1 1908.
ROLL P52 #9556 FCT COMM #21143 – Katie Deerinwater – 34

10389. JOE GROUNDHOG,   Tahlequah, Okla
Admitted. 1st cousin of #2271. Father of applicant enrolled
in 1851 in G. S. #544.
ROLL P68 #12741 FCT COMM #26091 – Joe Groundhog – 24
     12742   29265 – Nancy (wife) – 20
                    (App 14697)

10390. ADA LAURA FOREMAN,   Claremore, Okla
Admitted. Niece of #1816.
ROLL P62 #11521 FCT COMM #12603 – Ada Laura Foreman – 25

10391. SARAH L. LIPE and 3 children,   Talala, Okla
Admitted. Niece of #1816.

```
ROLL P90 #17123 FCT COMM #12177 - John G. Lipe      - 42
                                 (App 32593)
         17124          12178 - Sarah L. (wife) - 31
         17125          12179 - Flora F. (dau)  -  7
         17126          12180 - Ada C. (dau)    -  5
         17127           664m - De Witte (son)  -  2
```

10392. POLLY SUGGS,   Audubon, Ga
Rejected. Mother of #16319.

10393. SARAH GILLISPI,   Calhoun, Ga
Rejected. It does not appear that applicant or ancestors were
enrolled with the Cherokees, or parties to treaties of 1835-6
or '46. Misc. Test. P. 1297.
MISC. TEST. P. 1297. No 10393 - Sarah Gillispi:
    "My name is Sarah Gillispie; I was born in Union Co., Ga.
1853; I claim Indian blood through my mother; I make no claim
of Indian blood through my father; my mother's maiden name was
Rebecca Mathis; I think my mother was born in White Co., Ga.
1835; my mother claimed her Indian blood through both her father and mother; my mother's father's name was William Mathis;
my mother's mother's maiden name was Elizabeth Henson; I think
my grandfather was born in S. C., I do not know the district
or when; I never saw the grandfather through whom I claim; my
mother's mother was born in S. C.; I do not know just exactly
when she was born; in 1835 my mother and the ancestors through
whom I claim were living in Union Co., Ga.; in 1851 my mother
and her mother lived in Union Co., Ga.; I have been told that
my grandfather, William Mathis, was enrolled; I do not know on
what roll; I do not know whether my mother or her parents ever
lived with the Indians as a member of the tribe or not; none
of the ancestors through whom I claim were ever held in bondage; none of the ancestors through whom I claim ever had an
Indian name that I know of; I have been told that my grand
mother, Elizabeth Mathis (nee Henson) was enrolled and enrolled her whole family so I have been told; I have been told
that my cousin, Jesse Carroll, went to the Ind. Terr. and drew
land; he is the grandson of Elizabeth Mathis, my grandmother."
SIGNED: Mrs. Sarah "X" Gillispi, Calhoun, Ga., Jul 9 1908.
EXCEPTION CASE. Rejected.   Total number of exceptions filed
in this group -- 2. Original recommendation renewed.

10394. AMY A. GRAY and 4 children,   Quinton, Okla
Rejected. Claims thru same source as #9629.

10395. JAMES A. CROW and 3 children,   Center, Okla
Rejected. Claims thru same source as #9629.

10396. PATSY BATT,   Stilwell, Okla
Admitted. 1st cousin to 1386. Father "426 Tahl. Mose Ketcher"
ROLL P26 #4390 FCT COMM #15606 - Jack Batt   - 23 (App 12502)
         4391   18327 - Patsy (wife) - 21

                           39
```
```

10396. PATSY BATT (Cont)
      4392 FCT COMM #2566m - Earthy (son) - 2
      4393   2567m - Daniel (son) - 1

10397. POLLY RUSSELL,   Sallisaw, Okla
Admitted. Applicant's father enrolled by Drennen 1852, George
Guess S. B. 320. Misc. Test. P. 2934. [For Testimony See App
1252, Vol. 1]
ROLL P121 #23353 FCT COMM #3255 - Polly Russell - 53

10398. BETSY RUTHERFORD,   Wauhillau, Okla
Admitted. 1st cousin of #862.
ROLL P121 #23371 FCT COMM #1487 - Betsy Rutherford - 40

10399. JAMES SANDERS and 3 children,   Wauhillau, Okla
Admitted. 1st cousin to #862.
ROLL P122 #23521 FCT COMM #20747 - James Sanders - 34
        23522   20748 - Rachel (wife) - 28
                         (App 16892)
        23523   20749 - Charles E. (son) - 10
        23524   20751 - May (dau)   - 4
        23525   4402m - Lucinda J. (dau) - 2

10400. TOOKA BOWLIN,   Cookson, Okla
Admitted. Applicant enrolled by Drennen Fl. #603 as Two-ker.
ROLL P32 #5562 FCT COMM #20132 - Tooka Bowlin - 76

10401. JACK CRITTENDEN and 1 child,   Baron, Okla
Admitted. Brother of #1783.
ROLL P48 #8799 FCT COMM #25816 - Jack Crittenden - 30
        8800   25818 - Luke (son)   - 6

10402. MINNIE M. WATKINS,   Catoosa, Okla
Admitted. Sister of #781 and claims thru same source.
ROLL P147 #28492 FCT COMM #5687 - Minnie M. Watkins - 25

10403. FANNIE WATKINS   Catoosa, Okla
      by Cyrus A. Watkins, Gdn.
Admitted. Sister of #781 and claims thru same source.
ROLL P147 #28475 FCT COMM #5690 - Fannie Watkins - 16
                  by Cyrus A. Watkins, Gdn.

10404. FELIX CRITTENDEN,   Baron, Okla
Admitted. Brother of #1783.
ROLL P48 #8778 FCT COMM #29704 - Felix Crittenden - 25

10405. WILLIAM WATKINS,   Catoosa, Okla
      by Cyrus A. Watkins, Gdn.
Admitted. Brother of #781 and claims thru same source.
ROLL P147 #28511 FCT COMM #5691 - William Watkins - 14
                  by Cyrus A. Watkins, Gdn.

10406. LOUISA F. CANDLE and 4 children,   Tecumseh, Okla
Rejected. it does not appear that any ancestor was ever enrolled or that any ancestor was a party to the treaties of
1835-6 or '46. Shows no connection with the Eastern Cherokee.
Misc. Test. P. 2576.
MISC. TEST. P. 2576. #43952-10406 - Joseph C. Terry:
     "That I am 55 years of age. I claim my Indian descent
through my mother; my father was full blooded white man. My
first wife was claimed to be a Chickasaw. I made application
before the Dawes Commission but never got on the roll. This
application was for my first children by my first wife. My
second wife is a white woman. My mother claimed Indian through
her father and he through his mother. My mother was born in
1834 in Putnam Co., Tenn. She left there in 1870. Up to that
time she was living in Putnam Co., Tenn. Her parents lived
there too. My mother nor her parents never lived with the Indians as members of the tribe and were never on any rolls that
I know of. I am recognized as a white man in the community
where I live. I did not heard of this fund until last October
and that is when I filed my claim. I have two brothers who
married Choctaws."
SIGNED: Jos. C. Terry, Ardmore, Okla., Sep 3 1908.

10407. MARY E. WICKETT,   Muskogee, Okla
Admitted. Applicant claims thru mother, Annie Wickett, en-
rolled in Tahl. 6 Group. Applicant's sister Juliett also
Tahl. #6.
ROLL P150 #29124 FCT COMM #25580 - Mary E. Wickett - 50

10408. JOHN C. DAVISON,   Tolson, Okla
Rejected. Brother of 9266.

10409. WILLIAM SMALLWOOD, Duplicate of #1669.

10410. MARY L. RALEY, Duplicate of #4029.

10411. LOCKIE OSBORN,   Apple Grove, N C
Rejected. Sizemore Case. See special report #417.

10412. MANDA BROOKS and 2 children,   Weasel, N C
Rejected. Sizemore case. See special report #417.

10413. FIELDEN OSBORN and 4 children,   Apple Grove, N C
Rejected. Sizemore case. See special report #417.

10414. AR-LICK WELCH,   Birdtown, N C
Admitted. Applicant claims thru father Oo-tah-ne-yah-tah,
enrolled with his parents Oo-la-nuh-hih and A-nih, Chapman
751, C. 749 and C. 750. [For Roll information See App 6508,
Vol. 3]

41

10415. SUSIE REED and 4 children,   Basin, W Va
Rejected. Sizemore case. See special report #417.

10416. ELIZABETH MILLER,   Weasel, N C
Rejected. Sizemore case. See special report #417.

10417. MARY MILLER,   Weasel, N C
Rejected. Sizemore case. See special report #417.

10418. SAMUEL SMALLWOOD, Duplicate of #1668.

10419. ROBERT E. WEST and 7 children,   Warner, Okla
Admitted. Half brother of 5238 and claims thru same source.
ROLL P149 #28905 FCT COMM # 5896 - Robert E. West   - 35
            28906   5897 - William E. (son)   - 13
            28907   5898 - Walter T. (son)   - 11
            28908   5899 - Martin L. (son)   - 9
            28909   5900 - Elizabeth D. (dau)   - 7
            28910   5901 - Valeria E. (dau)   - 5
            28911   1539m - Robert I. (son)   - 3
            28912   1540m - Richard E. (son)   - 1/4

10420. KATE TAYLOR and 4 children,   Ahniwake, Okla
Rejected. Father of children was a white man. Niece of #3551.
Claimant's mother under the name of Lucinda Terrell on O. S.
Roll, Tahlequah #113.

10421. JIM FALLING and 1 child,   Spavinaw, Okla
Admitted. Applicant claims thru father Choo-noo-la-hus-ke enrolled in Del. #724. Grandparents Lewis Cul-ca-los-ke and Ah-
te-the-e, 724 Del. Misc. Test. P. 3836.
MISC. TEST. P. 3836. #13257 (#10421) - Nick Falling...thru
Martin Squirrel, Interpreter:
    "My name is Nick Falling. I was born in Saline District in
1876. I was not enrolled by the Dawes Commission and never received an allotment of land. I am a full-blood Cherokee. None
of my brothers and sisters were enrolled in 1851.   My father
and mother were not married in 1851. My father was enrolled in
Saline District in 1851 with his parents. My mother was enrolled with her parents in Saline District in 1851. My father
is living at the present time and was notified to appear at
Pryor Creek, Okla about Oct 10th, 1908. He is an applicant for
a part of this money. My father had a brother by the name of
Jo-sah-ye, a sister by the name of Nancy, a brother by the
name of Gau-hun-tis-ke. (See 724 Del. for father, grandparents
on fathers side and uncles and aunt.)   None of my ancestors
were Old Settlers. (See application of father and O. K. it)."
SIGNED: Nick Falling, Locust Grove, Okla., Oct 12 1908.
ROLL P59 #10852 FCT COMM #18602 - Jim Falling   - 35
            10853   32633 - Quaity (wife) - 23
                                 (App 17279)
            10854   32282 - Laura (dau)   - 8

10422. SNAKE L. MILLER and 2 children,   Tahlequah, Okla
Admitted. First cousin of #3461. Claimant's paternal grand
father enrolled in 1851 by Drennen G. S. #449.
ROLL P100 #19063 FCT COMM #28230 - Suake L. Miller - 37
          19064   28231 - Minnie L. (wife) - 34
                                 (App 26666)
          19065   28232 - Dicie G. (dau)   - 12
          19066   28233 - Henry S. (son)   - 9

10423. MARY WILLIAMS,   Mark, Okla
Admitted. Cousin of #317 and claims thru same source. See
Misc. Test. P. 3868-4283
MISC. TEST. P. 3868. 10423 - Mary Williams:
    "I am 42 years of age. I claim my Indian descent through
my mother. My father was a white man. My mother died in 1878
and was about 40 years of age when she died. My mother was a
half breed Cherokee. She derived her Indian descent from her
mother. My mother always claimed to be an Emmigrant. She and
her mother claimed to be on the Emmigrant Roll. I don't know
where my mother was born, but it was somewhere back in the Old
Nation. Think she was living back in the Old Nation in 51. My
mother's maiden name was Eldridges -- Manerve Eldridge. Her
mother's name at that time was Ailsey Eldridge. My grandmother
first married a man named Elridge, than about the war time she
married a man named Murphy. My mother had one brother living
in 51, some what older than she, named Jeff Elridge. She had
two sisters but I don't know their names. They were older than
she. Think Jef. Eldridge came west when the rest did. He died
along about 1879. He died up here west of Pryor Creek. I don't
know how old he was when he died but he was right grey. I am
enrolled by the Daws Commission number 6977. I received Strip
money in 1894. I have always been a member of the Cherokee
tribe since my birth. I am now living upon my allotment. I am
no relation to Peggy Murphy Sharp, Woodall or Wash-hand).   I
don't know who my Great Grandparents were. Think Jeff was
grown in 51. (See G. S. 191 ?) Thin[k] he always lived up
where he died after he came out here. That was Saline District before the war. Think I have a first cousin by the name
of Susan Cook living at Vinita. Her mother was my mother's
sister and her maiden name was Sanders, I think, but I don't
know her mother's given name. Susan Cook had a sister named
Polly Claws. She lived in Vinita to the last I heard of her. I
don't know what my grandmother's name was before she was married. I don't know when my Grandmother Eldridge died, but it
was after the war. Don't know where she was living when she
died. Don't know of anyone that can furnish any more information. My mother told me that they came out here on a Steamboat
with a lot of other Indians. I don't know much about my people, my mother died when I was small. I have a boy grown named
Tuskie [? several letters crossed out] Williams. He lives
right close to us. He has made application to. I haven't any
brother or sisters living. My mother was married the first

43

time before the War to a man by the name of Terrell. My moth-
er's Indian name was Tooker. Don't know of my grandmother having any Indian name. I never had any full brothers or sisters.
I had a half brother named Tom Terrill. He was killed along
about 1896. He was an Old Settler on his father's side. We
were related on our mother's side. His father was named Lige
Terrill."
SIGNED: Mary Williams, Locust Grove, Okla., Oct 8 1908.
MISC. TEST. P. 4116. John Sanders...in behalf of Mary
Williams, the wife of Leonard Williams:
    "Mary Williams lives at Rose, Okla. I am about 58 years of
age. I live at Claremore, Okla. Have lived here about 19
years. I was born in the Cherokee Nation. I am acquainted with
Mary Williams. She is about thirty years of age. She was born
in the Cherokee Nation. She gets her Indian blood from both
sides of the house. Her mother's name was Manerva Terrell nee
Eldridge. She has been dead some twenty years and was pretty
well up in years at the time of her death. She was living at
the time of her death in Ft. Gibson. She was born in the East.
Manerva was a Emigrant. Mary Williams has just one brother,
his name being Tom. He is dead and left no children. Jess
Eldridge, Jeff, Ibbie, Elmira (my mother) - she married
Sanders and that was her name in 1851. These were brothers and
sisters of Manerva Eldridge. (See G. S. 698) Also G. S. 191.
Manerva Terrell lived in G. S. District in 1851. I do not know
why she was not enrolled. Mary Williams' mother Manerva never
associated with any other tribe of Indians. She never drew any
Old Settler money. I know that Mary Williams has Eastern Cherokee blood. Mary Williams' mother was younger than my mother
but she was old enough to have been enrolled in 1851. Jess
started out with the emigrants but died on the road. The
Terrells were not Old Settlers. I do not know why she was not
enrolled, that is Manerva Terrell."
SIGNED: John Sanders, Claremore, Okla., Mar 10 1909.
MISC. TEST. P. 4283. #10423 - "See Testimony in case rela-
tive to Jefferson Eldridge who was applicant's full uncle.
This case must be grouped with #317 who is Ok thru Jefferson
Eldridge. It is impossible with the information at hand to
find Minerva mother of applicant on the roll. See #317 for
information as to mother of applicant."
SIGNED: H. W. Ketron [NOTE: Ketron was one of the Assistant
Commissioners of Guion Miller]
[For Roll information See App 2733, Vol. 2]

10424. KA-YOR-HE WHITEWALKER,   Locust Grove, Okla
Admitted. 1st cousin of #1687; claims thru same source. [No-
tation on roll "Whitewalker, Ka-yor-he. See Roll No. 27936"]
ROLL P144 #27935 FCT COMM #18561 - Dick Walker - 22(App 14191)
         27936   - Ka-yor-he (wife) - 26
         27937   - Bettie (dau)   - 1

44

10425. ANDREW CATCHER (KETCHER) & 1 child, Locust Grove, Okla
Admitted. 1st cousin to #1386. "Moses Te-cah-ne-ye-skee"
father "426 Tahl." [For Roll information See App 6975, Vol. 3]

10426. LIZZIE HAIR,   Hulbert, Okla
Admitted. 1st cousin to #1386. Father "Moses Te-cah-ny-ye-
skee 424 [sic - see entry above] Tahl." [For Roll information See App 9269, Vol. 4]

10427. JOHN WICKLIFFE,   Spavinaw, Okla
Admitted. Half brother of #462. Applicant enrolled as John
Wickliffe, Saline #216.
ROLL P150 #29140 FCT COMM #20889 - John Wickliffe   - 62
          29141   18528 - Nellie (wife)   - 35
                                 (App 10626)
          29142   18529 - Hattie TIGER (dau) - 13
                                 (App 14179)

10428. POLLY (WAL-LE) SMOKE & 3 children, Locust Grove, Okla*
Admitted. 1st cousin of #1687 and claims thru same ancestors.
See Misc. Test. P. 4334. [* Residence Spavinaw, Okla on roll]
MISC. TEST. P. 4334. #10428 - Wal-le Smoke...thru Tom Roach,
Interpreter:
     "I am 30 years old; I have four minor children living,
Chah-wah-you-gah, english Mary, 14 years Old, Oo-you-tih 8
years old, We-lick, William, 5 years old, - and I another
child about a year old now. I am a Night Hawk. (the Daws Com-
mission number of applicant and children is #32746 to 32748)."
SIGNED: Wal-le Smoke, Spavinaw, Okla., Mar 16 1909.
ROLL P130 #25045 FCT COMM #32745 - Lewis Smoke   - 29
                                 (App 11408)
          25046   32746 - Polly (Wah-le) (wife) - 30
          25047   32747 - Chah-wah-you-gah (dau) - 11
                                 (or Mary)
          25048   32748 - Oo-you-tih (son)   - 6
          25049   - William (son)   - 2

10429. CORA CHICKEN,   Locust Grove, Okla
Admitted. 1st cousin #1687; claims thru same ancestors.
ROLL P41 #7308 FCT COMM #32190 - Ned Chicken   - 31
                                 (App 10632)
          7309   32191 - Cora (wife)   - 33
          7310   32192 - Jackson (son) - 6
          7311   4827m - High (son)   - 3

10430. MARTHA BLACK,   Sterrett, Okla
Rejected. Enrolled as Chickasaw by marriage D. C. #644.

10431. LUCY G. ROSEBOROUGH and 3 children, Afton, Okla
Admitted. Applicant is a niece of #1056.
ROLL P119 #23016 FCT COMM #8409 - Lucy G. Roseborough - 45
          23017   8411 - Jesse F. (son)   - 18

45

10431. LUCY G. ROSEBOROUGH (Cont)
             23018 FCT COMM #8412 - Claude (son)   - 16
             23019   - Sarah L. (dau)   - 20
                          (App 23330)

10432. GEO. M. BALLARD,   Maysville, Ark
Admitted. Applicant is a nephew of #1056.
ROLL P25 #4095 FCT COMM #28697 - George W. Ballard - 50

10433. NANCY BROOKSHER and 5 children,   Dahlonega, Ga
Rejected. It does not appear that ancestors were enrolled or
were parties to the treaties of 1835-6 or '46. Applicant
shows no real connection with the Eastern Cherokees.

10434. WILLIAM BARRETT and 2 children,   Holcomb, N C
Rejected. Keziah Vann case. See special report #276.

10435. MARY DICKERSON and 4 children,   Athens, Tenn
Rejected. Applicant's father was a slave. See letter.
EXCEPTION CASE. Rejected. Total number of exceptions filed
in this group -- 2. Original recommendation renewed.

10436. JOSEPHINE H. CANNEFAX,   Enid, Okla
Rejected. It does not appear that any ancestor was ever enrolled or that any ancestor was a party to the treaties of
1835-6 or '46. Shows no real connection with the Eastern
Cherokees. Misc. Test. P. 2334 and 2335.
MISC. TEST. P. 2334.   APPL. #13842-10436 - Louvisa A. H.
Freeman:
     "My name is Louvisa A. H. freeman. I live 2131 Va. Ave.
Joplin, Mo. I was born in 1852 in Warren Co., Tenn. I claim
my Cherokee blood through my father, George Haley. He was
born in Warren Co., Tenn. in 1828. He always lived in Tenn.
until he came to Mo. in 1858. My grandmother's maiden name
was Callahan. She married a man by the name of Haley. I
don't know whether my father lived with the Indians or white
people in Tenn. He never lived with the Cherokee tribe. He
never was enrolled. He never received any money or land from
the Government on account of his Indian blood."
SIGNED: Louvisa A. H. Freeman, Carthage, Mo., Aug 27 1908.
MISC. TEST. P. 2335. Appl. #13825-10436 - Ruthie S. H.
Rawlings:
     "My name is Ruthie S. H. Rawlings. I live at 516 N.
Mineral Street, Joplin, Mo. I am the sister of 13842. I
claim through my great grandmother on my father's side,
Elizabeth Callahan. Her maiden name was Ralston. She was
trandferred [sic] from Ala. with the Cherokee Tribe to the I.
T. in 1836. My father was just ten years old. She never
reached I. T. She stopped first in Ill. then went back to
Tenn. to get some money that was coming to her. Then she went
back to Ill. and died there in 1855. She had two sons that
went to the I. T. and took up land and died there. Dave and

46

John Callahan. They died in I. T. They went on with the Indians. I could not tell you whether or not my father ever lived with the Cherokee tribe in Eastern Tenn. I don't think that he did."
SIGNED: Ruthie A. H. Rawlings, Carthage, Mo., Aug 27 1908.
EXCEPTION CASE. Rejected. Total number of exceptions filed in this group -- 28. Original recommendation renewed.

10437. RETTIE DICKSON and 6 children, Laurel Springs, N C
Rejected. Sizemore case. See special report #417.

10438. FRANKLIN GRITTS, Duplicate of #2339.

10439. JACK SPAINARD, Campbell, Okla
Rejected. Does not appear that applicant or ancestors were ever enrolled. Does not appear that they were living within the limits of the Cherokee domain in 1835-36 and 1846 as recognized members of the tribe. Failed to appear when notified to give testimony.

10440. GEORGE GOINS and 3 children, Vian, Okla
Rejected. 1st cousin of #10294 and claims thru same source.

10441. GIRTY JAMES and 1 child, Campbell, Okla
Rejected. 1st cousin once removed of #10294 and claims thru same source.

10442. NANCY COLEMAN, Gritts, Okla
Admitted. Sister of #2339. [NOTE: Applicant's husband's residence shown as Porum, Okla on roll and applicant's residence as Gritts, Okla]
ROLL P45 #8086 FCT COMM # 5328 - John Coleman - 77 (App 13995)
        8087   17605 - Nancy (wife) - 55

10443. ISABELLE LINTON and 3 children, Durant, Okla
Rejected. Sister to #9266.

10444. PEARL L. GEORGE and 2 children, Sterrett, Okla
Rejected. Sister to #9266.

10445. SARAH J. McCORMICK and 1 child, Henshaw, Ky
Rejected. Applicant born in 1850 but not enrolled. It seems that none of her ancestors are on the rolls. It appears that they were not parties to the treaties of 1835-6 or '46; failed to appear when notified and information in letters and application insufficient.
EXCEPTION CASE. 10445. Manerva F. Donaho & 1 child, App #10446, Lebanon, Tenn. Rejected. Total number of exceptions filed in this group -- 9. Original recommendation renewed.

10446. MINERVA F. DONAHO and 1 child, Lebanon, Tenn
Rejected. Sister to #10445.

10447. LAURA ASHMAN,   Chicago, Ill*
Admitted. Sister to #5375; claims thru the same source.
[* Also "116 North Clark St." on roll]
ROLL P5 #89 - Laura Ashman - 52

10448. GEORGE A. LLOYD,   Rome, Ga
Rejected. It does not appear that claimants are connected
with the "Water Hunter" on rolls of 1835. The ancestors of
claimants belonged to the McIntosh tribe of Creek Indians.
They show no real connection with the Eastern Cherokee. It
further does not appear that any ancestor was party to treaties of 1835-6 or 1846. They are recognized as white people.
Misc. Test. P. 903 and 904.
MISC. TEST. P. 903. #10448 - George A. Loyd:
    "That I am 56 years of age and live in Floyd Co., Ga. I
claim through my father; my mother was a full blooded white
woman. My father's mother claimed Indian. My grandfather on
my father's side was a full blooded white man. Susan Loyd
died in 1866. Her grandfather was a full blooded Cherokee
Indian; she was about 1/4. Her grandfather's Indian name was
Water Hunter. Don't know when he died - haven't any idea.
Susan Loyd's father was S. D. Parson; he was 1/2 blood. I am
about 1/16 Cherokee. I think my father was never on any roll.
I don't know whether his mother was or not. My father was
born in Coweta Co., Ga. He moved to Floyd Co., Ga. in 1835 or
1836. He lived amongst the Indians in Coweta Co., but I don't
know whether he lived with them as a member of the tribe. I
don't think the Indians were in Floyd Co. when my father came
here. My grandmother Loyd came with him when he came to this
county. I never heard of my great grandfather coming to this
country. He must have been dead when my father and grandmother came to Floyd Co. I am recognized as a white man in the
community. This is the only application I ever made for Indian benefits. My grandfather first moved to Fayette Co.,
Ga., then he went to Coweta Co. My grandfather and grandmother lived with the McIntosh tribe in Coweta Co., or Fayette
Co., Ga. They were a Creek tribe. I think my grandfather
Loyd came from S. C., am not sure, however. I have an uncle,
a brother of my father, Geo. W. Loyd - and he went to the
Territory about 1870. He came from Floyd Co., Ga. While out
there he made application for a portion of land being allotted
to the Cherokees. He came back here about 1878 to get evidence attempting to prove his Indian blood. The last record I
have of the claim it was turned over to the Dawes Commission.
Don't know when it was submitted to them. It was about 1896.
I here have a paper entitled In the U. S. Court, Ind. Ter.,
Northern Dist. at Muskogee, I. T., John G. Loyd, et al vs. the
Cherokee Nation, which is an application made by my uncle and
other immediate members of his family and reciting the proceedings had therein for the purpose of securing land and enrollment amongst the Five Civilized Tribes in I. T. and the
same is here marked Exhibit "A" and attached as a part of my

48

testimony. Charles A. Loyd and Mary Jane Stafford are cousins
of mine, they being the children of Jasper Loyd and claim
through the same source as I and through no other source. I
here also offer in evidence an affidavit made by James T.
Pullen, Sr., made in behalf of my sister and marked Exhibit
"B", which my said sister, Nora Loyd, had obtained when she
was about to go to Texas in 1896 and which was gotten with the
view of making application out West for Indian benefits in the
Cherokee Nation but she never filed her claim or did anything
further with it."
SIGNED: George A. Loyd, Rome, Ga., [date cut off]
MISC. TEST. P. 904. #10448 - Wilson Monroe Shropshire...in
behalf of George A. Loyd:
    "That I am 88 years of age and live in Floyd Co., Ga. I
knew Thomas Loyd and his wife, grandparents of applicant. Got
acquainted with them about 1840. They were then living south
of Rome, Ga., about three miles. I suppose they had been here
five or six years when I got acquainted with them. I think
they came from N. C. but I don't know what part. I have just
heard this. He lived with the Indians right here in this
country, Floyd Co., Ga. He was recognized as having Indian
blood but I don't know whether he took part in the Indian
councils or not. He claimed to be 1/4 Cherokee Indian. I
don't know how much Indian blood the wife of Thomas Loyd
claimed. They had a farm here at that time. They had been
living on the farm when I came here. There were not a great
many Indians here when I came. I never heard of Thomas Loyd
or his wife being on any roll. All I know is that they were
recognized as having Indian blood by the whites and by the
Indians. I knew Geo. Loyd who went to the Ter. He was the
son of Old Thomas Loyd."
SIGNED: Wm. Shropshire, Rome, Ga., Jul 2 1908.
EXCEPTION CASE. 10448. Minnie May Evans & 1 child, App
#10477, Duncan, Arizona. Rejected. Total number of excep-
tions filed in this group -- 60. Original recommendation
renewed.

10449. MARY JANE STOFFORD,   Rome, Ga
Rejected. Claims thru "Water Hunter". See #10448.

10450. LIZZIE LUMPKIN KANE and 4 children, Rome, Ga
Rejected. Claims thru same source as Water Hunter. See #10448

10451. THOMAS JOHNSON, minor child,   Afton, Okla
Admitted. Claims thru grandfather and grandmother enrolled as
Thomas and Quaty Woodward in Del. Dis. #402. Uncles enrolled
as Red Bird Woodward, Del. #74, Stocking Woodward Del. #72.
ROLL P82 #15556 FCT COMM #32452 - Thomas Johnson - 15
                              by George Johnson, Gdn.

10452. HIRAM BLAKELY,   Tug River, W Va
Rejected. Applicant or ancestors were never enrolled. Does

not appear that they were living within the limits of the Cherokee domain in 1835-6 and '46, as recognized members of the tribe. Applicant was born in Kentucky in 1833. Does not appear that they ever lived with the Cherokees as recognized members of the tribe.

10453. NEVA C. PIERCE,   Grassy Creek, N C
Rejected. Sizemore case. See special report #417.

10454. MAE PIERCE and 2 children,   Grassy Creek, N C
Rejected. Sizemore case. See special report #417.

10455. ELEANOR B. BELL, minor child   St. Elmo, Tenn
           by Ada Jane Bell
Admitted. Niece of #4119. Grandparent, Albina M. Rogers,
Chapman 1841.
ROLL P5 #185 - Elanor B. Bell - 18
           by Ada Jane Bell, Gdn.

10456. WILLARD BELL and minor children,   St. Elmo, Tenn
           by Ada Jane Bell, Gdn.
Admitted. Nephew of #4119. Grandmother "Albina M. Rogers,
1841 Chap."
ROLL P5 #196 - Willard Bell - 12
           by Ada Jane Bell, Gdn.

10457. RAYMOND B. BELL,   St. Elmo, Tenn
Admitted. Nephew of #4119. Grandmother "Albina M. Rogers,
Chapman 1841."
ROLL P5 #190 - Raymond B. Bell - 23

10458. GOLDIE POSLEY,   Grassy Creek, N C
Rejected. Sizemore case. See Special report #417.

10459. ISLA MAY BELL,   St. Elmo, Tenn
Admitted. Niece of #4119. Grandmother "Elbina [sic] M. Rogers,
Chapman 1841."
ROLL P5 #188 - Isla May Bell - 25

10460. HENRY C. BELL,   St. Elmo, Tenn
           by Ada Jane Bell, Gdn.
Admitted. Nephew of Mary Jane Bell (4119) and claims from the
same source.
ROLL P5 #187 - Henry Charlton Bell - 20
           by Ada Jane Bell, Gdn.

10461. WILLIAM H. STUART,   Warner, Okla
Admitted. Claims thru mother enrolled as Soo-ke-Path-killer.
Half brothers enrolled as Joseph and John M. McDonald McDaniel
S. B. #125. Grandfather and grandmother and uncles and aunts
enrolled S. B. #121. [For Roll information See App 5082, Vol.
3]

10462. SARAH J. GIBBONY and 6 children,   Texanna, Okla
Admitted. Niece of #10641 and claims thru same source.   Ap-
plicant's father enrolled S. B. #125.
ROLL P65 #12121 FCT COMM #32443 - Sarah J. Gibbony   - 31
        12122   32446 - Maggie SIMMONS (dau)   - 15
        12123   32447 - Columbus SIMMONS (son)   - 12
        12124   32444 - Laura May GIBBONY (dau) - 9
        12125   32445 - Russel GIBBONY (son)   - 7
        12126   32448 - John William GIBBONY   - 4
                                (son)
        12127   2357m - Mary E. GIBBONY (dau)   - 1

10463. ROSA KIDWELL and 2 children,   Chant, Okla
Admitted. Niece of #10461; claims thru same source.   Sister
of #10462. Applicant's father enrolled S. B. #125.
ROLL P86 #16244 FCT COMM #22890 - Rosa Kidwell - 28
        16245   22891 - Nora (dau)   - 10
        16246   2888m - Clella (dau) - 1

10464. SALLIE CHARLES,   Tug River, W Va
Rejected. Applicant nor ancestors were ever enrolled.   Does
not appear that they were living within the limits of the
Cherokee domain in 1835-6 and 1846 as recognized members of
the tribe. Applicant's father and grandparents thru whom she
claims were born in Virginia.

10465. ETHEL QUINTON,)   Texanna, Okla
       ISAAC QUINTON,) 1st cousin once removed to #3080
       NANCY QUINTON,) By Roxie Haney, Gdn. and mother of
       MARY QUINTON,) "A. J." [Admitted]
ROLL P114 #21866 FCT COMM #12071 - Ethel M. Quinton - 17
        21867   12072 - Isaac S. (bro)   - 15
        21868   12073 - Nancy E. (sis)   - 13
        21869   12074 - Mary E. (sis)   - 11
                                by Roxie Haney, Gdn.

10466. MAMIE MARTIN,   Pryor Creek, Okla
Rejected. This applicant claims thru her husband who died Dec.
16, 1902.

10467. JOHN EDGAR McELRATH,   Oakland, Okla*
Admitted. Uncle of #8048; claims thru same source. [* "5101
Dover St., Oakland, Cal." on roll]
ROLL P94 #17872 - John Edgar McElrath - 62
        17873 - Alden (son)   - 17
        17874 - Clifford (son)   - 15

10468. ECK ROSS and 2 children,   Locust Grove, Okla
Admitted. Cousin to #99.
ROLL P120 #23054 FCT COMM #25508 - Eck Ross   - 47
        23055   2178m - Neoma (dau)   - 4
        23056   2179m - Henry Pigeon (son) - 1

51

10469. JOE SANDERS and 1 child,   Lometa, Okla
Admitted. 1/2 brother of #407. Father and mother of applicant enrolled in 322 Tahl. [For Roll information See App
9425, Vol. 4]

10470. NELLIE RATTLINGGOURD,   Gideon, Okla
Admitted. Half sister of #8272. Applicant enrolled in 1851
as "Gah-dah-nah" by Drennen, Del. 526. [For Roll information
See App 10299]

10471. MARTHA A. C. MILLS,   Egirid, W Va
Rejected. Sizemore case. See special report #417.

10472. MARY E. MAY and 2 children,   Coalgate, Okla
Rejected. It does not appear that applicant's ancestors were
parties to the treaties of 1835-6 or '46, nor enrolled with
the Cherokees. Misc. Test. P. 2487.
MISC. TEST. P. 2487. No 10472 - Mary E. May:
     "My name is Mary E. May; my post-office is Coalgate; Okla;
I was born in Garden Co., Ga. in 1855; I claim relationship to
the Cherokee Indians through my father, James Browning and he
was a quarter; he was born in Ardel Co., N. C.; I do not know
the year; it was formerly known as Roane Co.; my father was
born about 1827; my father always lived in the eastern states;
he moved from North Carolina to Georgia, I do not know the
year; my father claimed back through the Ford family and
Buckaloo family; in know of [sic] no enrollment of my people
and they never received any money or land from the government." SIGNED: Mary "X" E. May, Coalgate, Okla., Aug 31 1908.

10473. WM. H. HAMPTON,   Oran, Ga
Rejected. Blythe case. See Special report #153.

10474. ROB. L. ROBINSON and 7 children,   Springplace, Ga
Rejected. Brother of #725 and claims thru same source.

10475. MARY E. GREGORY,   Aurora, Mo
Rejected. Cousin of #551 and claims thru same source.

10476. JULIA A. HOOD,   Sellwood, Ore
Rejected. Cousin of #2324.

10477. MINNIE MAY EVANS and 1 child,   Duncan, Ariz
Rejected. Claims thru "Water Hunter". See #10448.

10478. NOAH T. HICKS,   Sackville, Mo
Rejected. Claims thru Alex. Brown. See special report #35.

10479. JASON L. ROBINSON and 2 children,   Springplace, Ga
Rejected. Brother of #725; claims thru same source.

10480. SARAH ANN MULIMAX and 4 children,   Trion, Ga
Rejected. Neither applicant nor ancestors ever enrolled. Does
not establish fact of descent from person who was a party to
the treaties of 1835-6 or '46.

10481. LILLY EDWARDS and 1 child,   Springplace, Ga
Rejected. Sister of #725; claims thru same source.

10482. GEORGIA A. WAYBOURN,   [no residence given]
Rejected. Duplicate of #9829. Her child enrolled thru father's
side in Group #4453.
MISC. TEST. P. 2349. App No 10482-9829 - Georgia A. Wayburn:
    "My name is Georgia A. Wayburn. My age is 33 years old. I
live in Collinsville, Rogers Co., Okla. I have lived here 20
years. I came from Texas; was born and raised there. I am a
claimant under the Dawes Commission, but have not been allowed. My case is pending. I have never been enrolled before.
I did not get any bread or strip money. I got my blood from my
mother's side. My mother Alsey Jane Smart, Barber before marriage. She lived with me and is in this District. She was born
and raised in Texas. I think my mother was enrolled by the
Dawes Commission, but has not received anything. Her blood
came from her mother's side. Capt. John Rogers was my great
grandfather. My mother's mother was Joanna Barber before marriage. She was born in Arkansas but moved to Texas. Her father's name was John Petty and her mother's name Elizabeth
Petty, or "Betty" was the daughter of Polly Dawson, nee
Rogers, who was the daughter of Capt. John Rogers. The Dawsons
were enrolled by the Dawes Commission and got their land. I do
not know if any of my ancestors were enrolled in 1851.   I do
not know that they ever associated with any other tribe of Indians than the Cherokees.   The case of Joanna Barber was ap-
pealed from the decision of the Commissioner of the Five Civilized Tribes. The case is still pending. (Capt. John Rogers
was a party to the treaty of Nechota of 1835, and was one of
the Old Settler Cherokee Chiefs. Information furnished by Mr.
Starr. He was the grandfather of the present Chief Wm. C.
Rogers.) The Chief Wm. C. Rogers drew Old Settler money. My
daughter is about 8 years old. She claims through me and
through her father, Wilson L. Rayburn. Her name is Edna
Wayburn, Roll No. 29337, Dawes Commission. Her father has been
dead 4 years last April. He was enrolled by the Dawes Commission also; Cherokee Roll No 29336. He may have been on the '80
Roll. He never received any Old Settler money, nor any of his
ancestors. He got his blood from his mother's side. Her name
was Gage, and her father's name was DAvid Gage, and she had a
brother named John Gage. I do not know whether the Gages were
enrolled in 1851. I do not know whether his people ever associated with any other tribe of Indians. He had brothers, Bill
Bob and William Wayburn. I don't know his sisters names, but
they live in this District. I don't know any of his mother's
brothers and sisters. Royal Wayburn is a half-brother to this

53

child by a different mother, but he is dead."
SIGNED: Georgia A. Waybourn, Claremore, Okla., Aug 27 1908.

10483. EDNA A. WAYBOURN, minor child,   Collinsville, Okla
            by Georgia A. Waybourn, Gdn.
Admitted. This minor is good thru her father and not thru her
mother. "Mary Ann Gage", grandmother 1040 Del.
ROLL P147 #28587 FCT COMM #29337 - Edna A. Waybourn - 6
                            by Georgia A. Waybourn, Gdn.

10484. ROBER AVARY,   Olive, Okla
Rejected. Uncle to #744.

10485. JOSEPH A. ROBINSON and 4 children, Springplace, Ga
Rejected. Sister [sic] of #725; claims thru same source.

10486. LEONA A. HARVEY and 6 children,   Egeria, W Va
Rejected. Sizemore case. See Special report #417.

10487. DELLA P. WALKER,   Egeria, W Va
Rejected. Sizemore case. See Special report #417.

10488. ANNA BAILEY and 1 child,   Dott, W Va
Rejected. Sizemore case. See Special report #417.

10489. CEBERRY S. GRAHAM,   Egeria, W Va
Rejected. Sizemore case. See Special report #417.

10490. THOS. B. COOK and 8 children,   Pinoak, W Va
Rejected. Sizemore case. See Special report #417.

10491. WILLIAM M. VERNON and 3 children,   Waleska, Ga.
Rejected. Son of #10492 and claims thru same source.

10492. JOSIAH VERNON,   Cherokee, Ga
Rejected. It does not appear that any ancestor was a party to
the treaties of 1835-6 or 1846; nor does it appear that any
ancestor was ever enrolled. Misc. Test. P. 1101.
MISC. TEST. P. 1101. No 10492 - Josiah Vernon:
    "I am 59 years of age; was born in Forsythe County, Ga.;
have spent my life most around Cherokee County. I claim Cherokee Indian blood through both my mother and father.   I have
never received any Indian money from the government. My father
nor mother ever received any Indian money. I never heard them
speak of receiving any money in 1852. I do not think they ever
tried to get any Indian money. They did not live with the Indians. My father was a voter. My grandfather Stephen Hays was
part Indian. I remember him. He lived in Hall County. I do not
know that he ever lived with the Indians. My grandmother on my
father's side was Indian. I remember her. She spoke the Indian
language but were recognized white people. My grandfather also
spoke the Indian language. In 1882 I lived here in this part

54

of the country. I did not hear of Hester, the enrolling agent
about that time. I first heard my grandparents speak of their
Indian blood. My grandfather claimed to be quarter Indian and
my grandmother a quarter Indian also. My grandmother was born
in Virginia but do not know where my grandfather was born."
SIGNED: Josiah Vernon, Canton, Ga., Jul 7 1908.
EXCEPTION CASE. Mary Vernon, App #15130, Waleska, Ga.
Rejected. Total number of exceptions filed in this group --
1. Original recommendation renewed.

10493. JOHN C. VERNON and 5 children, Waleska, Ga
Rejected. Son of #10492, claims through same source.

10494. JOE RAY, Waleska, Ga
Rejected. Claims through same source as #690.

10495. GEO. W. ROGERS, Sutter, Okla
Rejected. It does not appear that ancestors of applicant were
parties to the treaties of 1835-6 and 1846. Applicant shows
no real connection with the Eastern Cherokees.

10496. ALEX. DOWNING, Baron, Okla
Admitted. Applicant's grandmother Oo-cah-yah-ster was enrolled
in 1851 in G. S. Dis. Group #387. For their ancestral connections see G. S. Dis. 385 and 351. See Misc. Test. of Edward
Walkingstick in Ap 10500 taken at Westville, Oklahoma, Mar.
27, '09. p. 4044.
MISC. TEST. P. 4044. 10500-10498 - Edward Walkingstick...in
behalf of Tom Downing:
"I am 59 years of age. I am acquainted with Tom Downing
and knew his father and paternal grandparents. Tom's father
was Ned Te-na-kee or Ned Downing. I am now sure [sic] whether
Ned was living at the time of the payment or not, he was born
along about that time. Ned's mother was named Oo-cah-yah-stee.
Oo-cah-yah-stee's father was named Doo-che-stuh. Oocha-yah-
stee had a brother named Te-gah-nuh-way-de-ske, which means
digging a hole deeper. Her sister were Choh-go-hih, Gah-de-
cloh-ih, and Gah-ke-law-stah. (For Ned's mother see G. S. 387.
For Ned's mother's father and brother and sister see G. S.
385). Ned never lived with his father his mother raised him.
They always lived in Going Snake District. I don't know who
Oo-wah-le-nah-ste was. Ned Downing's father was named Oo-de-
skul-le Downing or in the time of the war he was called Hider
Downing. Oo-dee-skul-le had a sister named Cah-ta-goo-guh. See
G. S. 351."
SIGNED: Edward Walkingstick, Westville, Okla., Mar 27 1909.
ROLL P54 #9876 FCT COMM #15999 - Alex. Downing - 26

10497. SAMUEL BECK, Cherokee City, Okla
Admitted. 2nd cousin of #2671.
ROLL P28 #4718 FCT COMM #6428 - Samuel Beck - 21

10498. JOSHUA DOWNING,   Baron, Okla
Admitted. Brother of #10496; claims through same source.
ROLL P54 #9975 FCT COMM #1173 - Joshua Downing - 13

10499. TOM JONES, by Bird Jones, Father and Gdn.   Minor son
of #5775.
MISC. TEST. P. 3748. 5775. Also 10499 - Bird Jones:
    "I am about 66 years of age. Think I was enrolled in 51
under the name of Che-squa-dah-lo-nih. Both of my parents were
Emmigrants and were living in Delaware District. I was enrolled with my father, Che-nah-quih. My mother wasn't living
in 51. I had two brother enrolled with me named Stu-ee-skih,
Te-gah-glu-gay-skih. I had still older brother that was enrolled by himself named Gah-lah-soo-gee-skih.   See Del. 222.
Tom Jones, number 10499, is my son. My Dawes Commission number
is 25912."
SIGNED: Bird Jones, Locust Grove, Okla., Oct 3 1908.
[For Roll information See App 5775, Vol. 3]

10500. TOM DOWNING,   Baron, Okla
Admitted. Brother of #10498; claims through same source.
ROLL P55 #10039 FCT COMM #1170 - Tom Downing - 19

10501. NANCY RICHARDSON,   Woodstock, Ga
Rejected. Claims through same source as #7812.

10502. ALLIE M. RICHARDSON,   Woodstock, Ga
Rejected. Claims through same source as #7812.

10503. DELILAH RICHARDSON,   Woodstock, Ga
Rejected. Claims through same source as 7812.

10504. GARNETT D. RICHARDSON,   Woodstock, Ga
Rejected. Claims thru same source as #7812.

10505. GEORGE M. RICHARDSON,   Woodstock, Ga
Rejected. Claims thru same source as #7812.

10506. WILLIAM E. RICHARDSON,   Woodstock, Ga
Rejected. Claims thru same source as #7812.

10507. MAUD L. RICHARDSON,   Woodstock, Ga
Rejected. Claims thru same source as #7812.

10508. FRANK P. RICHARDSON,   Woodstock, Ga
Rejected. Claims thru same source as #7812.

10509. ALVA RICHARDSON,   Woodstock, Ga
Rejected. Claims thru same source as #7812.

10510. ALVIN RICHARDSON,   Woodstock, Ga
Rejected. Claims thru same source as #7812.

10511. CHARLIE M. RICHARDSON,   Woodstock, Ga
Rejected. Claims thru same source as #7812.

10512. JAMES D. RICHARDSON,   Woodstock, Ga
Rejected. Claims thru same source as #7812.

10513. LILA RICHARDSON,   Woodstock, Ga
Rejected. Claims thru same source as #7812.

10514. LUTIE RICHARDSON,   Woodstock, Ga
Rejected. Claims thru same source as #7812.

10515. WESLEY RICHARDSON,   Woodstock, Ga
Rejected. Claims thru same source as #7812.

10516. HARVEY A. RICHARDSON,   Woodstock, Ga
Rejected. Claims thru same source as #7812.

10517. LEACIE RICE,   Holly Springs, Ga
        by her father John B. Rice
Rejected. Hillhouse case. See special report #9847.

10518. GEORGIA WOODS,   Holly Springs, Ga
Rejected. Hillhouse case. See special report #9847.

10519. BEN WOODS,   Holly Springs, Ga
        by his mother, Georgia Woods
Rejected. Hillhouse case. See special report #9847.

10520. GRADIE WOODS,   Holly Springs, Ga
        by his mother, Georgia Woods
Rejected. Hillhouse case. See special report #9847.

10521. WM. H. WHEELER,   Holly Springs, Ga
Rejected. 3rd cousin of #2780; claims thru same source.

10522. JAMES E. THOMAS and 6 children,   Rome, Ga
Admitted. Son of #9838.
ROLL P18 #2670 - James H. Thomas   - 35
        2671 - William H. (son) - 13 [? last digit blurred]
        2672 - Herbert H. (son) - 11
        2673 - Annie J. (dau)   - 9
        2674 - Stella (dau)   - 5
        2675 - Thomas A. (son) - 3
        2676 - Harlin E. (son) - 1

10523. WM. W. SHAW,   Rome, Ga
Rejected. Does not appear that ancestors were parties to the
treaties of 1835-6 or '46; or that ancestors were ever enrolled. Misc. T. P. 953.
MISC. TEST. P. 953. #10524-10523 - Susan Jane Shaw:
    "That I am 54 years of age and live in Floyd Co., Ga. I

claim my Indian descent through my mother; don't know whether
my father was a full blooded white man or not; hardly think he
was. My mother claimed 1/4; her father was 1/2 Cherokee Indian. My mother was born and raised in Floyd Co., Ga. She
moved from here to La. about 52 years ago; they started to the
Cherokee Nation but never reached there. I think Martha Shipp
was mixed with Indian, but an not sure. She was the wife of my
grandfather through whom I claim. My mother nor father were
never on any rolls. My mother never lived with the Indians as
a member of the tribe; don't know whether Benjamin Shipp did
or not, but he lived here among the Indians before they were
carried away. He died about 50 years ago, about the time my
folks went to La. Emily Shipp who married Urser, Jane who married Tovery were sisters of my mother. Jackson, John, Richard
and Joe were my mother's brothers. This is the only application I ever made for benefits by reason of my Indian blood.
About 1896 I filled out some papers with the Dawes Commission
and sent them in but never heard anything more from them. My
husband claimed Indian on both sides. His mother claimed
about 1/3 Indian. Never heard how much his father claimed. It
was the Cherokee blood they claimed. My husband was a little
younger than I. His father and mother were never on any rolls
that I know of. His father nor mother never lived with the Indians as a member of the tribe that I know of. I am recognized
as a white woman, and my husband was recognized as a white
man. If he was considered as having some Indian in him, people
never spoke of it. My husband's father, Johnnie Shaw, was
brought to this country an orphan boy; if he had any brothers
and sisters, he didn't know it. My husband's mother, Jane
Shaw, had a sister Mattie Phelps who married Cobb and then
Selman. She had another sister Nancy who married a Cobb also.
Another named Mary who married Smith."
SIGNED: Susan Jane "X" Shaw, Rome, Ga., Jul 3 1908.

10524. SUSAN J. SHAW,   Rome, Ga
Rejected. Mother of 10523; claims thru same source.

10525. MAUD L. SHAW, by her mother,   Rome, Ga
Rejected. Sister of #10523; claims thru same source.

10526. ELLIS J. SHAW,   Rome, Ga
Rejected. Brother of #10523; claims thru same source.

10527. JESSE E. SHAW,   Rome, Ga
Rejected. Brother of #10523; claims thru same source.

10528. ODESSA SESSION,   Rome, Ga
Rejected. Sister of #10523; claims thru same source.

10529. AMROSE SHAW,   Rome, Ga
Rejected. Brother of #10523; claims thru same source.

10530. OSCAR TEE GRAVELY,   Rome, Ga
Rejected. Applicant's proof of genuine connection with Eastern Cherokees insufficient. No ancestor was ever enrolled. It
does not appear that any ancestor was a party to the treaties
of 1835-6 or '46. Misc. Test. P. 889.
MISC. TEST. P. 889. #11355-10530 - Ellen Lenora Gravely:
    "That I am 64 years of age and live in Rome, Ga. I claim
through my mother; my father is a full blooded white man. My
mother's father claimed the Indian. My grandmother on my mother's side was white. My mother was born and raised in Marshall
Co., Ala. She was born in 1828. Don't know where my grand
father on my mother's side was born, but think it was in Ala.
or Ga. I don't know whether my mother ever lived with the Indians or not. Don't know how much Indian my mother claimed.
Never was on any roll myself and don't know whether my mother
was or not. I guess my mother's father was but I don't know
what roll it was. My grandfather never had any other name than
Kennedy that I know of. I am recognized as a white woman in
the community. I never lived amongst the Indians. This is the
only application I ever made by reason of my Indian blood."
SIGNED: Ellen Lenora "X" Gravely, Rome, Ga., Jul 2 1908.
EXCEPTION CASE. Ellen Elnora Gravely, App #11355, R. 3, Rome,
Ga. Rejected. Total number of exceptions filed in this group
-- 1. Original recommendation renewed.

10531. THOMAS A. GRAVELY,   Rome, Ga
Rejected. Brother of Oscar Tee Gravely (10530).

10532. GEORGE RAY,   Ferrobutte, Ga
Rejected. Claims thru same source as #690.

10533. ED RAY,   Nelson, Ga
Rejected. White mire case. See special report #2546.

10534. ANNA ELIZABETH PERRY and 5 children, Rome, Ga
Rejected. Claims thru "Water Hunter". See 10448.

10535. ROBERT LEE LLOYD and 5 children,   Rome, Ga
Rejected. Claims thru "Water Hunter". See 10448.

10536. NORA L. LLOYD,   Rome, Ga
Rejected. Claims thru "Water Hunter". See 10448.

10537. JAMES M. LLOYD,   Rome, Ga
         by James A. B. Lloyd, father and Gdn.
Rejected. Claims thru "Water Hunter". See 10448.

10538. JAMES ANDERSON B. LLOYD,   Rome, Ga
Rejected. Claimant is a brother of Geo. A. Lloyd #10448 and
is rejected for the reasons set forth in that case.

10539. HOMER M. LOYD,   Rome, Ga
Rejected. Claims thru "Water Hunter". See 10448.

10540. HARPER H. LOYD,   Rome, Ga
Rejected. Claims thru "Water Hunter". See 10448.

10541. GEORGE ALEXANDER LOYD,   Rome, Ga
Rejected. Claims thru "Water Hunter". See 10448.

10542. BESSIE LOYD,   Rome, Ga
Rejected. Claims thru "Water Hunter". See 10448.

10543. OSCAR DAVIS,   Lindale, Ga
Rejected. Applicant's proof of genuine connection with the
Eastern Cherokees insufficient. There is a Nancy Davis on the
roll but it appears that this is not the one thru whom these
people are claiming. No ancestors of these people were ever
enrolled. It appears that none of them were parties to the
treaties of 1835-6 or '46. Misc. Test. P. 893.
MISC. TEST. P. 893. #10544 with #10543 - Henry Davis:
     "That I am 56 years of age and live in Floyd Co., Ga. I
claim through my mother; my father was a full blooded white
man. It was my grandmother and great grandmother on my mother's side who were the Indians. My grandmother claimed to be
3/4 Cherokee. My grandmother was raised in the Indian Trial
[sic], N. C. - within a few miles of Raleigh. We first moved
from N. C. during the last year of the War. All of my ancestors were raised right there in N. C. My grandmother was connected with the Indian tribe as a member, to the best of my
knowledge. I have heard grandmother say she thought she was on
some roll, but I don't know what. My grandmother and mother
were in N. C. when this roll was made. My grandmother lived
several years after the war out in Indian Ter. She never received anything from the government that I know of. I am not
on any roll that I know of. I was born among the Cherokee Indians, near Raleigh, N. C. Some people call me part Indian and
some don't. I am recognized as a white man in the community. I
filed an application with the Dawes Commission in 1896, but I
never heard any more of it. I made my proof and that was the
last of it." SIGNED: Henry "X" Davis, Rome, Ga., Jul 2 1908.
EXCEPTION CASE.   Henry Davis, App #10544, Lindale, Ga.
Rejected. Total number of exceptions filed in this group --
1. Original recommendation renewed.

10544. HENRY DAVIS,   Lindale, Ga
Rejected. Father of Oscar Davis (10543) thru whom he claims.

10545. FANNIE HOMER COLLINS and 5 children, Rome, Ga
Rejected. Claims thru "Water Hunter". See 10448.

10546. WM. H. ATKINS,   Cartecay, Ga
Rejected. Whitmire Case. See special report #2516.

10547. WEBSTER B. ATKINS,   Waleska, Ga
Rejected. Whitmire Case. See special report #2516.

10548. GEORGE W. ATKINS,   Nelson, Ga
Rejected. Whitmire Case. See special report #2516.

10549. CALVIN V. ATKINS,   Nelson, Ga
Rejected. Whitmire Case. See special report #2516.

10550. BENJAMIN M. ATKINS,   Nelson, Ga
Rejected. Whitmire Case. See special report #2516.

10551. BERRY I. ATKINS,   Nelson, Ga
Rejected. Whitmire Case. See special report #2516.

10552. LILA G. ATHERTON and 1 child,   Nelson, Ga
Rejected. Applicant or ancestors were never enrolled. Does
not appear that they were living within the limits of the
Cherokee domain in 1835-6 and '46 as recognized members of the
tribe. Applicant failed to appear and answer notice to take
testimony. The person thru whom she claims was born in Virginia.
EXCEPTION CASE. Rejected. Total number of exceptions filed
in this group — 73. Original recommendation renewed.

10553. EDNA B. DOBBS,   Woodstock, Ga
Rejected. 3rd cousin to #2780; claims thru same source.

10554. MATTIE MAY DOBBS,   Woodstock, Ga
Rejected. 3rd cousin to #2780; claims thru same source.

10555. LESLIE LEE DOBBS,   Route #1, Woodstock, Ga
Rejected. 3rd cousin once removed of #2780; claims thru same
source.

10556. FANNIE O. DOBBS,   Woodstock, Ga
Rejected. 3rd cousin once removed of #2780; claims thru same
source.

10557. AUGUSTA A. HILLHOUSE,   Holly Springs, Ga
Rejected. Hillhouse case. See special report #9847.

10558. SUSAN HOWARD,   Holly Springs, Ga
Rejected. Hillhouse case. See special report #9847.

10559. JACKSON JORDAN,   Ft. Payne, Ala
Rejected. Claims thru same source as #7812.

10560. GEORGE KUY KENDALL,   Woodstock, Ga
Rejected. 3rd cousin of #2780. Claims thru same source.

10561. NORA LOVINGROOD,   Holly Springs, Ga
Rejected. Hillhouse case. See special report #9847.

10562. JAS. E. McGINNIS,   Marietta, Ga
Rejected. 3rd cousin twice removed to #2780; claims thru the
same source.

10563. JOHN N. McGINNIS,   Atlanta, Ga
Rejected. 3rd cousin of #2780; claims thru same source.

10564. WM. McGINNIS,   Marietta, Ga
Rejected. 3rd cousin once removed of #2780; claims thru same
source.

10565. LAWRENCE McGINNIS,   Marietta, Ga
Rejected. 3rd cousin twice removed of #2780; claims thru same
source.

10566. HARRIET MILLER,   Woodstock, Ga
Rejected. Great aunt of #7811 and claims thru same ancestors.

10567. AUGUSTUS MILLER,   Woodstock, Ga
Rejected. Cousin of #7811 and claims thru same ancestors.

10568. JENNIE MILLER,   Woodstock, Ga
Rejected. Cousin of #7811 and claims thru same ancestors.

10569. MARCUS MILLER,   Woodstock, Ga
Rejected. Cousin of #7811; claims thru same ancestors.

10570. PAUL REECE,   Marietta, Ga
Rejected. Claims thru Abraham Helton. See #2780.

10571. EMILY RICE,   Holly Springs, Ga
Rejected. Hillhouse case. See special report #9847.

10572. JOHN B. RICE,   Holly Springs, Ga
Rejected. Hillhouse case. See special report #9847.

10573. ADLAID RICE,   Holly Springs, Ga
        by her father, John B. Rice, Gdn.
Rejected. Hillhouse case. See special report #9847.

10574. GRACIE RICE,   Holly Springs, Ga
        by her father, John B. Rice
Rejected. Hillhouse case. See special report #9847.

10575. HANSELL RICE,   Holly Springs, Ga
        by his father, John B. Rice
Rejected. Hillhouse case. See special report #9847

10576. JAMES RICE,   Holly Springs, Ga
            by his father, John B. Rice
Rejected. Hillhouse case. See special report #9847

10577. JOSEPH RICE, JR.,   Holly Springs, Ga
            by his father, John B. Rice
Rejected. Hillhouse case. See special report #9847

10578. LUTHER RICE,   Holly Springs, Ga
            by his father, John B. Rice
Rejected. Hillhouse case. See special report #9847

10579. SARAH MARTINDALE,   Sallisaw, Okla
Rejected. Applicant's brothers and sisters living in 1851 enrolled as old settlers. See old settler Roll #222. This claimant, born in 1853, is conclusively of old settler descent.
Nothing shown in this case to establish an Emigrant Cherokee
right as her parents were not enrolled with such in 1851.

10580. SARAH MARTINDALE, Duplicate of #10579.

10581. RED BIRD BIG ACORN,   Southwest City, Mo
Admitted. The parents and one sister of the applicant were
enrolled in 241 Del. in 1851. See Misc. Test. P. 4304.
MISC. TEST. P. 4304. #10581 - Redbird Big Acorn...through Tom
Roach, Interpreter:
    "I am 49 years old; Both of my parents were Emigrants. My
father's name was Goo-la-guah. My mother's name was Wah-lee-
yuh. She also went by the name of An-nih. My parents were
living together in 1851; They were living in Delaware District; I had a sister by the name of Susie. I think that she
drew the money in 1851; (See 241 Del. for the enrollment of
the parents and sister of the applicant.) I have no brothers
or sisters living - nor any children living. I have never been
married. I am a Night Hawk. In have [sic] never been known by
any other name Red Bird Big Acorn of Taw-choo-wah Goo-la-
quuh." SIGNED: Redbird Big Acorn, Eucha, Okla., Mar 20 1909.
ROLL P29 #4971 - Red Bird Big Acorn - 47

10582. LACY SKAHGINNE, Duplicate of #1700.

10583. MANDA JACKSON 10 children,   Vinita, Okla
Admitted. Sister to Katie Silversmith #1735 and claims thru
same source.
ROLL P81 #15295 FCT COMM #26468 - Mauda Jenkins   - 38
          15296   26469 - Walter (son)   - 19
          15297   26470 - Fannie (dau)   - 17
          15298   26471 - Johnnie (son)   - 14
          15299   26472 - Levi (son)   - 12
          15300   26473 - Lizzie (dau)   - 11
          15301   26476 - Rufus (son)   - 10
          15302   26474 - Lulu (dau)   - 9

                            63

10583. MANDA JACKSON/JENKINS (Cont)
          15303 FCT COMM #26475 - Dolly (dau)   - 7
          15304   26477 - Otis (son)   - 5
          15305   2230m - Theodore (son) - 2

10584. JIM ELLICK and 2 children,   Southwest City, Mo
Admitted. Applicant's father and mother enrolled by Drennen
in Del. Dist. #232 under names of Allickey and Jinney.
ROLL P57 #10576 FCT COMM #19489 - Jim Ellick   - 56
          10577   19488 - Nellie (wife) - 55
                                   (App 10585)
          10578   19492 - Polly (dau)   - 19
          10579   19491 - Coon (son) - 18 (App 26064)
          10580   19492 - Johnson (son) - 14

10585. NELLIE ELLICK,   Southwest City, Mo
Admitted. Sister of #630; claims thru same source. See 13215
duplicate. [For Roll information See App 10584]

10586. OO-AQIW-NI OO-CHI-LA-TA,   Southwest City, Mo
Admitted. Claims thru self enrolled as Oo-scoo-ne mother enrolled as Lau-te-ti-ye. Brother enrolled as Culle-ska-we. Enrolled by Drennen in 1851 in Del. Dis. Group #228. [For Roll
information See App 10587]

10587. THOMPSON OO-CHI-LA-TA,   Southwest City, Mo
Admitted. Claims thru father and mother enrolled as Oo-lau-
kit-te and Warl-se-na.   Sisters enrolled as Te-gu-la-ske and
A-key. Applicant is probably enrolled as Oo-hearn-clau-e.
Del. #150.
ROLL P106 #20316 - Thompson Oo-chi-la-ta - 63
          20317 - Oo-squi-ne (wife)   - 64 (App 10586)

10588. JOSEPH SMITH,   Webbers Falls, Okla
Admitted. Brother to #9402.
ROLL P129 #24868 FCT COMM #17039 - Joseph Smith - 31

10589. SAMUEL J. STARR and 3 children,   Evansville, Ark
Admitted. Brother of #2204. [NOTE: only 1 child on roll -
The FCT Nos. of Geo. E. Starr (32911) and Martin C. Starr
(32912) fall between those of Saml J. & Joseph Starr]
ROLL P132 #25504 FCT COMM #1830 - Samuel J. Starr - 39
          25505   1834 - Joseph (son)   - 10

10590. LOUCINDA NEELEY, Duplicate of #5327.

10591. SALLIE BALLARD,   Braggs, Okla
Admitted. Niece of #4524. [For Roll information See App 10593]

10592. CLARENCE T. MADDEN, JACK J. MADDEN, Braggs, Okla
          JOSEPH HOWARD MADDEN, Minors, by William Ballard, Gdn.
Admitted. Grand nephew of #1596; claims thru same ancestors.

64

```
ROLL P95 #18175 FCT COMM #28235 - Clarence T. Madden  -  6
        18176            32018 - Jack J. (bro)         -  4
        18177                  - Joseph Howard (bro) -  1
                         by William Ballard, Gdn.
```

10593. WILLIAM BALLARD and 5 children,   Braggs, Okla
Admitted. Nephew of #1596; claims thru same source.

```
ROLL P25 #4142 FCT COMM #16774 - William Ballard  - 31
        4143           16775 - Sallie (wife)     - 27
                               (App 10591)
        4144           16776 - Thomas H. (son)   - 10
        4145           16777 - John J. (son)     -  8
        4146           16778 - Carrie M. (dau)   -  6
        4147           16779 - Donald L. (son)   -  4
        4148           2828m - Capitola L. (dau) -  2
```

10594. ELIZABETH CONRAD,   Braggs, Okla
Rejected. Special report below:
                    No #10594.
     The applicant and   others whose applications are grouped
herewith claim their right to participate in the fund arising
from the judgment of the Court of Claims in favor of the Eastern Cherokees thru one Samuel Martin who they claim was enrolled in 1835. Samuel Martin was the grandfather of the applicant. Applicant's mother was Minerva Davis, nee Martin.
Her father was the said Samuel Martin.
     Applicant's mother was living in 1851, but was not en-
rolled. The applicant and others, whose applications are
grouped herewith were refused allotments as Cherokees in Oklahoma. Samuel Martin was enrolled in 1835 in Tennessee. His
name is found on page 8 of the Roll of 1835 at the head of a
family of seven. There was one white person in this family,
associated by marriage; there were seven quarter bloods, no
half bloods, and no full bloods.
     "It is evident therefore, that Samuel Martin or his wife
was a white person. Then the other spouse must have been a
half blood, because of the fact that the other members of the
family, that it [sic] the children, were quarter bloods. It
can but be presumed that the half blood was the wife of Samuel
Martin and that she had died prior to the year 1835 and Samuel
Martin was enrolled at the head of the family and he is the
white person mentioned as being associated by marriage. If
Minerva Martin, the mother of the applicant, was one of the 7
mentioned on the 1835 Roll, then she would have been entitled
to enrollment in 1851 and her children would have been entitled to allotments in Indian Territory.
     The fact that Minerva Martin was not enrolled in 1851 and
that her children were refused allotments in Indian Territory
leaves but one conclusion, that is, that Samuel Martin, after
the death of his first wife, who was a half blood married a
white woman and that the said Minerva Martin was the offspring
of the second union. According to the Cherokee customs, if a

```
```

person married a Cherokee by blood and was thus associated
with the tribe by marriage and after the death of the spouse,
who was a Cherokee by blood, that party then married a white
person, or some one not a descendant of the Cherokees by
blood, he or she, then lost whatever rights he or she had with
the Cherokees by reason of the first marriage.

The applicant give Sallie Martin as the wife of said
Samuel Martin. Applicant #36506, who has been alloted land in
Oklahoma, gives as grandfather, Samuel Martin, and as his
grandmother, Catherine Martin. Therefore, Catherine Martin
must have been a Cherokee by blood and the first wife of
Samuel Martin and the said Sallie Martin, who is the grand
mother of applicant #10594, must have been a white person, or
a person not a descendant of Cherokee by blood. Therefore the
right to participate in this fund cannot be established by the
fact, that the party is a descendant of Samuel Martin but it
must be further shown that they claim thru a wife of the said
Samuel Martin, who was a Cherokee by blood; and it not appearing that these applicants were of such descent but appearing
that they are not Cherokee by blood, they and their ancestors
living in 1851 not having been enrolled and they, themselves,
refused allotments in Indian Territory, their applications to
participate in this fund are rejected. See Misc. Test. P. 3120
MISC. TEST. P. 3120. No 10594 – Elizabeth Conrad:

"I am 49 years of age; am not a Cherokee alotte. I was
born in Illinois District. My mother, Minerva Martin, was the
Indian. She came here after the Immigrants came. My grand father came here with the Immigrants. Ten years before the war
my mother lived in Illinois District. I have one older brother. He was born in Tennessee. He came here when my mother
came. My grandfather was killed just after the Immigrants came
west. My mother's mother was Lila Munday or Martin. She was
a white woman. My mother did not speak the Cherokee language.
Her father talked English and Cherokee. Her mother who was a
white woman raised her. My grandfather, Sam Martin, was a
Cherokee. He came to the Nation with the Immigrants. He was
killed shortly after the Immigrants came. We did not push our
allotment claim because we were unable to pay the lawyers. I
do not know why my mother was not paid if she was not paid in
1852. My mother stopped in Missouri for a year on her way out
here and that may have been the year of the payment."
SIGNED: Elizabeth Conrad, Muskogee, Okla., Sep 23 1908.
EXCEPTION CASE. Rejected. Total number of exceptions filed
in this group —— 3. Original recommendation renewed.

10595. GEORGE GRIMET,   Vian, Okla
Admitted. Son of #9377; claims thru same source.
MISC. TEST. P. 3028. Interpreter Used. App No 10595 – George
Grimet:

"My name is George Grimet. My age is 27 years. I have
Cherokee Indian blood. I was born and raised in Illinois District. I was enrolled by the Dawes Commission as they came

around, but I did not get an allotment. I got the strip money.
I am a full-blood. My mother is Wa-gie or Peggy Locust; or
Quakie or Peggy Locut. She is living. She is over 50 years
of age. I don't know whether she was enrolled by the Dawes
Commission. Got the strip money. I do not know where she lived
when a girl. She had brothers and sisters. Her brothers were
Gi-yan-ne or Gar-yar-ne; Ju-lah was next to the oldest; Chick-
ka-dih-lih or Chicken-fighter in English; it might be Chick-
aw-de-lee; she had sisters but I do not know their names. His
grandmother on mother's side was Ga-hu-nah or Ga-yuh-nee. They
lived in Flint District. My mother's father was Arch. He also
lived in Flint. I do not know if he had any brothers and sisters. I don't know whether he had any other name than Arch. My
father's name was Yan or Yo-nah meaning Bear Grimet. He was
killed about 23 years ago. I don't know whether he got money
in 1851. My father's mother's name was Ar-het-e meaning
Carried in English. She probably lived in Flint District. I
don't know whether she had any brothers and sisters. I don't
know my grandfather's name. I do not know where my ancestors
came from. I do not know if they were regarded as Old Settlers
or not. I don't know whether they ever joined any other tribe
of Indians. (Geo. Grimet Dawes No 25754 and Turner Grimet
#28445.) Turner is my brother. Do not know Polly Locust."
SIGNED: George Grimet, Sallisaw, Okla., Sep 19 1908.
ROLL P68 #12680 FCT COMM #25754 – George Grimet – 25
        12681   25750 – Ida (wife) – 24 (App 10671)

10596. GEORGE DEW,   Moodys, Okla
Admitted. Claims thru the father enrolled as O-see Ah-he-sah-
te-skee. Grandfather and grandmother enrolled as Ah-he-sah-ta-
skee (Dew) and Lucy. Aunts enrolled as Anna and Sally, G S 79.
ROLL P53 #9657 FCT COMM #18479 – George Dew – 18

10597. ROBERT W. WALKER, FRANK T. WALKER, Tahlequah, Okla
        JOHN W. WALKER, by their father, William H. Walker
Admitted. Nephew of #5793; claims thru same source. Duplicate of Suppl. of 7646. Minor children. [For Roll information See App 7646, Vol. 4]

10598. JAMES PUMPKIN and 1 child,   Moodys, Okla
Admitted. Son of #8259 and claims thru same source.
ROLL P113 #21830 FCT COMM #18884 – James Pumpkin – 33
        21831   18885 – Mary (wife) – 27
                               (App 10697)
        21832   18886 – Richard (son) – 12
                               (App 16085)
                         by George Pumpkin, Gdn.
[NOTE: son Richard's residence "Whitmire Ok", Geo. Pumpkin
(App 16098) is a brother of James]

10599. LUCINDA SMITH,   Stilwell, Okla
Admitted. Niece of #2339.

ROLL P129 #24904 FCT COMM #26964 - Lucinda Smith - 38

10600. WILLIS DAVIS,   Braggs, Okla
Rejected. Claims thru same source as 10594.

10601. JOE IRVING and 6 children,   Braggs, Okla
Admitted. Applicant's mother probably enrolled in 1851 as
"Nancy Lovell" Ill. #10 as she was first married to Lovett.
Maiden name "Hildebrand". Michael Hildebrand, grandfather
"1534 Chapman". Cousin of #859.
ROLL P80 #15105 FCT COMM #23121 - Joe Irving   - 43
          15106   23123 - Watie (son) - 16
          15107   23124 - Roy (son)   - 10
          15108   23125 - Grover (son) - 8
          15109   23126 - Samuel (son) - 6
          15110   2000m - Renie (dau) - 4
          15111   2001m - Venie (dau) - 2

10602. LUCY WEIGAND,   Braggs, Okla
Rejected. Half sister of 8764 ["#10715" crossed out].
EXCEPTION CASE. Rejected. Half-sister of #8764.

10603. JAMES LOVITT and 2 children,   Braggs, Okla
Admitted. Nephew of #4708; claims thru same source.
ROLL P91 #17325 FCT COMM # 5063 - James Lovitt   - 32
          17326   5064 - Irene (dau)   - 5
          17327   4748m - Ina Bell (dau) - 3

10604. CORNELIUS E. WRIGHT and 2 children, Christie, Okla
Admitted. Son of #1848; claims thru same source.
ROLL P154 #29963 FCT COMM #29437 - Cornelius E. Wright - 30
          29964   4635m - Jack (son)   - 4
          29965   4636m - Claude (son)   - 1

10605. CAROLINE ALEXANDER,   Westville, Okla
Admitted. Niece of #654; claims thru same source. [For Roll
information See App 2225, Vol. 2]

10606. ELIZA ANDRE,   Ft. Gibson, Okla
Admitted. 1st cousin of #8862.
ROLL P23 #3773 FCT COMM #5437 - Eliza Andre - 59

10607. JOHN S. McCAY and 4 children,   Inola, Okla
Admitted. 2nd cousin to #3080; claims thru the same source.
Father of applicant, William McCay, was enrolled in 1851, in
Disputed District No. 97.
ROLL P92 #17598 FCT COMM #11850 - John S. McCay   - 31
          17599   11852 - William L. (son) - 9
          17600   11853 - Claude R. (son) - 7
          17601   11854 - Watson B. (son) - 5
          17602   2371m - Ruth (dau)   - 2

10608. LEROY G. LOWTHER and 4 children,   Inola, Okla
Admitted. 1st cousin once removed to #3080. Mother of appli-
cant enrolled in 1851 under name of Jane McCay in Disputed
District No. 97. See letter herewith.
ROLL P91 #17438 FCT COMM #24736 - Leroy G. Lowther - 53
         17439   24739 - Wayne S. (son)   - 13
         17440   24740 - Lem M. (son)   - 10
         17441   4754m - Laura E. (dau)   - 4
         17442   4755m - Viola F. (dau)   - 2/3

10609. ELIZABETH A. A. HILL,   Norman, Okla
Rejected. It does not appear that any ancestor was ever enrolled or that any ancestor was party to the treaty of 1835-6
or '46. Shows no connection with the Eastern Cherokees.   It
appears that no ancestor has lived with the tribe since about
1789. See letters herewith.
MISC. TEST. P. 2029. No 14044-10609 - Elizabeth A. A. Hill:
    "My name is Elizabeth A. A. Hill; my post office is Nor-
man, R. F. D. No. 6, Okla.; Hasel Hill, No 14044 is a daughter
of mine, Niota B. Rees, No. 11715 is also a daughter, Edna H.
Chilton [?], No 14045 is also a daughter; Stella E. Allen No.
10885 is a second cousin of mine; I was born in the state of
Indiana at Carthage, Rush Co. in the year 1849; I make claim
to the Cherokee Indians through my father, Herman H. Allen; my
father claims through his mother, Anne Clark; my fa- ther was
born in North Carolina in Gilford Co.   I will have my aunt,
Nancy Dick, send her testimony giving the full family history
into Washington." SIGNED: Elizabeth A. A. Hill, Aug 20 1908.
EXCEPTION CASE. Isadell J. Sanders & 2 children, App #32800,
Chicago, Ill. Rejected. Total number of exceptions filed in
this group -- 2. Original recommendation renewed.

10610. JANE SUNDAY,   Tulsa, Okla
Admitted. Niece of #175.
ROLL P135 #26024 FCT COMM #12738 - Jane Sunday - 30

10611. ANDREW J. HENSON and 2 children,   Owasso, Okla
Admitted. Son of #72. Mother. She is enrolled by Chapman 1305.
ROLL P74 #13880 FCT COMM #11549 - Andrew J. Henson - 40
        13881   11550 - Chili (son)   - 17
        13882   - Joseph (son)   - 1/12

10612. JOHN W. HENRY and 1 child,   Longmont or Denver, Colo*
Admitted. Son of #138. [* Longmont, Colo on roll]
ROLL P74 #13832 FCT COMM #6196 - John W. Henry - 33
        13833   6197 - Almel (dau)   - 12

10613. THOMAS MILLER,   Verdigris, Okla
Admitted. Half brother of #2118 on father's side.
ROLL P100 #19067 FCT COMM #3306 - Thomas Miller - 28
         19068   3307 - Sarah (dau)   - 7

10614. JOHN PICAMAN,   Claremore, Okla
        for his (7) minor children,
[Admitted] Nieces and nephews of #248.
ROLL P111 #21375 FCT COMM #11344 - Clara M. Picaman - 18
           21376   11345 - Clarence M. (bro) - 18
           21377   11346 - Jennie (sis)   - 16
           21378   11347 - August C. (bro)   - 14
           21379   11348 - Julius W. (bro)   - 11
           21380   11349 - Dewey M. (bro)   - 8
           21381   11350 - Caroline S. (sis) - 6
                                 by John Picaman, Gdn.

10615. LOUIS C. BUTTRY and 6 children,   Claremore, Okla
Rejected. Cousin of #551; claims thru same source.

10616. SAM BUCKSKIN,   Kansas, Okla
Admitted. Son of #84. [Notation on roll "Redbird, Sam.   See
Roll No. 6136."]
ROLL P35 #6136 - Sam Buckskin - 26

10617. SIDENY R. NEAL,   Bartlelville, Okla
Rejected. Claims thru Benjamin and Gardner Green. See #5145.

10618. LOUISA JANE STARR,   Huntsville, Mo
Rejected. Claims thru Benjamin and Gardner Green. See #5145.

10619. SQUIRE JUDSON NEAL,   Tuscumbia, Mo
Rejected. Claims thru Benjamin and Gardner Green. See #5145.

10620. GEORGE A. McKENZIE,   Paunee, Okla
Rejected. Claims thru Benjamin and Gardner Green. See #5145.

10621. ALBERT FLOOD and 2 children,   Oran, Ga
Rejected. Grand son of #4809 and claims thru same source.

10622. ELIZABETH WATTS and 1 child,   Ft. Mountain, Ga
Rejected. Cousin of #4809 and claims thru same source.

10623. JOSEPHINE BEAVERS and 2 children,   Ft. Mountain, Ga
Rejected. Granddaughter of #4809 and claims thru same source.

10624. ELIZA BELLEW and 6 children,   Ft. Mountain, Ga
Rejected. Cousin of #4809; claims thru same source.

10625. JOSEPH HAWKINS,   Locust Grove, Okla
Admitted. Full brother of #8149.
ROLL P73 #13600 FCT COMM #18430 - Joseph Hawkins - 40

10626. NELLIE WICKLIFF and 1 child,   Spavinaw, Okla
Admitted. Applicant's parents were enrolled by Drennen in
Saline District #257. Misc. Test. P. 3882.
MISC. TEST. P. 3882. #10626-9608 - Nellie Wickliff:

70

"My name is Nellie Wickliff. I was born in Saline District
in 1871. I was not enrolled by the Dawes Commission. I am a
full-blood Cherokee. My father and mother were born in Georgia. My parents came from Georgia to the Indian Territory
during the Emigration. They came about 1839. Neither I nor any
of the ancestors thru whom I claim ever received any Old Settler. None of my ancestors were Old Settlers. My ancestors and
I have always remained with the Cherokee tribe. Both my parents were living in Saline District in 1851. They were enrolled at that time and drew Emigrant money. I do not know
what names my parents were enrolled under in 1851. I do not
know the names of my grandparents on my fathers side. They
died back in the Old Nation. My grandparents on my mother's
side came from the Old Nation to the Indian Territory with the
Emigrant Cherokees. They were enrolled in 1851 in Saline District. My grandfather's name was Dee-gah-hee-gee-skih and my
grandmother's Cherokee name was Oo-gah-wee-yih. My grandfather
and grandmother were not living together in 1851. Dee-gah-hee-
gees-skih was living in Delaware District. His wife at that
time was Chah-wah-you-cah. They had two children by the name
of Tau-you-we-se and Tau-yah. (See 259 Del) My mother had a
sister by the name of Tar-ne. Ool-sah-getah was Tar-ne's
child. I do not know who Nee-yernske was. (See 256 Sal) My
father and mother were also enrolled in Saline District. They
had a child by the name of Oo-taar-ne-yeh-teh who was enrolled
with them. (See Sal. 257 for mother and father and brother.)
I was enrolled for the Strip payment in 1894 and drew money at
that time."
SIGNED: Nellie Wickliff, Locust Grove, Okla., Oct 7 1908.
[For Roll information See App 10427]

10627. NIGHT CHICKEN, Locust Grove, Okla
Admitted. Brother of #10626 and claims thru same source.
ROLL P41 #7312 FCT COMM #32872 - Night Chicken - 42
        7313   32873 - See-kee (wife) - 24
                      (App 10649)

10628. GEORGE FENCE and 1 child, Kansas, Okla
Admitted. Claims thru grandfather and grandmother enrolled as
Arch Chu-dah-la and Aa-si. Uncle enrolled as Gah-law-ne-dah,
Del. #672. Mother was not born in 1851.
MISC. TEST. P. 3785. 10628 - George Fence:
"I am about 27 years of age. Both of my parents were emi-
grants. Think they were living in 1851. My mother may not have
been living in 51 but am pretty sure my father was. My moth-
er's parents were Arch Chu-had-la and Na-se. Gah-law-ne-dah
which in English means God was my mother's brother. See Del.
672. Madison Stover is my half brother on my mother's side. My
Daws Commission Roll Number is 32775."
SIGNED: George Fence, Locust Grove, Okla., Sep 28 1908.
ROLL P59 #10986 FCT COMM #32775 - George Fence - 23
        10987   4901m - Dick (son)   - 1

10629. ANDREW ROSS,   Locust Grove, Okla
Admitted. Brother of #99.
ROLL P119 #23027 FCT COMM #29500 - Andrew Ross - 34

10630. JOHN HICKORY,   Locust Grove, Okla
Admitted. Evidence shows that applicant and his mother were
emigrant Cherokees and are considered as such by every one
whom knows them. Applicant never drew any old settler money.
See Misc. Test. P. 4281.
MISC. TEST. P. 4281.   #10630 - Charley Ketcher...thru Martin
Squirrel, Interpreter:
    "I am 64 years old and have known John Hickory for more
than 30 years. I knew his mother and known that she was an
emmigrant Cherokee. I do not know about his father but I
thing [sic] that his father was an emmigrant also, but I am
sure that his mother was an emmigrant. John Hickory never
drew any Old Settler money."
SIGNED: Charley Ketcher, Locust Grove, Okla., Mar 12 1909.
ROLL P74 #13994 FCT COMM #17617 - John Hickory - 29

10631. JENNIE SIXKILLER,   Locust Grove, Okla
Admitted. Sister to #99. [For Roll information See App 684,
Vol. 1]

10632. NED CHICKEN and 2 children,   Spavinaw, Okla
Admitted. Brother of #10626; claims thru same source.
[For Roll information See App 10429]

10633. ESTER JANIE MARTIN and 8 children, Gainesville, Ga
                                              R F D #10
Admitted. Daughter of #159 and claims thru same source.
ROLL P13 #1649 - Ester Janie Martin - 32
         1650 - Van B. (son)   - 15
         1651 - David Lee (son)   - 14
         1652 - Gurley (son)   - 11
         1653 - Frances (dau)   - 10
         1654 - Lenar (son)   - 7
         1655 - Thomas E (son)   - 5
         1656 - Kate (dau)   - 3
         1657 - Smith A. (son)   - 1

10634. LEW M. HAYES,   Gainesville, Ga
Rejected. Applicant fails to show any genuine connection with
Eastern Cherokees. No ancestor on the rolls. No ancestor a
party to the treaty of 1835-6 or '46.
EXCEPTION CASE.   J. Norman Hayes & 4 children, App #21088,
Gainesville, Ga. Rejected. Total number of exceptions filed
in this group -- 1. Original recommendation renewed.

10635. JESSE JONES,   Long Creek, S. C.
Rejected. It does not appear that any ancestor was a party to
the treaty of 1835-36 or '46. Nor does it appear that any an-

cestor was ever enrolled. Misc. Test. P. 1546.
MISC. TEST. P. 1545. Witness in re App No 11830-10635 -
George Matheson:
"George Matheson is my name. I am about 45 years old. I
have lived here about 20 years. I am an Englishman. I did not
know their father. I know Rachel Jones, the mother. I do not
know of my own knowledge that she has Indian blood, but it is
generally known that they have Indian blood, and being an Englishman I was interested and questioned the mother, & she told
me that she was part Indian. She looked like an Indian to me.
She never told me anything about receiving any money from the
Government. They were a peculiar class of people and it was
hard to get them to understand about these things. I never
heard them talk about the treaties. The Indians used to visit
them and they were undoubtedly recognized in the community as
part Indian. They claimed it through their father. They said
his name was John B--dy [blurred letters]. I did not know him
myself. I do not know why they were not enrolled but judging
from my knowledge I do not think they knew anything about it.
From the mother I could readily understand that they might be
afraid to enroll for fear of being driven off. I have heard
that some of them were enrolled. They all lived here and did
not go west. Rachel Jones' mother was a Jones before marriage
but no relation to Elias Jones, the father of applicants."
SIGNED: Geo. Matheson, Walhalla, S. C., Jul 14 1908.

MISC. TEST. P. 1546. Appln. No 11830-10635 - Amanda Watkins:
"My name is Amanda Watkins. I am over 50 years of age. I
am a sister to Jesse Jones, Mary Jones, Sarah Woodall. I claim
Indian blood through my mother. Cherokee. My mother is not
living. She has been dead 3 or 4 years. She was about 90 when
she died. She lived in S. C. before I was born. She was Rachel
Brady before marriage, and Rachel Jones after marriage. I do
not think she was ever enrolled. We heard talk of their getting money but they were afraid of being carried off. I have
heard it said that if we enrolled they would be driven off. I
don't know that my mother ever lived with the Indians but they
visited her and she visited them. My mother was always recognized as a woman with Indian blood. My mother was pretty dark.
I think she got her blood from her father's side. His name was
John Brady. I never saw my grandfather. I have heard my mother
talk about her Indian blood. I never heard my mother speak of
the treaties but I have heard her speak of the Indians being
driven out of the country. This is all I know. Our great grand
father's name was also John Brady. They came from N. C.
SIGNED: Amanda "X" Watkins, Walhalla, S. C., Jul 14 1908.
EXCEPTION CASE. Rejected. Total number of exceptions filed
in this group -- 3. Original recommendation renewed.

10636. MARY JONES,   Long Creek, S. C.
Rejected. Sister of 10635; claims thru same source.

10637. LOUVENY MITCHAM and 7 children,   Algoma, W Va
Rejected. Sizemore case. See special report #417.

10638. EMMA TIGER,   Locust Grove, Okla
Admitted. Daughter of #339; claims thru same ancestors. [For
Roll information See App 10647]

10639. QUATIE VANN, Gdn. and 1 child,   Locust Grove, Okla
Admitted. Nephew of #4504 and claims thru same source.
ROLL P53 #9658 - George Dew - 18 by Quatie Vann, Gdn.

10640. WILSON RODGERS and 2 children,   Locust Grove, Okla
Admitted. Applicant's parents, brothers and sisters are en-
rolled in Del. Dis. Group #434. Misc. Test. P. 3858.
MISC. TEST. P. 3858. 526 - Beaver Ridge...through Tom Roach,
Interpreter:
     "I am about 59 or 60 years of age. I was about two years
of age in 51 and am on the Emmigrant roll. Adam Ridge is my
son. Wilson Rogers is Adam's uncle on Adam's mother's side.
Adam's mother was an Emmigrant and was living in 51 in Delaware District. His mother's name was Sahl-duh or Charlotte.
Her father was named Sam-mih or Sam, and her mother was Nu-gih
or Nancy. Charlotte had a full brother named La-sih or Lacy
and I think another by the name of Stephen, or Ste-wih. See
Del 434. Also See Del 862. I don't know whether Nancy ever had
another husband then or Sam another woman. If either of them
did I don't know their names. Think Adam's mother had a half
sister by the name of Ski-os-tih.   I have filed application
number 1574. My father's name was Ta-caw-naw-he-lih. My mother's name was Caty. My oldest brother was named Tee-kin-nih.
Another brother named Wah-sih or Mose. Another brother Ah-le-
chuh. A sister named Tar-ne and my name Taw-ya-nee-tuh. See
Del 285. Mose is still living at Cloeta, Okla. He goes by the
name of Mose Ridge. Adam's Commission number is 8895."
SIGNED: Beaver Ridge, Locust Grove, Okla., Oct 9 1908.
ROLL P119 #22975 FCT COMM #21454 - Wilson Rogers - 53
          22976   32078 - Susie (wife) -48(App 14062)
          22977   26011 - Jesse (son)   - 11
          22978   - Cullus (son) - 6

10641. ANDY YOUNGBIRD and 5 children,   Lometa, Okla
Admitted. Applicant's parents enrolled by Drennen 1852 [sic].
Del. 697. Ches-squa-ne-ta and Canyousa. Misc. Test. P. 2714.
MISC. TEST. P. 2714. Interpreter used - App No 10641 - Andy
Youngbird:
     "My name is Andy Youngbird. My age is 60 years. I was born
and raised in the Territory. I am a Cherokee Indian. I never
joined any other tribe. I applied to the Dawes Commission but
did not get an allotment. Went before some Commissioner but
did not know what was wanted. Don't understand. I got the
strip money and bread money. His father and mother are both
Cherokees. His Cherokee name is A-nit or A-nick. His mother

74

was Co-hin-nih or Co-hee-nee. I don't know any English name.
His mother's name may have been Co-hee-ne. She lived in Dela-
ware District, Honey Creek. (Co-he-nee.) My mother drew money
in 1851 from the Government at Fort Gibson. She drew Emigrant
money. His father's name was Youngbird. He lived in Delaware
District. The name may be Chees-qui-neet (Chees-quh-neet or
Chees-quah-neet. He drew money also at Fort Gibson with the
Emigrants. They came from the East but do not know what state.
They came out with the Emigrants in wagons. I recollect my
grandparents: Ga-nees-a or Geh-neesah, my mother's father.
They lived in Delaware District. (Gin-ne-sah) His wife was
Na-ke. Lived in same district. (Na-che) I cannot give my father's mother or father. I have no brothers or sisters. My
mother's sister was named Too-kah or Tu-ka. Another was named
Lucy or Lu-cie. They were from Delaware District. Father had a
sister Ann-nih or An-nih, and a brother, Ges-gah-ne, who also
lived in Delaware District. This is all I can remember as to
my relatives. I had a brother named Jack-rabbit which was a
nick-name, his name being Jack. Gin-ne-sah, my grandfather was
also called Jack-rabbit."
SIGNED: Andy Youngbird, Wagoner, Okla., Sep 9 1908.
ROLL P155 #30162 - Andy Youngbird - 60
            30163 - Sallie (wife) - 46 (App 10645)
**   30164 - Nakie (son)   - 19 **
            30165 - Elsie (dau)   - 17
            30166 - William (son) - 16
            30167 - Lossie (dau)   - 15
            30168 - Jack (son)   - 13
[** entire entry crossed out - no explanation]

10642. QUATIE JUNE-STOOT,   Locust Grove, Okla
Admitted. Aunt of #9007.
ROLL P83 #15814 FCT COMM #18525 - Quatie June-stoot - 66 [?]

10643. CE-NEE ALLEN,   Locust Grove, Okla
Admitted. Half sister of #9007.
ROLL P23 #3634 FCT COMM #18590 - Jefferson Allen - 52
                              (App 14146)
        3635   18591 - Ce-nee (wife) - 45
        3636   18592 - Sarah (dau)   - 19
        3637   18593 - Aaron (son)   - 17

10644. MAUD COCHRAN,   Locust Grove, Okla
Admitted. Niece of #195; claims thru same source. [For Roll
information See App 5285, Vol. 3]

10645. SALLIE YOUNGBIRD,   Lometa, Okla
Admitted. Claims thru father enrolled as John Butler, G. S.
#699. Misc. Test. P. 2713.
MISC. TEST. P. 2713. Interpreter Used...App No 10645 (Wife of
10641) - Sallie Youngbird:
    "Sallie Youngbird is my name. My age is [blank] I was born

and raised in the Territory. I was not enrolled by the Dawes
Commission. Did not apply. Did not know anything about it. I
got land. (They don't know what allotment.) I got strip and
bread money. I am straight Cherokee. Both parents full-floods.
Takie was my mother and father John Butler. I came from Going
Snake District. John Butler got killed at Tahlequah at time of
the war. I don't know whether they were married but they lived
together. Indian name John Gook or Goot. My father's brother
was Judge Butler. I don't remember my grandparents, on either
side. I have one sister, Ella Swan. I don't recollect whether
I had any that are dead. My mother's brothers were: Tom or
Tom-mih; Ga-das-kie or Gaw-daskie or Gaw-das-kee or Caw-dasie
or Co-daws-kie; lived in Going Snake; Cau-das-ke it may be;
De-ga-las-kee, or De-yah-lees-kee. I don't recollect, but they
drew Emigrant money. My father's brother were Ga-len or Jo
Butler; Judge Butler or Da-goo-disk, who lived in Going Snake
Dist. De-gu-dees-kie or Ti-goo-di-skie; De-go-gees-ke possi-
bly. They came from Georgia. Don't recollect when they came
out." SIGNED: Sallie Youngbird, Wagoner, Okla., Sep 9 1908.
[For Roll information See App 10641]

10646. ONIE FALLING, Locust Grove, Okla*
Admitted. Niece of #639; claims thru same source. Mother not
born in 1851. Misc. Test. P. 3835. [* Spavinaw, Okla on roll]
MISC. TEST. P. 3835. #10646 - Onie Falling...through Martin
Squirrel, Interpreter:
    "My name is Onie Falling. I was born in Delaware District
in 1880. I was not enrolled by the Dawes Commission and never
received an allotment of land. I am a full-blood Cherokee. I
do not know the English names of my parents. The Cherokee name
of my father and mother were Ock-sah-yah and Je-nah-yih. My
parents were not born in 1851. My father had no brothers and
sisters living in 1851. My mother had three brothers living in
1851. Their names were Skah-yoh-sti-ih, Tee-gah-noo-gaw-whe-
skee and Ska-guah. Ska-guah is living now and applied for this
fund under the name of Sam Squirrel, P. O. Spavinaw, Okla. He
never received a notice to appear to give testimony. (See this
application). My grandparents on my father's side were Ni-qui-
chi (Nick) and Ah-noo-you-he. They were enrolled together in
1851 in Delaware District. They had no children at that time.
(See 178 Del. Nick is very probably intended for Ni-qui-chi)
I nor any of my ancestors never received any Old settler money. All my ancestors have always been with the Cherokee tribe.
I was enrolled in 1894 and drew the Strip Payment."
SIGNED: Onie Falling, Locust Grove, Okla., Oct 12 1908.
ROLL P59 #10860 - Nick Falling - 29 (App 13257)
          10861 - Onie (wife) - 26
          10862 - Katie (dau) - 6
          10863 - John (son)   - 3
          10864 - Joe (son)   -- 5/12

76

10647. JOHN TIGER and 2 children,   Spavinaw, Okla
Admitted. Applicant's grandfather and grandmother enrolled by
Drennen as Dirt-thrower Tyger and Oo-tah-ye respectively in
Del. Dis. Group #654.
ROLL P140 #27047 FCT COMM #19364 - John Tiger   - 28
          27048   18056 - Emma (wife) - 29(App 10638)
          27049   - Ollie (son) - 5
          27050   - Jinnie (dau) - 1

10648. NANNIE WOLF and 1 child,   Oakes, Okla
Admitted. Claims thru father and mother enrolled as Choo-dah-
kah-hah and Nancy. Brothers and sister enrolled as Kih-wo-ah-
skee-sam Tih-no-na-lah-nee, Charles, Goo-we-slah, Rider and
Ah-ta-lih in G. S. #65.
MISC. TEST. P. 3873. #10648 - Nannie Wolf:
     "My name is Nannie Wolf. I was born in Going Snake Dis-
trict in 1852. I am a full-blood Cherokee. I never drew an
allotment of land. I had four brothers and sisters who drew
Emigrant money in 1852. I was not enrolled in 1851. My brothers and sisters were living in Going Snake District in 1851
and were enrolled in that District. I think my brothers and
sisters were enrolled with my parents in 1851. My fathers
Cherokee name was Guh-la-we-skee and my mothers Cherokee name
was Nancy. My brothers and sisters who were enrolled were Sah-
ny, Duh-naw-wha-lah-nih, Chee-nah-kee-luh-dih, A-se-ke and
Coo-wee-stah. I also had a brother by the name of Charles who
died before the payment but my parents drew his share of the
money. My father had a nick name Chee-dah-kah-hah. (Chee-nah-
kee-luh-dih means Rider in English) (See 65 G. S.) Louella
Sunday, App 16930 is my daughter. Sam Chee Wee is my son. His
application number is 16935."
SIGNED: Nannie Wolf, Locust Grove, Okla., Oct 8 1908.
ROLL P153 #29674 FCT COMM #20359 - Tom Wolf - 47 (App 16933)
          29675   20360 - Nannie (wife)   - 52
          29676   20361 - Sam CHUWEE (son of w) - 17

10649. SEE-KEE HULLY or CHICKEN,   Locust Grove, Okla
Admitted. Claims thru mother enrolled as Na-le. Grandfather
and grandmother enrolled as Te-la-he-la and Tar-ke. Aunt enrolled as Arl-ser, Del. #282. Misc. Test. P. 3813
MISC. TEST. P. 3813. 10649 - See-gih- Huh-lih or Hully...
through Martin Squirrel, Interpreter:
     "That I am 27 years of age. My parents were both Emmi-
grants and were living in 51. My father and mother were enrolled with their parents. My father's name was Huh-lih. I
don't know of him having any other name. If Hul-lih was anything in English it would be Harry. My father's father was
named Dee-guh-suck-skih. My father's mother died back in the
old country. My father was living with his father. My father's father wasn't living with any woman in 51. My father had
one brother living in 51 named Oo-luh-la-nuh. One sister
named Qua-dih. Another sister named Nah-chih. They were all

77

living in Delaware District.   My mother's name was   Na-lih or
Nellie. Her mother was named Dah-gih. Her father Duh-lay-
hay-lih. My mother had a sister living in 51 named Al-suh.
They were living in Delaware District. See Del. 282. My aunt
Al-suh has one girl living by the name of Celia Eh-daw-hih.
She lives near Eucha but I don't know her English name."
SIGNED: See-gih Huh-lih, Locust Grove, Okla., Oct 13 1908.
[For Roll information See App 10627]

10650. TI-A-NEE-LEVI,   Locust Grove, Okla
Admitted. Daughter of #5845; claims thru same source. Misc.
Test. P. 3186. [For Testimony See App 5845, Vol. 3. For Roll
information See App 4184, Vol. 2]

10651. DICK SMITH,   Locust Grove, Okla
Admitted. Applicant's parents enrolled at Del. #280. Father
of #5971.
ROLL P128 #24746 FCT COMM #18518 - Dick Smith - 51
          24747   25598 - Lizzie (wife) - 55
                          (App 16918) (Died Mar 25 1907)

10652. CLEM TREASURE,   Choteau, Okla
Admitted. Brother of #4296.
ROLL P141 #27253 FCT COMM #20737 - Clem Treasure - 23

10653. GEORGIA V. DELOZIER and 6 children, Adair, Okla
Admitted. Nephew of #356.   Father of claimant enrolled in
1851 by Chapman #1963.
ROLL P52 #9577 FCT COMM #13519 - Georgia V. Delozier - 38
         9578   13520 - Fountain G. (son)   - 18
         9579   13521 - Manford E. (son)   - 15
         9580   13522 - John Edward (son)   - 13
         9581   13523 - Ralph A. (son)   - 10
         9582   13524 - Hazel M. (dau)   - 8
         9583   13525 - Vivian (dau)   - 4

10654. ELIZA LONG,   Caney, Okla
Admitted. 1st cousin of #3080; claims thru the same source.
Applicant was enrolled with her mother Jane McCay in 1851,
Disputed Dis. #97.
ROLL P91 #17286 FCT COMM #29478 - Eliza Long - 57

10655. MARTHA E. WILSON and 5 children,   Bluejacket, Okla
Admitted. Niece of #579.
ROLL P152 #29508 FCT COMM # 9264 - Martha E. Wilson - 59
          29509   9265 - Elgin D. (son)   - 15
          29510   9266 - Martha E. (dau)   - 12
          29511   9267 - Clara E. (dau)   - 9
          29512   9270 - Dnithan A. (dau) - 6
          29513   2610m - Wade C. (son)   - 1/2

78

10656. AMELIA McDUFFIE and 2 children, Box 297, Columbus, Ga
Rejected. Applicant nor ancestors never enrolled. Applicant's mother and grandmother slaves. Misc. Test. P. 3482.
MISC. TEST. P. 3482. #32158-10656 - Suel J. McDuffie:
    "That I was born in 1878. I claim my Indian descent
through my mother; my father was a colored man. My mother
claimed through her mother. My mother was born before the
war. She claimed 1/4 Indian blood. Don't know who owned her.
She was living in Harris Co., Ga. That is where she was born
and raised. Don't know who owned her mother. Both she and
her mother were held in slavery in Georgia. This is the only
application I ever made. Did not make application to the
Dawes Commission. My wife is a colored woman."
SIGNED: Suel J. McDuffie, Muskogee, Okla., Sep 21 1908.

10657. PIGEON SANDERS,   Edna, Kans
Admitted. Great nephew of 3867.
ROLL P123 #23644 FCT COMM #11017 - Pigeon Sanders - 16
                        by Joanna Cooper, Mother & Gdn.

10658. JOE SANDERS,   Edna, Kans
Admitted. Great nephew of #867.
ROLL P122 #23553 FCT COMM #11018 - Joe Sanders - 14
                        by Joanna Cooper, Mother & Gdn.

10659. SEQUOYAH SANDERS,   Edna, Kans
Admitted. Great nephew of #867.
ROLL P123 #23667 FCT COMM #11016 - Sequoyah Sanders - 18
                        by Joanna Cooper, Mother & Gdn.

10660. SUBRINA T. JAMES and 7 children,   Fayetteville, Ark
Admitted. Applicant is a niece of #1056.
ROLL P81 #15276 FCT COMM # 7366 - Sabrina L. James - 41
        15277   7368 - Rex E. (son)   - 19
        15278   7369 - Ray B. (son)   - 17
        15279   7370 - Ethel N. (dau) - 15
        15280   7371 - Max A. (son)   - 13
        15281   7372 - Ruth G. (dau)   - 10
        15282   7373 - Fairy F. (dau) - 9
        15283   21187 - Harold F. (son) - 4

10661. NANNIE E. SHANKS,   Vian, Okla
          by John C. Cotner, Gdn.
Admitted. Claims thru grandmother enrolled as Mary Ann Brown.
Great grandfather enrolled as Robertson Brown. Great uncles
and aunts enrolled as John Robertson and Elizabeth Brown.
S. B. #39.
ROLL P126 #24264 FCT COMM #28346 - Nannie E. Shanks - 16
        24265   28345 - Jessie J. (Sis) - 17
                              (App 10663)
        24266   28348 - John Ed. (bro)   - 12
                              (App 10664)

79

10661. NANNIE E. SHANKS (Cont)
```
        24267           28347 - Narcissa (sis)  - 14
                        (App 10662)
                        by John C. Cotner, Gdn.
```

10662. NARCISSA SHANKS, Included in Application #10661.

10663. JESSIE J. SHANKS, Included in Application #10661.

10664. JOHN ED SHANKS, Included in Application #10661.

10665. ELIZA BARK,   Vian, Okla
Admitted. 1st cousin once removed of #6940. Paternal grand
father enrolled in 1851 by Drennen Flint #78.
ROLL P26 #4242 FCT COMM #29039 - Eliza Bark - 17

10666. EUGENIA THOMAS and 5 children,   Tulsa, Okla
Admitted. Cousin of #2910. Mother of applicant enrolled in
1851 under name of Jane Riley, Flint #613.
```
ROLL P138 #26664 FCT COMM #12750 - Eugenia Thomas  - 32
         26665           12751 - Viola B. (dau)  - 13
         26666           12752 - George H. (son) -  9
         26667           12753 - Arvol V. (son)  -  7
         26668           12754 - Theron T. (son) -  5
         26669           1785m - Gladys M. (dau) -  1
```

10667. SUSIE C. ANDREWS,   Tulsa, Okla
Admitted. Niece of #2977; claims thru same source.
```
ROLL P23 #3783 FCT COMM # 5819 - Susie C. Andrews - 27
         3784           3375m - Howard B. (son)  -  1
```

10668. EDWARD WILLIAMS and 3 children,   Oronogo, Mo
Rejected. Father of #4729; claims thru same source. [See
Exception Case 4729, Vol. 3]

10669. NOAH LANGLEY and 2 children,   Big Cabin, Okla
Admitted. 1st cousin of #805; claims thru same source. Father enrolled by "Chapman #1905" as Noah Langley.
```
ROLL P88 #16695 FCT COMM #28895 - Noah Langley      - 29
         16696           28896 - Hattie Lee (dau) -  6
         16697           3131m - Noah R. (son)     -  3
```

10670. MALDERINE E. VINCENT and 2 children, Foyal, Okla
Admitted. Applicant claims thru her father James Randolph
enrolled as James Adair with his mother Ailsey in 248 Flint
who after the death of her first husband married Adair. Misc.
Test. P. 4114.
MISC. TEST. P. 4114. App No 10670 - Malderine E. Vincent:
     "That I am 31 years of age. I was born in Indian Territory
and was enrolled by the Dawes Commission, No 13446. I got the
strip payment. I get my Indian blood from my father, James
Randolph. He was born in Indian Territory. He died when I was

just a month old and was about thirty years of age at that
time. James was living in Flint District in 1851. His step-
father raised him. His name was Andy Adair and I think that
James was enrolled as James Adair. James Randolph's mother was
named Ailsey and was married to Andrew Adair. James had a sister, Susan, Malderine or Mollie, Kate or Catherine, Betty or
Elizabeth. These were half-sisters by the same mother. There
was a brother named William (Fl. 248). Andy had a son named
Rufus who was a half-brother to my father."
SIGNED: Malderine E. Vincent, Claremore, Okla., Mar 11 1909.
MISC. TEST. P. 2412. Witness in re App No 10670 - Malderine
E. Vincent - George W. Vincent:
"My name is George W. Vincent. My age is 34 years. I did
not file an application. Malderine E. Vincent is my wife. She
is 32 years old. She lives in this county. She was born and
raised in Going Snake District. She left there about 12 years
ago. She was enrolled by the Dawes Commission, Cherokee Roll
#13446. My children were also enrolled by the Dawes Commis-
sion. She drew the '94 payment. Her blood comes from James
Randolph. She does not claim from her mother. Her father has
been dead over 32 years. He lived in Going Snake District. I
do not know whether he ever lived in any other District. He
was enrolled in 1851. He was known under a Cherokee name but
I cannot give it. I do not know the parents of J[a]mes
Randolph. I cannot assign any good reason for his not being
enrolled in 1851. My wife has two half-brothers, by her mother's side. She has one sister. Genie Hamilton, Randolph before
marriage. I do not know whether James Randolph had any brothers and sisters. They did not associate with any other tribe
of Indians. I do not know whether they are Emigrants or Old
Settlers. I don't know any ancestor back of the father. I have
heard that her father helped to bring the Indians from Georgia. He came from Georgia. This is all I know in this matter."
SIGNED: Geo. W. Vincent, Claremore, Okla., Aug 28 1908.
ROLL P144 #27878 FCT COMM #13466 - Malderine E. Vincent - 30
         27879   234m - Clausine R. (son)   - 3
         27880   235m - Robert B. (son)   - 2

10671. IDA GRIMET,   Vian, Okla
Admitted. Niece of #1124. Parents not living in 1851. [For
Roll information See App 10595]

10672. MINNIE SANDERS,   Stilwell, Okla
Admitted. Niece of Peter Doublehead and appl #3484; admitted
for same reasons.
ROLL P123 #23632 FCT COMM #19862 - Mose Sanders - 24
                                   (App 42179)
         23633   18381 - Minnie (wife) - 22

10673. JOHN YOUNG,   Marble, Okla
Admitted. Nephew of #4507.
ROLL P155 #30109 FCT COMM #2880 - John Young - 20

81

10674. TOM FOREMAN,   Vian, Okla
Admitted. Applicant's grandparents enrolled by Drennen in
Del. Dis. #153. (Sucker and Al-cy).
ROLL P63 #11645 FCT COMM #21181 - Tom Foreman - 34
        11646   19535 - Alice (wife) - 32
                         (App 25879)

10675. CLYDE HORN,   Stilwell, Okla
See father's application #5915; also enrollment card.

10676. FANNIE M. HORN,   Stilwell, Okla
Admitted. Claims Cherokee descent thru Minerva Keys, nee
Nave, who was enrolled by Drennen in 1851 in Tahl. Dis. Group
#143. [For Roll information See App 5915, Vol. 3]

10677. POLLY FENCER,   Oaks, Okla
Admitted. Daughter of 39946 and great niece of #5812. [For
Roll information See App 10684]

10678. CHARLEY CARROLL,   Oaks, Okla
Admitted. John Edwards, Gdn. Nephew of #1865.
ROLL P39 #6867 FCT COMM #29613 - Charley Carroll - 7
                                by John Edwards, Gdn.

10679. CHARLES VANN, Duplicate of #4643.

10680. DELE-YEH-IN BULLFROG,   Whitmire, Okla
Admitted. Applicant and her mother were enrolled by Drennen
in G. S. Dis. #528. Misc. Test. P. 3426.
MISC. TEST. P. 3426. #10680 - Tiana Bullfrog...through Tom
Roach, Interpreter:
    "My name is Tiana Bullfrog. I am 79 years old. I was
born in the Old Nation and came to the Indian Territory at the
time of the Emigration. I was enrolled in 1851 in Going Snake
District with my parents. I was enrolled under the name of
Dah-ya-nih. My fathers name was Geh-skuh-nih-hih and my moth-
er's name was Quait-cy. My mother lived with a man by the
name of Peach-eater. My father was called Stephen sometimes.
I had some brothers and sisters who were enrolled in 1851 with
my mother and father. My brothers and sisters were Ah-yah-
nih, Tau-choo-whuh Celia, Geh-chee-yeh-luh. (See 528 G. S.
for enrollment of applicant, her father, mother and sister)
John Peacheater was my step-father. (See 527 Del.) George
Bearwool, #14719 is my grandson. He died November 9, 1907.
(See Application)."
SIGNED: Tiana "X" Bullfrog, Locust Grove, Okla., Oct 13 1908.
ROLL P35 #6195 FCT COMM #18903 - Deh-yeh-ni Bullfrog - 73

10681. MADISON STOVER,   Oaks, Okla
Admitted. Half brother of #10628 and claims thru same source.
ROLL P133 #25815 FCT COMM #28286 - Madison Stover - 21

10682. ROY ISRAEL,   Oaks, Okla
Admitted. Nephew of #2045 and claims thru same source.
ROLL P80 #15129 FCT COMM #14984 – Roy Israel – 25

10683. JAMES WILSON and 4 children,   Whitmire, Okla
Admitted. Son of #10680.
ROLL P152 #29482 FCT COMM #30668 – James Wilson – 39
          29483 FCT COMM #30669 – Bettie (wife) – 50
                                  (App 11233)
          29484   30670 – Stealer (son) – 16
          29485   30671 – Will (son)   – 14
          29486   30672 – Nancy (dau)   – 10
          29487   32338 – Lizzie (dau) – 8

10684. SAM FENCER and 3 children,   Oaks, Okla
Admitted. Nephew of #1197 and claims thru same source.
ROLL P60 #10999 FCT COMM #   – Sam Fencer   – 39
          11000   6114 – Polly (wife) – 25(App 10677)
          11001   4901m – Dick (son)   – 5
          11002   – Gar–coo–s–der–dy (son) – 3
          11003   – Jesse (son)   – 1

10685. ALLISON DAVIS and 1 child,   Braggs, Okla
Rejected. Claims thru same source as #10594.

10686. LIZZIE NAKEDHEAD, Duplicate of #5329.

10687. JESSIE L. MARTIN and 2 children,   Muskogee, Okla
Admitted. by T. H. Martin, Gdn.Nieces and nephews of #3257.
ROLL P100 #19120 FCT COMM #6924 – Jessie L. Mills – 16
           19121   6925 – Cynthia E. (sis) – 14
           19122   6926 – Samuel H. (bro) – 12
                                  by T. H. Martin, Gdn.

10688. MITCHELL BIGFEATHER,   Maple, Okla
Admitted. Son of #2828; claims thru same source.
ROLL P30 #5039 FCT COMM #29827 – Mitchell Bigfeather – 30
          5040   29830 – Mary (wife) – 25 (App 27105)
          5041   29828 – Lucy (dau)   – 5
          5042   29829 – Gussie (son)   – 4
          5043   2868m – Jennie (dau)   – 2
          5044   2869m – Annie (dau)   – 1

10689. CLEM C. MOTON and 4* children,   Long, Okla
Admitted. Brother of #130. [* Only 2 children on roll – The
FCT# of Jesse J. Moton (28191) falls between Clem C. and Andy]
ROLL P102 #19603 FCT COMM #3845 – Clem C. Moton – 48
           19604   3848 – Andy M. (son)   – 18
           19605   3849 – Bert E. (dau)* – 17
[* "son" crossed out]

10690. JOSHUA ROSS, Same as #145.

83

10691. CHARLIE STARR,   Catoosa, Okla
Admitted. Applicant's grandfather enrolled as George Deerskin
in Illinois Dis. in Group 298 and his great grandmother,
Sallie Deerskin enrolled in the same district.   Grandson of
#895; claims thru same source.
ROLL P132 #25424 FCT COMM #30068 - Charlie Starr - 21

10692. ORLENA T. MYERS and 2 children,   Musquite, Tex
Rejected. It does not appear that any ancestor was enrolled
in 1835 or 1851; nor that any ancestor was a party to the
treaty of 1835-6 or '46. The case is given color by the testimony which is not borne out either by the rolls or the application. Misc. Test. P. 1963.
MISC. TEST. P. 1963. In re #10692 - Cordelia Edgar #24534:
     "My name is Cordelia Edgar, and I live at Mosquite, Tex. I
am 32 years old. I claim my Cherokee Indian blood through my
mother, Orlena T. Myers, who died the 2nd day of Aug. I have
heard my mother say that she was born either at Little Rock,
Ark. or in the Territory. She was 49 years old at the time of
her death. She got her Indian blood from her mother Mildred
Cherokee Hargrove (maiden name) and she married a Ray. Mildred
Hargrove was about 3/4 Cherokee. My grandmother was born in Ga
She must have come west when she was young. She was born in
1845 and died in 1898. Mildred C. Hargrove was the daughter of
Elizabeth Hargrove, nee Miller. Elizabeth also lived in Ga until she came West. She lived in Dalton, Ga. and came west, I
do not know just when but it was before the war, and she died
in the Indian Territory. I expect she died before I was born,
but she was right old when she died. My grandmother, Mildred
C. Hargrove got some bread money and other small payments on
account of her Indian blood. She was always recognized as
being an Indian. My mother, Orlena T. Myers, and I myself have
drawn Strip payments in Okla. We drew these payments on account of our Indian blood as recognized in us through my grand
mother as mentioned above. I have heard my mother speak of her
and us children drawing over $200 apiece in the Strip payment
in 1892. But I do not know whether grandmother drew in 1851 or
not." SIGNED: Cordelia Edgar, Dallas, Tex., Sep 8 1908.
EXCEPTION CASE. Orlena T. Myers (dec'd) & 2 children, by S. B.
Myers, Mesquite, Tex. Rejected. Total number of exceptions
filed in this group -- 6. Original recommendation renewed.

10693. WILLIAM STARR and 2 children,   Catoosa, Okla
Admitted. Brother of #10691, and claims thru same source.
ROLL P132 #25513 FCT COMM #29732 - William Starr - 23
            25514   29734 - Carl M. (son)   - 4
            25515   4234m - Ernest W. (son) - 2

10694. HARRISON WILLIAMS and 4 children,   Chelsea, Okla
Admitted. Uncle of #741. Applicant himself enrolled by
Drennen in Flint Dist. #525.

```
ROLL P151 #29327 FCT COMM #13121 - Harrison Williams  - 64
          29328          22007 - Emma S. (dau)         -  8
          29329          22008 - Harrison Jr. (son) -  6
          29330          1114m - Leonard (son)        -  3
          29331          1115m - Amanda P. (dau)     -  1
```

10695. WILLIE DEW,   Moodys, Okla
Admitted. Brother of #10596 and claims thru same source.
ROLL P53 #9668 FCT COMM #18477 - Willie Dew - 24

10696. ANNIE PUMPKIN and 1 child,   Tahlequah, Okla
Admitted. Daughter of #8259; claims thru same source.
```
ROLL P113 #21824 FCT COMM #18881 - Annie Pumpkin        - 18
           21825              - Charlotte HOGSHOOTER -  1
                               (dau)
```

10697. MARY PUMPKIN,   Moodys, Okla
Admitted. Sister of #10596; claims thru same source. [For
Roll information See App 10598]

10698. GEORGE LOCUST,   Vian, Okla
Admitted. Nephew of Jesse Locust Appl. #316 and is admitted
for same reasons.
ROLL P90 #17234 FCT COMM #21112 - George Locust - 26

10699. PLES K. MILLER and 7 children,   Webbers Falls, Okla
Admitted. Half brother of #2118.
```
ROLL P99 #19027 FCT COMM # 3381 - Ples Henry Miller - 37
           19028          3382 - Francis E. (dau)  - 16
           19029          3383 - Effie M. (dau)    - 14
           19030          3384 - George W. (son)   - 12
           19031          3385 - Eliza P. (dau)     -  9
           19032          3386 - John T. (son)      -  6
           19033          3387 - Belmont (son)      -  4
           19034          4441m - Ollie B. (dau)    -  2
```

10700. GEORGE HILDEBRAND, Duplicate of #1913.

10701. LIZZIE TITTLE and 7 children,   Gritts, Okla
Admitted. Sister of #8289.
```
ROLL P140 #27137 FCT COMM #25147 - Lizzie Tittle   - 34
            27138          25148 - Goldie (dau)     - 17
            27139          25149 - Clyde L. (son)   - 14
            27140          25150 - Omer A. (dau)    - 12
            27141          25151 - Bessie (dau)      -  9
            27142          25152 - Lelia (dau)       -  6
            27143          4377m - Willie V. (son) -  4
            27144          4378m - Thelma (dau)     -  2
```

10702. RICHARD BENGE,   Braggs, Okla
Admitted. Nephew of #1629; claims thru same source.
ROLL P29 #4880 FCT COMM #21059 - Richard Benge - 26

10703. JOHN VANN,   Fort Gibson, Okla
Admitted. Brother of #2182. Claims thru same source.
ROLL P143 #27724 FCT COMM #6110 - John F. Vann - 31

10704. CARRIE E. MARLOW and 3 children,   Braggs, Okla
Admitted. Applicant's grandfather was enrolled by Drennen in
G. S. #453. Misc. Test. P. 3471.
MISC. TEST. P. 3471. #10704 - Carrie E. Marlow:
    "That I am 33 years of age. I claim my Indian descent thru
both parents. I don't know how much Indian blood they claimed
but they were both Cherokees. My father was about 25 years old
when he died. Don't know how old my mother was when she died,
but guess she was about the age of my father. My grandfather
on my mother's side was an Old Settler, I think, but none of
my other ancestors were that I know of. My father got his Indian descent thru his father and mother.   Don't know how much
Indian Andrew Fields was. Betty Lovett was my grandmother on
my mother's side.   She was not an Old Settler. Curry Pettit
(O. S. G. S. 37) had a daughter named Aggie (O. S. G. S. 39).
Andrew Fields was living in the West in 1851, in Going Snake
District. Betsy Enloe was my great grandmother and she was
living in 1851, I think. Don't know whether Andrew Fields ever
received any Old Settler money or not. Elmira Fields (G. S.
454) was a sister of Andrew (G. S. 453) Elmira's name now is
Patrick. I think he also had a sister named Martha or Mattie
Fields. John Fields, who lives at Stilwell, is a brother of my
father. Andy is another, and he lives at the same place. Richard Fields is another and he is the oldest, I think. He lives
at the same place. Joe and Ben were also brothers of my father. I am on the Dawes Commission roll #5032 [?]. I have some
half brothers on my mother's side by the name of Hensley. John
(who lives at Eaton, Okla.), Tennie Hensley (married now lives
at Eaton, Okla.), Sam is another and he lives at Tahlequah.
Houston was another and he lives at Tahlequah. Jim Hensley is
another - lives at Tahlequah. Joe is another and he lives at
Tahlequah."
SIGNED: Carrie E. Marlow, Muskogee, Okla., Sep 22 1908.
ROLL P96 #18327 FCT COMM # 5032 - Carrie E. Marlow - 31
         18328   5033 - Minnie (dau)   - 9
         18329   5034 - Edna (dau)   - 7
         18330   1927m - Ruby (dau)   - 2

10705. RICHARD BALDRIDGE,   Sallisaw, Okla
Admitted. Uncle of #8280; claims thru same source. Dawes Commission #25696.   Full blood.   [For Roll information See App
7459, Vol. 4]

10706. ELIZA BALDRIDGE,   Hanson, Okla
Admitted. Sister of #8280; claims thru same source.
ROLL P25 #4021 - Eliza Baldridge - 26

10707. CAROLINE BALDRIDGE, Hanson, Okla
Admitted. Parents and aunts of claimant were enrolled by
Drennen in 1851 in Flint District Group No 604.
ROLL P25 #4060 FCT COMM #20555 - William Baldridge - 21
(App 16661)
4061 29147 - Caroline (wife) - 22

10708. MARTHA VANN, Brushby, Okla
Admitted. Mother of #226. Applicant enrolled in 1851 under
the name of Martha Hood, S. B. #130.
ROLL P143 #27756 FCT COMM #3084 - Martha Vann - 73

10709. JESSIE CHUCALATE, Vain, Okla
Admitted. Niece of #9468; claims thru same source.
ROLL P42 #7506 - Jessie Chucalate - 31

10710. JOHN BARK and 4 children, Vian, Okla
Admitted. First cousin of #6940. Applicant's father enrolled
in 1851 by Drennen, Flint #78.
ROLL P26 #4245 FCT COMM #21169 - John Bark - 51
4246 21170 - Lizzie (wife) - 45(App 17014)
4247 21171 - Richard (son) - 18
4248 21172 - Levie (son) - 15
4249 21173 - Louisa (dau) - 12
4250 21174 - Daisy (dau) - 7

10711. JAMES FOSTER and 4 children, Vian, Okla
Admitted. Applicant's mother Eliza Horn enrolled by Drennen
in Flint Dist. #102. Misc. Test. P. 3200 and 3268.
MISC. TEST. P. 3200. Interpreter Used. - App No 1839 - Eliza
Smith:
"My name is Eliza Smith. My age is 58 years. I was born &
raised in Flint District. I think I was enrolled in 1851 as I
drew money when a child. My father's name was John Horn; he
was an Old Settler. My first husband's name was Foster. My
maiden name was Eliza Horn. I got the bread and strip money. I
was enrolled by the Dawes Commission, Cherokee Roll #26963. I
guess he did draw Old Settler money in 1851. My mother's name
was Nellie or Nah-lie Horn. Before marriage Nellie Miller. My
mother had one brother; I think his name would be Jim in English; Chu-ah-nus-kie or Chu-ah-naw-ske, in Indian. He lived in
Flint District. My mother had a sister named A-key; she was
the oldest. (Chu-aw-naw-ske 448 Flint.) (306 Ills.) Brother to
mother. Nellie Miller was born in the East. I don't know when
they came out here. Nellie had some sisters; A-key was one;
she lived in Flint. She married a man by the name of Sanders,
Akey Sanders had one child, Ail-sey Sanders. My mother had another sister named Eliza Miller. She lived in Flint District.
She did not have any children. Peter Miller was the father of
Nellie; Que-ter Miller in Cherokee. I don't remember whether
he ever came to this country, but think he died back in the
old nation. Jack Miller was his brother's name. He lived in

87

Illinois District. He also lived in Flint District. Jack had a daughter by the name of Lucy. I don't know whether he was enrolled in 1851. Don't remember ever hearing him say he received money from the Government. I don't remember any other brothers; nor any sisters. Nellie Miller's mother's name was Wutty. My mother came here with the Emigration. None of my mother's people got Old Settler money in 1851. I claim 1/4 whole ["Cherokee" crossed out] blood. They have never associated with any other tribe of Indians."
SIGNED: Eliza Smith, Stilwell, Okla., Sep 25 1908.
MISC. TEST. P. 3268. Interpreter Used. App No 17025-1839 - Sam Leach:

"My name is Sam Leach. My age is about 25 years. I am enrolled by the Dawes Commission, Cherokee Roll No. 26970. I got the strip payment. I get Indian blood from both parents. (Evidence of Indian blood on his mother's side found in application #1839.) My father's name was Ned-sin-nih Leach. He is dead; never saw my father; he was somewhere in the 40's. I don't know whether he was enrolled in 1851. I don't know whether he ever got any money from the Government. He had one brother named Thompson Leach. Another brother by the name of Oo-la-nees-ke or Gau-la-nes-kee. He lived in Flint District. He had another brother but I do not recollect his name. My father's father's name was Ah-lee-sah. He lived in Flint District. I don't know of any other name or District. Don't know any brothers or sisters or other relatives of Ah-lee-sah or Ah-lee-cha. (581 Fl.) Wah-di-yah-hih is my father's mother's name. I don't know any brothers and sisters of Wah-di-yah-hihi. None of my father's people were Old Settlers. I don't know whether they ever got money from the Government in 1851 or not. They never associated with any other tribe that I know of." SIGNED: Sam Leach, Stilwell, Okla., Sep 28 1908.
[For Roll information See App 6669, Vol. 3]

10712. ISAAC CHRISTIE, Vian, Okla
          by Jas. Foster, Gdn.
Admitted. Nephew of 2687 and his grandfather Jackson Christie is enrolled from Flint Dis. #640.
ROLL P42 #7423 FCT COMM #29738 - Isaac Christie - 20
                                by James Foster, Gdn.

10713. CATHERINE TERRAPIN, Baron, Okla
Admitted. Sister of #256; claims thru same source. Applicant herself enrolled in G. S. #242 with mother Sallie Foreman.
ROLL P138 #26615 FCT COMM #14416 - Catherine Terrapin - 66

10714. CALEDONA MARTIN and 2 children, Claremore, Okla
Admitted. Half sister of #2118 on father's side.
ROLL P96 #18375 FCT COMM #22836 - Caledona Martin - 23
          18376   22837 - Jessie S. (dau) - 4
          18377   4379m - William E. (son) - 2

10715. THOS. D. SANDERS,   Braggs, Okla
Rejected. Nephew of #8764; claims thru same source.
EXCEPTION CASE. Admitted. Applicant's father on the 1851
Roll, #179 S. B., as Didimus Sanders. Applicant born in 1874.
SUPP ROLL #30762 FCT COMM #5299 - Thomas D. Sanders - 32

10716. WM. FOGG, Duplicate of #8079.

10717. HENRY N. NOLEN,   Big Cabin, Okla
       by James A. Nolen, Gdn.
Admitted. Cousin of #874. Maternal grandmother enrolled in
1851 by Drennen Del. 370.
ROLL P105 #20152 FCT COMM #27601 - Henry N. Nolen - 14
         20153   27600 - James A. Jr. (bro) - 19
                      (App 10719)
                      by James A. Nolen, Gdn.

10718. CHARLOTTE ROBERTS and 5 children,   McGrady, N C
Rejected. Sizemore case. See special report #417.

10719. JAMES A. NOLEN, JR.,   Big Cabin, Okla
       by James A. Nolen, Gdn.
Admitted. Cousin of #874. Maternal grandmother enrolled in
1851 by Drennen Del. 370. [For Roll information See App 10717]

10720. JENNIE FELTS and 6 children,   Springfield, N C
Rejected. Sizemore case. See special report #417.

10721. TOM PANTHER,   Marble, Okla
Admitted. Nephew of 4216. Grandfather of [sic] "Diver Glass",
G. S. #545.
ROLL P107 #20631 FCT COMM #19571 - Tom Panther - 13
                         by Martha Panther, Gdn.

10722. ALICE PANTHER,   Marble, Okla
Admitted. Niece of 4216. Grandfather "Diver Glass" G. S. 545.
ROLL P107 #20626 FCT COMM #19570 - Alice Panther - 16
                         by Martha Panther, Gdn.

10723. JESSIE C. SAMUELS,   Muldrow, Okla
Admitted. Sister of #4821 and claims thru same source.
ROLL P122 #23434 FCT COMM #26347 - Jessie C. Samuels - 22

10724. LOUTITIA ROBERSON,   Muldrow, Okla
Admitted. Sister of #4821; claims thru same source.
ROLL P118 #22633 FCT COMM #26348 - Lutitia Roberson - 20

10725. BIRD DOUBLEHEAD and 3 children,   Warner, Okla
Rejected. Applicant claims thru his mother but does not know
her name. He states that he drew old settler money for both
his father and mother.

10726. ZADEE BOON and 6 children,   Shibboleth, Okla
Rejected. Creek case. See Creek File #1139.

10727. ALEX WELCH and 1 child,   Muldrow, Okla
Admitted. Son of #1898.
ROLL P148 #28712 FCT COMM #28594 - Alex Welch   - 34
        28713   4004 - Victory (wife) - 29
                       (App 10728)
        28714   28596 - Maggie (dau)   - 12
        28715   4005 - Richard CHANDLER - 13
                       (son of w)

10728. VICTORY WASH and 1 child,   Muldrow, Okla
Admitted. Sister of #6592; claims for the same reasons. [For
Roll information See App 10727]

10729. AUSTIA L. BURKE,   Coffeyville, Kans
Admitted. 1st cousin of 562. Claims thru grandfather Anderson
Lowery Tahl. #536. Father probably not born in 1851.
ROLL P36 #6267 FCT COMM #10745 - Austia L. Burke - 16

10730. FRANCES COX,   Vinita, Okla
Admitted. The applicant claims thru her mother and maternal
grandparents. Her mother was born after 1851. It has been impossible to locate definitely the name of the maternal grand
parent of the applicant on the rolls of 1851. The father of
applicant's grandmother was Samuel Foster. He is enrolled in
16 Saline together with his wife and the great aunts and uncles of applicant. The names of applicant's ancestors do not
appear on the Old Settler Roll and the testimony taken in this
case proves the ancestors of applicant to be Eastern Cherokees
See Misc. Test. P. 4379, 3643.
MISC. TEST. P. 3643. Appl. #10732-10730 - Edward Fritz:
    "My name is Edward Fritz. I live at Vinita, Okla. 8613 is
my Dawes Commission number. I made my claim through my mother.
I don't think she was old enough to get money in 1852. My father was a white man. My mother's father's name was John Bigside. I don't know whether my mother's parents were living in
1852 or not. My mother's mother had a brother by the name of
Roastingear. Her mother's brother's name was Jeff Ballou. Jeff
Ballou did not get any money as I know of. My mother's mother
had the following brothers; -- Roastingear, Adam, and Stealer
(or Kar-nah-tse-sta-tse) and Sapsucker (or Ka-hyor-kah) I
don't remember any other names of my grandmother's brothers
and sisters. See Saline 16."
SIGNED: Edward Fritz, Vinita, Okla., Oct 12 1908.
MISC. TEST. P. 4379. #10732-10730 - Francis Fritz...in behalf
of Edward Fritz:
    "I am 72 years old. I am the step-father of Edward Fritz.
His own father's name was Harding Trot. He was an Emigrant
Cherokee. Harding Trott and my wife were never married but it
was the general saying in the community that Harding Trot was

the father of Edward Fritz. There was never any doubt about that fact. Edward Fritz was enrolled on the 1880 roll as Eddie Trot. The parents of Harding Trot were James Trot and Rachel Trot. Harding Trot had as brothers and sisters -- Ross, Oce or J. C., William, Benjamin, who was in the west in 1851, Mary, who married a man by the name of Steadman, Charlotte, Timothy or Tip (See Chapman 1670-77) James and Rachel were living in the east in 1851. I do not think that Harding Trot was born until his parents came out to the Territory. He was born after 1851. Edward's mother was named Aggie, and Aggie's father's name was Big sides but she always went by the name of Foster before her marriage. Aggie's mother was named Nancy Foster, but she went sometimes by the name of Ballou. She was a full sister of Jeff Ballou, who died about ten years ago. Jeff Ballou went a part of the time by the name of Jack Foster. I think that Jeff Ballou was old enough to be on the roll of 1851. His Cherokee name was Cun-dee-sta-chih or Wasp. The Cherokee name of Nancy Foster was Nun-chih. I do not know whether Nancy Foster was an Emigrant Cherokee. She was consid- ered to be a full-blood Cherokee. When the Old Settler payment was made in 1896 I made inquiry to see if there was any chance of getting in on the Old Settler payment and Old Jeff Ballou told me that Edward Fritz was a descendant of Emigrant Cher- okees. Nancy Foster was born in the East. I do not know when Nancy came out to the Indian Territory. I understand that Jeff Ballou came out here at the time of the Emigration. Jeff and Nancy had the following brothers and sisters, --- Roastingear Foster, Choo-wah-nee-guh, Adam, Sapsucker, Kar-nah-tse-sta-tse or Wasp, (this was the Indian name of Jeff Ballou) (See Saline 16) Cah-nee-gah or Black-haw, Ai-lin, or Ellen. Jeff Ballou and Nancy Foster's father was named Sam Foster or Sam Roast- ingear. Ta-ke is the mother of Blackhaw and Jess. Nancy was a good deal older the[n] Jeff Ballou. Nancy Foster died when Aggie was a little girl. I don't know the exact date. I do not know whether Nancy Foster ever was married to any other man than Bigsides or not. Nancy Foster lived in Saline District in 1851. Edward Fritz and Jeff Ballou, the grand son of Old Jeff Ballou are 2nd cousins, Edward's mother and young Jeff's fa- ther were first cousins. Elizabeth Hilderbrand, Fannie L. Hil- derbrand and Katie Fritz are half sisters to Edward Fritz."
SIGNED: Francis Fritz, Vinita, Okla., Mar 10 1909.
ROLL P48 #8628 FCT COMM #8371 - Frances Cox - 21

10731. KATIE FRITZ,   Vinita, Okla
          by Francis Fritz, Gdn.
Admitted. Half sister of #10730 and claims thru same source.
ROLL P64 #11899 FCT COMM #8372 - Katie Fritz - 17
                          by Francis Fritz, Gdn.

10732. EDWARD FRITZ,   Vinita, Okla
Admitted. The paternal grandparents and aunts and uncles of the applicant were enrolled by Chapman in 1670-71 in 1851.

Half brother of #10730 and claims thru same source. See Misc. Test. P. 4379, 3643. [For Testimony See App 10730. For Roll information See App 5967, Vol. 3]

10733. KATE BOLAND,   Texanna, Okla
Admitted. Father and mother enrolled as John and Eliza Eavin. Brother enrolled as Looney, Ill. #225. See Misc. Test. P. 4402
MISC. TEST. P. 4402.   #10733 - Katie Boland...thru J. C. Groves, Interpreter:
    "My father's name was John Gooden. His father's name was John Eaven. I do not think that his father was living in 1851. My father changed his name from Eaven to Gooden, but I do not know when. My mother's name was Eliza. I was the young- est child. The oldest childs name was Loony. See Ill. #225."
SIGNED: Katie Boland, Porum, Okla., Mar 22 1909.
MISC. TEST. P. 3093. No 10733 - Kate Boland:
    "I am 55 years of age; am a full blood Cherokee. I am a Cherokee alotte and my number is 17016. My father's name was John Goody. His Indian name was E-ju-la-ha. My mother's name was Lizzie Youngpuppy. My mother and father were both Immi- grants. I am the youngest child. There were three older than I. I was not living when the Immigrants were paid. I think none of my brothers and sisters were living then. My mother and father were not married then. My father lived in Delaware District. My father's father was named John Goody. I never saw my grandfather. I am sure he was living when the Immigrants were paid in 1852. My father was married before he married my mother. Hornet and Nanny Goodin were my father's sisters. I never drew any Old Settler money." "This case is O. K. through 598 Flint." [Notation added to end of testimony]
SIGNED: Kate Boland, Muskogee, Okla., Sep 22 1908.
[For Roll information See App 4081, Vol. 2]

10734. KATE BOLAND, Duplicate of #10733.

10735. KATE BOLAND, Duplicate of #10733.

10736. POLLY HARPER,   Texanna, Okla
Admitted. Cousin of #1583. Claimant's mother enrolled in 1851 by Drennen Tahl. #304.
ROLL P71 #13363 FCT COMM #30064 - Polly Harper - 18

10737. POLLY HARPER. Same as #10736.

10738. POLLY HARPER. Same as #10736.

10739. ROSA CHEEK and 8 children,   Akins, Okla
Admitted. Daughter of #8258 and claims thru same source.
ROLL P41 #7288 FCT COMM #3180 - Rosa Cheek   - 36
          7289   3182 - Myrtle (dau)   - 16
          7290   3183 - George (son)   - 15
          7291   3184 - Roy (son)   - 13

92

10739. ROSA CHEEK (Cont)
       7292 FCT COMM #3185 - Beatrice (dau) - 9
       7293   3186 - Nina (dau)   - 7
       7294   3187 - Margie (dau) - 6
       7295   3188 - Evie (dau)   - 4
       7296   125m - Seba (dau)   - 2

10740. NANNIE BALDRIDGE,   Maple, Okla
Admitted. Daughter of #8258; claims thru same source. [For
Roll information See App 8885, Vol. 4]

10741. CHARLES CARLILE,   Campbell, Okla
Admitted. 1st cousin of #4394.   Claimant's maternal grand
father enrolled in 1851 by Drennen, Del. #431.
ROLL P38 #6750 FCT COMM #17119 - Charles Carlile - 31

10742. JOSEPH J. LYNCH,   Woodville, Okla
Admitted. 1st cousin to 998. Father and grandfather of appli-
cant enrolled as Joseph Lynch #373 Saline.
ROLL P92 #17501 FCT COMM #5907 - Joseph J. Lynch - 32

10743. TEMPERENCE W. BAUGHMAN,   Campbell, Okla
       Deceased and 2 children, by W. D. Baughman, Gdn.
Admitted. Half sister of #5205; claims thru same source.
ROLL P27 #4415 FCT COMM # 1647 - Temperance W. Baughman - 24
       4416   2870m - Nannie L (dau)   - 4
       4417   2871m - Dora E. (dau) - 2 (App 10756)
(Tem. Baughman died June 18, 1906) by N. D. Baughman, Gdn.

10744. JOHN R. SMITH and 5 children,   Davis, Okla
Rejected. Brother of #322 and claims thru same source.

10745. JACOB WATTS, Duplicate of #3457.

10746. MARY A. JOHNSON and 1 child,   Porum, Okla
Admitted. Applicant's father Ellis Starr, and his grand
parents Thomas and Catherine Starr were enrolled by Drennen in
Canadian District #88.
ROLL P82 #15507 FCT COMM # 4251 - Mary B. Johnson - 18
       15508   4563m - L. W. (son)   - 2

10747. JACKSON BLYTHE,   Porum, Okla
Admitted. Claims thru grandfather enrolled as Jackson Blythe,
Chapman 155.
ROLL P32 #5406 FCT COMM #17200 - Jackson Blythe - 34

10748. FELIX LATTA,   Porum, Okla
Admitted. Applicant claims thru mother who was enrolled by
Drennen at Sal. #526. Misc. Test. P. 2165.
MISC. TEST. P. 2165. No 10748 - Felix Latta:
    "My name is Felix Latta; my post-office is Porum, Okla.; I
was born on the Grand River, Cherokee Nation, Indian Territory

in 1848; I claim to be three-quarter Cherokee Indian; I make
claim also through my mother, Peggy Latta, whose Indian name
was Wah-te, but she always went by the name of Peggy; my mother was born and raised in Tennessee; she came west with the
Indians in 1835; my mother married after she came to Indian
Territory; I was enrolled as a Cherokee by blood on the final
rolls of the Five Civilized Tribe and my number is 16849; my
daughter, Mary F. Latta was enrolled at the same time and her
number is 16850, and my son, Felix Latta was enrolled also at
the same time and his number is 25418. They filed application
for claim under the same as I did. We lived in what is known
as Saline District; my mother, Peggy Latta and my brothers,
Allen, David & Jefferson were on the rolls of 1851 but the
name was spelled Latty; I am also on the roll of 1851, my Indian name is given, namely Diver Latty. My cousin, Na-ne (English of which is Nannie Latty) is also on the roll of 1851."
SIGNED: Felix Latta, Ada, Okla., Aug 22 1908.
EXCEPTION CASE. 10748. Mary Francis Latta, Felix Latta,
Samuel Latta, by Felix Latta, parent and guardian, Porum,
Okla. Admitted. Minor children of No. 10748, Miller Roll No.
16766, and claims thru the same source. Formerly omitted thru
a clerical error.
ROLL P88 #16766 FCT COMM #16849 - Felix Latta   - 68
SUPP ROLL #30664 FCT COMM #16850 - Mary F. Latta   - 12
         30665   25418 - Felix (bro)   - 10
         30666   - Samuel (1/2 bro) - 3
                        by Felix Latta, parent & Gdn.

10749. NANNIE CRAIN and 4 children,   Porum, Okla
Admitted. Applicant's mother and grandmother were enrolled by
Drennen in Tahl. #170. Misc. Test. P. 2769.
MISC. TEST. P. 2769. #10753-10749 - Cynthia Peters:
    "That I am about 40 years of age. I claim my Indian de-
scent through both parents. I guess my father was a full blood
Cherokee. My mother was about 1/2 Cherokee. I think my parents
were living near Tahlequah in 1851. They were not Old Set-
tlers. Don't suppose my parents were married in 1851. Nannie
Campbell, Jim Campbell, George Crain and Nannie Crain are half
brothers and sisters on my mother's side. My mother was married several times. Before marriage she was Lizzie Hildebrand.
My mother was just a little girl in 1851. My mother was the
oldest child. I suppose her brothers and sisters were born after 1851. My grandmother's name was Mary Hildebrand (Tah. 170)
- Elizabeth Hildebrand (Tah. 170), mother. My father had an
Indian name but I don't know what it is. He may have been enrolled under that. He had no brothers and sisters that I know
of." SIGNED: Cynthia Peters, Stigler, Okla., Sep 10 1908.
ROLL P48 #8696 FCT COMM #17301 - Nannie Crain   - 29
         8697   17302 - Benie (dau)   - 14
         8698   17303 - Bessie May (dau)   - 12
         8699   1426m - Richard (son)   - 4
         8700   1427m - William Luther (son) - 2

94

10750. JIM CAMPBELL,   Porum, Okla
Admitted. Half brother of #10749 on the mother's side.
ROLL P37 #6568 FCT COMM #16859 - Jim Campbell - 19

10751. GEORGE CRAIN,   Porum, Okla
Admitted. Half brother of #10749 on the mother's side.
ROLL P48 #8691 FCT COMM #16858 - George Crain   - 25
        8692   1276m - Etter E. (dau) - 3
        8693   1277m - Eva May (dau) - 1

10752. DELILAH BIRD,   Briarstown, Okla
Admitted. Sister of #10748; claims thru same source.
ROLL P30 #5087 FCT COMM #16558 - Delilah Bird - 50

10753. CYNTHIA PETERS,   Porum, Okla
Admitted. Half sister of #10749 on the mother's side.
ROLL P110 #21149 FCT COMM #16855 - Cynthia Peters (dead) - 39
         21150   16857 - Henry RATLIFF (son)   - 15

10754. JENNIE MARTIN,   Porum, Okla
Admitted. Niece of #1724; and claims thru same source.
ROLL P96 #18433 FCT COMM #16958 - Jennie Martin - 23

10755. KATY McCLURE,   Porum, Okla
Admitted. The mother of the applicant enrolled by Drennen in
1851 in 351 G S as Darkey. The applicant was probably enrolled
as Kah-tah-goo-ga. See Flint 133 for great aunt Nelly & child.
See G. S. 2332 for enrollment of uncle, George Downing 3267.
ROLL P92 #17645 FCT COMM #5524 - Katy McClure - 55

10756. DORA A. BAUGHMAN,   Campbell, Okla
        by N. D. Baughman, Gdn.
Admitted. Half sister of #5205 and claims thru same source.
[For Roll information See App 10743]

10757. CHARLIE SUTAWAKEE and 2 children,   Campbell, Okla
Admitted. Son of #6597.
ROLL P135 #26065 FCT COMM #21088 - Charlie Sutawakee - 22
          26066   4909m - Gahoge (dau) - 4(App 17170)
          26067   4910m - A-to-la-ha (son) - 1
                                   (App 17169)

10758. NANNIE SHEARHART and 1 child,   Texanna, Okla
Admitted. Niece of #10755; and claims thru same source.
ROLL P126 #24315 FCT COMM #21608 - Nannie Shearhart - 23
          24316   4165m - Cale M. (son)   - 2

10759. ROBERT D. ROBERTS,   Major, Va
Rejected. Sizemore case. See special report #417.

10760. JAMES B. ROBERTS,   Major, Va
Rejected. Sizemore case. See special report #417.

10761. DOLLY NANCY ROBERTS,   Major, Va
Rejected. Sizemore case. See special report #417.

10762. SALLIE E. SCRAPER,   Baron, Okla
Admitted. Applicant is a sister of Nannie Watt #8956; claims
thru same source.
ROLL P124 #24003 FCT COMM #16689 - William Scraper - 26
                                   (App 16652)
        24004   22502 - Sallie E. (wife) - 22
        24005   29012 - Lula (dau)   - 4
        24006   3579m - Alice (dau)   - 3

10763. WILLIAM H. SWINFORD and 1 child,   Cleveland, Tenn
Rejected. Son of #25806 and claims thru same source.
MISC. TEST. P. 404. #25806-10763 - Mark L. Swinford:
     "That I am 53 years of age and live in Cleveland, Bradley
Co., Tenn. I claim my Indian descent through my mother and
her father. My grandfather went by two names. One of his names
was Jim Glass which was said to be his Indian name, and the
other was Jim Swofford. Don't know how he came to have two
names. He died along about 1870 but don't know when he was
born. He was in the war of 1812. My mother went by the name
of Glass before she was married. My mother nor her father was
never on any roll that I know of. My mother's oldest sister
was named Nancy Glass. She married an Awls. There was Clementine who never married. Julia Ann was another but I don't know
who she married. Elizabeth was another and married Jim Lawson.
Jack and Charlie were her two brothers. I don't know where my
mother and grandfather were born and raised.   My grandfather
they said went to the Indians when he was about 6 or 7 years
old and stayed with them until he was about 17 years of age.
They were the Cherokee and were in N. C. but I don't know what
part. My wife is a white woman. I don't know where my brother
Jim Swinford is. He used to live in Cleveland but he went to
Dalton, Ga. and I haven't heard from him since. I and my mother and her father were always recognized as white."
SIGNED: Mark L. "X" Swinford, Cleveland, Tenn., Jun 24 1908.

10764. CALLIE CREER,   Davis, Okla
Rejected. It does not appear that any ancestor was ever en-
rolled or that any ancestor was a party to the treaties of
1835, 6 or '46. Shows no connection with the Eastern Cher-
okees. Ancestors did not live in the Cherokee domain. Misc.
Test. P. 2304.
MISC. TEST. P. 2304. No 10765-10764 - Mrs. Rebecca Powell:
     "My name is Mrs. Rebecca Powell; my post-office is Davis,
Okla.; I was born in Grayson Co., Texas in 1860; I claim relationship to the Cherokee Indians through my father, Benjamin
Hinchee, who was one-quarter Cherokee; my father was born in
Bowling Green, Logan Co., Kentucky in 1831; he claimed through
his father Jona Hinchee, who was one-half Cherokee; my father
& his people lived in Kentucky until they moved to Texas some-

96

time prior to the Civil War; some of the family spell their
name Hinchee as Hinchey; my great-grandmother was Polly Clark,
and she was born and raised in Kentucky; the Hincheys shown on
the final rolls of the Five Civilized Tribe are relatives of
ours and they claim back through Polly Clark, full blood the
same as I do."
SIGNED: Mrs. Rebecca Powell, Sulphur, Okla., Aug 26 1908.
EXCEPTION CASE. 10764. Samuel K. Hinchee, App #11511,
Cunningham, Ky. Rejected. Total number of exceptions filed
in this group -- 2. Original recommendation renewed.

10765. REBECCA POWELL,   Davis, Okla
Rejected. Mother of #10764.

10766. JOHN T. BLEVINS and 3 children,   Crumpler, N C
Rejected. Sizemore case. See special report #417.

10767. CHARLES PATTERSON and 5 children,   Santa Luca, Ga
Rejected. Brother of #9947; claims thru same source.

10768. LULU STARR HASTING,   Tahlequah, Okla
Admitted. Sister to #8890; claims thru same source.
ROLL P72 #13533 FCT COMM # 1788 - William W. Hastings - 40
                              (App 23624)
        13534   1789 - Lula S. (wife)   - 33
        13535   1790 - Lucille (dau)   - 7
        13536   1064m - Mayme Starr (dau)   - 4

10769. MAY BELLE STARR,   Tahlequah, Okla
Admitted. Niece of #2204.
ROLL P132 #25495 FCT COMM #1878 - May Belle Starr - 21

10770. ELDEE STARR,   Tahlequah, Okla
Admitted. Niece of #2204.
ROLL P132 #25427 FCT COMM #1877 - Eldee Starr - 34

10771. MAGGIE E. STARR,   Tahlequah, Okla
Admitted. Aunt of #8890; claims thru same source.
ROLL P132 #25493 FCT COMM #22637 - Maggie E. Starr - 49

10772. MAGGIE STARR, Gdn. of 4 children,   Tahlequah, Okla
Admitted. Nieces and nephews of #2204.
ROLL P132 #25475 FCT COMM #1879 - Joel Mays Starr - 19
          25476   1880 - Callie L. (sis) - 17
          25477   1881 - J. Ruth (sis)   - 14
          25478   1882 - Ezekiel E. (bro) - 10
                              by Maggie E. Starr, Gdn.

10773. MARY E. GLAD and 3 children,   Manard, Okla
Rejected. Applicant's mother is an old settler and her father
is a white man. See application.

10774. TOM SWIMMER,   Wahhiyah, N C
Admitted. Claims thru father who was enrolled by Chapman
under name of Ah-yeh-he-neh #29 and mother under the name of
Ain-cih #258.
ROLL P18 #2604 - Tom Swimmer - 43

10775. FIDEL CHU-LO-AN-WE,   Big Cove, N C
Admitted. Father on Chapman #397.   Mother on Chapman #869.
Grandmother on Chapman #868. Misc. Test. P. 1741.
MISC. TEST. P. 1741. Witness re #10775 - James Blythe, in
behalf of Fidel Chu-li-au-wee,, #10775:
    "That I am acquainted with Fidel Chu-li-au-wee. His mother
was An-sih, enrolled by Hester as No. 667. Her father's name
was Wa-tah-too-kih. I have heard he went west. Fidel's father
was Choo-le-ah-wuh.   Fidel is no relation to Tom Swimmer,
#10774. SIGNED: James Blythe, Cherokee, N. C., Jul 21 1908.
ROLL P7 #492 - Fidel Chu-lo-an-we - 38

10776. FRANCES B. GIBSON,   Muskogee, Okla
Admitted. Sister of #7912; claims thru same source.
ROLL P65 #12139 FCT COMM #13832 - Frances B. Gibson - 19

10777. TENNESSEE F. JORDAN and 6 children, Molden Ridge, Tenn
Rejected. Ancestors were never enrolled. Does not prove
genuine connection with Cherokee tribe. Ancestors were not
parties to the treaties of 1835-6 or '46. Misc. Test. P. 441.
[? last digit typed over]
MISC. TEST. P. 441. No 10777 - Tennessee Jordan:
    "My name is Tennessee Jordan; I was born in Rhea Co.,
Tenn. in 1863; I am forty-five years old; I claim my Indian
blood through my father; my father, James Corvin, was born in
Va. in Withe Co., I think, about 1820; my father got his Indian blood from his father Thomas Corvin; I think my grand
father Thomas Corvin, was born in Va.; I never saw my grand
father, Thomas Corvin; I make no claim of Indian blood through
my mother; neither my father nor I were ever enrolled and never received any money or land that I know of; I do not know
why my father or grandfather were never enrolled ; my father
told me that I was part Cherokee, but he never told me how
much; both I and my father were always considered as white
people in the community in which we lived; I never heard of my
father or grandfather having an Indian name; my father never
lived with the Indians as a member of the tribe that I know
of." SIGNED: Tennessee "X" Jordan, Dayton, Tenn., Jun 24 1908.
MISC. TEST. P. 442. No 10781 - Pleasant M. Corvin:
    "My name is Pleasant M. Corvin; I was born in Meigs Co.,
Tenn. in 1845; I claim my Indian blood through my father; my
father's name was Philo Corvin. I think my father was born in
Withe Co., Va. in 1823; I think my father got his Indian blood
through his father, whose name was Thomas Corvin; I think his
grandfather was born in Va.; he came from Va. to Meigs Co.
Tenn. I also claim Indian blood through my mother; I think my

mother was born in Overton Co., Tenn. in (1825); my mother's maiden name was Margaret Teague; I think my mother got her Indian blood through her father, whose name was William Teague; neither I nor any of my ancestors were ever enrolled and never received any money or land that I know of; my father or mother never lived with the Indians as a member of the tribe; none of my ancestors through whom I claim were ever held as slaves or lived with the Indians. None of the ancestors through whom I claim ever had an Indian name that I know of. I learned from my parents that I was part Cherokee Indian, but they did not tell me how much. I was about ten years old when my mother died. I am always regarded as a white man in the community in which I live."
SIGNED: Pleasant M. Corvin, Dayton, Tenn., Jun 24 1908.
Henry Goin...deposes and says:
"My name is Henry Goin; I have known Pleasant M. Corvin since 1861; I knew the father of Pleasant M. Corvin. In the community in which they lived they were commonly regarded to be part Indian. I have heard the testimony of Pleasant M. Corvin and I have reason to believe that it is true."
SIGNED: Henry "X" Goin, Dayton, Tenn., Jun 24 1908.
EXCEPTION CASE. 10777. Pleasant N. Corwin, App #10781, Dayton, Tenn. Rejected. Total number of exceptions filed in this group -- 2. Original recommendation renewed.

10778. MARTHA E. CLOUSE and 4 children, Graysville, Tenn
Rejected. Niece of #4573; claims thru same source.

10779. MILLER GOINS, Graysville, Tenn
Rejected. 1st cousin of #6289; claims thru same source.

10780. JOSEPH H. EVERETT, Graysville, Tenn
Rejected. Nephew of #4573; claims thru same source.

10781. PLEASANT M. COWIN, Dayton, Tenn
Rejected. Niece of #10777.

10782. OLIVIER P. BREMER, Muskogee, Okla
Admitted. 1st cousin of # [blank] Father of applicant enrolled in 1851 in Illinois #263.
ROLL P33 #5760 FCT COMM #17588 - Oliver P. Brewer - 35

10783. MICHAEL O. GHORMLEY and 5 children, Tahlequah, Okla
Admitted. Brother of 2216. Applicant enrolled in 1851 in G. S. #544.
ROLL P65 #12101 FCT COMM #14517 - Michael O. Ghormley - 59
          12102   14518 - Nancy (wife) - 50(App 10784)
          12103   14520 - Lorenzo (son)   - 20
          12104   14522 - Rachel C. (dau) - 15
          12105   14523 - Lillie M. (dau) - 13
          12106   14524 - Stephen M. (son) - 11
          12107   14521 - Nancy J (dau) -20(App 27507)

10784. NANCY GHORMLEY,   Tahlequah, Okla
Admitted. Half sister on father's side of #8216. [For Roll
information See App 10783]

10785. LAURA W. WILLIAMS and 3 children,   Blairsville, Ga
Rejected. Cousin of #4748; claims thru same source.

10786. JENYMIRE C. BOLING,   Blairsville, Ga
Rejected. Cousin of #4748; claims thru same source.

10787. ELIZABETH S. DUNCAN,   Tahlequah, Okla
Admitted. Aunt of #14786 and claims thru same source. Appli-
cant enrolled as "Elizabeth Sanders 567 Flint."
ROLL P56 #10263 FCT COMM #14718 - Elizabeth S. Duncan - 74

10788. MATTIE S. THOMAS and 4 children,   Athens, Tenn
Rejected. Applicant or ancestors never enrolled. Applicant
claims thru her father and he was a slave. Misc. Test. P. 561.
MISC. TEST. P. 561. #19731-10788 - Mattie S. Thomas:
    "That I am 32 years of age and live in McMinn Co., Tenn. I
claim Indian descent through my father and his father. My
mother was a colored woman. My father was a Cherokee Indian,
but I don't know how much. My grandfather was 3/4 Cherokee.
A man by the name of Jackson owned my father. My father was
born in Jefferson Co., Tenn."
SIGNED: Mattie S. Thomas, Athens, Tenn., Jun 26 1908.

10789. WILSON PELONE,   Webbers Falls, Okla
Admitted. Uncle of #180.
ROLL P107 #20608 FCT COMM #29036 - Wilson Palone - 45

10790. GEORGE M. HUGHES,   Tahlequah, Okla
Admitted. Brother of #1619; claims thru same source.
ROLL P79 #14875 FCT COMM #14855 - George M. Hughes - 34
         14876   - Sue A (wife) - 38(App 11885)

10791. NICK SUNDAY,   Locust Grove, Okla
Admitted. Nephew of #175.
ROLL P135 #26033 FCT COMM #16215 - Nick Sunday - 21

10792. MOLLIE PIGEON,   Wauhillau, Okla
Admitted. Applicant's father and mother enrolled as Te-cha-
tah and Anna at Flint 610.
ROLL P111 #21448 FCT COMM #20866 - Milie Pigeon - 56

10793. DENNIS HOOD and 3 children,   Brushby, Okla
Admitted. Applicant's father and grandfather were enrolled by
Drennen in S. B. Dist. #130.
ROLL P77 #14549 FCT COMM #25894 - Dennis Hood   - 32
         14550   25895 - Lizzie (dau)   - 8
         14551   32085 - Hattie E. (dau) - 6
         14552   4863m - Tokay E. (son) - 4

10794. MAGGIE COOKSEY and 5 children,   McKey, Okla
Admitted. Information on this case can be had by reference to
the report upon which the Act of Congress roll was based. Applicant's mother probably enrolled on Act of Congress rolls as
Issiffi Still. Maternal grandmother on same roll as Sandell
Still. Maternal grandfather enrolled on 1835 roll. This application should go with #8067 when it is located.   See Misc.
Test. P. 3962. [For Testimony See App 3933, Vol. 2]
EXCEPTION CASE. Denied. Objection filed by J. L. Springston to
enrollment of applicants, Maggie Cooksey and 5 children. Said
objection does not set forth substantial ground for change of
former decision in case -- former decision confirmed.
ROLL P46 #8311 - Maggie Cooksey - 31
           8312 - Johnnie (son) - 14
           8313 - Benton (son)   - 12
           8314 - Nannie (dau)   - 10
           8315 - Robert (son)   - 9
           8316 - Floyd (son)   - 5

10795. ORA BULLOCK and 1 child,   Wichita Falls, Tex
Rejected. Sister to #10250.

10796. J. H. BELL and 2 children,   Atlanta, Ga
Rejected. Blythe case. See special report #153.

10797. SAMUEL R. HINCHE and 1 child,   Shawnee, Okla
Rejected. Uncle of #10764; claims thru same source.

10798. JAMES A. CURTIS,   Dickson, Tenn
Rejected. John Hatcher case. See #10798.

HATCHER-CURTIS GROUP #10798.

     There is a large number of cases in which the applicants
claim the right to share in the distribution of the Eastern
Cherokee fund, by reason of the fact that they are descendants
of one John Hatcher, who they allege, was an Eastern Cherokee
Indian. These applicants are scattered over a wide area, -
some in Texas, some in Tennessee, some in Indiana, and a number in several other states.   They claim through no other
source than John Hatcher. The name "Hatcher" does not appear
either on the roll of 1835 or 1851, nor do any of the descendants of John Hatcher appear on the Chapman Roll of 1851 or
the Hester Roll of 1884.   There is nothing in any of these
applications or in any of the letters received in regard to
these cases which would indicate that John Hatcher or any of
his descendants ever lived with the Cherokee tribe.   There is
nothing in any of these cases tending to show that John
Hatcher or any of his descendants were parties to the treaties
of 1835-6 and 1846. There is nothing in any of these cases to
show that John Hatcher or any of his descendants were enrolled. Some of the applicants do claim that John Hatcher

came from North Carolina to Tennessee in 1835, and some say
that he came from the "Cherry [sic] Nation", which does not
bespeak great familiarity with Cherokee affairs. There is
nothing in these applications to show the slightest connection
with the Eastern Cherokees, and for the reasons set forth, all
of the applicants who base their claims upon John Hatcher, are
rejected.
EXCEPTION CASE. Rejected. Total number of exceptions filed
in this group — 120. Original recommendation renewed.

10799. WILLIAM F. KEITH and 7 children,   Porum, Okla
Admitted. Nephew of #161; claims thru same source.
ROLL P84 #15957 FCT COMM #12592 - William F. Keith   - 35
             15958   12593 - Albert M. (son)   - 13
             15959   12594 - Paul (son)   - 10
             15960   12595 - Pearlie L. (dau)   - 8
             15961   12596 - Reuben M. (son)   - 6
             15962   12597 - Veror Azzeleen (dau) - 4
             15963   3487m - William Jr. (son)   - 2
             15964   3488m - Beulah B. (dau)   - 1/4

10800. THOMAS C. WEST and 2 children,   Briartown, Okla
Admitted. Half brother of #5238 and claims thru same source.
ROLL P149 #28920 FCT COMM #28333 - Thomas C. West   - 38
              28921   28334 - Tecumseh (dau)   - 5
              28922   4349m - William C. (son)   - 1/3

10801. LOUIS M. FRANKLIN,   Tennessee City, Tenn
Rejected. Does not show that parents were living within the
Cherokee domain in 1835-6, as recognized Cherokees. Ancestors
not enrolled. Misc. Test. P. 491.
MISC. TEST. P. 491. No 10801 - Louis M. Franklin:
    "I am 61 years of age; was born in Cherokee County, N. C.
I claim Cherokee Indian blood thru both my father and mother.
I never received any Indian money from the government nor did
my father and mother. I have never tried before to get any.
My father died before I remember. My parents lived with the
Indians before they left N. C. When they went away my mother
stayed in N. C. I do not know what became of my father but
think he died when I was small. Louisa Morgan was my aunt.
Two of her sisters went West with the Indians."
SIGNED: Louis M. "X" Franklin, Dickson, Tenn., Jun 25 1908.
A. Bishop, witness for Louis M. Franklin...deposes and says:
    "I know Louis M. Franklin; his mother said was Cherokee
Indian. When we were boys he was called Little Indian. His
parents lived in tents with the Indians so his mother said.
They came from Cherokee County, N. C. to Gilmore Co., Ga.,
when I was a small boy. His people came and bought adjoining
farms to my father. His father spoke the Indian language and
his mother also. I do not know if they ever received any Indian money from the government. His father went to Morganton,
N. C. and I never saw him again. This was a good while before

102

the war."
SIGNED: A. "X" Bishop, Dickson, Tenn., Jun 25 1908.
EXCEPTION CASE. Rejected. Total number of exceptions filed
in this group -- 2. Original recommendation renewed.

It does not appear that applicant was enrolled with the
Eastern Cherokees in 1851 or 1883, nor does the name of any
ancestor appear on the rolls of 1835 or 1851. It does not
appear that claimant's ancestors were recognized members of
the Eastern Cherokee Tribe in 1835 or 1846. Misc. Test. P. 491

10802. LOUIS M. FRANKLIN, Duplicate of #10801.

10803. Children of #7477. See #7477. [Vol. 4]

10804. JEFFERSON ARNEACH, Almond, N C
Admitted. Applicant's father Ah-quoo-ta-kih was enrolled by
Chapman #621. See letter herein.
ROLL P5 #66 - Jefferson Arneach - 32
        67 - Sarah (wife)   - 31 (App 15780)
        68 - David BIRD (son) - 13
        69 - Lizzie BIRD (dau) - 10
        70 - Bessie BIRD (dau) - 6

10805. DAVID BIRD, BELLE BIRD, BESSIE BIRD, Almond, N C
        by Jefferson Arneach.
Admitted. Nephew and nieces of #10020 and claims thru same
ancestors. Minor children of #15780 and enrolled as such.
[For Roll information See App 10804. NOTE: children's application numbers were not listed on roll]

10806. HENRY HORNBUCKLE, Birdtown, N C
Admitted. Uncle of #7651; claims thru same ancestors. This
applicant is dead.
ROLL P10 #1160 - Henry Hornbuckle (dec'd) - [age cut off]

10807. EMMA L. HYDEN, Atlanta, Ga*
Admitted. Niece of #3833; claims thru same source. [* Also
"54 Jackson St." on roll]
ROLL P11 #1243 - Emma L. Hyden - 30

10808. PETER NATTYTOM, Cherokee, N C
Admitted. Brother of #6642.
ROLL P14 #1763 - Peter Nottytom - 37
        1764 - Nancy (wife)   - 22 (App 10809)

10809. NANCY NATTYTOM, Cherokee, N C
Admitted. Sister of #7742; claims thru same source. [For
Roll information See App 10808]

10810. MARTHA SHEETS, Transon, N C
Rejected. Sizemore case. See special report #417.

10811. LULA SHEETS.   Beldon, N C
Rejected. Sizemore case. See special report #417.

10812. CARDOVIE SHEETS,   Beldon, N C
Rejected. Sizemore case. See special report #417.

10813. FORSTER SHEETS,   Beldon, N C
Rejected. Sizemore case. See special report #417.

10814. LUAIDER SHEETS,   Beldon, N C
Rejected. Sizemore case. See special report #417.

10815. LUE ELLEN SHEETS,   Transom, N C
Rejected. Sizemore case. See special report #417.

10816. JAMES F. SHEETS,   Beldon, N C
Rejected. Sizemore case. See special report #417.

10817. HATTIE V. SHEETS,   Transon, N C
Rejected. Sizemore case. See special report #417.

10818. U. S. GRANT SHEETS,   Beldon, N C
Rejected. Sizemore case. See special report #417.

10819. EDNA SHEETS,   Beldon, N C
Rejected. Sizemore case. See special report #417.

10820. HESTER SHEETS,   Beldon, N C
Rejected. Sizemore case. See special report #417.

10821. CECIL SHEETS,   Beldon, N C
Rejected. Sizemore case. See special report #417.

10822. VIRDIE MILLS,   Crumpler, N C
Rejected. Sizemore case. See special report #417.

10823. LOUISA HARRISON,   Neosho, Mo
Rejected. Sister to #3753; claims thru same source.

10824. WILLIAM J. GAMBILL and 7 children, Big Cabin, Okla
Rejected. Brother of #9353.

10825. BENJ. WILLIAMS,   Curtis, Tex
Rejected. Brother of #7786; claims thru same source.]

10826. BRUCE WILLIAMSON,   Joplin, Mo
Rejected. Cousin of #7040 and claims thru same ancestors.

10827. CORA SCOTT,   Denver, Colo
Rejected. It does not appear that any ancestor was ever enrolled or that any ancestor was a party to the treat of 1835-6
or '46. Ancestors did not live within the Cherokee domain.

Shows no connection with the Eastern Cherokees.

10828. JAMES M. ROWELL,   Flo, Tex
Rejected. Uncle of #7085; claims thru same source.

10829. MAGGIE E. PHARIS,   Leyden, Via Golden, Colo
Rejected. Aunt of #7038; claims thru same source.

10830. W. F. LEWIS,   McKinney, Tex
Rejected. It does not appear that any ancestor was ever enrolled or that any ancestor was a party to the treaties of
1835-6 or '46.   Shows no connection with the Eastern Cherokees. Misc. Test. P. 2491.
MISC. TEST. P. 2491. #10830 - Wm. Francis Lewis:
    "That I am 44 years of age. I claim my Indian descent thru
my mother; my father was a full blooded white man. My mother
was born in 1826 and died in 1889. She was born in Buncombe
Co., N. C. She left N. C. in 1845 and went to Cocke Co., Tenn.
She lived there until she died.   She claimed Indian descent
thru her mother. She was also born in N. C.   I think in Buncombe Co. My mother claimed to be 1/4 or 1/5 Cherokee. I don't
know whether my mother or her mother ever lived with the Indians as members of the tribe or not.   They lived there in
N. C. with them. Don't know whether either of them were ever
on any Indian rolls or ever received anything from the government. My mother was recognized as a mixed blooded woman. My
grandmother showed the Indian blood very much. This is the
only application I have ever made for Indian benefits. All of
us have married white people."
SIGNED: William Francis Lewis, McKinney, Tex., Aug 31 1908.
EXCEPTION CASE. Wm. Francis Lewis & 6 children, R. 1, Anna,
Tex. Rejected. Total number of exceptions filed in this
group -- 3. Original recommendation renewed.

10831. ALBERT L. LEWIS and 1 child,   McKinney, Tex
Rejected. Brother of #10830; claims thru same source.

10832. POLLY KUYKENDALL and 2 children,   Wealaka, Okla
Rejected. Sister of #923 and claims thru same ancestors.

10833. MRS. JANE EDWARDS,   Hortonville, Ind
Rejected. Sister to #8222; claims thru same source.

10834. MARTHA P. DALTON and 5 children,   Carter, Okla
Rejected. It does not appear that applicant's ancestors were
parties to the treaties of 1835-6 or '46, nor enrolled with
the Cherokees.

10835. REBECCA A. COLBERT,   St. Joseph, Mo
Rejected. Claims thru same source as #7053.

10836. JULIA BLACKWELL and 4 children,   McKinney, Tex
Rejected. Sister to #10830; claims thru same source.

10837. JOHN POLLARD ALLEN,   Fairview, Okla
Rejected. Brother to #8222; claims thru same source.

10838. CHARLES ANDREW ALLEN and 1 child,   Hortonville, Ind
Rejected. Brother to #8222 and claims thru same source.

10839. HELEN MEACHAIN and 2 children,   Cordova, N C
Rejected. "Indian Tom" case. See special report #3090.

10840. JESSE E. MEACHAIN and 1 child,   Cordova, N C
Rejected. "Indian Tom" case. See special report #3090.

10841. ELLIS B. MORSE and 1 child,   Cordova, N C
Rejected. "Indian Tom" case. See special report #3090.

10842. ETTIE J. MORSE,   Cordova, N C
Rejected. "Indian Tom" case. See special report #3090.

10843. NETTIE F. MORSE,   Cordova, N C
Rejected. "Indian Tom" case. See special report #3090.

10844. SHERWOOD THOMAS MORSE and 4 children, Cordova, N C
Rejected. "Indian Tom" case. See special report #3090.

10845. LIZZIE SIN CLAIR and 1 child,   Cordova, N C
Rejected. "Indian Tom" case. See special report #3090.

10846. JULIA A. BRAY and 3 children,   Cordova, N C
Rejected. "Indian Tom" case. See special report #3090.

10847. ANNIE GENTRY,   Grandview, N C
Rejected. Blythe case. See special report #153.

10848. WM. J. SLOAN and 2 children,   Springfield, Mo
Rejected. Claims thru Alex. Brown. See special report #35.

10849. LILLIE C. McGRATH and 3 children, Wichita Falls, Tex
Rejected. Sister of #10250.

10850. MATTIE BACON and 3 children,   Bowie, Tex
Rejected. 1st cousin and claims thru same source as #10250.

10851. AMELIA JANE CARNES,   Wichita Falls, Tex
Rejected. 1st cousin to #10250 and claims thru same source.

10852. MAUDE CARNES,   Wichita Falls, Tex
Rejected. Sister to #10250.

10853. WM. WASHINGTON LLOYD and 4 children, Duncan, Ariz
Rejected. Claims thru Water Hunter. See 10448.

10854. CORA GOODWIN and 3 children,   Rosebud, Tex
Rejected. It does not appear that any ancestor was ever enrolled or that any ancestor was a party to the treaty of 1835–
1836 or '46. Shows no real connection with the Eastern Cherokees.

10855. ELIZABETH MORSE and 2 children,   Artesie, N Mex
Rejected. Cousin of #551 and claims thru same ancestors

10856. DELORA JONES and 2 children,   Rosebud, Tex
Rejected. Sister to #10854 and claims thru same source.

10857. BENJ. M. DOCKERY and 4 children,   Brady, N C
Rejected. Blythe case. See special report #153.

10858. MARION W. MASON and 5 children,   Kyle, N C
Rejected. Son of #529 and claims thru same ancestors.

10859. EDWARD E. CARNES and 3 children,   Wichita Falls, Tex
Rejected. Brother to #10250.

10860. JACOB A. FRANKLIN and 5 children,   Chattanooga, Tenn
Rejected. 2nd cousin of #315; claims thru same source.

10861. JOHN L. LEGG,   Serena, W Va
Rejected. Sizemore case. See special report #417.

10862. MARTHA J. BIRD and 3 children,   Serena, W Va
Rejected. Sizemore case. See special report #417.

10863. REBECCA J. BROWN and 2 children,   Serena, W Va
Rejected. Sizemore case. See special report #417.

10864. WM. J. FITZWATERS,   Serena, W Va
Rejected. Sizemore case. See special report #417.

10865. SARAH A. KEITH,   Serena, W Va
Rejected. Sizemore case. See special report #417.

10866. ARMINTA J. HAMRICK and 3 children, Moroco, W Va
Rejected. Sizemore case. See special report #417.

10867. GEO. W. OSBURN,   Ira, W Va
Rejected. Sizemore case. See special report #417.

10868. MELISSA A. BROWN and 2 children,   Serena, W Va
Rejected. Sizemore case. See special report #417.

10869. MANERVA MARTIN and 2 children, Blaine, Ca
Rejected. Grandchild of Rebecca McGaha #4170.

10870. JAMES A. OSBURN and 2 children, Serena, W Va
Rejected. Sizemore case. See special report #417.

10871. BERTHA C. LEGG and 1 child, Serena, W Va
Rejected. Sizemore case. See special report #417.

10872. EMERY J. OSBURN and 2 children, Serena, W Va
Rejected. Sizemore case. See special report #417.

10873. SOLOMON OSBURN and 1 child, Ira, W Va
Rejected. Sizemore case. See special report #417.

10874. ELLA SIMMONS, Serena, W Va
Rejected. Sizemore case. See special report #417.

10875. GUY KEITH, Serena, W Va
Rejected. Sizemore case. See special report #417.

10876. JOHN T. OSBURN, Serena, W Va
Rejected. Sizemore case. See special report #417.

10877. WILBURN OSBURN, Serena, W Va
Rejected. Sizemore case. See special report #417.

10878. JOHN W. OSBURN and 6 children, Morocco, W Va
Rejected. Sizemore case. See special report #417.

10879. ANDREW J. MILLER and 1 child, Tahlequah, Okla
Admitted. 1st cousin of #3461. Claimant's father enrolled in
1851 by Drennen in G. S. #448.
ROLL P99 #18871 FCT COMM #25352 - Andrew J. Miller - 33
         18872   25353 - Mattie E. (dau) - 12

10880. ANNIE E. MILES, Nowata, Okla
Admitted. Niece of #1556; claims thru same source.
ROLL P98 #18842 FCT COMM #4711 - Annie E. Miles - 8
                              by William E. Miles, Gdn.

10881. JESSIE E. MILES, Nowata, Okla
Admitted. Nephew of #1556; claims thru same source.
ROLL P98 #18844 FCT COMM #4712 - Jessie Miles - 5
                              by William E. Miles, Gdn.

10882. LIZZIE DOWNING, Chauteau, Okla
Admitted. Aunt of #2141; claims thru same source. [Notation
on roll "Downing, Lizzie, with John Deerhead. See Roll No.
9537"]
ROLL P52 #9536 FCT COMM #6284 - John Deerhead - 31 (App 14287)
         9537   6285 - Lizzie (wife) - 47

108

10883. SUSIE BEAVER,   Marble, Okla
Admitted. Applicant's grandfather enrolled as Lewis Beaver,
by Drennen at Flint #577. Misc. Test. P. 3978.
MISC. TEST. P. 3978.   No 5957-5926 - William Young...through
D. M. Faulkner, Interpreter:
    "My name is William Young; my post-office is Marble City,
Okla.; I am about seventy-three years old; I knew George
Beaver, father of Linda Vann; Lindan [sic] Vann, No. 5957;
George Beaver's father was known as High Beaver, Indian name
Cah-lah-loh-tie, Flint 576; Cah-lah-loh-tie had a brother
named Ice Beaver, one named Lewis. (See Flint 574 and 577)."
SIGNED: William "X" Young, Marble City, Okla., Mar 18 1909.
ROLL P28 #4617 FCT COMM #20512 - Susie Beaver - 22

10884. HESTER McCOY,   Vian, Okla
Admitted. Niece of #4507.
ROLL P93 #17733 FCT COMM #20715 - Ned McCoy   - 29
                                  (App 13202)
         17734   2876 - Hester (wife) - 29

10885. STELLA E. ALLEN,   Wichita, Kans
Rejected. 2nd cousin of #10609; claims thru same source.

10886. ALAFORD WEAVER,   Madison, Wis
Rejected. Fully set forth in statement filed in application
#10886.
EXCEPTION CASE.   Ellen F. Shivers & 4 children, App #11474,
418 Mill St., LaCrosse, Wis. Rejected. Total number of exceptions filed in this group -- 103. Original recommendation
renewed.

10887. ROBERT E. BARNETT and 1 child,   Flint, Okla
Rejected. Claims thru the same source as #5141.
EXCEPTION CASE.   Admitted as to child, through mother. Rejected as to father. Bertha M. Barnett (minor) is a daughter
of Sarah F. Barnett, Miller Roll No. 4315. Omitted formerly
through a clerical error. Robert E. Barnett, father. In his
case original recommendation renewed. Exception discloses no
clerical error and sets forth no additional material facts.
SUPP ROLL #30509 FCT COMM #3349m - Bertha M. Barnett - 2
                          by Sarah F. Barnett, mother & Gdn.

10888. GEORGE H. WEST and 2 children,   Chocotah, Okla
Admitted. Half brother of #5238; claims thru same source.
ROLL P149 #28873 FCT COMM #17444 - George H. West   - 40
          28874   17445 - Berta May (dau)   - 5
          28875   2955m - Laura Annie (dau) - 3

10889. WM. L. MILLER,   Muskogee, Okla
Admitted. 1st cousin of #3461. Claimant's father is enrolled
by Drennen in 1851 in G. S. #448. [For Roll information See
App 5520, Vol. 3]

10890. THOMAS F. TAYLOR,   Tahlequah, Okla
Admitted. 1st cousin to #715. Mother of applicant, "Cora
Barnes" 169-1/2 Ill.
ROLL P137 #26509 FCT COMM #16318 - Thos. F. Taylor - 28

10891. ROBERT W. CRAIG,   Kingsburg, Cal
Admitted. Nephew of #9422.
ROLL P48 #8669 FCT COMM #9371 - Robert W. Craig - 28

10892. CHARLES S. CRAIG and 3 children,   Dixon, Cal
Admitted. Nephew of #9422.
ROLL P48 #8650 - Charles S. Craig - 49
          8651 - Annie T. (dau) - 20
          8652 - Charles A. (son) - 18
          8653 - Gladys P. (dau) - 5

10893. JACK W. McCRARY,   Vinita, Okla
          by his mother Laura Whittington, Gdn.
Admitted. Great nephew of #735 and claims thru same source.
Grandfather "N. B. McCrary 25 Delaware."
ROLL P93 #17751 FCT COMM #21672 - Jack W. McCrary - 11
                              by Laura Whittington, Gdn.

10894. SUSANNA WALKER, Included in application of mother
#10895.
MISC. TEST. P. 3651. App 10894 - Jennie Corntassell...through
her husband, John Corntassell:
    "My name is Jennie Corntassell. I live at at Vinita, Okla.
7922 is my Dawes Commission number. I am the mother and guardian of Suzanne Walker. I was not living in 1852. My mother
and father were Immigrants. My father was named John Buzzard.
He drew Immigrant money in 1852. I think he did. He lived in
Del. Dist. Her grandfather's name was Buzzard. Her mother's
name was Betsey. John Buzzard had brothers and sister; War-la-
loo, Katy, Alcey, and Ne-que-tieye. See Del. 471. My number is
10895. Susanna Walker was enrolled by the Dawes Commission.
Her number is (?) [sic]."
SIGNED: Jennie Corntassell, Vinita, Okla., Oct. 12 1908.

10895. JANE CORNTASSELL,   Vinita, Okla
Admitted. 1st cousin of #9496 and claims thru same source.
Applicant's father enrolled in Del. 417. Sister to #3818.
[For Roll information See App 1873, Vol. 2]

10896. JOHN M. INGRAM and 5 children,   Dawson, Okla
Admitted. Nephew of #361.
ROLL P80 #15075 FCT COMM #12693 - John M. Ingram   - 37
          15076   8655 - Mattie B. (wife) - 25
                              (App 21830)
          15077   12695 - Georgia L. (dau) - 13
          15078   12696 - Roy B. (son)   - 11
          15079   12697 - John M. Jr. (son) - 9

                         110

10896. JOHN M. INGRAM (Cont)
        15080 FCT COMM #12698 - Anna L. (dau)   - 7
        15081   4040 - Waunita (dau)   - 3

10897. LOUISA SUAGEE,   Vinita, Okla
Rejected. Claims only as a widow of David Suagee who died
Nov. 30, 1897.

10898. THOMAS SUAGEE, LOUISA AMANDA SUAGEE, Foyil, Okla
        by Louisa Suagee, Gdn.
Admitted. Nephew and niece of #714; claims thru same source.
Father "A-ve" or David, 83 Delaware.
ROLL P134 #25916 FCT COMM #7509 - Thomas Wilson Suagee - 19
        25917   7510 - Louisa Amanda (sis) - 16
                         by Louisa Suagee, Gdn.

10899. NELLIE M. HANNAR and 5 children,   Blujacket, Okla*
Admitted. Niece of #714 and claims thru same source. Father
"A-ve" or David "83 Del". [* Also "RFD #1" on roll]
ROLL P71 #13352 FCT COMM #13578 - Nellie M. Harnar - 27
        13353   13579 - Eulailiah (dau)   - 7
        13354   13580 - Ralph R. (son)   - 5
        13355   13581 - Claud R. (son)   - 4
        13356   2999m - Randall D. (son) - 2
        13357   - Clyde (son)   - 1/6

10900. MARIAH TAYLOR and 1 child,   Vian, Okla
Admitted. Claims thru father enrolled as Johnson Love. Moth-
er enrolled as Sally Love. Brother enrolled as Horsefly Love.
All of whom were enrolled by Drennen in 1851 in Tahlequah Dis-
trict, Group #308.
ROLL P137 #26430 FCT COMM #17532 - John Taylor   - 35
                         (App 23862)
        26431   17533 - Maria (wife)   - 37
        26432   17534 - Jesse DOWNING - 16
                         (son of w)

10901. JANIE ELLEN PITCH,   Leach, Okla
Admitted. Applicant enrolled as A-chee-nee and her father as
Kah-tah-la-nah at G. S. #66. Misc. Test. P. 3798.
MISC. TEST. P. 3798. #10901 - Annie Sanders:
    "My name is Annie Sanders. I have known Janie Ellen Pitch
for about 30 years. She is a fullblood Cherokee Cherokee.
[sic] She was enrolled by the Dawes Commission and received
her allotment. She was enrolled in 1851 under the name of A-
chin-nih Gah-dah-la-nuh or Big Feather -- English, Jennie Big
Feather. She was enrolled in Flint District. She had a brother
by the name of Johnson or Johnsinne. She had a sister by the
name of Nelly. I think all three were enrolled in 1851. They
were enrolled in Flint District. Her father was Gah-dah-la-nuh
and her mother was Gah-lee-stah-yah. There were living [sic]
in Flint District in 1851 and were enrolled. I do not remember

111

of seeing them but I think they were living in Flint District in 1851. I think they were living in 1851. (Above statement refers to sentence below) Her grandparents on her father's side were Oo-wah-hyuh-skee and Goo-dah-ye. Her grand parents on her mother's side were White Road and Nancy Whiteroad. I do not know the names of any of the uncles or aunts of Janie Ellen Pitch. I am positive that the ancestors of applicant, Janie Pitch, were Emigrant Cherokees. Her parents were brought out to the Indian Territory by the soldiers. None of them to my knowledge received any Old Settler money. She was enrolled and drew the Strip payment in 1894."
SIGNED: Annie Sanders, Locust Grove, Okla., Oct 14 1908.
ROLL P111 #21459 - Janie Ellen Pitch - over 56 [sic]

10902. JAMES PORTER,   Marble, Okla
Admitted. Son of #4205 and claims thru same ancestors.
ROLL P112 #21565 FCT COMM #25715? [sic] - James Porter - 29

10903. WOLFE PORTER,   Marble, Okla
Admitted with father #4205. [For Roll information See App 4205, Vol. 3]

10904. ALEX. McCOY, JR., and 2 children,   Vian, Okla
Admitted. Claims thru father enrolled as Jack McCoy, Ill Dist. Group #202. [For Roll information See App 7658, Vol. 4]

10905. SAM OWL and 5 children,   Wauhillau, Okla
Admitted. Brother of #5896 and claims thru same source.
ROLL P106 #20432 FCT COMM #28421 - Sam Owl   - 39
            20433   28422 - Ella (wife)   - 34
                                    (App 12498)
            20434   28423 - Charles (son)   - 12
            20435   28424 - Joseph (son)   - 9
            20436   28425 - Cat (son)   - 7
            20437   3946m - Daniel (son)   - 4
            20438   3947m - Washington (son) - 1

10906. WILLIAM PORTER,   Marble, Okla
Admitted in application of father #4205. [For Roll information See App 4205, Vol. 3]

10907. HOUSTON YOUNG,   Marble City, Okla
Admitted. Nephew of #4507.
ROLL P155 #30114 FCT COMM #2879 - Houston Young - 24

10908. JENNIE SPRINGWATER and 3 children, Stilwell, Okla
Admitted. Niece of #1894.
ROLL P131 #25276 FCT COMM #18933 - Jennie Springwater - 23
            25277   18934 - Lizzie (dau)   - 5
            25278   1234m - Eliza (dau)   - 4
            25279   - Richard (son)   - 1/12

10909. WALTER A. ALLEN and 2 children,   Stilwell, Okla
Admitted. Nephew of #2275. Mother of applicant enrolled in
1851 in Flint. #237.
ROLL P23 #3670 FCT COMM #1708 - Walter A. Allen - 47
          3671   1711 - Mary L. (dau)   - 14
          3672   1712 - Cephas (son)   - 12

10910. GEORGE LOWRY and 3 children,   Stilwell, Okla
Admitted. Unable to locate applicant's parents on either the
Eastern or Old Settler rolls. Applicant states that his fath-
er and paternal grand parents were emigrants and there is oth-
er evidence to that effect, but that his mother was an Old
Settler. Applicant's paternal grandmother is enrolled by
Drennen at Flint #36 as Annie Bigfeather. Applicant is a full
blood Cherokee and is enrolled as such by the Dawes Commission
at #25689. Misc. Test. P. 3344 and 3982.
MISC. TEST. P. 3344. Appli. 10910 - George Lowry...through L.
D. Walkingstick, Interpreter:
    "My name is George Lowry; I was enrolled by the Dawes Com-
mission under the name of George Lowry, #25689 as a full blood
Cherokee; I was born in Illinois District, 1851; my father's
Cherokee name was Ah-to-woh-skee; my mother's Cherokee name
was Wah-le-yah; my father and mother had no English names; my
father was an emigrant Cherokee, but my mother was an Old
Settler; my father's father's name was A-kil-lih; my father's
mother's name was Annie Lowry; my father's mother's Cherokee
name was Ah-nih; my grandparents on my father's side were
emigrant Cherokees; they came West with the Cherokees at the
time of the emigration; none of the parents on my father's
side were Old Settlers; both I and the ancestors through whom
I claim have always been with the Cherokees; my father and
grandparents on my father's side were enrolled in Flint District, in 1851; I had no brothers and sisters on my father's
side who were enrolled in 1851; I was enrolled and drew the
Strip payment; I am not certain about what district my father
and grandparents were enrolled; my father had three sisters,
Achillie, Susannah & Wah-lee-sah; Ta-ga-ta-skee, was the
brother of my father."
SIGNED: George Lowry, Stilwell, Okla., Sep 30 1908.
MISC. TEST. P. 3982. No 10910 - J. B. Adair:
    "I know George Lowery; I knew his father and his mother; I
think his mother was an Old Settler; his father was Wash
Lowery; and he was an emigrant Cherokee. Wash Lowery was a
son of Annie Bigfeather. (Flint No. 36)."
SIGNED: J. B. Adair, Stilwell, Okla., Mar 23 1909.
[For Roll information See App 3870, Vol. 2]

10911. MILLARD F. CARTER,   Hay Fork, Cal
Rejected. Nephew of #8694 and claims thru same source.

10912. ROBERT L. CARTER and 2 children, Weaverville, Cal
Rejected. Nephew of #8694 and claims thru same source.

113

10913. CLEMENT A. CARTER and 1 child,   Hay Fork, Cal
Rejected. Nephew of #8694 and claims thru same source.

10914. GEORGE W. CARTER and 2 children,   Hay Fork, Cal
Rejected. Nephew of #8694 and claims thru same source.

10915. FLORENCE E. SANBURN,   Hay Fork, Cal
Rejected. Niece of #8694 and claims thru same source.

10916. SUSIE FOSTER,   Afton, Okla
Rejected. Applicant failed to appear when notified to meet
field parties; cannot identify ancestors on emigrant rolls
with information at hand.

10917. WILLIAM MEEKS,   Vinita, Okla
Rejected. 1st cousin of #817 and rejected for same reasons.

10918. EDMOND FLEETWOOD and 7 children,   Sallisaw, Okla
Rejected. Brother of #818. Uncle of #817. The applicant was
not enrolled in 1851.

10919. MARY E. MONTGOMERY and 2 children, Hay Fork, Cal
Rejected. Niece of #8694 and claims thru same source.

10920. NANCY WYLY,   Maysville, Ark
Admitted. Daughter of #5905 and claims thru same source.
ROLL P155 #30035 FCT COMM #28031 - Nancy Wyly - 20

10921. CINTHA PARRIS,   Rose, Okla
Admitted. Niece of #130.
ROLL P108 #20758 FCT COMM #14454 - Cynthia Parris - 21? [sic]

10922. KATE SANGSTER, See #3459.   Claremore, Okla
Admitted. Niece of #205 and claims thru same source.
ROLL P123 #23709 FCT COMM #12809 [?] - Kate Sangster - 43

10923. MARY J. HARRIS,   Foyil, Okla
Admitted. Niece of #1539.
ROLL P72 #13439 FCT COMM #11885 - Mary J. Harris - 20

10924. ROXIE SCOTT and 5 children,   Rose, Okla
Admitted. Niece of #130.
ROLL P124 #23937 FCT COMM #23558 - Roxie Scott - 25
          23938   23561 - Buster (son) - 7
          23939   23562 - Edna (dau)   - 6
          23940   23563 - Eva (dau)   - 4
          23941   1873m - Ida (dau)   - 2
          23942   1874m - Rena (dau)   - 1

10925. JOHN A. STAMPER,   McGrady, N C
Rejected. Sizemore case. See special report #417.

10926. POLLY CROWDER, Duplicate of #836.

10927. SOAP DOUGHERTY and 2 children,   Stilwell, Okla
Admitted. Died in 1908. Grandson of #1463 and claims thru
same source.
ROLL P54 #9870 FCT COMM #19229 - Soap Dougherty - 23
                                (Died 1908.)
        9871   - Jimmie (son)   - 3
        9872   - Katie (dau)   - 1/3

10928. WALTER R. EATON and 3 children,   Claremore, Okla
Admitted. Son of #1335 and claims thru same ancestors.
ROLL P57 #10481 FCT COMM #11784 - Walter R. Eaton - 38
        10482   11786 - Mary E. (dau)   - 10
        10483   11787 - Raleigh (son)   - 8
        10484   11788 - Frank (son)   - 5

10929. GEO. ALEX HARLAND,   Westville, Okla
Admitted. Applicant's father Ellis Harland was enrolled in
1851 in G. S. dis. Group 554. Maternal grandmother Rachel,
enrolled in 553 G. S. Misc. Test. P. 4041.
MISC. TEST. P. 4041. #10929 - Edward Walkingstick...in behalf
of George Alexander Harland:
     "I am 59 years old; I have known George Harland as far
back as I can recollect. I also knew the parents of George A.
Harland. George claims his Cherokee blood thru his father; His
mother was a white woman; His father Ellis Harland was about a
half-blood Cherokee; He was an Emigrant. I think that Ellis
Harland drew the Emigrant money in 1851; I think that George
was the oldest child. I do not think that he was enrolled in
1851 or had any brothers and sisters enrolled at that time. I
think that Ellis was Living in Going Snake District in 1851. I
think that he was married in 1851 and was probably was living
with his wife who was a white woman. The mother of Ellis
Harland was married twice. In 1851 she was living with a man
by the name of Ka-skar-ne Pritchett. (See G. S. 553 for the
paternal grandmother of the applicant) Ellis Harland was living near a full-blood Cherokee by the name of Peacheater in
1851 (See 554 G. S. for the father of applicant and G. S. 556
for Peach-eater) I do not remember who Choo-coo-wah Harlin is.
Ta-kuh-kuh was another neighbor of Ellis Harland in 1851; His
wife's name was Darky. (See G. S. 554)." ["OK 554 G. S." handwritten notation at end of testimony]
SIGNED: Edward Walkingstick, Westville, Okla., Mar 27 1909.
ROLL P71 #13245 FCT COMM #1999 - Geo. Alex. Harland - 51

10930. NANNIE CHOOWEE,   Christie, Okla
Admitted. Niece of #42528. [Notation on Roll "Choowee, Nan-
nie. See Roll No. 12708", which is the entry for her aunt,
Nannie Gritts, App 42528; Cannot locate applicant on Roll]

10931. CLARA B. STROUP and 7 children,   Inola, Okla
Admitted. Applicant's mother and maternal grandmother en-
rolled at Del. #944.
ROLL P134 #25856 FCT COMM #11528 - Clara B. Stroup   - 36
            25857   11530 - Earl (son)   - 17
            25858   11531 - Theo. Pearl (dau) - 15
            25859   11532 - Jesse (son)   - 12
            25860   11533 - Ruby (dau)   - 9
            25861   11534 - Willie (son)   - 6
            25862   11535 - Johnnie (son)   - 4
            25863   4193m - Fredie (son)   - 1

10932. MILLARD F. HICKS,   Chelsea, Okla
Admitted. Duplicate of #3667-4668 [NOTE: 1st App. No. should
be #3767, however, that is applicant's granddaughter; App 4668
is Millard F. Hicks - See App 4668, Vol. 3]

10933. JOSIAH WATERS and 2 children,   Braggs, Okla
Admitted. Cousin of #10388 and claims thru same source.
ROLL P146 #28424 FCT COMM #29118 - Josiah Waters   - 27
            28425   29119 - Hattie (wife)   - 25
                                    (App 11188)
            28426   29121 - Richard (son)   - 3
            28427   - Anderson (son)   - 2
            28428   29120 - John SMITH (son of w) - 6

10934. TAKIE FOURKILLER,   Christie, Okla
Admitted. Applicant, her father and mother, brothers and sis-
ters enrolled in G. S. #353.
ROLL P63 #11736 FCT COMM #19649 - Takie Fourkiller - 65

10935. CHARLES McCOY and 2 children,   Sallisaw, Okla
Admitted. Brother of #5902 and claims thru same source.
ROLL P93 #17690 FCT COMM #28357 - Charles McCoy   - 33
           17691   28359 - Edward E. (son) - 11
           17692   28360 - Peachie (dau)   - 7

10936. ENORA TAPP,   Ft. Gibson, Okla
Admitted. Aunt of #4196 and claims thru same source. Mother
of applicant enrolled in 1851 under name of Polly Gearin, in
Ill. dis. #3.
ROLL P136 #26316 FCT COMM #4927 - Elnora Tapp - 60

10937. SALLY CHUCULATE,   Sallisaw, Okla
Admitted. Niece of #9715; claims thru same ancestors.
ROLL P42 #7538 FCT COMM #28361 - Sally Chuculate - 19

10938. WILLIAM RUNABOUT,   Maysville, Okla
            by mother, Annie Reed.
Admitted. Applicant's grandfather and grandmother enrolled by
Drennen under names of Gah-dee-las-kah, Del. 621 and Kah-te-
tlo-eh, Del. 620, respectively.

116

ROLL P121 #23272 FCT COMM #28044 – William Runabout – 12
by Annie Reed, Gdn.

10939. ALEX WHITE, Duplicate of #5992   Maysville, Ark
by Martha Tanner, Gdn.
Admitted. Grandson of #3250. [For Roll information See App
339, Vol. 1]

10940. NANCY WHITE, Duplicate of #5992,   Maysville, Ark
by Martha Tanner
Admitted. Granddaughter of #3250. [For Roll information See
App 339, Vol. 1. Given name "Okah" on roll.]

10941. SAGER WHITE,   Maysville, Ark
by Ben O'Fields, Gdn.
Admitted. Grandson of #3250.
ROLL P149 #29020 FCT COMM #18636 – Sager White – 14
by Ben O'Fields, Gdn. (son of 26302)*
[* Roll No., not application No.]

10942. THOMAS DAVIS,   Peggs, Okla
Admitted. Nephew of #5282; claims thru same source.
ROLL P52 #9438 FCT COMM #21289 – Thompson Davis – 44

10943. CHARLES STARR and 3 children,   Braggs, Okla
Admitted. 1st cousin of #4196 and claims thru same source.
Father of applicant enrolled in 1851 under name of Henry
Gearin in Ill. Dis. #3.
ROLL P131 #25414 FCT COMM # 4794 – Charles Starr   – 29
           25415   3405 – Georgia A. (wife)   – 26
                              (App 29864)
           25416   5795 – S. Pocahontas (dau) – 8
           25417   5796 – R. Juanita (dau)   – 6
           25418   38--m* – Jack R. (son)   – 1
[* FCT # blurred]

10944. NELLIE BEAVER and 1 child,   Bunch, Okla
Admitted. Applicant is a niece of Hunter & Buster #6752 and
claims thru same source. Her Dawes Commission # is [blank]
ROLL P28 #4611 – Nellie Beaver   – 36
           4612 – Jackson COLLAR (son) – 20

10945. E. ELENOR A. McANDREWS and 5 children, Oolagah, Okla
Admitted. Niece of #51; claims thru same source.
ROLL P92 #17547 FCT COMM #12169 – E. Eleanor A. McAndrews – 34
           17548   12170 – Nora E. (dau)   – 10
           17549   12171 – Mike C. (son)   – 7
           17550   12172 – David R. (son)   – 5
           17551   12173 – John F. (son)   – 3
           17552   1855m – Mary M. (dau)   – 1

117

10946. JOHN S. TROGLIN and 2 children,   Claremore, Okla
Rejected. Applicant was enrolled by the Dawes Commission as
1/4 blood #11445 but none of applicant's ancestors were enrolled in '51 or '35 under names given in application and testimony. Misc. Test. P. 2354.
MISC. TEST. P. 2354. App No 10947-10946 - Isaac M. Troglin:
    "My name is Isaac M. Troglin. I am about 48 or 49 years
old. I live in Coo-wee-scoo-wee District. I have been here a-
bout 15 years. I lived down here by Tahlequah awhile. I was
born near Knoxville, Tennessee. I was enrolled by by the Dawes
Commission. Roll No. 4791, the other 9573. My brothers here
was enrolled by the Dawes Commission, but David was not. I was
not enrolled any other time. Never applied before for bread or
strip money. I get my Indian blood from my father. He was part
Cherokee; about 1/4. He has been dead since '91 He was living
in this District at the time of his death. I do not remember
just when my father moved here. His name was Millican Troglin.
He was born in Tennessee in the Eastern part. He was not enrolled in 1851 to my knowledge, as I never heard him say anything about it. He never got any old settler money that I know
of. He never joined any other tribe than the Cherokees to my
knowledge. I have heard my father say that her name Patience
Lemon, or Lemons. They lived in the Old Cherokee nation in
Tennessee. I don't know whether my grandmother had any Indian
blood but he said she was a half-blood and came from Virginia.
I do not know about what time. I never heard my father say
whether she was enrolled in 1851 or 1835. I cannot give any
reason for their not being enrolled, if they were not. I never
heard my father say that his father had Indian blood but think
he said he came from Scotland. My father's brothers and sisters were: Ann, Sim and Dike, Peg. Aunt Peggy Wright was her
married name. I cannot give my mother's brothers and sisters.
My father died in 1901, and I think was enrolled by the Dawes
Commission. I do not know of any Indian names. I do not know
of my father joining any other tribe of Indians. This is all I
know about my case."
SIGNED: I. M. Troglin, Claremore, Okla., Aug 27 1908.
EXCEPTION CASE. Rejected. Total number of exceptions filed
in this group — 6. Original recommendation renewed.

10947. ISAAC M. TROGLIN,   Claremore, Okla
Rejected. Brother of #10946 and claims thru same source.

10948. JAMES H. TROGLIN and 1 child,   Claremore, Okla
Rejected. Brother of #10946.

10949. LOUISA TROGLIN,   Claremore, Okla
Admitted. Claims thru father enrolled as James Lovett, Ill.
Group #10.
ROLL P141 #27291 FCT COMM #11446 - Louisa Troglin - 23
          27292   11447 - Wesley T. (son) - 6
          27293   1106m - Thomas J. (son) - 3

10950. ANDREW J. ROGERS and 6 children,   Leach, Okla
Admitted. Brother of #201; claims thru same source.
ROLL P118 #22798 FCT COMM #23346 - Andrew J. Rogers - 40
          22799   23348 - Henry B. (son)   - 19
          22800   23349 - Levi H. (son)   - 15
          22801   23350 - Nannie (dau)   - 18
          22802   23351 - John (son)   - 13
          22803   23352 - George L. (son) - 7
          22804   23353 - Andrew (son)   - 4

10951. JAS. R. PEAK,   Southwest City, Mo
Rejected. Nephew of #9754. [See Exception Case 9754, Vol. 4]

10952. JOHN NED,   Muldrow or Sallisaw, Okla
Admitted. Applicant is recognized as of Emigrant Cherokee descent. He was enrolled by the Dawes Commission, Roll #19299.
See Misc. Test. of claimant and Thomas Proctor, [P.] 3923.
MISC. TEST. P. 3923.   No 10952 - Ellis Canoe...thru D. M.
Faulkner, Interpreter:
     "My name is Ellis Canoe; I am thirty-three years old and
live near Ramey, Okla.; I have filed an application; I am a
half-brother of John Ned, application No. 10952; we have the
same mother; her Indian name was Che-yan-sti; John Ned's father's name was Oo-na-ti."
SIGNED: Ellis "X" Canoe, Muldrow, Okla., Mar 9 1909.
Tom Proctor, thru D. M. Faulkner, Interpreter, deposes and
says:
     "My name is Tom Proctor; I live near Muldrow, Okla.; I am
about sixty years of age and I know John Ned who is something
over thirty years old; John Ned's mother was a sister to Ben
Bigfeather; she would be about fifty years old now; I understand that Oo-na-ti wa the father of John Ned; Oo-na-ti's
mother's name was Quai-ti and his father's name was Weaver or
Te-cah-yah-ski; Oo-na-ti was living in 1851 and they were emigrant Cherokees; my grandparents came here with them and my
people were emigrants."
SIGNED: Tom "X" Proctor, Muldrow, Okla., Mar 9 1909.
ROLL P104 #19911 FCT COMM #19299 - John Ned - 33

10953. SCOTT SEABOLT and 5 children,   Muldrow, Okla
Admitted. Applicant claims thru grandmother Betsy Seabolt enrolled in Flint #67. Uncles, Jeremiah and George are also enrolled in Flint #67. Misc. Test. P. 3502.
MISC. TEST. P. 3502. #10953 - Scott Seabolt...thru Tom Roach,
Interpreter:
     "That I am 33 years of age. I am a full blood Cherokee. My
father's name was Charlie Seabolt. His Cherokee name was Gah-
luh-gih. My father died about 32 years ago and was about 29
[? 2nd digit blurred] years of age when he died, at least, I
think he was old enough to be on the roll of 1851. His mother's name was Betsy (Flint 67) He had a brother named Jeremiah
and another named George and a sister named Sarah Ann. My

                            119

mother's name was Polly Ned and her mother's name was Ah-lih-kih. Her husband's name was Ned."
SIGNED: Scott Seabolt, Sallisaw, Okla., Sep 17 1908.
ROLL P125 #24098 FCT COMM # 3545 - Scott Seabolt   - 31
      24099   27264 - Levi Wofford (son) - 11
      24100   26351 - Lizzie (dau)   - 8
      24101   26352 - Charlie (son)   - 7
      24102   3049m - Ella May (dau)   - 4
      24103   3050m - Linnie Emma (dau) - 2

10954. GEORGE SILK,   Muldrow, Okla
Admitted. Claimant was enrolled by the Dawes Commission #27301 and is recognized as being of Cherokee descent. See Misc. Test. P. 3921 of Thomas Proctor and testimony of claimant.
MISC. TEST. P. 3918. No 10954 - George Silk...thru D. M. Faulkner, Interpreter:
"My name is George Silk; I live at Muldrow, Okla.; I am about fifty years old; my father's name was Cesar Silk; I do not know as much about my family as Tom Proctor who has already testified in my case. Betsy and Katie Silk are my daughters, application No. 16764."
SIGNED: George "X" Silk, Muldrow, Okla., Mar 9 1909.

MISC. TEST. P. 3921.   No. 10954 - Tom Proctor...thru D. M. Faulkner, Interpreter:
"I know George Silk, whose father was Ce-sah Silk; Cesah Silk had a brother Fog Silk, S. B. 212 and another brother named Wah-hbat-chee, Flint 469. Ce-sah Silk was an emigrant Cherokee and came here with Old Chief, John Ross; George Silk's mother was an emigrant Cherokee; her name was Dicey Soap." SIGNED: Tom "X" Proctor, Muldrow, Okla., Mar 9 1909.
ROLL P127 #24431 FCT COMM #27301 - George Silk - 45

10955. GEORGE DEER-INWATER,   Cookson, Okla
Admitted. Applicant's father and mother enrolled in Tahl. 134.
ROLL P52 #9551 FCT COMM #21116 - George Deerinwater - 50

10956. WILLIAM J. McKEE,   Tahlequah, Okla
Admitted. One half brother to Fanny E. Chandler #1723, and son of Eliza B. Sharp McKee 1188 C. [Chapman]
ROLL P94 #17977 FCT COMM #16525 - William J. McKee - 65

10957. KEENER DEERINTHEWATER,   Cookson, Okla
Admitted. Nephew of #10955 and claims thru same source.
ROLL P52 #9557 FCT COMM #21142 - Keener Deerinwater - 33

10958. CHARLES WICKET,   Cookson, Okla
Admitted. 1st cousin of #2687.
MISC. TEST. P. 3331. App 10958 - Charlie Wicket:
"My name is Charlie Wicket. 19575 is My Dawes Commission number. Both my father and mother were Immigrant Cherokees. My father's name was John Wicket. Both my mother and father were

living in 1851. My father had a sister Maria Wicket. She is
living now. My father was born in Ga. My father never moved
out to this country. I was mistaken my father did move out
here and died in Ill. Dist. My father died 20 years ago, and
was over fifty years old when he died. My father had a sister
named Sarah Wicket (or ed) See Chap. 1986."
SIGNED: Charlie Wicket, Tahlequah, Okla., Sep 30 1908.
"Could not find this appl. but appl. said he was notified to
appear this date." [Notation added to end of testimony]
ROLL P150 #29120 FCT COMM #19575 - Chas. Wicket - 36

10959. THOS. J. TADPOLE and 1 child, Tahlequah, Okla
Admitted. Uncle of #1204. [NOTE: Notation on roll "Brewer,
Thos. J. See Roll No. 26213." and "Brewer, Commodore P. See
Roll No. 26214." which are applicant and son]
ROLL P135 #26213 FCT COMM #16283 - Thos. J. Tadpole - 34
        26214   16284 - Commodore P. (son) - 11

10960. LOUISA STEWART,   Toronto, Kans
Rejected. Neither applicant nor ancestors were ever enrolled.
Does not establish fact of descent from a person who was a
party to the treaty of 1835-6 and 1846. Misc. Test. P. 3912.
MISC. TEST. P. 3912. 13555-10960 - Thomas K. McDonald:
    "I am 54 years of age past. I claim my Indian blood
through my mother. My father was more Irish and French than
anything else. My mother claimed to be about one-half Cherokee. The other half was German and French. My mother was
born not far from Nashville, Tenn. about the year 1824. She
lived near the place where she was born until about 1850 and
from there she went to Glassglow Ken. I don't know for sure
that my mother ever lived with the Indians but I have heard
her say that she was with them where she lived in Tennessee.
She never lived with them any after she went to Kentucky. She
derived her Indian blood from her father and she lived with
him but in what manner she lived with the Indians I couldn't
say. I have heard my mother say that she and her father were
on the Cherokee rolls of the early days made when she was a
child but I don't know the date or what roll it was. I think
my mother's father died along about 1840 in Tennessee. His
name was James Smith. My mother went to Tahlequah in about
1870 to be enrolled. She said when she went down there that
she didn't think there was much use to go down as all her papers were burned up when the rebels made a raid on her father's place back in Missouri. Anyway she went down and gave
what evidence she could before the Cherokee Council and they
told her to get some affidavits as to her children and they
would enroll her. She came back and took sick and died and
nothing further was done with it. I made application through
the Watts Association for enrollment with the Daws Commission
but I never heard anything from it. I made application for
citizenship with the Five Civilized tribes in 1887 through an
attorney at Afton, I. T. and he wrote me that my application

alright but I never heard anything further from it. I don't know whether my mother or her father ever received any land or money from the Government or not by reason of their Indian blood. I think my mother was living in Kentucky in 1851. I think that my mother's father was born there near Nashville but I am not certain about that. I don't know where his people came from. My mother had a brother named Harvey Smith, he was the oldest child. Another brother named John Smith, he was younger than my mother. Hervey was about two years older than my mother. My wife was a white woman. I have always passed for a white man in the community where I live but people that knew me knew that I was part Indian."
SIGNED: Thos. K. McDonald, Burlington, Kans., Oct 19 1908.

10961. SALLIE HICKS and 5 children, Chelsea, Okla
Admitted. Claimant's father, half brother and sister and aunt enrolled by Drennen in 1851, Del. #706. Paternal grandfather enrolled in Del. 821. See Misc. Test. P. 4326.
MISC. TEST. P. 4326. #15075 - 10961 - William Sweetwater in behalf of Polly Brown...thru Tom Roach, Interpreter:
"I am about 60 years old; I knew Polly Brown and her parents. I do not know whether the mother of Polly Brown was an Emigrant or not. I became acquainted with her after the enrollment of 1851; after the payment of 1852 Rachel lived with Jack Wickett; Rachel was an old woman in 1851; I do not know whether Jack Wickett was an Old Settler or not; I do not know his Cherokee name; he was called Ja-ke Choo-tah-gee-tah-lih or Blue-eye. He was about a quarter Cherokee. Rachel looked to be about a quarter Cherokee; I do not know when Rachel died; I think she died about the time of the war; Rachel took up with another man and went South the time of the war; the man she went with was Joe Summerfield; He was a part Cherokee Indian. Rachel was considered to be a Cherokee about the time of the war; Webb Wickett, #16445, is a full brother of Polly Brown; Anna Cordery is a half sister of Polly Brown on the mothers side; her father was Joe Summerfield. The father of Joe Summerfield was John Summerfield -- the wife of John Summerfield was Caty; (see Del 821) The Indian name of Joe Summerfield was Choo-guh-tah-tih. I think that Joe Summerfield had some children in 1851; He had a daughter by the name of A-ke. He also had a son by the name of Isaac, or A-sick-e. Josep Summerfield had a sister living with him by the name of Gah-daw-tluh-nuh in 1851." (See Del. 706) I think that Coo-lah-chih was the father of Rachel. I do not remember seeing the mother of Rachel. I do not know her name; I do not of [sic] Rachel living with any other man before she lived with Jack Wickett; I do not think that Coo-lah-chih was living in 1851; When Coo-lah-chih was living, he lived in Del. District. (See Del 908 ? [sic]) I do not know who Goo-lah-chih's wife was. The brothers and sisters of Rachel were Sallie, who was living with a man by the name of Oo-dah-nee-yuh-duh. She had a brother by the name of Nick. He had a wife by the name of Ailcey. I do not know the

names of any of Nicks children. He had some at that time; I
think Nick had sons by the name of We-le or William and Wah-
yih of Pigeon. (See Del 907 [? 2nd digit blurred])   I do not
know the names of any of the other brothers and sisters of
Rachel. I first became acquainted with Polly Brown in 1851;
she was about 10 years old at that time; She has always been
regarded as a Cherokee Indian; she was the oldest child. She
had a brother by the name of Webb."
SIGNED: Wm. Sweetwater, Eucha, Okla., Mar 18 1909.
[For Roll information See App 4668, Vol. 3]

10962. CALEB E. STARR and 2 children,   Stilwell, Okla
Admitted. Brother of #2204. [For Roll information See App
9133, Vol. 4]

10963. DANIEL BEARPAW,   Oaks, Okla
Admitted. Brother of #5784; claims thru same source. [For
Roll information See App 7464, Vol. 4]

10964. ANNIE BEARPAW SNAKE,   Oaks, Okla
Admitted. Sister to #5784; claims thru same source. [Nota-
tion on Roll "Snake, Annie. See Roll No. 25923." and one each
for husband and child]
ROLL P134 #25922 FCT COMM #20356 - Tom Suake   - 27
                                    (App 16498)
          25923   26061 - Annie Bearpaw (wife) - 35
          25924   20358 - Richard (Ezekiel)   - 11
                                    (son) (App 17669)

10965. ROBERT J. MANN for deceased children, Oaks, Okla
Rejected. See #4790. Applicant is an Old Settler. Children
died long prior to 1906.

10966. LUCINDA ROGERS and 1 child,   Lowery, Okla
Admitted. Daughter of #1210; claims thru same source. [For
Roll information See App 10968]

10967. ARCH GOINGSNAKE,   Oaks, Okla
Admitted. Half brother of #2139 on father's side. Del. 835.
ROLL P66 #12355 FCT COMM #20390 - Arch Goingsnake - 50

10968. DAVID ROGERS,   Oaks, Okla
Admitted. Half brother of #2041 and claims thru same source.
Mother, Susan, Saline Dis. #82.
ROLL P119 #22831 FCT COMM #15123 - David Rogers   - 36
          22832   15124 - Lucinda (wife)   - 46
                                    (App 10966)
          22833   15125 - Emma GALCATCHER - 14
                                    (dau of w)

10969. MINNIE L. BARKER and 2 children,   Grassy Creek, N. C
Rejected. Sizemore case. See special report #417.

123

10970. MARION HEATH,   Fleet, Va
Rejected. Sizemore case. See special report #417.

10971. CHARLES HEATH and 2 children,   Fleet, Va
Rejected. Sizemore case. See special report #417.

10972. ALES J. HELMS and 2 children,   Fleet, Va
Rejected. Sizemore case. See special report #417.

10973. LON HEATH,   Fleet, Va
Rejected. Sizemore case. See special report #417.

10974. JOHN HEATH and 5 children,   Fleet, Va
Rejected. Sizemore case. See special report #417.

10975. VIRGINIA A. MARTIN,   Chattanooga, Tenn
Rejected. No ancestors ever enrolled. No ancestors party to
the treaties of 1835 '36 or '64. Shows no real connection with
the Cherokee tribe.

10976. ELIZABETH F. MUNNICK,   Hill City, Tenn
Rejected. Sister of #10975; claims thru the same source.
MISC. TEST. P. 135. #10976 - Elizabeth F. Minnick:
     "That I am 65 years of age and reside in Hill City, Tenn.
I claim Indian blood through my father only. My great grand
mother was a full blood. Her name was Gourdie Mott. I don't
know when she died, but think it was shortly before 1840. She
was born in Va. and was raised and educated where the City of
Baltimore is now. I think my grandfather, Henry Jenkins, was
born in Va. The most of his life he lived here in Chattanooga.
I never was on any Indian roll. My grandfather drew Indian
money in Catoosa Co., Ga. when I was about 9 or 10 years. This
was about 1852 or 3. I don't know the object of the payment at
that time. My grandfather, Henry Jenkins, was the only child.
I think he died before the war -- just a few years. I never
knew of my father and grandfather living among the Indians,
but my father came with the Indians from Meigs Co. to Chattanooga about 1839. Helped to move the Indians here. I don't
know whether he was ever recognized as a member of the tribe.
My mother was a full blood white woman. My father was Indian
and English. I was never enrolled because my mother did not
like to have my father say anything about us being Indian and
wanted us to keep it quite on account of our white connections. I never made any application for money but always knew
that I had Indian blood in me. I don't think I am able to produce any other witnesses or add anything to the testimony already given."
SIGNED: Elizabeth F. Minnick, Chattanooga, Tenn., Jun 18 1908.

10977. ALBERT GAINS and 1 child,   Chattanooga, Tenn
Rejected. Nephew of #6290 and claims thru the same source.

124

10978. TENNESSEE GILLESPIE and 5 children, Chattanooga, Tenn
Highland Park
Admitted. 1st cousin to #6292. Nancy Davis mother of applicant enrolled by Chap. 1609.
MISC. TEST. P. 127.   #10978 for Tennessee Gillespie – Thomas Coward...in behalf of Tennessee Gillespie:

"I am 62 years of age and reside at Hill City, Tenn. I am acquainted with Tennessee Gillespie but did not know her mother, nor her grandparents. I have known Tennessee Gillespie since 1882. She is on the roll of 1882, was named Tennessee Davis at that time. This roll was made by Hester at Chattanooga, Tenn. I didn't know any of her brothers and sisters, though she might have had them. Tennessee Davis is less than a quarter Indian and the rest white. I don't remember when Nancy Reed died. She died prior to 1880."
SIGNED: Thomas Cowart, Chattanooga, Tenn., Jun 18 1908.
MISC. TEST. P. 128.   #10978 – C. D. Miller...in regard to claim of Tennessee Gillespie, #10978:

"That I am 67 years of age and live near Bartlebaugh, Hamilton Co., Tenn. I got acquainted with the applicant and her parents about 1866 and they were living at that time near Harrison P. O. in what is know now as James Co., Tenn. As far as I ever heard she and her mother and grandparents always resided right near Harrison, Tenn. She claims only through her mother, as I understand. I have heard that there was a tribe of Indians lived in that vicinity and the best I recollect they were known as the Reeds. Her grandparents never went by any other name than that of Reed, that I ever knew. I have heard that both of the Reeds possessed Indian blood but I don't know what tribe but I think the Cherokee. That is what I heard all the time everywhere. I have heard of them being enrolled but do not know what roll but think it was made sometime in the forties. I don't know what roll it was nor what it was for. Her grandparents were Indian and white. The applicant is between a quarter and a half blood and plainly shows her Indian blood in her features. The applicant and her mother were regarded as Indians in the neighborhood in which they lived. I cannot give any more information than I have about the roll mentioned or about the ancestry of the applicant."
SIGNED: C. B. Miller, Chattanooga, Tenn., Jun 18 1908.
ROLL P9 #943 – Tennessee Gillespie – 50
         944 – Marcus E. (son)   – 16
         945 – Grace (dau)   – 12
         946 – William R. (son)   – 10
         947 – James R. (son)   – 8
         948 – John W. (son)   – 8

10978. SALLIE TUCKER,   Cohutta, Ga
Rejected. It does not appear that any ancestor was a party to the treaties of 1835–36 or '46. Nor does it appear that any ancestor was ever enrolled. Misc. Test. P. 1390.

MISC. TEST. P. 1390.   No 10979 - Sallie Tucker;:
"My name is Sallie Tucker; I was born in Whitfield Co.,
Ga. 1841; I claim my Indian blood through my father; I make no
claim through my mother; my father's name was John Stancel; my
father was born in S. C. 1795; I do not know the district; my
father got his Indian blood through his mother; my grandmother's maiden name was Mille Hightower; my grandmother, Mille
Hightower, was born in S. C.; I do not know what district nor
when; I think she was born about 1741; I am unable to trace my
ancestry father back than my grandmother; my grandmother,
Millie Hightower, claimed to be a full blood Cherokee woman; I
never saw my grandmother through whom I claim; none of the ancestors through whom I claim were ever held in bondage; in
1835 my grandmother and father lived in either Haversham or
Cherokee Co., Ga.; in 1851 my grandmother was dead and my
father and I lived in Whitfield Co., Ga.; my father died in
1855; I do not know whether my father or grandmother were ever
enrolled or not; I do not know why; I do not know whether my
grandmother or father lived with the Indians as a member of
the tribe since 1800 or not; they lived among the Cherokee
Indians in Haversham and Whitfield Co., Ga.; I had two aunts,
my father's sisters, Tempie Ward and Sallie Wilson (nee
Stancel) who went West with the Indians when they left this
part of the country; they went to the Ind. Terr. and as members of the tribe; had also some cousins, by the name of John
Stancel and Sallie Stancel, the children of Hilman Stancel the
brother of my father, John Stancel, who went West with the Indians." SIGNED: Sallie Tucker, Dalton, Ga., Jul 10 1908.
EXCEPTION CASE. Rejected. Total number of exceptions filed
in this group -- 11. Original recommendation renewed.

10980. WM. V. GOINS, Duplicate of #6289.

10981. CHARLES GOODMAN,   Hill City, Tenn
Rejected. No ancestor was ever enrolled. No ancestor was a
party to the treaties of 1835-6 or 1846. Shows no real connection with the Cherokee Tribe.
MISC. TEST. P. 133. #10981 - Charles Goodman:
"That I am 52 years of age and was born in Blount Co.,
Tenn. I now reside in Hill City. I claim my Indian descent
thro my father. My grandfather was named Tommy Goodman. My
grandmother did not possess any Indian. Just thro my grand
father on my father's side that I claim. My paternal grand
father was born and raised in Haywood Co., N. C. Lived there
up to the time of his death. That's where my father was born.
He died in Blount Co. He moved to Blount Co. before the war -
before I was born. I never knew of my father or grandfather
being enrolled nor were they ever known by any other name than
that of Goodman. I never lived with the Indians. My father had
no brothers and sisters. I claim one-fourth Indian and the
rest Dutch."
SIGNED: Charles "X" Goodman, Chattanooga, Tenn., Jun 18 1908.

MISC. TEST. P. 134.   #10981 - G. W. Newberry...on behalf of
Charles Goodman, #10981:
   "That I am 48 years of age and reside in Chattanooga,
Tenn. I am acquainted with Charles Goodman and have known him
ever since we were boys. He was raised in Blount Co. I knew
his father. His father was living in Blount Co. when I got acquainted with him. They were considered part Cherokee Indians
in the community in which they lived. I never heard of him or
his father being on any roll, or claiming to be enrolled. Never heard of any enrollment until I came here. I have given all
the information I can in reference to his ancestry."
SIGNED: G. W. Newberry [signature very difficult to read],
Chattanooga, Tenn, Jun 18 1908.

10982. FRANCIS M. GOINS,   Bridgeport, Ala
Rejected. Brother of #6290 and claims thru the same source.

10983. MARY JANE JANEWAY and 3 children,   Whitewell, Tenn
Rejected. Cousin of #2194.

10984. BENJAMIN F. RIDGE & 3 children, Highland Park Station
                                        Chattanooga, Tenn
Rejected. Cousin of #2194.

10985. JOSEPH C. RIDGE and 7 children,   Hill City, Tenn
Rejected. Cousin of #2194.

10986. ESTHER JANEWAY and 3 children,   Highland Park Station
                                        Chattanooga, Tenn
Rejected. Cousin 2194.

10987. HIRAM RIDGE,   Chattanooga, Tenn
Rejected. Cousin of #2194.

10988. JAMES D. RIDGE and 8 children,   Whitfield, Tenn
Rejected. Cousin of #2194.

10989. ELIZABETH RIDGES,   Whitwell, Tenn
Rejected. Cousin of #2194.

10990. LAURA WOODRING and 6 children,   Newalla, Okla
Rejected. Aunt of #10764 and claims thru same source.

10991. MOLLIE M. ROBERSON and 2 children, Weaverville, N C
Rejected. Kesiah Vann case. See special report #276.

10992. ROBT. SHEPHERD and 2 children,   Just P. O. N. C.
Rejected. Kesiah Vann case. See special report #276.

10993. JONAH HINCHEE,   Haileyville, Okla
Rejected. Uncle of #10764; claims thru the same source.

127

10994. JUDSON SAPP and 2 children,   Dalton, Ga
Rejected. Claims thru same source as #5170.

10995. ROSA SAPP,   Dalton, Ga
Rejected. Claims thru same source as #5170.

10996. MARY SAPP,   Dalton, Ga
Rejected. Claims thru same source as #5170.

10997. NORA A. MONROE,   Lenox, Mass
Admitted. Niece of #6648; claims thru same source.
ROLL P13 #1713 - Nora A. Monroe - 26

10998. ELIZABETH MORGAN and 2 children,   Deckson, Tenn
Rejected. Applicant nor ancestors not enrolled. Does not appear that they were living within the Cherokee domain in 1835-
1836 or '46 as recognized members of the tribe. Claim not suf-
ficiently established. Misc. Test. P. 490.
MISC. TEST. P. 490. 10998 - Elizabeth Morgan:
    "I am 56 years of age; was born in Cherokee Co., N. C.; I
claim my Indian blood through my mother. Do not know when I
moved away from Cherokee County, I was small. My mother told
me that she was a half blood Cherokee Indian. She spoke the
Indian language. She never received any Indian money from the
government and never tried to get any. I have never tried to
get any Indian money from the government and never received
any. My mother lived with the Indians in N. C. My father who
is here with me now knows more about my people than I do. My
sister, Mary Ann Hicks, is now with me but knows no more about
my people than I do."
SIGNED: Elizabeth "X" Morgan, Dickson, Tenn., Jun 25 1908.
Jesse Morgan, father of Elizabeth Morgan...deposes and says:
    "Louisa Franklin, mother of Elizabeth Morgan, and Mary
Hicks, was my wife. She was a Cherokee Indian; think she was
about half. When I first knew her she lived in Cherokee County. She was born in Buncom County, N. C. and moved to Cherokee
County. She claimed her Indian blood through her father who
was very near full blood. He never received any Indian money
that I know of. When I knew him he was not living with the Indians in Cherokee County and the Indians left Buncomb County
before he did. He was a kind of a farmer."
SIGNED: Jesse "X" Morgan, Dickson, Tenn., Jun 25 1908.
EXCEPTION CASE. Rejected. Total number of exceptions filed
in this group -- 11. Original recommendation renewed.

10999. JAMES T. RAPER and 2 children,   Isabella, Tenn
Admitted. Brother to #335.
ROLL P15 #2058 - James T. Raper - 30
            2059 - Harvey L. (son) - 5
            2060 - Harley T. (son) - 3

11000. MANDY THOMAS,   Ducktown, Tenn
Admitted. Sister to #335.
ROLL P18 #2677 - Mandy Thomas - 33

11001. WILLIS ABERCROMBIE,   Loving, Ga
Rejected. It does not appear that any ancestor was a party to
the treaties of 1835-6 or 1846 - nor does it appear that any
ancestor was ever enrolled. Misc. Test. P. 1494.
MISC. TEST. P. 1494. #11001 - Willis Abercrombie:
"That I am 35 years of age and claim Indian descent for my
children who claim their descent through my wife. My wife
claimed her descent through her father, Jackson Lambert. Jackson Lambert's father, Hugh Lambert, claimed Cherokee descent.
I don't know whether Jack Lambert had any brothers and sisters
or not. Don't know whether Hugh Lambert had any brothers and
sisters. Don't know where Jackson Lambert was born but he
lived in Cherokee Co., N. C. I don't know whether my wife's
father or grandfather lived with the Indians as members of the
tribe or not. Jack Lambert was hung at Bryson City, N. C. for
killing a man, but don't know when that was. He was about 30
years old at that time and that was about 20 years ago. Never
heard that he had any other name than Jack Lambert. Jackson
Lambert had a brother named Hugh. Hugh Lambert, Jack Lambert's
father, went out to Washington (don't know what Washington)
about 30 or 40 years ago and was in the Indian service out
there. Don't know whether my wife's father had any sister by
the name of Nancy or Catherine. Don't know Hugh Lambert's address. My wife was 33 when she died and that was 1903. Don't
know how much Indian she claimed to be. She showed Indian very
much. She never told me that her father ever lived with the
Indians. Mattie Abercrombie, 12 years old; Sarah Elizabeth
Abercrombie, 10 years old and Thomas Solon Abercrombie, 7
years old, are my children."
SIGNED: Willis Abercrombie, Blue Ridge, Ga., Jul 13 1908.

11002. CATHERINE PARRIS and 1 child,   Culberson, N C
Admitted. Sister of #796 and claims thru same source.
ROLL P14 #1885 - Catharine Parris - 23
         1886 - Laura May (dau) - 1/12

11003. ANDREW J. SIVEANEY,   Tuscumbia, Mo
Rejected. Claims thru same source as #3935.

11004. LUTIE NEAL and 2 children,   Lizemore, W Va
Rejected. Sizemore case. See special report #417.

11005. HILEY UNDERWOOD,   RFD 1, Dayton, Tenn
Rejected. 1: no ancestors ever enrolled. 2: no ancestors
party to treaties of 1835-6 and 1846. 3: shows no connection
with Eastern Cherokees. See Misc. Test. P. 912.
MISC. TEST. P. 912. No 11005 - Hiley Underwood:
"My name is Hiley Underwood; I was born in McMinn Co.,

Tenn. in 1847. I am sixty-one years old; I claim my Indian blood through my father; my father was born in McMinn Co., Tenn. in 1809. My father is ninety-nine years old; my father's name was Thomas Riggins. My father never applied for participation in this fund. None of my brothers and sisters ever applied for this money. Neither my father nor I were ever enrolled. We never received any money, lands or other benefit as an Indian. Neither my father or any of the ancestors through whom I claim were ever slaves. In 1851 I resided in McMinn Co., Tenn. I do not know why my father was never enrolled. My father was always regarded as a white man in the community in which he lived. I am regarded as a white woman. My father's mother's name was Nancy Hazzard. That was her Indian name. Neither my father nor his mother, Nancy Hazzard never lived with the Indians as a member of the tribe. My father and my grandmother told me that I was part Cherokee. I think that they told me that I was a quarter Cherokee. I have seen my grandmother, Nancy Hazzard. I think I was about six years old when she died. I do not know where Nancy Hazzard was born. My grandmother, Nancy Hazzard, never lived with the Indians as a member of the tribe and associated with white people, who was always regarded as a white woman."
SIGNED: Hiley Underwood, Dayton, Tenn., Jun 23 1908.

11006. SAML. T. BURNS and 2 children,   Cumberland Gap, Tenn
Rejected. Betsy Walker case. See special report #500.

11007. JOHN HART and 4 children,   Saltville, Va
Rejected. See special report Sizemore #417.

11008. CHARLES O. FRYE,   Sallisaw, Okla
Admitted. Applicant claims through mother Nancy Frye enrolled in Skin Bayou 173. Brothers and sisters 173 Skin Bayou.
ROLL P64 #11923 FCT COMM #3097 - Charles O. Frye - 52
       11924   3099 - Roy (son)   - 19
       11925   3100 - Argyle (son)   - 17
       11926   3101 - Raymond (son)   - 14
       11927   3102 - Charles O. (son) - 12
       11928   3103 - Pliny S. (son)   - 9
       11929   3104 - Catherine (dau) - 7
       11930   3105 - Mamie (dau)   - 4
       11931   111m - Harriette (dau) - 2
       11932   - Thomas (son)   - 1/4

11009. SAM'L JOHNSON and 4 children,   Vian, Okla
[Admitted.] Nephew of #901. Paternal grandmother enrolled in 1851 by Drennen, S. B. 251. [For Roll information See App 3926, Vol. 2]

11010. WILLIAM W. WRIGHT and 4 children,   Baron, Okla
Admitted. Son of #1848 and claims thru same source. [For Roll information See App 6620, Vol. 3]

11011. MOLLIE L. BLACKSTONE,   Carona, Cal*
Admitted. First cousin of #4394.   Claimant's father enrolled
in 1851 by Drennen, Del. 431. [* "San Pedro" crossed out.
Also "282 1/2 4th St." on roll]
ROLL P31 #5243 FCT COMM #4254 - Mollie L. Blackstone - 25

11012. TOM BEAUER and 2 children,   Webbers Falls, Okla
Admitted. Enrolled as Oo-squa-lu-sker.   Mother enrolled as
Ta-kee, Fl. 544.
ROLL P28 #4621 FCT COMM #18227 - Tom Beaver   - 56
          4622   30465 - Alsie (wife) - 50 (App 11489)
          4623   18230 - Cherrie (dau)   - 16
          4624   18231 - Mary (dau)   - 12
          4625   30469 - Lila BANTY (dau of w) - 14
                               (App 17270)

11013. WILLIAM R. PROCTOR and 1 child,   Ballard, Okla
Admitted. Nephew of #5107 and claims thru same source.
ROLL P113 #21813 FCT COMM # 1213 - William R. Proctor - 34
          21814   18900 - Bell (wife) - 25(App 32292)
          21815   25628 - Willie Bell (dau)   - 4

11014. WILLIAM B. ANDERSON and 1 child,   Chance, Okla
Admitted. Nephew of #5107; claims thru same source.
ROLL P23 #3767 FCT COMM #16585 - William B. Anderson - 37
          3768   16586 - Lizzie (wife)- 28 (App 22976)
          3769   16587 - Willie May (dau)   - 5

11015. EZEKIEL PROCTOR, Duplicate of #3752.

11016. LOLA HARLESS and 2 children,   Siloam Springs, Okla
Admitted. Grandniece of #132.
ROLL P71 #13249 FCT COMM # 1099 - Lola Harless   - 25
          13250   3236m - Carr C. (son)   - 2
          13251   31572 - Luster L. (bro) - 10

11017. LEVENA ENGLAND,   Baron, Okla
Admitted. Grand nephew of Winnie Six Killer #177 and admitted
for same reasons.
ROLL P58 #10703 FCT COMM #20095 - Levena England - 19

11018. SALLIE WALKINGSTICK,   Marble City, Okla
Admitted. Applicant's father probably not born before 1851.
Grandfather Chickenroost and grandmother Chicko-te-you-hee and
several uncles and aunts all enrolled in 470 Fl. Misc. Test.
P. 2955 - 2938.
MISC. TEST. P. 2938. Appl. #17130-11018 - John Glass:
    "My name is John Glass. I live at Muldrow, Okla. I was
born in Flint District. I am 23 years old. My father's name
was John Glass. My father was born about the time of the war.
I am a son of Lizzie Deer-in-water #17344. Sallie Walkingstick is my sister."

131

SIGNED: John Glass, Sallisaw, Okla., Sep 19 [1908].
MISC. TEST. P. 2955.   No 11018 - Mrs. Sallie Walkingstick
...thru L. D. Walkingstick, Interpreter:
    "My name is Sallie Walkingstick; my post-office is Marble
City, Okla.; I am twenty-six years old and was born in Flint
District, Okla.; Cherokee roll No. 22847; maiden name Sallie
Killer; John Glass is my half-brother, we have the same mother; my mother's name is Lizzie Danewater; or Lizzie Deerinwater; application No. 17344 of Lizzie Deerinwater; Taylor
Chickenroost is the name of my father; he was about thirty
when he died; my father's father was named Chickenroost; my
father had one sister named Quallayou, one brother named
Chequakeh; Chick-a-youhee was Chickenroost's wife; my father's
brother was named Fox; (Flint 470) My father and mother was
fully recognized as man and wife; my father was living in
1851, I think but I am not sure. (See application 1890) My
father lived in Flint District; my mother lived there also."
SIGNED: Mrs. Sallie "X" Walkingstick, Sallisaw, Okla., Sep 19
1908. [For Roll information See App 4050, Vol. 2]

11019. FRANCIS L. DAMRON,   Webb City, Mo
Rejected. Sister of #10260.

11020. MATILDA E. MILLER,   Joplin, Mo
Rejected. Sister of #10260.

11021. ISADORA COWAN and 2 children,   Henryetta, Okla
Rejected. It does not appear that any ancestor was party to
the treaties of 1835-6 and 1846, nor does it appear that ancestors lived in the Cherokee domain. See M. S. T. P. 2824.
MISC. TEST. P. 2824.   No 11021 - Isadora Cowan:
    "I am 33 years of age. I claim Cherokee Indian blood
through my mother. She was born in Illinois. I have seen my
mother's parents. They lived in Arkansas. My grandfather was
the Indian. He was a farmer and a voter. He never got any
Indian money from the government. I am not a Cherokee alottee
and have never received any Indian money from the government.
My mother was not a full blood and did not live with the Indians. She attended the white schools. I claim no Indian
blood through my father. My grandfather was born in Illinois
and moved from there to Arkansas."
SIGNED: Isadora Cowan, Okmulgee, Okla., Sep 14 1908.

11022. MARY M. COLLINS and 5 children,   Black Gum, Okla
Admitted. First cousin once removed of #326 and claims thru
same source.
ROLL P45 #8155 FCT COMM #4420 - Mary M. Collins   - 28
         8156   4421 - Wyoming (son)   - 12
         8157   4422 - Sirl (son)   - 9
         8158   4423 - Lindsey (son)   - 8
         8159   4424 - U. Grant (son)   - 5
         8160   2465m - John Robert (son)   - 2

132

11023. NANNIE GUESS and 3 children,   Chilhowie, Va
Rejected. Applicant fails to show any genuine connection to
the Eastern Cherokees nor was ancestor ever enrolled. No ancestor was a party to the treaties of 1835-6 and 1846.
EXCEPTION CASE. Rejected. Total number of exceptions filed
in this group -- 1. Original recommendation renewed.

11024. SARAH FOSTER and 1 child,   Chilhowie, Va
Rejected. Sister to Nannie Guess (11023) and claims thru same
line.

11025. ANDREW OTTER and 5 children,   Birdtown, N C
Admitted. Applicant is brother of #3955 and claims thru same
source. Applicant on Hester Roll No 1153. [For Roll information See App 8422, Vol. 4]

11026. FANNIE L. HILDERBRAND,   Estella, Okla
Admitted. Half sister of #10730 and claims thru same source.
[For Roll information See App 2185, Vol. 2]

11027. ELIZABETH HILDEBRAND,   Estella, Okla
Admitted. Half sister of #10730 and claims thru same source.
[For Roll information See App 1920, Vol. 2]

11028. LUCY B. LOWERY,   Muskogee, Okla
Admitted. First cousin to #422. Claims thru grandmother enrolled in 1851, as Nancy Harnage, and mother Sarah Harange,
[sic], G. Snake No 728. [For Roll information See App 11029]

11029. ANDERSON LOWERY and 2 children,   Muskogee, Okla
Admitted. First cousin to #562. Claims thru "James Lowery",
father, #736 Tahl.
ROLL P91 #17344 FCT COMM #28843 - Anderson Lowery - 29
          17345   28844 - Lucy B. (wife) - 30
                               (App 11028)
          17346   225m - Wanetta (dau)   - 4
          17347   226m - Raymond (son)   - 2

11030. POLLY LEADER,   Texanna, Okla
Admitted. First cousin of #906. Mother enrolled as "Ka-ho-
ka" at F1 #89.
ROLL P88 #16837 FCT COMM #17229 - Polly Leader - 54

11031. POLLY LEADER, Duplicate of #11030.

11032. POLLY LEADER, Duplicate of #11030.

11033. POLLY LEADER, Duplicate of #11030.

11034. POLLY LEADER, Duplicate of #11030.

11035. POLLY LEADER, Duplicate of #11030.

11036. POLLY LEADER, Duplicate of #11030.

11037. POLLY LEADER, Duplicate of #11030.

11038. POLLY LEADER, Duplicate of #11030.

11039. POLLY LEADER, Duplicate of #11030.

11040. JESSIE H. PARKER and 1 child,   Tulsa, Okla
Applicant a Creek.   Accepted on allotment.   See ----Applica-
tion. [sic]

11041. MARY H. ROGERS,   Chelsea, Okla
Admitted.   Sister of #3154 and claims thru same source.
ROLL P119 #22891 FCT COMM #13232 - Mary K. Rogers - 54

11042. BETTY KEYS and 1 child,   Coffeyville, Kans
Admitted.   Applicant claims thru mother Stacy Taylor nee Welch
enrolled by Chapman 1287 [? 3rd digit blurred].   Grandfather
enrolled Chap. 1279.   Uncles and Aunts.   C. [Chapman]
1288--1278.
ROLL P85 #16149 FCT COMM #8860 - Betty Keys   - 45
          16150   8861 - Campbell L. (son) - 18

11043. BETTIE KEYS, Duplicate of #11042.

11044. BETTIE KEYS, Duplicate of #11042.

11045. BETTIE KEYS, Duplicate of #11042.

11046. BETTIE KEYS, Duplicate of #11042.

11047. BETTIE KEYS, Duplicate of #11042.

REJECTED
APP 11048 TO 11100 - SIZEMORE CASES - SEE SPECIAL REPORT #417

11048. LAURA C. FARRIS and 3 children,   Damascus, Va

11049. LELAH DOLINGER and 4 children,   Cole, Va

11050. ALICE M. BLEVINS,   Cole, Va

11051. WILDA DOLINGER,   Cole, Va

11052. MARY SHULER,   Cole, Va

11053. EMANUEL BLEVINS,   Cole, Va

11054. RHODA V. EDMONSTON,   Damascus, Va

11055. LUCINDA EDMONDSON,   Damascus, Va

11056. ISAAC A. EDMONDSON,   Damascus, Va

11057. MARTHA P. BLEVINS and 3 children, Seven Mile Ford, Va

11058. JOSEPHINE BLEVINS and 3 children, Seven Mile Ford, Va

11059. FRANKLIN C. HALL and 7 children, Seven Mile Ford, Va

11060. IRVING W. BLEVINS,   Green Cove, Va

11061. JOHN M. HALL and 4 children,   Park, Va

11062. GREEN C. BLEVINS and 2 children, Seven Mile Ford, Va

11063. MINTER F. BLEVINS,   Seven Mile Ford, Va

11064. NANNIE C. MARTIN and 2 children, Azen, Va

11065. ROBERT N. WIDNER,   Damascus, Va

11066. ELIZABETH BLEVINS,   Azen, Va

11067. MILLEY STURGILL and 2 children,   Azen, Va

11068. ALICE BISHOP and 3 children,   Cole, Va

11069. LOTTIE HENDERSON and 2 children, Azen, Va

11070. JOHN L. STAMPER and 5 children,   Lodi, Va

11071. HENRY C. BLEVINS and 3 children, Azen, Va

11072. SARAH S. TRIVETT and 1 child,   Azen, Va

11073. HUGH J. HART and 3 children,   Green Cove, Va

11074. SARAH BLEVINS and 3 children,   Azen, Va

11075. JOHN H. BLEVINS,   Green Cove, Va

11076. WAITIE E. TRENT and 8 children,   Damascus, Va

11077. SUSAN M. COOK and 6 children,   Damascus, Va

11078. ESTILLE E. BLEVINS,   Green Cove, Va

11079. GEORGE W. BLEVINS and 3 children, Worth, W Va

11080. NANCY REDAFORD,   Worth, W Va

135

APP 11048 TO 11100 – SIZEMORE CASES – SEE SPECIAL REPORT #417

11081. MARTHA A. WRIGHT and 5 children,   Lodi, Va

11082. MARY E. WIDENER and 1 child,   Damascus, Va

11083. CELEY HART,   Weasel, N C

11084. CHARLEY MILLER,   Weasel, N C

11085. ELI MILLER and 1 child,   Weasel, N C

11086. AILEY MILLER,   Weasel, N C

11087. WM. L. BLEVINS and 4 children,   Green Cove, Va

11088. ELON TAYLOR and 2 children,   Park, Va

11089. ELIZABETH BLEVINS,   Green Cove, Va

11090. BINNIE MILLER,   Weasel, N C

11091. CORA STRINGER and 2 children,   Geary, Okla

11092. GORDEN BLEVINS,   Green Cove, Va

11093. NANCY BARLOW,   Green Cove, Va

11094. MECA BARE and 3 children,   Green Cove, Va

11095. ETTIS BLEVINS,   Cole, Va

11096. ALLEY BLEVINS,   Cole, Va

11097. MARY E. BLEVINS,   Green Cove, Va

11098. MANERVIA C. BLEVINS,   Green Cove, Va

11099. DELILA EDMONSEY and 5 children,   Green Cove, Va

11100. SUSAN B. BLEVINS,   Elizabethtown, Ill

END OF CONSECUTIVE SIZEMORE CASES

11101. RICHARD DOWNING and 4 children,   Childers, Okla
Admitted. Brother of #885 and claims through same ancestors.
ROLL P55 #10014 FCT COMM #11092 – Richard Downing – 43
        10015   26635 – Roy (son)   – 12
        10016   26636 – Simpson (son) – 10
        10017   26637 – Susie (dau)   – 6
        10018   – Maggie (dau)   – 3

11102. JOHN LANG,   Vian, Okla
Rejected. Neither applicant nor any ancestors ever enrolled.
Does not establish fact of descent from a person who was a
party to the treaty of 1835-6 and 1846.

11103. ZOE and LEONARD McCLAUCHAN, Minors, Vian, Okla
        L. B. Cornelius, Gdn.
Admitted. Nephew and niece of Lucinda Flesher No 8307
MISC. TEST. P. 2904. No 11103 - Thomas B. Cornelius:
    My name is Thomas B. Cornelius; my post-office is Vian,
Okla.; I am appearing as guardian for Zoa McClanahan and
Leonard McClanahan; Cherokee Roll No for Zoa McClanahan 4366
and Leonard 4367. They claim their Indian blood through their
mother, Louisa Firekiller; Reese Hildebrand told me that their
mother's name was Louisa Firekiller before she was married;
Reese Hildebrand's address is Weber Falls, Okla.; Louisa Fire-
killer was about thirty-five years old when she died and she
died in 1903; Jackson Firekiller was the father of Louisa
Firekiller and Nellie Firekiller was her mother; these children are now living with me and have been living with me for
about five years; Louisa Firekiller has a sister Lucinda
Flesher, No. 8307."
SIGNED: Thomas B. Cornelius, Sallisaw, Okla., Sep 18 1908.
ROLL P92 #17611 FCT COMM #4366 - Zoe McClanahan - 11
         17612   4367 - Leonard (bro) - 7
                                   by T. B. Cornelius, Gdn.

11104. THOMAS McCOY,   Vian, Okla
Admitted. Cousin of #5300 and claims thru same source.
ROLL P93 #17738 FCT COMM #18083 - Thomas McCoy - 21

11105. FRANK F. HALL and 3 children,   Stilwell, Okla
Admitted. Uncle of #3789 and claims thru same source.
ROLL P70 #13012 FCT COMM # 2859 - William F. Hall - 35
         13013   2860 - Stella E. (dau) - 9
         13014   2861 - John W. (son)   - 6
         13015   4554m - Gracie (dau)   - 2

11106. SALLIE HILL,   Wahhiyah, N C
Admitted. Applicant enrolled herself by Chapman under name of
I-yos-tuh #415. [For Roll information See App 11111]

11107. SILL BIRD,   Wahhiyah, N C*
Admitted. Applicant enrolled in 1851 by Chapman #556 as Silih.
Aunt of #7754. ["Big Cove, N C" on roll]
ROLL P6 # 6668 - Tohiskie Bird - 64 (App 15825)
        30245 - Sill (wife)   - 57
        18984 - Quatie (dau) - 16

11108. ANDY STANDINGDEER,   Cherokee, N C
Admitted. Brother of #10037 and claims thru same source.
[For Roll information See App 6208, Vol. 3]

137

11109. AM HILL and 3 children, Wahhiyah,, N C
Admitted. Aunt of #7754 and claims thru same source. Appli-
cant enrolled by Chapman #554 as "A-he-kih".
ROLL P10 #1131 - Ann Hill   - [ages cut off]
            1132 - Nancy (dau)   -
            1133 - Hausley (son) -
            1134 - Kelley (son) -

11110. DICK DRIVER and 1 child, Wahhiyah, N C
Admitted. Uncle of #7754 and claims thru same source. Appli-
cant enrolled by Chapman 555.
ROLL P9 #785 - Dick Driver - 61
          786 - Nannie (dau) - 1

11111. JOHN HILL, Wahhiyah, N C
Admitted. Uncle of #7754 and claims thru same source.
ROLL P10 #1138 - John Hill   - [ages cut off]
            1139 - Sallie (wife) - (App 11106)

11112. SQUENCY TOONIGH, Cherokee, N C
Admitted. Applicant's parents enrolled as Too-ni-ih and Che-
low-wee-sih by Chapman at 291 and 292 respectively.
ROLL P18 #2743 - Squency Toonigh - 54
            2744 - Lydia (wife)   - 51 (App 15770)
            2745 - Mose (son)   - 16

11113. MAGGIE HORNBUCKLE, Cherokee, N C
Admitted. Sister of #10041.
ROLL P11 #1172 - Maggie Hornbuckle - 26

11114. REBECCA HORNBUCKLE, Cherokee, N C
Admitted. Mother of #10041; is enrolled in 1851 by Chapman
#588.
ROLL P11 #1173 - Rebecca Hornbuckle - 66

11115. OLLIE BIRD, Cherokee, N C
Admitted. Aunt of #6213 and claims thru same source. [For
Roll information See App 11118]

11116. WILLIAM H. BLYTHE, Cherokee, N C
Admitted. Uncle of #6223, and claims thru same source.
ROLL P6 #284 - William H. Blythe - 33

11117. CHARLOTTE WELCH, WILLIAM WELCH, Cherokee, N C
        JAMES WELCH, LUCINDA WELCH, by John Goins, Gdn.
Admitted. First cousin once removed of #613 and claims thru
same source. Applicant's grandfather Chapman #1370.
ROLL P19 #2911 - Charlotte Welch - 19
            2912 - William H. (bro) - 17
            2913 - James (bro)   - 15
            2914 - Lucinda (sis)   - 13
                by John Goins Welch, Gdn.

11118. BIRD C. BIRD,   Cherokee, N C
Admitted. Applicant enrolled by Hester at #128. Applicant's
father enrolled by Chapman at #1502 under name of Chees-quh-
neet (or Young Bird).
ROLL P6 #237 - Bird C. Bird - 36
            238 - Ollie (wife) - 33 (App 11115)
            239 - Nan (dau)   - 16
            240 - Colinda (dau) - 16
            241 - Dan (son)   - 8

11119. POLK SAUNOOKE and 2 children,   Cherokee, N C
Admitted. Son of Stilwell Suanooke (7749) and claims thru him.
ROLL P16 #2289 - Polk Sawnooka   - 32
             2290 - Nanny (dau)   - 9
             2291 - Wal-lin-ny (dau) - 1

11120. QUATIE W. TOI-NEE-TA,   Cherokee, N C
Admitted. Aunt of #10041. Claimant's parents enrolled in
1851 by Chapman #585 and 586. [For Roll information See App
6213, Vol. 3]

11121. JOHN WOLFE and 1 child,   Wahhiyah, N C
Admitted. First cousin once removed of #7742. Applicant's
father Oo-chun-tah is enrolled by Chapman #577.
ROLL P20 #3085 - John Wolfe   - 39
             3086 - Linda (wife) - 28 (App 11127)
             3087 - Walker (son) - 1

11122. JAMES M. LAMBERT and 6 children,   Ocona Lufty, N C
Admitted. Brother of No 6648 and claims through same source.
ROLL P11 #1351 - James M. Lambert   - 50
             1352 - Capter Moses (son)   - 20
             1353 - Minnie Hester (dau)   - 18
             1354 - Charles Jackson (son) - 16
             1355 - George Fred (son)   - 13
             1356 - Jesse James (son)   - 11
             1357 - Fritz Simmes (son)   - 9

11123. ANNA TO-NIGH and 2 children,   Soco, N C
Admitted. Applicant's father Teel-tut-ta-kih, C. 474; Fl. 402,
grandparents No-wat-tah and Do-ki-yos-tih. Chp. 469 and 470.
Hester #402.
ROLL P18 #2738 - Mike Toonigh - 32 (App 25980)
             2739 - Anna (wife) - 28
             2740 - Lige (son)   - 7
             2741 - Nancy (dau) - 4

11124. JOHN LOCUST,   Cherokee, N C
Admitted. Uncle of #10026 and admitted for same reasons.
[For Roll information See App 6198, Vol. 3]

11125. CAMBLE SCOT, Wahhiyah, N C
Admitted. Applicant claims thru mother Sallie, enrolled by
Chap. 166. Grandparents John Towih and Aul-kin-nih, Chap. 162,
163. Hester 778. Applicant mistaken as to his age in App.
ROLL P16 #2311 - Camble Scott - 40

11126. WILL DRIVER, Cherokee, N C
Admitted. First cousin of #7754 and claims thru same source.
Applicant's father enrolled by Chapman #555 as "Dicky".
ROLL P9 #801 - Will Driver - 34

11127. LINDA WOLFE, Wahhiyah, N C
Admitted. Niece of 6220. Applicant's grandparents enrolled by
Chapman in 1851, 82 & 83. [For Roll information See App 11121]

11128. ELIZA DRIVER and 3 children, Cherokee, N C
Admitted. Niece of #6212. Applicant's mother enrolled as Ka-
li-nih by Chapman #817.
ROLL P9 #786 - Eliza Driver - 36
         787 - Ned (son)   - 7
         788 - Adam (son)   - 4
         789 - Lucy (dau)   - 1

11129. JAMES B. MUMBLEHEAD, Almond, N C
       ROGERS L. MUMBLEHEAD, CHAS. B. MUMBLEHEAD, By John D.
Mumblehead, Gdn. These children are incl in App 11130

11130. JOHN D. MUMBLEHEAD and 3 children, Almond, N C
Admitted. This applicant was enrolled by Hester #1330 as the
bastard son of Ross Smith, who was enrolled by Chapman #1369.
[For Roll information See App 9117, Vol. 4]

11131. ANNIE WADASUTTA, Wahhiyah, N C
Admitted. Applicant was enrolled by Hester #829. Applicant's
grandfather was enrolled by Chapman 56 as Choo-luh or Fox.
Misc. Test. P. 1771.
MISC. TEST. P. 1771. Witness re #11131 - James Blythe...in
behalf of Annie Wadasutte:
       "I am acquainted with Anna Wadasutte. She is about 50
years of age. She is a full blood Indian. Her father is Wilson
or Wil-sin-nih, or Wah-he-yah-hah. Swimmer Fox and Sen-doo-
leh were full brothers of Wilson. Wilson Fox's father's name
was Choo-luh or Fox (Chapman 56). Choo-lah's wife's name Dah-
ah-gih. I do not know who Anna Wadasutte's mother was. She
and her father always lived with the Indians and were full
blood Cherokees."
SIGNED: James Blythe, Cherokee, N. C., Jul 22 1908.
[For Roll information See App 11132]

11132. WADASUTTE SUWAGGIE, Wahhiyah, N C
Admitted. Brother of #10034, and claims thru same source.
Applicant enrolled by Chapman #260.

ROLL P18 #2589 - Wadasutta Suwaggie   - 61
          2590 - Anna WADASUTTA (wife) - 43 (App 11131)

11133. CINDA SCREAMER,   Cherokee, N C
Admitted. Sister of #10027 and claims thru same source.
ROLL P16 #2313 - James Screamer - 47 (App 16272)
          2314 - Cinda (wife)   - 37
          2315 - Cain (son)   - 6
          2316 - Soggy (son)   - 3

11134. ANNIE DAVIS,   Wahhiyah, N C
Admitted. Applicant's father and grandparents enrolled by
Chapman #333, 334 and 337. [For Roll information See App
7747, Vol. 4]

11135. JOHN SAWNOOKA, JR.,   Cherokee, N C
Admitted. Nephew of #11134 and applicant's grandparents are
enrolled by Chapman #333 and 334. [For Roll information See
App 6033, Vol. 3]

11136. MANLY W. WHIPPERWILL,   Cherokee, N C
Admitted. Nephew of #6220. Applicant's mother enrolled by
Chapman in 1851 as E-wee or Eve, #85.
ROLL P19 #2962 - Manly W. Whipperwill - 22

11137. CILINDA BIRD,   Cherokee, N C
Admitted. Minor child of #1118 [should be #11118] and enrolled as such.
MISC. TEST. P. 1746. Witness in re #7556 and 11137 - Willie
West, in behalf of #7556 and 11137:
    "I am acquainted with Amy Armachain or Amy Jo-la-oo-go-
ooth. She was the daughter of my half sister. Her Indian name
is Uh-kee-lee. She was older than I am, and I am 58 years of
age. She did not have the same mother that I did, but her father was Ah-nee-che. I am acquainted with Golindy Bird. Amy is
the aunt of Golindy." SIGNED: Willie West, Cherokee, N. C.,
Jul 21 1908. "NOTE — Uh-kee-lee is Chapman 12, the father is
Chapman 10, and the above witness Chapman 16." [Notation added
to end of testimony]
[For Roll information See App 11118]

11138. LIZZIE YONAGUSKI,   Wahhiyah, N C
Admitted. First cousin of #7754 and claims thru same source.
Applicant's father enrolled Chap. #555 as "Dicky".
ROLL P20 #3126 - Lizzie Yonaguski - 36

11139. NANNIE BLYTHE and 1 child,   Whittier, N C
Admitted. Applicant's mother enrolled by Chapman 1851 #95.
Daughter of #6653.
ROLL P6 #274 - David Blythe   - 44 (App 16274)
          275 - Nannie (wife)   - 36
          276 - Jack JACKSON (son of w) - 13

                        141

11140. LUCY RATLEY,   Cherokee, N C
Admitted. Applicant enrolled by Chapman #448.
ROLL P15 #2100 - Lucy Ratley - 62

11141. ADAM SAWNOOKE,   Cherokee, N C
Admitted. Nephew of #11134 and applicant's grandparents are
enrolled by Chapman #333 and 334. Applicant's parents were
born after 1851.
ROLL P16 #2275 - Adam Sawnooka - 20

11142. JULIA V. GEORGE and 1 child,   Silver Creek, N Y
Admitted. Niece of #6648 and claims thru same source.
ROLL P9 #922 - Julia V. George   - 31
            923 - Charlotte B. (dau) - 2

11143. SALLIE WOLFE,   Wahhiyah, N C
Admitted. Sister of #7746 and claims thru same source. [For
Roll information See App 11145]

11144. LAURA ANN LEE and 4 children,   Birdtown, N C
Admitted. Sister of #6648 and claims thru same source.
ROLL P12 #1458 - Laura Ann Lee   - 43
            1459 - Samuel (son)   - 17
            1460 - Oberlander (son) - 14
            1461 - Edith (dau)   - 12
            1462 - Debrader (son)   - 10

11145. JOWEN WOLFE,   Wahhiyah, N C
Admitted. Enrolled as Cho-win-nih, Chapman #384. Father of
#10080.
ROLL P20 #3097 - Jowen Wolfe   - 47
            3098 - Sallie (wife) - 48 (App 11143)

11146. MATTIE SHELL,   Yellow Hill, N C
Admitted. Claims thru grandmother enrolled as Wah-lih. Half
uncles and aunts enrolled as Qua-kih, E-too-wih, Lok-kin-nih;
Sic-e-you-it and Ta-lis-kih. All enrolled by Chapman in 1851.
Nos. 60-1-3-4-6 and 7. Father enrolled by Chapman #1217.
Mother enrolled by Hester #28. [For Roll information See App
11148]

11147. SALLY SHELL,   Yellow Hill, N C
Admitted. Mother of 1146 [should be 11146] and claims thru
same source. [For Roll information See App 8769, Vol. 4]

11148. UTE SHELL and 3 children,   Cherokee, N C
Admitted. Son of #8769 and claims thru same source.
ROLL P16 #2364 - Ute Shell   - 29
            2365 - Mattie (wife) - 20 (App 11146)
            2366 - Joe (son)   - 5
            2367 - Bessie (dau) - 3
            2368 - Alice (dau)   - 1

142

11149. CORNELIA T. OWL,   Birdtown, N C
Admitted. Half sister of #9782 and admitted for same reasons.
MISC. TEST. P. 1747. #11149 - Cornelia T. Owl...through David
Owl, Interpreter:
    "That I am 50 years of age, and I live at Birdtown, N. C.
I was know[n] as Cor-ne-lih Tramper in 1884. My father's name
was Te-la-ska-skih. (Chapman 253)."
SIGNED: Cornelia "X" Owl, Cherokee, N. C., Jul 20 1908.
ROLL P14 #1820 - Adam Owl   - 45 (App 36132)
         1821 - Cornelia T. (wife) - 52
         1822 - Thomas (son)   - 19
         1823 - Mose (son)   - 16
         1824 - John (son)   - 14
         1825 - Davis (son)   - 9
         1826 - Samuel (son)   - 9
         1827 - Martha (dau)   - 6
         1828 - Quincy (son)   - 1

11150. JESS SKEE-KEE,   Cherokee, N C
         by Segillie Dah-leyiskee, Father
Admitted. Duplicate of child on #11151.

11151. SE-GIL-LIE DAH-LE-YE-SKEE, 1 child, Cherokee, N C
Admitted. Brother of #10035. Is enrolled in 1851 by Chapman
as "So-kil-lih" #1471. The child filed for by this applicant
is adopted by him. The child's name is Jesse Co-lo-na-has-kie
and his mother was enrolled by Hester at 1147 as Quailsie and
his grandfather as Ka-lo-na-hess-kee, at Hester #1146 and by
Chapman #746 as Ka-lo-na-hesk. (See letters herein marked
Exhibit A.)
ROLL P8 #664 - Se-gil-lie Dah-le-ye-skee   - 63
         665 - Jesse Co-lo-na-has-kie (Adson) - 15

11152. THOMAS OWL and 5 brothers,   Birdtown, N C
         and one sister, By Adam Owl, Gdn.
Admitted. Half brother and sister of #9986 and claims thru
same source. See Application #36132. [For Roll information
See App 11149 - NOTE: The application number for these children was listed as 36132]

11153. DAVID OWL,   Cherokee, N C
Admitted. Grandfather of #9986. Enrolled by Chapman in 1851
as David Owl, #1168.
ROLL P14 #1831 - David Owl - 74

11154. CHARLEY LAMBERT and 1 child,   Swayney, N C
Admitted. Nephew of #6215. Grandmother enrolled as No 415 by
Chapman.
ROLL P11 #1336 - Charley Lambert - 21
         1337 - Mary (wife)   - 20 (App 15859)
         1338 - Jackson (son)   - 1/3

143

11155. LILLIAN V. DUNCAN and 2 children,   Cherokee, N C
Admitted. First cousin of #613 and claims thru same source.
Applicant's father enrolled by Chapman #1368.
ROLL P9 #802 - Lillian V. Duncan - 30
          803 - Tommy POTTER (son) - 11
          804 - Sybal DUNCAN (dau) - 1

11156. KINSEY WOLFE,   Swayney, N C
Admitted. First cousin to #21.
ROLL P20 #3099 - Kinsey Wolfe - 21

11157. JOHNSON TOWNEY,   Cherokee, N C
Admitted. Applicant's mother enrolled by Chapman in 1851
#165.
ROLL P18 #2746 - Johnson Towey - 50
          2747 - Nancy (wife) - 44 (App 11159)

11158. ANNIE DEDAHLEEDOGEE,   Wahhiyah, N C
Admitted. Sister of #6203 and claims thru same source.
ROLL P8 #741 - Annie Dedahleedogee - 49

11159. NANCY TOWEY,   Cherokee, N C
Admitted. Applicant's father enrolled by Chapman at #82. Applicant's mother enrolled by Chapman at #502.   Applicant enrolled by Hester at #722. [For Roll information See App 11157]

11160. WM. L. WILDER,   Chouteau, Okla
Rejected. Applicant claims thru his wife who died 1878. See
letter.

11161. CHARLOTTE B. WILDER,   Chouteau, Okla
Rejected. Mother of applicant and claimant herself an old settler G. S. 77.   Father not enrolled.   He was not a party to
the treaties. Applicant states she put in application for her
husband who died in 1877. Misc. Test. P. 3606.
MISC. TEST. P. 3606. No 11161 - Charlotee B. Wilder:
     "I am 51 years of age.   My father and mother were both
Indians. My mother was an Old Settler and my father was an
Immigrant. He died before the roll was made. I put in this
claim for my husband. He died in 1877. I have no minor children."
SIGNED: Charlotte B. Wilder, Pryor Creek, Okla., Oct 9 1908.
EXCEPTION CASE. Rejected.   Total number of exceptions filed
in this group — 2. Original recommendation renewed.

11162. LINCOLN WOLFE and 2 children,   Leavenworth, Kans
Admitted. Brother of #2394.   Claims thru mother, Elizabeth
Jones (now Elizabeth Wolfe) enrolled in 1851, at 329 G. S.
Applicant in prison. See 16355, 2492-2394. [For Roll infor-
mation See App 10272]

11163. DAVE HENDRICKS,   Ochelata, Okla
        for his ward BEN STEELER,
Admitted. Half brother of #5604. Applicant's father Oo-lon-
nos-tee-skie is enrolled by Drennen in Flint Dist. Group #166.
ROLL P132 #25533 FCT COMM #29138 - Ben Stealer - 11
                                by Dave Hendricks, Gdn.

11164. LOVELLA E. WHITNEY and 2 children, Adair, Okla
Admitted. Niece of #2920. Applicant's mother is enrolled by
Drennen in 1851, G. S. 677, as Flora Scraper.
ROLL P150 #29092 FCT COMM #9805 - Louella E. Whitney - 38
        29093   9808 - Ethel (dau)   - 17
        29094   9809 - Bertha J. (dau)   - 6

11165. JOSEPH E. REED,   Pensacola, Fla
Rejected. See special report Creek File #1139.

11166. DAVID HENDRICKS,   Ochelata, Okla
Admitted. First cousin of 671. [For Roll information See App
10363]

11167. MIKE HENDRICKS, Minor,   Ochelata, Okla
        by father David Hendricks
Admitted. Duplicate #11116 [Should be 11166]

11168. MRS. J. G. SHULLTEWORTH and 3 children, Pensacola, Fla
Rejected. See Special Report Creek 1139.

11169. WILLIAM CLIFFORD and 4 children,   Warrington, Fla
Rejected. See Special Report Creek 1139.

11170. DIXON B. REED, JR.,   Pensacola, Fla
Rejected. See Special Report Creek 1139.

11171. CAPT. DIXON B. REED,   Pensacola, Fla
Rejected. See Special Report Creek 1139.

11172. JOHNSON QUINTON,   Brush, Okla
        by Letha Quinton, Gdn.
Admitted. Applicant is a cousin to Henry Dreadfulwater #2748
and claims thru same source.
ROLL P114 #21878 FCT COMM #3135 - Johnson Quinton - 18
                                by Letha Quinton, Gdn.

11173. GEO. HICKS, Duplicate of #7482.

11174. DELLA E. CHANCE and 5 children,   Temple, Ga
Rejected. Third cousin of #2780 and claims thru same source.

11175. SAPHRONIA S. LEDFORD and 3 children, Stilwell, Okla
Rejected. Claims thru John Tidwell. See special report #16.

11176. ROSS HENSON,   Evansville, Ark
Admitted. Applicant's mother enrolled by Chapman 1851, #1309.
ROLL P74 #13921 FCT COMM #1996 - Poss Henson - 52

11177. LEVY HEWING,   Stilwell, Okla
Admitted. Nephew of #1895 [? last digit blurred]
ROLL P74 #13971 FCT COMM #2381 - Levy Hewing - 24

11178. LUCY PHILLIPS and 2 children,   Vian, Okla
Admitted. Niece of #7450 and claims thru same source.
ROLL P111 #21327 FCT COMM # 3327 - Lucy Phillips   - 22
        213;28   3329 - Daniel J. (son) - 4
        21329   1319m - Henry (son)   - 3

11179. JEFFERSON C. BALES and 3 children, Keefeton, Okla
            by Matilda Schoonover, Gdn.
Rejected. Children claim thru their father who was not enrolled. Father's mother left Tenn. in 1831. Must be O. S.
See Misc. Test. P. 4172.
MISC. TEST. P. 4172. App. No. 11179 - Matilda Schoonover:
    "I am 57 years of age. I have been here 28 years. I am a
white woman and am making no claim through myself. This claim
is for my husband. His name was David Bales. He has been
dead 12 years and he was 59 years of age at the time of his
death. My husband was born in Arkansas. He got his Indian
blood through his mother, Tinsey Jane Craig. She married
Bales. She came from Red Clay, Tenn. in about 1831. My husband got no Indian blood through his father. None of my husband's people were enrolled in 1851. They were all born in
Arkansas. That is the reason they were not enrolled. My understanding is that people who lived in Arkansas were not enrolled. I am not on the Dawes Commission roll nor is my husband. My children are not enrolled by the Dawes Commission."
SIGNED: Matilda Schoonover, Muskogee, Okla., Mar 22 1909.

11180. ELIZABETH J. KEEFE,   Fairmount, Ga
Rejected. It does not appear that applicant's ancestors were
parties to treaties of 183-6 46, never shared in payments to
the Cherokees nor enrolled with them. See Also #16319; claims
thru same source; also #12945. Misc. Test. P. 1309 and 1431.
MISC. TEST. P. 1309. No 16319 (10392) - Elias M. Suggs:
    "My name is Elias M. Suggs; I was born in Gordon Co., Ga.
1851; I claim my Indian blood through my mother; I make no
claim through my father; my mother's maiden name was Polly
Cox; My mother was born in McMinn Co., Tenn. 1817; my mother
got her Indian blood through her father, John Cox; I never saw
my grandfather, John Cox; I do not know where or when he was
born; my grandfather, John Cox, got his Indian blood through
his mother; I do not know for certain what her maiden name
was, but I think it Was Polly Sprigmore; I do not know where
or when Polly Sprigmore was born; my mother never lived with
the Cherokees as a member of the tribe that I know of; my

146

grand father, John Cox, went with the Indians to the West; he
helped take the Cherokees away from Ga.; Newechota; neither my
mother nor my grandfather through whom I claim were ever enrolled that I know of; I learned from my father that my grand
father, John Cox, went West with the Indians; I also heard the
same report from old settlers; none of the ancestors through
whom I claim were ever held in bondage; I do not know the
names of any of the brothers and sisters of John Cox; none of
my ancestors through whom I claim ever had an Indian name with
the exception of my great grandmother, Polly Sprigmore; none
of my ancestors ever went West with the Indians with the exception of John Cox that I know of; in 1835 and 1851 my mother
through whom I claim lived in Gordon Co., Ga.; I was not enrolled in 1882 that I know of; Group 11180; Lottie C. Cox is
the sister of Polly Cox."
SIGNED: Elias M. "X" Suggs, Calhoun, Ga., Jul 9 1908.
Zachariah F. Wilson...deposes and says:
   "My name is Zachariah F. Wilson; I am eighty-eight years
old; I never knew John Cox personally, but I knew his wife;
his wife told me that John Cox went off with the Indians as a
member of the tribe in 1838; from Newechota, Ga.; Polly Cox
was always regarded as a white person with Cherokee blood; I
have heard that John Cox was a half breed Cherokee Indian; he
was so reputed to be in the community."
SIGNED: Zachariah F. Wilson, Calhoun, Ga., Jul 9 1908.

[NOTE: The following page of testimony is very dark and difficult to read]
MISC. TEST. P. 1431. No 12945 - George W. Cox:
   "My name is George W. Cox; I was born in Gordon Co., Ga.
1854 [?]; I claim my Indian blood through my father; I make no
claim of Indian blood through my mother; my father, Jacob Cox,
was born in McMinn Co., Tenn., to the best of my recollection,
1819; my father got his Indian blood from his father my grand
father's name was John Cox; I never saw my grandfather, John
Cox; I do not know where or when he was born; I think he was
born in East Tenn. in McMinn Co.; I heard that my grandfather
got his Indian blood from his mother, whose maiden name was
Polly Sprigmore; I do not know where or when she was born, but
she lived in Tenn.; my father never lived with the Cherokee
Indians as a member of the tribe; my grandfather, John Cox,
was a half Cherokee; my grandfather, John Cox, went West with
the Indians from Gordon Co., Ga.; I think he went to the Ind.
Terr.; I do not know the names of any of my father's brothers
or sisters [looks like foregoing line was crossed out and I
cannot read the rest of the sentence] in 1851, my father was
living in Gordon Co., Ga.; in 1835 father lived in Gordon Co.,
Ga1; none of the ancestors through whom I claim were ever held
in bondage; I never heard of the enrollment of 1882; --?--
Suggs is my cousin; his mother and my father were brother and
sister; (See cases examined in Calhoun, July 9th)"
SIGNED: George W. Cox, Springplace, Ga., Jul 11 1908.

147

EXCEPTION CASE. Rejected. Total number of exceptions filed in this group -- 13. Original recommendation renewed.

11181. LOTTIE C. WADDLE,   Fairmount, Ga
Rejected. Mother of 11180 and claims thru same source.

11182. JOHN W. PETTY,   Warner, Okla
Rejected. Claimant apparently makes no claim only thru his wife, who died in November 1876. None of his ancestors or claimant himself are on any roll. His son states in letter herewith that claimant is a white man.

11183. OLLIE ROGERS, Gdn. for 2 minor children
Duplicate of children in 11191.

11184. ANNIE NOBLES and 3 children,   Bedias, Tex
Rejected. Cousin of #10290.

11185. SALLIE M. ALFORD and 1 child,   Hanson, Okla
Admitted. Sister of #9183.
ROLL P23 #3614 FCT COMM # 2746 - Sallie M. Alford - 20
          3615   2849m - William D. (son) - 2

11186. BENJ. F. GOINS and 3 children,   Graysville, Tex
Rejected. Cousin of #6290 and claims thru same source.

11187. HENRY GOINS,   Graysville, Tex
Rejected. Brother of #10294 and claims thru same source.

11188. HATTIE WATERS,   Braggs, Okla
Admitted. Applicant's grandparents on father's side enrolled by Drennen in Sal Dist. Group 141 under name of John E-tow-ie and Lucy. Misc. Test. P. 3359. [NOTE: Should be 3369]
MISC. TEST. P. 3369. Witness for No 11188 - Johnson Waters, witness for Hattie Waters...through S. E. Parris, Interpreter:
    "Hattie Waters is the wife of my son, Joe Waters. She is a full blood. She never drew any Old Settler money. She drew Strip money. I knew her mother. She was an Immigrant. She was as old as I am. She drew money in 1852. She was a little girl then. I do not know her father's name. Hattie's mother's name was Ah-heh-stah. Hattie's father was a very old man when he died. His name was Oo-dah-yeh-day, or Oo-daw-ye-dau or Oo-taw-ye-daw." SIGNED: Johnson Waters, Tahlequah, Okla., Oct 1 1908. [For Roll information See App 10933]

11189. JAMES PHILLIPS and 3 children,   Braggs, Okla
Admitted. Uncle of #2181 and claims thru same source.
ROLL P111 #21309 FCT COMM #20614 - James Phillips - 40
           21310   20615 - Lizzie (wife) - 47
                                    (App 11481)
           21311   20616 - Nellie (dau)   - 16
           21312   20617 - Joseph (son)   - 12

11189. JAMES PHILLIPS (Cont)
          21313 FCT COMM #20618 - Thomas (son)   - 6

11190. LOONEY HAMMER and 3 children,   Braggs, Okla
Admitted. A nephew of #1224. Tom Smith Tah. 290 is grand
father of claimant and Ah-ne-na-ke Smith is mother. See Misc.
Test. P. 3464 [Should be 3463]. Applicant enrolled by Daws
Commission #23135.
MISC. TEST. P. 3463. #11190 - Looney Hammer:
    "That I am 41 years of age. I am a full blood. Both of my
parents were Cherokees.   That is the only Indian blood they
had. My father and mother were living in 1851. My parents were
not Old Settlers. My mother had a half brother on the father's
side by the name of James Smith, who is now living at Moody,
Okla. He is about 54 years of age. Peggy was living in Tahlequah in 1851. My mother's Indian name was Ah-ne-wa-kee Smith
(Tah. 290). Her parents' names were Tom and Susie Smith. My
mother had a sister named Quatie, another Nellie and another
Jennie and a half brother named James Smith. James is the one
living at Moody. My mother did not have any full sisters or
brothers; these given were half brothers and sisters.   Susie
was the step-mother of my mother. My mother's mother was dead
in 1851. My father had a step-mother by the name of Choo-gah-
wa-lees-kee (Flint 4?3 [2nd digit blurred]) and Aleeke was her
granddaughter whom she took to raise. Black Hammer was my father father's full brother. I don't know who John Hammer was.
I am on the Dawes Commission roll #23135"
SIGNED: Looney Hammer, Muskogee, Okla., Sep 22 1908.
[For Roll information See App 6674, Vol. 3]

11191. OLLIE ROGERS,   Braggs, Okla
Admitted. Niece of Coleman Dick #6753.
MISC. TEST. P. 3387. No 11183 - Ollie Rogers...through S. E.
Parris, Interpreter:
    "I am about 33 years of age. I am a Cherokee alottee. My
mother and father were both Cherokees. My mother was living at
the time of the Immigrant payment in 1852 with her mother and
father. Her name was Nannie. My mother had a sister living at
the time named Rachel Christy. They were living in Flint District. Rachel was my mother's first cousin not her sister. My
mother was Nannie Dick and her father was Wah-leh-he.   Her
mother was Gah-ne-yeh-ih. My mother was an Immigrant. My mother had a brother by the name of Richard and another named Cold
weather."
SIGNED: Ollie Rogers, Tahlequah, Okla., Oct 2 1908.
"This case is O. K. through applicant's mother Nan-ne Dick, 13
Tahlequah." [Notation added to end of testimony]
ROLL P119 #22901 FCT COMM #25958 - Ollie Rogers - 35
          22902*   25962 - Jim (son)   - 14
          22903   25961 - Lovely (son) - 6
          22904   4692m - Bessie (dau) - 1
[* Notation added to roll "Young, James. See Roll No. 22902"]

11192. JIM YOUNG, thru his mother and Gdn., now Ollie Rogers,
Duplicate of child in #11191.

11193. RICHARD D. PERDUE,   Cookson, Okla
Admitted. Brother of #10388 and claims thru same source.
ROLL P110 #21115 FCT COMM #20826 - 28

11194. JOHN W. SHARP and 5 children,   Tahlequah, Okla
Admitted. Brother of Fannie E. Chandler (#1723) and son of
Eliza Sharp-McKee.
ROLL P126 #24281 FCT COMM #8751 - John W. Sharp   - 53
             24282   8756 - Albert (son)   - 17
             24283   8757 - Caroline (dau)   - 15
             24284   8758 - Grover (son)   - 13
             24285   8761 - George W. (son) - 4
             24286   8755 - John (son)   - 20
                               (App 44338)

11195. GEORGE WASHINGTON and 4 children,   Cookson, Okla
Admitted. Applicant enrolled by Drennen in 1851, Saline 285.
Misc. Test. P. 3525 and 3526.
MISC. TEST. P. 3525.   No 11195 - George Washington...thru S.
E. Parris, Interpreter:
    "I was small at the time of the Immigrant payment but I
think I drew. I was about thirteen when the war started. I was
the oldest child."
SIGNED: George Washington, Tahlequah, Okla., Oct 5 1908.

MISC. TEST. P. 3526.   Witness for No 11195 - Mary Washington
(Bluebird):
    "John Washington was my husband. He died Nov. 1906. He
was on his death bed when papers were made out.   I have four
minor children by John Washington.   They are Bettie 11 years
old; Emmet 8 years old; Willie 6 years old and John 4 years of
age. I am an Immigrant Cherokee. My father was a white man.
My mother drew Immigrant money. Her name was Bettie Leavitt.
George Washington drew Immigrant money. My mother married a
Pettit and then a Dunbar. I never drew any Old Settler money.
My husband never drew any Old Settler money."
SIGNED: Mary Washington, Tahlequah, Okla., Sep 30 1908.
[For Roll information See App 10282]

11196. IDA MILLER,   Cookson, Okla
Admitted. Niece of #7450 and claims thru grandmother enrolled
Ill. #140.
ROLL P99 #18946 FCT COMM #3328 - Ida Miller - 20

11197. LARENDA BUSHYHEAD and 4 children,   Braggs, Okla
Admitted. Grandfather, Cah-sah-low-ee, enrolled in 1851 in
Skin Bayou #23.   Mother of applicant, Sarah Ann Miller,
enrolled in 1851 in Tahl. #200. Daws Comm. #32779. See Misc.
Test. P. 3459.

150

MISC. TEST. P. 3459. #11197 also #12212 - Larenda Bushyhead
...thru Tom Roach, Interpreter:
"That I think I was enrolled as 30 years of age by the
Commission; I don't know my exact age. Larenda Micco was before marriage. My roll number by the Dawes Commission is
32779. My son, Edward Swimmer, is enrolled #28406. My daughter, Lizzie Swimmer, is 28405. I am Cherokee and a little
white, but am enrolled as a full blood. My father, Jim Carselowey, is living in Sequoyah. His full name is James R. Carselowey. #13569 is his number by the Dawes Commission. He is very
old; I don't know just exactly how old he is. He is an emigrant, not an Old Settler. My mother was an emigrant. Both of
my parents were living in 1851. My father's Indian name is Al-
teesk Cah-se-low of Cah-se-low. My father's father's name is
Cah-sah-low-wee (S. B. 23) His wife's name was Cah-le-low-
hih. My father had a full brother named Tuh-see-lee, and Lewis
was a son of my father's brother Eli. Eli is living and goes
by the name of Eli Cah-sah-low. His post office is Stilwell,
Okla. My mother was enrolled in 1851 under the name of Sarah
Ann Miller (Tah. 200). She had a brother named Henry W.
Miller. My mother was living on the line of Skin Bayou and
Tahlequah. Wat Watts (12212) and Lizzie Watts (12213) is my
daughter. The father of these children is Jim Watts. He was my
first husband."
SIGNED: Larenda Bushyhead, Muskogee, Okla., Sep 23 1908.
ROLL P36 #6375 FCT COMM #32779 - Larenda Bushyhead   - 35
        6376*   28405 - Lizzie SWIMMER (dau) - 14
        6377*   28406 - Ned SWIMMER (son)   - 10
        6378   32780 - Jim MICCO (son)   - 6
        6379   4845m - Bessie MICCO (dau)   - 4
[* Notation on roll "Watts, Lizzie. See Roll No. 6376." and
"Watts, Watt. See Roll No. 6377."]

11198. ALBERT SOUR JOHN and 4 children,   Braggs, Okla
Admitted. Applicant claims thru father Oo-gow-se-dah, en-
rolled 1017 Del. Also see testimony of Jenny Bushyhead, Misc.
Test. P. 4200-4201.
MISC. TEST. P. 4200. App. No. 11198 - Albert Sour-john...thru
John Israel, Interpreter:
"I live at Braggs, Okla. and my Dawes Commission number is
21036. I am a full blood Cherokee. Oo-gaw-sit-tah was the name
of my father. He is dead - has been dead 29 years. He lived in
Delaware District. I don't know whether my father drew in 1851
or not. I am 37 years of age. I don't know whether my father
had any brothers and sisters or not. I don't know of anybody
named Lucy. I don't know my father's father's name. Never
heard of him. I don't know the name of my grand mother on my
father's side either. Cha-we-yu-kah was the name of my mother.
She lived in Canadian District. Dah-yu-chin-ih was my mother's
father's name. Oo-naw-dut-tah was the name of a brother of my
mother. She had no sisters. Bushy-head Severe was the English
name of that brother of my mother. My father's English name

151

was Sour-john. My mother was an Old Settler. I have been told
that my father was an Emigrant. My parents were never married.
They lived together. They lived in Canadian District and then
moved to Illinois District. My father died in Illinois District. My father had a first cousin named Sah-nee. I had an
uncle named Ned but that's all the name I knew him to have. I
did not draw Old Settler money but my mother drew at that
time. My parents lived together until my father died."
SIGNED: Albert Sourjohn, Braggs, Okla., Mar 26 1909.
MISC. TEST. P. 4201. App. No. 11198 - Jennie Bushyhead...thru
John Israel, Interpreter, in behalf of Albert Sour-john:
    "I am 75 years of age. I was born in Illinois District.
I am an Old Settler but his father was an Emigrant. Oo-gah-
sit-tah was the name of Albert's father. I think he was living in 1851. I don't know whether he drew money in 1851 or
not. I know that Albert's father was an Emigrant. He was
born in Delaware District. Both of Oo-gah-sit-tah's parents
were Emigrants. I don't know the name of applicant's grand
father. Never saw him. I don't know whether he was living in
1851 or not. Ail-sey was the name of the applicant's grand
mother on his father's side and she lived in Canadian District. She died there. Albert's grandparents lived in Delaware
District before they lived in Canadian. I don't know whether
applicant's grandparents were married or not but they lived
together. I don't know of any brothers and sisters that Oo-
gah-sit-tah had. Oo-gah-sit-tah had a wife named Wa-key. They
had a child but I don't know the name. (See Del. 1017)."
SIGNED: Jennie Bushyhead, Braggs, Okla., Mar 27 1909.
MISC. TEST. P. 3157. App #11198 - Albert Sour John...through
Tom Roach, Interpreter:
    "My name is Albert Sour John. I live at Braggs, Okla. I
have been enrolled by the Dawes Commission. My number is
#21038. I was told that my father drew Immigrant money, but I
don't know whether he did or not. His name was Sour John. He
was living in Delaware District at first, and then he went to
Canadian District. My mother drew Old Settler money. I could
not find out my grandfather's name on my father's side. My father had a half brother name Saun-nie [? 1st syllable blurred]
I don't know my grandmother's name on my father's side. I
don't know whether my father had any full brothers or not. I
don't know whether had [sic] any sisters or not. I was told
that my father an uncle [sic] by the name of Ned and another
named Rattlinggourd. I have no full brothers and sisters."
SIGNED: Albert Sourjohn, Annie L. Stephens, witness to mark,
[NOTE: No mark indicated] Muskogee, Okla., Sep 24 1908.
ROLL P130 #25151 FCT COMM #21038 - Albert Sourjohn - 33
          25152   - Oo-lu-ja (wife) - 30
                             (App 17044)
          25153   21040 - Levi (son)   - 11
          25154   21041 - Anderson (son) - 10
          25155   32650 - Silk (son)   - 5
          25156   - Charley (son)   - 2

                         152

11199. SUSIE RUNABOUT,   Braggs, Okla
Admitted. Applicant's mother and father enrolled in G. S. 259
under name of Anna and Choo-we-skah respectively.   Applicant
herself enrolled in same group as Susan. [See "NOTES" p. 436
this volume]
ROLL P121 #23270 FCT COMM #21141 - Susie Runabout - 60

11200. SARAH CHOOWEE,   Christie, Okla
Admitted. Father and brothers and sisters of applicant enrolled in Going Snake Dist. No 569 [?] by Drennen in 1851, under name of Fisher. Misc. Test. P. 4038.
MISC. TEST. P. 4038. #11200 - Edward Walkingstick...in behalf
of Sarah Choo-wee:
    "I have know Sarah Choo-wee ever since the year 1862; I am
59 years old. I knew the father of Sarah Choo-wee, Soo-uh-skee
or Fisher. It is my opinion that they came to this country
with the Emigrants, that is, the father of Sarah Choo-wee. The
mother of Sarah Choo-wee was a white woman and her father was
a full blood Cherokee. The general reputation of Sarah Choo-
wee was that of an Emigrant Cherokee.   I never heard of her
getting any Old Settler money. I think that her father was
probably enrolled in either Going Snake District or Flint in
1851; They lived right on the dividing line. I live about six
miles from Sarah Choo-wee and I was raised about seven miles
from her and I have been a [sic] position to know her well."
SIGNED: Edward Walkingstick, Westville, Okla., Mar 27 1909.
ROLL P41 #7376 - Sarah Choowee - 48

11201. PLEASANT S. DAVENPORT,   Blueridge, Ga
Rejected. First cousin once removed to #2877 and claims thru
same source.

11202. ROBERT T. KINCAID and 3 children,   Blue Ridge, Ga
Rejected. First cousin to #2877 and claims thru same source.

11203. YELL C. WARD and 7 children,   Siloam Springs, Ark
Rejected. Applicant's parents enrolled as Old Settlers.

11204. MITTIE Q. VERNON and 3 children,   Power Spgs., Ga.
                                            Route #16
Rejected. Applicant fails to show any genuine connection with
the Eastern Cherokees. No ancestors it appears were parties to
the treaties of 1835-6 or 46. No ancestor was ever enrolled.
Misc. Test. P. 971.
MISC. TEST. P. 971. #11204 - Mittie Q. Vernon:
    "That I am 31 years of age and live in Co., Ga. I claim my
Indian blood through my father; my mother is a white woman.
Both of my father's parents were of Indian descent. Ruthe
Maddox was my grandmother and her maiden name was Dabbs. My
grandparents were 1/2 Indian Cherokee. My father was 45 when
he died and has been dead 19 years. My father never was on any
Indian roll that I know of. I don't know whether any of my an-

cestors were or not. My father died when I was small. He never lived among the Indians as a member of the tribe. My grand parents died in Gwinnett Co., Ga. My grandmother has been dead about 7 years and my grandfather has been dead about 12 years. I think they were born in Gwinnett Co., Ga. Both of my great grandparents were buried in Gwinnett Co., Ga. I am recognized as a white woman in the community. My father never made any application for benefits and this is the only one I ever made. None of my brothers and sisters have made application to share in this fund."
SIGNED: Mittie I. Vernon, Marietta, Ga., Jul 6 1908.
EXCEPTION CASE. Rejected. Total number of exceptions filed in this group -- 1. Original recommendation renewed.

11205. MARION M. GREEN and 6 children,   Pine Log, Ga
Rejected. It appears conclusively that no ancestor was ever enrolled and that no ancestor ever lived with the Cherokee tribe. Applicant and his ancestors all passed as white. This claim is without merit. See Misc. Test. P. 1202.
MISC. TEST. P. 1202. No 11205 - Marion M. Green:
    "My name is Marion M. Grenn; I was born in Gordon Co., Ga. in 1864; I claim my Indian blood through my father; I make no claim through my mother; my father, John R. Green, was born in Ga. I think; I do not know what county; my father was born in 1839; my father got his Indian blood from his father; I think my grandfather through whom I claim was born in Ga., but I do not know what county; I do not know where my grandfather got his Indian blood; I have heard that my the [sic] great grandmother of your [sic] grandfather was a full blood Cherokee Indian; none of the ancestors through whom I claim ever lived with the Indians as a member of the tribe; none of my ancestors had an Indian name that I know of; none of the ancestors through whom I claim were ever enrolled and never received any money or land; in 1851 my father and grandfather lived in Dawson Co., Ga.; none of the ancestors through whom I claim ever went West with the Indians; none of my ancestors through whom I claim were ever held in bondage; I never heard of the enrollment of 1882; both I and the ancestors through I claim were always regarded as white people in the community in which we lived, but it was generally known that we were part Cherokee Indian."
SIGNED: Marion M. Green, Cartersville, Ga., Jul 8 1908.
EXCEPTION CASE. Marion M. Green and 6 children, Adairsville, Ga. Rejected. Total number of exceptions filed in this group -- 1. Original recommendation renewed.

11206. ROSCOE LAMBERT and 5 children,   Forney, Ala
Admitted. Nephew of #6648 and claims thru same source.
ROLL P12 #1368 - Roscoe Lambert - 31
          1369 - Albert (son)   - 9
          1370 - Georgia (dau) - 7
          1371 - William (son) - 6

11206. ROSCOE LAMBERT (Cont)
      1372 - Andrew (son)   - 4
      1373 - Finley (son)   - 2

11207. HUGH LAMBERT and 1 child,   Forney, Ala
Admitted. Nephew of #6648 and claims thru same source.
ROLL P11 #1344 - Hugh Lambert - 25
      1345 - Lee F. (son) - 2

11208. NANNIE LEMINGS and 1 child,   Forney, Ala
Admitted. Niece of #6648 and claims thru same source.
ROLL P12 #1466 - Nannie Lemings - 27
      1467 - Ollie (son)   - 2

11209. TILDEN LAMBERT,   Forney, Ala
Admitted. Nephew of #6648 and claims thru same source.
ROLL P12 #1387 - Tilden Lambert - 29

11210. LIZZIE WASHINGTON,   Braggs, Okla
Admitted. Applicant's mother Aley, enrolled in 1851 in Del.
Dist. #67. Applicant enrolled by the D. C. Did not draw O. S.
money. John Israel states applicant recognized as full blooded
Cherokee. Misc. Test. P. 4186.
MISC. TEST. P. 4186. App. No. 11210 - Lizzie Washington...
through John Israel, Interpreter:
    "I am 50 years of age. No. 21152 is my enrollment number
by the Dawes Commission. I am a full blood Cherokee. My mother
drew money in 1851 but I don't know whether my father did or
not. They were both Cherokees. Ail-sey was my mother's name.
That's all the name I know. She lived in Delaware District.
She had a sister but I don't know what her name was. She had
no brothers that I know of. My mother told me that she drew
money in 1851. I am sure that she was living in Delaware District in 1851. She was an Emigrant. I don't know the name of
my mother's mother. I don't know the name of my mother's father either. Ailsey has been dead about 30 years. My mother
was not an Old Settler. Ned Uh-stuh-quah [last syllable
blurred] was the name of my father. My parents were not married in 1851. My mother was a little girl. Taw-ju-wah and Gaw-
du-quah-skee were brothers of my father. Se-quah-ne-yah (Hogshooter) was the name of another brother of my father. Uh-
stuh-a-quah was the name of my father's father. I don't know
the names of any of my grandfather's brothers and sisters. I
don't know the name of my grandmother on my father's side. I
did not draw Old Settler money a few years ago. I have never
mixed with any other tribe of Indians than the Cherokees. I do
not know of any witness who could testify as to my grandparents. My grandfather on my father's side drew money in 1851,
but I don't know whether my father did or not. I don't know
whether it was Old Settler money or Emigrant money that my
grandfather drew. People have told me that it was Emigrant
money." SIGNED: Lizzie Washington, [no date or place]

"Interpreter states that he does not believe applicant drew
O. S. money. He states that she is a full blooded Cherokee
and is recognized as such." [Notation at end of testimony]
** ROLL P146 #28356 - Lizzie Washington - 50**
[** Entire line crossed out - no explanation - the preceeding
entry, also a Lizzie Washington, listed App #10282, but 20
years younger than applicant 10282 probably should have been
the entry crossed out]

11211. WILLIAM DAVIS and 3 children,   Blue Ridge, Ga
Rejected. Claims thru same source as #690.

11212. BENJ. DAVIS and 4 children,   Blue Ridge, Ga
Rejected. [NOTE: Nothing else on this application]

11213. MOLLIE STUBBLEFIELD,   Flats, N C
Rejected. It does not appear that any ancestor was ever enrolled or that any ancestor was a party to the treaties of
1835-6 and 46. Shows no connection with the Eastern Cherokees.

11214. OWENAH A. BAUER, Minor,   Bellaire, Ohio
        by John A. Schick, Gdn.
Admitted. First cousin once removed of #6223 and claims thru
same ancestors.
ROLL P5 #157 - Owenah A. Bauer - 11
        by John A. Schick, Gdn.

11215. MARY ELIZABETH BROOKS and 3 children, Goodman, Mo
Rejected. Sister to #3753 and claims thru same source.

11216. EVA TAYLOR and 4 children,   Christie, Okla
Admitted. Daughter of #5845 and claims thru the same source.
Grandmother enrolled.
ROLL P136 #26394 FCT COMM #28390 - Eva Taylor   - 36
            26395   28391 - Rider (son)   - 19
            26396   28393 - Shadock (son) - 12
            26397   28394 - Betsy (dau)   - 6
            26398   3830m - John (son)   - 1

11217. QUETIE REDBIRD,   Christie, Okla
Admitted. Applicant enrolled as "Quatey" in G. S. #358. Her
mother enrolled as Cha-yeh-yo-hee, head of same group. [For
Roll information See App 9691, Vol. 4]

11218. AGGIE KNIGHT, Duplicate of #1782.

11219. JEFF PICKARD,   Poplar Bluff, Mo
Rejected. Applicant's ancestors were not parties to treaties
of 1835-6-46. In 1835 they lived in Indiana several hundred
miles from Cherokee country. Never shared in payments to the
Cherokees or enrolled with them.

11220. ARCH COLEMAN and 6 children,   Vian, Okla
Admitted. Brother of #9377.
ROLL P45 #8069 FCT COMM #21115 – Arch Coleman   – 48
       8070   19344 – Peggie (wife)   – 40
                          (App 11221)
       8071   19436 – Emma (dau)   – 17
       8072   19347 – Chi (dau)   – 16
                          (Died January 21, 1909)
       8073   19348 – Esther (dau)   – 12
       8074   32299 – Ed (son)   – 9
       8075   32300 – Gooestah (son) – 6
       8076   – Samuel (son)   – 1
                          (Died June 24, 1906.)

11221. PEGGIE COLEMAN,   Vian, Okla
Admitted. Sister of #10904 and claims thru same source. [For
Roll information See App 11220]

11222. MITTIE ROWLAND and 1 child,   Webbers Falls, Okla
Admitted. First cousin of #4394. Mother of claimant enrolled
in 1851 by Drennen, Del. 431.
ROLL P121 #23250 FCT COMM #16986 – Mittie Rowland – 20
        23251   3862m – Mary (dau)   – 2

11223. ORPHA R. SLOAN,   706 Oak St., San Francisco, Cal
Rejected. Sister of #622 and claims thru same source.

11224. JULIA E. HILDEBRAND, minor,   Remy, Okla
        by Margaret E. Moton, Gdn.
Admitted. Applicant's grandfather enrolled 36 Tahl., Stephen
Hildebrand. Niece of #859.
ROLL P75 #14173 FCT COMM #22920 – Julia E. Hilderbrand – 13
                          by Margaret E. Moton, Gdn.

11225. JAS. J. LEVIER and 3 children,   Webbers Fall, Okla
Admitted. The applicant's mother Catherine Sevier nee Ore, is
enrolled by Drennen from Canadian Dist. under group #36. See
Misc. Test. P. 3474.
MISC. TEST. P. 3474.   #25673 – 11225 – Delia Brewer...in behalf of James J. Sevier:
"That I am 74 years of age. I was acquainted with the father of applicant. Applicant claims through his father and his
grandmother on his father's side. Applicant's father died in
May 1907. James J. was born in 1852. The grandmother of appli-
cant was born in 1831. Her name was Caroline Ore. She died in
1878 and was sometimes known as Catherine Ore.   The father of
applicant was the only child. Don't know whether Caroline or
Catherine was an Old Settler or not. His grand parents were
living near Webbers Falls in 1851. They were married in 1851.
Joe and Jim Ore were brothers of Catherine.   (Can. 33 and 35)
Lydia and John were brother and sister of Catherine (Can 34).
His grandmother Catherine was probably enrolled under the name

157

of Sevier as she was married in 1851 (Can 36). Catherine's
husband John was a full blood. They called him Hogshooter. Ap-
plicant is on the Dawes Commission roll #14774 and his father
is #14770. Nelson's number is #14778; Charles is #14776 and
Lee's is #14777, and Jerry's is #14773. Callie's is #14771 and
Alice's is #14775."
SIGNED: Delia Brewer, Muskogee, Okla., Sep 21 1908.
ROLL P125 #24197 FCT COMM #14770 - <u>Jos. J. Sevier</u>   - 48
          24198   14775 - Alice B. (dau)   - 19
                                   (App 25676)
          24199   14776 - Charles Fowler (son) - 18
          24200   14777 - Leo Earnest (son)   - 14
          24201   14778 - Nelson A. M. (son)   - 8

11226. MARY E. SCOTT and 1 child,   Tahlequah, Okla
Admitted. Enrolled as Letitia McClean 260 Ill. Sister to #4054
ROLL P124 #23923 FCT COMM #15981 - Mary E. Scott   - 54
          23924   15984 - Grover Harris (son) - 14

11227. MAY RHOMER and 4 children,   Webbers Falls, Okla
Admitted. Niece of #2175. Applicant's father Calvin Hanks, en-
rolled in 1851, by Chapman #1560.
ROLL P116 #22376 FCT COMM #17271 - May Rhomer   - 34
          22377   17272 - Emma N. (dau)   - 17
          22378   17273 - May F. (dau)   - 14
          22379   17274 - Maggie B. (dau) - 13
          22380   17275 - Fannie c. (dau) - 11

11228. EMMA H. BRANAN and 5 children,   Webbers Falls, Okla
Admitted. Father of applicant, Calvin Hanks, enrolled in 1851
by Chapman #1560.
ROLL P33 #5681 FCT COMM #17539 - Emma Branan - 29
          5682   17540 - Clifford B. (son) - 12
          5683   17541 - Edward H. (son)   - 10
          5684   17542 - William C. (son) - 7
          5685   49m - Virgil C. (son)   - 4
          5686   50m - Goerge F. (son)   - 2

11229. EMMA SPENCER,   Kansas, Okla
Admitted. Daughter of #4917 and claims thru same source.
MISC. TEST. P. 3811. 11229 - Emma Spencer:
    "I am about 26 years of age. My mother is still living
near Locust Grove. Her name is Elsie Jew-li-eh-wah. She has
filed Application Number 4917. I am a Night Hawk. I have a
half brother living on my mother's side named Sam Buckskin. My
mother's father was named Choo-le-ah-wah and her mother was
named Lucy. She had a sister named Susannah and a brother
named Jimmy. See Sal. 245."
SIGNED: Emma Spencer, Locust Grove, Okla., Oct 13 1908.
ROLL P131 #25251 FCT COMM #15990 - Emma Spencer - 24

11230. JESSE BIRD,   Whitmire, Okla
Admitted. Applicant's mother enrolled by Drennen in 1851,
Del. 908.
ROLL P30 #5099 FCT COMM #20783 - Jesse Bird   - 28
          5100   20312 - Sis (wife) - 24 (App 11238)
          5101   30600 - Charley SAND (son of w) - 5
          5102   - Sallie POORBOY (dau of w) - 2

11231. ELLA YOUNGBIRD,   Kansas, Okla
Admitted. Niece of #2041 and claims thru same ancestors.
Grandfather of applicant, Blue Batt, enrolled in 1851 in Sa-
line Dist. #82. [For corrected Roll information See p437,
Vol. 4, see also App 6621, Vol. 3.]

11232. AGGIE STRAINER,   Oaks, Okla
Admitted. Applicant enrolled as A-kee.   Mother enrolled as
A-lee. Sister enrolled as Ca-law-cuh and Susan-ne, Tahl. #191.
See Misc. Test. P. 4239.
MISC. TEST. P. 4239. #11232 Aggie Strainer...thru D. S. Mann:
    "I was living with my mother in 1851. Her name was A-lee.
She was living with a man by the name of Chin-a-que. I had a
sister by the name of Ca-haw-cuh and Susannah, and a brother
by the name of John. We were all living together in 1851 when
we got the money. My brother was an emmigrant Cherokee. He
never drew any old settler money. See Tahl. 191."
SIGNED: Aggie Strainer, Oaks, Okla., Mar 17 1909.
ROLL P134 #25825 FCT COMM #29509 - Aggie Strainer - 64

11233. BETTIE WILSON,   Whitmire, Okla
Admitted. Applicant's mother enrolled as Goo-we-stah by Drennen in G. S. Dist group 65. Grandfather and grandmother enrolled as head of same group. [For Roll information See App
10683].

11234. LUCY BLACK FOX,   Kansas, Okla
Admitted. Half sister of #469 and claims thru same source.
[For Roll information See App 10221]

11235. JOHN PIGEON,   Oaks, Okla
Admitted. Brother of #11232 and claims thru same source.
ROLL P111 #21441 FCT COMM #20369 - John Pigeon - 68
                             (Died in May, 1907)

11236. JACK RUSSELL and 3 children,   Kansas, Okla
Admitted. Applicant's father enrolled by Drennen in Del. Dist.
Group #641. Grandmother as head of same group. See App #1425.
ROLL P121 #23313 FCT COMM #30038 - Jack Russell   - 29
          23314   20806 - Ella (wife)   - 23
                                (App 16932)
          23315   32336 - Dave (son)   - 9
          23316   4824m - Emma (dau)   - 2
          23317   - Roscoe (son)   - 1

159

11236. JACK RUSSELL (Cont)
        28132   - Mollie YOUNG DUCK - 6
                                 (dau of w) (App 16931)

11237. DAVID RUSSELL,   Kansas, Okla
Admitted. Brother of #11236 and claims thru same source.
ROLL P121 #23303 FCT COMM #19736 - David Russell - 23
        23304   19736 - Sallie (wife) - 24
                                 (App 32383)

11238. SIS BIRD and 2 children,   Flint, Okla
Admitted. Daughter of #9623 and claims thru same source. [For
Roll information See App 11230]

11239. MELVEN E. WEAVER,   Shawano, Wis.
Rejected. Claims thru the same source as #10886.

11240. MAGGIE GOLECH,   Cherokee, N C
Admitted. First cousin, once removed, of #6223 and claims
thru same ancestors.
ROLL P10 #983 - Maggie Golech - 17

11241. JOHN G. BARKER,   Sheridan, Ind.
Rejected. Applicant claims to inherit Cherokee blood from his
great-great-grandmother who was born in 1752 and died in 1825.
Do not find name of applicant or any of his ancestors on any
of the rolls. Does not establish fact of descent from person
who was a party to the treaty of 1835-6 an 1846.

11242.   MARTHA E. MILLIKAN,   Sheridan, Ind
Rejected. Sister of #11241 and claims thru same source.

11243. JOHN G. ALLEN (Dec'd) and 5 children, Hortonville, Ind
Rejected. First cousin of #11241 and claims thru same source.

11244. IDA J. A. EMRY and 1 child,   Sheridan, Ind
Rejected. First cousin of #11241 and claims thru same source.

11245. EPHRAM B. PRUETT and 2 children, Roswell, Ga
Rejected. See special report Sizemore #417.

11246. JOHN S. PRUETT,   Roswell, Ga
Rejected. See special report Sizemore #417.

11247. JANE I. WITT,   Edwarto, Alberta Prov., Canada*
Admitted. Applicant enrolled in 1851 in Going Snake #409.
[* Residence Okoee, Okla. on roll]
ROLL P152 #29592 FCT COMM #7649 - Jane I. Witt - 62

11248. IDA L. SHEPHERD,   Just P. O., N C
Rejected. See special report Kesiah Vann #276.

11249. WM. H. SHEPHERD and 3 children,   Just P. O., N C
Rejected. See special report Kesiah Vann #276.

11250. FRANK L. DONCARLOS,   Wann, Okla
Rejected. Applicant's grandmother (Appl #35599) was Mary Cornwell or Mary Ward and her father, brothers and sisters were
enrolled on Old Settler Roll, Group #36 in Non-resident list.
EXCEPTION CASE. Rejected.   Total number of exceptions filed
in this group -- 1. Original recommendation renewed.

11251. JOHN BLACK,   Oktaka, Okla
Rejected. This applicant born in 1806 on the way from Georgia
to Arkansas. He and his parents were living in Arkansas in
1835 and 1851. They were not parties to the treaties of 1835-6
and 1846, and were never enrolled.

11252. WILLIAM H. HALL and 1 child, Rt. #3, Shawanee, Okla
Rejected. Neither applicant nor ancestors ever enrolled. Does
not establish fact of descent from person who was a party to
the treaty of 1835-6 and 1846. See Misc. Test. P. 3467.
MISC. TEST. P. 3467. #11252 - William H. Hall:
     "That I am 58 years of age. I claim my Indian blood
through my mother. My father was a white man. My mother was
about 58 years old when she died.   She claimed Indian through
her mother, Clarissa Burns. She never married - just lived Indian custom. I never knew the name of my grandfather. My mother was a half breed Cherokee. She was half Cherokee and half
white. If my mother was ever on any roll I don't know of it.
In 1851 my mother went by the name of Hall. My mother left
Cherokee Co., Ga. between 1835 and 1840.   My grandmother came
along too and they came to Missouri and Arkansas. Think they
started with the Cherokees. Don't know why my mother was never
enrolled, unless it was that she never lived here in the Cherokee country. My mother lived with the Indians up to the time
they left the old country.   My mother and grandmother talked
Indian all the time. They never had any other name than Burns.
Martin Burns was my mother's uncle - my grandmother's brother.
Don't know what became of him. Don't know whether there were
other brothers or not. Dent Burns, Jack and Jim were brothers
of my mother. Dent Burns died in Tahlequah. Don't know whether
he was enrolled or not. He has been dead several years. My
mother had no sisters. I have heard my mother speak of George
Burns, but I don't know just what relation he was. My mother
was not an Old Settler. I was not enrolled by the Dawes Commission. None of us applied. All of these people claim back
through my mother and grandmother - that is my children and my
brothers children."
SIGNED: Wm. H. Hall, Muskogee, Okla., Sep 22 1908.
EXCEPTION CASE. Rejected.   Total number of exceptions filed
in this group -- 19. Original recommendation renewed.

11253. CLARISY PANLEY and 6 children,   Oktaha, Okla
Rejected. Sister of #11252 and claims thru same source.

11254. GEO. M. D. SHEPHERD,   Just P. O., N C
Rejected. See special report Kesiah Vann #276.

11255. MITTY L. SHEPHERD,   Just P. O., N C
Rejected. See special report Kesiah Vann #276.

11256. ELIZA SHEPHERD and 4 children,   Just. P. O., N C
Rejected. See special report Kesiah Vann #276.

11257. JOHNSON FALLING,   Vinita, Okla
Admitted. Applicant was born in 1854 and his father John Fall-
ing was enrolled by Drennen, Del. #376 as John B. Falling.
[For Roll information See App 2154, Vol. 2]

11258. NICHOLAS S. SANDERS and 1 child,   Pryor Creek, Okla
Admitted. First cousin to #862.
ROLL P123 #23642 FCT COMM #6939 - Nicholas S. Sanders - 46
          23643   6940 - Irene (dau)   - 16

11259. JAMES WELCH and 1 child,   Miami, Okla
Admitted. Brother of #4361 and is admitted for same reasons.
[For Roll information See App 939, Vol. 1]

11260. SARAH QUINTON,   Fawn, Okla
Rejected. It does not appear that any ancestor was ever enrolled as an emigrant Cherokee.   Nor does it appear that any
ancestor was party to the treaties of 1835-6 and 1846. There
is a Lydia Quinton on the Old Settler Roll and she may be applicant's grandmother. Applicant can give no further information. Misc. Test. P. 2754.
MISC. TEST. P. 2754. No 11260 - Sarah Quinton:
     "My name is Sarah Quinton; my post-office is Fawn, Okla.;
I was born in McIntosh Co., Okla. in 1890; I claim relationship to the Cherokee Indians through my father, Moses Quinton;
He was born in Polk Co., Ark.; I know nothing further about
the family history as I was too young to know, but I have been
enrolled by the Commission of the Five Civilized tribes and my
number is 22076."
SIGNED: Sarah Quinton, Eufaula, Okla., Sep 10 1908.

11261. JOHN F. CONCH,   [no residence*]
Admitted. First cousin of #2679. [* Chelsea, Okla on roll]
ROLL P47 #8528 FCT COMM #12484 - John F. Couch - 39

11262. ELIZABETH HEFFLINGER,   Dawson, Okla
Admitted. Great aunt of #4291. Claimant's parents enrolled
in 1851 by Drennen #44 Del.
ROLL P73 #13705 FCT COMM #12363 - Elizabeth Hefflefinger - 54

11263. THOMAS S. FOSTER and 1 child,   Claremore, Okla
Admitted. Brother of #1350 and claims thru same source.
ROLL P63 #11724 FCT COMM #11523 - Thomas S. Foster - 31
          11725   643m - Emmett H. (son) - 1

11264. JOHN I. CHAMBERS,   Claremore, Okla
Admitted. Half brother of #9831 and claims thru same source.
ROLL P40 #7116 FCT COMM #28048 - John Q. Chambers - 25

11265. WILLIAM W. CHAMBERS for his children, Tiawah, Okla
           Leon and Joe Chambers.
Sons of #1371. Duplicate of #1371. These children are admitted
in supplemental application filed by their father, #1371.

11266. EZEKIEL P. CHAMBERS,   Tiawah, Okla
Admitted. Son of #1371. Father enrolled in 1851 in Tahl. #240
ROLL P40 #7105 FCT COMM #11478 - Ezekiel P. chambers - 31

11267. GEORGE S. CHAMBERS and 2 children,   Tulsa, Okla
Admitted. First cousin of #107 and claims thru same source.
Children of #11267 enrolled with Osages, therefore rejected.
ROLL P40 #7106 FCT COMM #31685 - George S. Chambers - 52

11268. JOHN T. LYLE,   Saltville, Va
Rejected. See special report Sizemore #417.

11269. JAS. B. COLLINS,   Kennison, Okla
Admitted. Second cousin of #2671.
ROLL P45 #8142 FCT COMM #24204 - James B. Collins - 21

11270. ABRAM WEAVER and 4 children,   Park, Va
Rejected. See special report Sizemore #417.

11271. ROBERT BECK,   Kennison, Okla
Admitted. Second cousin of #2671.
ROLL P28 #4707 FCT COMM #7746 - Robert Beck - 24

11272. SALLIE A. DAVIS and 4 children,   Bartlett, Kans
Admitted. Second cousin of #2671.
ROLL P52 #9419 FCT COMM # 9445 - Sallie A. Davis - 26
         9420   9446 - Edna G. (dau) - 9
         9421   9447 - Ellis L. (son) - 6
         9422   9448 - Mable B. (dau) - 4
         9423   1985m - Katie M. (dau) - 2

11273. MARTHA T. KIRKLAND and 1 child,   Yellow Creek, N C
Admitted. Niece of #423 and claims thru same source. Applicant
enrolled by Hester at #1939 as Lucinda Kirkland, his [sic]
mother enrolled by Chapman at #1891.
ROLL P11 #1332 - Martha T. Kirkland - 47
         1333 - Georgia E. (dau)   - 5

11274. JOHN H. MEIGS,   Hulbert, Okla
Admitted. Nephew of #1363.
ROLL P98 #18745 FCT COMM #15825 - John H. Meigs   - 47
         18746   15826 - Elinor M. (wife) - 44
                               (App 11275)
         18747   15827 - Carrie M. (dau) - 13
         18748   18528 - Charles R. (son) - 12
         18749   15829 - Elinor B. (dau) - 7
         18750   15830 - John H. (son)   - 5
         18751   3066m - Return J. (son) - 3

11275. ELINOR M. MEIGS and 3 children,   Hulbert, Okla
Admitted. Uncle [sic] of #7810 and claims thru same source.
[For Roll information See App 11274]

11276. CHARLES THROWER and 1 child,   Bunch, Okla
Admitted. Applicant's father, mother and sisters and brothers
enrolled as Chee-ta-kee and Nancy, etc., and applicant as Che-
o-cah in Tahl. 386.
ROLL P139 #27009 FCT COMM #25786 - Charles Thrower - 56
          27010   19836 - Nancy (dau)   - 9

11277. MARK A. BEANS,   Tahlequah, Okla
Admitted. First cousin of #537 and claims thru same ances-
tors. Father of applicant, Bruce Bean, enrolled in Tahl. Dist.
#594.
ROLL P27 #4514 FCT COMM #23184 - Mark A. Beans - 37

11278. ROBERT B. BEAN and 3 children,   Tahlequah, Okla
Admitted. First cousin of #537 and claims thru same ancestors. Father of applicant, Bruce Bean, enrolled in Tahl. Dist.
#594. [For Roll information See App 8317, Vol. 4]

11279. JAMES SCULLAWL, (Deceased)   Hulbert, Okla
          by Joe M. Tahay, Muskogee, Admr.
Admitted. Brother of #6781 and claims thru same source.
ROLL P125 #24035 FCT COMM #21290 - James Scullawl - 75 (Dec'd)
          by Joe M. Tahay, Admr., Claremore, Okla

11280. ANNIE TAHQUITTE, Duplicate of #1203.

11281. CHEROKEE FOREMAN,   Tahlequah, Okla
Admitted. Sister of #1619 and claims thru same source. [For
Roll information See App 11886]

11282. MARY ANN ELLIS,   McGrady, N C
Rejected. See special report Sizemore #417.

11283. ELZINA BROWN and 3 children,   McGrady, N C
Rejected. See special report Sizemore #417.

11284. ELIAS C. THORNE and 2 children,   Tahlequah, Okla
Admitted. Applicant's maternal grandfather enrolled by Drennen 1851 S. B. 188. See Misc. Test. P. 3231.
MISC. TEST. P. 3231. No 11885 - Sue A. Hughes:
    "I am 48 years of age. I am a Cherokee alottee and my num-
ber is 14127. My mother was an Old Settler. My father was
Charles Foreman and he was an Immigrant.   I am the oldest
child. My father has been dead ever since I was a little girl.
He was a young man when he died. I guess I saw my grandfather
but I was very small. My father's father was an Indian and his
mother was a white woman. My father had a brother by the name
of William, one named Charles and one named Samuel. My father
had a sister by the name of Minerva Thornton."
SIGNED: Sue A. Hughes, Tahlequah, Okla., Sep 26 1908.
ROLL P139 #26935 FCT COMM #13904 - Elias C. Thorne - 29
          26936   2935m - Lula (dau)   - 2
          26937   2936m - Oplala (dau)   - 1

11285. PETER AX,   Japan, N C
Admitted. Claimed for [by] mother in application #24443.
[Notation on Roll "Axe, Peter. See Roll No. 2938."]
ROLL P19 #2936 - Mary Welch   - 41 (App 24443)
         2937 - Lucinda AXE (dau) - 18
         2838 - Peter AXE (son)   - 12
         2839 - Mandy AXE (dau)   - 10
**   2840 - Lee WELCH (son)   - 8 **
[** entire entry crossed out]

11286. MANDA AX,   Japan, N C
Admitted. Claimed for by mother in Application #24443. [Nota-
tion on Roll "Axe, Mandy. See Roll No 2939." For Roll information See App 11285]

11287. CZAIMA V. McCAFFREE,   Vera, Okla
Admitted. Applicant's grandfather enrolled by Chapman as John
Rogers in 1840; mother enrolled by Daws Comm. as Cherokee in
11921. See Misc. Test. P. 427*. [* Should be P. 2427]
MISC. TEST. P. 2427. #11301-11287 - Georgia C. McCafree:
    "I am 42 years of age; was born in the Indian Territory,
Choctaw Nation. I claim Cherokee Indian blood through my father. My mother was a Choctaw.   She drew Choctaw money and I
have drawn Choctaw money. I am enrolled by the Dawes Commission as a Cherokee. I was allowed by the Dawes Commission to
enroll either as a Cherokee or Choctaw. I enrolled as a Cherokee. I also drew Cherokee strip money. I think my father came
west in 1858."
SIGNED: Georgia C. McCafree, Bartlesville, Okla., Aug 28 1908.
"There is a John Rogers, Sr. and a John Rogers enrolled by
Chapman as Nos. 1839 and 1840. This is the only John Rogers
who could possibly have been enrolled as her father. I am in-
clined these are her ancestors. See Ketron." [Notation added
to end of testimony]

EXCEPTION CASE. 11287. Bradley D., Barton A. and Laura V. McCaffree, by Czarina V. McCaffree, mother, Ramona, Okla. Admitted. Total number of exceptions filed in this group — 1. These children were omitted from the roll through a clerical error and should be placed thereon with their mother, who is enrolled at No. 17564, Miller Roll.

ROLL P92 #17564 FCT COMM #11925 - Czarina V. McCaffree - 22
SUPP ROLL #30677   11926 - Bradley D. McCaffree - 5
         30678   3396m - Barton A. (bro)   - 3
         30679   3397m - Laura V. (sis)   - 1
                    by Czarina V. McCaffree, mother & Gdn.

11288. ABBIE E. TALBERT,   Claremore, Okla
Admitted. Niece of #253 and claims thru same source. Applicant's mother Eunice D. Chamberlain enrolled by Drennen, Disp. Dist. #1. Applicant enrolled as Alice E. Disp. Dist. #1.
ROLL P136 #26244 FCT COMM #11267 - Abbie E. Talbert - 57

11289. LEANDER KELLY and 6 children,   Cleveland, Tenn
Rejected. Applicant nor ancestors were ever enrolled. Does not appear that they were living within the Cherokee Domain in 1835-6 and 1846 as a recognized member of the tribe. Does appear that applicant's grandfather came from Va. and were always recognized as white people. See Misc. Test. P. 502.
MISC. TEST. P. 502. #17396 with #11289 - Mrs. Nannie E. Evans and Leander Kelly:
    "That we are 49 and 44 years of age respectively and live in Cleveland, Tenn. We claim through our mother and grand mother on our mother's side. My great grandfather, William Evans, was supposed to be one-half Cherokee Indian. My grand mother was born in Virginia; I don't know what part. My mother was born in Pickens Co., Ga., I think. She may have been born in S. C. and raised in Ga. I think my great grandfather came from Virginia. I don't know whether my mother or any of my ancestors ever lived with the Indians and don't know whether they were ever on any roll. We are recognized as white people in the community in which we live, and so were our mother and grandmother. We never made application before to share in any Indian benefits." SIGNED: Nannie E. Evans, Leander Kelley, Cleveland, Tenn., Jun 25 1908.

11290. JASPER N. KELLEY and 2 children,   Cleveland, Tenn
Rejected. Brother of #11289.

11291. BENJ. M. CORNETT and 4 children,   Temple, Ga
Rejected. Claims thru Abraham Helton. See #2780.

11292. ELI DAY SPEARS and 2 children,   Melvin, Okla
Admitted. Cousin of #803 [? 2nd digit blurred].
ROLL P131 #25235 FCT COMM #28004 - Eli Day Spears   - 24
         25236   1671m - John Albion (son) - 2
         25237   1672m - Daniel Eli (son) - 1/3

11293. PEGGIE JOHNSON,   Melvin, Okla
Admitted. Niece of #2686 and claims thru same source. [For
Roll information See App 7692, Vol. 4]

11294. JENNIE DOWNING and 1 child,   Melvin, Okla
Admitted. Applicant is a sister of Besey Tucker, #3696. [For
Roll information See App 9800, Vol. 4.

11295. JACK CRAINFORD,   Melvin, Okla
Admitted. The paternal grandmother and aunts were enrolled by
Drennen in 1851 in #58 Ill. Paternal grandfather on O. S. Roll
ROLL P48 #8720 FCT COMM #16514 - Jack Crawford - 25

11296. CATY WOODALL,   Melvin, Okla
Admitted. Sister of #12259 and claims thru same source. 58 Ill
ROLL P153 #29806 FCT COMM #16515 - Caty Woodall - 21

11297. SEPTEMBER MOSE, Duplicate of #5533.

11298. TAYLOR HENSON,   Tahlequah, Okla
Admitted. Applicant's father enrolled by Drennen in 1851,
Tahl. 460. See Misc. Test. P. 3434.
MISC. TEST. P. 3434. 21153-11298 - Betsey Tucker:
    "I was about 8 years old at the time the war commenced.
My father was an Old Settler and my mother was an Emmigrant.
My father and mother were living together in Tahlequah District in 51. My father's name was Wash Henson and my mother's
name was Rachel Henson. They didn't have any children of their
own but my father had a child by another woman that was named
Jacob. My mother had a sister named Susannah and she had a
daughter named Nellie Henson that was living in 51. Susannah
was only a half sister of my mother on the father's side, but
her mother was an Emmigrant and was drove from the old nation
with them. My mother's mother was named Too-nih but she was
living over in Delaware District with old man Mouse. Old man
Mouse had two families. One wife was Too-nih and the other was
Quah-le-you-guh. They had several children. I have the following children. Hiram Woodall, George Woodall, Jim Woodall, Maggie Whitekiller, and Willie Whitekiller. I have been married
three times. Alsie Flying is my mother's full sister and still
living near Tahlequah or Melvin or maybe Peggs is her post office. I guess I am a Night Hawk. I refused to take my allotment. I am a full blood. See also Del 38. I was notified to
testify at Tahlequah but got my notice too late."
SIGNED: Betsy "X" Tucker, Locust Grove, Okla., Oct 14 1908.
ROLL P74 #13944 FCT COMM #21402 - Taylor Henson - 37

11299. ALBERT C. ALBERTY and 1 child,   Westville, Okla
Admitted. Nephew of #384.
ROLL P22 #3519 FCT COMM # 928 - Albert C. Alberty - 29
        3520   3785m - Julianna (dau)   - 7/12

                              167

11300. ELLIS R. ALBERTY and 4 children,   Tahlequah, Okla
Admitted. Grand nephew of #384.
ROLL P22 #3535 FCT COMM #22352 - Ellis R. Alberty - 34
         3536   27947 - Callie (wife)   - 31
                                  (App 25715)
         3537   27948 - Robert G. (son) - 14
         3538   27949 - James H. (son)   - 11
         3539   27950 - Lora May (dau)   - 9
         3540   3187m - Albert B. (son) - 4

11301. GEORGIA C. McCAFFREE and 4 children, Vera, Okla
Admitted. Mother of #11287.
ROLL P92 #17559 FCT COMM #11921 - Georgia C. McCaffree   - 41
         17560   11922 - Charles M. BRICE (son) - 19
         17561   11923 - Annie L. BRICE (dau) - 17
         17562   11924 - Walter J. BRICE (son) - 12
         17563   11926? - Louis A. BRICE (son) - 5
[NOTE: FCT # of Louis A. Brice as written]

11302. ELVIN P. DEMPSEY,   Talking Rock, Ga
Rejected. Proof of genuine connection with Eastern Cherokees
insufficient. It appears that no ancestor was a party to the
treaties of 1835-36-46.   No ancestor ever enrolled.   Misc.
Test. P. 1236.
MISC. TEST. P. 1236. #11307-11302 - Margaret G. Garrett:
    "That I am 60 years of age and live in Pickens Co., Ga. I
claim through my father. My mother was a white woman.   My
father's father was the Indian. All the rest of my grandparents were white. My father was born and raised in S. C. near
Charleston. My father's father was born and raised there too.
My grandfather did not come to this country, but my father
came here when I was about ten years old. I don't know whether
my father or grandfather ever lived with the Indians as a member of the tribe. They lived among the Indians but not after
they came to Georgia. My father claimed 1/2 Cherokee. Don't
know whether my father or his father were ever on any roll. I
nor my father never received anything from the government.
People regard me as white with some Indian blood.   They all
know that I have some Indian blood. My husband is a white
man."
SIGNED: Margaret C. "X" Garrett, Jasper, Ga., Jul 9 1908.

11303. THOS. W. CRAFT,   Toonigh, Ga
Rejected. Neither applicant nor ancestors ever enrolled. Does
not establish fact of descent from a person who was a party to
the treaty of 1835-6 and 1846.

11304. LULU L. CRAFT,   Toonigh, Ga
Rejected. Sister of #11303 and claims thru same source.

11305. CHARLEY A. CRAFT,   Toonigh, Ga
Rejected. Son of #11303 and claims thru same source.

11306. SALLY ARNOLD,   Talking Rock, Ga
Rejected. Niece to Elvin P. Dempsey (11302).

11307. MARGARET C. GARRETT,   Talking Rock, Ga
Rejected. Sister to Elvin P. Dempsey (11302).

11308. JOHN S. ATKINS,   Walesha, Ga
Rejected. See special report #2516.

11309. JAMES L. ATKINS,   Walesha, Ga
Rejected. See special report Whitmire #2516.

11310. ALICE ROBINSON,   Talking Rock, Ga
Rejected. Niece to Elvin P. Dempsey (11302).

11311. ELLER ROBINSON and 2 children,   Talking Rock, Ga
Rejected. Niece to Elvin P. Dempsey (11302).

11312. MATTIE A. SOSEBEE,   Woodstock, Ga
Rejected. Hillhouse Case No. -- [sic - should be 9847]

11313. CINTHIA M. SOUTHERLEN,   Woodstock, Ga
Rejected. It does not appear that any ancestor was ever enrolled or that any ancestor was party to the treaties of 1835-
1836 and 1846. Shows no real connection with the Eastern Cherokees. See Misc. Test. P. 1105.
MISC. TEST. P. 1105. No 11315 - Cynthia M. Sutherland:
    "I am 64 years of age; I claim my Indian blood through my
mother. I have never received any Indian money from the govern
ment and I never heard my mother say if she received any. She
lived right where the the Indians lived when they were carried
away. I tried to get land in the Territory but it was too
late. None of my people that I know of ever received any Indian money. My grandfather lived in McDowell County, N. C. He
was the Indian and his name was John Hunter. It seems to me I
remember hearing of a government agent through this part of
the country about twenty years ago taking the names of people
with Indian blood."
SIGNED: Cynthia M. Sutherland, Canton, Ga., Jul 7 1908.

11314. MARY JANE McCLURE,   Woodstock, Ga
Rejected. Hillhouse Case No -- [should be 9847]

11315. GEO SAMUEL MILLWOOD,   Woodstock, Ga
Rejected. Hillhouse Case No -- [should be 9847]

11316. JOHN HENRY MILLWOOD,   Woodstock, Ga
Rejected. Hillhouse Case No -- [should be 9847]

11317. F. M. OWENSBY,   Woodstock, Ga
Rejected. Brother of #11313 and claims thru same source.

169

11318. LULU E. GRIER,   Woodstock, Ga
Rejected. Claims thru Celia Gravet etc. (See #3991)

11319. S. E. GARRETT,   Talking Rock, Ga
Rejected. Nephew to Elvin P. Dempsey (11302)

11320. WARREN W. PRATHER,   Marble Hill, Ga
Rejected. Claims thru the same source as #10552.

11321. ELIZABETH A. REESE,   Jasper, Ga
Rejected. Claims thru the same source as #10552.

11322. MAY STEGALL,   Jasper, Ga
Rejected. Claims thru the same source as #10552.

11323. MAMIE T. STONER,   Jasper, Ga
Rejected. Claims thru the same source as #10552.

11324. DRED P. POOL,   Talking Rock, Ga
Rejected. Claims thru the same source as #10552.

11325. GIDEON R. PRATHER and 7 children,   Jasper, Ga
Rejected. Claims thru the same source as #10552.

11326. GEORGIA S. PRATHER,   Jasper, Ga
Rejected. Claims thru the same source as #10552.

11327. LEE W. PRATHER,   Jasper, Ga
Rejected. Claims thru the same source as #10552.

11328. ROBT. L. LANIER,   Lindale, Ga
        by his father and Nat. Gdn., Ernest T. Lanier
Rejected. Son of #11351 and claims thru same source.

11329. THOMAS E. LOYD,   Rome, Ga
Rejected. Claims thru "Water Hunter". See No 10448.

11330. MARY FRANCES LOYD,   Rome, Ga
Rejected. Claims thru "Water Hunter". See No 10448.

11331. ODESSA E. MOSS,   Marble Hill, Ga
Rejected. Claims thru the same source as #10552.

11332. LILA FITZSIMMONS,   Marble Hill, Ga
Rejected. Claims thru the same source as #10552.

11333. BIRDIE I. LANIER,   Lindale, Ga
        by her father and Gdn., Ernest T. Lanier
Rejected. Daughter of #11351.

11334. MINNIE R. LANIER,   Lindale, Ga
          by her father and Gdn., Ernest T. Lanier
Rejected. Daughter of #11351.

11335. OLA MAY LANIER,   Lindale, Ga
Rejected. Daughter of #11351 and claims thru same source.

11336. BESSIE CORN,   Marble Hill, Ga
Rejected. Uncle of #9446 and claims thru same source.

11337. HENRY CORN,   Marble Hill, Ga
Rejected. Nephew of #9446 and claims thru same source.

11338. LUDIE CORN,   Marble Hill, Ga
Rejected. Niece of #9446 and claims thru same source.

11339. THOMAS J. EUBANKS,   Holcomb, Ga
Rejected. Claims thru the same source as #10552.

11340. GEORGE CORN,   Marble Hill, Ga
Rejected. Brother of #9446 and claims thru same source.

11341. MARTIN V. BECK,   Brutsboro, Ga
Rejected. Reason for rejection hereto:

              IN RE APPLICATION THROUGH ELMINA A. BECK
                    AND COLEMAN J. DAVIS
                      Group No 11341

     Applicants herein claim that they are the children of the
descendants of Elmina A. Beck and Coleman J. Davis, son of
Daniel Davis, but that the said Elmina A. Beck and Coleman J.
Davis were never married. They claim to inherit Cherokee blood
from Coleman J. Davis. There is no claim that Elmina A. Beck
had Cherokee Indian blood. She was never enrolled. There is
no substantial evidence to prove that the applicants herein
are the children and descendants of Coleman J. Davis. None of
them have ever been enrolled, and if they had been considered
in 1851, 1869, or 1882 as having Cherokee Indian blood from
Coleman J. Davis they would have been enrolled by Chapman, by
Siler, or by Hester, or by all three, as applicants were living at those dates in counties and towns in which other persons, who were living there, were enrolled by those Agents, so
that persons claiming to be descended from Coleman J. Davis
and Elmina A. Beck, if applicants at those dates, were doubt-
less considered for enrollment by the Agents above mentioned
and rejected.
     Wherefore, and in consideration of the premises, the ap-
plications of all persons claiming jointly through Elmina A.
Beck and Coleman J. Davis must be rejected.
See Misc. Test. P. 1509.

                              171

MISC. TEST. P. 1509. Testimony in case of Martin V. Beck, #11341 - Lorenzo D. Davis:

"My name is Lorenzo D. Davis. I live at Dahlonega, Ga. I was born in 1855 in Lumpkin Co., Ga. My father's name was Lorenzo D. Davis. I had an uncle named Coleman J. Davis. My grandfather's name was Daniel Davis. I know Martin V. Beck. I knew what was supposed to be his father. His name was Coleman J. Davis. I suppose he is a first cousin of mine. I never heard Coleman J. Davis say whether he acknowledged him as his child or not. Coleman J. Davis did not support these children as I know of. I only know from hearsay as to whether he recognized these children as his. Coleman Davis was living around here in my time. I knew him. He was living with his wife, Eliza Huff, in Lumpkin Co. (Huff was her maiden name) when I knew him. I never heard my father speak of Coleman Davis having these children, and have never heard anyone say anything to Coleman Davis about these children, or I never heard Coleman Davis say anything about it."
SIGNED: Lorenzo D. Davis, Dahlonega, Ga., Jul 13 1908.
"I concur in the above statement of facts, and could not state anything more than is stated there."
SIGNED: Miller Davis, Dahlonega, Ga., Jul 13 1908.
"I feel satisfied that Coleman J. Davis was the father of Martin V. Beck & his brother but it is impossible to get any good evidence." [Notation added to end of testimony]
EXCEPTION CASE. Martin V. Beck and 2 children, Burtsboro, Ga. Recommended. Total number of exceptions filed in this group -- 1. From additional testimony taken in this case by H. W. Ketron under a commission, it is clear that Coleman J. Davis was the father of Martin V. Beck and Jeff Beck and that said Becks and their descendants are entitled to enrollment. Said Coleman J. Davis was enrolled by Chapman at #2027. (See testimony taken in this case in Nov. 1909 by H. W. Ketron). [NOTE: Field testimony ended in March, 1909, if the date mentioned is correct the testimony referred to above would be in the orignal file]
SUPP ROLL #30287 - Martin V. Beck - 57
         30288 - Lila May (dau) - 4
         30289 - Laura (dau)   - 3

11342. JOE RUTLEDGE,   Waleska, Ga
Rejected. It does not appear that applicant's ancestors were parties to treaties of 1835-6 and 1846. Never enrolled with the Cherokees, nor shared in their payments.

11343. JAMES WRIGHT and 1 child,   Pine Log, Ga
Rejected. See special report Whitmire #2516.

11344. SHOSHONIE REECE,   Jasper, Ga
         by her husband and agent, Cicero L. Reece
Rejected. It does not appear that any ancestor was a party to the treaties of 1835-36 or 1846 -- nor does it appear that any

ancestor was ever enrolled. Shows no connection with the Cherokees. See Misc. Test. P. 1141.
MISC. TEST. P. 1141. No 15216 with 11344 - Aaron P. Carney:
"I am 64 [54? blurred] years of age; was born in Lumpkin Co., Ga. and have lived in Georgia all my life. I claim Indian blood through my mother. I have never received any Indian money from the government and never tried to get any. My mother never received any Indian money from the government. Have heard my mother speak of the money paid to the Indians in 1852. My father was always opposed to our making any application for Indian money. I was not enrolled in 1882 by a government agent. My grandmother, Clara King was the Indian. I did not see her but once when I was small. My mother lived with the white people. I do not know if my grandmother lived with the Indians."
SIGNED: Aaron P. Carney, Canton, Ga., Jul 8 1908.
EXCEPTION CASE. Rejected. Total number of exceptions filed in this group -- 7. Original recommendation renewed.

11345. CICERO L. REECE, Jasper, Ga
Rejected. Claims thru same source as #10552.

11346. JAMES RAY, Nelson, Ga
Rejected. See special report Whitmire #2516.

11347. ALLIE REECE, Nelson, Ga
Rejected. Claims thru same source as #10552.

11348. CARTER REECE, Jasper, Ga
Rejected. Claims thru same source as #10552.

11349. KINSEY REECE, Ellijay, Ga
Rejected. Claims thru same source as #10552.

11350. FLORENCE REBECCA McLAIN and 9 children, Rome, Ga
118 Spring St
Rejected. Claims thru Water Hunter. See #10448.

11351. SARAH J. LANIER, Calhoun, Ga
Rejected. It does not appear that applicant's ancestors were parties to treaties of 1835-36 and 1846, never shared in Cherokee payments nor enrolled with them.

11352. THOMAS J. GRIFFIES, Rome, Ga
Rejected. Ancestors not on roll. No real connection shown with Cherokee tribe.

11353. PRESTON W. GROVELY, West Rome, Ga
Rejected. Brother of Oscar Lee Grovely, (10530)

11354. J. LEMMUEL GROVELY, Waleska, Ga
Rejected. The ancestor thru whom the applicant claims was

never enrolled. Not one a party to the treaties of 1835-6 and
1846. No genuine connection with the Eastern Cherokees. See
Misc. Test. P. -- [blank].

11355. ELLEN LENORA GROVELY,   Rome, Ga
Rejected. Mother of Oscar Lee Gravely (10530) thru whom he
claims.

11356. NANCY ANN GAYDON,   Burtsboro, Ga
Rejected. Sister of #9446 and claims thru same source.

11357. MARY E. GODDIS and 3 children,   Jasper, Ga
Rejected. Claims thru same source as #10552.

11358. HENRY T. FINDLEY,   Greeley, Ga
Rejected. See special report Whitmire #2516.

11359. JOHN DEBORD,   Waleska, Ga
Rejected. Applicant's ancestors do not appear on emigrant
rolls; were not parties to treaties of 1835-6 and '46 and show
no connection with Cherokees.

11360. MARY J. CULBERSON,   Adairsville, Ga
Rejected. Sister to #7603 and claims thru same source.

11361. JOHN H. CORBIN and 4 children,   Sharpton, Ga
Rejected. See special report Whitmire #2516.

11362. SUSAN L. CARNEY,   Sharpton, Ga
Rejected. Claims thru same source as #10552.

11363. SILAS K. CARNEY,   Nelson, Ga
Rejected. First cousin once removed of Shoshonie Reece, App
#11344 and claims thru same source.

11364. SCOTT CARNEY,   Sharpton, Ga
Rejected. Cousin of Shoshonie Reece, App #11344, and claims
thru same source.

11365. MILLIE BYRD,   Waleska, Ga
Rejected. Ancestor not on rolls. Slaves. See Misc. Test. P.
1115.
MISC. TEST. P. 1115. #11365 - Millie Byrd:
    "That I am 68 [? blurred] years of age and live in Cher-
okee Co., Ga. I claim my Indian descent through my mother; my
father was a colored man. My mother was a quarteroon Cherokee. I was owned by a man named Bob Moore and so was my mother and father. My husband is a colored man."
SIGNED: Millie Byrd, Canton, Ga., Jul 7 1908.
EXCEPTION CASE. Rejected. Total number of exceptions filed
in this group -- 2. Original recommendation renewed.

174

11366. SARAH A. BYARS,   Stamp Creek, Ga
Rejected. Claims thru same source as #690.

11367. SPARTAN S. ATKINS,   Walesha, Ga
Rejected. See special report Whitmire #2516.

11368. BIRTIE M. KILLINGWORTH and 1 child, Morrisville, Ga
Rejected. Claims thru Alex. Brown. See special report #35.

11369. JAS. A. EDDINGS and 2 children,   Iuka, Ill
Rejected. Claims thru Elizabeth Eddings, daughter of Dave
Weaver. See #45 special report.

11370. WM. R. EDDINGS and 3 children,   Iuka, Ill
Rejected. Claims thru Elizabeth Eddings, daughter of Dave
Weaver. See special report Dave Weaver #45.

11371. AMANDA M. CHERRY and 1 child,   Iuka, Ill
Rejected. Claims thru Elizabeth Eddings, daughter of Dave
Weaver. See special report Dave Weaver #45.

11372. JOHN A. COCHRUM and 2 children,   Claremore, Okla
Rejected. Claims thru Elizabeth Eddings, daughter of Dave
Weaver. See special report Dave Weaver #45.

11373. WESLEY S. EDDINGS and 3 children,   Iuka, Ill
Rejected. Claims thru Elizabeth Eddings, daughter of Dave
Weaver. See special report Dave Weaver #45.

11374. LOONEY McGUIRE and 4 children,   Andrews, N C
[Rejected] See special report Blythe Case #153.

11375. STRUMLOW N. HICKS and 6 children,   Saorille, Mo
Rejected. Claims thru Alex. Brown. See special report #35.

11376. NEWTON J. EDDINGS,   Iuka, Ill
Rejected. Claims thru Elizabeth Eddings, daughter of Dave
Weaver. See special report Dave Weaver #45.

11377. SAM A. DIXON,   Wilkerson, Ky
Rejected. Uncle of #4252.

11378. SAMUEL R. ROSS,   Prue, Okla
Rejected. Claims thru Elizabeth Eddings, daughter of Dave
Weaver. See special report Dave Weaver #45.

11379. WILLIAM B. SHERRILL and 4 children, Whittier, N C
Rejected. See special report Betsy Walker #500.

11380. PINA T. STOKES and 3 children,   Springfield, Mo
                                           2226 Travis St.
Rejected. Claims thru Alex. Brown. See special report #35.

11381. NANCY JANE LEDFORD,   Wolf Creek, N C
Rejected. Neither applicant nor ancestors ever enrolled. Does
not establish fact of descent from person who was a party to
the treaty of 1835-6 and 1846. Misc. Test. P. 1048.
MISC. TEST. P. 1048. Appln. No. 19582-423:
        "My name is Samuel Patterson. I am 82 years old. My
mother told me she was a half breed and that would make me
1/4. I lived in Gilmer Co., Ga. in 1851. I was not enrolled
as I did not know there was such a thing at that time. I never lived with the Indians although I have visited among them.
I claim through my mother, Martha Allen, before marriage. After marriage Martha Patterson. My grandmother, Sally Tucker
was born and raised in Tennessee. In 1835 my grandmother was
dead. I do not know that she ever lived with the Indians. My
mother lived in Lumpkin Co., in 1835 when the treaty was made.
I do not know why they did not take us away with them. The
first I heard about the enrollment was when Mr. Tucker got his
money. I do not know that Sally Tucker ever went to Indian
Territory. I don't know that Sally Tucker, my grandmother,
was related to John Tucker. My grandmother was recognized as
white, as were the other members of my family. I cannot remember that I told Mr. Bell that my grandfather's name was
Allen Tucker. I cannot remember that I told Mr. Bell that my
grandfather married Martha Scroggins. My mother's name is
Martha Allen and I cannot account for the name Martha Tucker
as my mother in the application."
SIGNED: Samuel Patterson, Gainesville, Ga., Jul 7 1908.
EXCEPTION CASE. 11381. Samuel Patterson, App. #19582, R. F.
D. #2, Murrayville, Ga. Rejected. Total number of exceptions
filed in this group -- 2. Original recommendation renewed.

11382. MILLEY M. CROW,   Dahlonega, Ga
Rejected. It does not appear that any ancestor was ever enrolled or that any ancestor was party to the treaties of 1835-
1836 and 46. Shows no connection with the Eastern Cherokees.
Misc. Test. PP. 1501 and 1506.
MISC. TEST. P. 1501. Appl #12375-12197 - Wm. Jasper Worley:
        "My name is Wm. Jasper Worley. I live at Dahlonega, Ga. I
was born in 1837 in Lumpkin Co., Ga. I claim through my mother
and her mother, and her mother. My mother was born in 1812, in
Pickens District, S. C. My grandmother was born and raised, I
suppose in S. C. My mother and grandmother lived with white
people in S. C. I could not tell you whether they were recognized as Indians or white people. My mother, grand mother and
I have never gotten any money or land on account our our Indian blood. I don't know whether my grandmother came here from
S. C. In 1851 my mother and I were living in Lumpkin Co., Ga.
I don't know why we were not enrolled with the Cherokees at
that time. In 1882 we were living here also. I did not hear of
any roll of the Cherokees at that time. I had a brother born
in 1835, he was born here in Dahlonega, Lumpkin Co., Ga. My
father did not have any Indian blood as I know of. I don't

know why my mother was not driven away in 1835 when the Indians were driven away. I have heard my mother speak of the time that the Indians were driven away. My father and mother were living with the white people here when my oldest brother and I were born. I have never heard my mother speak about living with the Indian tribe. I have heard her speak about their coming to the house and trading. I know Milley M. Crow. She is my first cousin. Her application number is 11382. So far as I know my mother, grandmother and I never got any money or land from the Govt. on acct. of our Indian blood."
SIGNED: Wm. Jasper Worley, Dahlonega, Ga., Jul 13 1908.

MISC. TEST. P. 1506. Appl #11382 - Milley M. Crow:
    "My name is Milley M. Crow. I live at Dahlonega, Ga., Route #3. I was born in Pickens Co., S. C. I claim Indian blood. I don't know what tribe my grandmother belonged to. If I ever heard I forgot it. I claim through my father. My father died in 1880. He was about 70 years old when he died. He was born in S. C. too. In Pickens Co., S. C. I claim through my father's mother. I don't know where she was raised, but she lived in S. C. I came to Ga. in 1847. My father, my grandmother and I have never gotten any money or land from the Govt. on account of our Indian blood. In 1882 I was living in Lumpkin Co., Ga. I did not know anything about an enrollment at that time. My father and I lived with white people, but the Indians were there. I never heard of my father living with the Indian tribe. When the Indians were carried off, I was living in Pickens Co., S. C. There were not Indians living there at that time. They had all come to Ga. My father did not got off [sic] with the Indians. I don't know why he did not go with the Indians. They did not drive him away. I have been taught all my life by my mother and uncles and aunt that I was part Indian. I claim through my great grandmother. Her name was Eaton. That was her name after she was married. I don't know her given name." SIGNED: Milley M. Crow, Dahlonega, Ga., Jul 13 1908.

11383. ONA ADAMS and 1 child,   Andrews, N C
Rejected. See special report Blythe #153.

11384. M. D. I. SMALLWOOD, St. Louis St., Chattanooga, Tenn
Rejected. Sister of #10480 and claims thru same source.

11385. ALBERT ADAMS,   Andrews, N C
Rejected. See special report Blythe #153.

11386. CLEMON C. PEAK and 8 children,   Pryor Creek, Okla
Rejected. Nephew of #9754.

11387. DOLLIE M. PEAK,   Pryor Creek, Okla
Rejected. Claims only as a descendant of Polly Murphy. See #119. [The Exception Case 119, Vol. 1, listed Dollie Peak's App No. as 11397, which is incorrect]

11388. DORA J. MASON,   Flats, N C
Rejected. Niece of #529 and claims thru same ancestors.

11389. MARY E. GRANT and 3 children,   Wesser, N C
Rejected. Niece to #529 and claims thru same source.

11390. WILLIAM ADAMS,   Andrews, N C
Rejected. See special report Blythe #153.

11391. ELLER WEST,   Andrews, N C
Rejected. See special report Blythe #153.

11392. W. B. GODFREY and 1 child,   Kensington, Ga
Rejected. Brother to #9110.

11393. WM. C. GRAHAM and 5 children,   Ducktown, Tenn
Rejected. Claims only as a descendant of Polly Murphy. See
#119.

11394. JAS. G. SLOAN and 8 children,   Morrisville, Mo
Rejected. Claims thru Alex. Brown. See special report #35.

11395. ROY SLOAN,   Morrisville, Mo
Rejected. Claims thru Alex. Brown. See special report #35.

11396. DAVID FORESTER and 4 children,   Alread, Ark
Rejected. Nephew of #529 and claims thru same source.

11397. AMEZETTA V. HENSLEY,   Tellico, Tenn
Rejected. Niece of #664 and claims thru same source.
MISC. TEST. P. 633. App No 13397 [sic -should be 11397] -
1067 - Armazetta V. Hensley:
    "My name is Armazetta V. Hensley. I am 23 years old. I was
born in Swain Co., N. C. My father was John Crisp. My mother
before marriage was Mary Delosier. I claim my Indian blood
through my mother. My grandfather and grandmother were Edward
and Elizabeth Delozier. I claim through the Delosier's and not
through the Poindexters. I don't know how old my mother was
when she died. I do not know when she was born. I never heard
of my grandfather or grandmother going out west. My aunt is
Sarah N. Mashburn and she lived in North Carolina. My mother
was a sister of Sarah M. Mashburn. She lives at Murphy, N. C."
SIGNED: Armazetta V. "X" Hensley, Madisonville, Tenn., Jun 26
1908.

11398. ADA ADAMS,   Andrews, N C
Rejected. See special report Blythe Case #153.

11399. JANE MURPHY and 1 child,   Unalsa, N C
Rejected. Claims only as a descendant of Polly Murphy. [Ad-
mitted by Exception Case #119, Vol. 1]

SUPP ROLL #30416 - Jane Murphy - 30
        30417 - Walter (son) - 9

11400. CHAS. A. MIDDLETON, 718 E. 7th St., E. St. Louis, Mo
Rejected. Claims thru Elizabeth Eddings, daughter of Dave
Weaver, See #45 special report Dave Weaver.

11401. MRS. MARY ROY,   Macon Co., N C
Rejected. It does not appear that any ancestor was a party to
the treaties of 1835-6 or 1846. Nor does it appear that any
ancestor was ever enrolled. Shows no real connection with the
Eastern Cherokees. See Misc. Test. P. 1364.
MISC. TEST. P. 1364. No. 11401 - Mary Roy:
     "My name is Mary Roy and I reside at Franklin, N. C. I
was born in Macon Co., N. C. in 1840. I claim relationship to
the Cherokee Indians through my mother, Elizabeth Morgan, who
was a quarter Cherokee Indian. My father's name was William
Dill, and the old neighbors have told me that he was part Indian. I do not know how much. My mother was born in Burke Co.,
N. C. about 1821. My father was born in Blount Co., Tenn. My
mother has often told me about the Indians and that she has
visited the Indians and the Indians visited us. My mother had
an uncle named Gideon Morgan and he lived in Tennessee. I have
often heard my mother speak of him. He had several children,
namely, Washington, Libbey, and Charity, and they all lived in
Tennessee. We were always taken for white people with Indian
blood. My mother had often told me that Gideon Morgan visited
her home when she lived in Tennessee, but not since she lived
in North Carolina. The Indians who used to visit us where
[sic] Cherokees and they recognized us as members of their
tribe. I do not know why my ancestors were never enrolled.
Back in 1840 and 1850 my father and mother owned their own
place and farmed it. My parents never received any money or
lands from the Government on account of being Indians."
SIGNED: Mary "X" Roy, M. L. Daley, Test., Franklin, N. C., Jul
10 1908.

11402. LULU M. BURKE and 3 children,   Payne, Okla
Rejected. First cousin of #1312.

11403. JIM BLACKBIRD and 3 children,   Southwest City, Mo
Admitted. Applicant's grandfather and probably father were
enrolled in 1851, under the name of Sequoyeh in Tahl. Dist.
Group #79. Misc. Test. P. 4063.
MISC. TEST. P. 4063. No 16116-11403 - Joseph Blackbird...thru
Richard L. Taylor, Interpreter:
     "My name is Joseph Blackbird; my post-office is Baron,
Okla.; I am thirty years old; my father's name was Blackbird;
my father lived in both Delaware and Saline District; my fath-
er's father was named Leech or Clah-noo-see; I am not certain
that my father was living in 1851; (See Tahl. 79)."
SIGNED: Joseph Blackbird, Westville, Okla., Mar 26 1909.

```
ROLL P30 #5177 FCT COMM #19458 - Jim Blackbird        - 35
       5178          19459 - Lucy (wife) - 23 (App 11458)
       5179          19460 - Jew-saw-lunt (son)      - 14
       5180          19461 - Oo-goo-ne-ya-chee (son) - 11
       5181                - Squai-eest (son)        -  3
```

11404. ELIZABETH LITTLE DANE,   Southwest City, Mo
Admitted. Niece of #653. Not living in 1851.
ROLL P90 #17158 FCT COMM #18185 - Elizabeth Littledave - 28

11405. LESE BUZZARD,   Cove, Okla
Admitted. Claimant's father, by the name of Oo-chun-tie,
father's mother and older brother enrolled by Drennen in 1851,
Del. 472. Misc. Test. P. 4295.
MISC. TEST. P. 4295. #11405 - Le-se Buzzard...thru Tom Roach,
Interpreter:
     "I am about 44 years; my parents were Emigrants; my fath-
er's name was Oo-chuh-duh.   His English name was John Sweetwater. He is still living. His P. O. is Zena, Okla. I do not
know with whom my father was living in 1851; my father's fathers name was Sweetwater or Ah-moo-gah-nah-stuh. My father's
mother was Gah-nuh-dee-skee. My father had one brother by the
name of Yo-lah-sa-chih, another by the name of Wah-hyah or
Wolf, they were half brothers on the mother's side. They had
different sisters [sic]. My father had a sister by the name of
Chick-a-yih; I was told that she drew money in 1851. (See 472
Del. for the enrollment of father's mother, older brother and
father of claimant.) My husband's name is Sam Buzzard. He has
filed application #11443. I have two children all the rest of
my children are grown. My husband included my minor children
in his supplemental application. The correct name of my husband is Sam Oo-law-nah-s-te-skee."
SIGNED: Le-se Buzzard, Southwest City, Mo., Mar 23 1909.
[For Roll information See App 11443]

11406. NANCY FROG,   Cove, Okla
Admitted. Claims thru grandparents Buck and Caty, enrolled in
1851, and also father, Moses, enrolled in Del. Dist. #464.
ROLL P64 #11900 FCT COMM #19424 - Nancy Frog - 32

11407. WINNIE WATERMELLON,   Southwest City, Mo
        (Included in 11426)
The grandfather and great aunt and great uncle of the applicant were enrolled by Drennen in 829 Del. Dist. in 1851, under
the name of Ie-cah-hoo-ges-ske, Quake and Mah-yah. Parents not
living in 1851.

11408. LEWIS SNAKE,   Southwest City, Mo
Admitted. This applicant's grandfather Watty Smoke and Ailee
Smoke his grandmother are both enrolled by Drennen from Del.
Dist. under group #1005. [For Roll information See App 10428
- Surname "SMOKE" on roll]

                          180

11409. OO-SQUI CHEATER, Jay, Okla
Admitted. Applicant's mother enrolled by Drennen in 1851, Del. 234. [For Roll information See App 11432]

11410. JESSE BUSHEYHEAD, Duplicate of #213.

11411. DAVIS A. McGHEE and 2 children, Southwest City, Mo
Admitted. Brother of #390. Claimant is enrolled by Drennen in 1851, Del. 142.
ROLL P94 #17899 FCT COMM #9630 - David A. McGhee   - 57
         17900   9636 - Florence E. (dau) - 14
         17901   9637 - Ambrose (son)   - 12

11412. CORNELIUS BUZZARD and 1 child, Carnee, Okla*
Admitted. Brother of #2342. Father of applicant enrolled in 1851 in Del. 319. [* "Cove Okla" on roll]
ROLL P37 #6445 FCT COMM #19367 - Cornelius Buzzard - 36
         6446   19368 - Lucy (wife) - 19 (App 11430)
         6447   4877m - Nancy (dau)   - 1

11413. FRANK C. GLENN, JESSE E. GLENN, Miles, Okla
         by Charles L. Clapper, Gdn.
Admitted. Brother of #1683 and claims thru same source.
ROLL P66 #12290 FCT COMM #8337 - Frank C. Glenn - 16
         12291   8338 - Jesse E. (bro) - 12
                              by Charles L. Clapper, Gdn.

11414. EDWARD R. BEAN and 5 children, Claremore, Okla
Admitted. First cousin of #537 and claims thru same ancestors. Mother of applicant, Jane Bean, enrolled in Tahl. Dist. #594.
ROLL P27 #4476 FCT COMM #11491 - Edward R. Bean - 48
         4477   26669 - Eliza E. (dau) - 18
         4478   26670 - Lorena (dau)   - 16
         4479   22671 - Tot (dau)   - 13
         4480   22672 - Dot (dau)   - 13
         4481   22274 - Jesse E. (son) - 2

11415. GEORGE W. WILKINS and 2 children, Chloeta, Okla
Admitted. Applicant's mother enrolled as Che-squa-ne-tah by Drennen at Del. #1006. (Misc. Test. P. 2728, also test. of applicant taken Mar 16 1909.)
MISC. TEST. P. 2728. Appl. 11415 - George W. Wilkins:
   "My name is George W. Wilkins. I live at Chloeta, Okla. My Dawes Commission number is 9113. I am about 31 years old. I claim my Cherokee Indian blood through my mother. I was about 8 or 9 years old when my mother died. I suppose she was somewhere about 35 years when she died. Her name was Caty Youngbird. Her married name was Caty Wilkins. I don't know the name of my mother's mother and father. My mother did not have any brothers and sisters as I know of. I don't know the names of any of her uncles and aunts. Simpson Bennett's wife knew my

181

mother, she lives near Muskogee. She was no relation to my
mother. Slater Cowet who lives at Muskogee knows my mother
also. I don't know whether my mother was living in 1851 or
not. My mother's Indian name was Chees-qui-nee-tah. I don't
remember an aunt Rachel. My cousin, Nannie E. Walker, appl.
#1603 has filed an appl. Her mother a relative of my moth-
er, second cousin, I think. Nannie E. Walker's name before
marriage was Howdeshell."
SIGNED: George W. Wilkens, Grove, Okla., Sep 9 1908.
MISC. TEST. P. 4337. #11415 - Geo. W. Wilkins:
    "I am 32 years old; my mother died about (1890) between
1885 and 1890 and she was between 30 and 40 when she died;
that is as near as I can come to it; I do not know the names
of my mother's parents; I only know that my mother's name was
Caty Youngbird; or Caty Little Youngbird; I lived with my
mother until the time of her death; my father's name was W. W.
Wilkins; I was on the roll of 1880; I received the strip payment; I did not share in the Old Settler payment of 1896; I
never heard my mother say that she was born before the payment
of 1851; I do not know where my mother was born whether in the
East or in the West; I was sent to the Orphans Asylum, the
Cherokee Asylum, at the time of my mother's death, and I lived
there until I was grown. My wife is a white woman. I have been
told that my mother had one sister but I do not know her name
or who she married; Slater Couch is my step-father and he
lives at Muskogee, Okla."
SIGNED: Geo. W. Wilkins, Spavina, Okla., Mar 16 1909.
ROLL P151 #29271 FCT COMM # 9113 - George W. Wilkins - 29
         29272   24187 - Ethel (dau)   - 5
         29273   2182m - Bertha (dau)   - 2

11416. LAURA TOWNSEND,   Proctor, Okla
Admitted. Niece of #2724 and claims thru same source. [For
Roll information See App 11417]

11417. GEORGE TOWNSEND,   Proctor, Okla
Admitted. Applicant's grandmother enrolled by Drennen in 1851
46 [no district given]. Misc. Test. P. 3232.
MISC. TEST. P. 3232. 11417 - Susan E. Parris, witness for
George Townsend:
    "George Townsend is my nephew. His father was an Old
Settler and his mother an Immigrant. His mother had several
brothers and sisters. Her mother, I think, was named Elmira.
Her brothers were William, George and Johnathan Roah; sisters
Nancy and Polly Ann. There was also a brother named James."
SIGNED: Susan E. Parris, Tahlequah, Okla., Sep 28 1908.
ROLL P141 #27222 FCT COMM #29956 - George Townsend - 35
         27223   29957 - Laura (wife)   - 27
                              (App 11416)
         27224   29958 - Adda (dau)   - 10
         27225   29959 - Walter (son)   - 8
         27226   29960 - Jesse (son)   - 3

11417. GEORGE TOWNSEND (Cont)
        27227 FCT COMM #4144m - Tommie (son)   - 1

11418. ALEXANDER PEAK & 4 children, Hazlewood, Pittsburg, Pa
Rejected. Sizemore case #417 special report.

11419. CORA NULL,   Seven Mile Pond, Va
Rejected. See special report Sizemore #417.

11420. CARNEALY PEAK,   Seven Mile Pond, Va
Rejected. See special report Sizemore #417.

11421. LEANDER PEAK,   Seven Mile Pond, Va
Rejected. See special report Sizemore #417.

11422. CAROLINE STUMP and 1 child,   Pittsburg, Pa
Rejected. See special report Sizemore #417.

11423. TIN CUP DE-GUA-DE-HI, Minor   [no residence]
Admitted. By Jennie Leaf.   See special #5675 (with #630.)
[For Roll information See App 5674, Vol. 3]

11424. ELIZABETH J. SMITH and 2 children, Braggs, Okla
Rejected. Claims thru the same source as #2844.
EXCEPTION CASE. Admitted.   Total number of exceptions filed
in this group -- 8.   Applicant is a daughter of Jane Butler,
enrolled by Drennen in 1851 in Canadian District, Group #2 and
of Edward Butler, enrolled in Canadian District, Group 104.
Applicant's grandfather and great grandfather, John and Wiley
enrolled in 1835. Dawes Commission No. 5701. Formerly rejected
thru a clerical error.
SUPP ROLL #30770 FCT COMM #5701 - Elizabeth J. Smith - 51
        30771   5707 - Junie (dau)   - 14
        30772   5708 - Jennie (dau)   - 11

11425. JOHN MORRIS and 4 children,   Edna, Kans
Admitted. Cousin of #4519.
ROLL P101 #19440 FCT COMM #10557 - John Morris - 40
        19441   10558 - William O. (son) - 15
        19442   10559 - Rosa A. (dau)   - 11
        19443   10560 - Bessie J. (dau) - 9
        19444   10561 - Ruby (dau)   - 6

11426. CHARLIE WATERMELON and 3 children, Southwest City, Mo
Admitted. Father of #11407 and claims thru same ancestors.
ROLL P146 #28385 FCT COMM #19690 - Charlie Watermelon - 44
        28386   19691 - Katie (wife)   - 23
                                (App 11431)
        28387   30562 - Bird (son) - 6 (App 11427)
        28388   19692 - Winnie (dau)   - 16
                                (App 11407)
        28389   - Lee (son)   - 1/12

183

11427. BIRD WATERMELLON,   Southwest City, Mo
(included with #11426) Half brother of #1140 [sic - should be
11407] and claims thru same ancestors.

11428. SAMUEL HOG DE-GUA-DE-HI,   [no residence]
Admitted. By Jennie Leaf. Suppl #5675 (with #630). [For Roll
information See App 5674, Vol. 3]

11429. BROWSTON DE-GUA-DE-HI, (Deceased),   Choloeta, Okla
Rejected. By his mother, Jennie Leaf. The child for whom this
application is made died ten or twelve years ago.   See Misc.
Test. P. 4336 - 4340. [For Testimony See App 5674, Vol. 3]

11430. LUCY BUZZARD,   Cove, Okla
Admitted. Sister of #11406 and claims thru same ancestors.
[For Roll information See App 11412]

11431. KATIE WATERMELON,   Southwest City, Mo
Admitted. Applicant's father enrolled by Drennen 1851, Del.
742. [For Roll information See App 11426]

11432. JOHN CHEATER,   Cove, Okla
Admitted. Half cousin of #1558 and claims thru same source.
Grandparents, Talen, enrolled as Lacy in 320 Del.
ROLL P41 #7279 - John Cheater   - 39
           7280 - Oo-squi (wife) - 48 (App 11409)

11433. AMEY DE-KA-HOO-GUS-SKY WATERMELON, So. West City, Mo
Admitted. Applicant enrolled in 1851 Drennen Del. 331. [For
Roll information See App 11434]

11434. DE-KA-HOO-SKY or WATERMELON,   Southwest City, Mo
Admitted. The applicant and his brother and sister were enrolled by Drennen (See Del 829) under the names of Se-cah-hoo-
ge-ske, Sua-ke and Wah-yah. This applicant is dead. See #11426
letter. Grandfather of #11407.
ROLL P52 #9569 FCT COMM #19448 - De-ka-hoo-gee-skie - 72
                                 (or Watermelon)
           9570   - Ancy (wife) - 74 (App 11433)

11435. LOUISA STRINGER,   Edna, Kans
Admitted. Aunt of #4519.
ROLL P133 #25734 FCT COMM #9799 - Louisa Stinger - 63

11436. ROBT. B. CARLILE and 1 child,   Campbell, Okla
Admitted. First cousin of #4394. Claimant's maternal grand
father enrolled in 1851 by Drennen Del. 431.
ROLL P38 #6761 FCT COMM #6089 - Robert B. Carlile - 32
           6762   6088 - Piercie J. (wife) - 29
                                    (App 11437)
           6763   685m - Senareste (dau) - 2

184

11437. PIERCY J. CARLILE,   Campbell, Okla
Admitted. Niece of #8353. Daughter of #8354. [For Roll information See App 11436]

11438. [?] SAM BONEY, Same as #370.   [NOTE: Sam Boney's name
was inserted between applications 11437 and 11439, but was
listed as #11347 which is incorrect - it is assumed it should
be 11438]

11439. ALEXANDER S. FOREMAN,   Vian, Okla
Admitted. Nephew of #8353 and claims thru same ancestors. Son
of #8354.
ROLL P62 #11523 FCT COMM #3018 - Alexander S. Foreman - 27

11440. MOLLIE E. STILL,   Hedley, Okla
Admitted. First cousin once removed of #850 and claims thru
same source. Father and sister and brother enrolled 1746 and
1746 [sic], Chapman, as Geo. and Sarah Langley and John C.
Langley.
MISC. TEST. P. 3365. Witness for No 11440 - Frank J. Still,
witness for his mother Mollie E. Still:
    "Mollie E. Still is my mother. She is an Immigrant Cher-
okee. Lock Langley was my mother's father and grandmother was
Sarah. I had an uncle named Bee Langley. I never saw my grand
father. My mother never drew Old Settler money about 14 years
ago. I did not get any."
SIGNED: Frank J. Still, Tahlequah, Okla., Oct 1 1908.
[For Roll information See App 2060, Vol. 2]

11441. NA-KE HILDEBRAND,   Cove, Okla
Admitted. Sister of #11406 and claims thru same ancestors.
ROLL P75 #14189 FCT COMM #19741 - Na-ke Hilderbrand - 28

11442. SA-KE BONEY and 2 children,   Southwest City, Mo
Admitted. Sister of #5059 and claims thru same source. [NOTE:
Applicant's roll information was listed with App 370, Vol. 1,
however, two children were inadvertently omitted - the entire
family follows:]
ROLL P32 #5489 FCT COMM #19411 - Sam Bone - 30 (App 370)
          5490   19412 - Sa-ka (wife)   - 32
          5491   30547 - Ollie (dau)   - 8
          5492   17803 - Bertha MILLER (dau of w) - 14
          5493   19413 - Emma MILLER (dau of w) - 11

11443. SAM BUZZARD and children,   Cove, Okla
Admitted. Brother of Nancy Buzzard, App #9292 and admitted
for same reasons.
ROLL P37 #6472 FCT COMM #19359 - Sam Buzzard   - 46
          6473   19360 - Lese (wife)   - 42 (App 11405)
          6474   30536 - John (son)   - 5
          6475   - Israel (son) - 3

185

11444. RACHEL STARR,   Cove, Okla
          by Na-ke Hildebrand, Gdn.
Admitted. Niece of #11406 and claims thru same ancestors.
ROLL P132 #25502 FCT COMM #19742 - Rachel Starr - 14
                          by Na-ke Hilderbrand, Gdn.

11445. AVA M. BONDS,   Chelsea, Okla
Admitted. Second cousin of #1208 and claimant's grandmother
Nancy Compton is on Chapman Roll, #1866. Mother was born after 1851. Duplicate of #8685 application, with the exception
that a supplemental application for two minors is filed herewith. [NOTE: Name should be Ora M. Bonds according to Index
and roll. - For roll information See App 8685, Vol. 4]

11446. MATTIE B. SURRELL and 2 children,   Atoka, Okla
Admitted. Niece of #2977, and claims thru same source.
ROLL P135 #26062 FCT COMM #16874 - Mattie B. Surrell - 22
          26063   3725m - Mildred D. (dau)   - 4
          26064   3726m - John R. (son)   - 2

11447. ELLEN STURGILL,   Park, Va
Rejected. See special report Sizemore #417.

11448. BERTIE BLEVINS,   Kipling, Va
Rejected. See special report Sizemore #417.

11449. MAUDIE MILLER,   Kipling, Va
Rejected. See special report Sizemore #417.

11450. CATHERINE HARD,   Sturgill, N C
Rejected. See special report Sizemore #417.

11451. JOHN F. HART and 7 children,   Sturgill, N C
Rejected. See special report Sizemore #417.

11452. COLUMBUS CLAY,   Fawn, Okla
Admitted. Applicant's father enrolled by Drennen 1851 Fl. 650.
ROLL P43 #7700 FCT COMM #5388* - Columbus Clay - 42
[* FCT # originally printed "3398" and crossed out - the new
number may be 5588 - difficult to read]

11453. JESSE GRAY,   Tahlequah, Okla
          by Horace Gray, Gdn.
Admitted. Nephew of Henry W. Moore, App #9693 and is admitted
for same reasons.
ROLL P67 #12531 FCT COMM #229930 - Jesse Gray - 8
                          by Horace Gray, Gdn.

11454. KATE CRAVEN,   Tahlequah, Okla
Admitted. Aunt of Henry W. Moore, App #9693 and is admitted
for same reasons.
ROLL P48 #8716 FCT COMM #29936 - Kate Craven - 49

11455. MARY CREEKKILLER and 2 children,   Southwest City, Mo
Admitted. Daughter of #630 and claims thru same source.
ROLL P48 #8743 FCT COMM #19419 - Mary Creek-killer - 40
        8744   19421 - Rachel (dau) - 15 (App 11459)
        8745   19422 - Lydia (dau) - 5

11456. A-WI SUMMERFIELD and 2 children,   Zena, Okla
Admitted. The father of the applicant was enrolled by Drennen
in 1851 in 149 Del. Dist. as Oo-law-noo-steat. Ky (See also
App #6989) The mother of the enrolled was (probably) enrolled
by Drennen in 1851 in 440 Del. under the name of An-i-ca (See
App #5975) Half sister of #6898.
ROLL P134 #25962 FCT COMM #25868 - A-wi Summerfield   - 54
         25963   25872 - Daisy (Cowati) (dau) - 17
         25964   25873 - Aggie (dau)   - 16

11457. CHIC-GU-WI BONEY,   Southwest City, Mo
Admitted. Sister of #8983 and claims thru same source.
ROLL P32 #55483 FCT COMM #18567 - Chi-gu-wi Boney - 56

11458. LUCY BLACKBIRD and 3 children,   Southwest City, Mo
Admitted. Aunt of #1558. [For Roll information See App 11403]

11459. RACHEL CREEK KILLER,   Southwest City, Mo
          by her mother Mary Creek Killer
Admitted. See #11455 in which Mary Creek Killer has already
filed suppl. for Rachel Creek Killer.

11460. LA-LE CREEK KILLER,   Southwest City, Mo
(included in 11455) Granddaughter of #630 and claims thru same
source. Duplicate of child in #11455.

11461. SUSAN TURNER,   Tahlequah, Okla
Admitted. Sister of #2972.
ROLL P142 #27447 FCT COMM #20920 - Susan Turner - 16
                              by J. T. Parks, Gdn.

11462. REBECCA C. ROBBINS,   Metory, Okla
Rejected. Applicant claims no Cherokee blood, has filed as
heir to one-half brother who has been dead eight years. See
Misc. Test. P. 3553.
MISC. TEST. P. 3553. No 11462 - Rebecca C. Robbins:
    "I am 63 years of age; am not a Cherokee Indian myself. I
am claiming for my half-brother who was an Immigrant Cherokee.
He has been dead about 8 years. I am the only heir of this
half-brother. He was my half-brother on my father's side and
got his Indian blood from his mother. His mother was not related to me."
SIGNED: Rebecca C. Robbins, Tahlequah, Okla., Oct 6 1908.

11463. SARAH PRICE,   Metory, Okla
Admitted. Sister of #2692 and claims thru same source.

ROLL P113 #21693 FCT COMM #5808 - Sarah Price - 50

11464. THOMAS WILLIAMS,   Metory, Okla
Admitted. Nephew of #2692 and claims thru same source.
ROLL P151 #29395 FCT COMM #14650 - Thos. Williams - 29

11465. CLEM CRITTENDEN and 1 child,   Proctor, Okla
Admitted. Brother of #2686 and claims thru same source. [For
Roll information See App 9249, Vol. 4]

11466. LILLIE HICKS and 3 children,   Tahlequah, Okla
Admitted. Applicant's grandfather enrolled by Drennen in 1851,
Tahl. 536. See Misc. Test. P. 3554.
MISC. TEST. P. 3554. No. 11699-11466 - Beatrice Hicks:
    "I am a Cherokee alottee and my number is 14439. My mother
was an Immigrant. I do not know if she drew Immigrant money in
1852. I saw my mother's mother. She was the Indian. Her name
was Nanny Lowrey. Daniel Lowrey was also an Indian. I never
drew any Old Settler money. Nanny Lowery [sic] has been dead
about 14 years. She was an Old Settler. I have heard her say
she drew money. My uncle Andy Lowrey has made application for
this money. He is my mother's uncle and my great-uncle. Dolly
was my mother's aunt also Dolly and James an uncle. These are
all I remember."
SIGNED: Beatice Hicks, Tahlequah, Okla., Oct 6 1908.
ROLL P75 #14048 FCT COMM #14596 - Lillie Hicks   - 26
          14049   14597 - Jennie M. (dau)   - 5
          14050   2660m - Beatrice I. (dau) - 3
          14051   2661m - George E. (son)   - 2

11467. FRANCIS SUSAN TWEEDLE,   Davis, Okla
Admitted. By Wm. Tweedale, Gdn. First cousin once removed of
#5319 and claims thru same source.
ROLL P142 #27483 FCT COMM #32822 - Francis Susan Tweedle - 12
                                    by William Tweedle, Gdn.

11468. IDA POWELL,   Blairsville, Ga
Rejected. Ancestors not enrolled nor parties to treaties of
1835, 36 and 46. Applicant fails to establish genuine connection with Cherokee Tribe. Applicant failed to appear to testify at Madisonville, Tenn., June 25 and 27, 1908. Also neglected to answer letter of inquiry in regard to family relationship. No official testimony taken in this case.
EXCEPTION CASE. Ida Powell, Cleveland, Ga. Rejected. Total
number of exceptions filed in this group -- 2. Original recommendation renewed.

11469. GEORGE W. ORTEN,   Wilcot, Ga
Rejected. Ancestor never enrolled. Never lived with the Indians as members of tribe. Did not take part in tribal affairs. Applicant fails to establish genuine connection with
Cherokee tribe. Misc. Test. P. 1498.

MISC. TEST. P. 1498. #11469 – 7880 – George N. Orten:
"That I am 70 years of age and live in Fannin Co., Ga. I
claim my Indian descent through my mother; my father was a
white man. I claim through my grandmother Coble or Cobble;
don't know her first name. My mother was born and raised in
Iredell Co., N. C. I think my grandmother was born there too
but am not sure. I don't know whether my mother or grand
mother lived with the Indians as members of the tribe or not.
I never lived with the Indians myself. My folks were living
in Iredell Co., N. C. when I was born and I was four years old
when they moved to Fannin Co., Ga. where they lived there until they died. It was then Union County, Ga. I was never on
any roll myself. My understanding is that my mother was on a
roll, but I don't know what roll it was. Never heard of either
my mother or grandmother receiving anything from the government. I nor my brothers nor sisters never received any money
from the government. I am recognized as white with some Indian
blood. My mother claimed to be 1/4 Cherokee. We farmed when
we came to Fannin Co., Ga. My father bought the farm from a
man named Gamble. My father never got any land from the government. This is the only application I ever made to the government. All of my brothers and sisters have married white
people. There is no one who know anything more than I do."
SIGNED: George N. Orten, Blue Ridge, Ga., Jul 13 1908.

11470. ABNER ORTEN and 3 children,   Padena, Ga
Rejected. Brother of #11469.

11471. JOHN COLLIER,   Thomaston, Ga
Rejected. Applicant and his mother were slaves. See application.

11472. SARAH E. HEINDSELMAN and 3 children, Chelsea, Okla
Admitted. First cousin of #587 and claims thru same source.
Sister of #1235.
ROLL P73 #13718 FCT COMM #24507 – Sarah E. Heindselman – 33
        13719   24508 – Ada E. (dau)   – 13
        13720   24509 – William R. (son)   – 9
        13721   2998m – Leon E. (son)   – 2

11473. EMMA MOSES and 3 children, 723 Mill St., LaCrosse, Wis
Rejected. Claims thru same source as #10886.

11474. ELEN FRANCES SHIVER and 4 children, LaCrosse, Wis
                                           723 Mill St.
Rejected. Claims thru same source as #10886. [See Exception
Case #10886]

11475. ELIZABETH WALDRON, 517 St. Cloud St., LaCrosse, Wis
Rejected. Claims thru same source as #10886.

11476. BURLETTA WALDRON LOVING, 729 Mills St., LaCrosse, Wis
Rejected. Claims thru same source as #10886.

11477. LYDIA WATERS,   Braggs, Okla
          by Johnson Waters, Father
Admitted. Cousin of #10388 and claims thru same source.
ROLL P147 #28437 FCT COMM #19922 - Lydia Waters - 5
                                   by Johnson Waters, Father

11478. JOHNSON WATERS,   Braggs, Okla
Admitted. Uncle of #10388 and claims thru same source.
ROLL P146 #28423 FCT COMM #19917 - Johnson Waters - 57

11479. TOM WATERS,   Braggs, Okla
Admitted. Cousin of #10388 and claims thru same source.
ROLL P147 #28461 FCT COMM #19920 - Tom Waters - 16

11480. NELLIE WATERS,   Braggs, Okla
Admitted. Cousin of #10388 and claims thru same source.
ROLL P147 #28452 FCT COMM #19921 - Nellie Waters - 14

11481. LIZZIE PHILLIPS,   Braggs, Okla
Admitted. Applicant claims thru mother Ellen Grove enrolled
as A-kee with a brother, James, 181 [? 2nd digit blurred]
Tahl. See Misc. Test. P. 4202.
MISC. TEST. P. 4202. No. 11481 - Lizzie Phillips...thru John
Israel, Interpreter:
    "I am about 50 years of age. My mother was named Ellen
Grove before marriage. My mother's father's name I don't know
but he was a Cherokee Indian. My mother's mother was a Creek
Indian. My father was a Cherokee. His name was Sam Carey. My
mother had no brothers that I know of. Jack Grove was a brother of my mother. He had a child named Ah-kil-lo-hee. James or
Jim was a brother of my mother. Wat-tih was their mother. She
was a Creek. My mother had been dead about thirty years, I
think. I am not sure about this. Su-yah-tah was a half-brother
of my mother. Nancy was the wife of Su-yah-tah. They had children as follows: Su-sah-na, A-chin-nee, A-lah-quah and Isaac.
(Tah. 304). My mother was not married to any other man. She
had no other name that I know of. My mother got no money from
the Creeks. She made application for Creek benefits but was
rejected. Her Indian name is Akee. They lived in Tahlequah
District. (Tah. 181)."
SIGNED: Lizzie Phillips, Braggs, Okla., Mar 27 1909.
[For Roll information See App 11189]

11482. ANNIE ALLEN,   Braggs, Okla
Admitted. Niece to #11481 and claims thru same source.
ROLL P23 #3616 FCT COMM #29133 - Annie Allen - 18

11483. SUSAN F. SCOTT and 4 children,   Sallisaw, Okla
Admitted. Daughter of #8625 and claims thru same source.

```
ROLL P124 #23954 FCT COMM #2960 - Susan F. Scott  - 35
        23955          2961 - Carry E. (dau)  - 10
        23956          2962 - Sue J. (dau)    -  7
        23957          304m - Arthur L. (son) -  3
        23958          305m - George S. (son) -  1
```

11484. LILLIAN CHOATE,   Sallisaw, Okla
Admitted. Daughter of #8625 and claims thru same source.
ROLL P41 #7359 FCT COMM #3138 - Lillian Choate - 30

11485. DANIEL MARTIN,   Sallisaw, Okla
Rejected. Applicant claims Cherokee blood thru mother who was
not enrolled by Chapman, though her husband and children (by
Duncan) were enrolled at that time. Applicant owns ancestors
[sic] were not parties to treaties of 1835-6 and 46. See Misc.
Test. P. 3090.
MISC. TEST. P. 3090. No 11662-11485 - Richard Martin:
"I am 50 years old; was born in Lumpkin County, Ga. I am
a Cherokee alottee and my number is 4648. I claim my Indian
blood through my mother. My father was a white man as far as I
know. My mother came west in 1871. She drew some Indian money
from the government but I do not know when. She had a brother
named Aaron Martin and some half brothers and sisters by the
name of Duncan. My grandfather, Joe Martin, was an Indian so I
have been informed. Charles Duncan was my mother's step-
father. She told me she never did marry Jackson Cawn. He was
my father. I do not know if he was an Indian. During the war
my mother lived in Georgia. She was not married before she
lived with my father that I know of. I was my mother's oldest
child. I have heard her say she was paid in 1852. My mother
had the same mother as her half brothers and sisters, Aaron,
John, William, Alonso, Martha, Marion and George"
SIGNED: Richard Martin, Muskogee, Okla., Sep 22 1908.
"This case is O. K. through Chapman 1793, 1794 and 1795. Half
brothers of mother. Mother was older than these half brothers
and was living with some man in 1852. Applicant named all of
the children of Chas. Duncan who are half brothers and sisters
of his mother." [Notation added to end of testimony]
EXCEPTION CASE. Recommended. Total number of exceptions
filed in this group -- 1.
     Applicant is enrolled by the Dawes Commission as a one-
sixteenth Cherokee. He was born in Lumpkin County, Ga. in
1860. He claims through his mother, Mary Martin and states
that he and his mother moved to the Indian Territory in
1870-1. Mary Martin was the daughter of Judy Martin, a white
woman and Joe Martin who is said to have been an Indian and
the son of Samuel Martin whose name appears on the roll of
1835. It is further claimed that Joe Martin started West with
the Cherokees prior to the Treaty and died on the way, when
his wife, Judy, with her two children then living, Aaron and
Mary, returned to Georgia, and Judy married Charles Duncan
prior to the Treaty. It is further claimed that Mary, and

191

Aaron are enrolled with Charles Duncan on the 1835 roll. Charles Duncan is there enrolled, page 38, from Etowah River, Ga. with two males under eighteen, one male over eighteen and one female under sixteen, with one affiliated white (probably Judy). The degree of blood is shown, four Cherokees, three of whom are half bloods and one quadroon. In 1851 Charles Duncan was enrolled with a large number of children, including Aaron, then reported to be twenty-three years of age and John, then sixteen years of age. Silar reports that Duncan had remarried since the Treaty to a white woman. It seems probable, however, that from the statements made and from the fact that John is reported to have been sixteen years of age in 1851 and is shown by the several applications to have been born in September 1835, that Charles Duncan and Judy were married prior to the Treaty and that John appears on the roll of 1835 as one of the males under eighteen. The difficulty in the case is that while Aaron and John with other children of Charles Duncan were enrolled in 1851 the name of Mary either as Duncan or Martin does not appear on the roll of 1851. Aaron appears as Aaron Duncan rather than Aaron Martin but that could be easily accounted for from the fact that he was said to have been living with his step father, Charles Duncan, though on the Chapman Roll Aaron is reported as the son of Charles.

In 1851 Mary Martin would have been about twenty years of age and it is entirely possible that she may have then been living with some one other than Charles Duncan and may have taken the name of the party with whom she was then living. One of the children of Charles Duncan and Judy, Martha Duncan, has filed application No. 357 and her name is found enrolled with her father in 1851 and she states in an affidavit that Mary Martin was her half sister and a full sister to Aaron who was enrolled in 1851, and that she is undoubtedly an Eastern Cherokee Indian. As Mary did not start West as is clearly shown, until 1870, if she is a Cherokee at all it is plain that she must have been an Eastern Cherokee, and that she was a Cherokee is a least prima facie established by the fact that she and her children have been enrolled as Cherokees in the West.

Marion Duncan in a letter dated Dec. 1., 1909 confirms the fact that his half sister, Mary Martin was the daughter of Joe Martin, a Cherokee Indian. It thus appears these claimants are entitled.
SUPP ROLL #30682 FCT COMM #17589 - Daniel Martin - 46

11486. THOMAS MARTIN and 2 children, Sallisaw, Okla Rejected. Brother to #11485.
EXCEPTION CASE. Recommended. Total number of exceptions filed in this group -- 1. Brother of No. 11485 and admitted for the same reasons.
SUPP ROLL #30691 FCT COMM #32367 - Thomas Martin - 32
          30692   32368 - Lora (dau)   - 7
          30693   4364m - Phronia (dau) - 3

11487. IDA SPRINGWATER and 1 child,   Long, Okla
Admitted. Niece of Jesse Locust, App #316 and is admitted for
same reasons.
ROLL P131 #25274 FCT COMM #19595 - Ida Springwater   - 25
        25275   32304 - Eli AUGERHOLE (son) - 7

11488. JOHNSON YAHOLA,   Braggs, Okla
Admitted. Cousin of #9587.
ROLL P155 #30061 FCT COMM #29107 - Johnson Yahola - 55
        30062   29108 - Polly (wife)   - 51
                              (App 11493)

11489. ALSIE BEAVER and 1 child,   Webbers Falls, Okla
Admitted. Daughter of #1716. [For Roll information See App
11012]

11490. NANNIE DEAN and 2 children,   Braggs, Okla
Admitted. Father, John McClean, 260 Ill. Niece of #4054.
ROLL P52 #9519 FCT COMM #23277 - Nannie Dean   - 32
        9520   23278 - Claud (son)   - 8
        9521   23279 - Bessie (dau) - 5

11491. MAGGIE FIELDS and 5 children,   Braggs, Okla
Admitted. The applicant's mother Nellie Leaf, App #12402 is
enrolled by Drennen from Ill. Dist. under group 9. See Misc.
Test. P. 3362-3466.
MISC. TEST. P. 3362. App. #12406 - Dick Justice:
"My name is Dick Justice. I live at Cookson, Okla. I was
not enrolled by the Dawes Commission. My father was born after 1851. His name was Arch Justice. My grandfather was an
Immigrant Cherokee. His name was Dan-tas-kee. My grandparents
lived in Flint Dist. (Da-nie Taskee). My grandmother drew money in 1851. Her name was Betsey Justice. My father and his
brothers and sisters were not born in 1851. My grand father on
my father's side drew money also. My grandmother's maiden name
was Nellie Sanders. Her father's name was George Sanders. Her
mother's name was Jinsy Sanders. See Ill. 49. Group No.
12402." SIGNED: Dick Justice, Tahlequah, Okla., Oct 1, 1908.
MISC. TEST. P. 3466. #11491 - Maggie Fields...thru Tom Roach,
Interpreter:
"That I am 36 years of age. I am a full blood Cherokee. My
father was living in 1851 and was on the 1851 roll. He came
with the big bunch of Indians that came here. My mother is
living at Cookson, Okla. Nellie Oo-ga-log is her name in Cherokee. Nellie Leaf is her name in English. She was on the 1851
roll but I don't know what name she was under. George was my
mother's father. Don't know any other name for him. Jency was
the name of my mother's mother. Lewis Tabb is the name my father went by. My mother's mother's folks went by the name of
Chicken. My mother had a sister named Susan Chicken. Susan had
a son named Squirrel (Ill. 42?) [sic] My mother has filed any
application in this fund. Neither my father nor mother ever

drew Old Settler money. Don't know my father's father's name.
Susie was my father's mother's name. My people were living in
Tahlequah District in 1851, that is, my mother's people. My
father's people lived in Illinois District. My father's Indian
name was Lewis Oo-sta-no-luh-tih. I was enrolled by the Dawes
Commission. I had a sister named Eliza Justus and she married
a man named Christie. She had a son by the first man named
Dick. Eliza is dead but her son Dick is still living. My half
brothers and sisters are on my mother's side. My Dawes Commission number is 29113. My children are 29114 to 29117 incl. My
husband is #29112."
SIGNED: Maggie Fields, Muskogee, Okla., Sep 22 1908.
ROLL P60 #11162 FCT COMM #29112 - Sam Fields - 51 (App 18145)
          11163   29113 - Maggie (wife) - 35
          11164   29114 - Jim (son)   - 14
          11165   29115 - Jinsie (dau) - 11
          11166   29116 - Betsy (dau)   - 7
          11167   29117 - Nancy (dau)   - 4
          11168   1878m - Willie (son)   - 2

11492. WILLIAM DREW,   Muskogee, Okla
Admitted. First cousin of #323 and claims thru same source.
ROLL P55 #10122 FCT COMM #28667 - William P. Drew - 26

11493. POLLY CROW, or YA-HO-LA,   Braggs, Okla
Admitted. Claimant's father, under name of Poorbear, enrolled
in Fl. 157, father's brother Fl. 156. Father's father in Ill.
183. See Misc. Test. P. 4189 and 3543.
MISC. TEST. P. 3543. App. #44016 - Polly Yahola:
   "My name is Polly Yahola. I live at Braggs, Okla. My moth-
er's name was Betsy Poorbear. I had a sister Lucy. I had a
brother named Mastee. My father's name was Poorbear. They
lived in Flint District in 1851. My Dawes Commission number
is 29108. See Flint 157."
SIGNED: Polly Yahola, Tahlequah, Okla., Oct 6 1908.
MISC. TEST. P. 4189. No 11493 - Polly Crow...thru Tom Young
and Annie Wildcat, Interpreters:
   "I am about 52 years of age. My enrollment number by the
Dawes Commission is 29108. I am the wife of Johnson Ya-ho-la.
I don't know whether I have any Creek blood or not. My parents
were Cherokees but I talk the Creek language and do not understand the Cherokee language. Yaw-noo-la-sott was my father.
That means Poorbear. He lived in Flint District. Wat-ta-du-ka
was the name of a brother of my father. He had a sister named
Lucy. Gah-do-wal-le was my father's father. The English meaning is "Clay". Gah-dah-qual-lih is the way to spell it, I
think. My grandfather on my father's side had a sister named
Jennie. Coo-wee-scoo-wee was my grandfather on my mother's
side. I don't know my grandmother's name on my father's side.
Quaitsey or Betsy was my mother's name. I don't know of any
other name that she had. She lived in Sequoyah District and
then she moved to Flint District. There were none of my moth-

er's brothers and sisters living at the time they came West. I
don't know when they came West. The English of Coo-wee-scoo-
wee is "Ross" and that was the name of my mother's father. I
have been told that my grandparents on my mother's side died
in the East. My parents were Emigrants. I have never associated with any other tribe than Cherokees, except the Creeks. I
talked Cherokee up until I was about 9 or 10 years old. Then
my parents died and I was raised by a family of Creeks, which
accounts for my speaking the Creek language."
SIGNED: Polly Crow, Braggs, Okla., Mar 25 1909.
"Tom Young, interpreter for above, states that applicant has
lived in the Cherokee Nation ever since he has known her and
that she associates with the Cherokees." [Notation added to
end of testimony]
[For Roll information See App 11488. Notation on roll "Crow,
Polly. See Polly Yahola."]

11494. LUKE CARTER,   Hulbert, Okla
Rejected. Applicant was a slave and was enrolled on the Freed-
man roll #1505.
EXCEPTION CASE. Rejected. Total number of exceptions filed
in this group — 1. Original recommendation renewed.

11495. MARY FRYAR and 4 children,   Braggs, Okla
Admitted. Father of [sic] John McClean, Ill. #260. Niece of
#40454.
ROLL P64 #11918 FCT COMM #32614 - Mary Fryar   - 30
        11919   32615 - Voisie (dau)   - 8
        11920   32616 - Andy (son)   - 6
        11921   32617 - Archie Severe (son) - 4
        11922   920m - Vancy (son)   - 1/3

11496. THOMAS HARRIS and 5 children,   Gritts, Okla
Rejected. This applicant's father Wm. Harris is enrolled as
an Old Settler.

11497. CARL L. SANDERS, minor,   Claremore, Okla
Admitted. By Annie Ward, Gdn. Applicant claims thru great
grandfather Eli Sanders 698 Going Snake. His grandfather
George was born in 1854. Grand nephew of #991.
ROLL P122 #23452 FCT COMM #21772 - Carl L. Sanders - 5
                                  by Annie Ward, Gdn.

11498. CHARLIE FODDER,   Braggs, Okla
Admitted. Nephew of #1590.
ROLL P62 #11468 FCT COMM #25885 - Charlie Fodder - 48

11499. NANCY BUSHYHEAD and 2 children,   Braggs, Okla
Admitted. Applicant's parents enrolled by Drennen 1851, Flint
577. See Misc. Test. P. 3099.
MISC. TEST. P. 3099. No. 11499 - Nancy Bushyhead:
    "My mother and father were both full blood Cherokees. My

195

father's name is Louis Beaver and my mother Sarah Beaver. They lives in Flint District, Cherokee Nation."
SIGNED: Nancy Bushyhead, Muskogee, Okla., Sep 23 1908.
"This case is O. K. through Lewis and Sarah Beaver, 577 Flint"
[Notation added to end of testimony]
ROLL P36 #6361 FCT COMM #20830 - George Bushyhead   - 51
                                (App 11774)
        6362   21212 - Nancy (wife)   - 52
        6363   21214 - Jennie RATTLINGGOURD   - 15
                                (dau of w) (App 17056)
        6364   21215 - John RATTLINGGOURD   - 13
                                (son of w) (App 17061)
        6365   21213 - Jack WALKER (son of w) - 20
                                (App 17057)

11500. CHAS. C. PRICE,   Inola, Okla
Admitted. Nephew of #1069. Father of applicant enrolled un-
der 287 Tahl., John Price.
ROLL P112 #21654 FCT COMM #12470 - Charles C. Price   - 36
          21655   12471 - Daisy E. (wife)   - 27
                                (App 11501)
          21656   12472 - Charles B. (son)   - 7
          21657   12473 - Clarence T. (son)   - 4

11501. DAISEY E. PRICE,   Inola, Okla
Admitted. Applicant claims thru mother who was probably not
living in 1851. Grandmother, Jane Fields and great grand
father Moses Fields enrolled in 1851, Del. 432. See Misc.
Test. P. 4122.
MISC. TEST. P. 4122. App. No. 11501 - Daisy E. Price:
    "That I am 29 years of age. I was born near Galena, Kan-
sas. I am now a recognized citizen of the Cherokee Nation. I
am enrolled by the Dawes Commission, No. 12471. I get my blood
from my mother, none from my father. My mother has been dead
five years. Her name was Emma E. Wells nee Rawles. My mother
was born in 1852. She got her Indian blood from her mother.
Mary Jane Field was the maiden name of my mother's mother. She
married a Rawles. In 1851 she probably lived in Del. District.
Augusta, Sarah Jane, Celeste and Serilda Rawles were the half-
brothers and sisters of my mother. They were older than my
mother. Rawles married two sisters. His name was John and he
was a white man. Catherine or Kate was the name of Augusta's
mother. Mary Jane and Catherine were full sisters. Mary Jane
Fields was the daughter of Moses and Elizabeth Fields. Moses
died in 1855. Think he lived in Del. District.   Jim and Sam
Fields were the brothers of Mary Jane. Margaret was a sister,
and Martha E. Fields was another, Sarah P. another, Laura V.
Fields, Moses A. Fields, Saphronia Fields and Susie Fields
were other brothers and sisters of Mary Jane.   Moses Fields'
first wife was Elizabeth Bigby and she died before 1851. His
second wife was Mahaley Cadle. She was a white woman.   Mary
Jane and Catherine were the daughters of Moses' first wife,

196

Elizabeth. (Del. 432)."
SIGNED: Daisy E. Price, Claremore, Okla., Mar 10 1909.
[For Roll information See App 11500]

11502. EDWARD McCOY and 1 child,   Sadie, Okla
Admitted. First cousin of 411 and claims thru same ancestors.
ROLL P93 #17701 FCT COMM #16943 - Edward McCoy - 35
          17702   1168m - Orlbie (son) - 2

11503. GEORGE COCHRAN and 1 child,   Stilwell, Okla
Admitted. Applicant enrolled in 1851 in Flint Dist. #334.
ROLL P44 #7941 FCT COMM #19003 - George Cochran - 72
          7942   19005 - Charlie (son)- 18 (App 12538)

11504. THOMAS SISSON,   Dalton, Ga
Rejected. Applicant is a nephew of Posey Sisson, #41618,
claiming thru the same source. Posey Sisson was born in Buncombe Co., N. C. in 1831 and they claim their Cherokee blood
thru Lucy Sisson nee Franklin. The claimant nor his father or
grandmother or great grandfather appear to have been enrolled
with the Cherokees in 1835 or at any time since. Claimant tes-
tifies that none of his ancestors ever had Indian names. Applicant states his father was regarded as a white man with Indian blood. See Misc. Test. P. 1378 and 1495. It appears from
application #17387 that Lucy Sisson was the granddaughter of
Gardner Green and this claim therefore groups back to #315.
MISC. TEST. P.. 1378. No. 11504 - Thomas Sisson:
    "My name is Thomas Sisson; I was born in Cherokee Co.,
N. C. 1852; I claim my Indian blood through my father; I make
no claim through my mother; my father was born in Cherokee
Co., N. C. 1830; my father got his Indian blood through his
mother; my grandmother's maiden was Lucy Franklin; my grand
mother was born in Cherokee Co., N. C. about 1810; my grand
mother, Lucy Franklin, got her Indian blood through her father, Patton Franklin; my great grandfather was born in Cherokee Co., N. C.; I do not know what year; I never saw my grand
mother or great grandfather through whom I claim; none of ancestors through whom I claim were ever enrolled that I know
of; in 1835 my father and grand parents lived in Cherokee Co.,
N. C.; James Sisson, Albert Sisson, Posie Sisson and William
are the brothers of my father and Emaline Sissin was my father' sister; none of the ancestors through whom I claim were
ever held as slaves; none of my ancestors ever had an Indian
name and none of them ever went West with the exception of my
grandmother, Lucy Franklin and my great grandfather, Patton
Franklin, who went as members of the tribe; I think they went
West of the Miss. River with the Indians; my great grand
father, Patton Franklin, was a full Cherokee Indian; my father
was regarded as a white man with Indian blood."
SIGNED: Thomas "X" Sisson, Dalton, Ga., Jul 10 1908.
MISC. TEST. P. 1495. #14373 - James Porter...in behalf of
Mrs. Julia Porter:

197

"That I am 54 years of age. Julia Porter is my daughter
in law and I am acquainted with her. She claims Indian descent
thru her father. Her mother was a white woman. Her father's
mother, Lucy Sissons, was a quarteroon Cherokee. Don't know
whether her father or grandmother ever lived with the Indians
or whether they were ever on any roll. John Henry Sisson
(41617) is a cousin of applicant and he was at the time of
making his application, lived in Gilmer Co., Ga. Julia Porter
had an uncle by the name of Posey Sisson, and she claims thru
the same source as he does and through no other. Julia Porter
is recognized as a white woman."
SIGNED: J. M. Porter, Blue Ridge, Ga., Jul 13 1908.

11505. SARAH J. PINSON and 1 child,   Dalton, Ga
Rejected. Applicant fails to establish a genuine connection
with Cherokee tribe. Ancestors not on rolls. Were not parties to treaties of 1835-6 and 1846. See Misc. Test. P. 1333.
MISC. TEST. P. 1333. No. 11505 - Sarah J. Pinson:
"My name is Sarah J. Pinson; I was born in Murray Co., Ga.
1853; I claim my Indian blood thru my father; no claim thru my
mother; my father got his Indian blood thru his father; my
grandfather thru whom I claim was born in Haversham Co., Ga.;
I never saw my grandfather thru whom I claim; I do not know
when; my grandfather, Aaron Bridges, got his Indian blood thru
both his father and mother; my great grandfather's name was
Obadiah Ksaw [?] Bridges; my grandmother's name was Coniheinie
Jerusha Bridges; she was a McDaniel before she was married;
none of the ancestors thru whom I claim were ever enrolled
that I know of; in 1835 my great grand parents lived in Haversham Co. Ga.; my grandfather was dead at that time; in 1851 my
father lived in Murray Co., Ga.; none of the ancestors thru
whom I claim were ever held in bondage; I do not know any of
the Indian names of any of my relatives; I was never enrolled;
My grandfather, Aaron Bridges, was taken away with the Cherokee Indians when they were taken away from Haversham Co., but
he came back soon after; my father went also but came back
soon after and settled in Ga.; my great uncle John Bridges,
also went West with the Indians at that time; my grandfather,
Aaron Bridges, was a half breed Cherokee, but married a white
woman." SIGNED: Sarah J. Pinson, Dalton, Ga., Jul 10 1908.

11506. MARY V. LANCE and 3 children,   Dalton, Ga
Admitted. Claims thru father enrolled as John Brackett, Chap-
man #1930.
ROLL P12 #1388 - Mary V. Lance   - 45
          1389 - John M. (son)   - 15
          1390 - Joseph M. (son) - 9
          1391 - Thomas J. (son) - 6

11507. WILEY W. ROOP and 7 children,   Laurel Bloomery, Tenn
Rejected. See special report Sizemore #417.

198

11508. MARTHA RAINS,   Claremore, Okla
Rejected. Applicant claims share of husband who died Nov. 9,
1888.

11509. ALSIE HAMILTON and 4 children,   Dewey, Okla
Admitted. Applicant's grandmother enrolled by Drennen 1852,
Ailsie Adair, 248 Flint. See Misc. Test. P. 2428.
MISC. TEST. P. 2428. No. 11509 - Alsie Hamilton:
    "I am 34 years of age; was born in Flint District, Chero-
kee Nation. I am a Cherokee alotee. I never drew any Old Set-
tler money and none of my people were Old Settlers that I know
of. I claim my Indian blood through my father. My mother was
a white woman." SIGNED: Alsie Hamilton, Bartlesville, Okla.,
Aug 29 1908. "This case is O. K. through Alsie Adair and James
Adair, 248 Flint." [Notation added to bottom of testimony]
ROLL P70 #13051 FCT COMM #12675 - Alsie Hamilton - 33
           13052   12676 - Hugh M. (son)   - 9
           13053   12677 - Clarence (son)   - 7
           13054   172m - James R. (son)   - 2
           13055   - George T. (son)   - 1

11510. ANNA CARDELL and 4 children,   Honolulu, T. H.*
Admitted. This applicant's father Wm. Long-knife and Barbury
Long-knife his mother are enrolled by Drennen from Del. Dist.
under group #120. [* "1520 Fort St, Honolulu, H. I." on roll]
ROLL P38 #6685 - Anna Carden   - 46
          6686 - William Thomas (son)   - 18
          6687 - John Joseph (son)   - 16
          6688 - Edward W. (son)   - 14
          6689 - Mary A. (dau)   - 11

11511. SAMUEL K. HINCHEE,   Cunningham, Ky
Rejected. Great uncle of #10764 and claims thru same source.

11512. ELIZA WARD,   Caddo, Okla
Rejected. Applicant applied with Choctaws; has Choctaw allotment. Enrolled as Choctaw by Mainage 485. See Misc. Test. P.
2600.
MISC. TEST. P. 2600. #11512 - Eliza Ward:
    "That I am 57 years of age. I claim my Indian descent thru
my mother; my father was a white man. My husband is 1/8 Choctaw. I am mistaken about that; he is 1/16 Choctaw and is a
Choctaw allotee. He lives here in the Choctaw Nation. My son
also received Choctaw allotment. I received about 200 acres of
land and my husband received about the same amount. All of my
children received land by their Choctaw blood. Osceola Allen
(11822) is my nephew, he being my sister Elizabeth's child. He
got a land allotment in the Cherokee Nation and never received
anything from the Choctaws. He has no Choctaw blood. I have a
minor child by the name of Henry William Ward. I have not
filed any separate application for him but he received Choctaw
allotment also. My mother claimed to be a full blood Cherokee.

199

She was born in Georgia but I don't know what county. Don't
know when she was born, but she was about 65 years old when
she died. She claimed thru her mother, Sulkinny Smith. Suppose
it is spelled Sah-kin-nah Smith. My grandmother was born and
raised in Georgia. I think I was about two years old when she
died. She died in the Cherokee Nation, I. T. My mother and her
mother came West when the Cherokees left Georgia. My mother
and her mother were on the roll but I don't know what date.
They received money when I three years old. That was at Ft.
Gibson. She (my mother) nor my grandmother never received any
Old Settler payment. Chah-wa-yu-ka was my mother's Indian
name. My mother went by the name of Martha Smith before marriage, and if she was enrolled that would be the name under
which she was enrolled. If my grandmother was enrolled it was
under the name of Sah-kin-nah Smith. My mother had two half
brothers by the names of Ave and William on the mother's side.
She had another half brother named Josiah Carter. In 1851 my
mother's name was Beck. She was living just north of Tahlequah. At the time my mother drew, I was just two or three
years old and she drew money for me and for my sister, Sarah
Ann Beck. I applied to the Dawes Commission with the Choctaws
as an intermarried citizen and I got land therefor. I here offer an evidence, copies of the decision, of the Dawes Commission, made upon hearing an exam- ination had before them and
which are marked Exhibits A and B. Osceola Allens's [sic]
mother died before the Dawes Commission was organized."
SIGNED: Eliza Ward, Durant, Okla., Sep 4 1908.
EXCEPTION CASE. Rejected. Total number of exceptions filed
in this group -- 7. Original recommendation renewed.

11513. ELIZA WARD, Duplicate of #11512.

11514. SOPHRONIA SWEANEY,   Tecumbia, Mo
Rejected. Claims thru the same source as #3935.

11515. IRA L. SWEANEY,   Tecumbia, Mo
Rejected. Claims thru the same source as #3935.

11516. JANE GREGORY and 1 child,   Russellville, Mo
Rejected. Claims thru same source as No 6526.

11517. JOSEPH C. VANN,   Freman, Okla.
Admitted. Although unable to identify positively applicant's
ancestors on rolls of emigrant Cherokees, their names do not
appear on Old Settler roll and from evidence in case and from
fact that applicant is enrolled by Daws Comm. on Cherokee roll
at No 3318, a full blood, it appears that applicant is entitled to enrollment. See Misc. Test. P. 3504.
MISC. TEST. P. 3504. #11517 also #8264 - J. C. Vann...through
Tom Roach, Interpreter:
    "That I am 50 years of age and am a full blood Cherokee.
My father's name was Will Vann. Will Go-way-lu was his Chero-

kee name. Ella Smith was the name of my mother before she was
married. She was only married once and her name after marriage was Ella Vann. El Go-way-lu was her Indian name. I understand that they received money in 1851. Don't know whether
they received any Old Settler money in 1851 or not. I don't
know exactly just when my parents were married. My father was
about 40 years old when he died, that is, making a rough guess
at it. My mother when she died must have been about 30 years
old. My parents were living here in the West in 1851. Don't
know what district they were living in at time but I was born
in Delaware District. My mother had a sister named Ge-wah-nih.
That is the only one I remember. Don't know whether she had
any brothers or not, but I don't know whether she did or not.
She had a full brother named Ge-wah-noo-ski. I think my mother
and father were married by 1851. Don't know the names of my
mother's parents. Don't know my father's parent's names. Guh-
yu-guh was the name of my mother's mother. I have been told
that my mother's father's name was Dah-ye-skee or skih. My father has a brother who is living now and his name is Dave
Vann. He lives about 3 1/2 miles from Euchee. Don't know
whether Dave has a middle name or not. My mother had a brother
named Jim and another named Dah-ge. I rather think my father
was enrolled under his Indian name in 1851. I have always gone
by the name of Vann. David was younger than my father; he is
about 64 years old now. My great grandmother on my mother's
side was named Le-sih or Lacy. I think she was living in 1851
in the West. It is said that Amos Vann is my son and I have
acknowledged him to be my son. I have never been married. The
mother of Amos Vann is named Sarah Vann, not Polly. Her father's name was Chew-wah-geh. Her mother's name was Se-lih. My
father had a brother named Arch Vann. Don't know whether he
had any children or not. Arch is dead. I was enrolled by the
Dawes Commission. My full name is Joseph C. My roll number is
3318 (Cherokee Roll). Amos Vann's number is 88297 by the Dawes
Commission." SIGNED: J. C. Vann, Sallisaw, Okla., Sep 17 1908.
ROLL P143 #27735 FCT COMM #3318 - Joseph C. Vann - 47

11518.   JOSEPH SHADE, Duplicate of #1291.

11519.   DAVE BLACKBIRD,   Locust Grove, Okla
              by Sarah Dreadfulwater, parent and Gdn.
Admitted.   Half brother of 4283 and claims thru same source.
ROLL P30 #5175 Dave Blackbird - 17 by Sarah Dreadfulwater, Gdn

11520.   ISAAC TUCKER and 2 children,   Moody, Okla
Admitted.   Applicant claims through mother Ailcey Tucker, enrolled in Flint 647. Grandfather John Tucker 647 Flint. Grand
mother Sallie Tucker, 647, Flint.   Uncle Stacy, Aunts Susan
and Anny, Flint, 647. See Misc. Test. P. -- [no page given]
ROLL P141 #27377 FCT COMM #18838 - Isaac Tucker - 34
              27378   18811 - Mary (wife) - 23
                                  (App 12633)

201

11520. ISAAC TUCKER (Cont)
            27379 FCT COMM #30498 - Cora (dau)   - 12
            27380   2977m - Sallie (dau) - 1

11521. ELIZA CAVALIER and 6 children,   Choteau, Okla
Admitted. Applicant claims through her father ["mother"
crossed out] Carter Markham enrolled as Marcrum in Saline 461.
See Misc. Test. P. 3747.
MISC. TEST. P. 3747. Eliza Cavalier:
    "I am about 35 years of age. I claim my Indian descent
through both parents. I am about 1/8 Cherokee.   I think both
of my parents were Emmigrants. My father and mother were living in 51. My father was named Carter Markham. It used to be
spelled years ago Marcrum. His mother was named Eliza and he
had three brothers named Jacob, James and John. He also had a
sister named Ruth but she wasn't born until after '51.   They
were living in Saline District. See Sal 461. My mother was
named Mary Halfacre before she was married. She had a sister
named Cynthia. See Dis. 6. Think my mother's parents were
dead in 51. I know my grandfather died about that time out in
California. My Grandmother died at about the same time in
Delaware District. My Daws Commission number is 8937 and my
brother's is 15562."
SIGNED: Eliza Cavalier, Locust Grove, Okla., Oct 3 1908.
ROLL P40 #7027 FCT COMM # 8937 - Eliza E. Cavalier - 33
            7028   8938 - Cicero T. (son) - 17
            7029   8939 - Theodore P. (son) - 15
            7030   8940 - Markham (son)   - 12
            7031   8941 - Scott (son)   - 10
            7032   8942 - Curtis (son)   - 8
            7033   2348m - Walter A. (son)   - 2

11522. EWING MARKHAM,   Locust Grove, Okla
Admitted. Brother of #10283. Father Jas. Marcrum, 461 Saline.
ROLL P96 #18315 FCT COMM #28300 - Ewing Markham - 23

11523. CLARENCE B. MARKHAM,   Locust Grove, Okla
Admitted. Brother of #10283.
ROLL P96 #18314 FCT COMM #28301 - Clarence B. Markham - 21

11524. LYDIA WILSON,   Locust Grove, Okla
Admitted. Granddaughter of #87 and claims through same source.
[For Roll information See App 1885, Vol. 2]

11525. SIMON PICKUP,   Locust Grove, Okla
Admitted. Grandson of No 87.
ROLL P111 #21408 FCT COMM #18668 - Simon Pickup - 25

11526. FRANK BUCKSKIN and 1 child,   Locust Grove, Okla
            by Littlebird Buckskin, Gdn. No. 2818.
Admitted.   Minor child of No. 2818 and enrolled with him.
MISC. TEST. P. 3766. 11526 - Little Bird Buckskin...through

Tom Roach, Interpreter:
"I am nearly 50 years of age. Both of my parents were Emmigrants and drew emmigrant money in 52. My father was named
Jesse Buckskin. Indian name Jehsi Oo-chuh-wah-dih of Oo-juh-
wah-dih. My father and mother were living together when they
drew this money. My mother's name was Chee-yaw-guh. English
name Katie Buckskin. My father and mother had three children
living at the payment in 52. The oldest was Celia or Se-lih.
The next was Al-sey. The next was a boy by the name of Ah-day-
yoh-ih. I come next, but I was born after the payment. Red
Bird comes after me and he is my full brother. George is the
youngest. Jesse's mother was living up to the time I can recollect. Her name was Gee-gih-eh. I don't know either one of
my mother's parents. My wife who is the mother of the two
children I have made application for was named Nancy Buckskin.
She is dead and I don't know who her parents were. The children I am making application for are named Sam Buckskin. He is
16 [15 ?]. The other is named Frank Buckskin. He is about 17.
They are both living with me. I haven't nay children by my
present wife. James (No. 14206) and Sam Buckskin (No 10616)
are my nephews, they being the children of my brother Redbird
Buckskin. Redbird and I had the same father and mother. My
own application number is 2818. My parents came out with the
big emmigration from Georgia. They were living in Saline District in 51 I think. My Daws Commission number is 29672. Sam's
is 18212. Frank's is 18211."
SIGNED: Little Bird Buckskin, Locust Grove, Okla., Oct 1 1908.
[NOTE: Frank & Smith Buckskin inadvertently omitted from
family's roll information App 181, Vol. 1]
ROLL P35 #6132 FCT COMM #29672 - Little Bird Buckskin - 44
                         (App 2818)
        6133   29673 - Katie LITTLEBIRD (wife) - 57
                         (App 181)
        6134   18211 - Frank BUCKSKIN (son)   - 14
        6135   18212 - Smith BUCKSKIN (son)   - 12

11527. JACK HAIR,   [No Residence]
Enrolled with mother, Nellie Buck, application No 469*.
[* Should be "468"] [NOTE: The children of this family were
inadvertently omitted from App 468, Vol. 1 - Note also that
Jack Hair's App # was not shown on roll - Residence on Roll
"Spavinaw, Okla"]
ROLL P35 #6085 FCT COMM # 6185 - Jumper Buck - 31 (App 27108)
        6086   26399 - Nellie (wife) - 41 (App 468)
        6087   26402 - Jefferson HAIR (son of w)- 17
        6088   26403 - Jack HAIR (son of w)   - 16
        6089   26404 - Lizzie HAIR (dau of w)   - 14
        6090   26405 - George HAIR (son of w)   - 11
        6091   26406 - Charlotte HAIR (dau of w)- 9

11528. MARY M. BROCK,   Pryor Creek, Okla
Rejected. Applicant died in 1904 and no one seems to be claim-

203

ing through her. See letter in 162 with 161.

11529. JACK GRIFFIN,   Porum, Okla
Admitted. Applicant claims through mother Wutty, enrolled 208
Skin Bayou. Grandmother Annie Fool No 208 S. B.
ROLL P68 #12651 FCT COMM #4039 - Jack Griffin - 29

11530. BETSEY JOHNSON or LANGLEY,   Porum, Okla
Admitted. Sister of No 10900 and claims through same source.
ROLL P81 #15370 FCT COMM #18695 - Betsey Johnson - 53

11531. MARTIN JOHNSON,   Porum, Okla
Admitted. Applicant's grandmother and grandfather and uncle
enrolled in 1851 in Tahl. Dist. #308. See Misc. Test. P. 2732.
MISC. TEST. P. 2732. #11531 - Martin Johnson or Langley:
    "That I am 20 years of age. I claim my Indian descent
through both parents. Don't know how much Indian my father
claimed. I think my mother was a full blood Cherokee. My father was of Cherokee blood too. My mother died in January
1908. Don't know whether she filed application or not. She
went by the name of Johnson, Betsy Johnson. She was about 52
or 53 years old when she died. My father was 45 or 46 years
old when he died. I don't remember the name of my grandfather
on my father's side. Don't know my father's mother's name.
Johnson Love was my mother's father. He was a Cherokee. My
mother's mother's name was Sallie Love. Horse-fly was the
name of one of my mother's brothers. He died in Tahlequah
District but don't know when. (Tah. 308) I was enrolled by
the Dawes Commission and got an allotment of 120 acres in the
Cherokee Nation. (Dawes Commission roll number probably 18696,
and a mistake made as to the sex). I usually go by the name
of Johnson. My mother went by the name of Johnson and my father by the name of Johnson, but my father's brother went by
the name of Langley. I don't know much about how it went."
SIGNED: Martin Johnson, Stigler, Okla., Sep 9 1908.
ROLL P82 #15506 FCT COMM #18696 - Martin Johnson - 18

11532. NELLIE REESE,   Muskogee, Okla
Rejected. Applicant's father a Creek. Applicant's mother Old
Settler. See Misc. Test. P. 3096.
MISC. TEST. P. 3096. No 16727-11532 - Elizabeth Watts:
    "I am about 49 years of age; was born in Canadian Dis-
trict. My mother was living at the time of the payment in
1851. Nancy Reese is my niece and Felix Reese is my nephew.
They are the children of Nellie Reese. My mother and all her
people were Old Settlers. My father was half Creek and half
white. He was not a Cherokee. My mother's first husband's
name was Lot. I drew Old Settler money. I have never gotten
any Creek money. I am a Cherokee alottee. My sister Nellie
Reese's number is 16832. Thomas Lott was part Creek and part
white. My mother drew Old Settler money. She first drew when
she was fourteen years old. Nellie Reese's father was not a

Cherokee. I do not know if he ever got any Creek money."
SIGNED: Elizabeth Watts, Muskogee, Okla., Sep 22 1908.
EXCEPTION CASE. 11532. Elizabeth Watts and 3 children, App
#16727, Muskogee, Okla. Rejected. Total number of exceptions
filed in this group –– 1. Original recommendation renewed.

11533. HATTIE BLISS and 3 children,   Spavinaw, Okla
Admitted. First cousin of #4361 and admitted for same reasons.
ROLL P31 #5361 FCT COMM #16489 – Hattie Bliss   – 40
            5362   16490 – Thos. H. MANKILLER (son) – 18
            5363   16491 – Beacher MANKILLER (son) – 15
            5364   2652m – Luria V. BLISS (dau)   – 2

11534. ANNIE STANLEY and 5 children,   Flint, Okla
Admitted. Niece of Sarah E. Sturdivant No 250.
ROLL P131 #25365 FCT COMM # 7725 – Annie Stanley   – 33
            25366   7726 – Bessie Ann (dau)   – 13
            25367   7727 – Jefferson H. (son) – 10
            25368   7728 – Mabel (dau)   – 7
            25369   3364m – Barney (son)   – 3
            25370   3365m – Alva (son)   – 1

11535. MARY SANDERS, Duplicate of No 1436

11536. JOHNSON WATT,   Dutch Mills, Ark
Admitted. Father of No 1782. Claimant himself enrolled in Go-
ing Snake No 270.
ROLL P147 #28538 FCT COMM #1519 – Johnson Watt – 59

11537. RACHEL SPEAK, Duplicate of No 1609. [Name "Rachel
Spade" in App 1609]

11538. NANCY A. MORTON,   Skirum, Ark
Rejected. Applicant's ancestors not on rolls. Applicant does
not offer genuine proof of her connection with Cherokee tribe.
Applicant failed to appear to testify.

11539. ISAAC LEE,   Dutch Mills, Ark
Admitted. The paternal grandparents and uncle of applicant
enrolled by Drennen in 1851 in No 382, Going Snake. Appli-
cant's father, through whom he claims, was born after 1851.
Nephew of No. 1690.
ROLL P89 #16917 FCT COMM #19678 – Isaac Lee – 19

11540. WILLIE BOLEN,   Brent, Okla
Admitted. Grandnephew of Charles Walkingstick, appl. No 4048
and is admitted for same reasons. Grandfather John Walkingstick, enrolled also as "Young Pig" 611, Going Snake (See No
4050) herewith.
ROLL P32 #5457 FCT COMM #20515 – William Bolin – 24

11541. DICK WATERS, Jr.   Marble City, Okla
Admitted. By Dave Bird, Gdn. Applicant's grandmother enrolled
in Flint Dist. Group No. 60. See testimony of Dave Bird, taken
at Marble City, Okla., Mar. 18, 1909. See Misc. Test. P. 3975.
MISC. TEST. P. 3975.   No 11541 - Dave Bird...through D. M.
Faulkner, Interpreter:
     "My name is Dave Bird; my post-office is Marble City,
Okla.; I am about forty-three years old; I have a child by the
name of Dick Waters living with me; Dick Waters father's name
was James Waters or Oo-war-yus-ki; Jim Waters was something
over twenty years old when he died and he died about eight
years ago; James Waters father was named Digging Waters; James
Waters' mother was named Betsy Runningbear; Betsy was old
enough to draw Eastern Cherokee money; Betsy Runningbear was
my mother; Betsy was living in Flint in 1851; Betsy's father
Dah-yes-ki the mother of Betsy Oo-squi-ni. Joe Bolen was the
father of Lizzie Bolen and he was Cherokee; Charlie Bolen is
his brother; Joe's brother Charlie drew Emigrant money and he
is here now; Charlie Bolen's name is Charlie Tee-hee; Flint
601; Joe's mother's name was E-yar-nie and she also had a son
named James and one named Shaw-ney."
SIGNED: Dave "X" Bird, Marble City, Okla., Mar 18 1909.
ROLL P146 #28405 - Dick Waters, Jr. - 12 by Dave Bird, Gdn.

11542. RACHEL L. HALL and 1 child,   Isabella, Tenn
Rejected. Claims as descendant of Polly Murphy.

11543. CHARLEY SIXKILLER, Duplicate of App No 5975.

11544. PETER NICKS (or NIX) and 5 children, Maysville, Ark
Admitted. Nephew of No 654 and claims through same source.
ROLL P105 #20095 FCT COMM #20566 - Peter Nicks (or Nix) - 49
        20096   20567 - Rachel (wife)   - 36
                               (App 11545)
        20097   20568 - Luisa (dau)   - 14
        20098   20569 - Huston (son)   - 12
        20099   20570 - Alford (son)   - 10
        20100   - Alvy (son)   - 8
        20101   4826m - Bessie (dau)   - 2

11545. RACHEL NIX,   Maysville, Ark
Admitted. Uncle [sic] of No 1561 and claims through the same
source. [For Roll information See App 11544]

11546. NANCY NIX,   Maysville, Ark
Admitted. Niece of No 654 and claims through same source.
ROLL P105 #20113 FCT COMM #19417 - Nancy Nix - 36

11547. MARIA MILLER,   Maysville, Ark
        by Nannie Miller, Gdn.
Admitted. First cousin once removed. Grandfather "David
Miller", No. 790, Del." [For Roll information See App 11550]

11548. ELLA MILLER,   Maysville, Ark
        by Nannie Miller, Gdn.
Admitted. First cousin once removed of No 1089. Grandfather
David Miller No 790 Del. [For Roll information See App 11550]

11549. BYRDIE MILLER,   Maysville, Ark
        by Nannie Miller
Admitted. First cousin once removed of No 1089. Grandfather
David Miller No 790 Del. [For Roll information See App 11550]

11550. JOSIE MILLER,   Maysville, Ark
        by Nannie Miler, Gdn.
Admitted. First cousin once removed of No 1089. Grandfather
David Miller No 790, Del.
ROLL P99 #19007 FCT COMM #26953 - Nannie Miller - 35
                                 (App 23978)
        19008   26954 - Josie (dau) - 15
        19009   26955 - Maria (dau) - 11 (App 11547)
        19010   26956 - Ella (dau) - 5 (App 11548)
        19011   2968m - Birdie (dau)- 3 (App 11549)

11551. ADA SIMMON,   Marble City, Okla
Admitted. Grand niece of Jack Walkingstick, App No 4048 and
is admitted for same reasons. Grandfather, John Walkingstick,
or "Young Pig" 611 Going Snake (See 4050 herewith).
ROLL P127 #24461 - Ada Simmon - 22

11552. JENNIE BOLEN,   Marble City, Okla
Admitted. Can not locate applicant's father on rolls — but
paternal grandfather is enrolled as "Winkle-sides", by Drennen
at Skin Bayou No 201. [NOTE: No Testimony was referred to but
the following is for this applicant]
MISC. TEST. P. 3976. No 11552 - Jennie Bolen...through D. M.
Faulkner, Interpreter:
    "My name is Jennie Bolen; my post-office is Marble City,
Okla.; I am about sixty years old; my father's name was Ga-
che-yah-li; my father was living in S. B. in 1851; Ah-ni-wa-ge
was my mother; I do not know where my father was born; I do
not know whether he was an emigrant or an Old Settler."
SIGNED: Jennie "X" Bolen, Elizabeth G. Smith, Test., Marble
City, Okla., Mar 18 1909.
Peter Bird...through D. M. Faulkner, Interpreter:
    "My name is Peter Bird; my post-office is Bunch, Okla.; I
am about fifty-four years old; I know Jennie Bolen; my mother
was a sister of Jennie Bolen's father; my mother's name was
You-que; my mother came to this country in 1838; Jennie's
father came at the same time; my mother's father was named
Wrinkle-side; Indian name, De-squa-da-na-ga-you-le (See S. B.
201)." SIGNED: Peter "X" Bird, Elizabeth G. Smith, Test.,
Marble City, Okla., Mar 18 1909.
ROLL P32 #5431 FCT COMM #18975 - Charley Bolen - 57(App 17004)
        5432   28420 - Jennie (wife) - 54

11553. JENNIE FAULKNER and 3 children,   Wauhillau, Okla
Admitted. Applicant is a niece of No 1050.   Father "Lewis"
641 Flint. Grandfather, George Blair and Nancy Blair, grand
mother, enrolled 641 Flint.
ROLL P59 #10933 FCT COMM # 3890 - Jinnie Faulkner - 43
         10934   3892 - John F. (son)   - 17
         10935   3893 - Joseph H. (son) - 9
         10936   3752m - Jennie M. (dau) - 2

11554. ALEX. DAVIS,   Cherokee, Ark
Admitted. Nephew of No 337.
ROLL P51 #9290 FCT COMM #19825 - Alex. Davis - 25

11555. LEVI F. LEWIS and 4 children,   Thaxton, N C
Rejected. Applicant fails to show any genuine connection with
the Eastern Cherokees. No ancestor ever enrolled. No ancestor
or party to the treaties of 18356 or 46. See Misc. Test. P. 82
MISC. TEST. P. 82. Misc. & Sizemore - No 11555 Levi F. Lewis:
     "I am 53 years of age, and live in Ashe County, N. C. I
have lived in Ashe County all of my life, having been born
there. I claim Indian blood through my father and mother.
They lived in Ashe County, N. C. -- they were both born in
Ashe County. I suppose my grandparents lived in Watauga County, N. C., and part of the time in Ashe County. I have seen
them several times, -- that is my grandparents on my father's
side. They were said to have Cherokee Indian blood. When I
was a small boy it was thrown up to me that I had Indian
blood, by my neighbors. When it was thrown up to us children,
my mother acknowledged that we might be related to the Indians. Neither my father nor my mother ever received any money from the Government as Indians, nor have I received any.
Before this, I never made application for Indian money. I never knew that there was anything of that kind. I never saw Ned
Sizemore. My grandparents on my mother's side were descendants of the Sizemores. My father and mother and my grand
parents never lived with the Indians that I know of. I have
an uncle who moved to the Indian Territory and lived with the
Indians. He may have been allotted land out there, although I
do not know. I learned from old man Sap that the Rourke name
leads back to the Arkeelook Indians. Ole man Sap lived in
North Carolina."
SIGNED: L. F. Lewis, Weasels, N. C., Apr 7 1908.
EXCEPTION CASE. Rejected. Total number of exceptions filed
in this group -- 1. Original recommendation renewed.

11556. AMBROSE LEWIS and 3 children,   Thaxton, N C
Rejected. Son of Levi F. Lewis (11555) and claims through the
same source.

11557. RUFUS LEWIS,   Thaxton, N C
Rejected. Son of Levi F. Lewis (11555) and claims through the
same source.

11558. JOHN LEWIS and 1 child,   Thaxton, N C
Rejected. Son of Levi F. Lewis (11555) and claims through the
same source.

11559. TURNER GRIMAT,   Marble, Okla
Admitted. Claims through grandfather and grandmother enrolled
as Te-coh-le-qua-ta-kee and Ah-ye-tah. Uncle enrolled as
Chick-a-u-ee. Flint No 583. Father and mother born after 1851.
ROLL P68 #12682 FCT COMM #28445 - Turner Grimet - 21
          12683   18964 - Mary (wife) - 19 (App 14275)

11560. LAFAYETTE F. YATES and 10 children, Jefferson, N C
Rejected. See special report Sizemore No 417

11561. RICHARD M. LOCKER,   Talala, Okla
Admitted. First cousin of No 587 and claims through the same
source. Mother enrolled as "Margaret T. Nicholson", Tahl. 480.
ROLL P90 #17229 FCT COMM #30772 - Richard Locker - 39
          17230   30773 - Lola R. (dau) - 10
          17231   30774 - Dallas C. (son) - 8
          17232   30775 - John S. (son) - 6
          17233   2246m - Edward V. (son) - 3

11562. MARTHA BLEVINS,   Park, Va
Rejected. See special report Sizemore No 417.

11563. MONROE BLEVINS and 5 children,   Park, Va
Rejected. See special report Sizemore No 417.

11564. WM. W. THOMPSON and 8 children, Laurel Bloomery, Tenn
Rejected. See special report Sizemore No 417.

11565. W. W. THOMPSON,   Laurel Bloomery, Tenn
Rejected. See special report Sizemore No 417.

11566. SARAH PORTER,   Texana, Okla
Admitted. Niece of No 71 and claims through same source.
ROLL P112 #21571 FCT COMM #4632 - Sarah Porter - 17

11567. WILLIAM S. COODY,   Cannon, Okla
Admitted. Nephew of No 71 and claims through same source.
ROLL P46 #8300 FCT COMM #4630 - William S. Coody - 22

11568. ELLA PAUL and 1 child,   Warner, Okla
Admitted. Niece of No 71 and claims through same source.
ROLL P109 #20956 FCT COMM # 4629 - Ella Paul   - 25
          20957   4384m - Bertha (dau) - 2

11569. JESSE COODEY,   Cannon, Okla
          by R. B. Butts, Gdn., Muskogee, Okla
Admitted. Niece [sic] of No 71 and claims through the same
source.

ROLL P46 #8278 FCT COMM #4631 - Jesse Coodey - 19
                              by R. B. Butts, Gdn.

11570. CALLIE COODEY,   Cannon, Okla
          by R. B. Butts, Gdn., Muskogee, Okla
Admitted. Nephew [sic] of #71 and claims through same source.
ROLL P46 #8273 FCT COMM #4634 - Callie Coodey - 11
                              by R. B. Butts, Gdn.

11571. ANNIE COODEY,   Cannon, Okla
          by R. B. Butts, Gdn., Muskogee, Okla
Admitted. Niece of No 71 and claims through same source.
ROLL P46 #8270 FCT COMM #4633 - Annie F. Coodey - 14
                              by R. B. Butts, Gdn.

11572. BESSIE COODEY,   Cannon, Okla
          by R. B. Butts, Gdn., Muskogee, Okla
Admitted. Niece of No 71 and claims through same source.
ROLL P46 #8272 FCT COMM #4635 - Bessie Coodey - 9
                              by R. B. Butts, Gdn.

11573. SUSIE FIELDS,, Minor,   Warner, Okla
          by John Hood, Gdn.
Admitted. Mother not living in 1851. Grandfather "Timothy
Fields, 290 Ill."
ROLL P60 #11179 FCT COMM #4682 - Susie M. Fields - 3
                              by John Hood, Gdn.

11574. MARY HOOD and 6 children,   Warner, Okla
Admitted. Sister of No 4106. Father of applicant "Tim Fields,
No 290 Illinois." [For Roll information See App 11577]

11575. NANNIE MURRAY,   Muskogee, Okla
Admitted. Applicant claims through mother Jane O'Riley enrolled 348 Tahl. Sister Elizabeth and Paty 348 Tahl. Applicant must be mistaken as to date of her birth.
ROLL P103 #19767 FCT COMM #27874 - Nannie Murray - 54

11575.5 WALTER CARVER, PEARL CARVER,   Muskogee, Okla
          by James F. Carver, Gdn.
Admitted. Grandchildren of No 11575 and claims through same
ancestors.
ROLL P39 #6935 FCT COMM #27878 - Walter Carver - 18
        6936   27879 - Pearl (sis) - 13
                              by James F. Carver, Gdn.

11576. ELIZABETH FRAZIER,   Warner, Okla
Admitted. Applicant's father probably enrolled as "James Hood"
at Skin Bayou No 61.   Grandfather James Downing on 1835 roll
(see App No 14732) (Misc. Test. P. 4215) (See Group No 10793)
MISC. TEST. P. 4215. #11576 - Emma Filmore:
    "I was born in 1851. My father's name was James Hood. He

                              210

had two full brothers by the name of Dick and Tillman Hood. I
do not know who my grand father was but I have been told that
his name was Sunday Downing. Emmit Starr told me that my grand
fathers name was Sunday Downing. My grand mother and my mother
were white women. My father had a half brother by the name of
John Hood. He was enrolled as an Old Settler. He had no children and I drew his old settler money in 1894. I was told that
my father was living in Can. District, but that he was enrolled in Sequoyah in 1851. My father raised his brother Dick.
I do not know where he was enrolled.   My father went by the
name of his mother's second husband, who was the father of
John Hood, the old settler. See S. B. #61? [sic]. Will this
group with 10793? [sic]"
SIGNED: Emma Filmore, Porum, Okla., Mar 24 1909.
[For Roll information See App 9997, Vol. 4]

11577. JOHN HOOD and 6 children,   Warner, Okla
Admitted. Brother of No 11576 and claims through same source.
ROLL P77 #14553 FCT COMM #4441 – John Hood   – 51
         14554   4442 – Mary (wife)   – 46
                               (App 11574)
         14555   4443 – Charley (son) – 19
         14556   4444 – Lizzie (dau) – 15
         14557   4445 – Jennie (dau) – 13
         14558   4446 – Jimmie (son) – 10
         14559   4447 – Kitty (dau)   – 7
         14560   4448 – Steve (son)   – 5

11578. A. B. CALDWELL and 6 children,   Patsey, Ky.
Rejected. See special report Sizemore No 417.

11579. SARAH SMITH,   Patsey, Ky
Rejected. See special report Sizemore No 417.

11580. LOUISA L. CALDWELL and 1 child,   Patsey, Ky
Rejected. See special report Sizemore No 417.

11581. THOMAS J. CALDWELL and 3 children,   Patsey, Ky
Rejected. See special report Sizemore No 417.

11582. CATHERINE CALDWELL,   Radical, Ky
Rejected. See special report Sizemore No 417.

11583. FLORA DARRALL and 2 children,   Patsey, Ky
Rejected. See special report Sizemore No 417.

11584. WILLIE C. DARRELL,   Patsey, Ky
Rejected. See special report Sizemore No 417.

11585. LUTHER B. CALDWELL and 2 children,   Patsey, Ky
Rejected. See special report Sizemore No 417.

11586. JOHN T. GOODSKY, Gdn. Ellay, Ga
Rejected. Ancestors not on rolls. Does not establish genuine
connection with Cherokee tribe. See Misc. Test. P. 1402.
MISC. TEST. P. 1402. #11586 - Sarah Jane Goolsby:
"That I am 36 [? digits typed over] of age. I claim my
Indian through my father; my mother was white. My husband is
a white man. My father's father claimed Indian. All of my
other grandparents were white. My grandfather was a full
blooded Cherokee. My father was born and raised in Cherokee
Co., N. C. He left there when I was small and went to Murray
Co., Ga. and lived and died there. He never lived in Madison
Co., Ga. that I know of. My father has been dead ten years.
I was 20 when my father died. He was about 50. My grand
father was born and raised in N. C. the same place my father
was, - this side of Murphy. I don't think my father ever lived
with the Indians as a member of the tribe. I think my grand
father Ridley lived with the Indians in N. C, in Cherokee Co.
He left there and went to Murray Co., Ga. at the same time my
father did. That was after the war. I don't know whether my
grandfather lived with the Indians up to the time he came to
Ga. I never heard that my father or grandfather were on any
rolls. My father and grandfather never had any other name than
Ridley. I don't know whether my father had any brothers and
sisters or not. Don't know whether my grandfather had any
brothers or sisters or not. I am recognized as a white woman
with some Indian blood. My husband is a white man."
SIGNED: Sarah Jane "X" Goolsby, Ellijay, Ga., Jul 10 1908.
EXCEPTION CASE. 11586. John T. Goolsby, Gdn. for 6 children, Ellijay, Ga. Rejected. Total number of exceptions
filed in this group -- 2. Original recommendation renewed.

11587. LYDIA K. RICE and 6 children, Yokon, Ga
Rejected. Ancestors not on rolls. Does not establish genuine
connection with Cherokee Tribe. See Misc. Test. P. 1411.
MISC. TEST. P. 1411. #11587 - Elizabeth Call...in behalf of
Lydia K. Rice:
"That I am 64 years of age and live in Gilmer Co., Ga.
Lydia Rice is my daughter. I am a full blooded white woman
myself and applicant claims her Indian blood through her father, Joseph Call. Joseph Call's mother claimed the Indian.
All the rest of applicant's grandparents were white. My husband was born and raised in Yancey Co., N. C. in 1833. He
left there about 1842 and came to Gilmer Co., Ga. My grand
mother Call was born and raised in Yancey Co., N. C. She came
with my father when he came. She died in 1865 in Murray Co.,
Ga. My husband was not on any roll before the war. His grand
mother, Polly Sanders, was on the roll. Don't know who she
married. Don't know what roll she was on. My husband's mother
was Jane Call. I think Polly Sanders was enrolled in 1851.
Don't know when Polly Sanders died. My husband's mother was
not on any roll. My husband never lived with the Indians as a
member of the tribe but I don't know about his mother. My

212

husband told me that none of his ancestors had ever received anything from the government. My husband was recognized as a white man with some Indian blood. He claimed to be Cherokee. His mother was 1/2 or 3/4 Cherokee."
SIGNED: Elizabeth "X" Call, Ellijay, Ga., Jul 10 1908.

11588. JOHN F. CALL and 2 children,   Yokon, Ga
Rejected. Brother of No 11587.

11589. J. W. WILSON, Gdn. for 5 children, Yokon, Ga
Rejected. Duplicate of No 11591

11590. W. M. ROSS, Gdn. for 4 children,   Lindale, Ga
Rejected. Children of Margaret C. Ross, App No 2661 & claims through same source.

11591. NANCY JANE WILSON and 7 children, Yokon, Ga
Rejected. Sister of No 11587. Application for minor children is filed by husband of No 11591.

11592. J. C. RICE, Gdn. for 5 children,   Yokon, Ga
Rejected. Nieces and nephews of No 11591.

11593. CALVIN I. CALL,   Yokon, Ga
Rejected. Brother of No 11587.

11594. SARAH J. GOODSBY,   Ellay, Ga
Rejected. Mother of children in application No 11586.

11595. JOHN BECK and 5 children,   Cherokee City, Okla [sic]
Admitted. Uncle of No 2671..

ROLL P28	#4685	FCT COMM #28886	– John Beck	– 37
	4686	28887	– Ida R. (wife)	– 27
			(App 11597)	
	4687	28888	– Ezekiel (son)	– 11
	4688	28889	– George (son)	– 9
	4689	28890	– Sabra (dau)	– 7
	4690	28891	– Cherry M. (dau)	– 5
	4691	46m	– Lillie B. (dau)	– 3

11596. JOHN F. CALL, Gdn. for 1 child,   Yokon, Ga
Rejected. Nephew of No 11587.

11597. IDA R. BECK,   Cherokee City, Ark
Admitted. Cousin of #866. [For Roll information See App 11595]

11598. THOMAS PARKER,   Tate, Ga
Rejected. Nephew of No 5041.

11599. DAVID M. FAULKNER and 3 children, Hanson, Okla
Admitted. Father of No 9183 enrolled by Drennen S. B. 182.
[For Roll information See App 9458, Vol. 4]

11600. JACK F. SQUIRREL,   Cookson, Okla
Admitted. Half brother of #4855; claims through same source.
ROLL P131 #25302 FCT COMM # 6200 - Jack F. Squirrel - 34
        25303   25965 - Jennie (wife)   - 36
                        (App 11665)

11601. MARY MOORE,   Sugar Valley, Ga
Rejected. It does not appear that applicant or ancestors were
ever enrolled with Cherokees [or] were parties to treaties of
1835-6 and 46. See Misc. Test. P. 1301.
MISC. TEST. P. 1301. No 11601 - Mary Moore:
    "My name is Mary Moore; I was born in Bradley Co., Tenn.
1840; I claim my Indian blood through my father; I make no
claim of Indian blood through my mother; my father was born in
N. C. 1813; I do not know what county; my father got his Indian blood from his father, Isaac Nicholson; I am unable to
trace my ancestry any farther back than my grandfather; I
think my grandfather, Isaac Nicholson, was born in N. C., but
I do not know when; I never saw my grandfather, Isaac Nicholson; my father lived with the Indians in N. C. as a member of
the tribe up to the time of his marriage; 1832; I think my
grandfather lived with the Indians as a member of the tribe;
in 1835 my father lived in Bradley Co., Tenn.; my grand father
was dead in 1835; none of the ancestors through whom I claim
were ever held in bondage; neither I nor any of the ancestors
through whom I claim were ever enrolled; I heard of the enrollment in 1851 and that of 1882, but never were enrolled; I
do no remember of any of my ancestors through whom I claim
ever having an Indian name; at the time of my father's marriage in 1832 my grandfather was dead; my father told me that
my grandfather through whom I claim was a full blood Cherokee
Indian." SIGNED: Mary "X" Moore, Calhoun, Ga., Jul 9 1908.

11602. WILLIAM GRITTS,   Cookson, Okla
Admitted. Nephew of No 10955 and claims through same source.
ROLL P68 #12733 FCT COMM #20761 - William Gritts - 29
[NOTE: 2 Wm. Gritts on roll - both reside Cookson, Okla. -
both with the same FCT # - the 2nd William's age is 31 and his
App # is 42195 - probably a duplicate.]

11603. JOHN H. COOKSON,   Cookson, Okla
Admitted. Uncle of No 859.   Applicant enrolled in 1851, in
Ill. Dist. No 4. Applicant's father enrolled in 1835.
ROLL P46 #8327 FCT COMM #15266 - John H. Cookson - 80

11604. ROSS OO-DE-LE-DA,   Maysville, Ark
Admitted. Nephew of No 1825.
ROLL P106 #20321 FCT COMM #15311 - Ross Oo-da-le-da - 26

11605. ROXIE SMITH,   Cherokee, N C
Admitted. First cousin of No 613 and claims through the same
source. Applicant's father enrolled by Chapman No 1373.

214

11606. BETTIE WELCH,   Chiwooco, Okla
Admitted. Niece of No 16823 and claims through same source.
Yah-choo-houmee-yuh or Bear Meat. See Misc. Test. P. 1769.
MISC. TEST. P. 1769.   #16823 with 11606 - Lydia Brown...
through John Mumblehead, interpreter:
    "That I am somewhere between 50 and 60 years of age -- I
do not know my exact age. My father's name was You-choo-he-
wee-yuh (Chapman 1527). My mother's Indian name is Le-sih.
Chuo-huh-loo-huh and Wa-loo-kih were my half brothers on my
fathers side. Ta-nee-lih is my full sister. Ko-he-na-ih is
my mother's brother. Peter Brown #15810 is my son by John
Brown. Cinda Saunooka is my sister, and she is dead. She
left only one child who is under age -- his name is Stillwell
Saunooka, and I would guess him to be about 15 years old.
Nancy and Racel Saunooka are sisters of Stillwell. Samuel
Saunooka and Sarah Arneach are brother and sister of Still-
well. Bettie Welch is a daughter of my full sister, Al-cih,
or Alsie Bearmeat. Jonas Brown is my son. John Brown was
known as John Greenleaf."
SIGNED: Lydia "X" Brown, Cherokee, N. C., Jul 22 1908,
"Father of Lydia Bearmeat, Chapman 1527. Lydia, Hester 1281."
[Notation added to end of testimony]
ROLL P148 #28720 - Bettie Welch - 24

11607. FLETCHER RAY,   Tate, Ga
Rejected. Nephew of No 5041.

11608. NANCY J. HOLMES,   Roswell, Ga
Rejected. Proof of genuine connection with the Eastern Cherokees insufficient. The Susan Williams on roll is not the one
referred to by this applicant. No ancestor was a party to the
treaties of 1835-6-46. No ancestor was ever enrolled. See
Misc. Test. P. 970.
MISC. TEST. P. 970.   #11608 - Nancy J. Holmes:
    "That I am 28 years of age and live in Cobb Co., Ga. I
claim Indian descent on my father's side and his mother. My
mother is white, and all of my other grandparents were white.
My grandmother's name was Susan Williams on my father's side.
She married a Blair. My father was 54 when he died and he has
been dead 16 years. He was never on any Indian roll . My
grandmother was enrolled in N. C. under the name of Williams.
She was enrolled before she married my grandfather. Don't
know when my grandmother Williams died but it was in the time
of the war. She had some brothers and sisters but I don't
know their names. I don't know the names of the parents of my
grandmother Williams. Susan Williams lived all her life in
Randolph Co., N. C. She was there in 1851. She was born,
raised and died there. She never went to the Ter. that I know
of. Don't know why my father was never enrolled. I am recognized as a white woman in the community. My husband is a full

blooded white man. My father never lived with the Indians as a member of the tribe that I know of. Don't know when my grand mother married my grandfather. It was a long time before my father was born, I think. My father never made application for Indian benefits. This is the only one I ever made."
SIGNED: Nancy J. "X" Holmes, Marietta, Ga., Jul 6 1908.
EXCEPTION CASE. Rejected. Total number of exceptions filed in this group -- 2. Original recommendation renewed.

11609. CYNTHIA HART, Laurel Springs, N C
Rejected. See special report Sizemore No. 417.

11610. EDNA EARL DURALL and 2 children, Welch, Okla
Admitted. Niece of No 9422.
ROLL P56 #10381 FCT COMM #24254 - Edna Earl Durall - 26
        10382   24255 - Benoni F. (son) - 8
        10383   24256 - George R. (son) - 6

11611. ROBERT G. & JOSEPH WELCH, Sallisaw, Okla
Admitted. First cousins of 4361 and admitted for same reasons.
ROLL P148 #28816 - Robt. G. Welch - 1? *
          28817 - Jos. (bro)   - 1? *
              by A. G. Welch, Gdn.
[* last digit of ages cut off]

11612. CORA MARTIN and 6 children, Porum, Okla
Admitted. Niece of No 256 and claims through same source.
ROLL P96 #18393 FCT COMM #17403 - Cora Martin - 33
        18394   17404 - John A. Jr. (son) - 15
        18395   17405 - George D. (son) - 13
        18396   17406 - Ada B. (dau)   - 12
        18397   17407 - Charles J. (son) - 10
        18398   17408 - Lilla May (dau) - 4
        18399   2504m - Fay (dau)   - 1

11613. MARY WELCH, Sallisaw, Okla
Admitted. First cousin of 4561 and is admitted same reasons.
ROLL P148 #28794 FCT COMM #2165 - Mary Welch - 21

11614. LAURA ADAIR and 4 children, Sallisaw, Okla
Admitted. First cousin of #4561 and admitted for same reasons.
ROLL P21 #3299 FCT COMM # 2538 - Laura Adair   - 32
        3300   2539 - Myrtle (dau)   - 14
        3301   2540 - Cornelius (son) - 11
        3302   2541 - Mamie (dau)   - 9
        3303   4677m - Gladys (dau)   - 2

11615. HELLEN McQUIRE and 5 children, Andrews, N C
Rejected. See special report Blythe No 153.

11616. ELIZABETH SIZEMORE and 5 children, Crumpler W Va.
Rejected. See special report Sizemore No 417.

11617. EVVIE FRANKLIN,   RFD No 2, Wills Point, Tex
Rejected. Niece of No 315 and claims through same source.

11618. CORA L. BELDER and 1 child,   Hiawatha, W Va
Rejected. See special report Sizemore No 417.

11619. SARAH J. BLACKWELL,   Catoosa, Okla
Rejected. Duplicate of No 12957. Niece of No 532.
MISC. TEST. P. 2482. Witness in re Henry J. Maynar and
Ardenia Manar. App #12946-12954-11619 - J. A. Manar:
    "My name is J. A. Manar. My age is 61 years. I live in
Sequyoah District, in the Cherokee Nation. I have lived here
about 14 years, and came from Missouri. I was born in Tennessee and moved to Missouri in 1861. I filed an application for
myself #532. I know Ardenia J. Manar. She is married to my
brother. Henry J. Manar is my nephew. They claim through my
mother, Sallie Lowery. She died before the war, in Kentucky.
I am not a recognized citizen of the Cherokee Nation. These
relatives are not recognized citizens of the Cherokee nation.
I was not enrolled by Dawes Commission; neither were any of
those present. We found out it was too late to enroll. I was
never enrolled at all. I was not here at the time of the bread
and strip payments. None of us were here at the time the strip
money was paid out. I lived in Tennessee in 1851 and was not
enrolled. I understand my mother was enrolled in 1835. I suppose the reason my mother was not enrolled was that my father
married my mother and she had no correspondence with her people. She lived in Kentucky at the time of death. She probably
lived in Tennessee at the time of the 1851 enrollment. I think
my father did not attend to her being enrolled. A woman in
Fourteen Mile Creek said my mother was enrolled in 1835. She
knew her in the East. She married Manar. I think my grand
father's name was Jim Lowery. He lived in North Carolina. My
grandmother's name was also Sallie Lowery. I have one sister
living; Betsey Ann Lowery. She lives in Oklahoma. She was born
in Tennessee. I had a brother, Jefferson Manar and James Henry
Manar. I had an uncle called Kit Lowery. I do not know any
brothers and and sisters other than the above. I do not know
of the name being spelled any other way. I do not know of
their ever being associated with any other tribe. I do not
know what year they left North Carolina and Georgia. They were
known as Emigrants. I never heard them talk about the treaties. I do not know whether my mother was a party to that
treaty of 1835."
SIGNED: J. A. "X" Manor, Claremore, Okla., Aug 31 1908.

11620. JINNIE ALLEN and 4 children,   Murphy, N C
Rejected. Sister of No 23058. Ancestors not on rolls. Applicant and her parents were not enrolled by Hester or Chapman
in 1884 and 1851.

217

11621. CONRAD E. WEAVER and 2 children,   Ducktown, Tenn
Rejected. Ancestor not on rolls. Does not show a genuine connection with Cherokee tribe. See Misc. Test. P. 1323.
MISC. TEST. P. 1323. 11621 - Conrad E. Weaver:
     "I am 57 years of age; was born in South Carolina. I claim
Cherokee Indian blood through my mother. I have never received
any Indian money from the government and never heard my mother
say if she received any. She died when I was small. She moved
from South Carolina to Georgia. My grandfather, Patrick Dutton, was my mother's father. I have been taught about my Indian blood all my life. My uncle raised me and he told me.
About 26 years ago I lived in Georgia, Union County. There was
a government man through there about that time. I got an affidavit at that time but never sent it in."
SIGNED: Conrad E. Weaver, Ducktown, Tenn., Jul 10 1908.

11622. LAURA HARDIN and 4 children,   Greenville, S. C.
Rejected. See special report Blythe No 153.

11623. JEROME B. OSBORN,   Standard, W Va
Rejected. See special report Sizemore No 417.

11624. LAURA PERKINS,   Kirbyville, Tex
Rejected. Niece of No 315 [? middle digit typed over] and
claims through same source.

11625. PEGGIE CLAYHORN,   Catoosa, Okla
Admitted. Grandfather Benj. Downing on Drennen roll No 539,
Tahl. Grandmother Peggie Downing on Drennen roll No 539, Tahl.
See Misc. Test. P. 2481.
MISC. TEST. P. 2481. Witness in re App No 16432-11625 - Louis
Bruere:
     "Louis Bruere is my name. I am 44 years old. I live in
Rogers County, formerly Coo-wee-scoo-wee District.   I have
lived in this county 17 years. Lived in Canadian District previously, about 21 years. I have not filed for myself but for
my children whose mother was a half-sister to Peggy Claghorne
on father's but full sister on mother's side as their parents
married brothers. They were enrolled by the Dawes Commission.
They were enrolled as Cherokees by blood. They got the strip
money, in 1894. I do not know about the bread money. My wife
is 36 years old and we are divorced. She got her blood on both
sides. Her mother was Susie Reese. She died in 1882. She lived
in Canadian District. I think she was born in that District
and she was also the mother of Peggy Claghoren. I think she
was enrolled in 1851, as she drew Old Settler money. On the
father's side they are Emigrants. Ben Downing is the grand
father of these women. William Downing was the father of my
wife. He was killed when she was a year old. He was a son of
Ben Downing. Charlie Downing was the father of Peggy Claghorn.
Both dead. They were both enrolled under the strip payment. He
lived in Canadian District when he died. I don't know whether

218

he had any other name. William also lived in Canadian District. I do not know where they lived before the war but think they came from Going Snake District. In 1886 they lived in Canadian District. There was a Katy Downing and Lucinda Downing; also Sarah, Elizabeth, when I knew them they all lived in Canadian District. There is Clarinda Downing, or Lowery. She lives at Briartown. I cannot tell you whether these people were enrolled in 1851. (Look up on 1851 Roll.) Their grand mother on their father's side was Peggy Rattlinggourd. I do not know if they had any Indian name. She had some brothers and sisters. I do not know whether he was ever known by any other name, - that is, Ben Downing. He was Sheriff in Tahlequah District. I do not know whether he had any brothers and sisters. (Look on 1851 Roll). Peggy Claghorn has a brother Ben, and her father had another set of children living in Illinois. There was a sister Elizabeth. The Downings are Emigrants. They never associated with any other tribe that I know of."
SIGNED: Louis Bruere, Claremore, Okla., Aug 31 1908.
ROLL P42 #7596 FCT COMM #12756 - Peggie Claghorn - 27

11626. SARAH PORTER, Marble, Okla
Admitted with father, No. 4205. [For Roll information See App 4205, Vol. 3]

11627. RIDER FALLING, Spavinaw, Okla
Admitted. Uncle of No 1907.
ROLL P59 #10865 FCT COMM #18568 - Rider Falling - 64

11628. TOM C. BURCKHALTER and 3 children, Vinita, Okla
Admitted. Nephew of No 2050 and claims through same source.
ROLL P36 #6251 FCT COMM # 7455 - Tom C. Burckhalter - 25
    6252   7456 - Opal L. (dau) - 6
    6253   21576 - Frances L. (dau) - 4
    6254   1554m - Tom C. (son) - 1

11629. CAROLINE HART, Laurel Springs, N C
Rejected. Sizemore case special report No 417.

11630. MAGNOLIA ADAIR, Denison, Tex*
   by C. R. Gross, Gdn.
Admitted. Grand niece of No 356. Grandfather enrolled by Chapman in 1851--1963. [* Also "RFD No 6" on roll]
ROLL P21 #3318 FCT COMM #7688 - Magnolia Adair - 5
          by C. F. Gross, Gdn.

11631. FANNY KIRKSEY, Sulphur Springs, Ala
Rejected. Applicant born in 1835 or '51 and never heard of Hester. There is a Lewis Tyner on the 35 roll, but though a large family not one appears on the 51 roll. See Misc. Test. P. 760. "Applicant born in 1831 and not enrolled either."
[Handwritten notation after summary]

MISC. TEST. P. 760. No 11631 - Fanny Kirksey:
"I am 76 years of age; was born in Hamilton County, Tenn.;
have lived my life in Georgia, Tennessee, and Alabama. I claim
Cherokee Indian blood.   I have always been told this by my
folks. I claim this through my father.   He lived in Hamilton
County, Tenn. I have never received any Indian money from the
government and never tried to get any prior to this time. My
father never received any Indian money that I know of. My father lived with the Indians when I was small. I do not know if
my father knew the Indian language, but he may have. My father
was a farmer. In 1852 I lived in Hamilton County, Tenn. I did
not hear of the Indian payment at that time nor of Chapman.   I
never heard of Hester, the enrolling agent.   None of my relatives ever received any Indian money. My brother, J. L. Tyner,
was given a claim by the Dawes Commission.   This was in 1897.
His children are living in the Cherokee Nation at the present
time. Ben Tyner, is my nephew and lives at Campbell Station,
Oklahoma. Ulysses Tyner lives at the same place. My brother
wrote to me after receiving his claim and said he would help
me if I would go out there. He went to the Nation in 1876. I
neglected to go to the Nation until my brother's death and
then did not care to go. My father was a recognized white man
and a voter."
     "This applicant had a brother named Louis Tyner who was
born in 1826. The name Louis Tyner appears on the 1835 roll as
being 7 years of age." [Notation added to end of testimony]
SIGNED: Fanny Kirksey, Ft. Payne, Ala., Jun 29 1908.
EXCEPTION CASE. Admitted. Total number of exceptions filed in
this group -- 1. Applicant is the aunt of Fannie Cummins, who
filed application #1963 and is enrolled as #9008, and both
claim through Lewis Tyner who was enrolled as an Eastern Cherokee in 1835. This claimant is the daughter of the said Lewis
Tyner, but was left in the East when her father moved West in
1850 and she was separated from the rest of the family. It is
now shown conclusively that she belongs to this family. (See
Misc. Test. P. 760, 3657, 3958-9 and 2748). Her claim is
admitted for reasons set forth in #1963. [For Testimony pp
3657, 3958-9 See App 1963, Vol. 2 - Test. P. 2748 is for an
applicant who is not connected with Fanny Kirksey]
SUPP ROLL #30365 - Fanny Kirksey - 74

11632. LINNIE SCOTT,   Chance, Okla
Admitted. Applicant's father enrolled as Oo-na-ga-dah in G. S.
No 103.   Grandparents on father's side enrolled as heads of
group G. S. No. 103.   Grandparents on mother's side enrolled
in G. S. No. 326.
MISC. TEST. P. 3430. #16599-11632 - Betsy Waker:
     "My name is Betsy Waker. I am the mother of Tom Waker (Tom
Snake -- See applications #17669 and 16498-11632) and Jim
Waker (See application 16599-11632) Neither I nor my children
were enrolled by the Dawes Commission. We were opposed to the
Allotment of land. I am a full-blood Cherokee and all my chil-

220

dren are full bloods. I have a daughter by the name of Mary Waker, #11925 (Mary Swake) and Lawyer Snake, #12614 is my son. (note: on the cards which the applicant presented there exists a conflict in the spelling of these names) Linnie Scott, #11632 is also my Daughter. I was born in Going Snake District in 1851. I was not enrolled in 1851 but my parents were. My father's name was Ned Foreman (Edward Foreman) and my mother's name was Sarah Foreman. They were enrolled together in Going Snake District in 1851. (See G. S. 326) My father had a sister by the name of Elizabeth. She married a man by the name of Johnson Proctor. They had two children by name of Margaret and Charles. (See G. S. 324). None of my ancestors ever received any Old Settler money. I was enrolled and received the Strip Payment in 1894."
SIGNED: Betsy "X" Waker, Locust Grove, Okla., Oct 13 1908.
ROLL P124 #23910 FCT COMM #20770 - Linnie Scott - 21

11633. WILLIAM R. MANEY and 3 children, Democrat, N C
Rejected. See special report Kaziah Vann No 276.

11634. LOUISA E. MULLINS and 3 children, Clay, W. V.
Rejected. See special report Sizemore No 417.

11635. MARY E. BEAN, Eureka, Okla
Admitted. Sister of No 3461.
ROLL P27 #4521 FCT COMM #16428 - Mary S. Bean - 50

11636. POLLY KNIGHT, Christie, Okla
Admitted. Mother of No 8118. Claimant's father enrolled in 1851 by Drennen G. S. 275.
ROLL P87 #16455 FCT COMM #20125 - Polly Knight - 46

11637. FRANK W. PARIS, JOHN C. PARIS, Catale, Okla
DELBERT C. PARIS, MARION F. PARIS, SUSIE O. PARIS
by Annie E. Paris, Gdn.
Admitted. Nephews and nieces of No 1099.
ROLL P107 #20635 FCT COMM #10070 - Frank W. Paris - 20
20636   10071 - John C. (bro)   - 18
20637   10072 - Delbert C. (bro) - 15
20638   10073 - Marion F. (bro) - 14
20639   10074 - Susie O. (sis)   - 9
                                    by Annie E. Paris, Gdn.

11638. MARTHA E. JOHNSON, Cartralia, Okla
Admitted. Enrolled by affidavits that applicant's mother and maternal grandmother were emigrants. See Misc. Test. P. 4366.
MISC. TEST. P. 4366. #11638 - Charlotte E. Bumgardner, in behalf of Martha E. Johnson et al:
"I am 49 years old; I am acquainted with Martha E. Johnson and I think that she was born about 1875. Her father was a white man and her mother was Eliza Deans, nee Ward. The father of Eliza Deans was John Ward and her mother was Betsy Pigeon.

221

John Ward was an Old Settler. John Ward was my father. But I had a different mother than Eliza. Both of my parents were Old Settlers. My parents have always told me that Betsy Pigeon was an Emigrant. I do not know who Betsy Pigeons parents were. John Ward and Betsy Pigeon were never married. So we have always understood. I don't think he ever lived with Betsy Pigeon. Eliza Ward was taken and raised up with us. Betsy Pigeon died when I was about 10 or twelve years old. I do not know of her having any brothers or sisters. I never heard of Betsy Pigeon ever having any other children than Eliza Ward. Elizabeth C. Ward is my father's sister. She is an Old Settler (See O. S. Roll) Martha Johnson's correct name before she was married was Martha E. Deans. Beside Martha, Clara Bowen and John Deans, there is still another child living named Abbie. I do not know what her married name is. She lives near Edna Kan" SIGNED: Charlotte E. Bumgardner, Vinita, Okla., Mar 11 1909.
Charles D. Kenney:
    "I am 53 years old; I knew Eliza Ward when she was a small child. I knew Betsy Pigeon; I first knew her in the fall of 1865. She was considered to be a full-blood Cherokee; I do not know whether she was considered to be an Emigrant Cherokee or not. Her child was always said to be the child of John Wards or Bryant Wards. I never knew Eliza Ward after she became grown. When I knew Betsy Pigeon she went by that name. She never went by the name of Ward. I have been told that she was related to the Squirrel family but I do not know what Squirrel family." SIGNED: Chas. D. Kenney, Vinita, Okla., Mar 11 1909.
ROLL P82 #15500 FCT COMM #7346 - Martha E. Johnson - 29

11639. JOHN M. THOMPSON for HIRAM P. THOMPSON, Niagria, Kans
Admitted. Grandson of No 1122. Applicant's father enrolled in 1851 by Chapman No 2090.
ROLL P138 #26773 FCT COMM #14472 - Hiram A. Thompson - 29
                                    by Jno. M. Thompson, Gdn.

11640. LYDIA S. THOMPSON for   Niagria, Kans
       FRANCIS B. THOMPSON, RICHARD L. THOMPSON,
       ALFRED D. THOMPSON
Admitted. Grandsons of No 1122. Applicant's father enrolled in 1851 by Chapman No 2090.
ROLL P138 #26759 FCT COMM #14508 - Francis B. Thompson - 19
           26760   14509 - Richard L. (bro)   - 17
           26761   14510 - Alfred D. (bro)   - 14
                                    by Lyda S. Thompson, Gdn.

11641. NANCY DICK and 1 child,   Welling, Okla
Admitted. The father of the applicant was enrolled in 567 G. S. in 1851 under the name of Ja-le-tah-ta-kee. See Misc. Test. P. 4088.
MISC. TEST. P. 4088. #11641 and #16094 - Nancy Dick...through her interpreter, William Eubanks:
    "I am about 50 years old; my father's name was Jumper of

222

Dee-lah-ta-da-gee and my mother's name is Wa-ke or Peggy. I
do not know whether my parents were living together in 1851 or
not; I have one living sister, Susannah or Susie Weel, P. O.
Welling, Okla I think; I do not think that I had any brothers
and sisters living in 1851; The father of Jumper, my father
was Gah-naw-skee-skee or Stealer and his mother was Annie or
An-nih. Annie was living with another man in 1851, Bird Chopper or Chee-squah-gah-loo-yah. I do not know whether my father
was living with his mother Annie in 1851 or not. Jumper had a
brother by the name of Josiah or Che-sah-yah, Choo-lah-suh-
tah, Katy. They were living in Tahl. Dis. in 1851; they may
have lived in Going Snake District in 1851. The husband of my
Aunt Caty was Arch Christy. (See G. S. 564. For Dee-lah-ta-
da-gee his mother and brother see G. S. 567. The father of the
applicant was enrolled as Ta-le-tah-ta-kee) I had a daughter
by the name of Wah-le-se Bear Paw. She died about the last
day of Jan. 1909. See App 16094. She left no children. She was
about 20 years old at the time of her death. I have one child
living yet by the name of Sooky Dick. She is about 15 years
old now. I made out one application and afterwards thought
that I had made a mistake and I afterwards made out another
application. I am a Night Hawk and was opposed to the allotment." SIGNED: Nancy "X" Dick, Tahlequah, Okla., Mar 30 1909.
ROLL P53 #9702 FCT COMM #20849 - Nancy Dick   - 47
          9703   20852 - Sooky (dau) - 13

11642. SARAH L. BOATMAN and 3 children,   Texana, Okla
Admitted. Applicant's grandfather enrolled by Drennen in 1852
[sic], S. B. 199, David Longfoot. See Misc. Test. P. 2756.
MISC. TEST. P. 2756. No 11642 - Mitchell Ellis:
     "My name is Mitchell Ellis; my post-office is Sallisaw,
Okla.; I was born in Cherokee Nation in 1855; I am appearing
as a witness for Sarah L. Boatman; she claims relationship to
the Cherokee Indians thru her mother, whose maiden name was
Lydia Ellis; she was about one-half Cherokee; she claims thru
her father, whose name was Dave Ellis but was also known as
Dave Longfoot; he had several brothers, namely James Longfoot,
Ned Longfoot and Samuel Longfoot and they lived in Skinbayou
District, Indian Territory; Mrs. Boatman was enrolled by the
Commission of the Five Civilized Tribe & her number is 12619."
SIGNED: Mitchell Ellis, Eufaula, Okla., Sep 10 1908.
ROLL P32 #5418 FCT COMM #12619 - Sarah L. Boatman - 24
          5419   12621 - Edgar (son)   - 4
          5420   1733m - Ocie E. (dau)   - 2
          5421   1734m - Dovie L. (dau) - 1

11643. JESSE RATTLINGGOURD, Duplicate of 1984.

11644. NELLIE M. SIMMONS and 1 child,   Westville, Okla
Admitted. Sister of No 805 and claims through same source.
ROLL P127 #24464 FCT COMM #22398 - Millie M. Simmons - 25
           24465   - Mamie (dau)   - 1/6

11645. ELIZA COMINGDEER, Duplicate of No 1757.

11646. THOMAS SMITH, Duplicate of No 864.

11647. LILLIE E. THRASHER and 1 child,   Childers, Okla
Admitted. Sister of No 8679.
ROLL P139 #27006 FCT COMM #4530 - Lillie E. Thrasher - 29
            27007   277m - Ella (dau)   - 1/4

11648. JAMES CORDREY,   Manard, Okla
Admitted. Applicant's father, Sebe Cordrey enrolled at Ill 119
ROLL P47 #8432 FCT COMM #5391 - James Cordrey - 24

11649. MARY J. ELLIS,   Centralia, Okla
Admitted. First cousin of No 8289 paternal grandmother en-
rolled by Drennen in 1851, Ill. 219.
ROLL P58 #10635 FCT COMM #8373 - Mary J. Ellis - 29

11650. JESSE S. CHAMBERS,   Tiamah, Okla
Admitted. Son of No 1371.   Father of applicant enrolled in
1851 in Tahl. No. 240.
ROLL P40 #7114 FCT COMM #27749 - Jesse S. Chambers - 22

11651. PARALEE REED and 5 children,   Claremore, Okla
Admitted. Aunt of No 709. Father of appl. "George McPherson"
"Going Snake" No 434.
ROLL P116 #22268 FCT COMM #12800 - Paralee Reed   - 47
             22269   12804 - Jack RATTLINGGOURD - 19
                                        (son)
             22270   12805 - George RATTLINGGOURD - 15
                                        (son)
             22271   12806 - Calvin RATTLINGGOURD - 13
                                        (son)
             22272   12807 - Sister RATTLINGGOURD - 11
                                        (dau)
             22273   12808 - Johnnie REED (son)   - 4

11652. DAVID C. FROGLIN and 3 children,   Claremore, Okla
Rejected. Brother of No 10946.

11653. ELIHUGH M. FROGLIN,   Claremore, Okla
Rejected. Brother of No 10946.

11654. UNDEEN GRIFFITH and 2 children,   Sallisaw, Okla
Admitted. Grandniece of No 920. Grandmother of applicant en-
rolled as Sally Byers at Flint No 387 1/2.
ROLL P68 #12671 FCT COMM # 2820 - Undeen Griffith - 21
            12672   3799m - William W. (son) - 2
            12673   3800m - Mary May (dau)   - 1
                                     (Died Mar 7, 1907)

11655. DAVID WESSON, McKey, Okla
by W. S. Wesson, Gdn.
Admitted. Applicant's grandmother enrolled by Drennen in 1852
[sic]. Flint No 366, Nancy Taylor. Misc. Test. P.. 2939.
MISC. TEST. P. 2939. App #11655 - W. S. Wesson:
"My name is W. S. Wesson. I am 38 years old, and was born
in Crockett Co., Tenn. I am guardian for David Wesson, who
claims through his mother, whose name was Peggy Wesson, and
who is dead. She was born in Flint District. She would be
about 57 years old if she was living. David Wesson's number
is 22060 on Dawes Commission. His mother has been dead about
nine years. She claims through both her parents, who were
Immigrant Cherokees. His grandmother's name is Nancy Taylor.
She lived in Delaware Dist. Nancy Taylor's father was a white
man. His wife was named Lizzie Taylor. Nancy had the following brothers and sisters: Polly and Betsey. Nancy's father's name was Joseph. See Flint 386."
SIGNED: W. S. Wesson, Sallisaw, Okla., Sep 19 1908.
ROLL P149 #28858 FCT COMM #22060 - David Wesson - 12
by W. S. Wesson, Gdn.

11656. JOHN HANNAH RIGSBY and 5 children, Sallisaw, Okla
Admitted. Grand niece of No 920. Grandmother of applicant
enrolled as Sally Byers at Flint No 387 1/2.
ROLL P117 #22519 FCT COMM # 3028 - John Hannah Rigsby - 31
22520   3029 - James F. (son)   - 9
22521   3030 - Jessie (dau)   - 7
22522   3031 - Tiny (dau)   - 5
22523   1263m - Mary L. (dau)   - 2
22524   - Joe (son)   - 1/6

11657. CATHARINE WESSON, McKey, Okla
Admitted. Sister of No 8683 and claims through same source.
ROLL P149 #28857 FCT COMM #22059 - Catherine Wesson - 27

11658. RACHEL TALON, Briggs, Okla
Admitted. Mother of No 2234. Applicant enrolled in 1851 in
Flint Dist. No 283.
ROLL P140 #27147 FCT COMM #18075 - Rachel Tolan - 57
27148   18077 - Watt WILSON (son) - 16
(App 11659)

11659. RACHEL TOLEN, Gdn., Included in No 11658.

11660. EDWARD McLAIN, Braggs, Okla
Admitted. Son of McLain, enrolled 260 Ill. Nephew of No 4054.
ROLL P94 #18015 FCT COMM #5902 - Edward McLain - 34

11661. RICHARD MORRIS, Braggs, Okla
Admitted. Nephew o No 2198.
ROLL P102 #19493 - Richard Morris - 24

225

11662. RICHARD MARTIN and 2 children,   Braggs, Okla
Rejected. Brother to No 11485.
EXCEPTION CASE. Recommended. Total number of exceptions
filed in this group — 1. Brother of #11485 and admitted for
the same reason.
SUPP ROLL #30688 FCT COMM #4648 - Richard Martin   - 48
         30689   4652 - Octavia (dau)   - 13
         30690   4654 - Sanford M. (son) - 8

11663. JESSE McLAIN,   Braggs, Okla
Admitted. Nephew of No 4054. Grandmother, Della McLain en-
rolled 260 Ill. [* FCT # blurred on roll]
ROLL P94 #18037 FCT COMM #5518* - Jesse McLain - 29

11664. SARAH SILK, Minor, Included in No 4404. Duplicate

11665. JENNIE SQUIRREL,   Cookson, Okla
Admitted. Niece of No 1245, and claims through same ancestors.
Father of applicant enrolled in 1851, in Saline Dist. No. 103,
under name of Ter-ger-wor-se. [For Roll information See App
11600]

11666. WILLIAM J. LANGLEY and 1 child,   Alluwe, Okla
Admitted. First cousin of No 805 and claims through the same
source. Father Noah Langley 1905 Chapman.
ROLL P88 #16731 FCT COMM #16628 - William J. Langley - 32
         16732   2366m - Andrew J. (son)   - 1

11667. CHARLES L. STARR,   Stilwell, Okla
Admitted. Nephew of No 2204.
ROLL P131 #25419 FCT COMM #15694 - Charles L. Starr - 28
          25420   4788 - Amy (wife)   - 24
                                 (App 27911)
          25421   3260m - Cherry (dau)   - 4
          25422   3261m - Ezekiel (son)   - 3
          25423   3262m - Lula (dau)   - 1

11668. NANCY OWL,   Stilwell, Okla
Admitted. Mother of No 5896. Enrolled as Nancy, Flint, No 307.
ROLL P106 #20427 FCT COMM #1856 - Nancy Owl - 65

11669. SCOTT WELCH,   Dragger, Okla
Admitted. Nephew of No 132.
ROLL P148 #28819 FCT COMM # 946 - Scott Welch - 4?*
          28820   947 - Elizabeth (dau) - 1?
          28821   948 - Mary (dau)   - 1?
          28822   949 - Charlotte (dau) - 1?
          28823   950 - John (son)   - 1?
          28824   4617m - George (son)   - under 10
          28825   4618m - Ollie (dau)   - under 10
[* last digit of ages cut off]

226

11670. MARY M. McCAUSLAND and 1 child,   Rose, Okla
Admitted.   Applicant claims through grandmother Elizabeth
Fields enrolled No 32 Disp. Mother not living in 1851. D. C.
7060 1/16. See Misc. Test. P. 2836. [NOTE: Should be P. 3826]
MISC. TEST. P. 3826.   25567 - Also 11670 - Henry Sitsler:
    "I am about 53 years of age. I do not claim any Indian
blood myself but made application for minor children who claim
Indian blood through my deceased wife. Mary M. McCausland
Appl. No. 11670 is a full sister to my minor children and made
application for herself. My wife died about nine years ago.
She was born either in 61 or 62. She was nearly a half breed
Cherokee. My children and Mrs. McCausland are all alloted by
the Daws Commission. Mrs McCausland's number is 7060. The
children are James Lewis, 30136. George W. 30135. I just have
the two minor children. My wife derived her Indian blood from
her mother, Elizabeth Field or sometimes known as Goodfield.
My wife's mother married a man by the name of Bashears. He was
a white man. It was after 51 that she married him. Elizabeth's
father was named Richard Field or sometimes called Goodfield.
Elizabeth had one sister but I don't know her name. I don't
know just where Elizabeth was living in 51 but it was in the
Cherokee nation up towards the Kansas line. I think Richard's
wife was a white woman. Think Elizabeth was born in the Old
Nation back East. Don't know when she came out here. I don't
know when Richard Fields died or whether he was living in 51
or not. Elizabeth never had but the one half sister that I
know of and no brothers. My wife was a recognized citizen of
the Cherokee Nation and I think her mother was before her.
Don't know of any brothers or sister that Richard Field ever
had. My wife shared in the Strip payment and received bread
money before that. None of her people ever received any Old
Settler money that I know of. I can't tell what District
Elizabeth was living in in 51 or who she was living with and
don't know who to go to to find out."
SIGNED: Henry Sitsler, Locust Grove, Okla., Oct 13 1908.
ROLL P92 #17582 FCT COMM # 7060 - Mary McCausland   - 26
         17583   3241m - Fannie Bell (dau) -   2

11671. WILLIAM BELL,   Ballard, Okla
Admitted. Grandnephew of No 132.
ROLL P28 #4794 FCT COMM #30318 - William Bell - 22

11672. ANNIE BAT SANDERS,   Draggers, Okla
Admitted. Sister of No 5780 and claims through same source.
MISC. TEST. P. 3775. 11672-5780 - Annie Sanders...through Tom
Roach, Interpreter:
    "I am about 54 years of age. My father had a half sister
by the name of Sah-dah-ye on the mother's side. Her father's
name was Nee-chee and my father's mother was named An-nih. See
G. S. 142. They lived in Going Snake District. My grandfather
on my mother's side was a white man. My father's name was O-
see or Osee Dragger or Cun-seen. (Possibly Saline 31) My moth-

227

er's name I-yeh-guh. Her English name was Malinda. My mother
had a sister by the name of Julia. Never knew of her having
any other name. I never knew of her having any other brothers
or sisters. I am enrolled by the Daws Commission as Annie Bat
Number 27958."
SIGNED: Annie Sanders, Locust Grove, Okla., Sep 29 1908.
ROLL P122 #23451 FCT COMM #27958 - Annie Bat Sanders - 52

11673. GEORGE JUSTICE,   Cookson, Okla
Rejected. Ancestors on fathers side do not appear to be on
the rolls. Mothers side Old Settlers. See letter herein.

11674. ROXIE CANNON,   Dragger, Okla
Admitted. Grandniece of No 132.
ROLL P38 #6612 FCT COMM #22374 - Claud Cannon - 23 (App 23501)
        6613   30319 - Roxie (wife)   - 20
        6614   30324 - Mattie E. (dau) - 4
        6615   2790m - Effie L. (dau) - 2

11675. JOHN W. McPHERSON,   Pryor Creek, Okla
Admitted.   Paternal grandfather John V. McPherson, who has
filed application herein No 5197, enrolled by Drennen in 1851
G. S. 436. See Misc. Test. P. 436. [NOTE: Misc. Test. P. 436
is an unrelated case.] First cousin once removed to No. 384.
MISC. TEST. P. 4358.   #11675 - George W. Mayes, in behalf of
John W. McPherson, et al:
     "I am 60 years old;   I am acquainted with John McPherson;
Beatrice is a full sister of John; They are half-brother and
half-sister to Lewis L. McPherson, on the father's side; The
mother of Lewis was Cherokee. The mother of John and Beatrice
was white; The father of these children died in about 1901 and
was about thirty years old when he died; The father of these
children got his Indian blood thru both his parents; They were
living in 1851, that is, the grandparents of these children on
their father's side; He is still living, the grandfather of
these children on their father's side near Stilwell, Okla.
That is his P. O.   I have heard that Silas McPherson was a
brother of the Grandfather. (See G. S. 436)."
SIGNED: Geo. W. Mayes, Pryor Creek, Okla., Mar 12 1909.
ROLL P95 #18138 FCT COMM #16546 - John W. McPherson - 6
                              by Ida McPherson, Gdn.

11676. BEATRICE McPHERSON,   Pryor Creek, Okla
Admitted. Full sister of No 11675.
ROLL P95 #18127 FCT COMM #16545 - Beatrice McPherson - 8
                              by Ida McPherson, Gdn.

11677. LEWIS L. McPHERSON,   Pryor Creek, Okla
Admitted. Half brother on father's side of No 11675 and claims
through same source.
ROLL P95 #18139 FCT COMM #16544 - Lewis L. McPherson - 18
                              by George W. Mays, Gdn.

11678. C. VERNER McPHERSON,   Pryor Creek, Okla
Admitted. Half brother on the father's side to No 11675.
ROLL P95 #18128 FCT COMM #16543 - C. Verner McPherson - 20

11679. McDUFF ROSS and 4 children,   Texanna, Okla
Admitted. Cousin of No 99.
ROLL P120 #23127 FCT COMM #18057 - McDuff Ross   - 51
          23128   30799 - Dot (dau)   - 15
          23129   30800 - Kit (son)   - 14
          23130   30801 - Lola (dau)   - 11
          23131   30802 - McKinley (son) - 8

11680. PERRY B. BALENTINE,   Tahlequah, Okla
Admitted. Applicant's mother not living in 1851. Grandmother
enrolled as Nancy Balentine, Disp No 2. Uncle Hamilton 2 Disp.
See letter herein.
ROLL P25 #4066 FCT COMM #14124 - Perry B. Balentine - 20

11681. JOHANNA WEBB,   Muskogee, Okla
Admitted. Sister of No 11680 and claims through the same
ancestors.
ROLL P148 #28654 FCT COMM #14125 - Johanna Webb - 18

11682. LOUISA RAY,   Tate, Ga
Rejected. Niece of No 5041.

11683. MALINDA PARKER,   Tate, Ga
Rejected. Niece of No 5041.

11684. WILLIAM BIRD, Jr.   Tahlequah, Okla
Admitted. Son of No 3800 and claims through same source.
ROLL P30 #5118 FCT COMM #18257 - William Bird, Jr. - 20

11685. HENRIETTA JACKSON and 3 children,   Fort Gibson, Okla*
Admitted. Niece of No 4054. Mother enrolled as Letitia McLain
afterward called "Mary" No 260 Ill. (Twice married).
[* Residence "McLain, Okla" on roll]
ROLL P80 #15176 FCT COMM #17304 - Henrietta Jackson - 51
          15177   17306 - Wilson (son)   - 17
          15178   17305 - Anna May (dau)   - 17
          15179   17307 - Susan Ethel (dau) - 15

11686. SABINA ADAIR,   Dutch Mills, Ark
Admitted. Sister of No 8289.
ROLL P21 #3367 FCT COMM #27083 - Sabina Adair - 31

11687. JOHN DANIEL, ALYCE DANIEL,   Afton, Okla
        ADOLPHUS DANIEL, KATIE DANIEL
          by William Buzzard, Gdn.
Admitted. Jennie Daniel Grandmother of children enrolled as
Jane Welch 187 Del. Great grandmother Celia, 187 Del. Parents
not old enough to be on the '51 roll.

229

```
ROLL P50 #9131 FCT COMM #18642 - John Daniel    - 12
         9132            18643 - Alyce (sis)     - 10
         9133            18644 - Adolphus (bro) -  8
         9134            18645 - Katie (sis)     -  6
                              by William Buzzard, Gdn.
```

11688. JESSIE PETER USSERY and 3 children, Aubrey, Tex
Rejected. Ancestors do not appear on the rolls. They were
not parties to the treaties of 1835-6-46. If they are Cherokees at all they must be Old Settlers. See letter herein.
EXCEPTION CASE. 11688. John F. Ussery, App 43910, Miami,
Okla. Rejected. Total number of exceptions filed in this
group -- 3. Original recommendation renewed.

11689. MOSES FEELING,   Tahlequah, Okla
Admitted. The grandfather of the applicant on his father's
side was enrolled in Tahlequah Dist. by Drennen in 1851 under
the name of Oo-too-lah-ta-nah. See letter in application. Duplicate of #2989. [For Roll information See App 10304]

11690. ELVIA E. PARRIS,   Tahlequah, Okla
Admitted. Niece of No 361. [For Roll information See App 8315,
Vol. 4]

11691. JOHN W. ROUP and 1 child,   Whitehead, N C
Rejected. See special report Sizemore No 417.

11692. PAIRLEE ADOLPH and 3 children,   2500 Madison Ave
                                          Kansas City, Mo
Rejected. Does not appear that applicant or her ancestors were
ever enrolled. Does not appear that they were living within
the limits of the Cherokee Domain in 1835-6 and 1846 as a recognized member of the tribe. Does not appear that they ever
lived with the Cherokees as recognized members of the tribe.

11693. ELON HOPPERS and 7 children,   Ratler, N C
Rejected. See special report Sizemore No 417.

11694. NAN HART,   Laurel Springs, N C
Rejected. See special report Sizemore No 417.

11695. GUY McNEIL or WASHINGTON & 2 children, Charlotte, Tenn
Rejected. Applicant and both of his parents were slaves. See
application.

11696. JOHN B. MAYFIELD, TRIXIE V. MAYFIELD, Rowland, Okla
          by Amanda C. Mayfield, Gdn.
Admitted. Claims through grandfather enrolled as Carter V.
Mayfield, Going Snake No 311.
```
ROLL P98 #18657 FCT COMM #3741 - John B. Mayfield - 10
         18658            3742 - Trixie V. (sis)  -  9
                              by Amanda Mayfield, Gdn.
```

11697. MARY HILDERBRAND,   Braggs, Okla
          by Geo. Meeker, Gdn.
Admitted. Applicant's father enrolled Tahl. "Stephen Hilde-
brand" 36.
ROLL P75 #14187 FCT COMM #26997 - S. Mary Hilderbrand - 13
                                    by Geo. Meeker, Gdn.

11698. GEO. C. MEEKER,   Braggs, Okla
Admitted. Cousin once removed of No 859. Mother probably not
born until after 1851. Grandfather Joseph Hildebrand Ill. 11.
Great grandfather Michael, Chapman 1534. See letter of J. H.
W. in 3005.
ROLL P98 #18709 FCT COMM #23269 - George O. Meeker - 28
          18710   21888 - Bertha (wife)   - 23
                                  (App 23227)

11699. BEATRICE HICKS and 1 child,   Tahlequah, Okla
Admitted. Sister to No 11466.
ROLL P75 #14002 FCT COMM #14439 - Beatrice Hicks   - 21
          14003   1175m - Mary Bell (dau) - 3

11700. SARAH BOLYN and 4 children,   Cookson, Okla
Admitted. This applicant's mother Nelly Taylor or Tail is en-
rolled by Drennen from Flint Dist. under group No 623.
[For Roll information See App 10303]

11701. SARAH E. WATERS and 4 children,   Checotah, Okla
Rejected. Cousin of No 923, and claims through same ancestors.

11702. CHARLES L. MORRIS, Duplicate of No 17.

11703. FRANCES PARRIS and 3 children,   Chance, Okla
Admitted. Niece of No 5107 and claims through same source.
ROLL P108 #20803 FCT COMM #941 - Jesse R. Parris - 35
                                  (App 29771)
          20804   942 - Frances (wife) - 36
          20805   943 - Fannie (dau)   - 12
          20806   944 - Elizabeth (dau) - 10
          20807   945 - Josie B. (dau) - 6

11704. CALLIE CRITTENDON,   Proctor, Okla
Admitted. Niece of No 10 and claims through same source.
[For Roll information See App 9231, Vol. 4]

11705. JASPER N. ADKINSON and 6 children, Tahlequah, Okla
Admitted. First cousin of Maud Lane No 2379 and is admitted
for the same reasons.
ROLL P22 #3466 FCT COMM #16642 - Jasper N. Adkisson - 38
          3467   16643 - Susie (wife) - 34 (App 29238)
                                  (Died Dec. '06)
          3468   16644 - Clarence M. (son) - 14
          3469   16645 - Thomas E. (son)   - 11

                              231

11705. JASPER N. ADKINSON (Cont)
            3470   16646 - Kittie (dau)   - 9
            3471   16647 - Paralee (dau)   - 7
            3472   16648 - Callice M. (dau)   - 5
            3473   3840m - Susie D. (dau)   - 3

11706. GEORGE L. SMITH,   Tellico Plains, Tenn
Admitted. First cousin of No 613 and claims through the same
source. Applicant's father enrolled by Drennen No 1370. [Prob-
ably should by Chapman No 1370.]
ROLL P17 #2404 - George L. Smith - 25

11707. KATE WRIGHT and 2 children,   Coffeyville, Kans
Admitted. Niece of No 6792 and claims through same ancestors.
ROLL P154 #29988 FCT COMM #10780 - Kate Wright   - 32
            29989   10781 - Shelley K. (son) - 6
            29990   10782 - William J. (son) - 4

11708. BETTIE BUSH,   Marble City, Okla
Admitted. Niece of No 1070.   [For Roll information See App
9639, Vol. 4]

11709. JAS. R. CAMP,   Chattanooga, Tenn
Admitted. Second cousin of #1208, and claimant's grandmother
Nancy Compton is on Chapman roll No 1866. Mother was born af-
ter 1851.
ROLL P7 #424 - Jas. M.* Camp - 24
[* "R" crossed out]

11710. GEORGE MIXWATER,   Bartlesville, Okla
Admitted. Brother of No 2392.
ROLL P100 #19196 FCT COMM #20705 - George Mixedwater - 36
            19197   25946 - Nellie (wife)   - 23
                                  (App 18490)

11711. EMMA PARKER,   Jasper, Ga
Rejected. Niece of Geo. W. Parker (4067).

11712. OSCAR PARKER,   Jasper, Ga
Rejected. Nephew to Geo. W. Parker (4067).

11713. AMERICA R. SALTFIELD and 6 children, Blainsville, Ga
Rejected. Sister of No 4748 and claims through same source.

11714. LAVENA GAYLOR COODEY,   Eufaula, Okla
Admitted. Cousin of No 4008 and claims through same source.
ROLL P46 #8279 FCT COMM #12627 - Lavena Gaylor Coodey - 24

11715. NIOTO B. [or E.] REES,   Santa Cruz, Cal
Rejected. Daughter of No 10609 and claims through the same
source.

232

11716. KATY VANN and 2 children,   Leach, Okla
Admitted. Applicant's mother, Nancy, was enrolled by Drennen
in Del. Dist. No 800. See Misc. Test. P. 3832.
MISC. TEST. P. 3832.   11716 – Tom Chuc–ku–luch...through Tom
Roach, Interpreter...in behalf of Katy Vann:
   "I am about 68 years of age. Katy Vann is my wife's daughter. Her mother used to be Nancy Vann but now goes by the name
of Nancy Chuc–ku–luck. Nancy is an Emmigrant. She just went by
the name of Nancy in 51. Think she was living with her oldest
sister Oo–Loo–cha in 51, her parents were dead. Oo–loo–cha's
husband was named Gah–lay–nee–skih. They were living in Delaware District. They had a boy by the name of George. Jesse was
a brother of Nancy and Oo–loo–cha and lived with them.   See
Del. 800. Katy Vann's Daws Commission Number is 32553."
SIGNED: Tom Chuc–ku–luch, Locust Grove, Okla., Oct 12 1908.
ROLL P143 #27737 FCT COMM #32553 – Katy Vann   – 32
            27738   32554 – Oo–kil–lie (son) – 7
            27739   3015m – George (son)   – 5

11717. NANNIE MUSH,   Rose, Okla
Admitted. Applicant's paternal grandparents enrolled by Dren-
nen in 1851, Saline No 273. See Saline 64.
ROLL P103 #19784 FCT COMM #20779 – Nannie Mush – 26

11718. JAMES H. HARRIS,   Collbran, Colo
Admitted. Brother of No 11721 and claims through same source.
ROLL P72 #13413 – James H. Harris – 43

11719. WILLIAM DUKE and 5 children,   Box No 3 RFD No 6
                                           San Antonio, Tex
Admitted. Applicant in the Act of Congress Roll as "William
Duke" and his mother "Matilda Duke", also in Act. of Congress
Roll.
ROLL P56 #10240 – William Duke   – 58
          10241 – Mahala E. (dau)   – 18
          10242 – Jesse Bowen (son) – 16
          10243 – William H. (son) – 14
          10244 – Robert E. (son)   – 11
          10245 – Buford A. (son)   – 8

11720. EMMA VANN,   Pryor Creek, Okla
            by Jess H. Vann, Gdn.
Admitted. Niece of No 11721 and claims through same source.
ROLL P143 #27658 FCT COMM #6901 – Emma Vann – 16
                         by Jess H. Vann, Gdn.

11721. MATILDA A. SNODGRASS,   2310 Wilson St.*
                                           Denver, Colo
Admitted. Applicant's mother and grandmother on Act of Congress as "Orethea and Matilda Elliott." [* "Welton" St. on
roll]
ROLL P130 #25118 – Matilda A. Snodgrass – 49

11722. EVA M. HARRIS,   Pryor Creek, Okla
              by Mary S. Guartney, Gdn.
Admitted. Niece of No 1172 [should be 11721] and claims thru
same source.
ROLL P72 #13404 - Eva M. Harris - 13
              by Mary S. Gwartney, Gdn.

11723. GEORGE W. DAVIDSON and 3 children, Edith, Tex
Admitted. Applicant's mother "Matilda Duke" in the Act of
Congress Roll.
ROLL P51 #9279 - George W. Davidson - 42
         9280 - Earl (son)   - 10
         9281 - Roxie (dau)   - 7
         9282 - Dollie (dau)   - 4

11724. DORTHY M. MATHEWS and 2 children,   Nubia, Tex
Admitted. Applicant's mother Mahala Killingsworth in Act of
Congress Roll.
ROLL P97 #18526 - Dorothy M. Mathews - 47
         18527 - Morda (dau)   - 15
         18528 - Herles (son)   - 12

11725. MISSOURI J. FREEMAN and 2 children, Mount Judea, Ark
Admitted. Applicant's mother enrolled as "Mary Killingsworth
and father enrolled as "Matthew Killingsworth".   First cousin
of No. 11724.
ROLL P64 #11840 - Missouri J. Freeman - 46
         11841 - Rhoda A. (dau)   - 15
         11842 - William H. (son)   - 12

11726. MAHALA BOWEN,   Prairie Lea, Tex
Admitted. Sister of No 11723 and claims through same source.
Applicant in Act of Congress Roll as "Mahala Duke".
ROLL P32 #5556 - Mahala Bowen - 56

11727. JOSEPH L. HILLIN,   Pryor Creek, Okla
Admitted. Nephew of No 11733 and claims through same source.
ROLL P76 #14257 - Joseph L. Hillin - 37

11728. IDA L. LONG and 1 child,   Pawnee, Okla
Admitted. Cousin of No 3906 and claims through same source.
[NOTE: no child on roll]
ROLL P91 #17287 - Ida L. Long - 25

11729. DOMITILIA MILLER,   Pryor Creek, Okla
              ISABELLA I. MILLER, LUCY D. MILLER
              by Alex. Miller, Gdn.
Admitted. First cousins once removed of No 3906 and claims
through same source.   James I. Miller is rejected as he was
born in August 1906.
ROLL P99 #18918 - Domitilia Miller - 6
         18919 - Isabela L. (sis) - 4

11729. DOMITILIA MILLER, et al (Cont)
          18920 - Lucy O. (sis)   - 2
               by Alex. A. Miller, Gdn.

11730. ALEX. A. MILLER and 3 children,   Pryor Creek, Okla
Admitted. First cousin once removed of No 3906 and claims
through same source.
ROLL P98 #18856 FCT COMM #   - Alex. A. Miller - 39
          18857   21798 - Charles E. (son) - 7
          18858   3567m - Carrie E. (dau) - 4
          18859   - Ed (son)   - 1

11731. JOHN W. VAUGHN and 5 children, Duplicate of No 3906.

11732. WILLIAM HILLIN,   Sapulpa, Okla
Admitted. Nephew of No 11733 and claims through same source.
See Misc. Test. 4351. Grandmother Mahala Hilliam and fathers
brothers and sister on Act of Congress Roll.
MISC. TEST. P. 4351. #11732 - David I. Elliot:
     "I am 55 years old; I am a cousin of William Hillim [sic];
His grandmother Mahala Hillim and my father were brother and
sister. I am a second cousin of William Hillim; my father's
name was David Elliot; William Hillim gets his Indian blood
thru his father. The brothers and sisters of Andy Hillim were
James, Jesse, Thomas, Winfred, Nancy. Both the wives of Andy
Hillim were white women; The first wife was the mother of
William. She died just after he was born and his grandmother,
Mahala Hillim raised him; They were living in Jackson Co.,
Ala. at that time. I think that they came out here in about
1853; William was the only child Andy had by his first marriage; The first wife of Andy Hillim died before 1851; I do
not know whether Andy Hillim came out to the Indian Territory
or not; The rest of his brothers and sisters did. James Hillim
is still living at Pine Hills, Texas; William Hillim is living
now at Sapulpa, Okla. I do not know when or where Andy Hillim
died; The children of Andy Hillim by his second wife are all
living her[e] in the Cherokee Nation; One of them Bettie
Lunigan lives near Webbers Falls, Okla.; I think that Andy was
the oldest child of Mahala Hillim; if Andy Hillim is not on
the roll of 1851 I do not know why he wasn't; I do not know
where he was at that time.   Mahala Hillim was a one eight
Cherokee; and Mahala's father was Joseph Elliot and Joseph
Elliot's father was also named Joseph Elliot.   The old Joseph
Elliot was a white man and married a half breed Cherokee
woman; my father had a place in Jackson Co., Ala. and in 1838
he was paid for his improvements under the treaty of 1835; my
fathers got $92.82 per capita money, for himself, and each of
the minor children; William Hillin is not enrolled by the Daws
Commission on the ground that none of his ancestors were on
the rolls of the Cherokee Indians; I was not enrolled for the
same reason; our cases rested on the same testimony."
SIGNED: David I. Elliott, Pryor Creek, Okla., Mar 13 1909.

ROLL P75 #14259 - William Hillin - 56

11733. JAMES B. HILLIN,   Rusk, Tex
Admitted. Applicant enrolled as "James Hilliain" in act of
Congress Roll. Applicant's mother enrolled as "Mahala Hilliam"
ROLL P76 #14244 - James B. Hillin - 75

11734. PINKNEY H. HILLIN,   Hereford, Tex
Admitted. Nephew of No 11733 and claims through same source.
ROLL P76 #14258 - Pinkney H. Hillin - 39

11735. DAISY V. HARRIS,   320 Emery St., Longmont, Colo
Admitted. First cousin once removed of No 3906 and claims
through same source.
ROLL P71 #13395 - Daisy V. Harris - 25

11736. LOUISA J. LIGON,   Snyder, Tex
Admitted. Applicant enrolled on Act of Congress Roll as
"Lucia Elliott".
ROLL P90 #17051 - Louisa J. Ligon - 68

11737. HARRIETT HOWARD,   Pinehill, Tex
Rejected. Claims through deceased husband.

11738. WILLIAM VAUGHN,   Chatsworth, Cal
Admitted. First cousin No 3906 and claims through the same
source. Applicant's father enrolled "Josiah E. Vaughn" on Act
of Congress Roll.
ROLL P144 #27828 - William Vaughn - 44

11739. JESS CRITTENDEN,   Chance, Okla
Admitted. Applicant's mother, Maria Bull-frog and his grand
father Bull-frog were enrolled by Drennen G. S. 148. See Misc.
Test. [no page given].
MISC. TEST. P. 3429. #11739 - Betsy Waker:
    "My name is Betsy Waker. I know Jess Crittenden. We live
in the same house. He was not enrolled by the Dawes Commission. He was opposed to the allotment of land. He is a full-
blood nearly -- his mother was a full-blood and his father
about a half Cherokee. His father's name was Sam Crittenden
and his mothers name was Mariah Crittenden. I do not know
whether they were enrolled in 1851. I do not know whether they
were born or not. He had an uncle by the name of Dun-a-waws
Bullfrog -- a brother of his mother. I think that they would
have been enrolled in Going Snake District if enrolled in
1851. I do not know the maiden name of Mariah Crittenden. The
grandmothers of Jess Crittenden were Dah-ne on the father's
side and An-nie on the mother's side. I do not know the names
of the grandfathers of Jess Crittenden.
    "I have know this boy ever since he was a small child. He
is now about 30 years old. He never drew any Old Settler money
and neither did his parents to my knowledge. His parents were

236

always regarded as Emigrant Cherokees. I knew personally the grandmothers of applicant. They were born I have always been told in the Old Nation. His parents and grandparents have always been with the Cherokee tribe. He was enrolled and drew the strip payment in 1894.

"I think that the grandparents (grandmothers of applicant were enrolled in Going Snake District in 1851. (See G. S. 128) I think that the husband of Dah-nee was Ned. (This testimony was taken without the application before me. See application in connection with this testimony.)"
SIGNED: Betsy "X" Waker, Locust Grove, Okla., Oct 13 1908.
ROLL P49 #8812 FCT COMM #19653 - Jess Crittenden - 39

11740. SIDNEY J. LANGLEY and 8 children, Baptist, Okla
Admitted. Brother of No 805 and claims through same source.
ROLL P88 #16715 FCT COMM #22577 - Sidney J. Langley - 36

16716	22578 - Joseph B. (son)	- 15
16717	22579 - Alice L. (dau)	- 14
16718	22580 - Lock (son)	- 14
16719	22581 - Ollie H. (son)	- 12
16720	22582 - William J. (son)	- 8
16721	22583 - Lillie J. (dau)	- 6
16722	22584 - John C. (son)	- 4
16723	- Katie E. (dau)	- 1/6

11741. JOSEPH H. LANGLEY, Westville, Okla
Admitted. Brother of No 805 and claims through same source.
ROLL P88 #16676 FCT COMM #22400 - Joseph H. Langley - 23

11742. ALICE A. WOODS, Westville, Okla
Admitted. Sister of No 805 and claims through same source.
ROLL P154 #29906 FCT COMM #22401 - Alice A. Woods - 20

11743. GEORGE W. SIZEMORE and 4 children, Exkman, W Va
Rejected. See special report Sizemore No 417.

11744. GEORGE HURD and 5 children, Nowata, Okla
Rejected. Applicant's grandfather seems to be the only ancestor enrolled and he is enrolled as an Old Settler in Del. Dist No 41.

11745. THOMAS B. FRENCH and 2 children, Inola, Okla
Admitted. Applicant claims through father Thos. F. French, whose mother Margaret French, was enrolled in Ill. Dist. 83. Her maiden name Fields. Applicant not entitled through James Kell, tho an Emigrant, as his daughter. Applicant's mother Alice Kell, was an Old Settler.
ROLL P64 #11885 FCT COMM #11645 - Thomas B. French - 37

11886	11646 - Lila (wife)	- 29
	(App 13422)	
11887	11647 - Thomas F. (son)	- 11
11888	1988m - Walter P. (son)	- 2

237

11746. RUSSELL P. JONES,   RFD No 2, Lethia Springs, Ga
Rejected. Neither applicant nor ancestors were ever enrolled.
Does not establish fact of descent from a person who was a
party to the treaty of 1835-6 and 1846. (See Misc. Test. P.
1081).
MISC. TEST. P. 1081. Testimony in case of Russell Perry
Jones, #11746 - Alfred D. Jones:
   "My name is Alfred D. Jones. I live at Lithia Springs,
Ga. I am 58 years old. I know Russell Perry Jones. He is my
brother. We claim our Indian blood through my mother and her
mother and father. I have always been taught that I had Cherokee blood. My mother died in 1890 and was between 60 and 70
years old. My mother was born in Lumpkin Co., Ga. I don't
know where my grandmother came from. My mother and grand
parents as far as I know lived separate with themselves. My
grandfather's name was Hampton Perdue. I never heard of my
mother or her parents getting any money or land from the Government on account of their Indian blood. I never heard of
them being enrolled. My mother and her parents lived and died
here. One of my aunts went west, went to Texas. In 1882 I
was living in Hall County. My father was a white man. I never
heard of him having any Indian blood in him. My father and
mother so far as I know always lived with the white people. I
never heard my mother speak of a Treaty in 1835. I have heard
of the Indians being driven away from this country. I could
not say why my mother was not driven away with the Indians."
SIGNED: Alfred D. Jones, Atlanta, Ga., Jul 7 1908.
EXCEPTION CASE. 11746. Russell P. Jones, Austell, Ga. Rejected. Total number of exceptions filed in this group — 11.
Original recommendation renewed.

11747. HATTIE C. PAYNE,   Tahlequah, Okla
          for David R. Trainor, Deceased
Rejected. Applicant's husband died Jan. 7, 1895. See No. 4594
- 361*. [* Should be 741]

11748. ARCH L. WELLS,   Inola, Okla
Admitted. Brother to 11501 and claims through same source.
ROLL P149 #28841 FCT COMM #12463 - Arch L. Wells - 22

11749. WILLIAM E. SWEANEY and 2 children, Jefferson City, Mo
Rejected. Claims through same source as No 3935.

11750. N. L., BIRD and EMMA WELLS,   Inola, Okla
          by Volney E. Wells,
Admitted. Brother and sister to No 11501 and claims through
same people.
EXCEPTION CASE. 11750. Effie M. Wells, by Volney E. Wells,
father, Inola, Okla. Admitted. Total number of exceptions
filed in this group — 1. Effie M. Wells is of unsound mind
and her father applied for her along with his three minor
children, but being of age she was not allowed, which was a

238

clerical error. Brother on Miller Roll No. 28848.
ROLL P149 #28848 FCT COMM #12465 - N. L. Wells - 15
          28849   12466 - Burl (bro) - 12
          28850   12467 - Emma (sis) - 10
                         by Volney E. Wells, Gdn.
SUPP ROLL #30848 FCT COMM #12462 - Effie M. Wells - 32
                         by Volnie E. Wells, Committee

11751. SAMUEL J. ELROCK and 7 children,   Isabella, Tenn
Rejected. Ancestors not on rolls. Does not show a genuine
connection with Cherokee Tribe. See Misc. Test. P. 1316.
MISC. TEST. P. 1316. No 11751 - Samuel J. Elrod:
     "I am 51 years of age; was born in Polk County, Tenn.;
have spent my life in North Carolina, Georgia, and Tenn.   I
claim Cherokee Indian blood through my mother. I have never
received any Indian money from the government nor did my mother. My mother never tried to get any Indian money that I know
of. I did not live with the Indians and do not speak the Indian language. About twenty years ago I lived in Floyd Co.,
Ga. I do not remember a government agent enrolling people at
that time. About twelve years ago there was a man through
here. I think he was from the Territory. I filed a claim.
My mother's grandfather was the Indian. I never saw my grand
father. My mother's grandfather was Thomas Duke. My grand
mother, Martha or Patsy Duke, was the Indian. She did not
live with the Indians when I knew her."
SIGNED: Samuel J. Elrod, Ducktown, Tenn., Jul 10 1908.
EXCEPTION CASE.   11751.   Samuel J. Elrod and 9 children,
Isabella, Tenn. Rejected.   Total number of exceptions filed
in this group -- 4. Original recommendation renewed.

11752. STAND W. McCOY,   Stilwell, Okla
          by Nancy Sixkiller, Gdn.
Admitted. Cousin of No 5300 and claims through same source.
ROLL P93 #17737 FCT COMM #19328 - Stand W. McCoy - 11
                         by Nancy Sixkiller, Gdn.

11753. EVALEY MORRIS and 1 child,   Stilwell, Okla
Admitted. Brother of No 9380. Cousin of No 5919 and claims
through same ancestors.
ROLL P101 #19411 FCT COMM # 4220 - Enoley Morris   - 33
          19412   1606m - Thomas P. (son) - 1/4

11754. MAGGIE SIXKILLER, Duplicate of No 2873.

11755. WILL GREECE,   Braggs, Okla
Admitted. Half brother on mother's side of No 3147.
[For Roll information See App 9173, Vol. 4]

11756. ANDREW J. LANGLEY and 3 children, Westville, Okla
Admitted. Nephew of No 205 and claims through same source.

239

ROLL P88 #16659 - Andrew J. Langley - 42
            16660 - John J. (son)   - 15
            16661 - Robert E. (son)   - 15 [?]
            16662 - Rena Ellen (dau)   - 12

11757. THURSEY A. FORSYTHE,   Dayton, Tenn
Rejected. Ancestor not enrolled. Does not show a genuine connection with Cherokee tribe. Applicant failed to appear to
give testimony. Also neglected to answer letter of inquiry in
regard to family relationship.

11758. SARAH J. GARBER and 4 children,   Graysville, Tenn
Rejected. Niece to No 4572 and claims through same source.

11759. MARTHA E. LEMMONS and no children, Graysville, Tenn
Rejected. Niece to No 4572 and claims through same source.

11760. FLORENCE MICKLE and 1 child,   Claremore, Okla
Admitted. Great niece of No 253 and claims through the same
source. Applicant's grandfather, Milo A. Hoyt, enrolled by
Drennen, Disp. Dist. No. 38.
ROLL P98 #18817 FCT COMM #6247 - Florence Mickle - 21
            18818   171m - Hoyt (son)   - 2

11761. SUE G. WILLIAMS and 2 children,   Claremore, Okla
Admitted. Aunt of No 1208 and Thos. J. Harris father of the
claimant is enrolled by Chapman No 1860. [NOTE: only 1 child
on roll]
ROLL P151 #29393 FCT COMM #6246 - Sue G. Williams - 38
            29394   230m - Sid (son)   - 1

11762. SUE HOYT,   Claremore, Okla
            by Sue G. Williams, Gdn.
Admitted. Great grandniece of No 253 and claims through same
source. Applicant's grandfather, Milo A. Hoyt enrolled by
Drennen, Disp. Dist. No. 38.
ROLL P79 #14815 FCT COMM #6284 - Sue Hoyt - 14
                                by Williams, Sue G., Gdn.

11763. POWHATAN HENSON,   Skiatook, Okla
Admitted. First cousin of No 326. Grandfather "William Hen-
son", Chapman No 1307.
ROLL P74 #13922 FCT COMM #28364 - Powhatan Henson - 33
            13923   28365 - Mariah (wife)   - 34
                                   (App 17439)
            13924   28366 - Jack (son)   - 16

11764. ELSIE YOUNG,   Marble, Okla
Admitted. Claims through mother enrolled as Chu-ker-tah and
Sally. Uncles enrolled as En-eyou-yaw-hee and Wa-le-too-kee.
All were enrolled by Drennen in 1851 in Flint Dist. Group No
416. See Misc. Test. No 3014-5.

MISC. TEST. P. 3014. Interpreter used in this case - Witness
in re: App No 11764-9474 - Elsie Young - William Young:
"I am about 68 years old. I live in this or Illinois District. I am her father-in-law. I knew her mother. Her name
was Selsie or Celsy. She was a full-blood Cherokee Indian. I
don't know positively that she was an Old Settler but think
she was. I don't know if they drew money at that time, but
she lived in Skin Bayou at that time. She had two sisters living; cannot remember their names; do not know about any brothers. Her mother was named Sallie Ju-ka-tah, after marriage.
Her husband's name was just Ju-ka-tah. Charley Foreman was
Elsie Young's father. Do not know whether he had any brothers
and sisters. He looked pretty old when he died. Don't know
whether he was on the roll of 1851. His father was Tom Foreman. Do not know, but think his mother was Ailcey, or Ailcy.
They lived in Illinois District. His Indian name was Ave
Sooker or Sucre, or A-we Sugar. They never associated with any
other Indians."
SIGNED: William Young, Sallisaw, Okla., Sep 17 1908.

MISC. TEST. P. 3015. Interpreter used in this case - Witness
in re: App No 11764-9474 - Elsie Young - Mose Chuculate:
"My name is Mose Chuculate. My age is about 100 years,
according to Dawes Commission. Elsie Young is about 30 years.
She lives in Sequoyah District. She was enrolled by the Dawes
Commission, Cherokee Roll # [blank]. She got the strip money.
She gets her blood from both parents. Selcie is her mother's
name. Or Selse. That was all the name I ever knew. She is
dead; died about 14 years ago. She was about 40 years old. I
don't know whether she was enrolled in 1851. Her mother had
sisters and brothers A-licke, or Ellick; he lived in Sequoyah
District; Duck Sau-nicke or Duck Saw-neck was an uncle; he
either lived in Sequoyah or Flint. A sister by the New-yor-he
or Ne-yah-he; do not know where he lived but it was probably
Sequoyah or Flint District; her grandfather's name Juk-ta or
Juc-ta or Joct-ta; he lived in Sequoyah District. These are
all I know. Her father was Charley Foreman, and A--wih or
A-wee was his Indian name; he lived in Sequoyah District. She
does not know any brother and sisters of her father. I don't
know any either. Do not know her grandparents on her father's
side. Her people were not Old Settlers."
SIGNED: Mose, Chuculate, Sallisaw, Okla., Sep 17 1908.
ROLL P155 #30155 FCT COMM # 2877 - Tom Young - 26 (App 16595)
        30156   25635 - Elsie (wife) - 28

11765. ANNIE DANIEL and 3 children,   Pryor Creek, Okla
Admitted. Claimant's mother, Sally, and maternal grandmother
Che-caw-nee-lah enrolled by Drennen in 1851, Del. 804. Father
enrolled in Del. 845. Father Del. 833. See Misc. Test. 4188.
MISC. TEST. P. 4188. App No 11765 - Annie Deer-in-water or
Annie Birdtail...through John Israel, Interpreter:
"My present name is Annie Daniel. I have no Creek blood.

241

I am about 45 years of age. I am enrolled by the Dawes Commission No 21025. I am a full blood Cherokee. Sallie Pigeon-
roost was the name of my mother. I married James Birdtail and
then Deer-in-water and now Daniel. I was not married to Deer-
in-water - just lived with him. I don't know whether Sallie,
my mother, had any brothers and sisters or not. Wau-you-kih
was Sallie's father. He lived in G. S. District. Che-gaw-na-
lah was my grandmother's name on my mother's side. I do not
know of anyone by the name of Darkey Oo-lah-naw-te-ske. I
don't know in what district my grandparents lived. My grand
parents came to this country from the east but I do not know
to what part of the country they came. My grandmother had no
brothers and sisters that I know of. Wau-kih was the name of
my father. Can-you-wau-kih was the name of my father's father.
Nancy was the name of my father's mother. Qua-li-uke was the
name of my father's sister and she is living in the Saline
District now. Her postoffice is Rose, Okla., I think (Look up
this application). My parents drew money in 1851. My people
are Emigrants. I have never associated with any other tribe
of Indians. My postoffice is at Pryor Creek now. I can get
no witness to testify for me."
SIGNED: Annie Deer-in-water [No date or location]
"John Israel states in behalf of the above applicant: I am acquainted with the above applicant. She is regarded as a Cherokee in this community. I don't know whether she is an Old
Settler or an Emigrant." [Notation added to end of testimony].
ROLL P52 #9541 FCT COMM #21025 - Annie Deerinwater - 42
          9542   21027 - John BIRDTAIL (son) - 19
                               (App 17107)
          9543   21028 - Dave BIRDTAIL (son) - 13
          9544   21029 - Sam BIRDTAIL (son) - 11

11766. KATIE DICK,   Braggs, Okla
Admitted. Half aunt of No 2234. [For Roll information See App
6753, Vol. 3.]

11767. GEORGE D. WARD,   Afton, Okla
Admitted. Brother of No 9 and claims through same source.
ROLL P145 #28202 FCT COMM #23787 - George D. Ward - 59

11768. MARY A. HARRISON,   Afton, Okla
Admitted. Sister of No 5594.
ROLL P72 #13479 FCT COMM #8059* - Mary A. Harrison - 69
[* last digit of FCT # blurred]

11769. MARTHA C. WETZEL and 4 grandchildren, Maysville, Ark
Admitted. Sister of No 5594 and guardian of grandchildren.
ROLL P149 #28944 FCT COMM #23711 - Martha C. Wetzel - 65
          28945   32457 - Claud C. (Gson) - 19
          28946   32458 - Ida May (Gdau) - 17
          28947   32460 - Eddie (Gson) - 12
          28948   32459 - Oliver (Gson) - 16

11770. MATTIE LUELLA VICKS and 2 children, Roanoke, Tex
                                    c/o J. M. Johnson
                                    RFD No 1
Rejected. Ancestors were not parties to the treaties of 1835-
1836 46. No ancestor was enrolled on the 1835 and 1851. Applicant was born in Columbus, S. C. outside of the Cherokee
Indian Domain. See Misc. Test. P. 1977.
MISC. TEST. P. 1977. #11771 - Wm. E. Sneed:
    "My name is Wm. E. Sneed, and I live in Fort Worth, Tex.
I am 42 years old. I claim my Indian descent through my father, Isaac Sneed. My father died in Ardell County, N. C.
about 21 years ago, at the age of 86. I came West 16 years
ago from N. C. My father was born in Columbia, S. C. I think
my father was 1/2 Cherokee. I have heard him talk quite a lot
about his Cherokee blood. I never heard him say anything about
the money paid in 1851. My father was an orphan at a tender
age and I know nothing about his people, but I do remember
that he showed his Indian blood very strongly. My father was
never out of the two states of N. C. and S. C. I do not know
just where he was living in 1835. I believe that in 1851 he
was living in S. C. I have never made any claims save this
one on account of my Indian rights."
SIGNED: Wm. E. Sneed, Fort Worth, Tex., Sep 10 1908.
EXCEPTION CASE. 11770. William E. Sneed, App 11771, 1604
Holt St., Ft. Worth, Tex. Rejected. Total number of exceptions filed in this group -- 1. Original recommendation renewed.

11771. WM. EDWARD SNEED,   Fort Worth, Tex
Rejected. Evidence insufficient. Ancestors were not parties
to the treaties of 1835-6 and 46. No ancestor was ever enrolled on the 1835 or 1851. Applicant was born in Columbia,
S. C. outside the Indian Cherokee Domain. See Misc. Test. P.
1977. [See App 11770 for Test. and exception case.]

11772. THOMAS L. SNEED & 3 children, Sta. A, Fort Worth, Tex
Rejected. Brother to No 11770 and claims through same source.

11773. ALEXANDER RATTLINGGOURD & 3 children, Claremore, Okla
Admitted. Applicant claims through father Daniel R. Gourd,
enrolled 239 Tahl. Several brothers in 478 Tahl. Some in group
good through No 434 G. S. See Misc. Test. P. 4146.
MISC. TEST. P. 4146. App No 15619 - 11773 - Paralee Reed...in
behalf of Alexander Rattlinggourd:
    "I am 50 years of age. I was born in the Cherokee Nation
West. I know Alex Rattlinggourd or Alex Gourd. They sign
their names both ways. He is the uncle of my son, Daniel.
Sarah Rattlinggourd is Looney Rattlinggourd's daughter.
Looney, Thomas and Alex are brothers. Daniel, my son, is the
son of Tom Rattlinggourd. The old man Daniel Rattlinggourd is
the father of Alex, Looney, Tom, John and Timothy. Alex is
not quite as old as I am; don't know his exact age. Daniel

Rattlinggourd lived in Tahlequah District before I knew him.
Then he came to Coo-wee-scoo-wee District and lived there
until he died. Don't know when Daniel came from the Eastern
States. My husband was two years older than me, born about
1856. I have heard my husband, Thomas, say that Daniel, his
father, drew money in 1851. I think Daniel Rattlinggourd came
from the Eastern States. I was acquainted with Daniel Rattlinggourd. He was often called Gourd. John, Jackson and
Looney, I think, were brothers to old man Daniel. That is
what I have heard my husband say. I never knew any of them
and never saw any of them. There was one named Charlie too.
Jackson lived in Tah. District. Never heard of any sisters of
Daniel. I have heard Thomas say that his mother drew Old Settler money. Her name was Eliza but I don't remember her maiden
name. Thomas' father was not an Old Settler. My husband often spoke about his mother being an Old Settler and that his
father was an Emigrant. (See Tah. 478). None of my people
never associated with any other tribe than the Cherokees.
Ellis Rattlinggourd is some relation to my husband. I have
seen him and have also heard my husband speak of him. I think
he was a cousin of my husband but I am not sure of this.
    "I get my blood from George McPherson, my father. I have
filed an application to share in this fund. Silas was a brother of George and lived in Flint District, to the best of my
knowledge. Hughey was another brother; Alex was another. Lucy
was a sister. Christie was another. John was also a brother
of my father. (G. S. 434)."
SIGNED: Paralee Reed, Claremore, Okla., Mar 12 1909.
ROLL P115 #22074 FCT COMM #30262 - Alexander
                              Rattlinggourd   - 43
        22075   30263 - Artemiss (dau)   - 20
        22076   30265 - Susie (dau)   - 17
        22077   32064 - Andrew (son)   - 12

11774. GEORGE BUSHYHEAD,   Braggs, Okla
Admitted. Applicant's mother probably Cah-ta-yah. Enrolled
by Drennen in 1851. S. B. No 19. Grandfather Kah-to-yah, or
Stand enrolled in 1851 by Drennen in Going Snake No 48. Misc.
Test. P. 4199.
MISC. TEST. P. 4199. App No 11774 - Jennie Busyhead...through
John Israel, Interpreter...in behalf of George Bushyhead:
    "I am 75 years of age. I know the applicant. I raised him.
His father was named Gah-lah-daw-la-duh and he lived in Sequo-
yah District. I don't know his English name. He had no broth-
ers that I know of. The applicant got the name of Bushyhead
because I raised him. I don't know whether applicant's mother
was an Old Settler or an Emigrant. Gah-naw-hih was her name.
Da-gah-daw was the name of applicant's grandfather on his
mother's side. I don't know the name of his grandmother. Da-
gah-daw-ga means "Stand". He had no brothers that I know of.
He had a sister named Too-ni-yih. Applicant's father was an
Old Settler but his mother was an Emigrant. I don't know any

brothers and sisters that applicant's mother had."
SIGNED: Jennie Bushyhead, Braggs, Okla., Mar 27 1909.
[For Roll information See App 11499]

11775. JENNIE GIRTY and 1 child,   Webbers Falls, Okla
Admitted. Claimant's mother not born until after '51. Mater-
nal grandmother enrolled by Drennen in 1851, Can. 72.
ROLL P66 #12207 - Jennie Girty - 26
             12208 - Stan (son)   - 3

11776. MARGARET McEACHIN and 1 child,   Sallisaw, Okla
Admitted. Niece of No 2175. Father of applicant, Cabin Hanks,
enrolled in 1851, by Chapman No 1560.
ROLL P94 #17866 FCT COMM #2957 - Margaret McEachin - 39
             17867   2958 - Martha (dau)   - 12

11777. LIZZIE BUCKHORN,   Tahlequah, Okla
Admitted. First cousin of No 5549 and claims through the same
source. [For Roll information See App 4597, Vol. 3]

11778. SILAS SUNDAY,   Cookson, Okla
            by R. C. Fuller, Gdn.
Admitted. Applicant's grandfather was enrolled by Drennen in
Ill. Dist. No 19.
ROLL P135 #26035 FCT COMM #25384 - Silas Sunday - 19
                              by R. C. Fuller, Gdn.

11779. JOHN HASKINS, Duplicate of No 9219.   [NOTE: Surname
"Horsekin" App 9219]

11780. ROBERT E. BUTLER and 1 child,   Muskogee, Okla
Rejected. Claims through same source as No 2844.
EXCEPTION CASE. Muskogee, Okla. Admitted. Total number of
exceptions filed in this group -- 1.   Brother of #11424.
Formerly rejected through a clerical error.
SUPP ROLL #30547 FCT COMM #26111 - Robert E. Butler - 40
             30548   5738 - Willie E. (son) - 9

11781. LUCINDA JOHNSON and 5 children,   Verdigris, Okla
Admitted. Aunt of No 3644. Mother of applicant enrolled in
1851 in Skin Bayou No 308.
ROLL P82 #15485 FCT COMM #28117 - Lucinda Johnson   - 33
             15486   28118 - Daniel E. MOORE (son) - 19
             15487   28119 - Davie MOORE (son)   - 16
             15488   28120 - Charlie MOORE (son)   - 10
             15489   28121 - Lizzie MOORE (dau)   - 4
             15490   1816m - Cordelia JOHNSON (dau) - 1

11782. SUE M. ALBERTY and 5 children,   Claremore, Okla
Admitted. Sister of No 1335 and claims through same source.

```
ROLL P22 #3556 FCT COMM #7005 - Sue M. Alberty   - 44
           3557          7006 - Cecil E. (son)   - 18
           3558          7007 - Nannie W. (dau)  - 14
           3559          7008 - Maggie M. (dau)  - 11
           3560          7009 - Bernice L. (dau) -  6
           3561          673m - James R. (son)   -  1
```

11783. JOHN W. JOHNSON,   Claremore, Okla
Admitted. Applicant's mother was enrolled by Drennen in G. S.
Dist. No 654.
ROLL P82 #15460 FCT COMM #30439 - John W. Johnson - 46

11784. JAMES W. ELLIOTT and 5 children,   Pinehill, Tex
Admitted. Applicant's father Davis Elliott on Act of Congress
Roll.
```
ROLL P58 #10601 - James W. Elliott - 49
           10602 - Molllie V. (dau) - 18
           10603 - David I. (son)   - 14
           10604 - Emma H. (dau)    - 10
           10605 - Fannie M. (dau)  -  5
           10606 - John H. (son)    -  1
```

11785. DOLLY J. SUGGS and 4 children,   Pryor Creek, Okla
Admitted. Niece of No 11790 and claims through same source.
Applicant's father John Elliott enrolled on Act of Congress
Roll.
```
ROLL P134 #25935 - Dolly J. Suggs  - 32
            25936 - William A. (son) - 12
            25937 - Zelma G. (dau)   - 10
            25938 - F. M. (son)      -  7
            25939 - Elliott (son)    -  1
```

11786. RILEY ELLIOTT, ADDIE ELLIOTT,   Pryor Creek, Okla
            by Lizzie Griffin, Gdn. and Mother
Admitted. Nephew and niece of No 11790 and claims through the
same source. Applicant's father John Elliott on the Act of
Congress Roll.
```
ROLL P58 #10612 FCT COMM #17268 - Riley Elliott - 16
           10613          17269 - Addie (sis)   - 10
                          by Lizzie Griffin, Gdn.
```

11787. WILLIAM T. ELLIOTT,   Pryor Creek, Okla
Admitted. Nephew of No 11790 and claims through same source.
Applicant's father John Elliott enrolled in Act of Congress
Roll.
ROLL P58 #10620 FCT COMM #17267 - William T. Elliott - 20

11788. JESSE T. PRUETT and 3 children,   Terrell, Tex
Admitted. Niece of No 11780 and claims through the same
source. Applicant's mother enrolled on Act of Congress Roll
as "Catherine Elliott."

ROLL P113 #21817 - Jesse T. Pruett - 40
         21818 - I. Mabel (dau)   - 11
         21819 - J. Lillian (dau) - 5
         21820 - C. Glenn (son)   - 4

11789. DAVID I. ELLIOTT,   Pryor Creek, Okla
Admitted. Brother of No 11790 and claims through same source.
Applicant's father David Elliott on Act of Congress Roll.
EXCEPTION CASE. Denied. The exception filed by J. W. Springton
to the enrollment of applicant is denied. (Exception is filed
under Martha A. Davis, Appli. #11790).
ROLL P58 #10589 - David I. Elliott - 53

11790. MARTHA A. DAVIS,   Nocona, Tex
Admitted. Applicant on Act of Congress Roll as "Martha A.
Elliott." First cousin once removed of No 3906.
EXCEPTION CASE. Denied. The exception filed by J. W. Springton
to the enrollment of applicant is denied.
ROLL P52 #9404 - Martha A. Davis - 71

11791. MARTHA REDFEARN and 2 children,   Saulsbury, Tenn
Admitted. Niece of No 11790 and claims through the same
source. Applicant's mother enrolled on Act of Congress Roll
as "Catherine Elliott."
ROLL P15 #2134 - Martha Redfearn   - 28
         2135 - John Earl (son)   - 5
         2136 - Jesse Dewitt (son) - 2

11792. RUFUS SEVEN,   Grove, Okla
Admitted. Applicant's grandfather was enrolled by Drennen in
Del. Dist. No 70. For other side of house see Del. 198. See
Misc. Test. P. 2992.
MISC. TEST. P. 2992. No 11792 - Rufus Seven:
    "My name is Rufus Seven; I was born in Delaware District,
1877; I am three-quarters Cherokee; I claim my Indian blood
through both my father and mother; my father was born in Delaware District, 1845; my mother was born in Delaware District,
1852; my father's father's name was George Seven; I do not
know where my grandfather, George Seven, was born; I do not
know the name of my father's mother; my mother's father was
born in the Old Cherokee nation in the East; none of my people
ever received any Old Settler payment and have never affiliated with any tribe of Indians other than the Cherokees; I
was enrolled by the Dawe's Commission under the name of Rufus
Seven (#32381); I think my father was enrolled in Delaware
District or Saline District, but I think it was Delaware; I
think my grandfather, Daniel Muskrat, was enrolled in Delaware
District; I do not know the year."
SIGNED: Rufus Seven, Grove, Okla., Sep 8 1908.
ROLL P125 #24178 FCT COMM #32381 - Rufus Seven - 29

11793. DAVE BUCKET,   Grove, Okla
Admitted. Brother of No 8983 and claims through same source.
[For Roll information See App 1740, Vol. 2]

11794. ARAMINTA R. FOREMAN,   Vinita, Okla
Admitted. Sister of No 1816.
ROLL P62 #11524 FCT COMM #14635 - Araminta R. Foreman - 28

11795. ELBERT G. GODDARD,   Chelsea, Okla
        STILES H. GODDARD, IRVINE E. GODDARD
           by James W. Goddard, Gdn.
Admitted. Nephews and niece of No 375-6 and claims through
same source.
ROLL P66 #12334 FCT COMM #28152 - Elbert G. Goddard - 11
        12335   28153 - Stiles H. (bro) - 8
        12336   28155 - Irene E. (sis)   - 6
                             by James W. Goddard, Gdn.

11796. WM. H. WALKER,   Kipling, Va
Rejected. See special report Sizemore No 417.

11797. MAHALA E. WALKER and 3 children,   Kipling, Va
Rejected. See special report Sizemore No 417.

11798. HARDEN H. TROTT, BELLE TROTT,   Vinita, Okla
           by W. L. Trott, Gdn.
Admitted. Nephew and niece of 615 and claims thru same source.
ROLL P141 #27306 FCT COMM #27560 - Harden H. Trott - 18
         27307   27595 - Belle (sis)   - 16
                             by W. L. Trott, Gdn.

11799. LEWIS E. MURRELL,   Bayou Goula, La
Admitted. First cousin of No 90 and claims through the same
source. Applicant's mother Amanda Ross enrolled by Drennen,
Saline 459.
ROLL P103 #19777 - Lewis E. Murrell - 33
         19778 - George M. (son) - 8
         19779 - Richard C. (son) - 6

11800. JENNIE R. MURELL,   Bayou Goula, La
Admitted. Sister of No 145. Enrolled by Drennen, Tahl. 236
in 1851.
ROLL P103 #19776 - Jennie Ross Murrell - 69

11801. CARRIE B. FREEMAN,   Maysville, Ark
Admitted. Niece of No 2652
ROLL P64 #11825 FCT COMM #203 - Carrie B. Freeman - 24

11802. WM. D. FREEMAN,   Maysville, Ark
Admitted. Nephew of No 2652.
ROLL P64 #11844 FCT COMM #204 - William D. Freeman - 21

248

11803. GIRLIE L. FREEMAN,   Maysville, Ark
Admitted. Niece of No 2652.
ROLL P64 #11834 FCT COMM #205 - Girlie L. Freeman - 20

11804. ELIZA J. McMURRY,   Porum, Okla
Admitted. First cousin of No. 4395 [? last digit blurred].
Claimant's father enrolled in 1851 by Drennen, Del. 431.
ROLL P95 #18105 FCT COMM #16982 - Louisie McMurty - 61

11805. CHARLES RIDER,   Talala, Okla
Admitted. Uncle of No 781 and claims through same source.
ROLL P117 #22442 FCT COMM #10711 - Charles Rider - 41

11806. JOHNSON GROVE,   Porum, Okla
Admitted. Cousin of No 1583. Claimant's father enrolled in
1851 by Drennen, Tahl. 304.
ROLL P68 #12744 FCT COMM #16312 - Johnson Grove - 28

11807. JOHNSON GROVE, Same as No 11806.

11808. MARY J. RICHARDSON,   Laurel Springs, N C
[Rejected]. See special report Sizemore No 417.

11809. AARON OSBORN and 2 children,   Laurel Springs, N C
Rejected. See special report Sizemore No 417.

11810. ROBERT J. TESTERMAN and 4 children, Major, Va
Rejected. See special report Sizemore No 417.

11811. WILLIAM BLEVINS,   Laurel Springs, N C
Rejected. See special report Sizemore No 417.

11812. HENRY L. WATERS,   Laurel Bloomery, Tenn
Rejected. See special report Sizemore No 417.

11813. EVELYN WALKER,   Oolagah, Okla
Admitted. Father enrolled as John S. Tucker, Del. 918.
ROLL P144 #27950 FCT COMM #11815 - Evelyn Walker - 23

11814. PEGGIE A. MOORE,   Braggs, Okla
Admitted. Applicant's father enrolled Tahl. No 36. Cousin once
removed of No 859.
ROLL P101 #19301 FCT COMM #26996 - Peggie A. Moore - 18

11815. GUY TUCKER,   Oolagah, Okla
Admitted. Claims through father enrolled as John S. Tucker,
Del. No 918. Brother of No 11813.
ROLL P141 #27376 FCT COMM #11814 - Guy Tucker - 26

11816. CANZADA BARE and 4 children,   Burut Hill, -- [sic]
Rejected. See special report Sizemore No 417.

249

11817. MARTHA L. HARRIS and 4 children,   Collinsville, Okla
Admitted. First cousin of No 567 and claims through the same
source. Applicant's mother enrolled Tahl. 480 as "Margaret T.
Nicholson".
ROLL P72 #13432 FCT COMM #29397 - Martha L. Harris - 41
        13433   29399 - Johnnie A. (dau) - 16
        13434   29400 - Robert P. (son) - 13
        13435   29401 - Nellie M. (dau) - 9
        13436   29402 - William M. (son) - 6

11818. SUSIE FARINGTON,   Crumpler, N C
Rejected. See special report Sizemore No 417.

11819. EPHRAM OSBORN,   Ratler, N C
Rejected. See special report Sizemore No 417.

11820. LEONA WOODIE and 2 children,   Furches, N C
Rejected. See special report Sizemore No 417.

11821. ROZINA WOODY,   Furches, N C
Rejected. See special report Sizemore No 417.

11822. OSCEOLA ALLEN and 1 child,   Foyil, Okla
Admitted. Applicant's grandmother enrolled by Drennen in 1852
[sic] as Chah-wa-yi-ka, G. S. No 67. See Misc. Test. P. 2600.
[For Misc. Test. See App 11512]
ROLL P23 #3653 FCT COMM #21774 - Osceola Allen - 29
        3654   28133 - Georgia (wife) - 21
                            (App 28841)
        3865   773m - Velma (dau)   - 3

11823. FRANKIE C. BAILEY,   Waxahachie, Tex
Rejected. See special report Sizemore No 417.

11824. SARAH LAFON and 8 children,   Bartlett, Kans
Admitted. Cousin of No 4519. [NOTE: This entire entry hand-
written]
ROLL P87 #16534 FCT COMM #9496 - Sarah Lafon   - 37
        16535   9497 - Amos (son)   - 18
        16536   9498 - Claude (son)   - 18
        16537   9499 - Flossy (dau)   - 15
        16538   9500 - Essie (dau)   - 13
        16539   9501 - Mayes (son)   - 11
        16540   9502 - Clark (son)   - 8
        16541   9504 - Ambrose (son)   - 6
        16542   9503 - Beverly (dau)   - 6

11825. LIZZIE PETTIT and 2 children,   Braggs, Okla
Admitted. Sister of No 9468 and claims through same source.
Applicant enrolled as Lizzie, Flint No 496.

ROLL P110 #21191 FCT COMM #17633 - Lizzie Petitt - 63
** 21192 17634 - Jenny (dau) - 15 **
** 21193 17635 - Susie (dau) - 10 **
[** Both entries crossed out entirely - no explanation]

11826. ANDREW J. PETIETT, Minor   Wimer, Okla
Admitted. Nephew of No 319 and claims through same source.
Duplicate child in No 1958 [sic - should be 1058]. (See Misc.
Test. P. 2134).
MISC. TEST. P. 2134. Mother, witness in re No 11826 Andrew
Pettit, Lafelia Lee:
    "My name is Lafelolia Lee. I am 32 years old. I live about
15 miles from here. I have lived there about 10 years. I was
partly raised in Texas. I claim to have some Indian blood of
the Cherokee tribe. I was enrolled by the Dawes Commission as
a Cherokee, No 7596. Census card 3067. I was enrolled before
but cannot say when. My father enrolled me but I do not remember at what time. I have been twice married. My maiden name
was Wicket. I claim my blood through my father, John Wichet.
He has been dead -- [? blurred] years and lived in Indian Territory and moved from Texas when I was about 10 years old.
Newt Wicket, Albert Wicket, Baden Wicket are my brothers. My
father's brother was Lem Wicket. He lived in the Territory
since I can remember. My father's sisters and brothers lived
in Georgia. Originally my father and mother came from Georgia.
My father was 56 when he died. My father had a sister Becky
Wicket. I have never associated with any other tribe than the
Cherokees. My father did not associate with any other tribe
of Indians that I know of. I never heard my father say whether
he ever received any money from the Government. My first husband was Andrew Pettiett. He as been dead about 7 years. He
was about 27 years old when he died. He always lived in the
Territory. He got his Indian blood from both sides. He was
enrolled at one time. He mother was Polly Pettiett, before
marriage Polly Beck. She has been dead about 6 years. I think
she was enrolled with every enrollment of the Cherokee nation.
My husband's father was Frank Pettiett. He lives in Indian
Territory and has always lived there as far as I know. He was
enrolled by the Commissioner of the Five Civilized tribes but
witness does not know his roll number. I do not know that he
was ever enrolled at any other time. Frank Pettiett had brothers and sisters, Amelia and Bill Pettiett. My husband's brothers and sisters were, Joanna Pettiett, Amelia Pettiett and
Cynthia Pettiett, and Robert Pettiett, Jo Pettiett, and Andrew
Pettiett. They live in Illinois District. My child's father
had Indian name but I cannot recall it."
SIGNED: Lafelia Lee, Lenapah, Okla., Aug 21 1908.
[For Roll information See App 1058, Vol. 1]

11827. MORG. J. CRITTENDEN,   Warner, Okla
Admitted. Sister of Katie A. Cooper (9775) and claims through
same source.

251

ROLL P49 #8828 FCT COMM #26039 - <u>Mary</u> J. Crittenden - 14

11828. JAMES W. CRITTENDEN,   Warner, Okla
Admitted. Brother of Katie A. Cooper (9775) & claims through
same source.
ROLL P49 #8811 FCT COMM #26038 - James W. Crittenden - 16
                              by Margaret Hence, Gdn.

11829. LEROY CRITTENDEN,   Warner, Okla
        Margaret Hence, Gdn.
Admitted. Brother of Katie A. Cooper (9775) & claims through
same source.
ROLL P49 #8824 FCT COMM #26040 - Leroy Crittenden - 10
                              by Margaret Hence, Gdn.

11830. AMANDA WATKINS,   Battle Creek, S C
Rejected. Sister of No 10635 and claims through same source.

11831. JOSEPH JONES,   Deer Court, S C
Rejected. Brother of No 10635 and claims through same source.

11832. SARAH WOODALL,   Long Creek, S C
Rejected. Sister of No 10635 and claims through same source.

11833. SARAH R. JONES,   Battle Creek, S C
Rejected. Niece of No 10635 and claims through same source.

11834. WILLIAM BEEMON, et al,   Deer Court, S C
Rejected. Nephew and nieces of 10635, claims thru same source.

11835. WM. JESSE WATKINS and 3 children,   Battle Creek, S C
Rejected. Nephew of No 10635 and claims through same source.

11836. WM. W. JONES,   Mineral Bluff, Ga
Rejected. Brother of No 10635 and claims through same source.

11837. JOHN P. WATERS,   Laurel Bloomer, Tenn
Rejected. See special report Sizemore No 417.

11838. JOHN P. WATERS,   Laurel Bloomery, Tenn
Rejected. 1 - No ancestor ever enrolled. 2 - No ancestor was
party to the treaties of 1835-6-46. 3 - Shows no real connection with the Cherokee Tribe. 4 - On mother's side is a Sizemore and has filed application claiming as a Sizemore, Duplicate No. 11837.

11839. MOSES TROTTINGWOLF and 2 children, Swayney, N C
Admitted. Uncle of No 21.
ROLL P18 #2759 - Moses Trottingwolf - 60
         2760 - Jennie (wife)   - 48 (App 12773)
         2761 - Martha (dau)   - 17
         2762 - Johnnie (son)   - 13

[NOTE: The names John R. Trott and Wm. R. Trott crossed out and wife and daughter's names handwritten at bottom of page – under "CLERICAL CORRECTIONS TO BE MADE ON THE ORIGINAL ROLL" is the following information: "2759. After this number change roll numbers 3160 and 3161 to 2760 and 2761. Also change names opposite these numbers from John R. Trott to Jennie Trottingwolf, and from Wm. R. Trott to Martha Trottingwolf."

11840. NELCINA WOLFE and 6 children,   Swayney, N C
Admitted. Half sister of No 7754 and claims through the same source. Applicant's mother enrolled Chapman No 556. [For Roll information See App 11842]

11841. ANNIE TROTTINGWOLF,   Swayney, N C
Admitted. Aunt of No 21.
ROLL P18 #2757 – Annie Trottingwolf – 48

11842. JACOB WOLF,   Swayney, N C
Admitted. First cousin of 21 and claims through same source.
ROLL P20 #3075 – Jacob Wolf   – 35
         3076 – Nelcena (wife) – 33 (App 11840)
         3077 – Laura (dau)   – 16
         3078 – Rachel (dau)   – 13
         3079 – James (son)   – 10
         3080 – Joseph (son)   – 9
         3081 – Jesse (son)   – 7
         3082 – Abel (son)   – 3

11843. JENNIE MOSS and 7 children,   Cunningham, Ky
Rejected. First cousin of once removed [sic] of No 10764 and claims through same source.

11844. SAMUEL A. HINCHEE and 2 children,   Cunningham, Ky
Rejected. First cousin once removed of No 10764 and claims through same source.

11845. FORD E. HINCHEE,   Cunningham, Ky
Rejected. First cousin once removed of No 10764 and claims through same source.

11846. CHERRY OO-YER-SAT-TAH,   Oaks, Okla
Admitted. Brother of No 9444 and claims through same source.
ROLL P106 #20328 FCT COMM #20400 – Cherry Oo-yu-sut-tah – 22

11847. MINK DRYWATER and 2 children,   Oaks, Okla
Admitted. Son of No 540 and claims through same source. See Misc. Test. P. 3871.
MISC. TEST. P. 3871. #11847 – Mink Drywater:
"My name is Mink Drywater. I was born in Tahlequah District in 1871. I am a full-blood Cherokee. I was enrolled by the Dawes Commission and received my allotment. I was enrolled under the name of Mink Drywater, #20365. My father's Cherokee

name was Jah-ne Oo-tah-deh-gee-skee. My mother's Cherokee name
was Na-lih. I have been told that my father was enrolled in
Saline District in 1851 with his mother. That my mother was
enrolled in Going Snake District with her mother.

"My father had a brother by the name of Jesse and a sister
by the name of Lydia. (See Sal. 66)

"My father John Drywater is living at the present time. He
never received any notice to appear anywhere to give testimony. His application number is 540. (Se Sal. 66)."
SIGNED: Mink Drywater, Locust Grove, Okla., Oct 8 1908.
[For Roll information See App 9663, Vol. 4]

11848. WILLIAM McCRARY,   Kansas, Okla
          by Louisa McCrary
Admitted. Great nephew of No 735 and claims through the same
source. Grandfather John H. Crary Sr. 25 Del.
ROLL P93 #17754 FCT COMM #7944 - William McCrary - 15
                          by Louisa McCrary, Gdn.

11849. WILLIE JOE,   Oaks, Okla
Admitted. Applicant's father and grandfather were enrolled by
Drennen in Del. Dist. No 676. See Misc. Test. P. 3809.
MISC. TEST. P. 3809. 11849 - Willie Joe...through Tom Roach,
Interpreter:
"I am about 41 years of age. Both of my parents were Emmigrants and so where [sic] their parents. My parents were
not living together then. My father was living with his parents in Delaware District. My father's name was Jo-wuh or Joe
Davis. My father's father was named Davis. I don't know his
first name. His Indian name was Da-we-sih. My father's mother
was named Ah-qua-lih. Don't know of her having an English
name. My father had a brother younger than he that was living
in 51 named Dave or Da-wih. My father had a sister named
O-nih. He also had a brother named James but I think he was
born after the payment. I wasn't enrolled by the Daws Commission because I am opposed to making allotments. My aunt O-nih
is still living and goes by the name of Ona Wofford and lives
at Cherokee City, Ark. Squanih Joe is my son but Charlie Bluebird and Jackson Loman are my step children they being the
children of my present wife, Go-yeh-ne-e. She has filed application number 9946."
SIGNED: Willie Joe, Locust Grove, Okla., Oct 14 1908.
[For Roll information See App 9946, Vol. 4]

11850. RUFUS OO-YU-SAT-TAH,   Oaks, Okla
Admitted. Brother of No 9444 and claims through same source.
ROLL P106 #20331 FCT COMM #25913 - Rufus Oo-yu-sut-tah - 31

11851. ELIZA STONE for her child,   McDaniel, Ga
          WILLIAM PITMAN,
Rejected. No ancestor enrolled. It appears that no ancestor
was a party to the treaties of 1835-36 and 46. Proof of gen-

254

uine connection with the Eastern Cherokees insufficient. See
Misc. Test. P. 1231.
MISC. TEST. P. 1231. #11851 - William Pitman:
"That I am 19 years of age and live in Pickens Co., Ga. I
claim my Indian descent through my father and his mother and
her name was Prince - Jane Prince. My father was born in Tenn.
but I don't know what part. Don't know where my grandmother
was born. Never heard that my father or grandmother were on
any roll. Think my grandmother Prince claimed to be 1/2 Cherokee. I think she had brothers and sisters but I don't know
their names. I don't much or anything [sic] about my Indian
ancestry."
SIGNED: William "X" Pitman, Jasper, Ga., Jul 9 1908.
EXCEPTION CASE. Rejected. Total number of exceptions filed
in this group -- 1. Original recommendation renewed.

11852. NELLIE RUSTER,   Wauhellau, Okla
Rejected. Does not appear from application that applicant or
ancestors were ever enrolled. Does not appear that they were
living within the limits of the Cherokee Domain in 1835-6 and
'46 as recognized members of the tribe. Fails to answer letter of inquiry and failed to appear when notified to give testimony.

11853. TRANNA FIELDS, Duplicate of No 715. [Given name shown
as Texanna in App 715]

11854. SALLIE COCHRANE and 1 child,   Manard, Okla
Admitted. Applicant's grandmother was enrolled by Drennen in
Disp. Dist. No 87. Misc. Test. P. 3213.
MISC. TEST. P. 3213. App #11854 - Sallie Cochrum:
"My name is Sallie Cochrum. I live at Manard, Okla. My
father and mother were both Cherokee. My father was an Immi-
grant Cherokee. My father is still living. His name is David
Whitewater. His appl. is #4060. My father was born here, I
think in Illinois District. They called my grandfather
["Rider" crossed out] Whiteman Killer. My father had the fol-
lowing brothers and sisters, William, Johnson, Charlie Rider &
Susie and Nancy Rider. I think my father's sisters were younger than my father. My father did not draw Immigrant money. He
drew Old Settler money. (See Canadian 206 (?) O. S. Can. 204)
My mother's maiden name was Parrot. Seabolt was my grandmother's maiden name. My grandfather on my mother's side was named
William Parrott. My mother never received any Immigrant money.
My mother did not have any brothers and sisters. I don't know
what District Wm. Parrott lived in. My grandmother had a sister named Katy Seabolt. My mother has been dead nine years and
was about 38 or 39 years old. See Disputed 87. I have a sister
named Alice Disney #11855."
SIGNED: Sallie Cochrum, Tahlequah, Okla., Sep 26 1908.
ROLL P45 #8033 FCT COMM #21099 - Sallie Cochrum - 19
         8034   1270m - James A. (son) - 4

255

11855. ALIDE DISNEY and 1 child,   Manard, Okla
Admitted. Sister of No 11854.
ROLL P53 #9773 FCT COMM #18233 - Alice Disney - 26
       9774   3064m - Minnie (dau) - 2

11856. CARRIE WHITEKILLER,   Rex, Okla
Admitted. First cousin of No 781 and claims thru same source.
ROLL P150 #29035 FCT COMM #4747 - Carrie Whitekiller - 18

11857. HATTIE WHITE,   Braggs, Okla
Admitted. Applicant's grandfather was enrolled by Drennen in
Flint Dist. No 454. See Misc. Test. P. 3056.
MISC. TEST. P. 3056. No 11857 - Hattie White:
    "I am 19 years of age; I am a Cherokee alottee. My father
was the Indian. My grandfather was an Immigrant. I have seen
my grandfather. He died when I was small. My grandfather's
name was Wat Augerhole. I have never gotten any Old Settler
money. I have never gotten any land but Cherokee land and no
money but Cherokee money."
SIGNED: Hattie White, Muskogee, Okla., Sep 21 1908.
"This case is O. K. through grandfather, Wat Augerhole, 454
Flint." [Notation added to end of testimony]
ROLL P149 #28996 FCT COMM #4657 - Hattie White - 17

11858. THOMAS J. CORDREAY,   Fort Gibson, Okla
Admitted. Brother of No 11858 and claims through same source.
Duplicate of No 36558.
ROLL P47 #8410 FCT COMM #23240 - Thomas J. Cordery - 27
       8411   21606 - Ada B. (dau)   - 8
       8412   21607 - Josie Ann (dau)   - 7
       8413   4697m - James B. (son)   - 1/3

11859. ALICE VANN,   Modasha*, Okla
Admitted. Cousin of J. W. Jordan (1442) and claims through
same source. [* "Neodesha" on roll]
ROLL P142 #27609 FCT COMM #28339 - Alice Vann - 47

11860. ELLEN KELLY,   Manard, Okla
Admitted. Sister of No 11858 and claims through same source.
ROLL P84 #16017 FCT COMM #4869* - Ellen Kelly - 34
[* last digit FCT # blurred]

11861. LUCINDA GONZALES,   Braggs, Okla
Admitted. Great niece of No 1224. Grandfather and grandmother, Tom and Susan Smith, 290 Tahl. Probably father born after
1851.
ROLL P66 #12380 FCT COMM # 6061 - Lucinda Gonzales - 22
       12381   26396 - John (son)   - 4
                         (App 12815)

11862. LEE SMITH, ARCH SMITH, MATTIE SMITH, Braggs, Okla
          by Sarah Smith, Gdn.
Admitted. Grandparents No 290, Tahl. [For Roll information
See App 11865]

11863. NANNIE SMITH,   Braggs, Okla
Admitted. Applicant's grandfather was enrolled by Drennen in
Canadian Dist. No 17. See Misc. Test. P. 3097 and 3560.
MISC. TEST. P. 3097. No 11863 - Nannie Smith:
    "I am 23 years of age. I am enrolled by the Dawes Commis-
sion. I have an allotment and my number is 30428.   I have
never gotten any Old Settler money. I do not know if either
my mother or father was an Old Settler. My father lived at
Kingston. My mother has been dead 18 years. My father is
about 64. I never heard him say anything about getting any
Immigrant money. My grandfather was named Whitewater.   I am
three quarters Cherokee. My father was part white. I drew
strip money. My father is an Old Settler."
SIGNED: Nannie Smith, Muskogee, Okla., Sep 22 1908.
"This case is O. K. through Whitewater, 17 Canadian."
[Notation added to end of testimony]

MISC. TEST. P. 3560. No 11865-11863 - Sarah Smith...through
S. E. Parris, Interpreter:
    "My mother and father were both Cherokees. They are both
dead. I do not know if they drew Immigrant money. They were
not very old when they died. I am 44 years old. My mother
died when I was two and my father when I was eight. My mother
was Sallie Whitewater. Her Indian name Sah-lih A-me-nah. My
father was John Whitewater. I do not know his father's name
or his mother's name. My mother's mother was Sarah Bigcabin
and her father was Bigcabin. My father's father was named
Chickenroost. I have seen him. I am three-quarters Cherokee.
My mother was more white than Cherokee I think. I am a Cherokee alottee and my number is 6060."
SIGNED: Sarah Smith, Tahlequah, Okla., Oct 6 1908.
ROLL P129 #24941 FCT COMM #30428 - Nannie Smith - 22

11864. SUSAN ROGERS and 2 children,   Braggs, Okla
Admitted. Niece of No 1224. Grandparents Thomas and Susan
Smith, 290 Tahl. Father probably born after 1851.
ROLL P119 #22943 FCT COMM #13281 - Susam Rogers - 24
         22944   12384 - George (son) - 7
         22945   1218m - Hoke (son)   - 3

11865. SARAH SMITH and 3 children,   Braggs, Okla
Admitted. Aunt of No 11863. Claimant's father enrolled by
Drennen in 1851, Can. 17.
ROLL P129 #24982 FCT COMM #6060 - Sarah Smith - 40
         24983   6063 - Lee (son)   - 16
         24984   6064 - Archie (son) - 13
         24985   6065 - Mattie (dau) - 10

[NOTE: Children also enrolled same page #24881-24883 & crossed off with explanation "Duplicate of Nos. 24983- 24985" - They were each listed as 1 year older on the other enrollment]

11866. RICHARD M. FIELDS, Duplicate of No 716.

11867. NETTIE JOHNSON,   Fort Gibson, Okla
Admitted. Sister of No 759 and claims through same source.
ROLL P82 #15522 FCT COMM #5257 - Nettie Johnson - 22

11868. MARY, SARAH and CHARLOTTE CORDERY, Fort Gibson, Okla
          by John B. Smith, Gdn.
Admitted. Brothers and sisters of No 11858 and claims through
same source.
ROLL P46 #8402 FCT COMM #27385 - Mary Cordery   - 13
          8403   27386 - Sarah (sis)   - 11
          8404   27387 - Charlotte (sis) - 9
                              by John B. Smith, Gdn.

11869. JOHN STARNES and 6 children,   Fort Gibson, Okla
Admitted. Uncle of No 759 and claims through same source.
ROLL P131 #25394 FCT COMM # 5239 - John Starnes - 47
          25395   5243 - Bessie (dau) - 17
                              (App 24718)
          25396   5240 - Thomas (son) - 19
          25397   5241 - Mary E. (dau) - 13
          25398   5242 - Emma (dau)   - 11
          25399   5244 - Lelia (dau)   - 7
          25400   2644m - Maggie (dau) - 1

11870. KATE WALKER,   Braggs, Okla
Admitted. Applicant's father and grandmother were enrolled by
Drennen in Tahl. Dist. No 142. [For Roll information See App
11871]

11871. EDWARD A. WALKER and 4 children,   Braggs, Okla
Admitted. Brother of No 13 and claims through same source.
ROLL P144 #27941 FCT COMM #17234 - Edward A. Walker - 50
          27942   17235 - Kate (wife) - 46(App 11870)
          27943   17239 - John H. (son)   - 16
          27944   17240 - Jennie (dau)   - 12
          27945   17241 - Jack O. (son)   - 11
          27946   17242 - Susie (dau)   - 9

11872. HENRY DEPEW,   McLain, Okla
Admitted. Applicant's mother and grandfather were enrolled by
Drennen in Ill. Dist. No. 305.
ROLL P89 #16962 FCT COMM #18226 - Henry Lefew - 31

11873. MARION R. SHINN,   Webber Falls, Okla
          by W. H. Shinn, Gdn.
Admitted. Niece of No 11872. Claimant's maternal grandmother

258

enrolled in 1851 by Drennen, Tahl. 305.
ROLL P126 #24402 FCT COMM #4306 - Marion R. Shinn - 18*
                                   by W. H. Shinn, Gdn.
[* age crossed out and "8" written in]

11874. MARTIN MILLER,   Ft. Gibson, Okla
Admitted. Brother of No 3461.
ROLL P99 #18986 FCT COMM #16217 - Martin Miller - 39
         18987   16218 - Alice (wife) - 24
                              (App 32557)

11875. CALVIN J. HANKS and 7 children,   Webbers Falls, Okla
Admitted. Applicant's mother and grandmother were enrolled by
Drennen in Tahl. Dist. No 9.
ROLL P70 #13149 FCT COMM #25456 - Calvin J. Hanks - 48
         13150   25457 - Ora May (dau)   - 15
         13151   25458 - James Otto (son) - 13
         13152   25459 - Maud K. (dau)   - 12
         13153   25460 - Grace (dau)   - 11
         13154   25461 - Fannie (dau)   - 9
         13155   25462 - Annie (dau)   - 7
         13156   237m - Emma (dau)   - 2

11876. GOBACK CHRISTIE,   Wauhillan, Okla
Admitted. Uncle of No 2234. Father of applicant enrolled in
1851 in Flint Dist. No 283.
ROLL P42 #7421 FCT COMM #29158 - Goback Christie - 41
         7422   29159 - Susan (wife) - 25 (App 11877)

11877. SUSAN CHRISTIE,   Wauhillau, Okla
Admitted. First cousin once removed of No 700. [For Roll information See App 11876]

11878. LUKE FOREMAN,   Stilwell, Okla
Admitted. This applicant's grandfather, Thos. Young is en-
rolled by Drennen from Going Snake Dist. under group No 634.
ROLL P62 #11593 FCT COMM #20752 - Luke Foreman - 20

11879. LOUISA J. HOOD and 1 child,   Wagoner, Okla
Rejected. Applicant born in 1844 at Ft. Emory, N. C., never
enrolled, though father, Sam Morgan, was born in Monroe Co.,
Tenn. residing in Polk Co., Tenn. in 1851, never enrolled.
Grandfather Wesley Morgan born in N. C. do not know what part.
Resided in Tenn. in 1851, never enrolled.
    Great-grandfather, Gideon Morgan––no information given a-
bout him; enrolled by Chapman 1549 but does not appear to be
applicant's great grandfather as the Gideon Morgan on Chapman
roll is the ancestor of the applicants in group No 18. and
applicants in that group and those herein do no appear to be
related.
    Gideon Morgan, ancestor of applicants in group No 18 was a
white man who married a Cherokee woman and he was enrolled for

that reason.

Applicants in this group (11878) may possibly be the descendants of the Gideon Morgan who was enrolled by Chap. and
some white woman, and for that reason were never enrolled. It
is a fact that none of the applicants herein have ever been
enrolled and do not establish any ground for enrollment for
participation. They are therefore rejected.
EXCEPTION CASE. Rejected. Total number of exceptions filed
in this group -- 3. Original recommendation renewed.

11880. NANCY WOODS,   Dickson, Tenn
Rejected. It does not appear that the applicant or any of her
ancestors were ever enrolled. It does not appear that they
were living within the Cherokee Domain in 1835-6 to 1846 as
recognized members of the Cherokee Tribe. It does appear that
they were living outside the limits of the Cherokee tribe.
See Misc. Test. P. 539.
MISC. TEST. P. 539. #26421 - Mrs. Watson Gordon:
"I am 42 years of age; was born in Nashville, Tenn., have
lived all my life in Dickson and Davidson Counties, Tenn. I
claim Cherokee Indian blood through my mother. She said my
great-grandfather was a full blood Indian. My mother said my
grandfather, Henry Hale, moved from Cherokee Nation, N. C., to
Tennessee. I never saw my grandfather, Henry Hale. I never
saw my great grandfather, Michael Hale. None of my relatives
ever received any Indian money from the government that I know
of. I never received any Indian money and never tried before
to get any. None of my people were ever held as slaves that I
know of. George Hale, my uncle, who is here with me now was
living in slavery time and not held as a slave so I suppose my
mother was not. My great grandfather lived in an Indian hut
and used to keep my mother there with him so my mother said.
I never heard of Hester, the enrolling agent in 1884."
SIGNED: Mrs. Watson Gordon, Dickson, Tenn., Jun 25 1908.
George Hale:
"I am 53 years of age; was born in DeKalb County, Tenn.,
have spent all my life in Tennessee. I claim Cherokee Indian
blood through my father. My grandfather was a full blood Cherokee Indian. I have never received any Indian money from the
government and never tried before to get any. I never heard
of Hester, the enrolling agent in 1884. I have seen my grand
father, Michael Hale, in DeKalb County, Tenn. He was an old
gray haired man with gray beard. My grandfather fished and
dug herbs. I never heard my grandfather say where he came
from. He wore feathers in his head and carried a tomahawk part
of the time. When I knew my grandfather I was small. My mother
would take me to see him and sometimes he would come after me.
He spoke both Indian and English. I do not know whether my
mother could speak Indian or not. I cannot. I never heard my
grandfather say anything about getting any Indian money."
SIGNED: George Hale, Dickson, Tenn., Jun 25 1908.

EXCEPTION CASE. 11880. Lizzie Holland and 4 children, App 26806, Dixon, Tenn. Rejected. Total number of exceptions filed in this group -- 2. Original recommendation renewed.

11881. KATE STEALEE and 1 child,   Marble, Okla
Admitted. Cousin of No 7661 and claims through same source.
[For Roll information See App 11995]

11882. ROSS SCACEWATER,   Stilwell, Okla
Admitted. Enrolled in 17103. First cousin of No 8289. Paternal grandmother enrolled in 1851 Drennen, Ill. No 219.
[Enrolled under App #17103]
ROLL P123 #23763 FCT COMM #3340 - Ross Scarcewater - 18
          23764   3341 - Jimmie (bro)   - 16
                              by Wm. E. McConnell, Gdn.

11883. JAMES SCACEWATER and 3 children,   Stilwell, Okla
Admitted. First cousin of No 8289. Applicant's paternal grand mother enrolled in 1851 by Drennen, Ill. No 219.
ROLL P123 #23758 FCT COMM # 2069 - James Scacewater - 29
          23759   27155 - Murtie M. (wife) - 27
                                (App 11913)
          23760   22663 - Lucien B. (son) - 6
          23761   2847m - Clara E. (dau)   - 4
          23762   2848m - Jack (son)   - 1

11884. EDNA MORRIS,   Stilwell, Okla
Admitted. Sister of No 9380 and Cousin of No 5919.
ROLL P101 #19397 FCT COMM #2304 - Edna Morris - 18

11885. SUE A HUGHES,   Tahlequah, Okla
Admitted. Aunt of No 11284. [For Roll information See App 10790]

11886. THOMAS W. FOREMAN and 3 children, Tahlequah, Okla
Admitted. Uncle of No 11885.
ROLL P63 #11640 FCT COMM #13728 - Thomas W. Foreman - 46
         11641   13729 - Cherrie (wife)   - 36
                                (App 11281)
         11642   13730 - William E. (son) - 20
         11643   13731 - Watie C. (son)   - 16
         11644   13732 - Thomas A. (son)   - 12

11887. EMILY HARRIS and 3 children,   Coffyville, Kans
Admitted. Applicant's mother and grandmother were enrolled by Drennen in Tahl. Dist. No 269.
ROLL P72 #13400 FCT COMM #10869 - Emily Harris   - 51
         13401   10872 - Fred A. (son)   - 20
         13402   10873 - Minnie (dau)   - 18
         13403   10874 - Charles J. (son) - 15

11888. LOONEY RATTLINGGOURD, Duplicate of No 5357.

11889. THOS. JONES,   Baxter, Ga
Rejected. Cousin of No 9876 and claims through same source.

11890. WILLIAM C. HICKS,   Chelsea, Okla
          by Eddie Hicks
Admitted. Cousin of No 7407 and claims through same source.
ROLL P75 #14098 FCT COMM #12930 - William C. Hicks - 15
                              by Eddie Hicks, Gdn.

11891. LONNIE HICKS,   Chelsea, Okla
Admitted. Cousin of No 7407 and claims through same source.
MISC. TEST. P. 2595. App No 11891-9485 - Lonnie Hicks:
   "My name is Lonnie Hicks. My age is 26 years. I was born
and raised in Illinois District. Dawes Commission #12927. My
brother was also enrolled by the Dawes Commission. I claim
through my father. Andrew J. Hicks was my father's name. My
father lived in Illinois District. I have lived here 18 years.
My father was enrolled by the Dawes Commission and the enroll-
ments for bread and strip money. I think he was born in this
country. He lived in Illinois and Coo-wee-scoo-wee District.
During the war they lived in the Choctaw nation. My grandfather's brother Oo-was-kie-ke and sister Qua-ki Oo-was-kie-ke.
My father's sister was Rachel Merrell. My father's father and
mother were both Indians. Their names were: grandfather Oo-
scun-eh and grandmother Minerva Hicks, nee Pettit. We put in
for Elizabeth Armstrong and Oo-scun-eh, filing applications in
their name. I think my people were parties to the treaties of
1835 and 1846. I think they were enrolled in 1851. My great
grandfather lived in the Cherokee nation prior to 1835. I do
not know whether they ever associated with any other tribe. I
do not know the date when my ancestors left the Old Nation.
Ool-was-kie-ke may be the name. They drew money ever since
there was any. My father drew Old Settler from heirship on his
mother's side. I think it was in the '90's. My great grandfather was Mike Hildebrand from Tennessee. Great grand mother
was Elizabeth Armstrong, or Pettit and her maiden name was
Hildrebrand. I got this information from the Cherokee Rolls
from Emmett Starr. My father gave him the information about my
grandfather being Mike Hildebrand."
SIGNED: Lonnie Hicks, Chelsea, Okla., Sep 4 1908.
ROLL P75 #14052 FCT COMM #12927 - Lonnie Hicks - 25

11892. EDDIE HICKS,   Chelsea, Okla
Admitted. Cousin of No 7407 and claims through same source.
ROLL P75 #14006 FCT COMM #13250 - Eddie Hicks - 29

11893. HENRY COLLINS and 3 children,   Kennison, Okla
Admitted. Second cousin of No 2671. [For Roll information See
App 7705, Vol. 4]

11894. ELJEIRY FLEETWOOD and 8 children,   Long, Okla
Rejected. Uncle of No 817. Ancestors no on rolls. (See No.

817 for reasons for the rejection of this claim).

11895. MAY LEVIN,   Dallas, Tex
Admitted. Niece of No 615 and claims through same source.
ROLL P89 #17015 FCT COMM #27594 - May Levin - 20

11896. CHARLES B. HUGHES and 5 children,   Vinita, Okla
Rejected. It does not appear that any ancestor was ever enrolled or that any ancestor was party to the treaties of 1835-
1836 and 46. Shows no real connection with the Eastern Cherokees. See Misc. Test. P.. 3642.
MISC. TEST. P. 3642. No 11896 - Chas. B. Hughes:
   "I am 43 years of age; was born in Polk County, Tenn. I
claim my Indian blood through my mother. I have never gotten
any land or money out here. My mother came here when I did.
She never got any land or money. I do not know where she was
born. She came here when I was five years old. My mother's
father was the Indian. I never saw him. I do not know where
he lived. He lived back east somewhere. None of my relatives
that I know of ever got any Indian money or land. My mother
did not speak the Cherokee language. She passed as a white
woman. I think my grandfather died during the war. I have
heard of my Indian blood ever since I can remember."
SIGNED: Chas. B. Hughes, Vinita, Okla., Oct 12 1908.

11897. ALICE W. LANDRUM,   [No Residence]
            by Charlotte J. Landrum
Admitted. First cousin of No 2847. Duplicate of child on No
5646. [For Roll information See app 5646, Vol. 3]

11898. WILLIAM L. CRAIG and 5 children,   Pinole, Cal
Admitted. Nephew of No 9422.
ROLL P48 #8671 - William L. Craig - 41
          8672 - Claud M. (son)   - 17
          8673 - Hazel O. (dau)   - 15
          8674 - Harry G. (son)   - 13
          8675 - Arthur O. (son) - 11
          8676 - Lucinda A. (dau) - 8

11899. ELIZA J. WALFFORD and 1 child,   Peggs, Okla
Rejected. Sister of No 11896 and claims through same source.

11900. SIS ANN FOREMAN,   Peggs, Okla
Rejected. Sister of No 11896 and claims through same source.

11901. JAMES HENRY HUGHES,   Vinita, Okla
Rejected. Brother of No 11896 and claims through same source.

11902. A. J. WATERS and 7 children,   Laurel Bloomery, Tenn
Rejected. Applicant is a daughter of and claims through Ned
Sizemore and is rejected for reasons stated in the Sizemore
case. [App 417, Vol. 1]

11903. AVERY J. WATERS, Duplicate of No 11902.

11904. AMANDA G. RUPARD and 8 children, Laurel Bloomery, Tenn
Rejected. See special report Sizemore No 417.

11905. MARY J. RUPARD,   Laurel Bloomery, Tenn
Rejected. See special report Sizemore No 417.

11906. MARY J. RUPARD,   Laurel Bloomery, Tenn
Rejected. See special report Sizemore No 417.

11907. JONATHAN R. WRIGHT,   Christie, Okla
Admitted. Son of No 1848 and claims through same source.
ROLL P154 #29987 FCT COMM #22473 - Johnathan R. Wright - 25

11908. THOS. BELT and 3 children,   Leach, Okla
Admitted. Mother enrolled as Jane. Grandfather enrolled as
Swimmee [sic], Del. No 688. See Misc. Test. P. 4249.
MISC. TEST. P. 4249.   #11908 - Tom Belt...through W. A.
Downing, Interpreter:
    "My mother's name was Ah-yer-noo-lah or Jennie. Her fa-
ther's name was I-hu-ah-neh or swimming or swimmer. Her moth-
er's name was Ga-tah-ne. They lived in Saline or G. S. in 1851
See Del. 688."
SIGNED: Tom(as) Belt, Rose, Okla., Mar 15 1909.

MISC. TEST. P. 3802.   #11908 - Thomas Belt...through Tom
Roach, Interpreter:
    "My name is Thomas Belt. I am 39 years old. I was enrolled
by the Dawes Commission as a full-blood and received my allotment of land. My father and mother were enrolled in 1851. I do
not know whether they were married at that time or not. My father was living in Going Snake District in 1851. I do not know
with whom he was enrolled. My mother was enrolled in Saline
District in 1851. My fathers and mothers names were Do-choo-
la-nah and Jen-nie. I made a mistake when I made out my application. My mother was enrolled I think with her parents in
1851. My grandparents on my fathers side were Gah-luh-nuh-duh
and Betsy or Quait-sy. I do not know where she was enrolled in
1851. My grandparents on my fathers side were emigrant Cherokees. My grandparents on my mother's side were Ah-hyuh-he-nuh
or Swimming and Gah-tah-nih. My grandparents on my mothers
side were enrolled I think in Saline District in 1851. My
grandparents on my mothers side came from the Old Nation. My
grandmother on my mothers side was born after her parents came
to the Indian Territory. None of my ancestors were Old Settlers. My ancestors have always been with the Cherokee tribe.
I was enrolled and drew the Strip payment in 1894. I do not
know the names of any of the aunts or uncles on my fathers
side who were enrolled in 1851. My mother had a sister by the
name of N-ake -- another by the name of Quait-cy -- a brother
by the name of Ool-skun-ne. They were enrolled in Saline Dis-

trict in 1851. They might have been enrolled in Delaware District." SIGNED: Thos. Belt, Locust Grove, Okla., Oct 14 1908.
ROLL P28 #4801 FCT COMM #18629 - Thos. Belt   - 37
          4802   18631 - Liddy (dau)   - 7
          4803   18632 - Scoo-wee Scoo-wee (son) - 5
          4804   3649m - Nancy (dau)   - 1

11909. FRENCH TAIT and 3 children,   Leach, Okla
Admitted. Father enrolled as Gah-ne-doo. Half sister
enrolled as Ma-le.   Del. No 600.   Evidence shows that
applicant is an emigrant Cherokee. See Misc. Test. P. 4252.
MISC. TEST. P. 4252. #11909 - Soggie Sanders...through W. A.
Downing, Interpreter:
    "I am 68 years old. I know Frenck Tail and have known his
people for a long time. I served in the Civil war with his father. His father's name was Cah-ne-too.   He had grown daughters in 1865. I only know the name of one of them, that was
Ma-le. See Del. 600. I know that Frenck Tails father was an
emigrant Cherokee. He never received any old settler money."
SIGNED: Soggie Sanders, Rose, Okla., Mar 15 1909.
Charley Hughes:
    "I am 60 years old. I known [sic] French Tail and have
always understood that he was an emigrant Cherokee.   I helped
to make the old settler payment in 1894 and I know that he did
not draw any old settler money at that time."
SIGNED: Charley Hughes, Rose, Okla., Mar 15 1909.
ROLL P136 #26237 FCT COMM #20773 - French Tail   - 38
          26238   20774 - Lucy (wife)   - 36
                               (App 26515)
          26239   30636 - Jim or Ezekiel (son) - 6
          26240   4642m - Lewis (son)   - 2
          26241   4643m - Eli or Cusarnee (son) - 1
          26242   20775 - Maggie Manus   - 14
                               (dau of w)

11910. MARY F. TRUEMAN and 2 children,   Cherokee City, Ark
Admitted. Aunt of No 1604.
ROLL P141 #27350 FCT COMM #1419 - Mary F. Trueman   - 59
          27351   1422 - Samuel O. (son)   - 15
          27352   1423 - Benjamin O. (son)   - 15

11911. NAOMI A. SITTEN and 2 children,   Maple, Okla
Admitted. First cousin of No 642. Father of applicant en-
rolled by Chap. No 1687.
ROLL P127 #24515 FCT COMM #31698 - Naomi A. Sitten - 24
          24516   31699 - Theo. L. (son)   - 5
          24517   3128m - Jeannie I. (dau)   - 1

11912. SAMUEL B. LANGLEY and 3 children,   Westville, Okla
Admitted. Brother of No 805 and claims through same source.
ROLL P88 #16711 FCT COMM #27953 - Samuel B. Langley - 29
          16712   27954 - Clarebe B. (son)   - 5

11912. SAMUEL B. LANGLEY (Cont)
      16713 FCT COMM #2435m - Fannie L. (dau) - 3
      16714   2436m - Manerva L. (dau) - 1

11913. MURTIE MAY SCACEWATER,   Stilwater, Okla
Admitted. Sister of No 9380 and cousin of No 5319. [For Roll
information See App 11883]

11914. ISAAC BEARPAW,   Stilwell, Okla
Admitted. Applicant's father enrolled by Drennen in Flint
Dist. No 290.
ROLL P27 #4580 FCT COMM #20702 - Isaac Bearpaw - 32

11915. SANDERS COCHRAN,   Stilwell, Okla
Admitted. First cousin of No 1071. Father enrolled in 1851
in Flint No 334.
ROLL P44 #8012 FCT COMM #19251 - Sanders Cochran - 27
        8013   19000 - Nancy (wife) - 22 (App 12535)
        8014   19001 - Jesse (son)   - 7

11916. NANCY MANKILLER,   Stilwell, Okla
Admitted. Applicant's mother, Polly, and grandmother Alsey
Rat, enrolled by Drennen in Flint 234 [? blurred]. See Testi-
mony of Nancy taken at Stilwell Mar 1904 [sic] p. 4034
MISC. TEST. P. 4034. No 11916 - Nancy Mankiller...through D.
M. Faulkner, Interpreter:
    "My name is Nancy Mankiller; my post-office is Stilwell,
Okla.; I am over forty years old; I claim my Indian blood thru
both my father and my mother; my father's name was Oo-squah-
lih Sequiche; Sequiche was my grand-father and Ailsey was liv-
ing with him; they lived close by here in Flint Dis- trict;
Polly was my mother and she drew emigrant money; Polly's fa-
ther was named Oo-tsa-te-yah-ta Darchursi & his wife was named
Ailsey Rat, Indian name Che-sta-chi; my father and mother were
both emigrants; my mother had a brother named John; my mother
also had a half brother named Wilson; Flint 234."
SIGNED: Nancy "X" Mankiller, Stilwell, Okla., Mar 19 1909.
[For Roll information See App 11991]

11917. POLLY MANKILLER,   Stilwell, Okla
Admitted. Applicant's father Scar-yah-du-gee, was enrolled in
Tahl. 469. See Testimony of applicant and that of Lucy Shooter
taken at Stilwell, March 19, 1909, p. 4033 and also Misc.
Test. P. 3127.
MISC. TEST. P. 3127. Interpreter Used - App No 11917 - Polly
Mankiller:
    "My name is Polly Mankiller; my age is 54 years about. I
was born in Flint District. I got the bread and strip pay-
ments. I was enrolled by the Dawes Commission, Cherokee Roll
No 29859. I am a full-blood Cherokee. My parents were not
Old Settlers. My father's name was Scar-yah-du-gee. Dead;
been dead a long time. He lived in Flint, I think. He came

from North Carolina with the Emigrants. I never heard him say about getting [sic] any money from the Government as I was too small when he died. My father's name may be Sca-yah-doo-ga. I don't know whether he ever lived in Tahlequah. I don't know whether he ever had any other name. He had one brother named Redbird in English, Chees-quah-gee-gah-ga, in Indian. I was told that he lived in Flint. Ches-quah-dee-gah-geh may be the name. I don't know my father's father's name. I don't know the name of my father's mother, but think it was Sal-lih or Sallie. My mother's maiden name was Ju-sun-tees-key. She had a brother by the name Ta-tes-ky or Tah-tas-key. Another named Da-gun-wak-sey. They lived in Flint District. It might be Da-guh-walk-sey. Another brother named Ben, Quanee in Indian. All lived in Flint District. A sister named A-sin-ni, or A-chin-nih. My mother's mother's name was Sarah. De-sun-ste-ske, was my mother's father's name. I don't know any of my grandparents brothers and sisters. I had a brother who was a baby when we drew money, Gah-nah-gees-ky, or Gah-nah-dees-ky. My grandmother had a brother Ah-nah-loo-ques-kee. I had a cousin named Ja-key. He lived in Flint too. My grandmother told me that we were Emigrants and we never associated with any other tribe of Indians."
SIGNED: Polly Mankiller, Stilwell, Okla., Sep 23 1908.
MISC. TEST. P. 4033. No 11917 - Polly Mankiller...through D. M. Faulkner, Interpreter:
"My name is Polly Mankiller; my post-office is Stilwell, Okla.; I am over fifty years old; my mother's mother was named Sah-li; my mother had one child older than I am named Gah-nar-desk; my father's name was Scar-nar-du-gee; this child Gah-nar-des-ki was a child of the same mother and different father; my mother was named Sallie; my mother and father were both emigrants, I think; my mother's father was Oo-sar-te-ski"
SIGNED: Polly "X"Mankiller, Stilwell, Okla., Mar 19 1909.
Lucy Shooter...through D. M. Faulkner:
"My name is Lucy Shooter; my post-office is Bunch, Okla.; I am about seventy years old; I know Polly Mankiller; I knew her father; he was an emigrant Cherokee."
SIGNED: Lucy "X" Shooter, Stilwell, Okla., Mar 19 1909.
[For Roll information See App 11998]

11918. WEBSTER HALFBREED (or PIGEON), Rose, Okla
        (1 child)
Admitted. Sister of No 497 and claims through same ancestors.
ROLL P69 #12958 FCT COMM #17573 - Webster Halfbreed - 37
        12959   3850m - Thomas C. (son) - 2

11919. SALLIE SHELL,   Stilwell, Okla
Admitted. Applicant's grandmother Tah-lah-tee is enrolled by Chapman on No 252. See Misc. Test. No. 3140.
MISC. TEST. P. 3140. Appli. 11924 (11919) - Idia Eagle... through L. D. Walkingstick, Interpreter:
    "My name is Idia Eagle; I was born in Flint District,

267

1866; I am a full blood Cherokee and was enrolled by the Dawes
Commission and received my allotment of land; I was enrolled
as Idia Eagle; (See Index 18792) (Also 19943) My father's
name was Standing Shell; he was also called Stand Backwater.
I do not know my mother's English name, but my mother's Cherokee name was Dah-too-skee-ste; my father and mother were born
in the old nation in the East; I don't know when they came to
the Ind. Terr.; my grandparents on my father's side were Ah-
man-tsuh and my grandmother Sah-lah-tee; my grandparents lived
in the Ind. Terr., but I do not know when they came West; I
don't know whether any of my people ever drew any Old Settler
money or not; I was small, but I do not think that any of them
were Old Settlers. None of my ancestors through whom I claim
have ever taken up rights with any other tribe of Indians other than the Cherokees. I don't remember of my parents ever
being enrolled, for I was a small child when my parents died.
My parents lived in Flint District; my father had a brother by
the name of Te-lah-ska-skih. (See Chapman 252 and 253).
SIGNED: Idia Eagle, Stilwell, Okla., Sep 23 1908.
ROLL P126 #24339 FCT COMM #18798 - Sallie Shell - 46
        24340   18800 - Arch (son) - 18

11920. MARY GLASS,   Stilwell, Okla
Admitted. This applicant's father Looney Glass is enrolled by
Drennen from Flint Dist. under the group No 496.
ROLL P66 #12275 FCT COMM #22713 - Mary Glass - 18

11921. ARCH SHELL, Minor son of No 11919.

11922. JOSHUA NOFIRE and 3 children,   Long, Okla
Admitted. Claimant was enrolled by the Dawes Comm. No 18787
and is recognized as being of emigrant Cherokee descent. See
Misc. Test. of Thomas Proctor page 3921.
MISC. TEST. P. 3921. No 11922 - Tom Proctor...through D. M.
Faulkner, Interpreter:
    "I know Joshua Nofire whose mother was Annie Proctor, a
daughter of George and Darkey Proctor; Annie had a sister Che-
coo-a and a brother Chu-wa-loo-kee and another brother Claw-
se-ny; S. B. #10. Annie was not living in 1851."
SIGNED: Tom "X" Proctor, Muldrow, Okla., Mar 9 1909.
ROLL P105 #20134 FCT COMM #18787 - Joshua Nofire - 30
         20135   18789 - Mary (dau)   - 6
         20136   18790 - Sequoyah (son) - 4
         20137   3816m - Nannie (dau)   - 2

11923. LUCY GLASS,   Stilwell, Okla
Admitted. Sister of Mary Glass App No 11920 and is admitted
for same reasons.
ROLL P66 #12274 FCT COMM #22712 - Lucy Glass - 19

11924. IDA EAGLE and 2 children,   Stilwell, Okla
Admitted. Daughter of No 11919 and claims thru same source.

ROLL P57 #10411 FCT COMM #18792 - Ida Eagle   - 37
          10412   18795 - Josiah (son) - 13
          10413   18796 - William (son) - 5

11925. MARY SNAKE,   Chance, Okla
Admitted. Sister of No 11632 and claims through same source.
ROLL P134 #25921 FCT COMM #19660 - Mary Suake - 17
                              by Betsy Suake, Mother

11926. LINNIE M. SIXKILLER,   Chance, Okla
Admitted. Niece of No 5107 and claims through same source.
[For Roll information See App 6694, Vol. 3]

11927. TENNESSEE V. BRILEY and 3 children, Black Gum, Okla
Admitted. Grand niece of No 920. Grandfather of applicant
enrolled as George Byers at Flint No 387 1/2.
ROLL P34 #5804 FCT COMM # 3763 - Tennessee V. Briley - 23
          5805   3764 - William E. (son)   - 8
          5806   3765 - Nettie M. (dau)   - 6
          5807   3898m - Lela E. (dau)   - 1

11928. ELLEN MORGANS,   Oolagah, Okla
Admitted. Niece of No 175.
ROLL P101 #19371 FCT COMM #24702 - Ellen Morgan - 19

11929. EDWARD SUNDAY,   Oolagah, Okla
Admitted. Brother of No 175.
ROLL P134 #26018 FCT COMM #24698 - Edward Sunday Sr. - 52

11930. EDWARD SUNDAY,   Oolagah, Okla
Admitted. Nephew of No 175.
ROLL P134 #26017 FCT COMM #24701 - Edward Sunday Jr. - 21

11931. LOU POLSON and 4 children,   Oolagah, Okla
Admitted. Niece of No 175.
ROLL P112 #21523 FCT COMM #11816 - Lou Polson   - 29
          21524   11817 - John M. (son) - 9
          21525   11818 - Eddie (son)   - 7
          21526   1317m - Willie E. (son) - 3
          21527   1318m - Jewell (son)   - 1

11932. WILLIAM SUNDAY,   Oolagah, Okla
Admitted. Nephew of No 175.
ROLL P135 #26051 FCT COMM #24700 - William Sunday - 28

11933. SARAH C. BALDRIDGE,   Empire City, Kans
Rejected. Applicant's ancestors were not parties to treaties
of 1835-6-46. Were never enrolled with Cherokees. See Misc.
Test. P. 2102.
MISC. TEST. P. 2102. No 11933 - Sarah C. Baldridge:
    "I am 67 years of age; was born in Union Co., Georgia. I
claim Cherokee Indian blood through my father, John Hudgkins.

I first heard of my Indian blood 38 years ago. A cousin of my
father told me. Her name is Geannie Ward and she lived in the
Indian nation. I have never received any Indian money from the
government and never tried to get any before this time. I left
Georgia in 1863. In 1851 I was living in Georgia. I think some
of the Indians were paid money at that time but I did not get
any nor did any of my people. I went to Illinois from Georgia,
then to Missouri and and from Missouri to Kansas.   I lived in
the Indian country one summer. I never tried to get an allotment and never went before the Dawes Commission. My father was
born in Habersham County, Ga. I never saw my grandparents. My
father parents lived in Habersham County, Ga. My grandfather's
name was Phillip Hudgins."
SIGNED: Sarah C. Baldridge, Columbus, Kans., Aug 21 1908.
EXCEPTION CASE. Rejected.   Total number of exceptions filed
in this group -- 2. Original recommendation renewed.

11934. EMMA INSCORE and 4 children,   Round Peak, N C
Rejected. It does not appear that any ancestor was ever en-
rolled or that any ancestor was a party to the treaties of
1835-6 and 46.   Shows no connection with the Eastern Cher-
okees. Does not know to what tribe ancestors belonged.   See
Misc. Test. P. 31.
MISC. TEST. P. 31. No 15178 - William P. Doby:
     "My name is Wm. P. Doby; I am 53 years old; I live at R.
F. D. #1, Rockford, Surry Co., N. C. I have been in Surry Co.
I think about 25 years. Before coming here, I lived near Old
Town, Grayson Co., Va. I was born in Davidson Co., N. C., and
moved to Grayson Co. when I was about 6 years old. According
to what my mother said, I have Indian blood in my veins. She
has been dead about 25 years; she died in Surry Co., N. C. She
came here with me from Va. The Indian blood came through my
father's side. He died in 1867 in Grayson Co., Va., near Old
Town. He lived there from the time I was 6 years old until the
second year after the surrender.   My mother said that my father's father was half Indian. I just really could not just
say positively to what tribe he belonged. I never heard that
my grandfather was enrolled, nor my father, either. I never
heard my father talk anything about it; I was young when he
died. I do not know where my grandfather was born; he died in
Davidson Co., N. C. I do not know whether or not he was an old
man. My father was about 50 when he died. My father was born
in Davidson Co., N. C. I don't know whether my father voted or
not; I suppose he did. He took an interest in politics, as
well as I can recollect. This is my brother with me, Charlie
Doby (14635), and I have other brothers and sisters applying
for this fund -- John Doby (15171), Jas. (19088), and sister
Jennie (25411), Sarah McGlothern (14633), Emma Inscore
(11934), Pulina Vernon (14640). They all claim Indian blood,
the same as I do. I do not know whether my father ever lived
with the tribe or not, but I suppose not. Nor do I know whether my grandfather ever lived with the tribe."

270

SIGNED: W. P. Doby, Pilot Mt., N. C., Mar 23 1908.
Charley Doby...brother of Wm. P. Doby...deposes and says:
    "My name is Charley Doby; I am about 45 years old; my
P. O. is Low Gap, N. C. I have heard the testimony of my
brother, as given above, and it is substantially correct, as
far as I know." SIGNED: Charles "X" Doby, Winifred E. Ayers,
Attest., Pilot Mt., N. C., Mar 23 1908.
EXCEPTION CASE. 11934. Emma Inscore and 4 children, Sanders,
Idaho. Rejected. Total number of exceptions filed in this
group -- 2. Original recommendation renewed.

11935. MARGARET L. LONG and 5 children,   Oottewah, Tenn
Rejected. Applicant nor ancestor never enrolled. It does not
appear that they were living within the Cherokee Domain in
1835-6 and '46 as recognized members of the tribe. It does
not appear that they never lived with any tribe of Indians.
See Misc. Test. P. 385.
MISC. TEST. P. 385. #11935 - Margaret L. Long:
    "That I am 51 years of age and live about three miles from
Ooltewah, Tenn. I claim my Indian descent thru my mother and
her mother. My grandfather on my mother's side was a full
blooded white man. I don't know how much Indian I am. I don't
know how much Indian my mother claimed. My grandmother was
born and raised in N. C. I think it was near Boone, N. C. but
I don't know just exactly where. My grand mother and grand
father moved to Tenn. when my mother was quite small. They
moved to Johnson Co. I don't know that any of my people ever
lived with any Indian tribe. I am Indian and white and am recognized as a white person. My husband is a white man. My
mother's sisters are: Louvenia Turner, never married; Margaret
Turner married Snodgrass, Eliza Turner who married Butler,
Mary Turner who was my mother and who married Reece. She was
married in 1855. My mother's brother was Thomas Turner. He
is living at Bristol, Tenn. My mother is living at Binnfield.
One of my great uncles was Burton Johnson. I have been to his
house in N. C. but I was so small I don't remember just the
part of N. C. My mother had another brother by the name of
Abraham Johnson. There was an Abraham Johnson, my great grand
father and an Abraham Johnson my great uncle. I don't know of
any of these parties ever being on any Indian roll. They never
had any Indian names that I know of, always went by the names
of Johnson and Turner. I don't know whether it was Abraham or
Annie Johnson who claimed the Indian blood but I think it was
Abraham. My mother and grandmother were living in Johnson Co.,
Tenn. in 1835 and 1851 - lived there until they died. My mother when I would ask her anything about it would say she got
her Indian blood thru Pocohontas. Don't know where Pocohontas
lived but it is the same Pocohontas we read of in history."
SIGNED: Maggie L. Long, Ooltewah, Tenn., Jun 23 1908.
EXCEPTION CASE. 11935. Mary A. Reece, App 30900, 423 W. 3rd
St., Morristown, Tenn. Rejected. Total number of exceptions
filed in this group -- 1. Original recommendation renewed.

11936. GEORGE TUCKER and 3 children,   Tulsa, Okla
Rejected. No connection with Del. No 383, see appl. No 4671.
Applicant notified to appear and testify but failed to do so.
Letter remained unanswered. Information in application insuf-
ficient.

11937. JENNIE HOLLAND,   Birmingham, Ala
                        410 35th St. & 5th Ave, N.
Rejected. Claims through the same source as No 5170.

11938. ROSE A. SHELTON and 5 children,   Volney, Va
Rejected. See special report Sizemore No 417.

11939. ROSA A. McCARTHY and 1 child,   Laurel Bloomery, Tenn
Rejected. See special report Sizemore No 417.

11940. ROSA A. McCARTHY,   Laurel Bloomery, Tenn
Rejected. See special report Sizemore No 417.

11941. JAMES J. BLACKBURN,   Homer, Ga
Rejected. Ancestor not enrolled. Does not establish genuine
connection with Cherokee tribe. See Misc. Test. P. 1259.
MISC. TEST. P. 1259. App No 11941 - James J. Blackburn:
    "My name is James J. Blackburn. I was born in 1844, in
Gilmore Co. Have always lived in Georgia. My father died when
I was about 3 years old, and we went to live with my grand
father. I never lived with the Indians, but my grand father
and mother lived among them or in the neighborhood with them.
I claim through my mother. My mother's name was Fanny Lucinda
Brown before marriage, and Blackburn after marriage.   If my
mother was enrolled I never knew it. I reckon old man Blackburn was enrolled. My mother visited the Indians and they
visited her. My mother got her blood from her father, Jimmy
Brown. He was living in Banks Co. in 1851. He has been dead
30 odd years. Fisher Brown was the father of Jimmy Brown and
was a full-blood Cherokee Indian. My mother had one brother
James but he died when 7 or 8 years old. If Jimmie Brown ever
lived anywhere else but Georgia I never knew it. I lived with
him 19 years, and never heard him mention it. My people have
always been recognized as white and also been called Indians.
I never heard my people talk about the treaties. I do not know
whether they were parties to the treaties of 1835-6 and 1846."
SIGNED: James J. "X" Blackburn, Maysville, Ga., Jul 9 1908.
EXCEPTION CASE. 11941.   James Jackson Blackburn, R F D #1,
Homer, Ga. Rejected. Total number of exceptions filed in
this group -- 2. Original recommendation renewed.

11942. ALBERT GRIFFITH,   Homer, Ga
Rejected. Applicant claims through his mother who was a slave.
See letter herein.

11943. HARRISON MOSS and 2 children,   Hollingsworth, Ga
Rejected. Applicant's parents were slaves. See letter.
EXCEPTION CASE. Rejected. Total number of exceptions filed
in this group — 4. Original recommendation renewed.

11944. NATHANIEL CROW,   [No residence]
Rejected. Grand nephew of No 8395 and claims through the same
source. [See Exception Case 8395, Vol. 4]

11945. CORNELIA WASHBURN,   Homer, Ga
Rejected. Sister of No 8395 and claims through same source.

11946. RUTH SIMMONS,   Hollingsworth, Ga
Rejected. Applicant's ancestors were not parties to the treaties of 1835-6--46 nor enrolled with them.

11947. SUSAN WHITE,   Commerce, Ga
Rejected. It does not appear that applicant's ancestors were
parties to the treaties of 1835-6 and 46, never shared in payments to Cherokees nor enrolled with them.

11948. RANSON O. SIMMONS,   Hollingsworth, Ga
Rejected. Ancestors were not enrolled. Were not parties to
treaties of 1835-6 and 46. Does not establish genuine connection with Cherokee tribe.
MISC. TEST. P. 1243. App No 11948 - Ransom O. Simmons:
    "My name is Ransom A. Simmons. I am 68 years old. I live
in Banks County, Ga. I have lived here 35 years, before that
in Franklin Co., N. E. part of Ga. I was born in Jackson Co.
In 1851 I was in Habersham Co., I was not enrolled at that
time we knew nothing about it. I never heard of the enrollment. I never got any money from the Government. Never tried
to get any. I claim Cherokee about 1/8. I claim through my
mother Catherine Smith, before marriage. She was born in Hall
Co. She was not enrolled as she knew nothing about it. I never
lived with the Indians and never attended their councils.   I
have always been recognized as a white man with Indian blood.
I have always voted. My mother claimed through her father,
Samuel Smith, his mother was Annie Marr, a full-blood. Samuel
Smith lived here in Hall Co.   I do not know that he was ever
enrolled. He died in 72. He was an old man at his death.   My
folks always told me I had Indian blood. I do not know that
Samuel Smith ever lived anywhere except here in Georgia.   I
never heard anyone say that he ever lived anywhere else.   I
don't know that Samuel Smith ever lived with the Indians.   I
was never known by any other name. He was sometimes called
Samuel Marr. They were uneducated and never knew anything
about the enrollment. I do not know any one who knows any more
about my case than I do.   I am a second cousin to James C.
Smith and we both claim Indian blood through the same line.
(11947)."
SIGNED: Ransom O. Simmons, Maysville, Ga., Jul 9 1908.

                          273

11949. WILLIAM CROW,   Baldwin, Ga
Rejected. Brother of No 8395 and claims through same source.
[See Exception Case No 2637, Vol. 2]
MISC. TEST. P. 1256. App No 11949-2637 - William Crow:
    "My name is William Crow. I am about 45 years old. I live
in Banks Co., Ga. Have always lived in Ga. I claim Cherokee
Indian blood. I have heard my family say so. I never got any
money. Never applied for any. I claim through my father Alfred
Crow. He is dead. Died about 18 [16?] years ago. He was quite
old. My father was not a slave. I do not know where my father
lived in 1851. My father was raised in Spartansburg, N. C. My
father was not enrolled that I know of. I do not know of any
reason why he was not. He did not live with the Indians that
I know of. I never heard of him attending any of their meet-
ings or councils. My father got his blood from his mother,
Maria, who was living with a man by the name of Farr. Samuel
Farr was his name.   My mother's father's name was Looney
Wattee. My mother's name was Cassie Cash. She was owned by
this one man only. The same man owned me. I know nothing more
about Looney Wattee. I am a brother to Cornelia, and Mandy
Crow, and Alfred Crow."
SIGNED: William "X" Crow, Maysville, Ga., Jul 9 1908.
MISC. TEST. P. 1257.   Witness in re 11949-2637 - William
Brown:
    "My name is William Brown. I am 58 years old. I have al-
ways lived in Georgia. I have known applicants since immedi-
ately after the war. They claim from their father and have
always claimed Cherokee blood. I do not know that their father
ever enrolled. I do not know that he ever applied. I never
heard any reason why their father was not enrolled. His mother
was owned by Samuel Farr. Their father looked like an Indian
and was proud of it. Alfred Crow claimed through his mother,
Maria Farr. This is all I know about this claim."
SIGNED: W. D. Brown, Maysville, Ga., Jul 9 1908.

11950. J. C. SMITH,   Mt. Airy, Ga
Rejected. Second cousin of No 11948.
MISC. TEST. P. 1527. #11950 - James C. Smith:
    "My name is James C. Smith and I reside at Mt. Airy, Ga.
I was born in Habersham Co., Ga. in 1841. I claim relation-
ship to the Cherokee Indians through my father, William Rylee
Smith, who was a quarter blood Cherokee Indian. He claimed
through his mother, Ellen Smith, who was a half-blood Cherokee
Indian; she claimed through her mother, Annie Marr, who was a
full blood Cherokee Indian. My mother and grandmother have
told me of my connection and also about living among the Indians; my grandmother has told me that she remembers when the
Indians were driven off and my father went as far as Chattanooga, Tenn. with them. I remember some of the Indians coming
back to this country and they would stop at our house. My
grandmother could speak the Indian language and my mother
could to some extent. The Indians recognized my grandmother

as one of their tribe. I know of no enrollment and do not know
of my people ever receiving any money or lands from the Government. I do not know where my father was born, but I think
it was at Greenville, S. C. My father was a child when he
moved over into Habersham County, Ga. My grandmother had one
brother, Sam Smith, and he stayed among the Indians until they
were taken away. I cannot tell why he didn't go West with the
Indians; he married a full blood white woman and remained in
this county. My father had two sisters, Nancy Smith and Betsy
Smith, but they staed [sic] in this country and died here.
None of my people, as far back as I know, ever went West. My
people were always recognized as white."
SIGNED: James C. "X" Smith, M. L. Daley, Test., Clarksville,
Ga., Jul 13 1908.

11951. ALFRED CROW,   Hollingsworth, Ga
Rejected. Brother of No 8395 and claims through same source.

11952. LARRY CASH,   Hollingsworth, Ga
Rejected. Applicant or ancestors never enrolled. Applicant's
ancestors through whom he claims were slaves. Misc. Test. P.
1265.
MISC. TEST. P. 1265. Witness in re: Appl. No 20205 - Larry
Cash:
    "My name is Larry Cash. I am 52 years old. I have always
lived in Georgia. I have always known Eliza Scott. I have
known her ever since her birth. She claims Indian blood. I
have heard it from her grandparents. Cherokee Indian blood
from her father. His name was Bird Cash. He was never enrolled. He never got any money from the Government. Old man
Wm. Warford owned Eliza Scott's father. Dan Cash was a full-
blooded Indian, and Charles Cash was half Indian. Eliza
Scott's mother was a slave. Reuben Jorden owned her. She was a
slave from her birth. I am an uncle of Eliza Scott's. I reckon
I have a claim in but I did not get a notice."
SIGNED: Larry Cash, Maysville, Ga., Jul 9 1908.
EXCEPTION CASE. Rejected. Total number of exceptions filed
in this group -- 1. Original recommendation renewed.

11953. MARY MORRIS,   Bellton, Ga
Rejected. Niece of No 11952 and claims through same source.

11954. HENRY COLUMBUS BROWN,   Homer, Ga
Rejected. 1: No ancestor was ever enrolled. 2: No ancestor
was party to the treaties of 1835-6-46. 3: Applicant claims
through his grandfather who was a slave.

11955. MANDA CROW,   Lula, Ga
Rejected. Sister of No 8395 and claims through same source.

11956. BIRD JAMES WASHBURN,   Homer, Ga
Rejected. It does not appear that applicant's ancestors were

parties to the treaties of 1835-6-46, never shared in payments to Cherokees no enrolled with them.

11957. CORA E. PATTIE, FREDERICK H. PATTIE,
        SOPHIE F. PATTIE, Duplicate of children in No 11958.

11958. LOTTIE A. CLARK and 3 children,   Sumas, Wash
Admitted. First cousin of No 613 and claims through the same source. Applicant's father enrolled by Chapman No 1368.
ROLL P43 #7637 – Lottie A. Clark   – 37
          7638 – Cora E. PATTIE (dau)   – 4
          7639 – Frederick H. PATTIE (son) – 3
          7640 – Sophie F. PATTIE (dau)   – 1

11959. AMANDA ELLISON,   Gibbsville, Ga
Rejected. Applicant was a slave. See letter.

11960. JESSE SIXKILLER, Gdn. Duplicate of No 2228.

11961. WILLIAM P. THORNE for   Tahlequah, Okla
        JACOB H. THORNE and WALTER THORNE,
Admitted. The grandmother of applicant on her mother's side was enrolled by Drennen in Del. Dist. 35, under the name of Martha A. Daniel. The maternal grandfather was enrolled in Going Snake district under the name of Jacob Woodall, Going Snake 236.
MISC. TEST. P. 3522. App #11961 – William P. Thorne:
    "My name is Wm. P. Thorne. I live at Tahlequah. I am guardian for Jacob H. and Walter Thorne, my children who claim through their mother who is dead. They are enrolled by the Dawes Commission #25225, and 25226. I think these childrens' mother was an Immigrant Cherokee. Her name was Emma B. Woodall. She was not living in 1851. Her father's name was Jacob H. Woodall. He was living in 1851. I could not say whether he had any children living then or not. His wife was name Anna Woodall. She had a brother by the name of Robert. I don't know what Dist. they were living in 1851.   I suppose in Delaware Dist. I don't know whether Ann Daniel had any sisters or not. She had a brother Robert Daniel. A brother named Ezekiel. She had a sister Nicy. Ann Daniel's mother's name was Mary Daniel. In 1852 Ann Daniels was living with her mother. She had a brother named John. See Del. 35 Emma B. Woodall's father's name was Jacob H. Woodall. He had a brother named Isaac, one named Abrah, and a sister named Peggy, and a sister named Nancy. See G. S. 236."
SIGNED: Wm. P. Thorne, Tahlequah, Okla., Oct 5 1908.
ROLL P139 #26938 FCT COMM #25225 – Jacob H. Thorne – 19
          26939   25226 – Walter (bro)   – 18
                                      by Wm. P. Thorne, Gdn.

11962. GEO. HALE,   Dickson, Tenn
Rejected. Uncle of No 11880.

11963. MACK MUSKRAT, Duplicate of No 10152.

11964. OO-SQUIN-NI RIDER,   Southwest City, Mo
Admitted. Aunt of No 1558. [For Roll information See App 8373,
Vol. 4 - Surname "Dirtseller" on roll]

11965. LUCINDA SUL-SAH, Duplicate. Same as No 380.

11966. ANNIE GOODMONEY and 1 child,   Southwest City, Mo
Admitted.   Claimant's father   under name   of We-le;   father's
parents and brothers enrolled by Drennen in 1851, Del. 299.
See Misc. Test. P. -- [no page number listed]
MISC. TEST. P. 4297.   #11966 - Annie Goodmoney...through Tom
Roach, Interpreter:
     "I am about 36 years old; my father and mother were both
Emigrant Cherokees; They both drew money in 1852; my father is
still living and his name is Will June-stoo-te.   My father's
mother was Wah-le. (See Del. 299) My father had a brother by
the name of Thompson. He drew the money in 1852 but died be-
fore the Civil War. I am a full-blood Cherokee. I am a Night
Hawk. I only have one child. His name is Webster. He is now 6
years of age."
SIGNED: Annie Goodmoney, Southwest City, Mo., Mar 25 1909.
ROLL P67 #12418 - Annie Goodmoney - 33
         12419 - Webster (son)   - 3

11967. CORNELIUS KETCHER,   Eucha, Okla
Admitted. Cousin of Darcus Wilson, App No 5653 and is admitted for same reasons.
EXCEPTION CASE. 11967. Susanna Ketcher, by Cornelius Ketcher,
father, Eucha, Okla. Rejected. Total number of exceptions
filed in this group -- 1. Exception filed for minor child born
after May 28, 1906.
[For Roll information See App 640, Vol. 1]

11968. JEREMIAH FEATHERHEAD, minor son on No 6499.

11969. BILL ARROW, Duplicate of No 7455.

11970. SUSIE SNELL,   Southwest City, Mo
Admitted. Sister of No 3055. [For Roll information See App
5030, Vol. 3]

11971. POLLIE TOWIE,   Tahlequah, Okla
Admitted. Applicant claims through grandfather Te-sah-ta-skee
enrolled in 1851 in Going Snake dist. No 140. See Misc. Test.
P. 3413.
MISC. TEST. P. 3413. No 11971 - Pollie Towie...through S. E.
Parris, Interpreter:
     "I drew Immigrant money in 1852. I was living with my
mother at the time. My father and mother were not living to-

gether. I had 2 [? typed over] half brothers older than I. We
lived in G. S. District at the time of the payment. Te-sah-ta-
skee was my grandfather; Little Deer, Jinney, Moses and Che-
nah-wee were my mother's brothers and sisters."
SIGNED: Pollie Towie, Tahlequah, Okla., Oct 3 1908.
ROLL P141 #27210 FCT COMM #18079 - Jeff Towie - 41 (App 12676)
       27211   18080 - Pollie (wife) - 59

11972. LID-DI STUDY and 5 children,   Southwest City, Mo
Admitted. Sister of Katie England No 4873 (Appl) and is admit-
ted for same reasons. [Notation on Roll "(For John and Wm.
Chunestudy and families, see Roll No. 25866 - et seq.)"]
ROLL P134 #25866 FCT COMM #19385 - Bill (William) Study - 54
                     (App 13090)
      25867   19386 - Lid-di (Lydia) (wife) - 44
      25868   19387 - Benjamin (son)   - 19
      25869   19388 - Andy (son)   - 16
      25870   19389 - Robert (son)   - 12
      25871   30543 - Katie (dau)   - 8
      25872   30544 - Ka-ya-ji (Guyuche)   - 6
                     (dau)

11973. AGNESS CAYWOOD,   Southwest City, Mo
Admitted. Daughter of No 14062 Susie Rogers, and is admitted
for same reasons.
MISC. TEST. P. 4289.   #11973 - Agnes Caywood...through Tom
Roach, Interpreter:
    "I am 26 years old; Both of my parents were Emigrant Cher-
okees; I do not know whether they were living in 1851 or not;
my mother is still living; Susie Rogers, P.O. Eucha, Okla. is
her name. Her husbands name is Wilson Rogers. My fathers name
is John Spaniard. His father name was ---- I do not know. My
father's mother's name was Sal-lih. My fathers brothers and
sisters were We-le, a full brother. He was older than my father. He had not [sic] sisters. They lived in Flint District.
I do not know whether my father drew money in 1852 or not. My
mother's name is Susannah Rogers. I do not know with whom my
grandmother on my father's side was living in 1851; The parents of my mother were Chah-lih; I do not know his last name.
My mother's mother was named Sal-lih also. My mother's people
lived in Flint District in 1851; My mother had a brother by
the name of Tom. He was a full-brother. He was older than my
mother. My mother has been living with her present husband,
Wilson Rogers, about 20 years. I was about 5 years old when
they commenced living together. I do not know whether I am enrolled by the Dawes Commission or not. I am a Night Hawk. I
have four minor children; I have made application for my minor
children. I have been married to my present husband about ten
years. The names and ages of my children are as follows - Aggie, ten years old, the next, Ida, 8 years old, the next, Tom,
6 years old, and Lee, 2 years old. My youngest child, Lee was
born Dec ? [blurred], 1906. I first made out an application

for myself and then I made a supplemental application for myself. My mother has never gone by any other name than Rogers
that I know of. I never drew the Old Settler money in 1896.
I have received all the Cherokee payments but the Old Settler
money I never got. I have always gone by the name of Agnes
Caywood since my marriage. I have never been called anything
else."
SIGNED: Agnes Caywood, Southwest City, Mo., Mar 24 1909.
ROLL P40 #7034 FCT COMM #19818 - Joe Caywood - 28 (App 31365)
       7035   20591 - Agnes (wife)   - 26
       7036   30624 - Agie or Cartayah (dau) - 8
       7037   30625 - Wolfe or Ool-skas-te (son)- 5
       7038   4950m - Dah-me or John Davis (son)- 3

11974. JOHN WATERMELON,   Southwest City, Mo
Admitted. Brother of No 11407.
ROLL P146 #28390 FCT COMM #20698 - John Watermellon - 26
      28391   19814 - Laura E. (wife) - 34
                     (App 11975)
      28392   - Kate (dau)   - 1
      28393   - Lillie M. PEAK - 13
                     (dau of w)

11975. LAURA E. WATERMELLON & 2 children, Southwest City, Mo
Admitted. Applicant's father enrolled by Drennen 1851 G. S.
No 319. [For Roll information See App 11974]

11976. SARAH R. AUSTIN and 1 child,   Pryor Creek, Okla
Admitted. Daughter of Eva Ofield (10087) and claims through
her.
ROLL P24 #3896 FCT COMM #12456 - Sarah R. Austin - 25
      3897   2781m - Lucinda (dau) - 3

11977. JOHN F. WOODALL,   Big Cabin, Okla
Rejected. Brother of No 4222.

11978. JOEL J. MORTON and 7 children,   Sallisaw, Okla
Admitted. Nephew of No 5650. Father of claimant enrolled by
Drennen in 1851, Dis. 91.
ROLL P102 #19564 FCT COMM #26308 - Joel J. Morton - 54
       19565   26309 - Robert L. (son) - 15
       19566   26310 - Grover C. (son) - 14
       19567   26311 - William H. (son) - 12
       19568   26312 - Mary B. (dau)   - 11
       19569   26313 - Flossie (dau)   - 5
       19570   3814m - Junia C. (dau) - 3
       19571   3815m - Maudie A. (dau) - 1

11979. FLORA R. AUDD and 7 children,   Checotah, Okla
Rejected. Applicant is enrolled on Creek Roll by the Dawes
Comm. His No is 2429. Other applicants grouped herewith on
same roll, Nos. 2422-3.

11980. TAYLOR DUNCAN and 6 children,   Stilwell, Okla
Admitted. Half brother of No 1991 and claims through the same
source.
ROLL P56 #10335 FCT COMM #27139 - Taylor Duncan - 52
            10336   27140 - Lydia (wife) - 46
                                    (App 31191)
            10337   27144 - Hubert (son) - 19
            10338   27145 - Sallie (dau) - 17
            10339   27146 - Emma (dau)   - 15
            10340   27147 - Annie (dau)   - 13
            10341   27148 - Felix (son)   - 11
            10342   27149 - Charlie (son) - 9

11981. LAURA CLARK and 10 children,   Catale, Okla
Rejected. It does not appear that any ancestor was ever en-
rolled or that any ancestor was party to the treaties of 1835-
1836 and 48 [sic]. No connection with the Eastern Cherokees
is shown either in the application or the testimony. See Misc.
Test. P. 2598.
MISC. TEST. P. 2598. Witness in re App No 11981 Laura Clark -
J. B. Young:
   "My name is J. B. Young. My age is 77 years. I live in
Craig County, Oklahoma. I have not always lived in the Terri-
tory but came from Kansas 16 years ago. I know Laura Clark.
She is about 44 years old. She claims to have Indian blood.
Mrs. McDonald, this lady's grandmother said that she was an
Eastern Cherokee and came from Georgia. She was not enrolled
by the Dawes Commission and did not try to be. I don't think
she had ever been enrolled. She claims through her mother,
Margaret Puffer, or Margaret Smith before marriage, or Bolton.
I don't think that she was enrolled, because her people were
indifferent to the enrolling, but the enrolling officer told
her, after looking at her papers, that if she would come back
in the morning he would enroll her, but her step father ob-
jected and would not look after it. Her grandmother was
Lucinda Smith before marriage, and Lucinda McDonald after. She
lived on the East border of Kansas. It was about 1851 or 1852.
I don't know whether she ever got any money from the Government. She came from Georgia to Missouri. I don't know whether
they are Old Settlers or Emigrants. I frequently heard them
speak of the treaties of 1835-6 and 1846 and claim to be parties to them. I never heard of their joining any other tribe.
Annie Shoemake and and John Shoemake were kin to her parents.
Margaret Puffer had a sister Luvicy Brown; her husband was
George Brown. I do not know any other brothers and sisters."
SIGNED: J. B. Young, Chelsea, Okla., Sep 4 1908.

11982. MARY L. NILAGES and 3 children,   Jefferson City, Mo
Rejected. Claims through the same source as No 3935.

11983. TOM HAND,   Marble, Okla
Admitted. Both applicant's parents were emigrant Cherokees

                          280

but cannot locate them on the Rolls. From evidence submitted however, applicant is entitled to enrollment. (See Misc. Test. P. 3982)
MISC. TEST. P. 3982. No 11983 - J. B. Adair:
"My name is J. B. Adair; my post-office is Stilwell, Okla; I am sixty six years old; I know Tom Hand and have known him since he was a little child; I knew his father and his mother. They were both emigrant Cherokees. I was raised up with them."
SIGNED: J. B. Adair, Stilwell, Okla., Mar 23 1909.
MISC. TEST. P. 3983. 11983 in re Tom Hand - J. B. Adair:
"I know Tom Hand; his father's name was Chu-wah-yah; his mother was Lila Char-wah-you-ka; they were both emigrant Cherokees; the father of Chu-wah-yah was Chees-quah-lah-tah; they were in S. B. District."
SIGNED: J. B. Adair, Stilwell, Okla., Mar 24 1909.
ROLL P70 #13132 FCT COMM #19173 - Tom Hand - 21

11984. JOHN PATHKILLER,   Proctor, Okla
Admitted. Cousin of No 1677 and claims through same source.
[For Roll information See App 9609, Vol. 4]

11985. JIM DEW,   Moodys, Okla
Admitted. Brother of No 10596 and claims through same source.
ROLL P53 #9667 FCT COMM #18478 - Jim Dew - 23

11986. FRANK L. SWEANEY,   Tucumbia, Mo
Rejected. Claims through the same source as No 3935.

11987. NETTIE HUTCHINS and 5 children,   Claremore, Okla
Admitted. Daughter of No 139.
ROLL P80 #15037 FCT COMM #11254 - Nettie Hutchins   - 34
         15038   11255 - Lou W. (son)   - 14
         15039   11256 - Ralph B. (son)   - 13
         15040   11257 - Uhal R. (son)   - 11
         15041   11258 - Ethel D. (dau)   - 9
         15042   1659 - Williard B. (son) -   3
[NOTE: youngest child's FCT # probably should be 1659m]

11988. SULLEY WILKINS and 1 child,   Muskogee, Okla
Admitted. Sister of No 6477. Father of applicant enrolled in 1851 in Del. No 495.
ROLL P151 #29274 FCT COMM #17376 - Sally Wilkins - 21
         29275   731m - Mary (dau)   - 2

11989. MARY CATRON for her brother,   Welling, Okla
       a minor, JOHN DICK
Admitted. Nephew of Coleman Dick No 6753.
ROLL P53 #9694 - John Dick - 15 by Mary Catron, Gdn.

11990. MARTY CATRON and 3 children,   Welling, Okla
Admitted. Niece of No 6753, Coleman Dick. [Only 2 children on roll - the 3rd could have been her brother App 11989]

ROLL P40 #7019 FCT COMM #25924 - Mary Catron - 28
     7020   - Peggie (dau) - 3
     7021   - Maggie (dau) - 1

11991. WILLIAM MANKILLER and 4 children,   Stilwell, Okla
Admitted. Applicant's father Ah-mah-doo-ih; Kah, was enrolled
by Drennen in 1851 in Flint Dist. Group No 141. For other members of this family, see Flint Dist. Group Nos 137, 138, 139
and 140. See Misc. Test. of Arch Mankiller taken at Stilwell,
March 23, 1909, P. 4004.
MISC. TEST. P. 4004.   No 11998-11991 - Arch Mankiller...
through J. B. Adair, Interpreter:
    "My name is Arch Mankiller; my post-office is Stilwell,
Okla.; I am about fifty-two years old; I was born in Flint
District, Oklahoma Territory; my mother and father were living
together in 1851; I am the oldest child; I couldn't say positively that they were living together in 1851; my mother was
an Old Settler and my father was an emigrant; my mother's name
was Anna Matcy, Ezekiel Matcy was her father; my father had a
brother Ka-scoo-ni (Flint 139); my father's sister married Eli
Smith (Flint 137); A-quo-sa was my father's sister (Flint 138)
my father also had a sister named Chow-a-you-kee (Flint 140);
my father's name was Umer-ta-you-ker (Umma-too-kah) (Flint
141). William Mankiller is my brother."
SIGNED: Arch "X" Mankiller, Stilwell, Okla., Mar 23 1909.
MISC. TEST. P. 3135.   Appli. #11991 - William Mankiller...
through L. D. Walkingstick, Interpreter:
    "My name is William Mankiller; I was enrolled by the Dawes
Commission under the name of William Mankiller #19181; I was
born in Flint District, 1860; my father had no English name;
my mother's maiden name was Annie McCoy; my parents were born
in the old nation in the East; my parents came to Ind. Terr.
at the time of the emigration; my grandfather on my father's
side was Ah-nee-skah-yah-tee and my grandmother on my father's
side was Sah-lee; my grandmother on my mother's side was Se-
gee-lee [Se-ge-kee ?]; my grandparents were born in the old
nation East and came at the time of the emigration of the
Cherokees; they lived in Flint District and were enrolled
there; my mother drew Old Settler money; my mother drew the
Old Settler money in 1851; my father drew emigrant money, but
did not draw any Old Settler money; my mother's father might
have been a half-blood Cherokee; neither I nor any of the ancestors through whom I claim have ever taken up rights with
any tribe of Indians other than the Cherokees."
SIGNED: Wm. Mankiller, Stilwell, Okla., Sep 23 1908.
ROLL P95 #18229 FCT COMM #19181 - William Mankiller - 51
     18230   19182 - Nancy (wife)   - 43
                     (App 11916)
     18231   19183 - Synthia (dau)   - 16
     18232   19184 - Bessie (dau)   - 13
     18233   - Hester (dau)   - 8
     18234   - William, Jr. (son) - 5

11992. RILEY BRADFORD,   Baron, Okla
        by Joe Bradford, Gdn.
Admitted. First cousin once removed of No 6935. Claimant's
maternal grandmother enrolled in 1851 by Drennen G. S. 500.
ROLL P33 #5638 FCT COMM #14450 - Riley Bradford - 4
                                by Joe Bradford, Gdn.

11993. MAMIE BRADFORD,   Baron, Okla
        by Joe Bradford, Gdn.
Admitted. First cousin once removed on No 8935* [Should be
"6935" - see previous entry]. Claimant's maternal grandmother
enrolled in 1851 by Drennen G. S. 500.
MISC. TEST. P. 3051. App 11993 (11992) - Joseph Bradford:
    "My name is Joseph Bradford; I am the father of Mamie,
Riley and Buff Bradford; they claim their Cherokee blood
through their mother and none through me. I am a white man. My
wife was born in Going Snake District, 1872. My wife was about
a half Cherokee. She claimed her Cherokee blood through both
of her parents; my wife's maiden name was Susie Walkingstick.
I have seen both of the grandparents of my children, but do
not know where or when they were born. My wife received money
from the Strip payment. None of my wife's people were Old Settlers and never received any Old Settler money. My wife was
enrolled by the Dawe's Commission under the name of Susie
Bradford, #14450. My children were also enrolled y the Dawe's
Commission under the names of Mamie, Riley and Buff, Nos.
14447, 14448 and 14449. I do not know whether my wife's parents were born in the Ind. Terr. but they were descendants of
the Eastern Cherokees. The grandparents of my children were
enrolled in Going Snake District. Neither my wife nor any of
the ancestors through whom my children claim their Cherokee
blood have ever affiliated with any tribe of Indians other
than the Cherokees. Isaac Walkingstick had a brother James and
a sister Nellie. (See Going Snake 500)."
SIGNED: Joseph Bradford, Stilwell, Okla., Sep 21 1908.
ROLL P33 #5637 FCT COMM #14448 - Mamie Bradford - 9
                                by Joe Bradford, Gdn.

11994. BUFF BRADFORD,   Baron, Okla
Admitted. First cousin once removed of No 6935. Claimant's
maternal grandmother enrolled in 1851 by Drennen, G. S. 500.
ROLL P33 #5636 FCT COMM #14449 - Buff Bradford - 7
                                by Joe Bradford, Gdn.

11995. GEORGE STEALER,   Marble, Okla
Admitted. Applicant's father enrolled by Drennen in 1852,
Stealer 526, G. S. See Misc. Test. P. 2916.
MISC. TEST. P. 2916. No 11995 - George Stealer...through L.
D. Walkingstick, Interpreter:
    "I am 29 years of age; born in the Cherokee Nation. My
mother and father were both full bloods. I do not know if my
parents were Old Settlers or Immigrants. My parents both died

283

in the year of 1895. I never drew any Old Settler money. I think my people were Immigrants. I was left an orphan and know nothing about my people. I know of no one who knew my people. I was enrolled by the Dawes Commission as 18971."
SIGNED: George Stealer, Sallisaw, Okla., Sep 18 1908.
"This applicant is a full blood Cherokee. Has never affiliated with any other tribe. After inquiring of older people I am satisfied that his ancestors were Immigrants. His parents were not living in 1852 and he doesn't know the names of his grandparents. Cannot find out their names from any one. I think this case should be O. K." [Notation added to end of testimony]
ROLL P132 #25534 FCT COMM #18971 - George Stealer   - 28
          25535   18972 - Kate (wife)   - 28
                               (App 11881)
          25536   18974 - William Angel (son) - 4

11996. TAYLOR W. FOREMAN and brother,   Claremore, Okla
       by Ada C. Foreman, Gdn.
Admitted. Nephews of No 1818.
ROLL P63 #11634 FCT COMM #12605 - Taylor W. Foreman - 18
        11635   12606 - Perry A. (bro)   - 16
                               by Ada C. Foreman, Gdn.

11997. ALEXANDER D. DAVIS,   Ramona, Okla
Admitted. Applicant's grandmother enrolled by Drennen in 1852 No 29 G. S. See Misc. Test. P. 2432.
MISC. TEST. P. 2432. No 11997 - Alexander D. Davis:
    "I am 31 years of age; was born in the Indian Territory. I am a Cherokee alotee. I claim my Indian blood through my mother, Lucy Tiner. She was an immigrant. My father was not an Indian. My grandfather Alexander Tiner was an Old Settler. I have never drawn any Old Settler money nor did my mother. My grandmother, Katie Tiner was an Indian and an immigrant. Her maiden name was Katie Smith. I had an uncle Joseph Smith and an aunt named Polly Smith. My mother was the only child of Katie Smith. I am the only child of my mother, Lucy Tiner."
SIGNED: Alexander D. Davis, Bartlesville, Okla., Aug 29 1908.
"This case seems O. K. through 29 G. S. See 1757 and ask Ketron about this case." [Notation added to end of testimony - Ketron was an assistant to Special Commissioner.]
ROLL P51 #9291 FCT COMM #26628 - Alexander D. Davis - 30

11998. ARCH MANKILLER,   Stilwell, Okla
Admitted. Brother of No 11991.
ROLL P95 #18216 FCT COMM #29860 - Arch Mankiller - 52
        18217   29859 - Polly (wife)   - 50
                               (App 11917)

11999. HENRY WALKER,   Willing, Okla
Admitted. Nephew of No 2271. Parents not living in 1851.
ROLL P144 #27958 FCT COMM #20955 - Henry Walker - 26

284

12000. JNO. A. PATTERSON and 2 children,   Marble City, Okla
Admitted. Brother of No 8347 and claims through same source.
ROLL P109 #20905 FCT COMM # 2190 - John A. Patterson - 29
        20906   2191 - Joseph (son)   - 8
        20907   3513m - Kinney V. (son)   - 4

12001. JOHN G. TIDWELL,   105 Fortress Avenue, Atlanta, Ga
Rejected. Claims through John Tidwell. See #16.

12002. THOMAS G. TEMPLES,   Tindale, Ga
Rejected. Proof of genuine connection with the Eastern Cherokees insufficient. It appears that no ancestor was a party
to the treaties of 1835-36-46. No ancestor was ever enrolled.

12003. TULA TEMPLES,   Tindale, Ga
Rejected. Brother to Thomas E. Temples (12002) and claims thru
same source.

12004. GERTRUDE TEMPLES,   Tindale, Ga
Rejected. Sister to Thomas E. Temples (12002) and claims thru
same source.

12005. GENERAL S. TEMPLES,   Tindale, Ga
Rejected. Brother to Thomas E. Temples (12002) and claims thru
same source.

12006. ANNIE TEMPLES,   Tindale, Ga
Rejected. Sister to Thomas E. Temples (12002) and claims thru
same source.

12007. THOMAS T. TEMPLES,   Tindale, Ga
Rejected. Brother to Thomas E. Temples (12002) and claims thru
same source.
MISC. TEST. P. 894. #12007-12002 - Thomas T. Temples:
    "That I am 59 years of age and live in Floyd Co., Ga. I
claim through my father's side and both of his parents. My
father claimed 3/4 Cherokee. My mother is a full blooded white
woman. My father was born in N. C., near Shelving Rock -
that's said to be the old Indian ball ground. Don't know when
my father was born. My father left N. C. before the war. My
mother is about 80 years of age now and my father came to
Pickens Co., Ga. when my mother was about 16 years of age and
married her then. My father lived among the Indians in N. C.
but he never lived with them after he came to Ga. He was carried away to the War, that is, he was drafted and forced to go
in the army. My grandfather died on the way to the Indian Territory when I was a very small boy, right after the war. He
never received anything from the government but he wanted to
go out to Ind. Ter., so he started out for it. My father nor
grandfather were never on any roll that I know of. My father
never went by any other name than that of Temples. My wife is
white. I am recognized as white man with some Indian blood. I

285

was never on any roll and never lived with the Indians. There is no one living who can tell more than I have. I filed a claim about 11 years ago. All I heard from it was that my claim was good by my lawyer died, and I never got anything."
SIGNED: Thomas T. "X" Temples, Rome, Ga., Jul 2 1908.

12008. ROMIE LEE STRICKLAND,   Dallas, Ga
Rejected. Claims through John Tidwell. See #16.

12009. MARY ANN STRICKLAND,   Dallas, Ga
Rejected. Claims through John Tidwell. See #16.

12010. ELLA ESTELLE STRICKLAND,   Dallas, Ga
Rejected. Claims through John Tidwell. See #16.

12011. MONROE T. REECE,   Talona, Ga
Rejected. Claims through same source as 10552.

12012. RACHEL RAY,   Waleska Ga.
Rejected. Claims through same source as #690.

12013. JOHN W. McINTOSH,   Rome, Ga
Rejected. Ancestor not enrolled. Does not show a genuine connection with Cherokee tribe. Applicant failed to appear to testify. Also neglected to answer letter of inquiry in regard to family relationship.

12014. REBECCA A. McCOY,   Waleska, Ga
Rejected. It does not appear that applicant's ancestors were parties to the treaties of 1835-36-46. Never shared in payment to Cherokee, nor enrolled with them.

12015. MISSIE MAYHUGH,   Sutaller, Ga
Rejected. Daughter of 10492 and claims through same source.

12016. LIZZIE LAWRENCE,   Dallas, Ga
Rejected. Claims through John Tidwell. See #16.

12017. JOSIE CAROLINE LAWRENCE,   Dallas, Ga
Rejected. Claims through John Tidwell. See #16.

12018. GEORGIA BELL LAWRENCE,   Dallas, Ga
Rejected. Claims through John Tidwell. See #16.

12019. ROBERT H. LAWRENCE,   Dallas, Ga
Rejected. Claims through John Tidwell. See #16.

12020. HULDA HAYNES,   Waleska, Ga
Rejected. Whitmire Case.

12021. E. LINDER M. GODFREY,   Calhoun, Ga
Rejected. Claims through same source as 10552.

12022. MARY E. GRAHAM,   Alice, Ga
Rejected. Claims through same source as 10552.

12023. JERRY DEMPSEY and 3 children,   Talking Rock, Ga
Rejected. Son of Elvin P. Dempsey (11302).

12024. PEARL DAVIS,   Tindale, Ga
Rejected. Sister to Oscar Davis (10543) and claims thru same
source.

12025. LILLIE DAVIS,   Tindale, Ga
Rejected. Sister to Oscar Davis (10543) and claims thru same
source.

12026. GUSSIE DAVIS,   Tindale, Ga
Rejected. Sister to Oscar Davis (10543) and claims thru same
source.

12027. HENRY DAVIS,   Tindale, Ga
Rejected. Brother to Oscar Davis (10543) and claims thru same
source.

12028. ALLEN DAVIS,   Tindale, Ga
Rejected. Brother to Oscar Davis (10543) and claims thru same
source.

12029. FREEMAN CARNEY,   Sharp Top, Ga
Rejected. Cousin of Shoshonie Reece, applicant #11344 & claims
through same source.

12030. CICERO A. CARNEY,   Sharp Top, Ga
Rejected. Cousin of Shoshonie Reece applicant #11344 & claims
through same source.

12031. J. PAD CLARK,   Waleska, Ga
Rejected. It does not appear that applicant's ancestors were
parties to treaties of 1835-6-46. Never shared in payments to
the Cherokees nor enrolled with them. Misc. Test. P. 902.
MISC. TEST. P. 902. #12034 - 12032 - C. H. Brown...as guardian
in case of Laura Brown, et al:
    "That I am 44 years of age and live in Floyd Co., Ga. I am
a full blooded white man. My wife claim Indian on her mother's
side. Her grandmother claimed to be 1/2 Indian, Cherokee. My
wife was about 45 years old when she died and she has been
dead about 7 years. My wife never lived among the Indians as
a member of the tribe. She was recognized as a white woman.
Eliza Giles died about 12 years ago and was 57 when she died.
She was not enrolled that I know of. I have heard her talk
about the Indians but don't know that she ever lived among
them.   All of my wife's ancestors were white except Eliza
Giles. She was born in Ga. and lived the most of her life in
Murray Co., Ga. She had a brother Dock Giles. Don't know

                              287

whether he ever lived with the Indians or not."
SIGNED: C. H. "X" Brown, Rome, Ga., Jul 2 1908.

12032. LAURA BROWN,   RFD #10, Rome, Ga
Rejected. 1: No ancestors ever enrolled. 2: no ancestors party to the treaties of 1835-6.

12033. INEZ BROWN,   RFD #10, Rome, Ga
Rejected. Sister of #12032, and claims through the same ancestors.

12034. EDDIE BROWN,   RFD #10, Rome, Ga
Rejected. Brother of 12032, and claims through the same ancestors.

12035. JOHN R. BROWN,   Sharp Top, Ga
Rejected. It does not appear that applicant's ancestors were
parties to treaties of 1835-6-46. Never enrolled with the
Cherokees nor shared in any of their payments.

12036. BARNUM L. BROWN,   Bull Ground, Ga
Rejected. Claims through same source as #12035.

12037. LON ETTA BONE,   Dallas, Ga
Rejected. Claims through John Tidwell. See #16.

12038. BESSIE BONE,   Dallas, Ga
Rejected. Claims through John Tidwell. See #16.

12039. ALBERT BONE,   Dallas, Ga
             by his mother, Etta Bone
Rejected. Claims through John Tidwell. See #16.

12040. FRANCIS ATKINS,   Waleska, Ga
Rejected. Whitmire case.

12041. SOLOMON W. ATKINS,   Waleska, Ga
Rejected. Whitmire case.

12042. DOROTHY ROBERTS and 4 children,   Marietta, Ga
Rejected. Applicant fails to show any genuine connection to
the Eastern Cherokees. It appears that no ancestor was a
party to the treaties of 1835-36-46. No ancestor was ever
enrolled.

12043. AGNES ROBERTS,   Woodstock, Ga
Rejected. Sister to Dorothy Roberts (12042) and claims thru
same line.

12044. GEORGE WILLIAMS,   Canton, Ga
Rejected. Brother to Dorothy Roberts (12042) and claims thru
same line.

12045. MARGARET WILLIAMS,   Canton, Ga
Rejected. Mother of Dorothy Roberts (12042) through whom the
letter [sic] claims.

12046. FANNIE B. PICKENS,   Marietta, Ga
Rejected. Ancestors were never enrolled. Does not establish
genuine connection with Cherokee Tribe. (Misc. Test. P. 1108)
MISC. TEST. P. 1108. #15331-12046 - Wm. B. Bramlett:
    "That I am 40 years of age and live in Cherokee Co., Ga.
I claim my Indian through my mother and father. I don't know
how much Indian they claimed. They were both Cherokee descent.
My mother is living but has not filed application. My father
was born and raised in Pickens Co., Ga. My father would be
about 75 years old now if he was living. My mother is at present about 80 years old. My grandfather Miles Bramlett was a
white man, and my grandmother Howell was a white woman. Anna
Ray has been dead about 14 years. Grandfather Howell died in
S. C., since the war. I don't know whether my father and mother ever lived with the Indians as members of the tribe or not.
Don't know about my grandparents either. I don't know whether
my parents or any of my ancestors were ever enrolled. Never
heard them say. I am recognized as white. They all know that
I have Indian blood. This is the only application I ever made
for Indian benefits. Neither my father nor mother never received any money from the government; don't know why they were
never on any roll. My Grandmother Ray was living in Pickens
Co., Ga., in 1835. My grandfather Howell lived in Anderson
Co., S. C. in 1835. I don't know whether my grandparents ever
had any other names than Ray and Howell. My wife has filed
application to participate in this fund. She claims through
her grandfather James Moore. She claims thro' her father. Her
mother is white. I think old man Moore came from S. C. to
Gwinett Co., Ga. I don't know whether any of them were on any
rolls or not. Don't know how much Indian my wife claims. She
nor her father nor grandfather never received anything from
the government. She is recognized as a white woman."
SIGNED: William B. Bramlett, Canton, Ga., Jul 7 1908.
EXCEPTION CASE. 12046. Wm. B. Bramlett and 6 children, App
15230, Porterdale, Ga. Rejected. Total number of exceptions
filed in this group -- 1. Original recommendation renewed.

12047. HENRY PADEN,   Woodstock, Ga
Rejected. 1: No ancestor ever enrolled. 2: No ancestor party
to treaties of 1835-6 and 1846. 3: Shows no connection with
Eastern Cherokees. 4: Parents were slaves.

12048. AMANDA R. McCLURE,   Alltoona, Ga
Rejected. Hillhouse Case.

12049. MAY B. GIBSON,   Marietta, Ga
Rejected. Sister of 12046.

12050. GEORGE CLEVELAND,   RFD #1, Woodstock, Ga
Rejected. Applicant's father and paternal ancestors were negroes and slaves. Mother and maternal ancestors not slaves.
Never enrolled with Eastern Cherokees however and does not
establish fact that he is a descendant of a person who was a
party to the treaty of 1835-6-1846. (Misc. Test. P. 1095)
MISC. TEST. P. 1095. No 12050 - George Cleveland:
    "I am 39 years of age; was born in Haversham County, Ga.;
have lived most of my life in Cherokee County. I claim my Indian blood through my mother. My mother was not a slave. I
remember her parents. They were not slaves and lived in Haversham County. Mother has been dead about seven years. She never received any Indian money from the government and never
tried to get any. In 1852 she lived in Haversham County. Do
not know where mother's parents were born. I heard my mother
say her father was part Indian & her mother was a full blood.
My grandmother was married. My mother spoke the Indian language some. My grandfather's name was Bud Thomas. I have never been enrolled by a government agent."
SIGNED: George Cleveland, Canton, Ga., Jul 7 1908.

12051. TILDA E. BRAMLETT,   Marietta, Ga
Rejected. Sister of 12046.

12052. ESTHER SMITH,   Poe, W. Va
Rejected. See full report in #417. Sizemore case.

12053. VICTORIA A. NEAL and 7 children,   Vaughan, W. Va
Rejected. See full report in #417. Sizemore case.

12054. MELVIN M. WILLIAMS and 6 children,   Zela, W. Va
Rejected. See full report in #417. Sizemore case.

12055. MARIAH E. FOWLER and 9 children,   Vaughan, W. Va
Rejected. See full report in #417. Sizemore case.

12056. DONIA J. BROWN,   Poe, W. Va
Rejected. See full report in #417. Sizemore case.

12057. ELIZABETH J. WILLIAMS and 1 child, Poe, W. Va
Rejected. See full report in #417. Sizemore case.

12058. MICHAEL I. WILLIAMS,   Mucklow, W. Va
Rejected. See full report in #417. Sizemore case.

12059. JOHN W. TARPLEY,   Weaverville, Cal
Rejected. Brother to #3282.

12060. CHARLES H. TARPLEY,   Junction City, Cal
Rejected. Brother to #3282.

12061. EDWARD L. TARPLEY and 1 child,   Junction City, Cal
Rejected. Brother to #3282.

12062. W. W. SHOOK and 7 children,   Hayfork, Cal
Rejected. Applicant or ancestors were never enrolled. Does
not appear that they were living within the Cherokee Domain in
1835-6 and 1846 as recognized members of the tribe. Does not
appear that they were ever recognized members of the tribe.

12063. JOHN WALKER CARTER,   Hayfork, Cal
Rejected. 1: No ancestor ever enrolled. 2: No ancestor party
to treaties of 1835-6 and 1846. 3: Shows no connection with
Eastern Cherokees. 4: Claimed only through [nothing else]

12064. PRECIOUS M. TURLEY and 1 child,   Broken Arrow, Okla
Rejected. First cousin of #2904. Claims through same source.

12065. MARGARET N. APPLEMAN,   Blue Jacket, Okla
Rejected. Daughter of #12078. 1st cousin of #9020.

12066. MRS. OVA A. TURNER,   Wagner, Okla
Rejected. First cousin of #2904. Claims through same source.

12067. LITIA J. TIMMONS,   Cuthand, Tex
Rejected. Cousin of #7085. Claims through same source.

12068. MANEY STILLWELL,   Blue Jacket, Okla
Rejected. Brother of #9020.

12069. ABIGALL J. STILLWELL,   Blue Jacket, Okla
Rejected. Aunt of #9020.

12070. ELLEN STAGG,   Blue Jacket, Okla
Rejected. Applicant was held as a slave of white people.
(Misc. Test. P. 3680).
MISC. TEST. P. 3680. No 12070 - Ellen Stagg:
    "I am 51 years of age. I am not a Cherokee Freedman. I
was owned by a man named Baker."
SIGNED: Ellen Stagg, Vinita, Okla., Oct 14 1908.

12071. ANDERSON STAGG,   Blue Jacket, Okla
Rejected. Applicant was a slave (See test.) (Misc. Test. P.
3679)
MISC. TEST. P. 3679. No 12071 - Anderson Stagg:
    "I was born in 1836 in Tennessee. I was owned by a man
named Spivey. I was born in Williamson County, Tenn."
SIGNED: Anderson Stagg, Vinita, Okla., Oct 14 1908.

12072. CATHERINE SMITH,   Hollow, Okla
Rejected. Sister to #9020.

12073. WM. T. SHEWMAKE and 1 child,   McKinney, Tex
Rejected. It does not appear that any ancestor was ever enrolled or that any ancestor was party to the treaties of 1835-
1836 and 46. Shows no real connection with the Eastern Cherokees. (Misc. Test. P. 2496)
MISC. TEST. P. 2496. #12073 - Wm. T. Shewmake:
     "That I am 40 years of age. I claim my Indian descent
thro' my father. My mother was a white woman. My wife is
white. My father claimed Indian blood through his mother. Her
name was Barnes, but I don't know her first name. My father
was born in 1831 in Perry Co., Tenn. He lived there until he
was 22 years of age and then went to south-west Missouri. He
stayed in Mo. 24 years and then he came to Texas. He died in
this state. He never lived with the Indians as a member of
the tribe that I know of and was never on any roll. He nor
none of us ever made application to the Daws Commission. This
is the first application I have made. My father claimed to be
1/4 Cherokee Indian. My father was recognized as a white man
but was considered to have some Indian blood. His mother died
in Tenn. She was not on any roll that I know of. Never heard
of either my father or grandmother receiving land or money
from the government. I am the only one of the family who has
filed application. I have a brother and sister living. I suppose that all of my father's brothers and sisters are dead."
SIGNED: Wm. T. "X" Shewmake, McKinney, Tex., Aug 31 1908.
EXCEPTION CASE. 12073. Wm. T. Shewmake and 1 child, R R #6,
McKinney, Tex. Rejected. Total number of exceptions filed in
this group -- 1. Original recommendation renewed.

12074. EMILY G. ROWELL,   Cuthand, Tex
Rejected. Cousin of #7085. Claims through same source.

12075. MARY MAPES,   Lexington, Okla
Rejected. 1st cousin of 6252; claims through same source.

12076. DAISY R. HATFIELD,   Nowata, Okla
Rejected. 1st cousin of #7715.

12077. JESSE A. ELMORE,   Chetopa, Kan
Rejected. Brother to 8226.

12078. SARAH A. CURRY,   Elmore, Okla
Rejected. Aunt of #9020.

12079. ROSY E. CURRY,   Blue Jacket, Okla
Rejected. Ancestors not on rolls. Were not parties to trea-
ties of 1835-36-46. Does not establish genuine connection with
Cherokee tribe. (Misc. Test. P. 2188).
MISC. TEST. P. 2188. No 14947-12079 - William N. Corbitt:
     "I am 54 years of age; was born in Illinois. I claim Cher-
okee Indian blood through my mother. She was born in Hickman
County, Tenn. I have seen my mother parents. They lived in

Illinois. I do not know when they moved there. I have never gotten any Indian money from the government and never tried to get any prior to this time. My mother never got an Indian money from the government. I made application before the Dawes Commission for an allotment but was turned down. Do not know why. My mother died here in the Cherokee Nation. We left Illinois in 1866. None of my family ever shared in a payment to the Cherokees."
SIGNED: William N. Corbitt, Miami, Okla., Aug 24 1908.

12080. ROBERT M. CURRY, Blue Jacket, Okla
Rejected. Daughter of #12078. 1st cousin of #9020.

12081. LOUVINA CUNDIF, Hollow, Okla
Rejected. 1st cousin to #9020.

12082. SARAH F. BRIGANCE and 2 children, Fort Worth, Tex
Rejected. Sister of 9355 [? last 2 digits blurred]

12083. REBECCA J. BILYEN, Stillwater, Okla
Rejected. Aunt of #2904. Claims through same source.

12084. LIZZIE BAYS, Colorado Springs, Colo
1012 N Walnut Street
Rejected. First cousin once removed of #2904. Claims through same source.

12085. DAVID C. BAYS and 3 children, Wagoner, Okla
Rejected. Uncle of #2904. Claims through same source.

12086. JAMES WATER, Sutherland, Tenn
Rejected. Applicant claims through Ned Sizemore - See special report in #417.

12087. A. G. WATERS, Southerland, Tenn
Rejected. No ancestor ever was enrolled. No ancestor was party to the treaties of 1835-6 or 46. Shows no real connection with the Cherokee tribe. Claims on his mother's side as a Sizemore and has filed duplicate application No 12068 which is in the Sizemore group.

12088. A. G. WATERS, Duplicate of 12087 - in regard to this application special report in the Sizemore case #417.

12089. MARY WATERS, Southerland, Tenn
Rejected. Applicant claims through Ned Sizemore - see report in #417.

12090. JOSIE HAND, Damascus, Va
Rejected. Applicant claims through Ned Sizemore - see report in #417.

12091. JAMES WATERS,   Southerland, Tenn
Rejected. No ancestor ever enrolled. No ancestor was party
to the treaties of 1835-6 or 1846. Shows no real connection
with the Cherokee tribe. Claims on mother's side as a Sizemore. See duplicate #12086.

12092. MARY WATERS for minor children,   Southerland, Tenn
Rejected. No ancestors ever enrolled. No ancestors were parties to the treaties of 1835-6 or 1846. Shows no real connection with the Cherokee tribe. Claims as a Sizemore on Mother's
side. See duplicate #12089.

12093. EBBIE TRAUTHAM,   Topton, N C
Rejected. Applicant claims through Blythe case - see report
#417. [should be 153]

12094. MARY M. COURTNEY,   Bartlesville, Okla
Rejected. Claims through Alex. Brown see #35.

12095. J. E. LANE,   Oklahoma City, Okla
Rejected. Husband of 744.

12096. MARGARET SIZEMORE PRIVETT & 4 children, Crumpler, W Va
Rejected. Applicant claims through Ned Sizemore - see report
in #417.

12097. LUCRETIA E. TINDELL,   Springfield, Mo
Rejected. None of the ancestors of applicant are enrolled
with the Eastern Cherokees. The grand father of applicant was
born in Kentucky. Ancestors not proven to be parties to treaties of 1835-6-1846.

12098. ED. A. TINDELL,   529 W Turner St., Springfield, Mo
Rejected. Claims through Alex. Brown. See #35.

12099. JIM PAYNE,   Nina, N C
Admitted. Brother of #745, claims through same source.
ROLL P14 #1923 - Jim Payne - 19

12100. MOSES S. HOWELL,   Merit, Tex
Rejected. It does not appear that any ancestor was ever enrolled or that any ancestor was party to the treaties of 1835-
1836 1846. Shows no connection with the Eastern Cherokees.
(Misc. Test. P. 2458)
MISC. TEST. P. 2458. #12100 - Moses S. Howell:
    "That I am 46 years of age. I claim my Indian descent
through my mother; my father was a white man. My mother
claimed through her mother, Martha Quails nee Binum or Bynum.
My mother was born in Georgia, close to Hall Co. - I think.
She was born about 1820. She died in 1903. My mother never
left Georgia. She lived and died there. Don't know how much
Indian blood she claimed but she was of Cherokee. I don't know

whether my mother or her mother ever lived with the Indians as a member of the tribe or not. My mother was recognized as a white woman in the community and I am recognized as a white man. I have heard that my grandmother drew script but never did locate the land. She died before they located the land. She died about 1840. She drew this by reason of her Indian blood. Never heard that my mother was on the roll. She never received any land or money from the government. My mother and father were married sometime about 1835 or 1836. My wife is a white woman. I did not apply to the Dawes Commission for enrollment. This is the only application I ever made. Don't know of my mother ever having made any application. I understand that my sister, Mary Smith, who lives near Ardmore, Okla may have made application but I don't know for sure. I know that her husband has made application."
SIGNED: Mosses S. Howell, Greenville, Tex., Aug 29 1908.

12101. ELISHA PAYNE, Vina*, N C
Admitted. Brother of #745, claims through same source.
[* "Nina, N C" on roll]
ROLL P14 #1908 - Elisha Payne - 25

12102. CATHANEY SIZEMORE HALSEY & 2 children, Pierpoint, W Va
Rejected. Applicant claims through Ned Sizemore - see report in #417.

12103. MIRA SIZEMORE MILLER, Saulsville, W Va
Rejected. Applicant claims through Ned Sizemore - see report in #417.

12104. JOHN R. SIZEMORE, Pineville, W Va
Rejected. Applicant claims through Ned Sizemore - see report in #417.

12105. RICHARD SIZEMORE, Pineville, W Va
Rejected. Applicant claims through Ned Sizemore - see report in #417.

12106. JAMES ADAMS and 2 children, Andrews, N C
Rejected. Applicant claims through Blythe case - see report in #153.

12107. MARY JANE PAYNE, Unaka, N C
Admitted. Sister of #745, claims through same source.
ROLL P14 #1925 - Mary Jane Payne - 28

12108. JOHN PAYNE, Nina, N C
Admitted. Brother of #745, claims through same source.
ROLL P14 #1924 - John Payne - 15

12109. FRANK L. SIZEMORE, Jared, W Va
Rejected. Applicant claims through Ned Sizemore - see report

in #417.

12110. MACK E. PRICE,   Sallisaw, Okla
Admitted. Grand-nephew of #920, grandmother of applicant en-
rolled as Sally Byers at Flint #387 1/2.
ROLL P113 #21687 FCT COMM #2819 - Mack E. Price - 23

12111. FRANK SAPP and 1 child,   Nashville, Tenn
                                                 1501 Phillips St.
Rejected. Claims through same source as 5170.

12112. MARTHA RUSH & 7 children, Westmoreland, Sumner Co, Tenn
Rejected. Sister of #10445.

12113. JEFFERSON D. PARKER,   Shawnee, Okla
Rejected. Applicant claims through Blythe case. See report
in #153.

12114. JONATHAN C. PARKER,   Shawnee, Okla
Rejected. Applicant claims through Blythe case. See report
in #153.

12115. RILEY LEDFORD and 3 children,   Almond, N C
Admitted. Applicant's mother enrolled by Chapman 1851 #1143.
ROLL P12 #1451 - Riley Ledford - 28
           1452 - Joe (son)   - 6
           1453 - Kiney (son)   - 4
           1454 - Eave (dau)   - 1

12116. MALINDA C. HARRIS,   Russelville, Ky
Rejected. Sister of #10445.

12117. HIRAM H. SIZEMORE and 2 children,   Jared, W Va
Rejected. Applicant claims through Ned Sizemore - see report
in #417.

12118. ALONZO LEE and 1 child,   Silver Creek, N Y
Admitted. Nephew of No 6648 and claims through Ned Sizemore -
See report in #417. [NOTE: Application 6648 is an admitted
case and is not related to Sizemore's at all - see Vol. 3]
ROLL P12 #1456 - Alonzo Lee   - 32
           1457 - Alice M. (dau) - 5

12119. MARY SNOWDEN and 2 children,   Patsey, Ky
Rejected. Sizemore case. [Entire entry handwritten]

12120. ROSA M. CHAMBERS and 1 child,   Richmond, Va
                                             417 W. Grace Street
Admitted. 1st cousin of #90 and claims through same source.
Applicant's mother Amanda enrolled by Drennen Sal. 459.
ROLL P7 #458 - Rosa M. Chambers   - 39
          459 - William A. Jr. (son) - 3

296

12121. MINNIE WILLIAMS and 4 children,   Clarence, Okla
Admitted. First cousin of #1208, and the daughter of Thos.
Harris who was enrolled by Chapman #1860.   [NOTE: Only 3
children on roll]
ROLL P151 #29373 FCT COMM # 6251 - Minnie Williams - 37
               29374   6252 - DeWitt (son)   - 18
               29375   6254 - Sue (dau)   - 13
               29376   2143m - Anna (dau)   - 3

12122. JAMES C. GROVE, Duplicate of 16551.

12123. JAMES C. GROVE, Duplicate of 16551.

12124. JAMES C. GROVE, Duplicate of 16551.

12125. JAMES C. GROVE, Duplicate of 16551.

12126. JAMES C. GROVE, Duplicate of 16551.

12127. JAMES C. GROVE, Duplicate of 16551.

12128. JAMES C. GROVE, Duplicate of 16551.

12129. JAMES C. GROVE, Duplicate of 16551.

12130. LULA M. ROBERTSON and 4 children,   Porum, Okla
Rejected. Applicant claims through mother who drew Old Set-
tler money and was enrolled on Old Settler roll at group #6 in
Skin Bayou District.
MISC. TEST. P. 2768. #13886-12130 - Eliza Catherine Redding:
    "That I am about 58 years of age. I was born in Scott Co.,
Ark. I had a sister older than I and her name was Mary Ann.
She is dead. My father and grandfather were both dead in 1851.
I claim my Indian descent through my father and his father. I
have an uncle who raised me and his name is Andrew Ross. He
and my grandfather Gentry went down to Ft. Smith to enroll me
in 1851. They were drunk and enrolled me under the name of my
sister, Mary Ann. She was dead at that time. Andrew had a son
named George and a daughter named Hannah. He had a son named
Benjamin. He also had a daughter named Margaret and a son
named Jesse T. Andrew Ross drew a little over $200.00 for me
in 1851. I had an aunt Hannah, my father's sister. I also had
an aunt Caroline, and an uncle named Frank Ross. Don't know
whether Frank was living in 1851 or not. My uncle Andy Ross
told me of having enrolled me. I have received Old Settler
money at Ft. Gibson about 12 or 14 years ago. I got a little
over a hundred dollars ($100.00). Never received any after
that. My number by the Dawes Commission is 29364. I got 90
acres of land. All of my children have married white people."
SIGNED: Eliza C. Redding, Stigler, Okla., Sep 10 1908.
MISC. TEST. P. 2772. #17243-12130 - Siller J. Welter:
    "That I am 36 years of age. I claim my Indian descent

through my mother; my father was a full blooded white man. My husband is a white man. My mother claimed Indian through her father, Joe Ross. Templeton Ross was Joseph Ross' father. During the Old Gold payment my mother was about three years old. She was living in Sevier Co., but I don't know just where. She was born in Arkansas. My mother's father was dead in 1851. Andy Ross was my mother's father's brother and he raised my mother. My mother had only one sister, Mary Ann. She had no brothers. Mary Ann only lived four years. Templeton Ross was not living in 1851. I think it was $280.00 that was drawn for my mother in 1851 at Ft. Smith That was an Old Settler payment. Old man Gentry and Andy Ross were drunk at the time the roll was made and I don't know just how my mother was enrolled. She had a good many different nick-names. I and my children were all enrolled by the Dawes Commission on Cherokee roll #29369. I have land allotment with the Cherokees. My mother also has an allotment with the Cherokees. My mother claims to be 1/8 Cherokee. Templeton Ross came West when a small boy at the time the Indians came from Georgia. Andy Ross has a son named Jesse."
SIGNED: Siller J. Welter, Stigler, Okla., Sep 10 1908.
EXCEPTION CASE. Rejected. Total number of exceptions filed in this group -- 4. Original recommendation renewed.

12131. JAMES C. GROVE, Duplicate of #16551.

12132. JAMES C. GROVE, Duplicate of #16551.

12133. CHAS. J. McCLURE and 4 children,   Porum, Okla
Admitted. Brother of #161 and claims through same ancestors.
ROLL P92 #17624 FCT COMM #5813 - Charles J. McClure - 42
	17625	5815 - Francis (son)	- 19
	17626	5816 - Della (dau)	- 16
	17627	5817 - Hattie (dau)	- 14
	17628	5818 - Douglas (son)	- 10

12134. WM. J. McCLURE,   Porum, Okla
Admitted. Brother of #161, and claims through same ancestors.
ROLL P93 #17651 FCT COMM #17069 - William J. McClure - 60

12135. SLATER COWART and 6 children,   Muskogee, Okla
Admitted. Brother of #628, claims through same source.
ROLL P47 #8603 FCT COMM #21541 - Slater Cowart - 53
	8604	21543 - John (son)	- 18
	8605	21544 - Alice (dau)	- 15
	8606	21545 - Cynthia (dau)	- 12
	8607	21546 - Mary (dau)	- 10
	8608	21547 - Collins (son)	- 8
	8609	21548 - Nettie (dau)	- 6

12136. MARY B. GRINSTEAD,   Coffeyville, Kan
Admitted. Applicant's grandmother enrolled by Drennen 1851

Del. 953.
ROLL P68 #12686 FCT COMM #24460 - Mary B. Grinstead - 23

12137. ADELINE HIPES and 10 children, Horsepen, Va
Rejected. Applicant claims through Ned Sizemore - see report
in #417.

12138. NANCY SIZEMORE and 2 children, Jared, W Va
Rejected. Applicant claims through Ned Sizemore - see report
in #417.

12139. MARGARET NEWMAN and 2 children, Horsepen, Va
Rejected. Applicant claims through Ned Sizemore - see report
in #417.

12140. HENRY OWENS, Webbers Falls, Okla
Admitted. Nephew of #1724, and claims through same ancestors.
Father of applicant enrolled under name of Oo-na-stil-ler, in
Del. District No 327.
ROLL P106 #20405 FCT COMM #21599 - Henry Owens - 34

12141. FANNY M. HUGHES, 712 Court St., Lynchburg, Va
Admitted. 1st cousin of No 90 and claims through same source.
[NOTE: Son's address listed 1000 Court St., Lynchburg]
ROLL P11 #1223 - Fanny M. Hughes   - 42
          1224 - Geo. M. ALEXANDER (son)   - 17
          1225 - Jeanie M. ALEXANDER (dau) - 14

12142. JOSEPH ALEXANDER, Box 27, Fort Smith, Ark
Admitted. 1st cousin to #3923. Applicant's mother, "Cherokee
Thompson, 1047 Del."
ROLL P23 #3592 FCT COMM #3680 - Joseph Alexander - 34

12143. THOMPSON ALEXANDER, Chaffee, Mo
Admitted. 1st cousin to #3923. Applicant's mother "Cherokee
Thompson, 1047 Del."
ROLL P23 #3604 FCT COMM #Thompson Alexander - 37

12144. IRENE ALEXANDER DICKENS and 1 child, Alexandria, La
Admitted. 1st cousin to 3923. Mother "Cherokee Thompson, 1047
Del."
ROLL P53 #9725 FCT COMM #29443 - Irene Alexander Dickens - 30
          9726   29444 - Miriam Cherokee (dau)   - 10

12145. SUSIE GROVE, Porum, Okla
Admitted. Sister of #1583.
ROLL P68 #12746 FCT COMM #5657 - Susie Grove - 26

12146. SUSIE GROVE, Duplicate of #12145.

12147. FANNIE GROVE, Duplicate of 12147 [sic]. Sister of 1583
[Admitted.]

ROLL P68 #12747 FCT COMM #5653 - Fannie Grove - 17

[NOTE: No entry for 12148 - skips to 12149]

12149. NED GROVE,   Porum, Okla
Admitted. Brother of #1583.
ROLL P68 #12745 FCT COMM #5652 - Ned Grove - 24

12150. NED GROVE, Duplicate of #12152.

12151. EVEN E. GROVE, Duplicate of #12152.

12152. EVAN GROVE,   Porum, Okla
Admitted. Brother of #1583.
ROLL P68 #12743 FCT COMM #16870 - Evan E. Grove - 28

12153. WM. H. DOWNING and 2 children,   Chelsea, Okla
Admitted. 1st cousin of 7641, and claims through grandparents
enrolled as John and Jane Downing, Sal. #381.
ROLL P55 #10070 FCT COMM #13166 - William H. Downing - 30
             10071   13167 - Lewis W. (son)   - 6
             10072   13168 - Anna L. (dau)   - 4

12154. WM. H. FRY,   Claremore, Okla
Admitted. Brother of 5373, and claims through same source.
ROLL P64 #11913 FCT COMM #11551 - William H. Fry   - 38
             11914   11552 - Paul W (son)   - 16
             11915   11553 - Robert E. (son)   - 9
             11916   11554 - Victorine C. (dau) - 7
             11917   11555 - Mary (dau)   - 4

12155. CATHERINE LANGLEY,   Claremore, Okla
Admitted. Sister of 5373 and claims through same source.
ROLL P88 #16684 FCT COMM # 961 - Lock Langley   - 32
                                  (App 15028)
             16685   30292 - Catherine (wife) - 32
             16686   90m - Catherine (dau)   - 3

12156. CULLIE FRY,   Claremore, Okla
Admitted. Brother of 5373 and claims through same source.
ROLL P64 #11904 FCT COMM #12541 - Cullie Fry   - 28
             11905   12542 - Gertrude (dau)   - 8
             11906   12543 - Cecil R. (son)   - 6
             11907   12544 - Lettie Marie (dau) - 4

12157. MARY JANE HAYHURST,   Douglas, Arizona
Admitted. Sister of 5373, and claims through same source.
ROLL P73 #13642 FCT COMM #12006 - Mary Jane Hayhurst - 30

12158. GEO. W. HAUSE, 5 bros. & 4 sisters, Claremore, Okla
            by Daniel M. Hause, Gdn.
Admitted. Nieces and nephews of 4911, and claims through same

300

source. Grandmother enrolled.
ROLL P72 #13561 FCT COMM #12211 - George W. Hause   - 18
         13562   12212 - Sarah R. (sis)   - 16
         13563   12213 - Joseph M. (bro)   - 15
         13564   12214 - Caleb W. (bro)   - 14
         13565   12215 - Ruth E. (sis)   - 13
         13566   12216 - Thomas Oliver (bro)   - 11
         13567   12217 - Mabel E. (sis)   - 9
         13568   12218 - Daniel M., Jr. (bro) - 7
         13569   12219 - Maria V. (sis)   - 6
         13570   512m - Benjamin F. (bro)   - 1
                        by Daniel M. Huse, Gdn.

12159. NANNIE E. CHAMBERS and 1 child,   Claremore, Okla
Admitted. Applicant's father Walker Coney and [sic] Drennen
roll Tahl. Grandfather on mother's side Aaron Downing on 1835
roll page 36. (Misc. Test. P. 2477.)
MISC. TEST. P. 2477. App No 12159 - Nannie E. Chambers:
    "My name is Nannie E. Chambers. My age is 46 years. I live
in Rogers County and have always lived in the Territory. I was
enrolled by the Dawes Commission, Roll #11839, Cherokee Roll.
I was enrolled for the bread and strip money. My Indian blood
comes from both sides. Mother was Malinda Downing and she married first, Wofford, and the next Carey. She died in this
county and came from Canadian to Tahlequah District and from
there here. She got the bread and strip money. She was enrolled on the Roll of 1851. Her name was Carey then. A-na-wa-
ki or Ah-ne-wa-ki. She had one brother, Mose Downing. He died
when a mere boy. My grandfather was Aaron Downing, and my
grandmother Lizzie Downing. She afterwards married a man by
name of Hogshooter. He lived (Aron) in the Eastern part of the
nation. One of Aaron's brothers was James. He lived in Tahlequah District. An aunt by the name of Judy; she would be a
great-aunt; also Katie. She lived in Tahlequah District at the
time I knew her. My mother's people were Emigrants. They never
associated with any other tribe of Indians. My mother came
from Georgia. My father was Walker Carey. He was Emigrant too.
He lived in different parts of the nation; he lived in Illinois District and Tahlequah and Canadian. He had one brother
Shade Carey. He had no sisters that I know of. Father and
James Cary. He got his blood from his mother, Nancy Pheasant.
I cannot tell whether these people on my father's side were
ever enrolled. My father's brother, Shade Carey was an Old
Settler, but my father was not. I do not know where Nancy
Pheasant lived. She had brothers and sisters but I cannot give
their names. (Look on 1851 Roll) Nancy Pheasant may have been
Nancy Carey or Nancy Too-stoo, in 1851."
SIGNED: Nannie E. Chambers, Claremore, Okla., Aug 31 1908.
ROLL P40 #7147 FCT COMM #11838 - William E. Chambers - 44
                        (App 41772)
         7148   11839 - Nannie E. (wife)   - 44
         7149   11842 - Teesey (son)   - 12

                        301

12160. MAXWELL FRY and 4 children,   Claremore, Okla
Admitted. Brother of 5373 and claims through same source.
ROLL P64 #11908 FCT COMM #12016 - Maxwell Fry   - 35
         11909   12017 - Pearl (dau)   - 11
         11910   12018 - Merritt L. (son) - 6
         11911   12019 - Cora V. (dau)   - 4
         11912   3500m - Robert L. (son)   - 1

12161. WM. LYMAN,   Romana, Okla
Admitted. Nephew of 1117. Applicant's claim through father
enrolled as John Lyman.
ROLL P92 #17482 FCT COMM #21104 - William Lyman - 29

12162. PATRICK LYMAN,   Talala, Okla
Admitted. Brother of 12161. Applicant's father enrolled in
1851 in Tahlequah #230.
ROLL P92 #17478 FCT COMM #12098 - Patrick Lyman - 26

12163. SAMUEL SAWNOOKA,   Altoona, Pa
Admitted. Nephew of 16823.
ROLL P16 #2294 - Samuel Sawnooka - 28

12164. JNO. F. METCALF and 7 children,   English, N C
Rejected. Keziah Van case. Applicant claims through Keziah
Van case. See report in #276.

12165. HIRAM METCALF and 4 children,   Trust, N C
Rejected. Applicant claims through Keziah Van case. See report #276.

12166. JOHN W. CRY,   Athens, Tenn
Rejected. No ancestors ever enrolled. No ancestors party to
treaties of 1835-6 and 1846. Shows no connection with Eastern
Cherokees.
MISC. TEST. P. 710. #12166 - John W. Cry:
     "That I am 46 years of age and live in McMinn Co., Tenn.
I claim my Indian descent through my father and his father. My
father was born and raised in Cherokee Co., N. C., I think. He
went from N. C. to Ga. somewhere between the Mexican and Civil
Wars. I think he went to Red Clay, Ga. and then he came to
Tenn. My grandfather was born and raised in Cherokee Co.,
N. C. My grandfather left N. C. between the two wars. I don't
know whether my father lived with the Indians as a member of
the tribe. My grandfather lived amongst the Indians but I
don't know whether he was a member of the tribe. Neither my
father nor grandfather were on any roll, nor were any of my
ancestors that I know of. My grandfather sometimes went by the
name of Croye. I don't know where my father was in 1835. My
grandfather claimed 1/2 Cherokee. I am recognized as a white
person. My wife is a white woman. James Ritchie who has filed
application #19729 is a cousin of mine and claims through
William Cry too. That is the only source he claims through."

SIGNED: John W. Cry, Athens, Tenn., June 27 1908.
EXCEPTION CASE. Rejected. Total number of exceptions filed
in this group -- 1. Original recommendation renewed.

12167. LEANDER D. HALL,　　　　　RFD #1, Hays, N C
Rejected. No ancestor ever enrolled. No ancestor party to
treaties of 1835-6 and 1846. Shows no connection with Eastern
Cherokees.
MISC. TEST. P. 81. No 12167 - Esom Fuguette:
　　"I am 46 years of age, and was born and raised in Wilkes
County, near Round Mountain. My father was Esom Fuguette, and
he had a daughter Jane who married Leander Hall. I think she
had a son named Leander Hall. I do not remember ever seeing
my father. I heard my mother and my older brother and sister
speak about there being some Indian blood. Some spoke as if
we were very near half Indian if not quite. I never heard the
name of the Indians. We passed as White people in the community. My father also passed as White. I do not know where my
father was born."
SIGNED: Esom "X" Fuguette, Wilkesboro, N. C., Mar 29 1908.

12168. ELIZABETH GARLAND, Duplicate of #3198.

12169. CORNELIA METCALF,　　　　　Little Creek, N C
Rejected. Keziah Van case. See report #276.

12170. LEE METCALF,　　　　　Little Creek, N C
Rejected. Applicant claims through Keziah Van case. See report #276.

12171. JESSE A. WOODARD,　　　　　Baileyton, Ala
Rejected. No ancestor ever enrolled. No ancestor party to
treaties of 1835-6 and 1846. Shows no connection with Eastern
Cherokees.

12172. SUSIE HOLMES and 1 child,　　　　　Collinsville, Okla
Admitted. Sister of #10949 and claims through same source.
ROLL P77 #14515 FCT COMM #25525 - Susie Holmes　- 22
　　　　　14516　　　　　2671m - Patrick (son) -　2

12173. SAMUEL ADAIR, Duplicate of #9979.

12174. GEO. B. WINEMAN, Gdn. for 1 child,　Macon, Ga
　　　　　　　　　　　　　　　319 Hazel Street
Admitted. Applicant 's grandfather enrolled by Chapman 1851
No 1782.
ROLL P19 #2908 -- Jennie E. L. Weinman - 9
　　　　　　　by Geo. B. Weinman, Gdn.

12175. ELLA N. RING,　　　　　Macon, Ga
Admitted. Aunt of #12174.
ROLL P16 #2162 - Ella N. Ring - 35

12176. GEO. W. RING,   Macon, Ga
Admitted. Uncle of #12174.
ROLL P16 #2163 - George W. Ring - 38

12177. CHAS. H. RING,   Macon, Ga
Admitted. Uncle of #12174.
ROLL P15 #2161 - Charles H. Ring - 35

12178. SALLE E. HANCOCK,   Rome, Ga
Admitted. Aunt of #12174.
ROLL P10 #1038 - Sallie E. Hancock - 39
        1039 - Ralph J. (son)   - 17
        1040 - Glennis R. (dau) - 11

REJECTED
APP 12179 TO 12195 - SIZEMORE CASES - SEE SPECIAL REPORT #417

12179. DAVIS S. WYATT,   City, N C

12180. REEVES OSBORN,   City, N C

12181. JOHN E. OSBORN,   City, N C

12182. ROBERT HEATH and 7 children,   Fleet, Va

12183. ANNA L. BROWN,   Herndon, W Va

12184. ELI OSBORN,   Furches, N C

12185. IDA WITHERSPOON,   Park, Va

12186. MARY E. WITHERSPOON and 4 children,   Park, Va

12187. LURA MYERS and 4 children,   City, N C

12188. CHARITY MABE and 1 child,   Anna, N C

12189. MARY BOWERS,   City, N C

12190. ESTELE MABE,   Anna, N C

12191. LILLIE BOWERS,   City, N C

12192. JESSIE OSBORN and 8 children,   Orddell, Va

12193. CALVIN OSBORN,   City, N C

12194. MARY J. DANEY and 8 children,   City, N C

12195. MARGARET OSBORN,   City, N C

END CONSECUTIVE SIZEMORE CASES

304

12196. FRANCES L. HACKER and 4 children,   Claremore, Okla
Admitted. Niece of #1539.
ROLL P69 #12840 FCT COMM #11892 - Frances L. Hacker - 25
        12841   32860 - Almon R. (son)   - 8
        12842   4394m - Alexander G. (son) - 3
        12843   4395m - Frank (son)   - 1
                          (died Aug 22, '06)

12197. COLUMBUS W. WORLEY and 3 children,   Carrolton, Ga
Rejected. Cousins of #11382, and claims through same source.

12198. RACHEL HOLLAND and 3 children,   Wann, Okla
Admitted. Applicant claims through father, Dah-ma-gah, enrolled in 1851 in Delaware #784.   Dawes Commission #10417.
Misc. Test. P. 2158.
MISC. TEST. P. 2158. App No 12198 - Rachel Holland:
    "My name is Rachel Holland. I am 30 years old. I was born
in Oklahoma and have lived here ever since.   I claim both
through my father and mother. I was enrolled by the Daws Commission as a full-blood. Roll No. 10417, I don't know whether
I was enrolled before. I drew in Cherokee Strip payment. My
mother's name Cynthia Turner before marriage, and she married
Wat Horsefly. She is not living, as she died when I was small.
She lived in Spavinaw, Delaware District. She lived there many
years. I think she was born in the Territory. My mother got
her Indian blood from both sides. I don't know my grandmother's full name on my mother's side but it was Mixwater. She
lived where my mother lived. My people came from North Carolina. My mother's mother came from North Carolina. They drew
money in 1850 or thereabouts.   About 1850 my mother's mother
drew money while living in Delaware District, at Spavinaw. The
Indian for Mixwater is Oo-ma-suy-ah. My uncle was Mink Mixwater. My mother's father was Isaac Turner. Asick as near as
I can spell it was his Indian name. He lived in Delaware District. I do not know any more about him. I do not know that
my mother's people ever associated with any other tribe of Indians. They were not Old Settlers. Alone was grandmother's
name. My father is Wat Horsefly in English, and Indian name
Wah-dee Dah-ma-gah. Peggy Horsefly is a sister to my father,
Indian name Wagy Dah-mah-gah.   My grandfather on my father's
side was Horsefly and Indian name Dah-mah-gah. A-lee Dah-mah-
gah is my uncle. Wah-lee-ne Horsefly was an aunt. I don't know
when my father's people came from the East. They were enrolled. They drew money in 1852. My mother's mother's brother
adopted me after the death of my mother and they called me
Mixwater and I was enrolled under that name. I think my father
and grandfather were living in the Delaware District in 1851."
SIGNED: Rachel Holland, Lenapah, Okla., Aug 22 1908.
ROLL P77 #14486 FCT COMM #10416 - William G. Holland - 38
                          (App 24769)
        14487   10417 - Rachel (wife)   - 29
        14488   10418 - Jesse W. (son)   - 19

12198. RACHEL HOLLAND (Cont)
      14489 FCT COMM #10419 - Robert L. (son)   - 16
      14490   2361m - Charles T. (son)   - 4
      14491   2362m - Florence M. (dau)   - 2
      14492   - Claude J. (son)   - 1/12

12199. RACHEL HOLLAND, Duplicate of #12198.

12200. MARGARET A. McGUIRE,   Peachtree, N C, via Murphy
Rejected. Claims through the same source as 5050.

12201.   MARION LANKFORD,   Riceville, Tenn
Rejected. Claims through same source as 5050.

12202.   ELLA DENSON,   Dayton, Tenn
Rejected. It does not appear that applicant ancestors were
parties to treaties of 1835-6 and 46. Never shared in
payments to Cherokees nor enrolled with them.
EXCEPTION CASE. Rejected. Total number of exceptions filed
in this group -- 1. Original recommendation renewed.

12203. BUNK GOINS,   Jasper, Tenn
Rejected. Niece of #10294, claims through same source.

12204. DAVID QUINTON,   Sallisaw, Okla
Admitted. Applicant is a cousin of Henry Dreadfulwater #2748.
ROLL P114 #21864 FCT COMM #3137 - David Quinton - 31
      21865   - Emma L. (dau) - 9
                (App 12206)

12205. OLIVER HOGG and 1 child,   Sallisaw, Okla
Admitted. Uncle of #5229. Claimant is enrolled in 1851 by
Drennen, Flint 385.
ROLL P76 #14328 FCT COMM #2976 - Oliver Hogg - 59
      14329   2977 - John (son) - 9

12206. EMMA L. QUINTON,   Sallisaw, Okla
      by Dave Quinton, Gdn.
Admitted. Included in Father's app #12204.

12207. FEILDEN H. HENSLEE,   RFD No 5, Sweetwater, Tenn
Rejected. Claims through same source as 5050.

12208. SARAH A. McKEEHAN,   Athens, Tenn
Rejected. Claims through same source as 5050.

12209. WM. R. HENSLEE and 5 children,   Murphy, N C
Rejected. Claims through same source as 5050.

12210. CHARLEY RATTLINGGOURD,   Braggs, Okla
Admitted. Nephew of 4524.
ROLL P115 #22084 FCT COMM #16780 - Charley Rattlinggourd - 25

12211. ROBERT V. COLLINS and 1 child,   Paris, Okla*
Admitted. 1st cousin of #226. Mother enrolled in 1851 Skin
Bayou #130. [* "Paris, Ark" on roll]
ROLL P45 #8170 FCT COMM #4705 - Robert V. Collins - 49
        8171   2949 - Dave (son)   - 10

12211.5 ANDY COLLINS and 2 children,   Sallisaw, Okla
Admitted. 1st cousin once removed of #226. This application
was filed under the same number as that of the father Robert
V. Collins, father of applicant was not living in 1851.
ROLL P45 #8114 FCT COMM #4706 - Andy Collins   - 25
        8115   107m - William R. (son) - 3
        8116   108m - Caroline (dau)   - 1

12212. WATT WATTS,   Braggs, Okla
         by Lorenda Bushyhead, Gdn.
Admitted. Son of #11197, and enrolled with her. [NOTE:
Surname "Swimmer" on roll]

12213. LIZZIE WATTS,   Braggs, Okla
         by Lorenda Bushyhead, Gdn.
Admitted. Daughter of #11197, and enrolled with her. [NOTE:
Surname "Swimmer" on roll]

12214. CAT BARNOSKE,   Campbell, Okla
Admitted. Applicant's grandmother "Mahage" was enrolled by
Drennen in 1851 in Skin Bayou Dist., Camp No 273. See Misc.
Test. of Charlie Barnoskie and Lucy McCoy taken at Vian, Okla,
Mar 13 '09 Mist. Test. P. 3963.
MISC. TEST. P. 3963.   No 12551 - Charlie Barnoskie...through
Wallace Thornton, Interpreter:
    "My name is Charley Barnoskie; my post-office is Vian,
Okla.; I am about twenty-three years old; I claim my Cherokee
blood through both my father and mother; my father's name was
Barnoskie; Barnoskie was about fifty-six years old when he
died; he was killed about 1889; Mage Banoski was my mother;
before marriage Mage Lawler."
SIGNED: Charley "X" Barnoskie, Vian, Okla., Mar 13 1909.
Lucy McCoy...through Wallace Thornton:
    "My name is Lucy McCoy, my post-office is Vian, Okla.; I
am about fifty-eight years old; I know Charley Barnoskie;
Charley Barnoskie's mother was named Mage Lawler before
marriage; I knew Mage Lawler's mother and she was named
Mahage; her first husband was named Wolf-going; Mahage had two
sisters, Jinnie and Arly and Susannah was another sister;
S. B. 273."
SIGNED: Lucy "X" McCoy, Vian, Okla., Mar 13 1909.
ROLL P26 #4318 FCT COMM #21062 - Cat Barnoske - 27

12215. SALLIE PORTER and ? [sic] children, Vian, Okla
Rejected. Applicant failed to establish claim. See testimony
of Dick Waters, taken at Vian, March 16 '09. Misc. Test. P.

3940.
MISC. TEST. P. 3940. No 12215 - Dick Waters...through Wallace
Thornton, Interpreter:
     "My name is Dick Waters; my post-office is Vian, Okla.; I
am about seventy years old; I know Sallie Porter and I knew
her father; his name was Ta-gu-ka-lar this is the name for
Crane; he was a full blood Cherokee; I do not know whether he
was an Old Settler or Emigrant but I know they failed to find
his name on the Old Settler roll when they were paying the Old
Settlers."
SIGNED: Dick "X" Waters, Vian, Okla., Mar 16 1909.
EXCEPTION CASE. Sallie Porter and 3 children, Vian, Okla.
Rejected. Total number of exceptions filed in this group --
1. Original recommendation renewed.

12216. DAVID ROGERS and 1 child,   Keefeton, Okla
Rejected. Applicant only claims Cherokee blood from mother
who was enrolled with the Old Settlers Flint 10.

12217. ELLA T. MULLEY,   Braggs, Okla
Admitted. Sister of #6066.   Father of applicant enrolled in
1851 in Skin Bayou #278.
ROLL P103 #19698 FCT COMM #21066 - Ella T. Mulley - 30

12218. JOSIE BRAMLET and 5 children,   Culberson, N C
Rejected. Daughter of #3682 and claims through same source.

12219. MARTHA M. BAKER, Gdn. for [?] children, Culberson, N C
Rejected. Sons and daughters of #3682 and claims through same
source.

12220. LAURA J. RICH,   East Bend, N C
Rejected. Applicant claims through Poindexter case.   See report #664.

12221. NANCY J. F. WHITE, Duplicate of #623.

12222. WM. H. McCAY,   Claremore, Okla
Admitted. 2nd cousin to 3080 (claims through same source.)
Father of applicant Wm. McCay, was enrolled in 1851 in Dis-
puted District, No 97.
ROLL P92 #17605 FCT COMM #13348 - William H. McCay - 28

12223. JOHN N. SWEANEY and 1 child,   Collinsville, Ill
Rejected. Claims through same source as 3935.

12224. ANNIE TINDLE and 5 children,   Stilwell, Okla
Admitted. Sister of #1328.
ROLL P140 #27094 FCT COMM #15554 - Annie Tindle   - 34
            27095   15557 - Henry C. (son)   - 15
            27096   15558 - Alexander (son)   - 13
            27097   15559 - Jensie (dau)   - 10

12224. ANNIE TINDLE (Cont)
            27098 FCT COMM #15560 - Jeff (son)   - 5
            27099   2136m - Nancy Ellen (dau) - 3

12225. JENNIE BLAIR,   Cookson, Okla
Admitted. Sister of #1328. [For Roll information See App
9640, Vol. 4]

12226. PLUTINA R. LAKEY and 6 children,   East Bend, N C
Rejected. Applicant claims through Poindexter case.   See report in 664.

12227. KATE BACON and 3 children,   Verdegris, Okla
Admitted. Claims through William and Betsy Mills, Ill 173.
An Uncle Nelson also enrolled 173 Ill. Misc. Test. P. 2889 -
2891.
MISC. TEST. P. 2889. No 17105 - in re Clifford Sharp - George
Waters:
    "My name is George Waters; I am appearing as a witness for
Clifford Sharp; I am sixty-two or three years of age; I know
the mother of Clifford Sharp, Anna Mills and her father's name
was William Mills; he lived in the Ill. District and his moth-
er's name was Betsy Mills; I do not know whether Betsy Mills
was an old settler or an emigrant, but know that she was a
Cherokee; This is all I know."   SIGNED: George Waters,
Sallisaw, Okla., Sep 17 1908. "See Ill. 173 and also examine
application 12227." [Notation added to end of testimony]

MISC. TEST. P. 2891.   No 17105 - In re Clifford Sharp -
Wallace Thornton:
    "My name is Wallace Thornton; I am appearing as a witness
for Clifford Sharp; I knew that Anna Mills was the mother of
Clifford Sharp and her father's and mother's names were William and Peggy Mills, and they lived in Ill. District; I knew
them when a boy and they were then about thirty-five or forty
years of age; I am now fifty-three years old; I know William
Sharp; he is not an Indian; Peggy and William Mills were both
Cherokee Indians; Peggy Mills was an Old Settler; Annie drew
old settler money for her mother, but I do not know whether
her father was an old settler or not, but I think he was an
emigrant; William Mills had an Indian name; William Mills had
a son, Samuel Mills; This is all I know."
SIGNED: Wallace Thornton, Sallisaw, Okla., Sep 17 1908.
ROLL P24 #3945 FCT COMM #12425 - Kate Bacon   - 48
            3946   12427 - William GANT (son)   - 17
            3947   12428 - Mattie GANT (dau)   - 16
            3948   12429 - Chas. Fount GANT (son) - 12

12228. SAM KEYS,   Cookson, Okla
Admitted. 1st cousin of #642. Father of applicant enrolled
by Chapman #1687. [For Roll information See App 5618, Vol. 3]

12229. LOREN P. GUTHRIE and 4 children,   Cookson, Okla
Admitted. 1st cousin once removed of No 2714 and claims thru
same source. Applicant's mother enrolled in Flint No 399.
ROLL P69 #12824 FCT COMM #16500 - Loren P. Guthrie - 44
          12825   25379 - Myrtle (dau)   - 9
          12826   25380 - William (son)   - 6
          12827   4648m - Maud (dau)   - 3
          12828   4649m - Odie B. (son)   - 1

12230. JAMES HENSON and 5 children,   Cookson, Okla
Admitted. Brother to 316, and claims through same source.
ROLL P74 #13894 FCT COMM #15473 - James Henson   - 39
          13895   15474 - Pearlie (dau)   - 13
          13896   15475 - Dulcemore (dau) - 10
          13897   15476 - Vestie (dau)   - 6
          13898   15477 - Hugh (son)   - 5
          13899   1882m - Eliza (dau)   - 3

12231. WASH HENDON,   Cookson, Okla
          James Henson, Gdn.
Admitted. Sister to #326, and claims through same source,
ROLL P74 #13946 FCT COMM #28290 - Wash Henson - 21

12232. MAY HENSON,   Cookson, Okla
          James Henson, Gdn.
Admitted. Sister to #316, and claims through same source.
ROLL P74 #13910 FCT COMM #28292 - May Henson - 17
                              by James Henson, Gdn.

12233. SUSAN SCOTT,   Sallisaw, Okla
Rejected. Applicant died before May 28, 1906. Misc. Test. P.
2948. [For Testimony See App 1702, Vol. 2]

12234. MIRTIE A. SIZEMORE,   Sizemore, Ala
Rejected. Applicant claims through Ned Sizemore, see report
#417.

12235. MARGARET C. SIZEMORE,   Sizemore, Ala
Rejected. Applicant claims through Ned Sizemore, see report
#417.

12236. WOODS M. SIZEMORE,   RFD #2, Winfield, Ala
Rejected. Applicant claims through Ned Sizemore, see report
#417.

12237. DANIEL W. SIZEMORE,   Sizemore, Ala
Rejected. Applicant claims through Ned Sizemore, see report
#417.

12238. DICK WATERS,   Blackgum, Okla
Admitted. Applicant's mother enrolled by Drennen in 1851 as
Nic-oo-tr-ee Waters S. B. 170. Misc. Test. P. 2926.

MISC. TEST. P. 2926. No 12239 (9580) - Eva Young:
    "My name is Eva Young; I was born in Illinois District,
1870; my father was born in Sequoyah District, 1839; I think
my mother was born in Flint District; my mother died in about
1877; I don't know when my mother was born; I think my grand
parents were born in the old nation; I don't know when they
came to the Ind. Terr., but they were all emigrant Cherokees;
none of my people have ever been Old Settlers; neither I nor
any of the ancestors through whom I claim have ever affiliated
with any tribe of Indians other than the Cherokees; I was opposed to the allotment and never accepted my allotment. I never heard my father say anything about being on the rolls, but
I guess my parents and grandparents were enrolled in Sequoyah
District; my father's brothers and sisters were Nick-quoh-tee-
yah Waters, Ona-wak-kee Waters, Co-yo-teh Waters, Blanket
Waters, Elijah Waters, Kah-kil-lah-wee-stah Waters, Conie
Waters and Dirt-hunter. (See Skin Bayou 170)."
SIGNED: Eva Young, Sallisaw, Okla., Sep 18 1908.
ROLL P146 #28404 FCT COMM #18100 - Dick Waters - 66

12239. EVA YOUNG and 1 child,   Blackgum, Okla
Admitted. Niece of 12238 claiming through same source.
ROLL P155 #30104 FCT COMM #17288 - Eva Young   - 35
            30105   17289 - James (son) - 10

12240. WM. P. BECK for his 3 children,   Tahlequah, Okla
            his minor children, James, Cogin, and Tom Beck
Admitted. 1st cousins of 2671 [? 2nd digit blurred].
ROLL P28 #4679 FCT COMM #6426 - James Beck   - 7*
          4680   6427 - Cogin (bro) - 11
          4681   6424 - Tom (bro)   - 18
                              (By Wm. P. Beck, Gdn.)
[* "13" crossed out]

12241. ELLIS HARP,   Cookson, Okla
Admitted. Nephew of #2926. Claimant's mother enrolled in
1851 by Drennen, Flint 375.
ROLL P71 #13358 FCT COMM #4219 - Ellis Harp - 30

12242. ROBERT WILLIAMS,   Westville, Okla
            by Robert Williams, Gdn.
Admitted. Grand-nephew of #384.
ROLL P151 #29387 FCT COMM #924 - Robert Williams - 11
                              by Robert Williams, Gdn.

12243. THOMAS WILLIAMS,   Westville, Okla
Admitted. Grand-nephew of #384.
ROLL P151 #29396 FCT COMM #926 - Thomas Williams - 6
                              by Robert Williams, Gdn.

12244. OMA WILLIAMS,   Westville, Okla
           by Robert Williams, Gdn.
Admitted. Grand-nephew of #384.
ROLL P151 #29383 FCT COMM #925 - Oma Williams - 9
                               by Robert Williams, Gdn.

12245. SUSIE HENDRIX,   Vian, Okla
Admitted. Mother of #7432, and enrolled by Drennen in 1851,
Tahl. #383.
ROLL P74 #13810 FCT COMM #18283 - Susie Hendrixx - 59

12246. THOMAS S. HOBGOOD,   Marion Station, Miss
Rejected. "Indian Tom" case - see special report in #3090.

                           REJECTED
APP 12247 TO 12265 - SIZEMORE CASES - SEE SPECIAL REPORT #417

12247. PHEBY SHULTS,   Kipling, Va

12248. DOSKA EDWARDS,   Whitehead, N C

12249. ROBERT L. OSBORN,   Laurel Springs, N C

12250. REBECCA PRUITT and 5 children,   Laurel Springs, N C

12251. MARSHALL OSBORNE,   Springfield, N C

12252. TROY OSBORNE and 7 children,   Springfield, N C

12253. CANDACE ROBERTS and 3 children,   McGrady, N C

12254. REBECCA ABSHER and 1 child,   McGrady, N C

12255. MARTHA COX,   Gray, N C

12256. MALINDA PAYNE,   Springfield, N C

12257. TENNESSEE OSBORNE,   City, N C

12258. POLLY OSBORN,   City, N C

12259. WILLIE OSBORNE,   Laurel Springs, N C

12260. FIELDS OSBORNE and 4 children,   Laurel Springs, N C

12261. JOHN COX,   Gray, N C

12262. ALIE HAYNES and 4 children,   Halls Mills, N C

12263. JOHN H. WAGONER and 2 children,   Halls Mills, N C

12264. JAMES STAMPER,   Springfield, N C

12265. ARTHUR STAMPER,   McGrady, N C

END CONSECUTIVE SIZEMORE CASES

12266. REUBEN H. HYATT and 4 children,   Bryson City, N C
Rejected. Betsy Walker case. [App 500, Vol. 1]

12267. ELLEN S. EVANS and 8 children,   Lookout, N C
Rejected. Nephew [sic] of 219 and claims through same source.

12268. A. M. HANEY and 4 children,   Lookout, N C
Rejected. Nephew of 219 and claims through same source.

12269. M. THOS. and ALICE V. HANEY,   Lookout, N C
Rejected. Nephew and niece of 219 and claims through the same
source.

12270. ROBERT B. SHEPPARD,   Guthrie, Okla
Rejected. No ancestor ever enrolled. No ancestor party to
treaties of 1835-6 and 1846. Shows no connection with Eastern
Cherokees. Party and ancestors were slaves.

12271. JOSEPH H. MARSH,   1316 T St., Lincoln, Neb
Rejected. No ancestor ever enrolled. No ancestor party to
treaties of 1835-6 and 1846. Shows no connection with Eastern
Cherokees. Ancestors never lived in Cherokee domain.

12272. JANE WILLIAMS,   Wichita Falls, Tex
Rejected. It does not appear that any ancestor was ever enrolled or that any ancestor was party to the treaties of 1835-
1836 and 1846. Shows no real connection with the Eastern
Cherokees.

12273. ELIZABETH FENDER,   Okesa, Okla
Rejected. Sister of #8411 and claims through same source.

12274. ISHAM H. COURTNEY and 2 children, Okesa, Okla
Rejected. Claims through Alex. Brown. See #35

12275. NETTIE MAY BYRON and 2 children,   Nowata, Okla
Rejected. Claims through Alex. Brown. See #35.

12276. ARZELIA P. QUEEN, Duplicate of #1306.

12277. VIRGINIA CLEVINGER and 6 children, Jumbo, W Va
Rejected. Applicant claims through Ned Sizemore - See report
in #417.

12278. JOHN ADAMS and 3 children,   Andrew, N C
Rejected. Applicant claims through Blythe case. See report
in 153.

12279. SARAH J. OWENBY,   Blue Ridge, Ga
Rejected. Daughter of #117.

12280. FIDILLE REE, c/o Supt. State Farm, Halifax, N C
Admitted. 1st cousin of 6223 [? 2nd digit blurred] and claims
through same ancestors.
ROLL P15 #2138 - Fidille Reed - 32

12281. MELISSA KILLIAN,   Murphy, N C
Rejected. Applicant claims through Blythe case.   See report
in #153.

12282. PASSEY J. CARVER and 3 children,   Jasper, Ga
Rejected. Nephew to Rebecca McGaha (4170).

12283. ROSA MARTIN and 1 child,   Jasper, Ga
Rejected. Grand child of Rebecca McGaha 4170.

12284. IDA M. OWENBY,   Blue Ridge, Ga
Rejected. Daughter of #117.

12285. BENJ. HENRY,   Blue Ridge, Ga
Rejected. No ancestor ever enrolled.   No ancestor party to
treaties of 1835-6 and 1846. Shows no connection with Eastern
Cherokees.

12286. MARY A. HENRY,   Blue Ridge, Ga
Rejected. Sister of #12285, and claims through the same ancestors.

12287. CHARLEY HENRY and 6 children,   Blue Ridge, Ga
Rejected. Brother of #12285, and claims through the same ancestor.

12288. CALLY J. OWENBY,   Blue Ridge, Ga
Rejected. Daughter of #117.

12289. MARTHA HENRY COLLET,   Blue Ridge, Ga
Rejected. Sister of #12285, and claims through same source or
ancestors.

12290. IRENE VERHINE,   Rout [sic] 28, Kennesaw, Ga
Rejected. Claims through same source as 7812.

12291. ROBERT L. HILLHOUSE,   Holly Springs, Ga
Rejected. Hillhouse case.

12292. GEO. C. ARNOLD,   Talking Rock, Ga
Rejected. Great nephew to Elvin P. Dempsey (11302)

12293. HOWARD VERHINE,   Rout 28, Kennesaw, Ga
Rejected. Claims through same source as 7812.

314

12294. ETHEL VERHINE,   Rout 28, Kennesaw, Ga
Rejected. Claims through same source as 7812.

12295. ELMO VERHINE,   Rout 28, Kennesaw, Ga
Rejected. Claims through same source as 7812.

12296. ANNIE VERHINE,   Rout 28, Kennesaw, Ga
Rejected. Claims through same source as 7812.

12297. THOMAS SPEAR,   Holly Springs, Ga
Rejected. No ancestor was ever enrolled. No ancestor part to
the treaties of 1835-6 and 1846. Ancestors did not live with
the Cherokee tribe. Shows no connection with the Eastern
Cherokees.

12298. PEGGY STELLS,   RFD #2, Woodstock, Ga
Rejected. Applicant claims through Biddy case.

12299. MELVIN M. HILLHOUSE,   Holly Springs, Ga
          by his father, Robert L. Hillhouse
Rejected. Hillhouse case. See special report 9897.

12300. RUBY STELLS,   RFD #2, Woodstock, Ga
          by Peggy Stells, Gdn.
Rejected. [No reason stated]

REJECTED
APP 12301 TO 12314 – HILLHOUSE CASES – SEE SPECIAL REPORT #9897

12301. MATTIE HILLHOUSE,   Holly Spring, Ga
          by her father Joshua R. Hillhouse

12302. JOSHUA R. HILLHOUSE,   Holly Springs, Ga

12303. JOSEPH J. HILLHOUSE,   Holly Springs, Ga
          by his father Robert L. Hillhouse

12304. JESSIE L. HILLHOUSE,   Holly Springs, Ga
          by her father Robert L. Hillhouse

12305. JAMES W. HILLHOUSE,   Holly Springs, Ga
          by his father, James S. Hillhouse

12306. ELIAS E. HILLHOUSE,   Holly Springs, Ga
          by his father Robert L. Hillhouse

12307. JAMES S. HILLHOUSE,   Holly Springs, Ga

12308. GEORGE W. HILLHOUSE,   Holly Springs, Ga
          by his father J. S. Hillhouse

315

12309. FANNIE P. HILLHOUSE,   Holly Springs, Ga
      by her father Robert L. Hillhouse

12310. ETHEL HILLHOUSE,   Holly Springs, Ga
      by her father Robert L. Hillhouse

12311. ERNEST D. HILLHOUSE,   Holly Springs, Ga
      by his father Joshua R. Hillhouse

12312. ANNIE B. HILLHOUSE,   Holly Springs, Ga
      by her father Robert L. Hillhouse

12313. GLENN HILLHOUSE,   Holly Springs, Ga
      by his father Joshua Hillhouse

12314. BELLE HILLHOUSE,   Holly Springs, Ga
      by her father James S. Hillhouse

END CONSECUTIVE HILLHOUSE CASES

12315. VERNIA FOWLER,   Holly Springs, Ga
Rejected. Daughter of #12321 and claims through the same ancestors.

12316. VENETA FOWLER,   Holly Springs, Ga
Rejected. Daughter of #12321, and claims through the same ancestor.

12317. ILER FOWLER,   Holly Springs, Ga
Rejected. Daughter of #12321, and claims through the same ancestors.

12318. JULIA FOWLER,   Holly Springs, Ga
Rejected. Daughter of #12321, and claims through the same ancestors.

12319. ESTELLE FOWLER,   Holly Springs, Ga
Rejected. Daughter of #12321, and claims through the same ancestors.

12320. EMORY H. FOWLER,   Holly Springs, Ga
Rejected. Son of 12321, and claims through the same ancestors

12321. MARY A. FOWLER,   Holly Springs, Ga
Rejected. It does not appear that ancestors were ever enrolled, or were parties to the treaties of 1835-6 and 1846.
Applicant shows no real connection with Eastern Cherokees.
Misc. Test. P. 1100.

MISC. TEST. P. 1100. #12321-12315 - Mary A. Fowler:
"I am 54 years of age; was born in Cobb County, Ga.; have
spent my life in Forsythe and Cherokee Counties. I claim my
Indian blood through my father. My grandfather never received
any Indian money that I know of. I remember my grandfather.
He lived in that county. I do not know if he lived with the
Indians. My father did not live with the Indians that I know
of. My father first told me of my Indian blood. He said his
mother and sister were Cherokee Indians. They were curious
looking. Did not look like my mother's people. My grandmother was a small woman. They were dark. My grandfather was a
small fleshy man. I do not think he had a beard. He was a
farmer. I cannot remember if he spoke the Indian language.
He died in 1875. I have never tried to get any Indian money
prior to this time."
SIGNED: Mary A. Fowler, Canton, Ga., Jul 7 1908.
EXCEPTION CASE. Rejected. Total number of exceptions filed
in this group -- 13. Original recommendation renewed.

12322. LUNIE FOWLER,   Holly Springs, Ga
Rejected. Daughter of 12321, and claims through the same ancestors.

12323. GRADY STELLS,   RFD #2, Woodstock, Ga
        by Peggy Stells, Gdn.
Rejected. Applicant claims through Biddy case. See special
report 7615.

12324. CLARA STELLS,   RFD #2, Woodstock, Ga
        by Peggy Stells, Gdn.
Rejected. Applicant claims through Biddy case. See special
report 7615.

12325. LILLY E. SIMPSON,   RFD #2, Woodstock, Ga
        by Angil Simpson, Gdn.
Rejected. Applicant claims through Biddy case. See special
report 7615.

12326. ANGIE SIMPSON,   RFD #2, Woodstock, Ga
Rejected. Applicant claims through Biddy case. See special
report 7615.

12327. ANDREW SIMPSON,   RFD #2, Woodstock, Ga
        by Angie Simpson, Gdn.
Rejected. Applicant claims through Biddy case. See special
report 7615.

12328. MARION H. SAMS,   RFD #2, Woodstock, Ga
Rejected. Applicant claims through Biddy case. See special
report 7615.

12329. LOUSEILLE SAMS,   RFD #2, Woodstock, Ga
        by Marion H. Sams, Gdn.
Rejected. Applicant claims through Biddy case.   See special
report 7615.

12330. SANFORD RICHARDSON,   Chattahooche, Ga
Rejected. Claims through same source as 7812.

12331. RALPH VERHINE,   Rout 28, Kennesaw, Ga
Rejected. Claims through same source as 7812.

12332. JOE FOWLER,   Holly Springs, Ga
Rejected. Son of 12321, and claims through same source.

12333. ARTHUR FOWLER,   Holly Springs, Ga
Rejected. Son of 12321, and claims through same source.

12334. ALICE FOWLER,   Holly Springs, Ga
Rejected. Daughter of 12321, and claims through the same ancestors.

12335. HATTIE COVINGTON,   Canton, Ga
Rejected. Hillhouse case. See report 9897.

12336. THOMAS COLE,   Holly Springs, Ga
Rejected. Hillhouse case. See report 9897.

12337. NOAH COLE,   Holly Springs, Ga
Rejected. Hillhouse case. See report 9897.

12338. WM. CLINE,   RFD #2, Woodstock, Ga
        by Jane Cline, Gdn.
Rejected. Applicant claims through Biddy case, #7615.

12339. JANE CLINE,   RFD #2, Woodstock, Ga
Rejected. Applicant claims through Biddy case, #7615.

12340. GARRISON CLINE,   RFD #2, Woodstock, Ga
Rejected. Applicant claims through Biddy case, #7615.

12341. MARY CAGLE,   RFD #2, Woodstock, Ga
Rejected. Applicant claims through Biddy case, #7615.

12342. HENRY L. CAGLE,   RFD #2, Woodstock, Ga
        by Mary Cagle, Gdn.
Rejected. Applicant claims through Biddy case, #7615.

12343. ROY VERHINE,   Kennesaw, Ga
Rejected. Claims through same source as 7812.

12344. LEON RICHARDSON,   Chattahooche, Ga
Rejected. Claims through same source as 7812.

12345. MARY E. BISHOP, Holly Springs, Ga
Rejected. Granddaughter of 12321, and claims thru same source.

12346. GLENN RICHARDSON, Chattahooche, Ga
Rejected. Claims through same source as 7812.

12347. CLAUDIE RAGSDALE, Holly Springs, Ga
Rejected. Applicant claims through the Hilman [sic - should be Hillhouse] case. See report 9897.

12348. MATTIE PINYAN, Holly Springs, Ga
Rejected. Applicant claims through Hillhouse case. See special report in 9897.

12349. SAMUEL S. HOWARD, Woodstock, Ga
Rejected. Applicant claims through Hillhouse case. See special report in 9897.

12350. ELLA BISHOP, Holly Springs, Ga
Rejected. Daughter of 12321, and claims thru same ancestors.

12351. WILLIAM L. HILLHOUSE, Holly Springs, Ga
        by his father Robert L. Hillhouse
Rejected. Applicant claims through Hillhouse case. See special report in 9897.

12352. THOMAS HILLHOUSE, Holly Springs, Ga
        by his father James S. Hillhouse
Rejected. Applicant claims through Hillhouse case. See special report in 9897.

12353. ROBERT T.* BRAMLETT, Holly Springs, Ga
Rejected. Claims through same source as 9783. [* "L" in index]

[NOTE: Skips to 12355 - Index shows App 12354 as Lucy Bramlett, by Gdn. Robt. L. Bramlett, Residence Ga.]

12355. TULA* ARNOLD, Talking Rock, Ga
Rejected. Great niece of Elvin P. Dempsey (11302). [* "Lula Arnold" in index]

12356. JAMES M. ARNOLD, Talking Rock, Ga
Rejected. Great nephew of Elvin P. Dempsey (11302)

12357. SUSAN F. HILLHOUSE, Holly Springs, Ga
        by her father, Robert L. Hillhouse
Rejected. Applicant claims through Hillhouse case. See special report in 9897.

12358. AMANDA E. PITTMAN, Stidham, Okla
Rejected. Applicant is enrolled as a Creels [sic] by blood on Dawes Commission Roll #2424.

319

12359. ALLEN M. MARKHAM,   1006 Holmes St., Kansas City, Mo
Admitted. Claims through grandmother enrolled as Martha Riley,
Aunts and uncles enrolled as Ruthy and George Drew, Nancy F.,
Richard and Martin Riley - Sal. #450.
ROLL P96 #18302 FCT COMM #28297 - Allen M. Markham - 23

12360. WM. S. COODEY,   Eufaula, Okla
Rejected. Brother of #11797, and claims through same source.

12361. MINNIE V. ISLAND,   Stidham, Okla
Rejected. Sister of 11979 and claims through same source.

12362. HENRY G. STARR,   Muskogee, Okla
Admitted. 1st cousin to #4196. [For Roll information See App
9376, Vol. 4]

12363. BETTIE GLENN,   Tobaccoville, N C
Rejected. No ancestor ever enrolled. No ancestor party to
treaties of 1835-6 and 1846. Shows no connection with Eastern
Cherokee. Parents were slaves.

12364. ADNA S. BENGE,   Fort Gibson, Okla
Admitted. 1st cousin of #4196, and claims through the same
source. [For Roll information See App 7895, Vol. 4]

12365. SARAH COODY,   Eufaula, Okla
Rejected. Sister of 11979 and claims through same source.

12366. EULA M. WALKER and 4 children,   Stidham, Okla
Rejected. Sister of 11979 and claims through same source.

12367. FAMOUS WHITWATER and 2 children,   Braggs, Okla
Admitted. The paternal grandparents of applicant were enrolled by Drennen in 1851 in Skin Bayou Dist. under the names
of Red, and W-ki- Red.
ROLL P150 #29044 FCT COMM #21160 - Famous Whitewater - 34
            29045   21148 - Betsy (wife)   - 24
                                  (App 13790)
            29046   4817m - Lizzie (dau)   - 2
            29047   4818m - Ross (son)   - 1

12368. JERRY HAUSER,   Tobaccoville, N C
Rejected. Brother to 12363, and claims thru same ancestors.

12369. SARAH VENERABLE,   Winston Salem, N C
Rejected. No ancestor ever enrolled. No ancestor party to
treaties of 1835-6 and 1846. Shows no connection with Eastern
Cherokee. Ancestors did not live in Cherokee domain.
MISC. TEST. P. 3. App #12369 - Sarah Venerable:
    "I am 61 years of age, and live at Winston-Salem, N. C. I
claim Indian blood through my grandmother and grandfather, who
are dead. I never heard them say to what tribe of Indians they

320

belonged. I never lived with the Indians. I was never enrolled
or paid any moneys, although I have heard of Indians being enrolled. That was 25 or 30 years ago. My father and mother were
not held as slaves. I was never held as a slave. I lived in
Surry county before the War. My mother was raised in Forsythe
County. My father was born in Halifax Courthouse, Va. My mother is alive and living near Stony Ridge in Surry County, and
is 107 years old. I remember by grandparents on my mother's
side. My grandparents on my mother's side lived in Forsythe
County. I never heard them say whether they lived with Indians. The Indians were carried away from here before I can
remember. My father and mother never received any Indian money. I was not married before the war. I have heard my father
talk of the Catawba Indians. I have heard him speak of the
Cherokee Indians. He said I was kin to the Indians, but did
not say any special tribe. I was free born. Malinda Scales of
Donaha, Forsythe County, N. C. is my sister."
SIGNED: Sarah "X" Venerable, Winston-Salem, N. C., Mar 18
1908.
EXCEPTION CASE. 12369. Joseph Sawyer and 2 children, App
14154, East Bend, N. C. Rejected. Total number of exceptions
filed in this group -- 2. Original recommendation renewed.

12370. WILEY HAUSER,   Tobaccoville, N C
Rejected. Brother to #12363, and claims through the same
ancestors.

12371. JAMES RUFUS SCALES,   Tobaccoville, N C
Rejected. No ancestor ever enrolled. No ancestor party to
treaties of 1835-6 and 1846. Shows no connection with Western
[sic] Cherokees. Ancestors never lived in Cherokee domain.
MISC. TEST. P. 11. No 16492 - Martha Ann Scales:
    "My name is Martha Ann Scales; I am 38 years old; my post-
office is Tobaccoville, N. C. I was born in Forsythe Co.,
N. C. I claim to be Indian through both mother and father. I
don't know what tribe of Indians either mother or father belonged. I have heard that my father's father was an Indian. My
father's mother and and my mother's mother were colored. My
father and mother were both slaves. I don't know what Indian
blood my father's father had. My brothers and sisters did not
file claims."
SIGNED: Martha Ann "X" Scales, Winston-Salem, N. C., Mar 19
1908.
No. 12371 - James Rufus Scales...deposes and says:
    "My name is James Rufus Scales; I live at Tobaccoville,
N. C.; am 41 years old. Was born in Forsythe Co. My mother
is living, and I claim Indian blood through her. She lives at
Tobaccoville & has filed a claim; her name is Emily J. Scales
(16484). I don't know that my father had Indian blood. My
mother got her Indian blood through her mother and father. My
father was held as a slave. I don't know whether my mother was
held as a slave or not; I think she was called "free issue"

and don't think she was held as a slave. I don't think my grandmother on my mother's side was held as a slave. My mother always said she was mixed with Indians, but never heard her just say what Indian. My mother came from Caswell Co., N. C. I think that her people came from Va."
SIGNED: James R. Scales, Winston-Salem, N. C., Mar 19 1908.

12372. NOAH GLENN,   Donnoha, N C
Rejected. No ancestor ever enrolled. No ancestor party to treaties of 1835-6 and 1846. Shows no connection with Eastern Cherokees. Party and ancestors were slaves.
MISC. TEST. P. 5. App No 12372 - Noah Glenn:
    "My name is Noah Glenn; I am 48 years old; I live at Donnohoo; I was born in Yadkin Co., N. C. I claim my Indian blood through my mother who was a slave. I was born a slave. My mother was an Indian on both her mother's and father's side. She belonged to the Cherokees. My mother was born in Yadkin Co." SIGNED: Noah Glenn, Winston-Salem, N. C., Mar 19 1908.

12373. JAMES H. WORLEY and 3 children,   Dahlonega, Ga
Rejected. Cousin of #11382 and claims through same source.

12374. MARY E. SHASTEEN and 2 children,   Winchester, Tenn
Admitted. 1st cousin of #642. Applicant enrolled in Tahlequah #224.
ROLL P16 #2348 - Mary Shasteen   - 5? [last digit blurred]
          2349 - Eliza E. (dau) - 20
          2350 - Nannie B. (dau) - 17

12375. WILLIAM JASPER WORLEY,   Dahlonega, Ga
Rejected. Cousin of 11382, and claims through same source.

12376. TIMOTHY H. WORLEY and 2 children,   Dahlonega, Ga
Rejected. Cousin of 11382, and claims through same source.

12377. SARAH E. KINYOUN,   East Bend, N C
Rejected. Applicant claims through Poindexter case. See report #464.

12378. GEO. WASHINGTON WILLIAMS,   RFD #2, Charlotte, Tenn
Rejected. No ancestor ever enrolled. No ancestor party to treaties of 1835-6 and 1846. Shows no connection with Eastern Cherokees. Ancestors were slaves.

12379. GUY WASHINGTON, Duplicate of #11695.

12380. JESSE SUGG,   RFD #2, Charlotte, Tenn
Rejected. No ancestor ever enrolled. No ancestor party to treaties of 1835-6 and 1846. Shows no connection with Eastern Cherokees. Party and ancestor were slaves.

12381. AMANDA CUNNINGHAM,   RFD #2, Charlotte, Tenn
Rejected. No ancestor ever enrolled. No ancestor party to
treaties of 1835-6 and 1836 [sic]. Shows no connection with
Eastern Cherokees. Ancestors never lived in Cherokee domain.
Ancestors were slaves.

12382. WILLIAM P. ATHINS and 5 children,   Chestnut Gap, Ga
Rejected. It does not appear that any ancestor was party to
the treaties of 1835-6-46. Shows no real connection with the
Eastern Cherokees. It does not appear that any ancestor was
ever enrolled. Misc. Test. P. 1449.
[NOTE: The following page of testimony is extremely dark and
difficult to read]
MISC. TEST. P. 1449. No 12382 - Wm. P. Atkins:
    "I am 57 [37?] years of age. I was born in Raburn County,
Ga. I claim Indian blood through my mother. Neither my
mother nor myself ever received any Indian money. My mother
claims her Indian blood through her father, Pleasant Brown
[?]. He looked to be an Indian. He could talk the Indian
language. I do not know where he was born. He lived in
Raburn County when I knew him. He was a farmer. He was a
dark looking man with black beard and hair. I do not know if
I have ever been enrolled. Twenty-five years ago my name was
not taken by a government agent. Never heard the name Hester.
I do not know if grandfather was a voter or not. I have always
voted." SIGNED: Wm. P. Atkins, Blue Ridge, Ga., Jul 11 1908.

12383. SUSIE SPLITNOSE and 3 children,   Porum, Okla
Admitted. Duplicate of #1153. [NOTE: Should be 1553]

12384. JAS. W. VANN,   Porum, Okla
Admitted. Son of #9191. 1st cousin of #4106. Mother "Mary
Rogers", enrolled 290 Ill.
ROLL P143 #27696 FCT COMM # 5012 - James W. Vann   - 34
          27697   5013 - Florence (wife)   - 29
                               (App 12389)
          27698   5014 - Mary E. (dau)   - 8
          27699   5015 - Charlotte A. (dau) - 5
          27700   3869m - Lester D. (son)   - 4

12385. RAY. P. MARKHAM,   Muskogee, Okla
Admitted. Brother of #12359, and claims through same source.
ROLL P96 #18319 FCT COMM #28298 - Ray P. Markham - 21

12386. MARY A. BARKER and 4 children,   Welch, Okla
Admitted. 1st cousin of #1912.
ROLL P26 #4261 FCT COMM #10061 - Mary A. Barker   - 46
          4262   10065 - Sequoyah (son)   - 17
          4263   10066 - Artemus B. (son) - 14
          4264   10067 - Dennis (son)   - 12
          4265   10068 - Emelese (dau)   - 10

12387. DAVE BARKER, Duplicate of #10198.

12388. MALINDA SUNDAY, Duplicate of #1556.
MISC. TEST. P. 2694. #12388-1553 - Malinda Sunday:
    "That I am about 50 years of age. I am a full blood Cher-
okee. My father's name was Catch-a-coon. His name was De-gah-
ne-ske or De-gah-nee-skih. My mother's name was Su-sih. Kun-
lih or Coon was my grandfather on my father's side. Uh-wah-
dih was my grandmother's name on my father's side. Da-lih-
skih was the name of my mother's father. A-gih was my grand
mother's name on my mother's side. My father had a twin brother by the name of Je-sih or Jessie. He has a sister living yet
at Oaks and her name is Che-ga-you-ih. He has a half sister on
the mother's side and she lives at Oaks, Okla. Her name is
Lit-tih. My father's brother was Jus-ca-yoh-ih. Dick Coon
was another of of his brothers. My folks were living in the
West in 1851. They were living in Going Snake District. I was
enrolled by the Dawes Commission and got 90 acres of land. My
number is 17203 in the Dawes Commission. I and my parents always lived with the tribe. None of them ever received any Old
Settler money. I have an older sister named An-nih."
SIGNED: Malinda "X" Sunday, Stigler, Okla., Sep 8 1908.

12389. FLORENCE VANN and 3 children,   Porum, Okla
Admitted. Niece of #278 and claims through same source. Applicant's mother Mary R. Gourd enrolled by Drennen, Tahl. District #478. [For Roll information See App 12384]

12390. LOUIS HARLESS, REED & RUFUS HARLESS, Pryor Creek, Okla
         by sister, Annie L. Abbott
Admitted. Grandnephews and grandnieces of #132.
ROLL P71 #13252 FCT COMM #23427 - Louisa Harless   - 15
         13253   23426 - Reed Warren (bro) - 17
         13254   23425 - Rufus (bro)   - 19
                              by Annie L. Abbott, Gdn.

12391. ANNIE L. ABBOTT and 2 children,   Pryor Creek, Okla
Admitted. Grandniece of #132.
ROLL P21 #3175 FCT COMM #23424 - Annie L. Abbott - 21
         3176   1396m - Louisa J. (dau) - 3
         3177   1397m - Leona M. (dau) -   1

12392. MARTHA ANN LLOYD,   Lindale, Ga
Rejected. Claims through "Water Hunter". See #10448.

12393. VIRGINIA I. LLOYD,   Lindale, Ga
Rejected. Claims through "Water Hunter". See #10448.

12394. ALICE ELIZA LLOYD,   Lindale, Ga
Rejected. Claims through "Water Hunter". See #10448.

12395. WHITLEY CICERO LLOYD and 7 children, Rome, Ga
Rejected. Claims through "Water Hunter". See #10448.

12396. JAMES ALFRED LLOYD and 8 children, Rome, Ga
RFD #2
Rejected. Claims through "Water Hunter". See #10448.

12397. JAMES A. B. LLOYD and 3 children,
#2 Oak Ave
Rejected. Claims through "Water Hunter". See #10448.

12398. ALLEN LATTA, Duplicate of #169.

12399. WILLIAM CRITTENDEN, Stilwell, Okla
Admitted. Brother of 5234, and claims through same source.
ROLL P49 #8855 FCT COMM #1919 - William P. Crittenden - 54

12400. MOSES F. SANDERS and 1 child, Sallisaw, Okla
Admitted. 1st cousin of #14786 and claims through the same
source. Applicant's father "46 Skin Bayou, Ellis, Sanders".
ROLL P123 #23634 FCT COMM #15127 - Moses F. Sanders - 40
23635   3827m - Mary L. (dau)   - 2

12401. SUSIE PERDUE and 1 child, Cookson, Okla
Admitted. Niece of #11493. Claims through same source. See
Misc. Test. P. 4193.
MISC. TEST. P. 4193. App No 12401 - Polly Crow...through John
Israel, Interpreter, in behalf of Susie Perdue:
  "Claimant is a full blood Cherokee. She was enrolled by
the Dawes Commission. Cucumber Ross is the father of applicant. Gah-nee-yaw-ih was the name of her mother. I knew her.
Oo-dee-sa-dee-et-tah was a brother of her mother. She had a
sister named Jinnie. Car-se-low-ee was another brother. Gaw-
se-low-ee was the grandfather on the mother's side. Cha-wee-
yu-ka was the grandmother on the mother's side and she lived
in G. S. District. I don't think she had any brothers and sisters. Claimant's mother never drew Old Settler money, but I
have heard that she drew money in 1851. Gah-nee-yaw-ih was
never known by any other name that I know of. Gaw-se-low-ee
lived near the Arkansas line, Sequoyah or Flint District."
SIGNED: Polly Crow, Braggs, Okla., Mar 27 1909.
[For Roll information See App 12413]

12402. NELLIE LEAF and 2 children, Cookson, Okla
Admitted. Illinois #49. Mother of Maggie Fiels [sic] App. No
11491, and is admitted for same reasons.
ROLL P89 #16860 FCT COMM #20646 - Nellie Leaf - 57
16861   20647 - Mary (dau) - 16
16862   20648 - Adam (son) - 15

12403. ROBERT H. EVANS, Cookson, Okla
Admitted. Brother of 385.

ROLL P58 #10785 FCT COMM # 2277 - Robert H. Evans - 26
      10786   27234 - Elizabeth (wife) - 26
                      (App 12404)
      10787   3804m - Katie M. (dau)   - 5/6

12404. ELIZABETH EVANS and 1 child,   Cookson, Okla
Admitted. Niece of #2687 and her grandfather Jackson Christie
is enrolled from Fl. Dist. 640. [For Roll information See App
12403]

12405. SEQUICHIE SQUIRREL and 4 children, Cookson, Okla
Admitted. Half-brother of #4855, and claims through the same
source. [For Roll information See App 3550, Vol. 2]

12406. DICK JUSTICE,   Cookson, Okla
Admitted. 1st cousin of Maggie Fields App #11491 and is admitted for same reason. Grandmother Nellie Leaf #12402, enrolled Illinois #49, as Nelly Sanders.
ROLL P83 #15816 - Dick Justice - 21

12407. JOHN GRIMETT,   [No residence]
      by Wm. Grimett, Gdn. & parent
Duplicate Inc. in 12412. See Application of father #10301.
[For Roll information See App 10301]

12408. SALLY DICK,   Cookson, Okla
Admitted. Niece of 9672 and claims through same source.
ROLL P53 #9719 FCT COMM #25949 - William Dick - 34
                    (App 41510)
      9720   25950 - Sally (wife) - 25
      9721   32072 - Jennie (dau) - 8
      9722   25951 - Maggie (dau) - 4
      9723   4812m - Henry (son) - 1

12409. BENJ. F. MEIGS,   Park Hill, Okla
Admitted. Nephew of 1363. [For Roll information See App 9462,
Vol. 4]

12410. COOIE MEIGS,   Park Hill, Okla
Admitted. Nephew of 1363.
ROLL P98 #18734 FCT COMM #27815 - Cooie Meigs - 23

12411. FLOREIN N. MEIGS,   Cookson, Okla
Admitted. Nephew of 1363. [For Roll information See App
10188]

12412. NANCY HOOPER,   Cookson, Okla
Admitted. Daughter of #10301.
ROLL P77 #14577 FCT COMM #20606 - James Hooper - 26
                    (App 13325)
      14458   18931 - Nancy (wife) - 22

12413. CHARLES PERDUE,   Cookson, Okla
Admitted. Wife 12401 has filed for one child. Brother 10388,
and claims through same source.
ROLL P110 #21110 FCT COMM #21093 - Charles Perdue   - 26
          21111   21094 - Susie (wife)   - 36
                                   (App 12401)
          21112   2115m - Star DEER-IN-WATER - 1
                                   (son of w)

12414. ELLEN WHITEWATER and 2 children,   Cookson, Okla
Admitted. Applicant's parents enrolled by Drennen as Black-
hawk & Wahlee Tah. 302.
ROLL P150 #29041 FCT COMM #21137 - Ellen Whitewater - 51
          29042   21138 - Sally (dau)   - 17
          29043   21139 - Mary (dau)   - 14

12415. LIZZIE ELK,   Cookson, Okla
Admitted. Sister of 9672, claims through same source.
ROLL P57 #10569 - Lizzie Elk - 52

12416. SUSIE BEAVER and 1 child,   Vian, Okla
Admitted. Applicant is a daughter of Nannie Buster, App 12552
and claims through same source.
ROLL P28 #4618 FCT COMM #32073 - Susie Beaver   - 23
          4619   32074 - Eliza Daugherty (dau) - 6

12417. AKEY McCUEN,   Atkins, Okla
Admitted. Applicant's father enrolled as Drinker at G. S. 614.
MISC. TEST. P. 3497. #12417 - Akey McCuen:
     "That I am 46 years of age. I am 3/4 Cherokee. My mother
was 1/2 breed. My father was a full blood; both Cherokees.
Don't know when my father was born but he died in the time of
the war. He was about 25 years old when he died. My mother
was in the fifties when she died. My father had a brother
named Levi Walkingstick. My father had a sister named Che-wah-
nih. Levi's Indian name was Gul-stoo-hus-kee. Jack Walkingstick was a cousin of mine; not an uncle. He was the son of
one of my father's brothers, but I don't know which one. My
mother's Indian name was Quatsey. Don't suppose she was married in 1851. My mother was on the Old Settler roll. My father
was an emigrant Cherokee. My mother received Old Settler money. My mother had a sister named Rachel (O. S. roll Group 79
- mother Group 18 Flint).   Ah-dee-tus-kee was the name of my
father. Al-kin was the name of my father's mother. I have a
sister named Sarah Foreman. She is sixty some odd years old.
Her name before marriage was Ross. She is a half sister on the
mother's side. I am the only child I know of on the father's
side. I am on the Dawes Commission roll (Cherokee roll 2609).
Virgie (2613 Dawes), William (2614 Dawes), Sarah (2615 Dawes)
are my children. My husband is a half breed Cherokee. Jack
Walkingstick is a distant relation of mine - possibly a cousin. We call cousins uncles in Cherokee lots of times. My

father went by the name of Drinker often.   I don't know who
Katy Drinker is. Ah-daw-la-nus-ky was the name of my father's
father."
SIGNED: Akey McCuen, Sallisaw, Okla., Sep 19 1908.
[For Roll information See App 2822, Vol. 2]

12418. JESS CHRISTIE,   Cookson, Okla
Admitted. Nephew of 2687 and his grandfather Jackson Christie
is enrolled Fl. Dist. #640.
ROLL P42 #7439 FCT COMM #27235 - Jess Christie - 20

12419. AKEY PROCTOR and 1 child,   Cookson, Okla
Admitted. Applicant claims through grandmother on mother's
side. Grandmother Su-sar-ne U-ha-ler, was enrolled in Skin
Bayou #273 [? 2nd digit blurred].
ROLL P113 #21778 FCT COMM #21103 - Daniel Proctor - 32
                                         (App 13379)
          21779   28518 - Akey (wife)   - 22
          21780   - Charley (son) - 2

12420. ELLA COON and 3 children,   Nowata, Okla
Admitted. Sister of #1537.
MISC. TEST. P. 2258. App No 12421-1537 - Ella Coon:
    "My name is Ella Coon. My age is 41 years. I live in Nowa-
ta County. Have lived here 8 years. Previously lived in Claremore. I was born and raised in Coo-ee-scoo-wee District. I was
enrolled by the Dawes Commission, Cherokee Roll # [blank] I do
not know my Roll number, and did not bring my certificate. We
have always drawn money ever since I can remember. I think we
were on every Roll. My father told us we were Cherokees and we
got it from both father and mother. My mother was Ruth Nicholson, Bible after marriage. My mother lived south of Alluwee,
in Rogers Co. I don't know where my mother was born. My father
was an Old Settler and my mother an Emigrant. I don't know
whether she was ever enrolled; she died when we were all
small. She was in the 30's when she died.   She had sisters:
Elnora and Harriett. Elnora lived in Tahlequah District. My
mother's father was Jacob Nicholson. Elenora married a man by
the name of Bigby. There was a sister Martha.   She lives in
Tahlequah District. I don't know whether my mother or her people ever associated with any other tribe of Indians. I don't
know where my grandfather lived. He died when my mother was
small. I know Arthur A. Bible. He is my brother. I know he was
enrolled. He is enrolled by the Dawes Commission, Cherokee
Roll #2633. My father was Lewis Bible but I don't know much
about his side."
SIGNED: Ella Coon, Nowata, Okla., Aug 25 1908.
ROLL P46 #8351 FCT COMM #12355 - Ella Coon   - 39
          8352   12356 - Alice (dau) - 13
          8353   12357 - Bertha (dau) - 11
          8354   12358 - Annie (dau) - 8

12421. ELLA COON, Same as 12420.

12422. CHAS. A. BRACKETT,   Claremore, Okla
Admitted. Brother of 8847 and claims through same source.
ROLL P33 #5598 FCT COMM #29528 - Charles A. Brackett - 22

12423. MARY J. FOSTER and 1 child,   Tiawah, Okla
Admitted. 2nd cousin of 3080, and claims through the same ancestors. Father of applicant William McCay was enrolled in
1851 in disputed District, #97. Claim for minor child, Vernie,
not allowed as said child was born after May 28, 1906.
ROLL P63 #11703 FCT COMM #11855 - Mary J. Foster   - 26
         11704   534m - Samuel E. DUGGER (son) - 3

12424. WM. H. McCLAIN and 3 children,   Claremore, Okla
Admitted. Nephew of 317 and claims through the same source.
Grandparent enrolled.
ROLL P92 #17607 FCT COMM #12780 - William H. McClain - 36
         17608   12782 - Robert (son)   - 9
         17609   12783 - Addie (dau)   - 8
         17610   21851 - William E. (son)   - 4

12425. JAMES E. SMITH and 2 children,   Longacre, W Va
Rejected. Sizemore case. See report #417.

12426. JOHN H. HARLIN and 1 child,   Welch, Okla
Admitted. 1st cousin of 1352 and claims through same source.
Father of applicant, John B. [?] Harlin, enrolled in 1851 in
Flint District #341.
ROLL P71 #13292 FCT COMM #24432 - John H. Harlin   - 31
         13293   24433 - Miriam Louise (dau) - 5

12427. SOPHRONIA HEREFORD and 4 children, Webbers Falls, Okla
Admitted. Sister (1/2) of 2791, and claims through 1st cousin
on 2158, same source. Father, Thomas Monroe, Disp. 27.   1st
cousin of #2158.
ROLL P74 #13955 FCT COMM #4450 - Sophronia Hereford - 47
         13956   4453 - Robert (son)   - 16
         13957   4454 - Jessie (son)   - 16
         13958   4455 - Burk (son)   - 12
         13959   4457 - Ross B. (son)   - 8

12428. LEE A. PETTY,   Furches, N C
Rejected. Sizemore case. See report #417.

12429. LEE A. PETTY and 6 children,   Furches, N C
Rejected. Sizemore case. See report #417.

12430. GREENY PETTY and 2 children,   Furches, N C
Rejected. Sizemore case. See report #417.

12431. SALLY & MARY WHITEWATER,   Cookson, Okla
Admitted. Enrolled with mother 12414.

12432. NORAH HYATT and 6 children,   Barnardsville, N C
Rejected. Keziah Van case. See special report #276.

12433. CYNTHIA A. BRADLEY and 5 children, Hanson, Okla
Admitted. Applicant is a sister of 1053.
ROLL P33 #5640 FCT COMM #2592 - Cynthia A. Bradley - 50
           5641   2596 - Robert (son)   - 20
           5642   2597 - Benjamin (son)   - 16
           5643   2598 - Frederick (son)   - 16
           5644   2599 - Walter (son)   - 13
           5645   2600 - George (son)   - 11

12434. LOUISA J. WATTS,   Muldrow, Okla
Rejected. Does not appear that applicant was ever enrolled.
Does not appear that they were living within the limits of the
Cherokee Domain in 1835-6-46, as recognized members of the
tribe.

12435. CALEB S. GONZALES,   Braggs, Okla
Rejected. Claims through mother enrolled as Old Settler.
Grandmother enrolled as Old Settler. See O. S. Fl. 16. Great
grandparents Samuel and Polly Adair enrolled as Old Settlers,
see O. S. Fl. 13. See Misc. Test. P. 3303.
MISC. TEST. P. 3303. App #12815-12435 - John A. Gonzales:
    "My name is John A. Gonzales. My age is 32 years. I was
born and raised in Flint District. I got the strip payment.
I am enrolled by the Dawes Commission. I did not bring my number with me. I get my Indian blood from my mother. She is
dead. She has been dead about 19 or 20 years. She was middle
aged when she died. I don't know whether she was enrolled in
1851. Her name was Margaret Pettitt; Gonzales after marriage.
I think it was Margaret; her nick-name was Ar-neech. She had
a brother Sam Six-killer, Walter, Jinnie and Lula; half-brothers and sisters. I don't know her father's name, and she has
no full brothers and sisters. My mother's mother's name was
Charlotte Adair. She married Six-killer. I think my mother
was a child in 1851. Charlotte Adair must have been Charlotte
Six-killer in 1851. I think she lived in Flint District. John
B. Adair and Delia were her brothers and sisters. Samuel Adair
I think was my great grandfather's name. (Samuel and Charlotte 244 Fl.) but never heard anything about remainder of
group. After she (Charlotte) married Sixkiller, she also lived
in Flint District. John B. Adair said that my grandfather on
my mother's side was Charley Pettiett. Ben was my great-grandfather. I think he must have lived in Flint District. I do
not know whether my great-grandfather Benjamin Pettiett was
living in 1851 or not. (53 Fl). I don't know whether all were
Old Settlers but I drew Old Settler money through my mother.
I don't know which side of my mother's parents were Old Set-

tlers. I don't know whether they ever joined any other tribe of Indians."
SIGNED: John A. Gonzales, Stilwell, Okla., Sep 29 1908.

12436. JESSE J. McLAIN, McLain, Okla
Admitted. Son of #4054. [* FCT # blurred on roll]
ROLL P94 #18038 FCT COMM #15597* - Jesse J. McLain - 26

12437. JACKSON ADAMS and 7 children, Rugby, Va
Rejected. Sizemore case. See report #417.

12438. JOHN A. ADAMS and 5 children, Grassy Creek, N C
Rejected. Sizemore case. See report #417.

12439. CATHERINE ADAMS, Rugby, Va
Rejected. Sizemore case. See report #417.

12440. JOEL SUTTON, by Bettie Sutton Hanson, Okla
Admitted. Applicant is a nephew of 1050. Applicant's grandfather Geo. Blair 641 Flint. Duplicate of child on 13773. [For Roll information See App 12441]

12441. PEARLEY SUTTON, Hanson, Okla
Admitted. Applicant is a niece of 1050. Applicant is grand father [sic] Geo. Blair "641 Flint".
ROLL P135 #26081 FCT COMM #3602 - Bettie Sutton   - 44
                                  (App 13773)
          26082   3605 - Pearlie (dau)   - 19
          26083   3606 - Joel E. (son)   - 17
                                  (App 12440)
          26084   3607 - Esther F. (dau) - 15
                                  (App 12443)
          26085   3608 - Anna L. (dau)   - 11
                                  (App 12442)

12442. ANNAH L. SUTTON, Hanson, Okla
          by Bettie Sutton
Admitted. Applicant is a niece of 1050. Applicant's grandfather, Geo. Blair "641 Flint". Duplicate of child on 13773. [For Roll information See App 12441]

12443. ESTHER F. SUTTON, Hanson, Okla
          by Bettie Sutton, Gdn.
Admitted. Applicant is a niece of 1050. Applicant is grand father [sic] Geo. Blair, "641 Flint". Dupl. of child on 13773. [For Roll information See App 12441]

12444. ALONZO RUSSELL, Kansas, Okla
          by Louis C. Horner, Gdn.
Admitted. Brother of 11236, and claims through same source.
ROLL P121 #23296 FCT COMM #32517 - Alonzo Russell - 4
                                  by Louis C. Horner, Gdn.

331

12445. GEO. SIMMONS and 6 children,   Bunch, Okla
Rejected. Do not find names of ancestors of applicant on Cherokee rolls. J. B. Adair stated to the commissioner applicant and ancestors for the most part were Creeks.

12446. W. H. DREW,   Chanute, Kans
Admitted. Nephew of 5226. Applicant enrolled as Henry Drew, G. S. #227.
ROLL P55 #10115 FCT COMM #10118 - William H. Drew - 63

12447. WM. HEADRICKS and 5 children,   Texanna, Okla
Admitted. Applicant enrolled at Del. #705. Deceased June 9, 1907 ["1909" crossed out]
ROLL P74 #13802 FCT COMM # 4435 - William Hendricks - 63
             13803   4436 - Rosy (dau)   - 9
             13804   4437 - Ruthy (dau)   - 7
             13805   4438 - Susie (dau)   - 5
             13806   4772m - Annie (dau)   - 3
             13807   4773m - Charlie (son)   - 1

12448. ANNIE E. STURGEON and 4 children,   Cassaway, W Va
Rejected. Sizemore case. See report #417.

12449. OCAL FOSTER,   Gauley Bridge, W Va
Rejected. Sizemore case. See report #417.

12450. DAVID A. OSBORN and 6 children,   Scotford, W Va
Rejected. Sizemore case. See report #417.

12451. BEULAH FOSTER,   Gauley Bridge, W Va
Rejected. Sizemore case. See report #417.

12452. ELIZABETH ROSE,   Baileysville, W Va
Rejected. Sizemore case. See report #417.

12453. ROBERT S. COOK,   Lashmeet, W Va
Rejected. Sizemore case. See report #417.

12454. OCA McCOMMIS and 4 children,   Morocco, W Va
Rejected. Sizemore case. See report #417.

12455. Z. T. SIZEMORE and 3 children,   Diana, W Va
Rejected. Sizemore case. See report #417.

12456. EDWARD ROSE,   Baileysville, W Va
Rejected. Sizemore case. See report #417.

12457. JAMES L. DIXON,   Blalock, Ga
Rejected. Uncle of #4252. [See Exception Case 4252, Vol. 3]

12458. MONROE DIXON,   Quartz, Ga
Rejected. Uncle of #4252.

12459. SHERMAN TRUSTY,   Burton, Ga
Rejected. Aunt of 4252.

12460. LUTHER GRAVE and 1 child,   Murphy, N C
Rejected. Blythe Case. See special report in 153.

12461. W. R. J. HELTON and 4 children, Rt 6, Lafayette, Ga
Rejected. Brother of 10480 and claims through same source.

12462. ERVINE Mc E. HILTON,   Rockyford, Ga
Rejected. Claims through Abraham Helton. See #2780.

12463. EDGAR RYDER,   Middletown, Cal
Rejected. Grandson of 3595 [NOTE: App 3595 was an admitted
case] and claims through same source.

12464. MARY M. ADKINS,   Collinsville, Okla
Rejected. It does not appear that any ancestor was a party to
the treaties of 1835-6-46 nor does it appear that any ancestor
was ever enrolled. Shows no real connection with the Eastern
Cherokees. Misc. Test. P. 3361.
MISC. TEST. P. 3361. App #12464 - Mary Melviney Adkins:
    "My name is Mary M. Adkins. I live at Gideon, Okla. I nev-
er was enrolled by the Dawes Commission. I applied but was rejected. I claim my Indian blood through my mother, whose maid-
en name was Polly Steven. She was born in Ky. My grandfather
died in 1830 in Ky. We moved from Ky. to Ark. My mother was
in Ky. with the Indians. I could not say whether my mother was
a recognized member of the tribe. She never lived any place
else but Ky. except Ark."
SIGNED: Mary Melviney Adkins, Tahlequah, Okla., Oct 1 1908.

12465. HENRY V. DOKE,   RFD #1, Morrisville, Mo
Rejected. Claims through Alex. Brown. See #35.

REJECTED
APP 12466 TO 12477 - SIZEMORE CASES - SEE SPECIAL REPORT #417

12466. JACOB PRUITT and 15 children,   City, N C

12467. ELLEN BURCHETT and 4 children,   Marion, Va

12468. JESSIE BLEVINS,   Beldon, N C

12469. JAMES W. OSBORNE,   Gale, N C

12470. JESSIE ORSBEN,   Laurel Springs, N C

12471. COLUMBUS PRUITT and 1 child,   Ravin, Va

12472. TALTON OSBORNE and 2 children,   Beldon, N C

333

APP 12466 TO 12477 - SIZEMORE CASES - SEE SPECIAL REPORT #417

12473. JOHN OSBORNE and 2 children,   Beldon, N C

12474. NANCY WILLIAMS and 4 children,   Laurel Springs, N C

12475. SUSAN A. BOWLIN,   Beldon, N C

12476. DAVID OSBORNE,   Laurel Springs, N C

12477. DAVID A. OSBOURNE,   Beldon, N C

END CONSECUTIVE SIZEMORE CASES

12478. GEO. W. BARNETT,   Leach, Okla
Rejected. Claims through same source as 5141.

12479. MINT VIERS and 3 children,   Campbell, Okla
Rejected. 1st cousin once removed of 10294 and claims through
same source.

12480. BUSH GOINS,   Campbell, Okla
Rejected. 1st cousin once removed of 10294, and claims thru
same source.

12481. MINNIE GOINS,   Campbell, Okla
Rejected. 1st cousin once removed of 10294, and claims thru
same source.

12482. RICHARD D. HILL,   Blue Ridge, Ga
Rejected. Neither applicant nor ancestors ever enrolled. From
letter herein it appear that applicant was negro for most part
and lived with negroes - says however that none of his people
were slaves. Does not establish fact of descent from a person
who was party to the treaty of 1835-6-46.

12483. BETTIE ADAIR,   Sallisaw, Okla
Rejected. Applicant's father enrolled on Old Settler roll as
"Joseph Clyning [?].   Applicant probably enrolled as "Betsy
Pumpkin Pile" with her mother and sisters. Misc. Test. P. 3024
MISC. TEST. P. 3024. App No [blank] - Jackoline Welch:
    "My name is Jackoline Welch. My age is 42 years. I live
in Sequoyah County. I was born and raised in Flint District.
I am enrolled by the Dawes Commission Cherokee Roll No. 2169.
I got the bread and strip payments twice. I claim to be a
Cherokee Indian. I have never associated with any other tribe.
I get Indian blood from both mother and father. My mother was
a full-blood Cherokee Indian. She is still living. Her name
is Betty Adair. She was enrolled by the Dawes Commission and
got the bread and strip money.   I do not know how old she is
and do not think she knows herself. I think she was enrolled

in 1851. Her father was called Joe Mitchell a whole lot but
my mother went by the name of Betty Clingan. She had a Cherokee name Di-ya-ni or De-ya-ne. She has a half-sister Janie
Downing, Johnson Downing's wife. She is older. My mother's
mother's name was Katy Clinging I reckon. She lived about 14
Mile Creek. She has been dead a great many years. My mother
drew Old Settler money but not as long ago as 1851. I don't
remember any other brothers and sisters of my mother. It has
been more than ten years since she drew Old Settler money. My
father was Newt Adair but he signed his name J. B. Adair. My
father drew Old Settler money at the same time my mother did.
I don't know whether he was enrolled in 1851. My father had a
brother George Adair. He lived in Flint District. He was older
than my father. My father and mother are living at Stilwell,
Okla. He is somewhat over 60 years. I had two aunts who are
dead, Charlotte and Delia Adair before marriage. Charlotte
married Watt Sixkiller. She lived in Flint. Delia married a
Gonsalis. She lived in Flint District. My father's mother's
name was Polly Adair, Huse or Hughes before marriage. She was
from Georgia and lived in Flint District. I don't know just
when she came from Georgia. I don't know whether she was regarded as an Old Settler. One of Polly Adair's sister was
named Betsey, and she married a Row. Catherine Adair was my
uncle George's wife's name. My father's father's name was
Samuel Adair. I think Samuel had a brother Andy; and that is
all I can recollect. He had a sister called Katy or Catherine
who married a Bigby. Samuel lived in Flint District. (244 and
250 Flint). I have a sister Lizzie Housebug, who is five years
older than I am. I don't know when these people came from the
Eastern States. I think before I was born. I have a brother
Samuel and others. John F. Adair is now dead. He was killed
last June. I have 7 children."
SIGNED: Jackoline "X" Welch, Sallisaw, Okla., Sep 19 1908.
"On Old Settler Roll" [Notation added to end of testimony]

12484. CUCUMBER ROSS and 4 children,   Braggs, Okla
Admitted. Brother of #11493. Claims through same source.
MISC. TEST. P. 4182. App No 12484 - Cucumber Ross...through
John Israel:
    "I am about 65 years of age. I am the son of Chief John
Ross. William Ross of Welling, Okla. is my first cousin. His
father was named John Ross and my father was named Chief Ross.
They were brothers. I have no brothers. I got land from the
Dawes Commission. I did not draw Old Settler money. I was born
in Tahlequah District. My father was not known by any other
name than Chief that I know of. My father lived in Tahlequah
District in 1851. My father drew Old Settler money. It was
along about 1851 and was Old Settler money. Quaitsy or Betsy
Ross was my mother. She lived in Tahlequah District. I don't
know whether my mother drew Old Settler money or not. I have
been told that she drew Old Settler money. I am not sure about
this. It is what I have been told. I don't know of any broth-

ers that my father had. I don't know of any brothers and sisters of my mother. I don't know whether my father ever lived
in any other District or not. I don't know who Jarratt Ross
was. Silas Ross was an uncle of mine and he raised me. He
lived in Tahlequah District. Lewis was a brother of Silas.
There was a sister named Le-sih or Lizzie. I don't know the
name of Silas Ross' father. My father was a brother to Silas'
father. (Applicant again states that he thinks his father drew
Old Settler money. He doesn't know about his mother but people
have told him that her people drew O. S. money too.)"
SIGNED: Cucumber Ross, Braggs, Okla., Mar 26 1909.
ROLL P120 #23043 FCT COMM #32320 - Cucumber Ross - 49
              23044   32322 - Minerva (dau) - 17
              23045   32323 - Annie (dau)   - 14
              23046   32324 - John (son)   - 11
              23047   32325 - Rachel (dau) - 8

12485. T. F. SIZEMORE,   Sizemore, Okla
Rejected. Sizemore case. See report #417.

12486. CALLIE COOKS and 1 child,   Blue Ridge, Ga
Rejected. Daughter of 32 and claims through same source.

12487. SARAH CHUCULATE,   Sallisaw, Okla
Admitted. Claimant's parents Tucksey Halt [sic] or Tarrapin
Holt and Sarah Holt were enrolled by Drennen in 1851 in Going
Snake Dist. Group No 548. [For Roll information See App 5927,
Vol. 3]

12488. ALBERT JOHNSTON, by Charley Johnston, included in
mother's application #9634.

12489. SUSAN ZACHARY,   San Francisco, Cal
Rejected. Betsy Walker case. See special report in #500.

12490. ROBT. P. HYDE,   San Francisco, Cal
Rejected. Betsy Walker case. Duplicate of 3908. See special
report in #500.

12491. SAMUEL ENGLAND,   Afton, Okla
Admitted. A once removed cousin of Fanny E. Chandler, 1723,
and great grand son of Gideon Morris.
ROLL P58 #10714 FCT COMM #11864 - Samuel England - 18
                                    by R. L. England, Gdn.

12492. SUSIE LEE ENGLAND,   Afton, Okla
Admitted. A cousin once removed of Fanny E. Chandler (1723).
Daughter of Eliza J. Morris.
ROLL P58 #10719 FCT COMM #11865 - Susie Lee England - 15
                                    by R. L. England, Gdn.

12493. JOHN ANNA DAVIS,   Afton, Okla
Admitted. A once removed cousin to Fanny E. Chandler 1723,
and great grand son of Rebecca Morris.
ROLL P51 #9375 FCT COMM #11863 - John Anna Davis - 20

12494. NANNIE SCOTT and 1 child,   Ft. Gibson, Ind. Ter.
Rejected. Ancestor never enrolled as Eastern Cherokee. Ancestor never party to treaties of 1835-6-46. Ancestors are old
settlers. See O. s. Ill. 14 - 15 & 264.

12495. DE WITT LIPE,   Claremore, Okla
Admitted. Applicant's mother enrolled at head of group #472
Flint. Applicant's maternal grandmother as Catherine Gunter.
Applicant enrolled probably as "Daniel W. C. Lipe".
ROLL P90 #17119 FCT COMM #11274 - De Witt Lipe - 66

12496. JOHN C. SEABOLT,   Hanson, Okla
Admitted. Applicant's father and paternal grandmother en-
rolled at Flint #67.
ROLL P125 #24078 FCT COMM #3690 - John E. Seabolt - 35

12497. ELVIRA SEABOLT and 1 child,   Hanson, Okla
Admitted. Sister of 12496.
ROLL P125 #24066 FCT COMM #3691 - Elvira Seabolt   - 31
            24067   3693 - Myrtle C. QUINTON (niece) -5

12498. ELLA OWL,   Cookston, Okla
Admitted. Applicant's father and mother enrolled as "Ah-ma-
de-ske" and "Che-na-ge" at Del. #637. Misc. Test. P. 3367.
MISC. TEST. P. 3367.   Witness for No 12498 - Ella Owl - Eva
Hawkins...through S. E. Parris, Interpreter:
     "I am about 50 [? blurred] years of age. I did not draw
Immigrant money in 1852. I had one brother older than I. He
drew Immigrant money. Ella Owl is my sister. My brother that
drew money was Gah-le-dah. My mother and father both drew Immigrant money. I was born in Delaware District. Mother's name
was Che-na-ye and my father's name was Ah-ma-de-ske.   They
lived in Delaware District."
SIGNED: Eva Hawkins, Tahlequah, Okla., Oct 1 1908.
[For Roll information See App 10905]

12499. CICERO W. ADDINGTON and 2 children, Stilwell, Okla
Admitted. Nephew of 774 and claims through same source.
ROLL P22 #3442 FCT COMM # 2335 - Cicero W. Addington - 31
          3443   2336 - Mollie E. (wife)   - 31
                                (App 27772)
          3444   2337 - Clarence G. (son)   - 5
          3445   20205 - Frederick E. (son)   - 4

12500. MINNIE PORTER,   135 Venable St., Atlanta, Ga
Rejected. Neither applicant nor any of her ancestors on any
of the Eastern Cherokee rolls. Does not establish fact that

she is a descendant of a person who was a party to the treaty
of 1835-6-46. Misc. Test. P. 1090.
MISC. TEST. P. 1090. App #12500 - Minnie Porter:
    "My name is Minnie Porter. I live at 135 Venerable St.,
Atlanta, Ga. I was born in 1875 in Gilmor County, Ga. I claim
to be connected to the Cherokee Tribe of Indians through my
father and his mother. My father died in 1898 and was about 75
years old when he died. He was born in Buncombe County, N. C.
My grandmother's maiden name was Morning Brown. She came from
N. C. My father and grandmother were recognized as Indians.
I don't know whether they lived with the Indian Tribe in N. C.
or not. My father and his mother never got any money or land
from the Government on account of their Indian blood. They
never were enrolled with the Cherokee tribe. In 1882 my father and I were living in Gilmor Co., Ga. I don't know why we
were not enrolled with the Cherokees at that time.   I never
heard of an enrollment at that time. I had an uncle Jesse
Burrell, Simpson Burrell, Timothy Burrell, Spence Burrell. My
aunts were: Sarah, Julia Ann, Mary Ann Burrell. I never heard
my father speak of a Treaty the Government made with the Indians in 1835. My sister, Mary Cowart, Vine Souther and Joe
Burrell, Tylus Burrell & Sarah Reed also filed applications."
SIGNED: Minnie Porter, Atlanta, Ga., Jul 7 1908.
"See Siler Roll 972-4" [Handwritten notation on side of page]

12501. ELLIS BATT and 4 children,   Stilwell, Okla
Admitted. Nephew of 1245 and claims through same ancestors.
Father of applicant enrolled in 1851 under name of Ter-gen-
wor-se Bat, in Saline District #103.
ROLL P26 #4377 FCT COMM #15604 - Ellis Batt   - 52
          4378   15608 - James (son)   - 15 (App 12503)
          4379   15609 - Hennie (dau)   - 11
          4380   2187m - Daylight (son) - 3
          4381   2188m - Lucy (dau)   - 2

12502. JACK BATT and 2 children,   Stilwell, Okla
Admitted. Included in card of Ellis Batt, #12501. [For Roll
information See App 10396]

12503. JAMES BATT,   Stilwell, Okla
Admitted. Included in card of Ellis Batt, #12501. [For Roll
information See App 12501]

12504. THOMAS HUMMINGBIRD and 3 children, Stilwell, Okla
Admitted. Half brother of 1349, and claims through same an-
cestors.
ROLL P79 #14959 FCT COMM #20188 - Thomas Hummingbird - 51
          14960   20189 - Nancy (wife)   - 25
                                   (App 15961)
          14961   20191 - Drunker (son)   - 8
          14962   20192 - Annie (dau)   - 5
          14963   4157m - William (son)   - 1

338

12505. SISSIE WALKER, James Horsefly, Gdn., Vinita, Okla
Admitted. 1st cousin once removed of 323 and claims through
same source.
ROLL P144 #28025 FCT COMM #28018 - Sissie Walker - 6
                                        by James Horsefly, Gdn.

12506. ANNIE TOLBERT and 5 children,   Claremore, Okla
Admitted. Niece of 317 and claims through same source. Grand
parent enrolled.
ROLL P140 #27149 FCT COMM #11965 - Annie Tolbert   - 31
         27150   11966 - Roscoe (son)   - 11
         27151   11967 - Otto (son)   - 8
         27152   11968 - Jennie (dau)   - 6
         27153   1344m - Hazel A. (dau)   - 2
         27154   1345m - Fay Leona (dau) -   1

12507. MYRA McCLAIN,   Claremore, Okla
Admitted. Niece of 317 and claims through same source. Grand
parents enrolled.
ROLL P92 #17606 FCT COMM #11465 - Myra McClain - 34

12508. MAGGIE THORNE and 1 child,   Muskogee, Okla
Admitted. 1st cousin to 715. Mother Corn Barnes, 169 1/2 Ill
ROLL P139 #26949 FCT COMM #13778 - Maggie Thorne   - 30
         26950   170m - Georgia E. (dau) -   1

12509. DEE-KI-LAS-KY COON,   Vian, Okla
Rejected. Applicant's father was a Creek and his mother's
mother was Creek and white. Is unable to connect himself with
any names on the Cherokee roll. See misc. test. p. of claimant
and Lucy McCoy taken at Vian, March 15, 1909, p. 3950.
MISC. TEST. P. 3950.   No 12509 - Deekilasky Coon...through
Wallace Thornton:
    "My name is Deekilasky Coon; my post-office is Vian, Okla;
I am about fifty-five years old; I am enrolled by the Dawes
Commission, No 20835; I am Cherokee on my mother's side; in
1851 my mother's name was Semma-hey-yah, she lived in Ill.
District; my mother was part Creek; my mother was born in the
east, but I do not know where; I think my mother was married
in the east; my father was a Creek; my mother's father was a
Cherokee and I do not know what her mother was; my daughter,
Annie's mother is a Creek."
SIGNED: Deekilasky "X" Coon, Vian, Okla., Mar 15 1909.
Lucy McCoy...through Wallace Thornton, interpreter:
    "My name is Lucy McCoy; my post-office is Vian, Okla.; I
am about fifty-eight years old; I know Deekalasky Coon; his
mother's mother was Farney, an old lady; I always understood
that she was part Creek and part white; I did not know Chener-
que, the husband of Farney but I have heard that he was a
Cherokee." SIGNED: Lucy "X" McCoy, Vian, Okla., Mar 15 1909.
EXCEPTION CASE. Rejected. Total number of exceptions filed
in this group -- 3. Original recommendation renewed.

12510. JENNIE MORRIS,   Muskogee, Okla
Admitted. Sister of 9380. Cousin of 5319.
ROLL P101 #19430 FCT COMM #2303 - 20

12511. BERT WEAVER,   Eau Claire, Wis
Rejected. Claims through same source as #10886.

12512. NETTIE PHILLIPS CHRISTIE,   Locust Grove, Okla
Admitted. Cousin of 2181. Claims through same source.
ROLL P42 #7451 FCT COMM #25922 - Nellie Phillips Christie - 22

12513. GEORGE DOWNING,   Estella, Okla
Admitted. Claimant's mother enrolled by Drennen in 1851 under
name of Sally, Flint 660. Maternal grandparents enrolled in
Flint 659.
ROLL P54 #9923 FCT COMM # 7936 - George Downing   - 32
       9924   15165 - Mollie (wife)   - 26
                                (App 13062)
       9925   7938 - John (son)   - 10
       9926   7939 - Zuma (dau)   - 9
       9927   31993 - Adam (son)   - 4
       9928   1561m - Noyah (son)   - 2
       9929   28717 - Lucy HAWK (dau of w) - 13

12514. MARY PORTER and 1 child,   Rose, Okla
Admitted. Sister of #8011. Father of applicant enrolled in
1851 in Going Snake #227.
ROLL P112 #21569 FCT COMM #7043 - Mary Porter   - 24
         21570   7044 - Mildred M. (dau) - 5

12515. ELIZA BLACKSTONE,   San Pedro, Cal
Admitted. 1st cousin of 4394. Father of claimant on roll of
1851 Drennen, Del. 431.
ROLL P31 #5233 FCT COMM #4255 - Eliza Blackstone - 21

12516. VINA MURRELL,   118 E 5th St., Davenport, Iowa
Rejected. Claims through same source as #10886.

12517. FRANK BLACKSTONE,   San Pedro, Cal
Admitted. 1st cousin of 4394. Claimant's father enrolled by
Drennen in 1851, Del. 431.
ROLL P31 #5234 FCT COMM #4256 - Frank S. Blackstone - 16

12517.5 WM. F. KINCAID and 2 children, Box 51, Blue Ridge, Ga
Rejected. 1st cousin once removed to 2877. Claims through the
same source.

12518. MARY F. CHASTAIN,   Box 151, Blue Ridge, Ga
Rejected. 1st cousin, once removed to 2877. Claims through
same source.

12519. REBECCA MINEY and 2 children,   Muskogee, Okla
Rejected. Applicant claims for herself and two minor children
through her husband J. C. Flying, deceased, no information
given in application of ancestors of husband and his name does
not appear on 51 roll. Applicant failed to appear to testify
although notified to do so.
EXCEPTION CASE. 12519. Linda A. Flying, Jessie J. by Rebecca
Miney, parent and Gdn., Oglesby, Okla. Recommended. Total
number of exceptions filed in this group -- 1. The mother of
these children is white and their claim is through their father. In her application previously filed for these children
the mother failed to give any of her husband's family history
and also failed to appear and testify when notified to do so
and so that it was impossible to properly consider her claim.
She applies for another child, Johnnie, but her claim for him
is rejected, as he died in 1904. (See Appli. #32426) These
children are enrolled by the Dawes Commission as half blood
Cherokees at No's. 5627 & 5628.
SUPP ROLL #30590 FCT COMM #5627 - Linda A. Flying - 10
         30591   5628 - Jessie J. (bro) - 8
                             by Rebecca Minew, parent & Gdn.

12520. JAMES H. OSBURN and 7 children,   Serena, W Va
Rejected. Sizemore case. See special report #417.

12521. MARTHA L. WATERS,   Canton, Ga
Rejected. Claims through same source as 9783.

12522. GEO. L. CANNEFAX,   Garber, Okla
Rejected. Applicant or ancestors were never enrolled. Does
not appear that they were living within the Cherokee Domain in
1835-6-46 as recognized members of the tribe. Does not appear
that they ever lived with the Cherokees as recognized members
of the tribe. See letter inside.

12523. SEABORN BURRELL,   Oak Hill, Ga
Rejected. Nephew of Jesse Burrell Jr., App #6917 and claims
through same source.

12524. OSCAR BURRELL,   Oak Hill, Ga
         Seaborn Burrell, Gdn.
Rejected. Nephew of Jesse Burrell Jr., App #6917 and claims
through same source.

12525. SIMPSON BURRELL JR.,   Cartecay, Ga
Rejected. Son of Jesse Burrell, Jr., App 6917 and claims thru
same source.

12526. ELIZA LIVER and 5 children,   Brushy, Okla
Admitted. Niece of 2235 [1st & 4th digit typed over]. Father
of claimant enrolled in 1851 as Ta-any by Drennen, Flint 429.

341

```
ROLL P90 #17185 FCT COMM # 3359 - Eliza Liver   - 31
         17186             3360 - Lizzie (dau) - 14
         17187             3361 - Felix (son)  - 12
         17188             3362 - Susie (dau)  -  9
         17189             3363 - Martha (dau) -  6
         17190            3854m - Lydia (dau)  -  2
```

12527. LEWIS ROGERS,   Bluejacket, Okla
Admitted. 1st cousin of 1912.
ROLL P119 #22878 FCT COMM #24075 - Lewis Rogers - 23

12528. SAMUEL SIZEMORE and 3 children,   Jared, W Va
Rejected. Sizemore case. See report in #417.

12529. ELIZA LOWERY,   Muskogee, Okla
Admitted. 1st cousin of 562. Claims through father "James
Lowery, 536 Tahlequah."
ROLL P91 #17363 FCT COMM #17169 - Eliza Lowery - 27

12530. ELSIE J. LOWERY, ANDREW LOWERY,   Muskogee, Okla
       HENRY G. LOWERY, by Susie Lowery, Gdn. & Mother
Admitted. Claim through father "James Lowery 536 Tahl." 1st
cousin of 562. [For Roll information See App 12533]

12531. RAPHAEL LOWERY and 1 child,   Muskogee, Okla
Admitted. 1st cousin of 562. Claims through father James
Lowery, 536 Tahl.
ROLL P91 #17376 FCT COMM #27818 - Raphael Lowery - 31
         17377   4662m - Henry C. (son) - 2

12532. MINNIE REID,   Muskogee, Okla
Admitted. 1st cousin to 562. Claims through father James M.
Lowery, 536 Tahlequah.
ROLL P116 #22338 FCT COMM #17175 - Minnie Reid - 19

12533. SUSIE LOWERY and 5 children,   Muskogee, Okla
Admitted. Claims through father enrolled as John Vickary.
Enrolled by Drennen in 1851 in Illinois District, Group #284.
Applicant's mother and brothers and sisters were enrolled as
Old Settlers in 1851 in Ill. Dist. Group #22. Grandmother en-
rolled as Charlotte Vickrey C. #1879. H.C.B. [NOTE: Last
child enrolled under App #12533]
```
ROLL P91  #17409 FCT COMM #17172 - Susie Lowery - 48
           17410            17176 - Susie (dau)  - 17
           17411            17177 - Jennie (dau) - 14
           17412            17178 - Andrew (son) - 11
           17413            17179 - Henry (son)  -  7
ROLL P142  27444            483m - Marion Lowrey TURNER -  1
                                   by Susie Lowrey, Gdn.
```

12534. STAR KILLER and 4 children,   Bunch, Okla
Admitted. Nephew to #1606.

MISC. TEST. P. 3266. App #12534 - Starr Killer:

"Starr Killer is my name. My age is 36 years. I was born and raised in Sequoyah District. I was enrolled by the Dawes Commission. I have not my roll number with me. I am a full-blood Cherokee Indian. My father's name was Gah-nah-he-lee. His English name was Jackson Killer. These are the only names I know. He had a sister named Sallie Killer. Chi-ne-lah-kih was another sister. Chi-ne-lah-kih married Eli. Sallie married a man by the name of Tom Proctor. Che-ne-lah-kee was the name. She lived in Sequoyah District. Sun-necoo-yah or Sun-negoo-yeh, was her brother. He lived in Flint. He used to live in Sequoyah. I think they were the only two. My father's father's name was Law-lih or Lau-lee, or La-lee. He lived in Flint District. My father's mother's name I cannot give. Gar-da-ter-ter was my mother's name; Ella Killer in English. Ah-daw-see-neh or Proctor in English is a brother to my mother. There was a sister named Chi-cow-wee; she lived in Sequoyah. There was one named Annie. My mother's father's name was George Chu-les-kanas-kee or Chu-les-ka-nas-kah. My mother's mother's name I do not know. They came out here with the Emigration. I don't think my mother drew money in 1851, but I think my uncles on the Proctor side, Ah-claw-see-nee Proctor, drew at that time. I think my grandfather drew in 1851. He drew with the Emigrants. They never associated with any other tribe of Indians."

SIGNED: Starr Killer, Stilwell, Okla., Sep 28 1908.
"Look for application" [Notation added to end of testimony]

ROLL P86	#16263	FCT COMM	#19849 - Starr Killer	- 34
	16264		21744 - Kate (wife)	- 30
			(App 42197)	
	16265		19856 - Betsey (dau)	- 8
	16266		19857 - Crawfish (son)	- 6
	16267		- Lawler (dau)	- 4
	16268		- Ga-yo-he (dau)	- 2

12535. NANCY COCHRAN and 1 child,   Stilwell, Okla
Admitted. Niece of Peter Doublehead App 3484 and admitted for same reasons. [For Roll information See App 11915]

12536. MARY A., ORA A. CRITTENDEN,   Stilwell, Okla
and THOS. C. CRITTENDEN, by Sanders Crittenden, Gdn.
Admitted. Enrolled with father Sanders Crittenden #12537. James E. Crittenden rejected as he is of age and filed no separate application.

12537. SANDERS CRITTENDEN and 3 children, Stilwell, Okla
Admitted. Brother of 5234 and claims through same source.

ROLL P49	#8846	FCT COMM	#2287 - Sanders Crittenden	- 52
	8847		2289 - Mary A. (dau)	- 16
	8848		2290 - Ora A. (dau)	- 13
	8849		2291 - Thomas C. (son)	- 10

343

12538. CHARLIE COCHRAN,   Stilwell, Okla
1st cousin of 1071. This applicant is admitted in application
of father 11503. [For Roll information See App 11503]

12539. SARAH WALTERS and 3 children,   Afton, Okla
Admitted. 1/2 sister of 2342. Father of applicant enrolled
in 1851, in Del 319.
ROLL P145 #28153 FCT COMM #19365 - Sarah Walters   - 28
            28154   30537 - John SIMSON (son)   - 6
                                    (SIMERSON)
            28155   4291m - Wilbur WALTERS (son) - 1
            28156   - Glee WALTERS (son)   - 1/12

12540. JENNIE CORNSILK, Duplicate of 2271.

12541. SARAH FOURKILLER,   Stilwell, Okla
Admitted. Daughter of 2271. Parents of applicant not living
in 1851. [For Roll information See App 8367, Vol. 4]

12542. JOHNSON CORNSILK,   Stilwell, Okla
Admitted. by his mother Jennie Cornsilk. Son of #2271.
Enrolled on mother's card 2271. Moth- er of applicant not
living in 1851. [For Roll information See App 2271, Vol. 2]

12543. WM. CORNSILK,   Stilwell, Okla
Admitted. Son of 2271. Parents of applicant not living in 1851
ROLL P47 #8486 FCT COMM #19280 - William Cornsilk   - 25
            8487   1477 - Kate (wife) - 30 (App 26356)
            8488   1478 - Emma SCOTT (dau)   - 10
            8489   1479 - Mary SCOTT (dau)   - 11
            8490   1480 - John SCOTT (son)   - 6
            8491   1481 - Buelah SCOTT (dau) - 4

12544. MINNIE B. CRITTENDEN,   Claremore, Okla
Admitted. Niece of 317 and claims through same source. Grand
parents enrolled.
ROLL P49 #8832 FCT COMM #11499 - Minnie B. Crittenden - 30

12545. ADA THURMAN and 3 children,   Foyil, Okla
Admitted. Sister of 8847, and claims through same source.
ROLL P140 #27012 FCT COMM #21741 - Ada Thurman   - 29
            27013   21742 - Elizabeth M. (dau) - 5
            27014   1107m - William E. (son)   - 3
            27015   1108m - Samia (son)   - 1

12546. MARY ADAIR,   Lenapah, Okla
Admitted. 1st cousin of 4361, and is admitted for same reasons. [For Roll information See App 411, Vol. 1]

12547. JENAHYE CAHSALAHWE,   Stilwell, Okla
        or CHE-HAN-YE TEREPEN,
Minor daughter of 2701 and enrolled as such.

344

12548. CHARLEY FOURKILLER,   Stilwell, Okla
Admitted. Son of 6971. Claims through same source.
ROLL P63 #11727 FCT COMM #25776 - Charley Fourkiller - 25

12549. CONSEE BARNOSKE and 1 child,   Vian, Okla
Admitted. Applicant is a brother of Cat Barnoske #12214 and
claims through same source.
ROLL P26 #4321 FCT COMM #21065 - Conseen Barnoske - 28
         4322   4730m - Lizzie (dau)   - 1

12550. NANCY BARNOSKE,   Vian, Okla
Admitted. Applicant is a sister of Cat Barnoske #12214 and
claims through same source.
ROLL P26 #4324 FCT COMM #21064 - Nancy Barnoske - 22

12551. CHARLIE BARNOSKE,   Vian, Okla
Admitted. Applicant is a a brother of Cat Barnoske 12214, and
claims through same source.
ROLL P26 #4319 FCT COMM #21063 - Charlie Barnoske - 26

12552. MAMIE BUSTER and 3 children,   Vian, Okla
Admitted. Applicant claims Cherokee descent through her moth-
er Susanah enrolled by Drennen in 1851 in Skin Bayou Dist 273.
ROLL P37 #6403 FCT COMM #28517 - Nannie Buster   - 45
         6404   28519 - Nannie WILSON (dau)   - 11
         6405   28520 - Watt MORRIS (son)   - 9
         6406   - Emma Yahola MORRIS (dau) - 3

12553. ALEXANDER BLEVINS,   Laurel Springs, N C
Rejected. Sizemore case. See report in #417.

12554. FELIX OSBORNE and 4 children,   Beldon, N C
Rejected. Sizemore case. See report in #417.

12555. ELIZABETH BAKER and 1 child,   Collinsville, Okla
Admitted. Sister of 878.
ROLL P24 #3987 FCT COMM #24919 - Elizabeth Baker - 51
         3988   24921 - Webster C. (son) - 17

12556. ALTON F. BOWLEY, Minor son of #12558.

12557. EDNA V. DORGELOH,   731 Fulton St., San Francisco, Cal
Admitted. Daughter of 12558 and claims through same source.
ROLL P54 #9849 - Edna V. Dorgeloh - 28

12558. LAUREL F. NEBEL and 1 child,   San Francisco, Cal
                                          1280 46th Ave
Admitted. Claims through mother enrolled as Nancy Ann Blythe,
Dl. [Del?] #943.
ROLL P104 #19912 - Laura F. Nebel   - 34
          19913 - Alton F. BOWLEY (son) - 16 (App 12556)

345

12559. ANNIE LAURA ROHRER,   204 Utah St., San Francisco, Cal
Admitted. Daughter of 12558, and claims through same source.
ROLL P119 #22984 - Annie Laura Rohrer - 26

12560. ALEXANDER OSBORNE,   City, N C
Rejected. Sizemore case. See report #417.

12561. NOAH OSBORNE,   City, N C
Rejected. Sizemore case. See report #417.

12562. STEPHEN OSBORNE and 2 children,   City, N C
Rejected. Sizemore case. See report #417.

12563. ZEDEKIA ORSBORN,   City, N C
Rejected. Sizemore case. See report #417.

12564. MARY H. STEPHESON and 3 children,   Murphys, Cal
Admitted. Sister of 12558 and claims through same source.
ROLL P132 #25565 - Mary H. Stephens   - 43
         25566 - James Raymond (son) - 20
         25567 - Earl Benjamin (son) - 17
         25568 - Della Ann (dau)   - 12

12565. CLARENCE COCHRAN,   Chelsea, Okla
Admitted. Cousin of 4291. Claimant's father enrolled in 1851
by Drennen, Del. 44.
ROLL P44 #7924 FCT COMM #13661 - Clarence Cochran   - 22
         7925   972 - Minda L (wife) -33(App 36556)
         7926   973 - Andrew Z. HALL (son of w) -16

12566. JESSE COCHRAN, Jr.,   Chelsea, Okla
Admitted. Cousin of 4291. Claimant's father enrolled in 1851
by Drennen, Del. 44.
ROLL P44 #7970 FCT COMM #13249 - Jesse Cochran Jr. - 32
         7971   6805 - Lettie J. (wife) - 25
                           (App 14777)

12567. CLINTON COCHRAN,   Chelsea, Okla
Admitted. Cousin of 4291. Claimant's father enrolled in 1851
by Drennen, Del. 44.
ROLL P44 #7927 FCT COMM #13659 - Clinton Cochran - 24

12568. JOHN OER and 1 child,   Campbell, Okla
Admitted. Brother of 3930 and claims through same source.
ROLL P105 #20224 FCT COMM #2628 - John Oer   - 24
          20225   470m - Emma May (dau) - 2

12569. ELIZA PHILLIPS and 1 child,   Braggs, Okla
Admitted. Minor's great grandmother enrolled by Drennen, 1852
[sic], Ill. 87.
ROLL P111 #21295 FCT COMM #21033 - Eliza Phillips - 22
          21296   - Steve (son)   - 4

346

12570. JENNIE ROSE and 4 children,   Braggs, Okla
Admitted. Claimant's father under name of Chu-con-nun-tole,
and paternal grandparents enrolled by Drennen 1851, Fl. 205.
Maternal grandparents and aunt enrolled in Ill. 75.
ROLL P119 #23011 FCT COMM # 5571 - Jennie Rose   - 30
              23012   5572 - Pearl (dau)   - 13
              23013   5573 - Joseph (son)   - 11
              23014   5574 - Henrietta (dau) - 8
              23015   2624m - J. Warren (son) - 3

12571. SARAH GRASS,   Midland, Ark
Rejected. Ancestors no on roll. Were not parties to treaties
of 1835-6-46. Does not establish genuine connection with Cherokee tribe. Misc. Test. 2836.
MISC. TEST. P. 2836. No 12571 - Sarah Cross:
    "My name is Sarah Cross; I was born in Alabama, 1841; I
don't know what part; I claim my Indian blood through my mother; I make no claim through my father, he was a German; my
mother's maiden name was Frances Emaline Hood; I don't know
when or where my mother was born; I was about twelve years old
when my mother died; my mother died in Louisiana; she died in
1853; my mother claimed her Cherokee blood through her father,
Trammel Hood; I don't know where my grandfather was born; in
1835 I don't know where my mother and her father were living;
in 1851 my mother living in Mississippi; my grandparents were
dead at that time; I think; neither I nor any of the ancestors
through whom I claim were ever enrolled or ever received any
money or land that I know of; I don't know whether my mother
ever lived with the Cherokees as a member of the tribe or not;
I think my grandfather lived with the Cherokees, but I do not
know at what place; I have never made application before the
Dawe's Commission; my grandfather was a half Cherokee."
SIGNED: Sarah "X" Cross, Greenwood, Ark., Sep 14 1908.

12572. BARBRA SMITH and 1 child,   Midland, Ark
Rejected. Claimant was born in 1843 in Indiana, her parents
were also born in that state. Claimant nor any of her ancestors do not appear on any Cherokee roll and no showing is made
that they ever lived with the tribe, and if they ever did they
left long prior to 1835.
EXCEPTION CASE.   12572.   Barbra E. Smith and 1 child,
Hartford, Ark. Rejected. Total number of exceptions filed in
this group -- 3. Original recommendation renewed.

12573. KATIE DOWNING, Gdn for 2 minor children, Texanna, Okla
Admitted.   Claimant's minors maternal grandfather and his
grandfather's parents and grandfather's brother and sisters
enrolled by Drennen in 1851 Fl. 222.
ROLL P32 #5438 FCT COMM #27420 - Leo B. Boles - 8
         5439   27421 - Richard (bro) - 5
                        by Katie Downing, Gdn.

347

12574. CHARLES D. GLASS and 1 child,   Braggs, Okla
Admitted. Nephew of #254 and claims through same source. Applicant's mother, Sarah Downing, enrolled in Tahlequah District #539, Sarah Downing. [For Roll information See App 9170, Vol. 4]

12575. DAVE DOWNING,   Vian, Okla
Admitted. Great uncle of 125173. Father of applicant enrolled in 1851 in Flint #222.
ROLL P54 #9897 FCT COMM #19513 - Dave Downing - 62

12576. JAMES BALDRIDGE and 2 children,   Porum, Okla
Admitted. Applicant's father and grandmother were enrolled by Drennen in Skin Bayou District #295. Misc. Test. P. 2767.
MISC. TEST. P. 2767.   #12576 - James Baldridge...through Wm. Smallwood:
    "That I am about 43 years of age. I am a full blood Cherokee. I was enrolled by the Dawes Commission and my roll number is 29312. My father's name was George Baldridge. His Indian name was Oo-wah-tee-skih. He was on the emigrant roll of 1851. I have 8 acres of land in the Cherokee Nation. My father was in Sequoyah District in 1851. My mother is on the emigrant roll of 1851 under the name of Oo-gah-yah-stah. My father's mother was Dah-gih. She had no English name. My father's name was Wolf-standing or Standing-wolf. His Indian name was Wah-yuh-gah-daw. Both of my grand parents were living in 1851. My grandfather's name of my mother's side was Ah-wih-gah-daw. My father did not have any brothers and sisters. I have none. My wife is a white woman. She is dead."
SIGNED: Jas. Baldridge, Stigler, Okla., Sep 10 1908.
ROLL P25 #4041 FCT COMM #29312 - James Baldridge - 41
       4042   29313 - William (son) - 9
       4043   29314 - Charles (son) - 7

12577. MARY HICKS,   Vian, Okla
Admitted. Great aunt of 12573. Father of applicant enrolled in 1851 in Flint #222.
ROLL P75 #14055 FCT COMM #18691 - Mary Hicks - 66

12578. GEO. G. and MAUD DOWNING,   Texanna, Okla
         by Katie Downing, Gdn.
Admitted. Enrolled with mother 12580.   [For Roll information See App 12580]

12579. SUSIE TONEY,   Porum, Okla
Admitted. Mother of applicant Sally Guess, enrolled on Skin Bayou, #320. Misc. Test. P. 27773 [sic]
MISC. TEST. P. 2773.   #12579 - Susie Toney...through Wm. Smallwood:
    "That I am 42 years of age. I am a full blooded Cherokee. My father's name was Seven Puppies (in English) and he also went by the name of Seven Fields. His Cherokee name was Gal-

348

quah-gih-ke-lih-uh-ne-ta. He was enrolled in the Sequoyah District. My mother's maiden name was Sallie Guess. She married my father about 1866 or about 64. My grandfather on my mother's side was named Tee-se Guess. (Can. 101). Wok-tee-yah Langley was his first wife. (S. B. 320). George Guess, Choo-wah-nos-kee Guess, Wah-la-ne-tah Guess, Wah-la-loo Guess, Lydia, Crawfish Guess were all children of my grandfather by his first wife - half brothers and sisters of my mother. Tee-se Guess was not an Old Settler, but my grandmother was. My father was an Old Settler. Katy Downing is my mother's full sister." SIGNED: Susie Toney, Stigler, Okla., Sep 10 1908.

ROLL P140 #27171 FCT COMM #17008 - Levi Toney - 46 (App 12917)

27172	17009 - Susie (wife) - 41	
27173	17011 - Cicero (son) - 19	
27174	17012 - Betty (dau) - 14	
27175	17013 - Kate (dau) - 11	
27176	17014 - Sallie (dau) - 11	

12580. KATIE DOWNING and 2 children,   Texanna, Okla
Admitted. Niece of #12579 and claims through same source.
ROLL P54 #9986 FCT COMM #5642 - Katie Downing - 55

9987	5645 - George H. (son) - 20
	(App 12578)
9988	5646 - Maud (dau) - 16

12581. DAISY M. WALKER,   Braggs, Okla
Admitted. Cousin of Geo. O. Meeker (11698) and cousin of #859 once removed. Claims from the same source. Mother probably born after 1851.
ROLL P144 #27939 FCT COMM #6111 - Edmond Walker - 29

	(App 26073)
27940	5659 - Daisy M. (wife) - 22

12582. MARY E. McCRACKER,   Braggs, Okla
Admitted. Cousin of Geo. O. Meeker 1169 [sic] and cousin once removed of #859. Claims from same source. Mother probably born after 1851.
ROLL P93 #17746 FCT COMM #29998 - Mary E. McCracken - 34

12583. NANNIE SLEEPER and 3 children,   Fort Gibson, Okla
Admitted. Half-sister to 11745. Claims through same source.
ROLL P128 #24669 FCT COMM #15249 - Nannie Sleeper - 23

24670	15250 - Nannie (dau) - 5
24671	579m - Margaret (dau) - 3
24672	580m - Louis (son) - 2

12584. LOONEY GOING TO SLEEP,   Oaks, Okla
Admitted. Claimant's parents enrolled by Drennen in 1851 Fl. 8. Father, stepmother and half brothers and sisters in Fl. 9.
ROLL P66 #12363 FCT COMM #21236 - Looney Going-to-sleep - 35

12364	32580 - Nancy (wife) - 47
	(App 12585)

12585. NANCY GOING TO SLEEP, Oaks, Okla
Admitted. The parents of applicant were enrolled in 33 Going
Snake in 1851 by Drennen. [For Roll information See App 12584]

12586. DAVE NEUGIN and 1 child, Hulbert, Okla
Admitted. 1st cousin of 1386. Son of 2448.
ROLL P105 #20190 FCT COMM #15097 - Dave Nugin or Neugin - 34
     20191   16540 - Alice (wife)   - 22
                 (App 26855)
     20192   15098 - Titus (son)   - 9

12587. ALICE BEAMER, Duplicate of 8045.

12588. GENNIE SCOTT, Grandniece of 1841. Duplicate of child
in 5688.

12589. NANCY SCOTT, Grandniece of 1841. Duplicate of child in
5688.

12590. LIZZIE FRAZIER, Duplicate of 11576.

12591. EUGENE M. ABBOTT and 2 children, Tahlequah, Okla
Admitted. Cousin of 385.
ROLL P21 #3179 FCT COMM #11951 - Eugene M. Abbott - 28
     3180   4532 - Netty M. (wife) - 25
                (App 12635)
     3181   4196m - Mary E. (dau)   - 3
     3182   - Gertrude (dau) - 1/12

12592. ANNIE DIRT EATER and 1 child, Moody, Okla
Admitted. Niece of #10 and claims through same source.
MISC. TEST. P. 2774. 12592 - Annie Dirteater...through S. E.
Parris, Interpreter:
    "Rosa Rogers is my daughter. She is 18 years of age. She
is the only child I have under 21 by Rogers. My daughter has
not made application for this money and I did not name her in
my application."
SIGNED: Annie Dirteater, Tahlequah, Okla., Oct 6 1908.
[For Roll information See App 480, Vol. 1]

12593. WM. ROSS BADGET, MARY BADGE, Vinita, Okla
       GEO. M. BADGET, Minors, by Wm. R. Badget, Gdn.
Admitted. Nephews and niece of 1361, claims thru same source.
ROLL P24 #3955 FCT COMM #24163 - Wm. Ross Badget - 16
     3956   24164 - Mary (sis)   - 15
     3957   24165 - George (bro) - 10
                by Wm. R. Badget, Gdn.

12594. MARY and JOHN FOSTER, Wauhillan, Okla
       Betsy Foster, Gdn.
Admitted. These minor wards claim through their grandmother
Eliza Foster, daughter of John Horn, enrolled in the family of

Wesley Gribbs in 1851 in Flint Dist. Group 102. [For Roll information See App 12599]

12595. LIZZIE CAMERON, Gdn. for 2 children, Wauhillan, Okla
Rejected. Ancestors cannot be identified on Emigrant rolls.
Guardian failed to appear when notified to do so. Rejected for
lack of information.

12596. ALCIE CAMERON and 3 children,   [No residence]
Admitted. 1st cousin once removed of #730. [Entire entry
handwritten and inserted.]
ROLL P37 #6546 FCT COMM #20870 – John Cameron – 40 (App 15956)
        6547   20871 – Olse (wife)   – 44
        6548   20875 – Will (son)   – 10
        6459   20876 – Susie (dau)   – 6
        6460   – Andrew (son)   – 3
        6461   20872 – Josie FLUTE (dau)   – 18
        6462   20873 – Charlotte FLUTE (dau) – 15
        6463   20874 – Aikey (Aggie) FLUTE   – 10
                            (dau)

12597. OLCIE CAMERON, Duplicate of 12596.

12598. CELIA ROSS,   Wauhillan, Okla
Admitted. Niece of #728. Mother and father "Quh-la-leet, and
Aul-cin-nih #1058 and 1059 Chapman." Grandmother and grand-
father "Kuh-see-hif and Jennie #979 and 980."
ROLL P120 #23034 FCT COMM #2485 – Celia Ross – 51

12599. BETSY FOSTER and 2 children,   Wauhillan, Okla
Admitted. 1st cousin once removed of #730, and claims through
same source. Mother #12598. Grandmother and grandfather "Quh-
la-leet, and Aul-cin-nih" 1058 and 1059 Chapman.
ROLL P63 #11684 FCT COMM #2482 – Betsy Foster – 32
        11685   2483 – Mary (dau)   – 13
        11686   2484 – John (son)   – 10

12600. HAY WHITE,   Hinton, W Va
Rejected. Sizemore case. See report in #417.

12601. SALLIE G. HUNT,   Ft. Smith, Ark
Admitted. 1st cousin of #2847.
ROLL P80 #15009 FCT COMM #17558 – Sallie G. Hunt – 18

12602. HARRISON HARLIS,   Choteau, Okla
            by father, Wm. Harlis
Admitted. Grandnephew of #132.
ROLL P71 #13300 FCT COMM #6678 – Harrison Harlis – 14
                            by William Harlis, Gdn.

12603. GEO. RAY,   Fate, Ga
Rejected. Nephew of 5041.

12604. CLAUD RAY,   Fate, Ga
Rejected. Nephew of 5041.

12605. LUTHER RAY,   Fate, Ga
Rejected. Nephew of 5041.

12606. LIZER JAN HALL,   Powder Springs, Ga
Rejected. Applicant shows no genuine connection with the Eastern Cherokees. No ancestor was ever enrolled. It appears that
no ancestor was a party to the treaties of 1835-36-46. Misc.
Test. P. 972.
MISC. TEST. P. 972. #12606 - Lizer Jane Hall:
    "That I am 56 years of age and live in Cobb Co., Ga. I
claim my Indian descent through my mother; my father was a
white man. My mother's mother was the Indian. All the rest
of my grandparents were white. My grandmother's name was
Cynthia Gothard and she married a Ashworth. My mother was born
and raised in Cherokee Co., Ga., near the edge of Forsythe Co.
She lived there all her life. She was 83 when she died and she
died in 1887. My mother nor I were never on any Indian roll,
nor any of my ancestors that I know of. My mother nor I never
lived with the Indians as members of the tribe. Joshua Ashworth, Jim, Joab, John Ashworth were my mother's brothers.
Betsy who married a Burdick, Nancy who married a Praither -
sisters of my mother. I am recognized in the community as a
white woman."
SIGNED: Lizer Jane "X" Hall, Marietta, Ga., Jul 6 1908.
EXCEPTION CASE. Lizer Jane Hall, Powder Springs, Ga.
Rejected. Total number of exceptions filed in this group --
2. Original recommendation renewed.

12607. EULA B. HENRON and 2 children,   Row, Okla
Admitted. 1st cousin of 866.
ROLL P74 #13811 FCT COMM # 1255 - Ula B. Hendron - 24
          13812   3632m - Beulah (dau) - 3
          13813   3633m - Nina (dau)   - 1

12608. GRADY RAY,   Fate, Ga
Rejected. Nephew of 5041.

12609. JOHN PROCTOR, by Betsy Snake,   Chance, Okla
Admitted. Grandson of #3752, claims through same source.
ROLL P113 #21800 - John Proctor - 5
                by Betsy Snake, Gdn.

12610. MARY CRITTENDEN,   Flint, Okla
Admitted. Applicant enrolled as Kah-lon-eh-skee, Going Snake
#71. Aunt of 2042 [? 1st digit blurred].
ROLL P49 #8827 FCT COMM #20275 - Mary Crittenden - 59

12611. LORA YOUNGBIRD,   Kansas, Okla
Admitted. Niece of 2041, and claims through same ancestors.

352

Grandfather of applicant, Bl[u]e Batt, enrolled in 1851, in Saline District, #82. [For Roll information See App 5810, Vol. 3]

12612. LYDIA MELLOWBUG and 2 children,   Oaks, Okla
Admitted. Niece of Dick Christy #2953. [For Roll information See App 9162, Vol. 4]

12613. BILL PORLONE, by Betsy Snake, Gdn.   Chance, Okla
Admitted. 1/2 nephew of #180. Minor child of Andy Perlone. [For Roll information See App 8109, Vol. 4]

12614. LAWYER SNAKE,   Ballard, Okla
Admitted. Brother of #11632, and claims through same source.
ROLL P134 #25920 FCT COMM #19661 - Lawyer Suake - 14
                                        by Betsy Suake, Mother

12615. ALEX. PHESANT,   Westville, Okla
Admitted. Applicant claims through her mother Mary Phesant enrolled in 1851 in G. S. dist. Group 682. See Misc. Test. of James Phesant taken at Westville, Okla., March 25, '09, p. 4067.
MISC. TEST. P. 4067.   No 15622-12615 - James Pheasant
...through J. B. Adair, Interpreter:
    "My name is James Pheasant; my post-office is Christie, Okla.; I am about thirty-four years old; my father's name was Jack Pheasant; he was too young to go into the war but I do not just [sic] how old he was; I have been raised in Going Snake but I do not know where my father was; my father's father was named Pheasant and my father's mother was named Aggie; my mother has two brothers living; my mother has a sister Jennie or Che-nar-se who is now living - she is living with a man named Jack Nugent and they live near Tahlequah; my mother has a brother named Coo-lau-qua or Big Drum - this brother is dead; he has been dead about twelve years; my mother has a brother Joe Threekiller who is now living about three miles beyond Christie - Christie is his post-office; he might be known as Joe Big Drum; my grandmother was named Che-yau-ni (G. S. 682) My mother's name was Coo-west-tah. Charlie Pheasant is my full brother - we have the same mother. Abraham Pheasant is my full brother - we have the same mother. Aleck Pheasant is also a full brother. My wife, Lula has a daughter Charlotte Bell for whom she never made application and we have a girl Jenanna Pheasant who is now about twelve years old for whom we have not made appl. They are both living with me. Dawes Commission numbers 20041 to 20044."
SIGNED: James "X" Pheasant, Westville, Okla., Mar 25 1909.

MISC. TEST. P. 3060.   App No 16463-12615 - Interpreter Used.
Charley Pheasant:
    "My name is Charley Pheasant. My age is [blank]. My mother is a sister to Nannie Bailey. Evidence on mother's side found

353

in 6678–6596. I was born and raised in Going Snake District. I
was enrolled by the Dawes Commission, Cherokee Roll #19635. My
father's name is Jack Pheasant. He is dead; I was small when
he died. I never heard whether he got any money in 8151. He
had a brother Ga-yah-nah. That is the only one I know of. His
sister's name was Chi-an-nuh-nah. Che-ah-nu-ah lived in Going
Snake District. She died in Going Snake. (136 S. B. Che-ah-
nun-ah). Think my father's mother was A-key. Don't know my father's father. Jack Pheasant's father was named Klon-desk, or
Clon-deisk. (Witness is young and does not know any of his ancestors.)"
SIGNED: Charley "X" Pheasant, Stilwell, Okla., Sep 22 1908.
ROLL P111 #21273 FCT COMM #20040 - Alex Pheasant - 23
       21274   - Susan (wife) - 28
                            (App 16580)
       21275   4866m - Nannie RATCLIFF - 3
                            (dau of w)
       21276   4867m - Wat RATCLIFF   - 2
                            (son of w)

12616. WILLIAM TURN,   Baron, Okla
Admitted. Claimant's father under name of Oo-hah-chu-sah
[? 1st syllable blurred], and paternal grandfather enrolled by
Drennen in 1851, G. S. 383.
ROLL P142 #27435 FCT COMM #25810 - William Turn   - 30
       27436   32020 - Lizzie (wife)   - 23
                            (App 12619)
       27437   32021 - Charles DOWNING - 6
                            (son of w)
       27438*   4056m - Pumpkin DOWNING - 1
                            (son of w)
[* Notation on roll "Pumpkin, Johny. See Roll No. 27438."]

12617. HENRY TURN,   Baron, Okla
Admitted. Brother of 12616. Father of applicant enrolled in
1851 in Going Snake #383.
ROLL P142 #27431 FCT COMM #25814 - Henry Turn   - 34
       27432   15985 - Sallie (wife)   - 29
                            (App 12618)
       27433   15986 - Alec (son)   - 4
       27434   4065m - Jennie Ann (dau) - 1

12618. SALLIE TURN and 2 children,   Baron, Okla
Admitted. Niece of #8259, and claims through same source.
[For Roll information See App 12617]

12619. LIZZIE TURN and 2 children,   Baron, Okla
Admitted. Niece of #8259, and claims through same source.
[For Roll information See App 12616]

12620. STEPHEN BELL,   Westville, Okla
Admitted. Claimant's father enrolled by Drennen in 1851 G. S.

492. Father's mother enrolled G. S. 490. Father's sister en-
rolled G. S. 491.
ROLL P28 #4783 FCT COMM #20029 - Stephen Bell - 41
        4784   20030 - Jennie (wife) - 32
                             (App 12621)
        4785   892 - Hooley (son) - 14
        4786   1735m - Jesse (son)   - 4
        4787   1730m*- John D. (son) - 5
[* FCT # blurred]

12621. JENNIE BELL and 2 children,   Westville, Okla
Admitted. Half sister of 11199, and claims thru same source.
[For Roll information See App 12620]

12622. JENNIE WATT,   Baron, Okla
Admitted. Sister of #12616. Father of applicant enrolled in
1851 in Going Snake #383. [For Roll information See App 12623]

12623. WM. WATT and 1 child,   Baron, Okla
Admitted. Applicant is a cousin of 1052.   Applicant's mother
"Margaret Reese", 161 Flint Dist.
ROLL P147 #28549 FCT COMM #28653 - William Watt - 26
         28550   19101 - Jennie (wife) - 25
                             (App 12622)
         28551   4690m - Peggie (dau) - 1

12624. JESSIE A. WEAVER,   Denver, Colo*
Admitted. Sister of #877. [* Also "3117 Stern St." on roll]
ROLL P147 #28632 FCT COMM #7409 - Jessie A. Weaver - 21

12625. OCTAVIA DILLARD and 3 children,   Mineral Bluff, Ga
Rejected. It does not appear that any ancestor was ever enrolled or that any ancestor was party to the treaties of 1835
1836, 46. Shows no real connection with the Eastern Cherokees.
Misc. Test. P. 1437.   [NOTE: This page of testimony is very
dark and difficult to read]
MISC. TEST. P. 1437. #12625 - ? - Tava Dillard:
    "I was born in Swain County, N. C.; am 35 [?] years of
age. I claim my Indian blood through my father.   He lives in
Fannin Co., Ga. I do not know if he made an application. I do
not know if he ever received any Indian money from the government. Never saw my grandparents. My mother told me I had Indian blood. She said my grandfather and great grandfather had
Indian blood in them. I do not remember if my father spoke the
Indian language. He lives with white people and is a voter.
Hester, the government agent never took my name that I know
of. I have never tried to get any Indian money prior to this
time." SIGNED: Tava Dillard, Blue Ridge, Ga., Jul 11 1908.
EXCEPTION CASE. Octavia Dillard and 3 children, Sweetgum, Ga.
Rejected. Total number of exceptions filed in this group --
1. Original recommendation renewed.

355

12626. MANDA C. KEYS and 1 child,   Ballard, Okla
Admitted. Sister of 805 and claims through same source. See
Supl. 8973.
ROLL P85 #16191 FCT COMM #1340 - Manda C. Keys   - 33
          16192   1341 - Lorenzo D. (son) - 11

12627. JAMES FLYING,   Braggs, Okla
          Looney Hammer, Gdn.
Admitted. Nephew of 1224. Mother Jennie Smith 290 Tahlequah.
ROLL P62 #11464 FCT COMM #5626 - James Flying - 16
                              by Looney Hammer, Gdn.

12628. NANNIE ELK,   Sallisaw, Okla
Admitted. Half-sister of #3645, and claims thru same source.
ROLL P57 #10561 FCT COMM #32064 - Nannie Elk   - 25
          10562   - Willie (son) - 1/4

12629. LUCY ADAIR,   Stilwell, Okla
Admitted. Father not born in 1851, grandparents enrolled as
Squirrel & Locinna. Aunt & Uncle enrolled as Susannah and To-
you-ne-tah, Fl. #203.
ROLL P21 #3307 - Lucy Adair - 24

12630. SU-SA-NI RATT and 4 children,   Bunch, Okla
Admitted. Claims through father enrolled as Ta-le-tah-ta-kee,
Uncle enrolled ass Josiah, Grandmother enrolled as Anny, G. S.
#567. [Notation on roll "Ratt, Susani - See Roll #4628"]
ROLL P28 #4627 FCT COMM #20700 - William Beaver   - 32
                              (App 13135)
          4628   25943 - Susani RATT (wife)   - 26
          4629   - Ola BEAVER (dau)   - 1
          4630   25945 - Polly RATT (dau of w) - 6
          4631   - John RATT (son of w)   - 3
          4632   - George HICKS (son of w) - 7

12631. CHARLES L. KEYS and 2 children,   Wauhillau, Okla
Admitted. Brother of #642. Applicant enrolled on Chapman
#1689. Father of applicant enrolled on Chapman #1686.
ROLL P85 #16159 FCT COMM #2378 - Charles L. Keys   - 55
          16160   2379 - Theodore S. (son) - 19
          16161   2380 - Wilson (son)   - 16

12632. LUCY MUSH,   Wauhillau, Okla
Admitted. Claims through grandfather, James Cameron, also
grandmother, Nancy Cameron, also mother, Peggy Cameron; all
enrolled 1851 by Drennen, in Tahlequah Dist. #39.
ROLL P103 #19783 FCT COMM #26147? [sic] - Lucy Mush - 20

12633. MARY TUCKER,   Moody, Okla
Admitted. Claimant's paternal grandparents enrolled by Drennen in 1851, G. S. 594. See Misc. Test. 3533. Claimant enrolled by Daws Com. under name of Coh-to-yah Young Duck, D. C.

18811 [? 3rd digit blurred], Full blood. Claimant's parents evidently not born until after 51.
MISC. TEST. P. 3533. No 12633 - Mary Tucker...through S. E. Parris, Interpreter:
"My mother and father were both Cherokees. I have heard them say they got Immigrant money in 1852. They lived in Going Snake District. My grandmother was named Ta-ya-ne. My grand father was called Young Duck."
SIGNED: Mary Tucker, Tahlequah, Okla., Oct 5 1908.
[For Roll information See App 11520]

12634. CALLIE TAUAPIN,   Wauhillau, Okla
Admitted. Applicant's grandparents enrolled by Drennen 1852 Fl. 610.
ROLL P136 #26318 FCT COMM #20934 - Charlie Tarepin - 30
                                   (App 13714)
         26319   20934* - Callie (wife)   - 30
         26320   - Henry W. (son) - 1/6
[* same FCT Nos. written for husband and wife]

12635. NETTIE M. ABBOTT,   Tahlequah, Okla
Admitted. Sister to 8679. For Roll information see App 12591]

12636. ANDY.SUNDAY and 4 children,   Peggs, Okla
Admitted. Nephew to #175.
ROLL P134 #26010 FCT COMM #28993 - Andy Sunday - 30
         26011   28994 - Mary (dau)   - 8
         26012   28995 - Elva (dau)   - 6
         26013   1762m - Lois (dau)   - 3
         26014   1763m - Laura (dau) - 1
                                  (Died Oct. 19, 1906)
         26015   16216 - Betsy (sis) - 14
                                  (App 17129)

12637. BETSY SMITH, Duplicate of #1211 [Should be 1223, half-sister of 1211]

12638. CYNTHIA WOLF,   Christie, Okla
Admitted. Niece of #1609.
ROLL P153 #29690 FCT COMM #1438 - Cynthia Wolfe - 18

12639. RICHARD WOLF,   Christie, Okla
Admitted. Nephew of #1609.
ROLL P153 #29668 FCT COMM # 1437 - Richard Wolf - 23
         29669   20114 - Nannie (wife) - 24
                                  (App 33148)
         29670   20115 - Hider (son)   - 4
         29671   4489m - Riley (son)   - 1

12640. MARY WOLF,   Proctor, Okla
Admitted. Niece of 6753. [For Roll information See App 6435, Vol. 3]

12641. QUAITSY WOLF,   Christie, Okla
Admitted. 1/2 Aunt of #2234. Father of applicant enrolled in
Flint Dist. #283.
ROLL P153 #29667 FCT COMM #27102 - Quaitsy Wolf - 36

12642. HUMMINGBIRD WOLFE,   Christie, Okla
Admitted. Nephew of 1609. Katy Wolfe mother of this child is
her Gdn.
ROLL P153 #29709 FCT COMM #1439 - Hummingbird Wolfe - 14
                                        by Katy Wolfe, Gdn.

12643. SARAH WOLFE,   Stilwell, Okla
Admitted. Niece of 1609.
ROLL P153 #29750 FCT COMM #1436 - Sarah Wolfe - 24

12644. GEO. GREESE, Duplicate of 3147.

12645. THOS. GRITTS,   Tahlequah, Okla
Admitted. Applicant's parents enrolled by Drennen 1851 G. S.
143.
ROLL P68 #12717 FCT COMM #25354 - Thos. Gritts   - 56
           12718   25355 - Agnes (wife)   - 40
                                    (App 17120)
           12719   25358 - Charlotte (dau) - 19
                                    (App 36486)
           12720   25359 - John (son)   - 16
           12721   25360 - Bernice (dau)   - 14
           12722   25361 - Steve (son)   - 12
           12723   25362 - Lily (dau)   - 10
           12724   25363 - Lizzie (dau)   - 7
           12725   25364 - Thomas (son)   - 4

12646. WM. WALKER,   Wauhillau, Okla
Admitted. Applicant's parents enrolled by Drennen 1852 Tah. 53
ROLL P145 #28035 FCT COMM #20193 - William Walker - 50
           28036   20194 - Mary (wife)   - 45
                                    (App 12663)

12647. CHAS. E. YOUNG,   Wauhillau, Okla
Admitted. Suppl. application see 1831.

12648. HENRY JOHNSON,   Stilwell, Okla
           Johnson Simmons, Gdn.
Admitted. Applicant's grandfather and great grandfather en-
rolled G. S. 604. Great nephew of #7025.
ROLL P82 #15420 FCT COMM #19083* - Henry Johnson - 18
                               by Johnson Simmons, Gdn.
[* FCT "13751" crossed out - NOTE: Under "CLERICAL CORRECTIONS
TO BE MADE TO ORIGINAL ROLL" is the following entry: "15420.
Henry Johnson - should have F.C.T. Com. No. 19083. He is the
son of Roll No. 5254." Roll #5254 was Annie Blackwood, App
2849 - See Vol. 2]

12649. JENNY AH–GUAH–TAKY,   Tahlequah, Okla
Admitted. 1st cousin of #5581.
ROLL P22 #3491 – Jennie Ah–quah–taky – 20

12650. TAYLOR CHRISTIE and 3 children,   Wauhillau, Okla
Admitted. Brother of 2687.
ROLL P42 #7462 FCT COMM #20597 – Taylor Christie – 45
         7463   20598 – Annie (wife) – 27 (App 17478)
         7464   20599 – Fannie (dau)   – 17
         7465   20600 – Albert (son)   – 16
         7466   20601 – Annie (dau)   – 13

12651. NANCY CHRISTIE,   Wauhillau, Okla
Admitted. Sister of 4507.
ROLL P42 #7448 FCT COMM #32588 – Nancy Christie – 62

12652. BETSY YOUNG, Duplicate of 1829.

12653. SUSAN SWIMMER, Duplicate of 1828.

12654. LIZZIE SMITH,   Stilwell, Okla
Admitted. Niece of 1828. [For Roll information See App 5062,
Vol. 3]

12655. MARY CARLILE,   Cookson, Okla
Admitted. Niece of 1828.
ROLL P38 #6760 FCT COMM #29778 – Mary Carlile – 19

12656. FRANCES E. LEE and 1 child,   Ahniwake, Okla
Admitted. Cousin of 671, claims through same source.
ROLL P89 #16915 FCT COMM #16057 – Frances E. Lee – 41
        16916   16058 – Almon (son)   – 9

12657. GEO. W. SHAMBLIN and 7 children,   Coffeyville, Kan
Admitted. Brother of 484, and claims through same source.
[NOTE: only 6 children on roll]
ROLL P126 #24248 FCT COMM #30259 – Geo. W. Shamblin – 41
          24249   10610 – Plese F. (son)   – 14
          24250   10611 – Stephen D. (son) – 11
          24251   10612 – Bert A. (son)   – 7
          24252   10613 – Annie E. (dau)   – 4
          24253   897m – Geo. Clark (son) – 2
          24254   – Arnold P. (son) – 1/12

12658. CHARLOTTE A. SANDERS,   Marble, Okla
Admitted. 1st cousin of #1?786 [? 2nd digit blurred], and
claims through same source. Father Samuel E. Sanders, 567 Fl.
ROLL P122 #23458 FCT COMM #3284 – Charlotte A. Sanders – 24

12659. JESSE WILLIAMS,   Moody, Okla
Admitted. Nephew of 1757 and claims through same source.

ROLL P151 #29340 FCT COMM #18486 – Jesse Williams – 21
         29341   7055 – Jennie (wife) – 22
                            (App 17068)

12660. THOS. ROWE,   Stilwell, Okla
Admitted. Son of #195 and claims through same source.
ROLL P121 #23247 FCT COMM #21938 – Thomas Rowe – 28
         23248   – Katie (wife) – 25
                                (App 12661)

12661. KATIE ROWE,   Stilwell, Okla
Admitted. Sister of 12629. Claims through same source. [For
Roll information See App 12660]

12662. JACOB MANKILLER and 7 children,   Stilwell, Okla
Admitted. Full brother of 6510 and claims thru same source.
ROLL P95 #18218 FCT COMM #25669 – Jacob Mankiller – 53
         18219   25670 – Susan (wife)   – 28
                            (App 13678)
         18220   25671 – John (son)   – 17
         18221   25672 – Lizzie (dau)   – 15
         18222   25673 – Jennie (dau)   – 13
         18223   25674 – Maggie (dau)   – 11
         18224   25675 – Calson (son)   – 9
         18225   25676 – Richard (son)   – 6
         18226   25677 – Mary (dau)   – 4

12663. MARY WALKER,   Wauhillau, Okla
Admitted. Full sister of 6510 and claims through same source.
[For Roll information See App 12646]

12664. VICY J. MITCHEN and 4 children,   Eckman, W Va
Rejected. Sizemore case. See special report in #417.

12665. MARY J. CRAWFORD and 6 children,   Kimball, W Va
Rejected. Sizemore case. See special report in #417.

12666. ELIZABETH HEFFLEFINGER, Same as #11262.

12667. RICHARE [sic] M. WOLFE, Duplicate of Supl. Appl. 4906.

12668. LOUIE M. WOLFE, Duplicate of Supl. Appl. 4906.

12669. NANIE HOUX,   Kinnison, Okla
Admitted. Sister of 12136. Parents of applicant not living in
1851.
ROLL P72 #13571 FCT COMM #24461 – Nanie Haux – 19

12670. FRANK BROWN and 2 children,   Welch, Okla
Admitted. Brother of 12136. Parents of applicant not living
in 1851.

360

```
ROLL P34 #5879 FCT COMM #24459 - Frank Brown      - 24
         5880           1268m - Geneva A. (dau)   -  2
         5881           1269m - Frederick C. (son) - 1
```

12671. DIANNA DOUGHERTY,   Stilwell, Okla
Admitted. Niece of 6732. Grandfather of 314 Flint "Eli",
Group 984.
ROLL P54 #9869 FCT COMM #29791 - Dianna Dougherty - 20

12672. NED PICKUP and 1 child,   Leach, Okla
Admitted. Cousin of 443, claims through same source.
```
ROLL P111 #21405 FCT COMM #32545 - Ned Pickup    - 33
          21406           32546 - Susie (wife)   - 33
                                  (App 26530)
          21407           2170m - Johnson (son) -  5
```

12673. JAMES RICH,   Boles, Kans
Rejected. Applicant or ancestors were never enrolled. Does
not appear that they were living within the limits of the
Cherokee Domain in 1835-6-46, as recognized members of the
tribe. Does appear that they never lived with the Cherokees
as recognized members of the tribe.
MISC. TEST. P. 744. No 39927 (12673) - Harvey Rich:
    "My name is Harvey Rich; I was born in Overton Co., Tenn.
in 1845; I claim my Indian blood through my father, Martin
Rich; my father was born about 1817; I do not know where my
father was born; I think my father was born in Tenn.; my father got his Indian from both his father and mother; my grand
father's name was Jesse Rich; my grandfather, Jesse Rich, was
born in N. C., but I do not know what part; my grandmother's
maiden name was Elizabeth Savage; I have seen my grand parents
through whom I claim; I do not know where my grandmother,
Elizabeth Savage, was born; I make no claim of Indian blood
through my mother; I never heard of any of the ancestors
through whom I claim ever living with the Cherokee Indians as
a member of the tribe. I am unable to trace my ancestry any
farther back than my grand parents; I have heard my grand
father through whom I claim say that his mother was a full
blood Cherokee woman [?]; I have heard that her name was Nancy
Hooker; neither I nor any of the ancestors through whom I
claim were ever enrolled and never received any money or land
that I know of; none of the ancestors through whom I claim
were ever held as slaves; in 1834-5 the ancestors through whom
I claim lived in Overton Co., Tenn.; I do not know where Nancy
Hooker lived in 1835; I do not know where she was born or when
she died; none of my ancestors through whom I claim ever went
West with the Indians and never had an Indian name that I know
of." SIGNED: Harvey Rich, Livingston, Tenn., Jun 29 1908.
EXCEPTION CASE. 12673. Harvey Rich and 4 children, App
39927, Hilham, Tenn. Rejected. Total number of exceptions
filed in this group -- 6. Original recommendation renewed.

12674. LINCOLN TOWIE and 3 children,   Tahlequah, Okla
Admitted. 1st cousin of 1902 and claims through same source.
Mother of applicant Sallie Towie (Vann) enrolled in Skin Bayou
Dist. #66. [For Roll information See App 8144, Vol. 4]

12675. WILSON TOWIE,   Tahlequah, Okla
Admitted. 1st cousin of 1902 and claims thru same ancestors.
Mother of applicant Sallie Towie (Vann) enrolled in Skin Bayou
Dist. #66.
ROLL P141 #27218 FCT COMM #18527 - Wilson Towie - 37

12676. JEFF TOWIE,   Tahlequah, Okla
Admitted. 1st cousin of 1902, and claims thru same ancestors.
Mother of applicant Sallie Towie (Vann) enrolled in Skin Bayou
Dist. #66. [For Roll information See App 11971]

12677. WALTER P. BREWER and 4 children,   Chapel, Okla
        by G. W. Brewer by power of attorney
Admitted. Brother of #3044. Claims through same source.
MISC. TEST. P. 4254. #12677 - G. W. Brewer:
    "I am the brother of Walter P. Brewer Appl 12677. I filed
his application for him by power of attorney. He never filed
an application for himself. He was living in California. His
minor children were living with me. I am sure that one of his
children Carrie B. Brewer, who is included in the supplemental
application that I filed for my brother, filed an application
for herself."
SIGNED: Geo. W. Brewer, Locust Grove, Okla., Mar 11 1909.
ROLL P33 #5768 FCT COMM #22115 - Walter P. Brewer - 42
        5769   6738 - Carrie B. (dau) - 19
        5770   6736 - William M. (son) - 17
        5771   6737 - John T. (son)   - 15
        5772   6739 - Mary G. (dau)   - 9

12678. GEO. W. BREWER and 4 children,   Locust Grove, Okla
Admitted. Brother of 3044. Father of applicant enrolled in
1851 in Ill. #263.
ROLL P33 #5742 FCT COMM #14971 - George W. Brewer - 48
        5743   14973 - Richard R. (son) - 10
        5744   14975 - Cherokee (dau)   - 8
        5745   14977 - Lucille G. (dau) - 5
        5746   2865m - Nannie M. (dau) - 4

12679. CHEROKEE BREWER,   Locust Grove, Okla
Rejected. Sister of 12494. Claims through same source and is
rejected.

12680. MARGARET D. PALMER and 4 children,   Collinsville, Okla
Rejected. Claimant is a full sister of #6958 and should be rejected for the same reasons. Claimant is enrolled by the Dawes
Commission #15467 as 1/8 blood and her husband is evidently a
white man as her children are enrolled as 1/16 bloods.

12681. JOHN M. RILEY and 4 children,   Chapel, Okla
Admitted. Uncle of 12359. Enrolled as Martin Riley Sal #450
[? last digit blurred].
ROLL P117 #22540 FCT COMM #6475 - John M. Riley - 55
        22541   6476 - Nannie E. (wife) - 46
                               (App 12682)
        22542   6480 - Welder (son)   - 16
        22543   6481 - Owen (son)   - 13
        22544   6482 - Mayme (dau)   - 11
        22545   6483 - Jack (son)   - 9

12682. NANNIE E. B. RILEY,   Chapel, Okla
Admitted. Sister of #3044. Father of applicant enrolled in
1851 in Ill. #263. [For Roll information See App 12681]

12683. JOHN COON, (Dec'd)   Stilwell, Okla
Admitted. Applicant claims through his father Dick Coon who
was enrolled by Drennen in 1851 in Tah. Dist., group #332. See
test. taken of Darkey Coon at Stilwell, Okla. Mar. 22, 1909,
p. 4005. J. B. Adair says Darkey Coon's father was an emi-
grant Cherokee.
MISC. TEST. P. 4005.   No 1263 - in re John Coon - Darkey
Coon...through J. B. Adair, Interpreter:
     "My name is Darkey Coon; my post-office is Stilwell,
Okla.; I am forty-two years old; I am the wife of John Coon
who died the 26th day of Feb. 1907; Ute Coon is the son of
John Coon but not my son; I have four children, all by John:
Boly Coon, 16 - Joe Coon, 14 - Chaw-wah-yoo-ka, she is 10 -
Turtle Coon, he is now five but has not been enrolled by the
Dawes Commission; my husband had an uncle named Wolf and an
aunt named A-chin-nee both of whom were younger than John's
father. (See Tahl. 332). My father was named James Stay-at-
home; he was born on the way out here; he was about sixty
years old when he died and he has been dead fourteen years; my
mother's name was Annie Dry before marriage; my father was an
Emigrant Cherokee and my father [sic] was also an Emigrant
Cherokee."
SIGNED: Darkey "X" Coon, Stilwell, Okla., Mar 22 1909.
ROLL P46 #8355 FCT COMM #1964 - John Coon   - 44
        8356   1965 - Dargery (wife)   - 40
                               (App 12685)
        8357   1966 - Boles (son)   - 17
        8358   1967 - Joe (son)   - 12
        8359   1968 - Chow-wee-yuk (son) - 9
        8360   3964m - Tarepin (son)   - 3

12684. HIRAM SIZEMORE,   Shraders, Va
Rejected. Sizemore case. See special report in #417.

12685. DARGEY COON and 4 children,   Stilwell, Okla
Admitted. Half-sister of 9928. [For Roll information See App
12683]

12686. MAUD HUNTER and 2 children,   So. McAlester, Okla
Admitted. Grandniece of 1953, claims through same source.
ROLL P80 #15012 FCT COMM #31700 - Maud Hunter   - 30
          15013   31701 - Florence I. (dau) - 9
          15014   4404m - Grace (dau)   - 1

12687. WILLIE MURRAY and 2 children,   Priddy, Tex
Rejected. Cousin of 10290.

12688. BANDIE MURRAY,   Priddy, Tex
Rejected. Cousin of 10290.

12689. RED PRICHETT,   Stilwell, Okla
Admitted. Claimant's mother, under name of I-ho-koli, maternal grandmother and mother's sister enrolled by Drennen in
1851, Flint 486.   Names identified by reference to applications and attached sheet in 13855 and 16920. Nancy the sister
of claimant's mother, was not born until 52. See group and
appl. 3210.
MISC. TEST. P. 3496.   13755-12689 - Tom Pritchett...through
Tom Roach, Interpreter:
     "That I am 41 years of age. I am a full blood Cherokee
Indian. My mother drew Old Settler money; guess it was along
about 1851. She was very small at that time. Don't know whether my father drew any money or not as an Old Settler. My father was a little over fifty when he died and he died in 1903.
I was named after my grandfather, his name being Tom Pritchett. Oo-gee-yah was the Indian name. Guess he was living in
1851. Mary Stand was the name of my father's mother. Da-gah-
daw was her Indian name. William Miller tells me that he knew
my father right after the war and that he was a pretty old man
then. George Oo-ge-yah was the name of my father."
SIGNED: Tom Pritchett, Sallisaw, Okla., Sep 19 1908.
Nancy Seabolt:
     "That I am 82 years of age. George Seabolt, the father
of applicant, was a grown man in 1851. He wasn't married at
that time. Thomas Pritchett, the grandfather of applicant, was
living here in the West in 1851. George lived with his father
until he married and then he came to Sequoyah District. It was
then called Skin Bayou District.   George had a sister named
Akey. Akey has a daughter who was up here yesterday.   Her
daughter's Indian name is Dah-kinny. Don't know her English
name.   John Little John (16920) is a half brother of Tom
Pritchett (13755). John's father is a white man. George was an
emigrant Cherokee, not an Old Settler.   I am certain that
George is on the emigrant 1851 roll. He was living in Flint
District. Think Lucy and Jinnie must have been sisters of
George. (See Tahl 67 [? blurred]) Old Tom Pritchett was living in 1851. Don't know anything about his wife, whether or
not she was living."
SIGNED: Nancy Seabolt, Sallisaw, Okla., Sep 19 1908.

```
ROLL P113 #21728 FCT COMM #19139 - Red Pritchett - 30
         21729          19140 - Fannie (wife) - 29
                               (App 12692)
         21730          19141 - Nannie (dau)  - 13
         21731          19142 - Philip (son)  - 10
         21732          19143 - Jesse (son)   -  7
         21733          3045m - Stephen (son) -  3
```

12690. ELLEN KILLER and 2 children,   Stilwell, Okla
Admitted. Georgianna Killer also on #3871 Sup. Duplicate.

12691. ELLEN KILLER FOR NANCY KILLER,   Stilwell, Okla
Admitted. Duplicate on supplemental app. 3871.

12692. FANNIE PRITCHETT,   Stilwell, Okla
Admitted. Applicant is a niece of Polly Step #2827 and claims
through same source. [For Roll information See App 12689]

12693. JENNIE PRITCHETT,   Stilwell, Okla
Admitted. Applicant is a niece of Polly Steps #2827 and claims
through same source.

```
ROLL P113 #21734 FCT COMM #25615 - Tom Pritchett  - 40
                               (App 13755)
         21735          25616 - Jennie (wife)  - 33
         21736          25617 - Annie (dau)    - 15
         21737          25618 - Eliza (dau)    - 16
         21738          25620 - John (son)     - 10
         21739          25621 - Narcissa (dau) -  5
         21740          3949m - Ollie (dau)    -  2
```

12694. GEO. DELLAS,   Uniontown, Ark
Admitted. The father of applicant was enrolled by Drennen in
1851 in Flint Dist. #339, under the name of Ta-kaw-tos-see.
Grandparents also enrolled in same Dist. and group. Misc.
Test. P. 2813.
MISC. TEST. P. 2813. No 12694 - George Dellus:
     "My name is George Dellus; I was born in Flint District,
1870; I am thirty-eight years old; I am a full blood Cherokee;
my parents were born in Flint District; I don't know the years
in which they were born; I never saw any of my grandparents; I
do not know the names of any of my grandparents.; I don't know
where they were born; my grandparents came from the East; I
think my parents were enrolled at Flint District; I don't know
under what names they were enrolled; I was enrolled by the
Dawe's Commission under the name of George Dellus, #6715; I
don't know whether my parents or grandparents ever received
any Old Settler payment; both I and my ancestors have always
belonged to the Cherokee Tribe and have never taken up rights
with any other tribe of Indians."
SIGNED: Geo. Dellus, Van Buren, Ark., Sep 12 1908.
ROLL P52 #9575 FCT COMM #4037 - George Dellus - 35

12695. EDWARD W. SANDERS,   Marble, Okla
             Mary Sanders, Gdn
Admitted. 1st cousin of 14736 [14786 ?] and claims thru same
source. Father, "Samuel Sanders, 567 Flint."
ROLL P123 #23628 FCT COMM #3282 - Mary Sanders   - 58
                                    (App 13416)
             23629   3286 - Edward W. (son) - 19

12696. JOHN McINTOSH,   Caroosa, Okla
Rejected. Applicant enrolled on Old Settler roll, Ill. Dist.
#179.

12697. LEVI ROGERS and no* children,   Braggs, Okla
Rejected. Claims through same source [as] #12216. "For children, see report in #13501" [Handwritten notation added]
[* "2" crossed out]
MISC. TEST. P. 3098. No 12697 with 12216 - Levi Rogers:
        "I am about 45 years of age; was born in Illinois Dis-
trict. I think my father was an Old Settler and my mother an
Immigrant. I drew Old Settler money when they made the payment
about two or three years ago. I drew about $800. I never saw
my grandparents on my mother's side. They died since the war.
I am the oldest child. I do not know if my mother drew Immigrant money in 1852. My cousin, George Sanders, told me my
mother was an Immigrant. My mother was dead when I drew $800
Old Settler money. My mother had one brother, Dave Sanders. I
never saw Mitchell or Polly Sanders. I do not know when they
died but do not think they were living at the time of the war.
I am a Cherokee alottee and my number is 12380."
SIGNED: Levi Rogers, Muskogee, Okla., Sep 22 1908.

12698. CHARLEY ACORN,   Stilwell, Okla
Admitted. Nephew of 4591, and claims through same source.
ROLL P21 #3199 FCT COMM #27185 - Charley Acorn - 22

12699. JOHN WILLIAM HILDERBRAND,   Needmore, Okla
Admitted. Nephew of 1351, and claims through same source.
ROLL P75 #14165 FCT COMM #9815 - John William Hilderbrand - 31

12700. JOHN SIX, minor,   Afton, Okla
             by John J. McGhee, Gdn.
Admitted. Child is nephew of 224 and claims thru same source.
Misc. Test. P. 3668, 4286. [For Testimony See App 224, Vol. 1]
ROLL P127 #24528 FCT COMM #17807 - John Six - 11
                                by Thomas M. McGlue, Gdn.

12701. JOHN HILDERBRAND,   Pryor Creek, Okla
             Geo. W. Mayes, Gdn.
Admitted. Nephew of 1351, and claims thru same source. Grand
father and uncles and aunts enrolled in 378 Delaware. Misc.
Test. P. 4359.

MISC. TEST. P. 4359. #12701 – George W. Mayes, Gdn.:
   "My name is George W. Mayes. I am 66 years old. I am
the Gdn. of John Hilderbrand; He is of age now; John is en-
rolled by the Daws Commission; His number is #27779; He was
born in March 4, 1888; I was appointed Gdn. by the Court. His
P. O. is still Pryor Creek."
SIGNED: Geo. W. Mayes, Pryor Creek, Okla., Mar 12 1909.
ROLL P75 #14162 FCT COMM #27779 – John Hilderbrand – 18
                                by Geo. W. Mayes, Gdn.

12702. MARY L. THOMAS and 3 children,   Afton, Okla
Admitted. Granddaughter of #112. Father of applicant enrolled
in 1857 [sic] Chapman #2090.
ROLL P138 #26694 FCT COMM #14638 – Mary L. Thomas – 25
          26695   14639 – Sopha E. (dau) – 10
          26696   14640 – Wm. B. (son)   – 9
          26697   14641 – Mable (dau   – 6

12703. RACHAEL THOMASON and 1 child,   Vinita, Okla
Admitted. Aunt of #1746 and claims through same ancestors.
Mother of applicant, Lucy Nidiffer, enrolled in Disputed Dist.
#9.
ROLL P138 #26711 FCT COMM #8880 – Rachel Thomason – 37
          26712   8882 – George L. (son) – 16
          26713   8881 – Bertha (dau)   – 18
                          (App 26844)

12704. JAMES P. LANDRUM and 1 child,   Cleora, Okla
Admitted. 1st cousin of #2847.
ROLL P87 #16614 FCT COMM #17560 – James P. Landrum – 28
         16615   4672m – Alice J. (dau)   – 2

12705. THOS. W. KEENER, Duplicate of 8800.

12706. RACHEL JANE McCULLOUGH, Duplicate of 1049.

12707. THOS. J. McGHEE, Same as #390.

12708. ELIZABETH REICHEL and 2 children, Jefferson City, Mo
Rejected. Claimant was born in 1850 and she nor any of her
ancestors appear on any Cherokee roll. Claimant #12709 herewith claims through same source was born in 1829 in Missouri
and she claims her Indian blood through her grandmother. If
these people ever had any Indian blood they were Old Settlers
or left the tribe long prior to 1835. No showing, however is
made that any of them ever lived with or were recognized at
any time as members of the Cherokee tribe.
EXCEPTION CASE. 12708. Barbara E. Washburn and 7 children,
App 12711, 232 Scott Ave., Kansas City, Mo. Rejected. Total
number of exceptions filed in this group —— 53. Original
recommendation renewed.

                          367

12709. VICINDA R. MOORE,   California, Mo
Rejected. Claims through same source as 12708.

12710. RACHEL W. HILL and 5 children,   Sedalia, Mo
Rejected. Claims through same source as 12708.

12711. BARBRAY E. WASHBURN and 7 children, Kansas City, Mo
Rejected. Claims through same source as 12708.

12712. RILEY L. MURRAY and 6 children,   Hume, Mo
Rejected. Claims through same source as 12708.

12713. JOHN W. MURRAY and 4 children,   Hume, Mo
Rejected. Claims through same source as 12708.

12714. EWING C. GHORMLEY and 5 children,   Adair, Okla
Admitted. Brother of #2216. Mother of applicant enrolled in
1851 in Going Snake #409.
ROLL P65 #12088 FCT COMM #8274 - Ewing C. Ghormley - 49
        12089   8275 - Ida N. (wife)   - 40
                          (App 27429)
        12090   8277 - Carrie E. (dau)   - 18
        12091   8278 - Bulah May (dau)   - 13
        12092   8279 - Hugh W. (son)   - 10
        12093   8280 - Lillian J. (dau)   - 8
        12094   8281 - Ewing M. (son)   - 6
        12095   2431m - Janice M. (dau)   - 1

12715. ADAIR E. FOWLER & BESSIE R. FOWLER, Owasso, Okla
        by Wesley E. Fowler, Gdn.
Admitted. Grandmother "Lovice Mitchell" enrolled 8 Ill. Dist.
Grandniece of 5107.
ROLL P63 #11751 FCT COMM #6328 - Ada E. Fowler   - 10
        11752   6329 - Bessie R. (sis) - 8
                          by Wesley E. Fowler, Gdn.

12716. SCOTT HEATH and 4 children,   Lodia, Va
Rejected. Sizemore case. See special report in #417.

12717. MARY A. TRENT and 1 child,   Lodi, Va
Rejected. Sizemore case. See special report in #417.

12718. MISSOURI EMILINE ROGERS,   Braggs, Okla
Admitted. Sister to Jack Quinton (16904) and claims through
same source.
ROLL P119 #22896 FCT COMM #23034 - Missouri Emeline
                                        Rogers - 47

12719. AMANDA C. RUPARD,   Laurel Bloomery, Tenn
     ted. Sizemore case. See special report in #417.

12720. JOHN MARION LOVELESS,   RFD #2, Booneville, Miss
Rejected. Cousin to H. J. Holcomb 3075, and claims thru same
source.

12721. J. M. LOVELESS & 7 children, RFD #2, Booneville, Miss
Rejected. Children are cousins of H. J. Holcomb, 3075 and
claims through same source.

12722. JOHN BROWN and 5 children,   Muskogee, Okla*
Admitted. Great uncle of 10661 [? 2nd digit blurred]. Enrolled as John Brown S. B. #39. [* Also "923 S. 2nd St." on
roll]
ROLL P34 #5921 FCT COMM #1851 - John Brown   - 59
             5922   6084 - Ollie (wife) - 26 (App 12724)
             5923   1852 - Jack (son)   - 19
             5924   1853 - Narcissa (dau) - 16
             5925   1854 - John Jr. (son) - 14
             5926   1855 - Kellah (dau)   - 12
             5927   2040m - Akie (dau)   - 3

12723. THOS. J. THORNTON,   923 So. 2nd St., Muskogee, Okla
Admitted. Brother of 330 and claims through same source.
ROLL P139 #26997 FCT COMM #498 - Thomas J. Thornton - 52

12724. OLLIE BROWN,   923 So. 2nd St., Muskogee, Okla
Admitted. Granddaughter of 1859. [For Roll information See
App 12722]

12725. BRADY PETTY and 2 children,   Furches, N C
Rejected. Sizemore case. See special report #417.

12726. DELILAH BREWER,   Muskogee, Okla
Admitted. Applicant enrolled by Drennen in Canadian Dist.
#13. Great aunt of 3858.
ROLL P33 #5741 FCT COMM #4324 - Delilah Brewer - 72

12727. CHERRIE B. JACKSON,   Muskogee, Okla
Admitted. 1st cousin of 3044. Father enrolled in 1851 in Ill.
Dist. 263.
ROLL P80 #15158 FCT COMM #4325 - Cherrie B. Jackson - 39

[NOTE: Under "CLERICAL CORRECTIONS TO BE MADE TO ORIGINAL
ROLL" are the following entries: "15158. For child see Roll
No. 15231." and "15231. Walter Jackson - son of Roll No.
15158."]

12727.5 WALTER JACKSON,   Muskogee, Okla
Admitted. 2nd cousin of 1208 and claimant's grandmother Martha
Jackson is on Chapman Roll 1866. Parents not born in 1851.
ROLL P81 #15231 FCT COMM #4326 - Walter Jackson - 5
                          by Cherrie Jackson, Gdn.

12728. ROBERT BROWN and 1 child,   Muskogee, Okla
Admitted. Great uncle of 10661. Enrolled as Robertson Brown,
S. B. #39.
ROLL P34 #5984 FCT COMM #32752 - Robert Brown - 56
          5985   32756 - Viola (dau) - 8 (App 42524)

12729. ALEXANDER PETTY and 4 children,   Furches, Okla
Rejected. Sizemore case. See special report in #417.

12730. TENNIE TALENT,   Patton, Ala
Rejected. Applicants or ancestors were never enrolled. Does
not appear that they were living within the Cherokee Domain in
1835-6-46 as recognized members of the tribe. Claims not suf-
ficiently established.
MISC. TEST. P. 450. No 12737-12730 - Mary Michael:
     "That I am 74 years of age and live in Bradley Co., Tenn.
I claim my Indian blood through my mother - she was 1/3 Cherokee. My husband is dead and he was 1/4 Cherokee Indian. My
mother's father was 1/3 Indian, I think. My mother's father's
name was Josiah Lemmons. He was born and raised in N. C. I
think it was in the Eastern part of N. C. but I don't know for
sure. He lived and died in N. C. My mother was born and raised
in Monroe and Bradley Counties, Tenn. She died when I was just
an infant. Her father died before she did. My mother nor her
father was never on any roll that I know of. We lived in kind
of a by [sic] settlement some 25 or 30 years ago when they
were getting up the land claims and making allotments to the
Cherokees. I never lived with the Indians. Don't know whether
my mother ever lived with them or not. My mother had four or
five brothers and sisters. One was Jesse, another Josiah, but
I don't know the rest. James Madison Ervin was one of my
brothers. Two others were Andrew Jackson and Joseph, and
Stephen Decatur, George Washington. They are only half-
brothers. They didn't have any Indian in them that I know of.
My husband was born and raised in Wilkes Co., N. C. His parents were Jacob Michael and Sarah Yates. Don't know where my
husband's parents were born and raised but think it was Wilkes
and Ash Co., N. C. Don't know whether they were on any rolls
or not. I was living in Cherokee Co., N. C. in 1851. Was not
enrolled at that time. Heard of an enrollment at that time. No
inquiry was made for my part."
SIGNED: Mary "X" Michael, Cleveland, Tenn., Jun 24 1908.
EXCEPTION CASE.   Tennie Talent, Vosburg, Miss.   Rejected.
Total number of exceptions filed in this group -- 9. Original
recommendation renewed.

12731. ELIZABETH PETTY and 7 children,   Alton Park, Tenn
Rejected. Sister of 12730. Claims through same source.

12732. MARTHA HUMPHREY and 3 children,   Alton Park, Tenn
Rejected. Sister of 12730, claims through same source.

370

12733. JACOB MICHAEL and 3 children,   Cleveland, Tenn
Rejected. Brother of 12730. Claims through same source.

12734. EMMA TALENT and 5 children,   Cleveland, Tenn
Rejected. Sister of 12730, and claims through same source.

12735. ABRAHAM L. MICHAEL and 4 children, Cleveland, Tenn
Rejected. Brother of 12730. Claims through same source.

12736. JOHN E. MICHAEL and 4 children,   Cleveland, Tenn
Rejected. Brother of 12730. Claims through same source.

12737. MARY MICHAEL,   Cleveland, Tenn
Rejected. Aunt of 12730, claims through same source.

12738. GEO. MICHAEL,   Cleveland, Tenn
Rejected. Brother of 12730. Claims through same source.

12739. LAZARUS RAPER and 6 children,   Cleveland, Tenn
Rejected. Applicant nor his ancestors were never enrolled
neither were any of them recognized as members of the Cherokee
tribe. Applicant is regarded as white man in community where
he resides. Misc. Test. 403.
MISC. TEST. P. 403. #12739 - Lazarus B. Raper:
     "That I am 53 years of age and live in Bradley Co., Tenn.
I claim my Indian blood through my father and his mother. The
rest of my ancestors were white people. Elizabeth Pitts was
born and raised in Cherokee Co., N. C. My father was was born
in Cherokee Co., N. C. and lived there until the war. He went
in the war and died at Nashville, Tenn. in 1865. My grand
mother was 1/2 Cherokee Indian. She was never on any roll that
I know of, nor was my father. My grandmother had some brothers
and sisters but I don't remember what their names were. None
of my father's brothers and sisters were ever enrolled that I
know of. My father was never known by any other name than
Raper and my grandmother was never known by any other names
than Pitts and Raper. Don't think my father or grandmother
ever lived with the Indians as a member of the tribe, although
they lived there in the Nation in Cherokee Co. I am recognized
as a white man. My wife is a white woman. My brother's wife is
also a white woman."
SIGNED: Lazarus B. "X" Raper, Cleveland, Tenn., Jun 24 1908.
EXCEPTION CASE. Rejected. Total number of exceptions filed
in this group -- 1. Original recommendation renewed.

12740. WM. RAPER,   Cleveland, Tenn
Rejected. Brother of Lazarus B. Raper #12739.

12741. JULIA RAY,   Oconee, Tenn
Rejected. Ancestors not on roll. There seems no genuine connection with the Cherokee (Eastern). Ancestors not parties to
the tribes [sic] of 1835-6-46. "(White See Misc. Test. P.

1212)" [handwritten notation] [For Testimony P. 1212 - See App
5041, Vol. 3]
MISC. TEST. P. 410-11. Witness in re #12741 - John W.
Hildebrand:
    "I did not know a Fed or a Bob Jackson."
SIGNED: John W. "X" Hildebrand, Benton, Tenn., Jun 24 1908.

12742. JOHN W. RAY and 6 children,   Oconee, Tenn
Rejected. Brother of 5041.

12743. ANDREW J. MORGAN and 3 children,   Benton, Tenn
Rejected. Brother of 3007 and claims through same source.

12744. ARMINDA WALKER and 4 children,   Cleveland, Tenn
Rejected. Sister of 11289.

12745. ADDIE MASON, Gdn. for 6 children,   Felker, Tenn
Rejected. Grandchildren of #529, and claims through the same
ancestors.

12746. MARY GRIFFITH,   Old Fort, Tenn
Rejected. Sister of 12747.
MISC. TEST. P. 410-11. Witness n regard #12746 - John W.
Hildebrand:
    "I knew a family of Mantooths and I believe they came from
Cocke ["Cobb" crossed out] Co., - they settled in the 4th Dis-
trict. I never heard them claim to be Cherokees, and they pass
as white people, and came here long after the treaty."
SIGNED: John W. "X" Hildebrand, Benton, Tenn., Jun 24 1908.

12747. ELIZABETH WELCH and 3 children,   Hughes, Ga
Rejected. Ancestors not enrolled, were not parties to treaty
of 1835-6-46. Does not show any connection with Cherokee tribe
MISC. TEST. P. 419. No. 12747-12746 - Elizabeth Welch:
    "My name is Elizabeth Welch. I am 61 years old. I was born
in Cocke Co., Tenn. I moved here when I was small. I claim my
Indian blood through my mother who was Elizabeth Mantooth. My
mother was born in Cocke Co. I do not know where she was born
or how old she was. She claimed her Indian blood through her
father, Thomas Mantooth. My great-grandfather, Thomas Mantooth, Sr., I have always heard was a full-blood Cherokee. I
do not remember where he lived. I do not remember when either
my grandfather or my great-grandfather died. They probably
died before I was born. I never lived the Indians. We have always been regarded as white people. We have never received any
money as Indians. I heard when I was small, that I had Indian
blood. My father and mother both spoke of it. They said that
they were Eastern Cherokees. The statements in my application
as to the time of the death of my grandfather and great grandfather I got from my parents. I never heard of either of them
being enrolled as Cherokees." SIGNED: Elizabeth "X" Welch,
Guion Miller, Test., Benton, Tenn., Jun 24 1908.

372

Mary Griffith...deposes and says that she has nothing to add to the testimony of her sister, Elizabeth Welch.
SIGNED: Mary "X" Griffith, Benton, Tenn., Jun 24 1908.

12748. MARY FEATHER and 1 child, Cherokee, N C
Admitted. Claims through father enrolled as Ah-ne-tah-nuh-uh and mother as Kul-le-nus-keh, Chapman #846-6. Niece of 10414.
[For Roll information See App 10027, Vol. 4]

12749. MARY GEORGE, RFD #1, Whittier, N C
Admitted. Claims through father Wesley Crow, enrolled by Chapman #1150, and through mother, Ahl-sah, enrolled by Chapman #509. Applicant was enrolled by Hester #690. Misc. Test. P. 17707 [sic].
MISC. TEST. P. 1707. #16325-12749 - Sallie Long Bigwitch:
    "That I am 31 years of age. I live in Jackson County, N. C. My mother's name was Elsie Thompson. My maternal grandmother's name was Caroline Thompson. My maternal grandfather's name was Thompson He-ah-doh-ka. I have understood that my father's name was Wesley Crow. I was raised at his house. We all lived there together. He died last summer. My maternal grandmother's name was Al-cuh. My mother's Indian name was Al-sih. The name Sah-la-nih was probably the name I was known by in Indian. (Hester 694)."
SIGNED: Sallie Long Bigwitch, Cherokee , N. C., Jul 20 1908.
"Note -- Wesley Crow (Chapman No 1150); Al-cuh, the grand mother (Chapman 50-" [remainder cut off - Notation added to end of testimony]
[For Roll information See App 12761]

12750. NANCY S. YOUNCE and 2 children, Birdtown, N C
Admitted. Sister to #6648 and claims through same source.
ROLL P20 #3127 - Nancy S. Younce - 54
            3128 - Nancy E. (dau) - 17
            3129 - Dasie M. (dau) - 15

12751. ALECK STANDINGWATER, Cherokee, N C
Admitted. The parents and brothers of applicant were enrolled by Chapman in 1851. Group 885.
ROLL P17 #2543 - Aleck Standingwater - 50
            2544 - Elsinnah (dau) - 12 (App 12759)

12752. GOING BIRD TOHISKIE and 1 child, Wahhiyah, N C
Admitted. Son of #15825. Nephew of #6629.
ROLL P6 #255 - Going Bird - 40
          256 - Wallie (wife) - 43 (App 12755)
          257 - Bettie (dau) - 10
          258 - Eli (son) - 13

12753. JENNIE CONLEY, Big Cove, N C
Admitted. Father of applicant is Scar-chih on Chapman roll #230. Applicant is wife of #7746. Applicant deceased Dec. 20,

1907. [For Roll information See App 7746, Vol. 4]
MISC. TEST. P. 1738. Witness in re #12753 - James Blythe...in
behalf of Jennie Conley::
    "That I was acquainted with Jennie Conley in her life
time. Jennie Johnson was her aunt. Jennie Johnson's mother's
name was Gah-dee-tla-a. She is No. 229 on the Chapman Roll.
Jennie Johnson is on the Chapman Roll as 223. I have heard of
Scot-chih as being a brother of Jennie Johnson."
SIGNED: James Blythe, Cherokee, N.C., Jul 21 1908.
"Note: Scot-chih, Chapman 230, Gah-dee-tla-a Chapman 229, Jen-
nie Johnson, Chapman 223" [Notation added to end of testimony]

12754. NANCY SAWNOOKA,   Whittier, N C
Admitted. Niece of #16823.
ROLL P16 #2287 - Nancy Sawnooka - 30

12755. WALLIE BIRD and 1 child,   Wahhiyah, N C
Admitted. Applicant's father enrolled by Chapman at 1500. Applicant's mother enrolled by Chapman at 1501. [For Roll information See App 12752]

12756. WATSON DICKEN,   Wahhiyah, N C
Admitted. Brother to Quattie Driver, 15819. Applicant says
was born after 51 enrollment.
ROLL P8 #752 - Watson Dicken - 55

12757. DALEESKEE CLIMBINGBEAR,   Wahhiyah, N C
Admitted. Nephew of 6215. Applicant's grandmother enrolled by
Chapman 415.
ROLL P7 #504 - Daleeskee Climbingbear - 31

12758. MORGAN CALHOUN,   Wahhiyah, N C
Admitted. Brother of 6215, and claims through same source.
ROLL P7 #412 - Morgan Calhoun   - 43
          413 - Sallie (wife)   - 44 (App 32303)
          414 - Wattie (son)   - 12
          415 - Lloyd (son)   - 10
          416 - Eve (dau)   - 8
          417 - Yenkeenee (dau) - 6
          418 - Lawrence (son)   - 4
          419 - Henry (son)   - 2
          420 - Godoquoskie (son) - 1

12759. ALECK STANDINGWATER,   Cherokee, N C
          father and guardian of Elsinne,
Admitted. Minor son of 12751. Enrolled as such. [For Roll
information SEe App 12751]

12760. SHELL GEORGE,   Cherokee, N C
Admitted. The father of the applicant was enrolled with his
parents in 1851 in 489-494 Chapman.
ROLL P9 #932 - Shell George - 47

12761. DAWSON GEORG[E] and 3 children,   Whittier, N C
Admitted. Brother of #12760.
ROLL P9 #901 - Dawson George - 45
        902 - Mary (wife)   - 45 (App 12749)
        903 - Manly (son)   - 19
        904 - Martha (dau)   - 15
        905 - Ollie (dau)   - 11

12762. JOHN PHEASANT,   Wahhiyah, N C
Admitted. Applicant enrolled Chapman 500. Half-brother 7753.
[For Roll information See App 10034, Vol. 4]

12763. WESLEY STANDINGDEER,   Cherokee, N C
Admitted. Brother of 10037 and claims through same source.
[For Roll information See App 10060, Vol. 4]

12764. JENNIE JOHNSON and 2 children,   Birdtown, N C
Admitted.   Claims through   father,   Oo-ga-tul-le-nowe-yeeh
Jesse, enrolled by Chapman #228. Applicant also enrolled by
Chapman 233, as Jen-e-lin-kih.
ROLL P11 #1279 - Stephen Johnson   - 64 (App 15843)
         1280 - Jennie (wife)   - 57
         1281 - Skeeg (son)   - 19
         1282 - Sim De Hart JESSANN (gson) - 3

12765. MARY S. STANDINGDEER,   Cherokee, N C
Admitted. 1st cousin of #613 and claims through same source.
Applicant's father enrolled by Chapman 1373. [For Roll infor-
mation See App 10025, Vol. 4]

12766. ANDY SHELL,   Whittier, N C
Admitted. This applicant is also known as "Andy Nute" and is
a duplicate of 15787. See letters.

12767. JACOB SMITH,   Cherokee, N C
Admitted. 1st cousin of #613 and claims through same source.
Applicant's father enrolled by Chapman #1373.
ROLL P17 #2407 - Jacob Smith - 27
         2408 - Olive Larch (wife) - 27 (App 16275)

12768. THOMAS SMITH,   Cherokee, N C
Admitted. 1st cousin of 613 and claims through same source.
Applicant's father enrolled by Chapman #1373.
ROLL P17 #2471 - Thomas Smith - 22

12769. HENRY BRADLEY,   Cherokee, N C
Admitted. Claims through his grandfather, Nick-ih, enrolled
by Chapman #206, and through his grandmother, Na-nih, enrolled
by Chapman #206. Misc. Test. P.. 1709.
MISC. TEST. P. 1709.   Witness re 12770-12769 - Van Daley
Bradley...in behalf of his daughter Lizzie Bradley, #12770:
    "That I am 58 years of age. I live in Jackson County,

N. C. I am the father of Lizzie Bradley. Her mother's name was
Lucinda Nick, or Lucinda Long, and her father's name was Nick
or Nick Long. Her grandmother was named Nai-nih or Nannie.
Lucinda Bradley was about 48 years of age when she died about
two years ago. Henry Bradley was a son of Lucinda Bradley."
SIGNED: Van Dalia "X" Bradley, Cherokee, N. C., Jul 20 1908.
"Note - Nick and Nai-nih are Chapman 206 and 207." [Notation
added to end of testimony]
ROLL P6 #352 - Henry Bradley - 23

12770. LIZZIE BRADLEY,   Cherokee, N C
Admitted. Sister of #12769, and claims through the same an-
cestors.
ROLL P6 #353 - Lizzie Bradley - 19

12771. LLOYD RATLIFF or RACKLEY,   Birdtown, N C
Admitted. Nephew of 8428, and claims through same source.
ROLL P15 #2101 - Loyd Ratliff - 30

12772. WM. RATLIFF and 2 children,   Birdtown, N C
Admitted. Nephew of 8428, and claims through same source.
ROLL P15 #2102 - William Ratliff - 33
             2103 - Lizzie (wife) - 28 (App 27172)
             2104 - Emma (dau)   - 5
             2105 - Jacob (son)   - 2

12773. JANNIE WOLFE,   Wahhiyah, N C
Admitted. Sister of 6215, and claims through same source.
[Notation on roll "Wolfe, Jennie. See Roll 2760" Roll #2760
is Jennie Trottingwolf, wife of Moses Trottingwolf, App 11839.
For Roll information See App 11839]

12774. SUSAN WOLFE and 1 child,   Wahhiyah, N C
Admitted. Mother of 7750 - enrolled as Susan, Chapman #426.
ROLL P20 #3114 - Susan Wolfe - 55
             3115 - Ward (son) - 14

12775. MARY SU-TE-GI,   Cherokee, N C
Admitted. Applicant's mother App 12776, enrolled by Chapman
under name of Sal-kin-nih at #482. Grandparent also enrolled
by Chapman #377-8. [For Roll information See App 6212, Vol. 3]

12776. SALLIE CLOUD,   Cherokee, N C
Admitted. Mother of 12775 and was enrolled by Chapman under
name of Sal-kin-nih at #482. Her parents enrolled by Chapman
at #377-8.
ROLL P7 #512 - Sallie Cloud - 83

12777. YORK CORNSILK,   Wahhiyah, N C
Admitted. Son of #15861. [For Roll information See App 6211,
Vol. 3]

12778. NANCY J. PASSMORE and 3 children,   Lookout, N C
Admitted. Niece of 6648 and claims through same source.
ROLL P14 #1891 - Nancy J. Passmore - 29
          1892 - Thomas (son)   - 5
          1893 - A. L. (dau)   - 4
          1894 - Cardie (dau)   - 2

12779. ANNIE CROW,   Soco, N C
Admitted. Sister of 3950. Applicant enrolled by Hester 1000.
ROLL P8 #631 - Joe Crow   - 39 (App 33905)
         632 - Annie (wife) - 46
         633 - Minnie (dau) - 13
         634 - Boyd (son)   - 12

12780. PIERSON LAMBERT,   Cherokee, N C
Admitted. Grandnephew of #6648, and claims through the same
source. See 15761.
ROLL P12 #1367 - Pierson Lambert - 6
              by Lucy A. Murphy, Gdn.

12781. FRANK MANEY and others,   Almond, N C
Rejected. Keziah Van case.

12782. ISIAH COLONAHESKI and 2 children, Wahhiyah, N C
Admitted. Claims through father, Co-lo-nah-hes-koh, enrolled
by Chapman #960.
ROLL P7 #539 - Isiah Colonaheski - 56
         540 - Martha (dau)   - 3
         541 - Mark (son)   - 1

12783. JOHN LOWEN,   Cherokee, N C
Admitted. Applicant enrolled by Hester roll at #661.   His
mother enrolled by Chapman at 614.   Grandmother on mother's
side enrolled by Chapman at #599.
ROLL P13 #1577 - John Lowen - 43
          1578 - Sis (wife) - 46 (App 12784)
          1579 - Katie COLONAHESKI (dau of w) - 18
          1580 - Nanny COLONAHESKI (dau of w) - 9

12784. SIS LOWEN and 2 children,   Cherokee, N C
Admitted. Sister of 12782, and claims through same ancestors.
MISC. TEST. P. 1708. #12784 with 12782 - Sis Lowen...through
David Owl, Interpreter:
    "I was about twelve or fourteen years of age at the time
of the war. My father was Col-o-ne-hes-ki. My grandfather's
name was Hah-we-sah-wah-yeh.   My two youngest children are
named Nannie, 11 years old, and Katie, about 17 years of age."
SIGNED: Sis "X" Lowen, Cherokee, N. C., Jul 20 1908.
[For Roll information See App 12783]

12785. JOSEPH SAWNOOKA,   Cherokee, N C
Admitted. Cousin of 15899 and claims through same source.

ROLL P16 #2283 - Joseph Sawnooka - 34

12786. WM. SAWNOOKA and 3 children,   Cherokee, N C
Admitted. Cousin of 15899 and claims through same source.
ROLL P16 #2305 - William Sawnooka - 36
        2306 - Stephen E. (son) - 6
        2307 - Osley B. (son) - 1
        2308 - Joseph A. (son) - 3

12787. DAVE REED,   Robbinsville, N C
Admitted. Son of 10063. Mother of applicant enrolled in 1851
by Chapman #11.
ROLL P15 #2137 - Dave Reed - 46

12788. STILWELL SAWNOOKA,   Whittier, N C
Admitted. Nephew of 16823.
ROLL P16 #2304 - Stilwell Sawnooka - 15 by John Sawnooka, Gdn.

12789. JOHN A. TAHQUETTE and 1 child,   Cherokee, N C
Admitted. Nephew of #2842. [For Roll information See App
10043, Vol. 4]

12790. JOHN SAWNOOKA,   RFD #2, Whittier, N C
Admitted. Applicant enrolled by Hester at 140. His father en-
rolled by Chapman at 25. His mother enrolled by Chapman at 11.
ROLL P16 #2278 - John Sawnooka - 51

12791. WILL LOCUST and 2 children,   Cherokee, N C
Admitted. Uncle of 10026 and admitted for same reasons.
ROLL P12 #1518 - Will Locust - 4? [2nd digit of ages cut off]
        1519 - Nellie (wife) - 4? (App 16259)
        1520 - Peter (son)   - 1?
        1521 - Tiney (dau)   - 1?

12792. JESSE TAYLOR,   Birdtow[n], N C
Admitted. The enrolled was enrolled by Hester 318 in 1884.
No answer to letter of inquiry. It is stated that he is recognized as a full blood by the Eastern Cherokee Band. His uncle
is enrolled in 696, Chapman. It appears that the ancestors of
applicant were parties to the treaties of 1835-6-46.
ROLL P18 #2626 - Jesse Taylor - 41
        2627 - Stacy (wife) - 46 (App 16837)

12793. SUSIE OOSOWIE,   Cherokee, N C
Admitted. The father and paternal grandparents, aunts and uncles are enrolled by Chapman in 1851. Group 169-175. Father
enrolled as Wa-ta-sat-tih 174. Chap.
ROLL P14 #1795 - Sam Oo-sowie - 46? [sic] (App 16825)
        1796 - Susie (wife) - 27
        1797 - Olise (dau) - 13
        1798 - Nicie (dau) - 13
        1799 - Paul (son)   - 6

12794. ANNIE WALKINGSTICK and 2 children,   Japan, N C
Admitted. Daughter of 6637.
ROLL P19 #2856 - Jasper Walkingstick - 34 (App 24574)
        2857 - Annie (wife)   - 25
        2858 - Nation (son)   - 2
        2859 - Maggie (dau)   - 1

12795. ELOWIH LITTLEJOHN,   Cherokee, N C
Admitted. Niece of 10060 and admitted for same reasons.
EXCEPTION CASE. 12795. Sally Anne Littlejohn, Sew-wah-nee,
Legilly (or Rachel Toonie) niece of wife, Goo-lah-gee, Soco,
N. C., by Elowhi Little John. Admitted. These children were
omitted through a clerical error. Children of Miller Roll 2743
ROLL P12 # 1488 - Elowih Littlejohn   - 28
SUPP ROLL #30378 - Sally Anne Little John   - 4
        30379 - Sow-wah-nee (bro)   - 2
        30380 - Legilly TOONIE (niece of wife) - 12
        30381 - Goo-lah-gee LITTLE JOHN (bro) - 7
                by Elowih Little John, parent & Gdn..

12796. JOSEPHINE SAWNOOKE,   Cherokee, N C
Admitted. Sister of 15899 and claims through same source.
ROLL P16 #2284 - Josephine Sawnooka - 14

12797. STELLA TATHAM and 1 child,   Bryson City, N C
Admitted. 2nd cousin once removed of 834. Grandmother "Stacy
Beck 2084 Chapman" mother not living in 1851.
ROLL P18 #2618 - Stella Tatham - 25
        2619 - Olive (dau)   - 2

12798. CATHERINE PETTY,   Furches, N C
Rejected. Sizemore case. See report in #417.

12799. RUTHIE CANNEFAX HERRON,   Monett, Mo
Rejected. Second cousin once removed of 12522. Claims through
same source.

12800. MILLER HINCHEE,   Cunningham, Ky
Rejected. 1st cousin once removed of 10764. Claims through
same source.

12801. HUNTER COMINGDEER, Duplicate of 7675.

12802. BEN WALKINGSTICK and 1 child,   Baron, Okla
Admitted. Applicant's uncles, grandmother enrolled by Drennen
in Going Snake Group 500. See test. of Ed. Walkingstick taken
at Stilwell, Mar. 23, 1909, p. 4002. Applicant is the great
grandchild of Rachel Soap #6730.
MISC. TEST. P. 4002. No 12802 in re Ben Walkingstick - Edward
Walkingstick:
    "My name is Edward Walkingstick; my post-office is Baron,
Okla.; I am fifty-nine years old; Ben Walkingstick's father

was my first cousin; I knew Ben Walkingstick's father and mother; his father's name was John Walkingstick; his mother's name was Lydia Crittenden; Lydia Crittenden's father's name was Isaac Crittenden; I don't think Lydia Crittenden was old enough to draw in 1851; my sister is now about fifty-six years old and she is the same age as Lydia; Nancy Soap was the wife of Isaac Crittenden; Katy Walkingstick was the mother of John Walkingstick and the grandmother of Ben; John Walkingstick, the father of Ben had a sister Nellie and brothers James and Isaac, (G. S. 500); John was not born in 1851."
SIGNED: Edward "X" Walkingstick, Stilwell, Okla., Mar 23 1909.
MISC. TEST. P. 3164. App [blank] Ben F. Walkingstick:
"My name is Ben F. Walkingstick. My age is 27 years. I was born and raised in Going Snake District. I got the strip payment. I was enrolled by the Dawes Commission, Cherokee Roll #16182. I have receipt card No. 12802, but am not the Ben Walkingstick who filed application No. 12802, as parents and grandparents named therein do not correspond to mine. There was another Ben Walkingstick who died about 6 weeks ago. We had the same post-office address and often got each other's mail. He was a cousin of mine. My mother was Sallie Walking-stick; her name was Bean before marriage. She is dead; died about two years ago. I do not know just how old she would be, but do not think it would be 60. Nancy Jane Bean was a sister of my mother's she married Edward Walkingstick. William Bean was my mother's brother; he lived in Coo-wee-scoo-wee District and was younger than my mother. Do not think he would be 60 years old. My mother got her blood from her mother Lydia Bean. She lived in Going Snake District and was born back in the old country and came here with the Emigrants. I could not say whether she had any sisters and brothers. I can't name any of my relatives on the Bean side. I don't know her father. (712 G. S. Lydia Bean.) My mother's father was William Bean. Lived in Going Snake District. I don't know whether he had any middle letter. I do not know whether he had any brothers and sister. (712 G. S.) My father was Edward Walkingstick. He lived in Going Snake District. One of his brothers was Flint Walk-ingstick; he is not 60 years old. He is dead. Jennie Walking-stick; she is not 60. Richard Ketcher, a half-brother, is 60 years old. Susan Walkingstick is my father's mother. (502 G. S. Susan and Edward.) My father's father was named Ben Walkingstick. I don't think he was living in 1851. He died before my grandmother. I have seen her. I can't name any brothers and sisters of my grandfather. Edward is living, my father. My grandmother has been dead a year and filed an application. I don't know whether they are enrolled in 1851. My mother and father both drew money; they said it was Emigrant money. My name is Benjamin F. Walkingstick. I don't know whether my people ever associated with any other tribe than the Cherokees. I don't know the number of the other application. Application for minor children #12802 is for my minor children."

380

SIGNED: Ben Walkingstick, Stilwell, Okla., Sep 24 1908.
[NOTE: The 2nd Ben Walkingstick, whose testimony appears
above, was applicant #6721. His summary appears in Vol. 3 and
his roll information can be found in App 1921, Vol. 2, however, his age was incorrectly listed as 33, it should have
been 26.]
ROLL P145 #28046 FCT COMM #18032 - Ben Walkingstick - 33
        28047   29043 - Lydia (dau)   - 9

12803. ANDREW REED and 8 children,   Bartlesville, Okla
Admitted. 1st cousin to 1386. Mother enrolled as Linny Vann
(nee Catcher) 292 G. S. Father enrolled as Johnson Reed, 291
G. S. Grandparents enrolled as Wm & Susan Reed 289 G. S.
ROLL P116 #22237 FCT COMM #10420 - Andrew Reed   - 48
        22238   29563 - Linnie L. (dau)   - 16
        22239   29564 - Nancy A. (dau)   - 14
        22240   29565 - Philatus L. A. (son) - 12
        22241   29567 - Alice L. V. (dau)   - 8
        22242   29566 - Alee M. (dau)   - 10
        22243   29568 - David A. (son)   - 4
        22244   1755m - Cleo F. (son)   - 2
        22245   1756m - Rena B. (dau)   - 7/12

12804. HONA N. MORRIS,   Tulsa, Okla
Admitted. A once removed cousin Fanny E. Chandler 1723, and
son of Eliza J. England.
ROLL P101 #19427 FCT COMM #11866 - Horra H. Morris - 26

12805. SARAH GUINN and 2 children,   Chetopa, Kan
Admitted. Daughter of 6062. See Misc. Test. P. 4376.
MISC. TEST. P. 4376. #12805 - Sarah Guinn:
    "My name is Sarah Guinn; I am 35 years old. James L. Guinn
is my husband. We were married in 1903; I have three three
children, Thomas B. Roach, Robert Roach, Jr. or George Roach,
Jr. and Ida Gertrude Guinn. George Roach was the father of the
children by the name of Roach. My husband and I are parted.
Thomas B. Roach lives with his father. George Roach lives in
Tahlequah. He never married again. Alma Lee Guinn my present
husbands oldest boy; The next is Charlie E. Guinn, James L.
Guinn, Jr. and Willie I. Guinn. They are all living at home
with me. The mother of these children is dead. My present husband's former wife was named Mary Lowry. Mary Lowry's parents
were Dan Lowery and Nannie Lowry. They were both Indians, he
about a quarter and she about three quarters. Dan Lowery has
a brother living whose name is Anderson or Andy Lowry whose
P. O. address is Manard, Okla. Dan had a sister named Susan
Roberson. I do not know who Dan's parents were. He had some
other brothers and sisters but I do not know their names. (See
Tahl. 536). My husband's former wife's mother was Nannie. I
do not know her maiden name. Lizzie Green was the name of the
half-sister of the first wife of my husband. She is living now
at Tahlequah. Bell Dawson is another half sister and she lives

381

at Talala, Okla. My husband's children have two older sisters who are living now at Tahlequah. Their name is Lille and Beatrice Hicks. They both married men by the name of Hicks."
SIGNED: Sarah Guinn, Vinita, Okla., Mar 11 1909.
ROLL P68 #12791 FCT COMM #16423 – Sarah Guinn   – 32
          12792   16425 – Robert George ROACH (son) –9
          12793   1440m – Ida G. GUINN (dau)   – 2

12805.5 JAMES L. GUINN for 4 children, Gdn. Chetopa, Kan
Admitted. Brothers of 11466, and claims through same ancestors. See also 11699. See Misc. Test. p. 4376. [For Testimony see application above]
ROLL P68 #12776 FCT COMM #14440 – Alma Lee Guinn   – 19
          12777   14441 – Charley E. (bro)   – 16
          12778   14442 – James L. Jr. (bro)   – 14
          12779   14443 – Willie I. (bro)   – 11
                                        by James L. Guinn, Gdn.

12806. CULL DOWNING,   Box 7 Ft. Leavenworth, Kan
Admitted. 1st cousin once removed of #2231.
ROLL P54 #9889 FCT COMM #20905 – Cull Downing – 27

12807. CULL DOWNING, Duplicate of 12806.

12808. HARVEY A. HYATT and 2 children,   Bryson City, N C
Rejected. Betsy Walker case.

12809. MARGARET M. WELSH,   Bryson City, N C
Rejected. Betsy Walker case. See special report in 500.

12810. ADALINE HARRIS and 9 children,   Flag Pond, Tenn
Rejected. Keziah Vann case. See special report in #276.

12811. LIZZIE BROSWELL and 1 child, RFD #3, Dallas, Ga
Rejected. Applicant's father and grandfather were living in Cherokee county in 1851 but were not enrolled there or at any other time. Does not establish fact of descent from a person who was a party to the treaty of 1835-6-46. Misc. Test. P. 1032.
MISC. TEST. P. 1032. No 12811 – Elizabeth Braswell:
    "My name is Elizabeth Braswell; I was born in Cobb Co., Ga. 1845; I claim my Indian blood through my father, Henry Guess; my father was born in Union Co., Ga. 1804; my father got his Indian blood from his father; my father's father's name was Abner Guess; my grandfather was born in Union Co., Ga.; I do not know what year; I never saw my grandfather through whom I claim; I claim no Indian blood through my mother; I am unable to trace my Indian ancestry back farther than my grandfather; none of the ancestors through whom I claim were ever held as slaves; I think my grandfather got his Indian blood from his father; my great grandfather's Indian name was Walking-stick; my father lived among the Cherokee Indians

382

in Ga., but I do not whether [sic] he lived as a member of the tribe or not; in 1835 my father lived in De Kalb Co., Ga.; in 1851 I and the ancestors through whom I claim lived in Cobb Co., Ga.; in 1882 I lived in Cobb Co., but I never heard of an enrollment at that time; none of my ancestors through whom I claim ever went West with the Indians that I know of; I have heard that my grandfather was a quarter Cherokee; both I and the ancestors through whom I claim were always regarded as white people with an admixture of Cherokee Indian blood."
SIGNED: Elizabeth "X" Braswell, Cedartown, Ga., Jul 7 1908.
EXCEPTION CASE. Rejected. Total number of exceptions filed in this group — 1. Original recommendation renewed.

12812. WM. P. WATTS,   Ranger, Ga
Rejected. The father of applicant was born in 1832 in Rabun Co., Ga. - out of Cherokee domain in 1835-6-46. None of the ancestors of applicant on the rolls. No genuine connection shown with Eastern Cherokees who were parties to treaties of 1835-6-46.
EXCEPTION CASE. Rejected. Total number of exceptions filed in this group — 1. Original recommendation renewed.

12813. HEAVY YAH-HO-LAH and 1 child,   Braggs, Okla
Admitted. Applicant's father enrolled by Drennen 1852 SB 276.
MISC. TEST. P. 3544. In re 12813 Heavy Yah-ho-la. Sul-le-coo-ke Yahola:
"I am the father of Heavy Yah-ho-la. I filed an application #15721. My father's name was Uck-saw-te-skee. My mother's name was Betsy. My name Sulle-coo-koo-hee. I had a sister named Akey. See S. B. 276." "Sul-le-coo-ke Yahola was enrolled as Johnson Yahola #29107 Dawes Com. Heavy Yah-olah Dawes Commission #29110" [Notation added to end of testimony.]
SIGNED: Sul-le-coo-kee Yahola, Tahlequah, Okla., Oct 6 1908.
ROLL P155 #30047 FCT COMM #29110 - Heavy Yahola - 21
         30048   - Joanna (dau) - 2

12814. JOHN ISRAEL and 2 children,   Braggs, Okla
Admitted. Claims through father enrolled as Quee-lee-kee in Going Snake #10. [NOTE: no children listed on roll]
ROLL P80 #15123 FCT COMM #28382 - John Israel - 32

12815. JOHN A. GONZALES and 1 child,   Braggs, Okla
Rejected. Brother of Caleb S. Gonzales #12435. Applicant's minor child is enrolled with his mother, App 11861. [For roll information of minor child See App 11861]

12816. TONEY A. BECK and 2 children,   Flint, Okla
Admitted. Cousin of 866.
ROLL P28 #4724 FCT COMM # 1274 - Toney A. Beck   - 35
        4725   1275 - Sarah A. (wife) - 35
                        (App 25987)
        4726   18137 - Chessie (dau)   - 6

12816.　TONEY A. BECK (Cont)
　　　　　4727 FCT COMM #3348m - Kermit (son)　　- 1

12817.　MARTHA F. SHACKELFORD & 2 children, Cherokee City, Ark
Admitted.　2nd cousin to 1604.
ROLL P125 #24212 FCT COMM #1407 - Martha F. Shackleford - 36
　　　　　24213　　　　　1409 - Effie E. (dau)　　　- 18
　　　　　24214　　　　　1410 - Charley L. (son)　　- 13

12818.　ZILLIE FOX and 5 children,　　　　　Park, Va
Rejected.　Sizemore case.　See special report #417

12819.　LEWIS LYMAN and 3 children,　　　　　Talala, Okla
Admitted.　Father of 12161.　Father of applicant　enrolled in
1851 in Tahlequah #230.
ROLL P92 #17472 FCT COMM #29484 - Lewis Lyman　　- 38
　　　　　17473　　　　　29485 - Elmira (dau)　　- 14
　　　　　17474　　　　　29486 - Levi (son)　　　- 13
　　　　　17475　　　　　29487 - Lewis A. (son) -　7

12820.　LEWIS LYMAN Gdn.　for 3 children, Niece and　nephew of
1117.　Dupl. of children in #12819.　Parent not living in 1851.

12821.　CORA SHARES and 3 children,　　　　　Furches, N C
Rejected.　Sizemore case.　See special report #417.

12822.　FROST FIVEKILLER,　　　　　　　　　Porum, Okla
Admitted.　The grandparents　of applicant enrolled in　1851 by
Drennen in 644 Flint.　Misc. Test. P. 3177.
MISC. TEST. P. 3177.　No 12822 - Frost Fivekiller:
　"I am 31　years old; am an allottee and my　number is 5641.
My parents died when　I was very　small.　My　grandfather Jack
Fivekiller was an Immigrant.　I never saw my grandfather nor my
grandmother.　Her name was Jinnie.　I am the only child."
SIGNED: Frost Fivekiller, Muskogee, Okla., Sep 24 1908.
[For Roll information See App 8985, Vol. 4]

12823.　FROST FIVEKILLER, Duplicate of 12822.

12824.　FROST FIVEKILLER, Duplicate of 12822.

12825.　FROST FIVEKILLER, Duplicate of 12822.

12826.　FROST FIVEKILLER, Duplicate of 12822.

12827.　FROST FIVEKILLER, Duplicate of 12822.

12828.　FROST FIVEKILLER, Duplicate of 12822.

12829.　JAS. or JOHN R. BLAIR and 3 children, Dunwoody, Ga
Rejected.　Brother to Nancy J. Holmes, 11608.

12830. HETTIE LEWIS and 2 children,   Inola, Okla
Rejected. Niece of 6054 [? blurred] and rejected for the same
reasons.
EXCEPTION CASE. 12830. Hettie Lewis & 2 children, Box 383,
Chetopa, Kans. Admitted. Total number of exceptions filed in
this group -- 1. Applicant was rejected through a clerical er-
ror and should have been admitted through father enrolled as
Henry Walkabout on Miller Roll, No. 27920.
SUPP ROLL #30668 FCT COMM #14082 - Hettie Lewis   - 27
              30669   2243m - Grace E. (dau) - 3
              30670   2244m - Ira A. (dau)   - 1

12831. BEULAH McCREADY,   Sallisaw, Okla
Admitted. L. L. McGrady, Gdn. Applicant claims through grandmother Celia Franklin, enrolled in 1851 Disputed 74. Celia
Franklins children William and Malinda are enrolled in Disputed 74 and her brothers and sisters in Disputed 75. Misc.
Test. P. 3487.
MISC. TEST. P. 3487. #13474-12831 - Georgie F. Hannah:
    "That I am 30 years of age. I claim my Indian descent thro
my mother; my father was a white man. My mother was 48 years
old when she died. She claimed her Indian descent through her
mother. Her maiden name was Choate, that is, my grandmother's
maiden name. My grandmother was on the 1851 roll under the
name of Franklin. Polly was a sister of my grandmother. Susie
was another and she married a Simpson. She may not have been
married in 1851; hardly think she was. Nancy was another sister. She was not married in 1851. Katy, Nancy, David, Susan
and Polly Choate (Dis. 73) were brothers and sisters of Celia
Franklin. John, James and Sanders were half brothers to Celia
(Dis. 75). Wm. Choate was a full brother to Celia, (Dis. 75).
Mary Franklin was Celia's step-daughter (Dis. 74). William
and Malinda were her own children (Dis. 74). I am on the Dawes
Commission Cherokee roll 2963. I have a second cousin by the
name of George Choate (8625). His father and my grandmother
were brother and sister, that is - half brother and sister,
but we are not related on the Indian side. Mack and Foster
McGrady are half brothers on my mother's side, and Beulah is a
half sister on my mother's side. Ethel Nix is a full sister."
SIGNED: Georgie F. Hannah, Sallisaw, Okla., Sep 18 1908.
ROLL P93 #17748 FCT COMM #2741 - Beulah McCrady - 10
                            by L. L. McCrady, Gdn.

12832. CHAS. L. KELL and 2 children,   Cherokee City, Ark
Admitted. 2nd cousin to 1604.
ROLL P84 #15965 FCT COMM #1417 - Charles L. Kell   - 35
              15966   1418 - Perry C. L. (son) - 6
              15967   4466 - Edith E. (dau)   - 3

12833. MACK McCRADY,   Sallisaw, Okla
Admitted. L. L. McGrady, Gdn. Brother to Beulah McCrady
(12831) and claims thru same source.

ROLL P93 #17750 FCT COMM #2739 - Mack McCrady - 18
                                by L. L. McCrady, Gdn.

12834. FOSTER McCR\DY,   Sallisaw, Okla
Admitted. L. L. McGrady, Gdn. Brother to Beulah McCrady 12831
and claims through same source.
ROLL P93 #17749 FCT COMM #2740 - Foster McCrady - 12
                                by L. L. McCrady, Gdn.

12835. LUCY SMITH and 2 children,   Blackgum, Okla
Admitted. Applicant states that her father, Richard, had a
brother Rider Fields and a half brother Arch Fields - that her
father was an old man before the war. The three names above
mentioned appear on 1835 roll - the name Richard Fields appears in three places on 1851 roll - in West Del. 935 and 941
and also Canadian 9 - also on Old Settler roll Fl. 49. The one
at Canadian #9 is probably applicant's father and also the
Richard on the roll of 1835. Rider Fields enrolled on Emmigrant roll Sal. #663. Applicant's mother's side Old Settlers.
Misc. Test. 12835 [sic]
MISC. TEST. P. 3011. App No 12835 - Son Interpreter - John R.
& Lucy Smith:
     "Lucy Smith is about 56 years old. She lives in Sequoyah
County, formerly Illinois District. She was born in Illinois
District. She was enrolled by the Dawes Commission, but never
filed her claim or allotment. She got the strip money and the
bread money. She gets her blood from both sides. Her name was
Eliza Brewer, and she married Fields. They lived in Illinois
District. Elizabeth Brewer had brothers and sisters; the oldest was Cynthia, Polly and Lydia; all lived in Illinois District; John and Tom Brewer were brothers. George Brewer was
her mother's father. (Ills. 263). Her father was Richard
Fields. He is dead. Died about 40 yrs. ago. Do not know in
what District he lived. He died in Washington, D. C. Before
he married her mother he had lived elsewhere than in Illinois
District. Lived on Honey Creek in Delaware District. His
brother was named Rider Fields. Sister Lucy or Lucinda Fields.
There were others but do not remember their names. Ju-wa-jar
or Ju-woo-jar-ga was the grandfather of Lucy Smith. Her father, Richard Fields was an agent or attorney for the Cherokees at Washington, after the war. (Del. 938 and 941). Arch
Fields was said to be a half-brother of Richard or Dick
Fields. Richard Fields was an old man in the time of the war.
Arch Fields, came to this country in 1837. Her father emi-
grated from the East.   Ellanora N. McLain is a daughter of
claimant; also John Smith, Sam Smith, Waters Smith and Richard
Smith, Tom Smith and George and Mose, Kiah, Stokes Smith. The
last two are dead. Susie Waters is a sister, Dick is her son."
SIGNED: Lucy Smith, Sallisaw, Okla., Sep 17 1908.
"17073 probably should be grouped with 12835." [Notation added
to end of testimony]

ROLL P129 #24907 FCT COMM #18098 - Lucy Smith - 53
         24908   18101 - Kiah (son) - 17
         24909   18102 - Stoke (son) - 15

12836. MRS. ELIZA TORBETT and 2 children, Crowder, Ind Terr
Rejected. Betsy Walker case. See special report in #500.

12837. JENNIE L. CONRAD,   Braggs, Okla
Admitted. The mother and father of enrolled were enrolled in
Canadian Dist. 93, by Drennen in 1851. Dead, see letter Geo.
Meeker, Adm.
ROLL P46 #8256 FCT COMM #6126 - George Conrad - 48 (App 13896)
       8257   5826 - Jennie L. (wife) - 53

12838. BERTIE PETTIE,   Furches, N C
Rejected. Sizemore case. See special report #417.

12839. WALTER L. WITHERSPOON,   Park, Va
Rejected. Sizemore case. See special report #417.

12840. ELIZA McDANIEL,   Warner, Okla
Admitted. Father of applicant enrolled in 516 Del in 1851.
Mother enrolled in 658 Del in 1851 by Drennen.
ROLL P93 #17803 FCT COMM #16869 - Eliza McDaniel - 50

12841. NANCY G. TIGUE,   Laurel Bloomery, Tenn
Rejected. Sizemore case. See special report #417.

12842. EUNICE BEL [?] and 3 children,   Furches, N C
Rejected. Sizemore case. See special report #417.

12843. ERMINA V. KENNEDY,   Talala, Okla
Admitted. Niece of 1816. [NOTE: age cut off on roll]
ROLL P84 #16029 FCT COMM #12604 - Ermina V. Kennedy - [?]

12844. FRANK HICKS,   Chelsea, Okla
Admitted. Cousin of 7407 and claims through same source.
ROLL P75 #14015 FCT COMM #12928 - Frank Hicks - 23

12845. GEO. ROSS MURRELL and 3 children, Bayou Goula, La
Admitted. 1st cousin of 90 and claims through same source.
Applicant's mother enrolled by Drennen Saline 459.
ROLL P103 #19772 - George Ross Murrell - 45
               19773 - Sarah G. (dau)   - 6
               19774 - Amanda R. (dau)   - 1
               19775 - Margaret G. (dau) - 1

12846. JOANNA LOUTHER and 1 child,   Claremore, Okla
Admitted. 1st cousin of 3080 & claims through same ancestors.
ROLL P91 #17313 FCT COMM #11353 - Joanna Louther - 50
        17314   11355 - William A. (son) - 15

12847. SAPHRONIA SHUGART,   Claremore, Okla
Admitted. 1st cousin once removed of 4?38 [blurred]. Grand
mother "Saphronia Bean, 274 Illinois."
ROLL P126 #24422 FCT COMM #11975 - Sophronia Shugart - 16

12848. ELIZ. L. FRANCIS and 6 children,   Garbers, Tenn
Rejected. Keziah Van case. See special report in 276.

12849. SAMUEL S. STARR,   Porum, Okla
Admitted. Uncle of 10746 and claims through same source.
ROLL P132 #25506 FCT COMM #4232 - Samuel S. Starr - 29
          25507*   4623 - Carrie E. (wife) - 27
                              (App 12850)
[* Notation on roll "Starr, Ellen C. See Roll No. 25507."]

12850. CARRIE E. STARR,   Porum, Okla
Admitted. 1st cousin once removed of 411, and claims through
same ancestors. [For Roll information See App 12849]

12851. THOS. McDANIEL and 4 children,   Warner, Okla
Admitted. 1st cousin once removed of 13022 and claims through
same source. Applicant's grandmother enrolled as "Martha Lee"
Can. 38.
ROLL P93 #17823 FCT COMM # 4409 - Thomas McDaniel - 30
         17824   4410 - Willis (son)   - 8
         17825   4411 - Louie T. (son) - 5
         17826   4928m - Noah (son)   - 3
         17827   - Susie (dau)   - 1

12852. F. E. THOMPSON, N. B. THOMPSON,   Warner, Okla
        N. F. THOMPSON, IRA THOMPSON, E. M. THOMPSON
        & M. M. THOMPSON,
Admitted. Claims through their mother Malinta [? blurred] D.
Thompson by their father John W. Thompson. 1st cousin once re-
moved of Oscar Jones, App 5614 and admitted for same reasons.
ROLL P138 #26753 FCT COMM #17281 - Florence E. Thompson - 15
          26754   17282 - Nora B. (dau) [sic]   - 14
          26755   17283 - Nellie F. (dau) [sic] - 12
          26756   17284 - Ira L. (son) [sic]   - 10
          26757   17285 - Ella M. (dau) [sic]   - 5
          26758   17286 - Mary M. (dau) [sic]   - 3
                              by John W. Thompson, Father

12853. THOMAS T. FLETCHER,   Braggs, Okla
Admitted. Nephew of 205 [? blurred] and claims through same
source.
ROLL P61 #11408 FCT COMM #32490 - Thomas T. Fletcher - 34

12854. SARAH JANE MANNING,   Braggs, Okla
Admitted. Niece of 1596 and claims through same ancestors.
ROLL P96 #18264 - Sarah Jane Manning - 40

12855. LOUISA PRUITT,   City, N C
Rejected. Sizemore case. See special report in #417.

12856. CALLIE OSBORN,   Laurel Springs, N C
Rejected. Sizemore case. See special report in #417.

12857. NINA OSBORN,   Laurel Springs, N C
Rejected. Sizemore case. See special report in #417.

12858. RUFUS B. OSBORN,   Laurel Springs, N C
Rejected. Sizemore case. See special report in #417.

12859. RUFUS MABE,   Laurel Springs, N C
Rejected. Sizemore case. See special report in #417.

12860. GEO. ORSBORN and 3 children,   Ratler, N C
Rejected. Sizemore case. See special report in #417.

12861. CICERO ORSBORN,   Laurel Springs, N C
Rejected. Sizemore case. See special report in #417.

12862. ROSIN MABE,   Laurel Springs, N C
Rejected. Sizemore case. See special report in #417.

12863. ROSINA MABE,   Laurel Springs, N C
Rejected. Sizemore case. See special report in #417.

12864. WM. C. WILLIAMS,   Oronogo, Mo
Rejected. Claims through same source as #12708.

12865. DAVIS WILLIAMS and 2 children,   California, Mo
Rejected. Claims through same source as #12708.

12866. SARAH L. ROBERTS and 1 child,   California, Mo
Rejected. Claims through same source as #12708.

12867. JOHN D. WILLIAMS,   California, Mo
Rejected. Claims through same source as #12708.

12868. ISAAC H. WILLIAMS and 5 children, California, Mo
Rejected. Claims through same source as #12708.

12869. THOS. C. WILLIAMS and 6 children, California, Mo
Rejected. Claims through same source as #12708.

12870. MARINA WILSON and 4 children,   Russellville, Mo
Rejected. Claims through same source as #12708.

12871. JOSEPH G. MURRAY and 7 children,   McGirk, Mo
Rejected. Claims through same source as #12708.

12872. ELIZABETH MURRAY and 3 children,   Versailles, Mo
Rejected. Claims through same source as #12708.

12873. BENJ. W. MURRAY and 7 children,   Mark, Okla
Rejected. Claims through same source as #12708.

12874. JOHN MURRAY and 7 children,   McGirk, Mo
Rejected. Claims through same source as #12708.

12875. FRED MURRAY,   California, Mo
Rejected. Claims through same source as #12708.

12876. CHAS. MURRAY and 5 children,   Russellville, Mo
Rejected. Claims through same source as #12708.

12877. TESSIE M. THORN,   Cottage Grove, Ore
Rejected. It does not appear that any ancestor was ever enrolled or that any ancestor was party to the treaties of 1835-
1836, 46. Shows no real connection with the Eastern Cherokees.
EXCEPTION CASE. 12877. Tessie May Thorn, Cottage Grove, Ore.,
by Mary J. Thorn, mother. Rejected. Total number of exceptions filed in this group -- 4. Original recommendation renewed. The father of applicant through whom claim is made was
enrolled as an Old Settler at Group #163 Canadian District.

12878. FRANKIE SHORTRIDGE and 3 children, Cottage Grove, Ore
Rejected. Sister of 12877 and claims through same source.

12879. MARY JANE THORN,   Cottage Grove, Ore
Rejected. Mother of 12877 and claims through same source.
(Deceased husband).

12880. JOHN W. THORN,   Cottage Grove, Ore
Rejected. Brother of 12877 and claims through same source.

12881. WILLIAM E. LINDSAY and 3 children, Rocky Face, Ga
Rejected. Ancestors not on rolls. Were not parties to trea-
ties of 1835-6-46. Did not part [sic] in tribal proceedings.
Applicant fails to show genuine connection with the Cherokee
tribe. Misc. Test. P. 1328.
MISC. TEST. P. 1328. No 12881 - William E. Lindsay:
    "My name is William E. Lindsay; I was born in Pickens Co.,
Ga. 1858; I claim my Indian blood through my father; I make no
claim through my mother; my father was born in Pickens Co.,
Ga. about 1832; my father got his Indian blood through his
mother, whose maiden name was Jane Mendenall; my grandmother
was born in Whitfield Co., Ga. 1783; I am unable to trace back
farther than my grandmother; I think my grandmother got her
Indian blood through her father; I do not know the given name
of my great grandfather; in 1835 my father and his mother
lived in Pickens Co., Ga.; in 1851 they lived in the same
place; I never heard of them being enrolled at that time; in

390

1882 I lived in Bartow Co., Ga.; I never heard of the enrollment of 1882; none of the ancestors through whom I claim ever
were held in bondage; my grandmother and father lived as white
settlers among Cherokee Indians; my grandmother was a half
blood Cherokee; none of my ancestors through whom I claim ever
went West with the Indians that I know of; my father never
lived with the Indians as a member of the tribe, simply as a
white settler, but was recognized as being part Indian, or a
quarter Cherokee. See Affidavits filed herewith."
SIGNED: William E. Lindsay, Dalton, Ga., Jul 10 1908.
EXCEPTION CASE. 12881. William E. Lindsay & 3 children, RFD
#1, Rocky Face, Ga. Rejected. Total number of exceptions
filed in this group -- 4. Original recommendation renewed.

12882. LIZZIE GRITTS,   Vian, Okla
Admitted. The mother and uncles of applicant were enrolled by
Drennen in 1851 in 394 Flint.
ROLL P68 #12691 FCT COMM #18091 - Anderson W. Gritts - 56
                                  (App 16722)
            12692   18092 - Lizzie (wife)   - 51

12883. RICHARD B. SANDERS,   Marble, Okla
Admitted. 1st cousin of 14786 and claims through same source.
Father "Samuel Sanders, 567 Flint."
ROLL P123 #23647 FCT COMM #3285 - Richard B. Sanders - 22

12884. RICHARD WILKERSON and 4 children,   Dewey, Okla
Admitted. The father and grandfather of applicant were en-
rolled by Drennen in 1851 in 602 and 603 Going Snake Dist.
ROLL P151 #29225 FCT COMM #12386 - Richard Wilkerson - 39
            29226   12387 - Annie (wife) -35(App 13053)
            29227   12388 - Ella M. (dau)   - 12
            29228   12389 - Katy (dau)   - 9
            29229   12390 - Oliver C. (son)   - 7
            29230   324m - William (son)   - 4

12885. HENRY B. McCLURE and 6 children,   Porum, Okla
Admitted. Brother of 161 and claims through same ancestors.
ROLL P92 #17636 FCT COMM #5798 - Henry B. McClure   - 50
            17637   5800 - Kathryn (dau)   - 18
            17638   5801 - Thomas (son)   - 16
            17639   5802 - Minnie F. (dau)   - 9
            17640   5803 - Hazel (dau)   - 5
            17641   517m - Ella (dau)   - 3
            17642   5804 - Vida E. JAMISON (gdau) - 6

12886. ANNIE CALDWELL,   Claremore, Okla
Admitted. Sister to Jack Quinton 16904 and claims through the
same source.
MISC. TEST. P. 4126. App No 12886-16904 - Annie Caldwell:
    "I am 47 years of age. I was enrolled by the Dawes Commis-
sion, No 18698. I get my Indian blood from my mother, Nellie

391

Quinton nee Langley. She lived in G. S. district. She died in
Ill. District. My father was an Osage and his mother was an
Osage. My grandfather was a white man. They never established
the Osage rights as they always lived among the Cherokees.
Bill and Sam Quinton, also Jim Quinton were my uncles. My
mother also lived in Canadian District. My parents were living
in Georgia in 1851. Lock Langley was my grandfather. Nellie
was in Georgia in 1851. They came here to the West with the
Indians and then went back to Georgia. Peggy Langley was my
grandmother's name. My grandfather was married twice, his
second wife being Sarah or Sallie. I never saw my grandmother;
she died before 1851. Lock Langley married Peggy's full sister, Sallie, the second time. The children of Lock and Sallie
were: Albert, Bayless M., Anna, Samuel, Thos., Susan, John,
Josiah, Caroline, Fannie and Lucy. Mary Ellen who married John
Williams was a daughter by the first wife. Margaret was another and she married Moore. Mary Ellen came to the Territory
about thirty years ago. There were two Lock Langleys and the
second one was a cousin of my mother. I have never affiliated
with any other tribe of Indians. I cannot explain why my grand
mother's children were not enrolled. (See Ch. 1916 and 1917).
Nellie, George and James were the other children of Lock and
Peggy. Missouri Emeline Rogers is my sister and is 46 years of
age." SIGNED: Annie Caldwell, Claremore, Okla., Mar 11 1909.
J. W. Leach in behalf of above, states:
    "I know Annie Caldwell, have known her about 20 years. I
knew her mother, Nellie Quinton. I can give no reason why Nellie Quinton was not enrolled in 1851. I have heard that they
drew Emigrant money in 1851. Mrs. Caldwell is recognized in
this community as an Emigrant Cherokee Indian."
SIGNED: J. W. Leach [probably same date and place]
ROLL P37 #6520 - Annie Caldwell - 47

12887. ALONA J. CANARY and 4 children,   Caney, Kan
Admitted. 2nd cousin of 3080, and claims through same ancestors. Grandmother of applicant, Rebecca Coeman [sic - should
be "Coleman"], enrolled in 1851, in Disputed Dist. 94.
ROLL P37 #6589 FCT COMM #26240 - Anola J. Canary - 34
           6590   26241 - Emma P. (dau)   - 15
           6591   26242 - Simeon C. (son) - 14
           6592   26243 - James H. (son) - 11
           6593   26244 - Elmira L. (dau) - 9

12888. STEPHEN M. McDANIEL, for minor wards, Warner, Okla
         ARCH & NARCIE MUSKRAT
Admitted. Half sister & brother of 12840.
ROLL P103 #19789 FCT COMM #28244 - Arch Muskrat - 18
          19790   25419 - Narcie (sis) - 16
                          by Stephen M. McDaniel, Gdn
12889. ROBERT E. WILLIAMS and 1 child,   Muskogee, Okla*
                                       511 S. B. Street
Admitted. Nephew of 929. Claims through same source.

392

[* Residence on roll "Yuma, Arizona, U. S. Constable"]
ROLL P151 #29388 FCT COMM #5542 - Robt. E. Williams - 30
          29389   - Hattie O. (wife) - 28
                               (App 29114)
          29390   6965 - Vera F. (dau)   - 9

12890. SARAH QUINTON, Duplicate of 11260.

12891. ANNIE E. PRIM and 1 child,   Miami, Okla
Admitted. Niece of 2919. Daughter of 8696.
ROLL P113 #21706 FCT COMM #10238 - Annie E. Prim   - 30
          21707   820m - Lawrence D. (son) - 1

12892. CICERO L. LYNCH, minor, Duplicate of 12893.

12893. JOHN B. LYNCH and 2 children,   Bunch, Okla
Admitted. Applicant's father "Leonida Lynch" enrolled 373
Saline. 1st cousin to #998.
ROLL P92 #17498 FCT COMM # 2354 - John B. Lynch - 38
          17499   2355 - Cicero L. Jr. (son) - 12
                               (App 12892)
**   17500   2718m - Nancy Esther (dau) - 1**
[** entire line crossed out - under "NAMES...TO BE STRICKEN
FROM THE ROLL" is the explanation that Roll #17500 is a dupli-
cate of Roll #17507, dau of Mariah Lynch, App 28387]

12894. DAVID J. FAULKNER and 3 children,   Claremore, Okla
Admitted. Brother of 9183.
ROLL P59 #10916 FCT COMM # 3712 - David J. Faulkner - 32
          10917   11540 - Jennie (wife) -28(App 12895)
          10918   26677 - Janice M. (dau)   - 5
          10919   1638m - Lavinah H. (dau) - 3
          10920   1639m - Frank F. (son)   - 1

12895. JENNIE FAULKNER,   Claremore, Okla
Admitted. Niece of 1816. [For Roll information See App 12894]

12896. EMMA LOVELESS TICE,   [no residence]
Rejected. Cousin to H. J. Holcomb 3075 and claims through the
same source.

12897. LONA L. NICHOLS & 2 children, RFD 2, Booneville, Miss
Rejected. Cousin to H. J. Holcomb, 3075 and claims through
the same source.

12898. SAM B. LOVELESS & 2 children, RFD 2, Booneville, Miss
Rejected. Cousin to H. J. Holcomb 3075 and claims through the
same source.

12899. DELLA LEE LOVELESS WINDHAM & 1 child, Booneville, Miss
                                           R F D #2
Rejected. Cousin to H. J. Holcomb 3075 and claims through the

same source.

12900. CATHERINE BUTLER and 3 children,   Tahlequah, Okla
Admitted. Sister of 4329.
ROLL P37 #6414 FCT COMM #27781 - Catherine Butler - 30
            6415   27783 - Daniel R. (son) - 16
            6416   27784 - James L. (son)   - 13
            6417   27785 - Pierce P. (son) - 8

12901. WENONA BARNES and 5 children,   Briartown, Okla
Admitted. Aunt of 10746, and claims through same source.
ROLL P26 #4292 FCT COMM #27389 - Wenona Barnes   - 43
            4293   27390 - Charles (son)   - 20
            4294   27392 - Cornelious (son) - 16
            4295   42393 - Oscar (son)   - 11
            4296   42395 - Bulah (dau)   - 5
            4297   27391 - Jamie (dau)   - 18

12902. WALTER POLECAT and 5 children,   Long, Okla
Admitted. Son of 2826. Grandparent "Polecat and Sealy 534
Del." Father says he was born in 1850, but thinks he may be
mistaken or under a different name.
ROLL P112 #21491 FCT COMM #3994 - Walter Polecat - 36
            21492   3995 - Lucy (wife)   - 34
                               (App 17053)
            21493   3996 - Betsey (dau)   - 13
            21494   3997 - Isaac (son)   - 11
            21495   3998 - Levi (son)   - 9
            21496   3999 - Sarah Ann (dau) - 6
            21497   3914m - Bethel (son)   - 2

12903. AKIE COLEMAN,   Long, Okla
Admitted. Niece of 2743 and claims through same source. Ap-
plicant's father enrolled in S. B. #29. Daughter of 9890.
ROLL P45 #8068 FCT COMM #3880 - Akie Coleman - 26

12904. MARY E. HOLT, Tuxie T.   Long, Okla
       and JACOB D. HOLT, by Sarah H. Holt, Gdn.
Admitted. Niece and nephew of 10278.
ROLL P77 #14534 FCT COMM #22938 - Mary E. Holt - 12
            14535   22939 - Tuxie T. (sis) - 10
            14536   22940 - Jacob D. (bro) - 8
                               by Sarah H. Holt, Gdn.

12905. FRANCES HOLT, Annie Holt, Gdn.   Long, Okla
This applicant included with mother 1892.

12906. CELIA SANDERS,   Long, Okla
Admitted. 1st cousin of 2743 and claims through same source.
Applicant's father enrolled S. B. #29. [For Roll information
See App 9184, Vol. 4]

12907. FLORENCE SANDERS MILLER and 6 children, Nanson, Okla
Admitted. Applicant is a sister of 1053.
ROLL P99 #18927 FCT COMM #3539 - Florence Sanders Miller - 36
         18928   3540 - Hettie L. (dau)   - 15
         18929   3541 - William J. J. (son)   - 12
         18930   3542 - Thomas F. (son)   - 10
         18931   3543 - Ida J. (dau)   - 7
         18932   3544 - Grayson N. (son)   - 4
         18933   3856m - Waitie H. (dau)   - 2

12908. JESSIE L. WILSON and 2 children,   Vian, Okla
Admitted. Applicant's mother born after 1851.   Grandparents
Benj. and Coty Drowning bear enrolled Saline 563.
ROLL P152 #29492 FCT COMM #5649 - Jessie L. Wilson - 27
         29493   5650 - Chas. A. (son)   - 5
         29494   558m - Keener C. (son)   - 1

12909. KATIE THOMPSON, Included in App 12912.

12910. GRACIE THOMPSON, Included in App 12912.

12911. WM. THOMPSON, Included in App 12912.

12912. NARCISSA COLLINS and 3 children,   Porom, Okla
Admitted. Great aunt of 10661, claims through the same source.
Applicant's father enrolled S. B. #39 as Robertson Brown.
ROLL P45 #8165 FCT COMM #27340 - Narcissa Collins   - 45
         8166   27341 - Willliam THOMPSON (son) - 17
         8167   27342 - Gracie THOMPSON (dau)   - 15
         8168   27343 - Katie THOMPSON (dau)   - 13

12913. EURA SCOTT,   909 Chestnut St., Porum, Okla*
Admitted.   Cousin of 8136. [* "St. Louis, Mo." on roll -
street address same]
ROLL P124 #23873 FCT COMM #22047 - Eura Scott - 26

12914. LUCINDA DAVIS,   Porum, Okla
Admitted. Aunt of 10746 and claims through same source. [For
Roll information See App 12916]

12915. GEORGIA A. DUNAGAN,   Porum, Okla
Admitted. Sister of 3707. Is enrolled in 1851 by Chapman 1750
ROLL P56 #10249 FCT COMM #25526 - Georgia Ann Dunagan - 58

12916. SAMUEL DAVIS,   Porum, Okla.
Admitted. Brother of 3707. Enrolled in 1851 by Chapman 1751.
ROLL P52 #9427 FCT COMM #17072 - Samuel Davis   - 56
         9428   17073 - Lucinda (wife) - 66
                      (App 12914)

12917. LEVI TONEY,   Porum, Okla
Admitted. Applicant's father enrolled by enrolled 1851 Saline

23. [For Roll information See App 12579]

12918. JOHN TONEY and 5 children,   Porum, Okla
Admitted. Brother of 12917.
ROLL P140 #27161 FCT COMM #18750 - John Toney   - 52
            27162   18754 - Mary (dau)   - 16
            27163   18755 - George (son) - 14
            27164   18756 - Jesse (son)   - 12
            27165   18757 - Famous (son) - 8
            27166   - Lela (dau)   - 3

12919. TASTING JESSE and 4? [sic] children, Maysville, Ark
Admitted. Applicant claims through father enrolled as Che-
ste-quo-le in Del. 60. Grandfather Wah-ne-naw-ha 60 Del.
ROLL P81 #15318 - Tasting Jesse - 49
          15319 - Jennie (wife) - 26 (App 12921)
          15320 - Nancy (dau)   - 16
          15321 - Fannie (dau) - 12
          15322 - Robert (son) - 4
          15323 - Annie (dau)   - 1/6

12920. ELIZABETH KUL-STOO-KER-SKY,   Southwest City, Mo
Admitted. Aunt of 1558. [Notation on roll "Leaf, Elizabeth.
See Roll No. 16487."]
ROLL P87 #16487 - Elizabeth Kul-stoo-her-sky - 41

12921. JENNIE JESSE,   Maysville, Ark
Admitted. Cousin of 1558. [For Roll information See App
12919 - Notation on roll "Drinker, Jennie. See Roll No.
15319." which is applicant's roll No.]

12922. IKE CHEATER,   Maysville, Ark
Admitted. Uncle of 1558.
ROLL P41 #7276 FCT COMM #19456 - Ike Cheater - 52
          7277   19457 - Jane (wife) - 61 (App 13359)

12923. GOODMONEY JESSE,   Maysville, Ark
Admitted. Son of 12919.
ROLL P67 #12420 - Jesse Goodmoney - 29

12924. SUSIE HOGSHOOTER,   Maysville, Ark
Admitted. Grandniece of 1245, and claims through same ances-
tors. Grandfather of applicant enrolled in 1851 under name of
Ter-ger-wor-se, in Saline Dist. #103.
ROLL P76 #14351 FCT COMM #28966 - Charley Hogshooter - 27
                                  (App 27658)
          14352   15605 - Susie (wife)   - 24

12925. CLAUDE CRUTCHFIELD and 2 children, Inola, Okla
Admitted. 1st cousin of 977. Claims through the same source.
Grandfather "John Crutchfield" 498 Del.

```
ROLL P49 #8961 FCT COMM #28099 - Claude Crutchfield - 26
         8962            28101 - Ray (bro)         - 18
         8963            28102 - Henry G. (bro)    - 16
```

12926. EZRA B. WEAVER,   1018 S. Race St., Marion, Ind
Rejected. Claims through same source as 10886.

12927. MARY E. SMITH & 3 children, 213 E 14th St, Marion, Ind
Rejected. Claims through same source as 10886.

12928. CHARITY MOORE,   645 E. Dayton St., Madison, Wis
Rejected. Claims through same source as 10886.
MISC. TEST. P. 1839. Alfred Weaver:
    "I am 78 years old, and I live in Grant County. I come
from N. C. I came in 1844. I am acquainted with Charity Moore,
she was my first wife. She lives now in Wis. I was divorced
from her about 30 years ago. Her father was Micaga Revels. I
knew him down in Howard County, Ind. He came from Guilford
County in 1840. He always claimed to be part Cherokee Indian
ever since I knew him. Charity Moore is the daughter of Revels
Mary E. Smith and Sinthy Prim are the daughters of Charity
Moore. I have heard Micaga Revels talk many a time about his
Indian blood. I do not know how he was recognized in N. C. in
regard to his Indian blood, as I have only known him since he
came here. He died up in Wisc. He died in 1883. He appeared
to be an Indian. I never heard him say that got [sic] any
money from the Government on account of his Indian blood."
SIGNED: Alfred Weaver, Marion, Ind., Aug 13 1908.

12929. CYNTHIA PRIM & 3 children, 1018 S Race St, Marion, Ind
Rejected. Claims through same source as 10886.

12930. MALINDA SMITH,   1302 S. Net St., Marion, Ind
Rejected. Claims through same source as 10886.

12931. ELLIS STARR,   Porum, Okla
Admitted. Father of 10746 and claims through same source.
ROLL P132 #25432 FCT COMM #5229 - Ellis Starr - 31

12932. SUSAN FOSTER,   Claremore, Okla
Admitted. 1st cousin of 1089. Grandfather "Joseph Miller,
904 Del." [For Roll information See App 12933]

12933. JOHN FOSTER and 6 children,   Claremore, Okla
Admitted. Brother of 1350, and claims through same source.
```
ROLL P63 #11695 FCT COMM #11290 - John Foster   - 37
         11696            11291 - Susan (wife)- 36(App 12932)
         11697            11292 - Jane (dau)     - 14
         11698            11293 - Margaret (dau) - 12
         11699            11294 - Annie (dau)    - 10
         11700            11295 - James (son)    -  5
         11701             507m - Joseph (son)   -  2
```

12933. JOHN FOSTER (Cont)
11702   - William (son) - 1/12

12934. ROSA J. SIZEMORE,   Pineville, W Va
Rejected. Sizemore case. See report in #417.

12935. DELPHIA M. SIZEMORE,   Pineville, W Va
Rejected. Sizemore case. See report in #417.

12936. BESSIE E. SIZEMORE,   Pineville, W Va
Rejected. Sizemore case. See report in #417.

12937. GEO. H. SIZEMORE,   Pineville, W Va
Rejected. Sizemore case. See report in #417.

12938. ELLIS N. COOKS and 1 child,   Matoka, W Va
Rejected. Sizemore case. See report in #417.

12939. MARY M. HORTON and 3 children,   Joe Branch, W Va
Rejected. Sizemore case. See report in #417.

12940. W. D. SIZEMORE,   Diana, W Va
Rejected. Sizemore case. See report in #417.

12941. ELIZA ANN REAGAN, Gdn. for 3 children, Mecca, Tenn
Rejected. Applicant nor ancestors never enrolled. Does not appear that they were living within the Cherokee Domain in 1835
1836-46 as recognized members of the tribe. Does not appear
that they ever lived with the Cherokee tribe. Misc. Test. P598
MISC. TEST. P. 598. #12941 - Eliza Ann Reagan:
     "That I am 52 years of age and live in Monroe Co., Tenn.
I am making claim for my children through their father.   His
name was Michael A. Reagan. His parents were William and Emeline Reagan. His mother was the Indian. His grandfather was
the Indian. His name was Henry Weise or Weice.   I don't know
where he was born and raised. I don't know where my husband's
mother was born and raised. Whenever I heard of her she lived
in Monroe Co., Tenn. She has been dead three years. Don't know
when Weice died. My husband's mother was 1/2 Cherokee. Don't
know whether she ever lived with the Indians or not, nor his
grandparents. None of them were on any rolls that I know of.
I can't give the names of my husband's uncles and aunts. I remember one, Dan Weise.   My husband was recognized as a white
man with Cherokee Indian blood. He never lived with the Indians. He has been dead two years and was 54 when he died. He
was never on any rolls that I know of. There is no one living
who can give any more information than I can. #15756 was also
filed by me and was made for the same purpose as 12941."
SIGNED: Eliza Ann Reagan, Athens, Tenn., Jun 24 1908.

12942. JAMES H. HELTON and 4 children,   Cedertown, Ga
Rejected. Brother of 10480, and claims through same source.

12943. STELLA M. SIZEMORE,   Pineville, W Va
Rejected. Sizemore case. See report in #417.

12944. ROBERT N. SIZEMORE,   Pineville, W Va
Rejected. Sizemore case. See report in #417.

12945. GEO. W. COX and 6 children,   Spring Place, Ga
Rejected. It does not appear that applicant's ancestors were
parties to treaties of 1835-6-46 nor enrolled with Cherokees.
Misc. Test. P. 1431. [For Testimony See App 11180]
EXCEPTION CASE. Rejected. Total number of exceptions filed
in this group -- 32. Original recommendation renewed. Note:
This case groups with Elizabeth J. Keefe, No. 11180 -- and
claims through the same source.

12946. HENRY J. MANER and 1 child,   Catoosa, Okla
Rejected. Applicant is a nephew of #532.

12947. JAMES COX and 10 children,   RFD, Rome, Ga
Rejected. Brother of 12945.

12948. LAURA ANN CARTER   RFD 6, Dalton, Ga
Rejected. Sister of 12945.

12949. ELMIRA BAKER and 3 children, RFD 5, Dalton, Ga
Rejected. Sister to 12945.

12950. NORA L. PHILLIPS and 1 child,   Bartlesville, Okla
Rejected. Claims through Alex. Brown. See #35.

12951. JAMES A. MANER,   Catoosa, Okla
Rejected. Nephew of 532.

12952. MARY BROWN and 2 children,   Spring Place, Ga
Rejected. Sister of 12945.

12953. JOHN A. COX and 4 children,   Spring Place, Ga
Rejected. Brother of 12945.

12954. ARDENIA J. MANER, Gdn. for   Catoosa, Okla
          CHAS., ALFORD P., JESSIE A. MANER
Rejected. Nieces and nephews of 532.

12955. CALLY JONES and 5 [?] children,   Spring Place, Ga
Rejected. Sister of 12945.

12956. ELLA V. CRAFT and 2 children,   Bartlesville, Okla
Rejected. Claims through Alex. Brown. See #35.

12957. SARAH I. BLACKWELL, Duplicate of 11619.

12958. HARVEY B. PEEK and 4 children,   Long Beach, Cal
Rejected. Nephew of 9754.

12959. WM. G. HARE,   Lodi, Va
Rejected. Sizemore case. See report in #417.

12960. HARVEY R. HART,   Lodi, Va
Rejected. Sizemore case. See report in #417.

12961. ELZINA BLEVINS and 3 children,   Park, Va
Rejected. Sizemore case. See report in #417.

12962. LOYD BLEVINS and 4 children,   Lodi, Va
Rejected. Sizemore case. See report in #417.

12963. FRANKLIN M. BLEVINS,   Park, Va
Rejected. Sizemore case. See report in #417.

12964. MARCALA [sic] and 1 child,   Green Cove, Va
Rejected. Sizemore case. See report in #417. [Name "Marcala
Blevins" in index.]

12965. NAOMY J. ANDERSON,   Burke, W Va
Rejected. Sizemore case. See report in #417.

12966. WM. R. BLEVIS and 5 children,   Green Cove, Va
Rejected. Sizemore case. See report in #417.

12967. NANCY J. WIDENER,   Lodi, Va
Rejected. Sizemore case. See report in #417.

12968. JENNIE PUMPKIN,   Whitmore, Okla
Admitted. Applicant's grandmother enrolled as Nancy Manns in
1851 in G. S. 636. Daughter of 10697.
MISC. TEST. P. 3551. Witness for 12968 - Mary Pumpkin, witness
for her daughter, Jennie Pumpkin:
    "Jennie Pumpkin is my daughter. She is about 24 years of
age. I have in an application for this money. Eli Pumpkin was
a full blood Indian. He is Jennie's husband. John Wildcat was
Jennie's father. He was not living at the time of the Immigrant payment. I was not living then either. I had some brothers that drew Immigrant money. My mother also drew. Her name
was Nancy Manus. My father was a white man. My oldest brother
was George, then next Bill, Sam, John and Wesley."
SIGNED: Mary Pumpkin, Tahlequah, Okla., Oct 6 1908.
[For Roll information See App 9246, Vol. 4]

12969. MARY M. THOMPSON, Arch Thompson, Gdn., Muldrow, Okla
Admitted. Grand nephew [sic] of 901. Claimant's maternal
grandfather enrolled in 1851 by Drennen S. B. 285.
ROLL P139 #26856 FCT COMM #3790 - Margy M. Thompson - 4
                              by Arch Thompson, Gdn.

400

12970. JOHN C. PETTY,   Blainsville, Ga
Rejected. Ancestors of applicant do not appear to be enrolled.
It seems that they were not parties to the treaties of 1835-6,
46. Information in application and letters insufficient.

12971. MARK BREWER and 1 child,   Black Gum, Okla
Admitted. Applicant born after 1851 probably. Mother Lydia
Griffin with children Andy and Emmer enrolled in Flint 380.
Father Isaac and Uncle James 127. S. B.
ROLL P33 #5758 FCT COMM #28367 - Mack Brewer - 45
         5759   2464m - Alice (dau) - 1

12972. MARY CATHERINE ANDERSON,   Robbinsville, N C
Rejected. Ancestors do not appear on the roll. It seems they
were not parties to the treaties. Information in application &
letters insufficient. Applicant failed to appear when notified

12973. MANUS SCREENER,   Cherokee, N C
Admitted. Father no[t] living in 1851. Grandmother Niche [?]
C. 347. Fathers brother Cho-co-na-leh 348 C. Fathers brother
Woseh-Moses 3500.
ROLL P16 #2317 - Manus Screamer - 24

12974. LUCINDA NIGAJACK,   Folcroft, Pa
Admitted. 1st cousin once removed of $200 [sic - should be
6200]. Applicant's grandfather enrolled by Chapman in 1851 as
Sie-quo-ih #248.
ROLL P13 #1760 - Lucinda Nigajack or Welch - 23

12975. JACKSON SAWNOOKE,   Cherokee, N C
Admitted. Nephew of 6645 and claims through same source.
ROLL P16 #2276 - Jackson Sawnooka - 24

12976. JONAS JACKSON,   Birdtown, N C
Admitted. Son of 6653. Brother of 11139.
ROLL P11 #1254 - Jonas Jackson - 24

12977. HENRY C. WILLIAMS, Duplicate of 7711.

12978. ROSA B. BORDERS and 1 child,   Wavahachie [sic], Tex
Rejected. Sizemore case. See report in #417.

12979. J. B. BAILEY,   Nevada [sic]
Rejected. Sizemore case. See report in #417.

12980. W. W. BAILEY,   San Antonio, Tex
Rejected. Sizemore case. See report in #417.

12981. MELVIN C. BAILEY,   Midlothian, Tex
Rejected. Sizemore case. See report in #417.

12982. WILLIAM C. HEMBREE and 7 children, Roswell, Ga
Rejected. Applicant born a slave. Mother a slave. Grandfather
a slave. See letter herein.

12983. AMANDA KIRK and 1 child,   Roswell, Ga
Rejected. Sister of 12982. Claims through same source.

12984. OCTAVIA HEMBREE and 6 (?) [sic] children, Roswell, Ga
Rejected. Ancestors not enrolled. They were not parties to the
treaties. Information in Application and letters insufficient.

12985. H. K. MILLER,   Beldon, N C
Rejected. Sizemore case. See report in #417.

12986. LAVANA MILLER and 6 children,   Beldon, N C
Rejected. Sizemore case. See report in #417.

12987. ELIZA OSBORN,   Harmon, N C
Rejected. Sizemore case. See report in #417.

12988. EMORY OSBORN,   Harmon, N C
Rejected. Sizemore case. See report in #417.

12989. HARRISON E. COLEMAN and 4 children, Birdtown, N C
Rejected. Brother to Bird Walk (9333) whose mother was a
slave. Appl. also a slave.

12990. PATSY J. BRENDLE,   Bryson City, N C
Rejected. Betsy Walker case. See special report in #500.

12991. JOHNSON LONG,   Birdtown, N C
Admitted. Claims through father enrolled as A-len-neh. Sisters
enrolled as Quee-neh and Sut-tah-ga-nee-tah, Chap. 1446-6 & 7.
ROLL P12 #1544 - Johnson Long - 46 [? ages cut off]
        1545 - Maggie (wife) - 36 [?] (App 12994)

12992. WINNIE E. PARTRIDGE,   Trough, S C
Admitted. Applicant claims through father David Partridge in
[sic] Da-wee-goo-qua enrolled by Chap. #820. The earlier
spelling Too-wih.
ROLL P14 #1890 - Winnie E. Partridge - 20

12993. MOSE PARTRIDGE,   Birdtown, N C
Admitted. Brother of 12992.
ROLL P14 #1887 - Mose Partridge - 23
        1888 - Sallie (wife) - 19 (App 28782)

12994. MAGGIE LONG,   Birdtown, N C
Admitted. Sister of #12992. [For Roll info. See App 12991]

12995. NELLY PARTRIDGE,   Birdtown, N C
Admitted. Applicant's mother Dakie enrolled as Akih, Chapman

402

#881. Grandmother Too-kah Chap. 879. Uncle E-lan-cih 832 Chap.
ROLL P14 #1889 - Nelly Partridge - 53

12996. AWEE S. FRENCH and 5 children,   Birdtown, N C
Admitted. The mother of applicant was enrolled as Sic-ou-ih
by Chapman in 1851, 423. Father probably enrolled by Chapman
as Sal-lah-lih as Squirrel 240.
ROLL P9 #842 - Awee S. French - 32
        843 - Maud (dau)   - 12
        844 - Maronie (dau)   - 9
        845 - Morgan (son)   - 7
        846 - Soggie (son)   - 5
        847 - George B. (son) - 2

12997. JOHN W. TUCKER and 1 child,   Weasel, N C
Rejected. Sizemore case. See report in #417.

12998. LAURA M. WAGONER and 2 children,   Weasel, N C
Rejected. Sizemore case. See report in #417.

12999. FRANKLIN SHEETS,   Harmon, N C
Rejected. Sizemore case. See report in #417.

13000. JESSE B. SHEETS and 6 children,   Harmon, N C
Rejected. Sizemore case. See report in #417.

13001. MARY SHEETS,   Harmon, N C
Rejected. Sizemore case. See report in #417.

13002. RUFUS SHEETS,   Harmon, N C
Rejected. Sizemore case. See report in #417.

13003. BENJ. F. PAYNE and 2 children, Tellico Plains, Tenn
Rejected. Neither applicant nor ancestors ever enrolled. Does
not establish fact of descent from a person who was a party to
the treaty of 1835-6-46. Claims through a daughter of Powhattan. (Misc. Test. P. 557.) [For Test. See App 3450, Vol. 2]
EXCEPTION CASE. 13003. George W. Payne, App #18339, Madisonville, Tenn. Rejected. Total number of exceptions filed in
this group -- 70. Original recommendation renewed.

13004. JOHN DOLINGER,   Rugby, Va
Rejected. Sizemore case. See report in #417.

13005. JOHN T. SIZEMORE and 4 children,   Jared, W Va
Rejected. Sizemore case. See report in #417.

13006. BENJAMIN H. HARRIS,   Ducktown, Tenn*
Admitted. Applicant claims through father not living in 1851
but the grandmother, Charlotte McDonald, is enrolled by Chap.
1289. [* "Wolf Creek, N C" crossed out]
ROLL P10 #1093 - Benjamin H. Harris - 26

13007. HOWARD PRICE,   Whitetop, N C
Rejected. Sizemore case. See report in #417.

13008. LEROY BRINEGAR and 2 children,   Airbellows, N C
Rejected. Sizemore case. See report in #417.

13009. EVERETT PRUETT,   Laurel Springs, N C
Rejected. Sizemore case. See report in #417.

13010. ANN ELIZA McCARTEY,   Jones, La
Rejected. It does not appear that any ancestor was ever enrolled or that any ancestor was party to the treaties of 1835-
1836 and 1846. Applicant don't know [sic] to what tribe of Indians ancestors belonged. Misc. Test. P. 1943.
MISC. TEST. P. 1943. #13010 - Annie E. McCarty:
    "My name is Annie E. McCarty, and I live at Jones, La. I
am 49 years old. I claim my Indian ancestry through my mother,
Dica [?] Ann Lewis. I think my mother was about 50 years old
at the time of her death. She died in Fla. in Calhoun County.
I myself was born down there, but I do not know just how long
my mother lived there. I was always told that my great grand
father, on my mother's side, was 1/2 Cherokee Indian. I think
my mother was born in Ga. but I have no knowledge of the County. My grandfather's name was Robert or Bob Lewis. He died in
Fla. when I was quite young. I just remember him. I left Fla.
and came to La. when I was about 15 years of age. My grand
father Bob Lewis must have been 1/4 Cherokee Indian. His father, my great grandfather, was 1/2 Indian. My mother and my
grandfather never got any money from the Government on account
of their Indian blood. My mother's sister who raised me, Eliza
Jane Lewis, often told me things about the Indians, and that I
myself was an Indian by blood. But she never told me just what
kind of Indian. She often told me that I was kin to the Indians. She lived in Calhoun County, Fla."
SIGNED: Annie McCarty, Montrose, Ark., Sep 1 1908.

13011. CYNTHA PARISH and 7 children,   Scottsville, N C
Rejected. Sizemore case. See report in #417.

13012. LULA PARISH,   Scottsville, N C
Rejected. Sizemore case. See report in #417.

13013. HAMPTON T. SHEETS,   Beldon, N C
Rejected. Sizemore case. See report in #417.

13014. VALE L. SHEETS,   Beldon, N C
Rejected. Sizemore case. See report in #417.

13015. JESSIE F. SHEETS,   Beldon, N C
Rejected. Sizemore case. See report in #417.

13016. JOHN C. LIPE,   Oolagah, Okla
Admitted. Brother of No 1632 and claims through same source.
ROLL P90 #17122 FCT COMM #10981 - John C. Lipe - 28

13017. MAGGIE E. LIPE,   Oolagah, Okla
Rejected. Claims through father and mother who were enrolled
as Richard and Elizabeth Thompson, sister enrolled as Nancy.
Applicant enrolled as Emma - O. S. - Ill. 16.

13018. CLARENCE LIPE,   Oolagah, Okla
             by Maggie E. Lipe, Gdn.
Admitted. Brother of No 1632 and claims through same source.
ROLL P90 #17117 FCT COMM #11713 - Clarence Lipe - 15
                                by Maggie E. Lipe, Gdn.

13019. DAGADOSE STANDINGDEER,   Wauhillah, Okla
Admitted. Brother of 6600.
ROLL P131 #25357 FCT COMM #25956 - Dagadose Standingdeer - 15

13020. MARY J. BOOKER and 1 child,   Goodway, Ala
Rejected. Creek Case. See special report in #1139.

13021. CLARK C. LIPE,   Oolagah, Okla
Admitted. Brother of No 1632 and claims through same source.
ROLL P90 #17118 FCT COMM #11712 - Clark C. Lipe - 19

13022. GEORGE DREW and 3 children,   Pueblo, Colo
Admitted. Claims through mother enrolled as Martha Lee. Grand
mother enrolled as Agnes Lee - Aunts and uncles enrolled as
Eliza, Jane, Lucy, Nelly, Laura and Nancy Lee. Canadian Dis-
trict No 38.
ROLL P55 #10107 FCT COMM #6743 - George Drew   - 34
             10108   6744 - Eugene H. (son) - 10
             10109   6745 - Richard E. (son) - 7
             10110   6746 - Eunis P. (dau)   - 4

13023. SIMPS ROBERTS,   Piedmont, Ala
Rejected. Applicant or ancestors were never enrolled. Applicant's father was a slave.

13024. MERRELL M. TAYLOR and 2 children, Minden, La
Rejected. It does not appear that any ancestor was ever en-
rolled or that any ancestor was party to the treaties of 1835-
1836 and 1846, nor does it appear that the ancestor through
whom this party claims ever lived in the Cherokee Domain.
Misc. Test. P. 1945.
MISC. TEST. P. 1945. #13024 - Merrill M. Taylor:
    "My name is Merrill M. Taylor, and I live in Minden, La.
I am 38 years old. I claim my Indian descent through my mother, Rebecca J. Monk. She died when I was a baby at Homer, La.
I think my mother was about 35 years old at the time of her
death. She was born in Harris County, Ga. She came west about

1848 with her mother and father. My mother got her Indian
blood through her farther, Merrill Monk. He was born in 1805,
near Darlington, S. C. We always understood that he was 1/4
Cherokee Indian. He died here in La. 1879. We never heard of
mother or grandfather ever getting any money from the Government on account of their Indian blood. Grandfather, Merrell
was know[n] as Captain Monk, he was under Jackson in the Fla.
war of 1835. My grandfather's mother was a Miss Flowers, she
was married near Darlington S. C. Grandfather has two daughters living, Mrs. Nettie Brown, at Arizona, La. and Mr. W. H.
Palmer at Arizona, La. also. They are very old ladies now.
They say that Merrell Monk had always claimed to be og [sic]
Cherokee Indian descent. Grandfather, Merrell Monk, was born
near Darlington, S. C. and went with his parents to Harris
County, Ga. when he was a baby."
SIGNED: Merrell Monk Taylor, Shreveport, La., Sep 3 1908.
EXCEPTION CASE. Rejected. Total number of exceptions filed
in this group -- 1. Original recommendation renewed.

13025. ANNIE HARLOW and 1 child,   Hominy, Okla
Admitted. Cousin of 833.
ROLL P71 #13304 FCT COMM #13977 - Annie Harlow - 31
        13305   13978 - Albert C. CRITTENDEN - 12
                               (son)

13026. JAMES SPEARS, by Mary J. Spearks, Gdn., Hominy, Okla
Admitted. Cousin of 833.
ROLL P131 #25238 FCT COMM #14222 - James Spears - 20
                            by Mary J. Spears, Gdn.

13027. JOE RUSK, Mary J. Spears, Gdn.,   Hominy, Okla
Admitted. 1st cousin once removed 833.
ROLL P121 #23295 FCT COMM #14223 - Joe Rusk - 6
                            by Mary J. Spears, Gdn.

13028. DENNIS S. SPEARS and 1 child,   Hominy, Okla
Admitted. Cousin of 833.
ROLL P131 #25233 FCT COMM #14219 - Dennis S. Spears - 27
        25234   4177m - Floyd (son)   - 2

13029. JOHN SPEARS,   Hominy, Okla
Admitted. Cousin of 833.
ROLL P131 #25239 FCT COMM #14220 - John Spears - 25

13030. URBANA LANE and 4 children,   Whitetop, Va
Rejected. Sizemore case. See special report in #417.

13031. WADE A. WEAVER,   Sturgill, N C
Rejected. Sizemore case. See special report in #417.

13032. NETTIE LADD and 5 children,   Wann, Okla
Admitted. Sister of #4922. Claims through same source.

```
ROLL P87 #16528 FCT COMM #10133 - Nettie Ladd      - 35
          16529          10134 - Percy H. (son)   - 13
          16530          10135 - Sadie D. (dau)   - 11
          16531          10136 - Roy (son)         - 9
          16532          10137 - Essie May (dau) -  7
          16533          2302m - Ethel (dau)      -  2
```

13033. DAVE HUGHES,   Hulbert, Okla
Admitted. Claims through grandfather enrolled as Otter-lifter
Hughes, Tahl. No 407. Father was not born in 1851.
ROLL P79 #14871 FCT COMM #16523 - Dave Hughes - 20

13034. ELLEN CARTER and 2 children,   Hulbert, Okla
Admitted. Sister of 3284 and claims through same source.

```
ROLL P39 #6899 FCT COMM #15621 - Ellen Carter        - 39
          6900          15622 - Maggie HUGHES (dau) - 18
          6901          15623 - Mattie HUGHES (dau) - 11
```

13035. MARY H. STEPHENS, Duplicate of 12564.

13036. DAVID SQUIRREL,   Birdtown, N C
Admitted. Brother of #12996; claims through same source.

```
ROLL P17 #2511 - David Squirrel - 32
          2512 - Nancy (wife)   - 31 (App 29398)
          2513 - Kimsey (son)   - 10
          2514 - Norah (dau)    -  8
          2515 - Dinah (dau)    -  6
          2516 - Daniel (son)   -  4
          2517 - Ollie (dau)    -  1
```

13037. GEORGE SQUIRREL,   Birdtown, N C
Admitted. Brother of #12996; claims through same source.

```
ROLL P17 #2519 - George Squirrel - 40
          2520 - Quattie (wife) - 36 (App 32045)
          2521 - Awee (dau)     - 17
          2522 - Sarah (dau)    - 13
          2523 - Nora (dau)     - 11
          2524 - Sequtteh (dau) -  9
          2525 - Mary (dau)     -  7
          2526 - Nancy (dau)    -  6
```

13038. JULIA EDWARDS and 5 children,   Pawhuska, Okla
Rejected. Enrolled as Osage - (see letter herein). Daughter
of #5613 and claims through same source.

13039. JOHN LONG, Jr.   Birdtown, N C
Admitted. Claims through mother enrolled as Ta-kin-nih. Grand
father and grandmother enrolled as Ten-la-whis-tah (or John
Cunnehect) and Ka-oo-chay. Chapman 1475, 6 and 8.

```
ROLL P12 #1542 - John Long  - 35
          1543 - Eve (wife) - 42 (App 13040)
```

13040. EVE LONG,   Birdtown, N C
Admitted. Claims through father and mother enrolled as E-low-
ih and Ain-ceh, C. #924-5. Brother enrolled as Choo-a-loo-kih
C. #928. [For Roll information See App 13039]

13041. HARLIN BECK and 1 child,   Row, Okla
Admitted. 1st cousin of 866. Minor child - Willie Orn Beck -
enrolled separately with mother as Gdn. See enrollment card
with #410.
ROLL P28 #4665 FCT COMM #28553 - Harlin Beck - 35

[NOTE: Notation on roll "For Willie Orien Beck, see Roll No
7808." Willie Beck is entered with his two half sisters by
their gdn., Laura Beck, residence Bloomfield, Ark. The two
girls App # is listed as "410", however, App 410 is for one
John Coats, Choteau, Okla., who was enrolled with wife and 1
child [See Vol. 1]. Neither the names of the half-sisters,
Willie Orien Beck, nor the guardian, Laura Beck, appear in the
index to applicants, their roll information is therefore
listed here.]
ROLL P43 #7806 FCT COMM #27570 - Canzadie Coats - 12 (App 410)
        7807   27571 - Novadia (sis)   - 11
        7808   4389m - Willie Orien BECK - 2
                              (1/2 bro) (App 13041)
                              by Laura Beck, Gdn.

13042. JOHN BECK,   Row, Okla
Admitted. Cousin of 866.
ROLL P28 #4692 FCT COMM #28555 - John Beck - 28

13043. WEATHERFORD BECK and 2 children,   Row, Okla
Admitted. 1st cousin of 866.
ROLL P28 #4732 FCT COMM # 1254 - Weatherford Beck - 25
        4733   22477 - John H. (son)   - 4
        4734   2954m - Lottie A. (dau)   - 2

13044. JEFFREY BECK,   Row, Okla
Admitted. 1st cousin of 866.
ROLL P28 #4682 FCT COMM #28552 - Jeffrey Beck - 37

13045. GUY BECK and 1 child,   Row, Okla
Admitted. 1st cousin of 866.
ROLL P28 #4663 FCT COMM # 1256 - Guy Beck   - 22
        4664   3733m - Arlilee (dau) - 2

13046. DIDD HOWERTON,   Row, Okla
Admitted. 1st cousin of 866.
ROLL P79 #14805 FCT COMM #7693 - Didd Howerton - 18

13047. ELIZABETH VANCE,   Superior, Neb
Rejected. Applicant and her brother were enrolled as Elizabeth, John and Randoph Denton - O. S. Sal. 127; sister en-

rolled as Neely Denton O. S. Sal. 129.

13048. ELIZABETH VANCE, Duplicate of 13047.

13049. MARGARET W. SPAINHOWER and 4 children, Pinnacle, N C
Rejected. Poindexter Case. See special report in #664.

13050. JERRY J. PATTERSON & 1 child, RFD #1, Gainesville, Ga
Rejected. First cousin once removed of 9947 and claims thru
same source.

13051. JOHN D. PATTERSON, RFD #1, Gainesville, Ga
Rejected. Nephew of #9947 and claims through same source.

13052. JAMES E. PATTERSON, RFD #1, Gainesville, Ga
Rejected. Brother of #9947 and claims through same source.

13053. ANNIE WILKERSON, Dewey, Okla
Admitted. 1st cousin of #168. [For Roll info. See App 12884]

13054. BEAR SKUL-LOR-LEE, Bartlesville, Okla
Admitted. Claimant is a brother of John Skul-lor-lee, #765
and claims through same source.
ROLL P128 #24652 FCT COMM #27715 - Bear Skul-lor-lee - 38

13055. PEGGY CHEATER, Duplicate of No 6995.

13056. LUCY CHEATER, Duplicate of 5982.

13057. BOB MIKE, Duplicate of No 6994.

13058. CELIA ALEX, Duplicate of #1823.

13059. LEWIS HITCHER, Southwest City, Mo
        by Nancy Hitcher, Gdn.
Admitted. Nephew of 11406, claims through the same ancestors.
ROLL P76 #14284 FCT COMM #30549 - Lewis Hitcher - 5
                                by Nancy Hitcher, Gdn.

13060. AGNES WARE and 6 children, Bartlesville, Okla
Rejected. Applicant has affiliated with Osages. Daughter of
#5613.

13061. GEORGE ADISON, Dayton, Tenn
Rejected. Ancestors not enrolled. Does not show genuine connection with Cherokee tribe. Applicant failed to appear to
testify. Also neglected to answer letter of inquiry in regard
to family relationship.

13062. MOLLIE DOWNING and 1 child, Estella, Okla
Admitted. Applicant's grandparents enrolled by Drennen 1852,
Del. 192. [For Roll information See App 12513]

13063. JENNIE FALLING and 1 child,   Foyil, Okla
Admitted. First cousin of No 6469 and claims through the same
source. Applicant's father enrolled, Sal. 506.
ROLL P59 #10835 FCT COMM #11280 - Calvin E. Falling - 28
                                 (App 42982)
          10836   12450 - Jennie (wife)   - 22
          10837   3524m - George (son)   - 1

13064. HENRY C. BALLARD and 5 children,   Vinita, Okla
Admitted. Applicant is a nephew of 1056. [For Roll information See App 1878, Vol. 2]

13065. JAMES F. BALLARD and 1 child,   Spavinaw, Okla
Admitted. Applicant is a nephew of 1056..
ROLL P25 #4105 FCT COMM #23488 - James F. Ballard - 48
          4106   23490 - Jno. C. (son)   - 8

13066. WINNIE DAVIS,   309 N. Compton Ave., St. Louis, Mo
Admitted. First cousin once removed of #3906. Claims through
same source.
ROLL P52 #9444 - Winnie Davis - 19

13067. CLARA POPEJOY,   Box 442, Ely, Nevada*
Admitted. First cousin once removed of 3906 and claims through
same source. [* "2112 Pine St., St. Louis, Mo." crossed out -
The St. Louis residence is shown on roll]
ROLL P112 #21555 - Clara Popejoy - 24

13068. ANNIE BARTHEL, et al, 516 Emporia St., Muskogee, Okla
          by Frank Barthel, Gdn.
Admitted. Claims through grandmother enrolled as Margaret -
Great grandmother enrolled as Eliza Taylor. Great uncles and
aunts enrolled as James, Cynthia and John. Fl. 508.
ROLL P26 #4346 FCT COMM #5335 - Annie Barthel   - 14
          4347   5336 - Frank, Jr. (bro) - 12
          4348   5337 - Mamie (sis)   - 10
          4349   5338 - William W. (bro) - 8
                             by Frank Barthel, Gdn.

13069. FRED B. DUNCAN and 1 child,   Chetopa, Kans
Admitted. Claims through mother enrolled as Martha Ann Fields.
Grandfather enrolled as Richard M. Fields. Del. No 938. Uncle
enrolled as James W. Fields, Del. 939.
ROLL P56 #10264 FCT COMM # 9857 - Fred B. Duncan   - 32
          10265   1254m - Inola Josephine (dau) - 1

13070. MARY N. DUNCAN,   Vinita, Okla
Admitted. Sister of No 13069 and claims through same source.
ROLL P56 #10316 FCT COMM #9856 - Mary N. Duncan - 33

13071. ANNIE B. JOHNSON and 5 children,   Spavinaw, Okla
Admitted. First cousin of #1687, claims through same source.

```
ROLL P81 #15359 FCT COMM #32001 - Annie B. Johnson - 22
        15360          32002 - Bertha M. (dau)  -  7
        15361          2161m - Andrew A. (son)  -  5
        15362          2162m - Roy C. (son)     -  3
        15363          2163m - Robert L. (son)  -  2
        15364                - Truly V. (dau)   - 1/6
```

13072. HIRAM T. LANDRUM,   Cleora, Okla
Admitted. First cousin of #2847.
ROLL P87 #16609 FCT COMM #17557 - Hiram T. Landrum - 24

13073. LUCINDA C. CLARK and 3 children,   Checotah, Okla
Admitted. Great aunt of #3080 and claims through same ances-
tors. Mother of applicant, Lucinda Coleman enrolled in 1851,
Disputed District No 94.

```
ROLL P43 #7641 FCT COMM #5048 - Lucinda C. Clark - 55
        7642          5053 - Austin (son)      - 19
        7643          5054 - Elita (dau)       - 16
        7644          5055 - Ruth (dau)        - 11
```

13074. LIZZIE HAIR,   Tahlequah, Okla
Admitted. Daughter of 8151.
ROLL P69 #12929 FCT COMM #18247 - Lizzie Hair - 17
                                   by Jennie Hair, Gdn.

13075. THOMAS McLEMORE,   Welling, Okla
Admitted. Brother of #4596.
ROLL P95 #18091 FCT COMM #2586 - Thomas McLemore - 30

13076. THOMAS RATTLINGGOURD, Duplicate of #10386.

13077. MARIAH RATTLINGGOURD, Duplicate of #3144.

13078. FRANK FOREMAN,   Tahlequah, Okla
Admitted. Cousin of #3206 and claims through same source.
Grandmother enrolled.
ROLL P62 #11551 FCT COMM #22159 - Frank Foreman - 11
                                   by Houston B. Tehee, Gdn.

13079. HOUSTON B. TEHEE,   Tahlequah, Okla
Admitted. Son of #13383 and claims through same source.
ROLL P137 #26577 FCT COMM #14727 - Houston B. Teehee - 32

13080. SUSAN A. E. FOREMAN,   Tahlequah, Okla
Admitted. Cousin of #3206 and claims through same source.
Grandmother enrolled.
ROLL P63 #11626 FCT COMM #22157 - Susan A. E. Foreman - 21

13081. JOHN D. R. FOREMAN,   Tahlequah, Okla
          by Houston B. Tehee, Gdn.
Admitted. Cousin of #3206 and claims through same source.

ROLL P62 #11571 FCT COMM #22158 - John D. R. Foreman - 19
                                 by Houston B. Tehee, Gdn.

13082. WILLIAM ASKWATER,   Tahlequah, Okla
Admitted. Brother of #8151.
ROLL P24 #3887 FCT COMM #21437 - William Askwater - 52

13083. COWIE JONES,   Webbers Falls, Okla
Admitted. Brother of Oscar Jones application No 5614, and is
admitted for same reasons.
ROLL P83 #15627 FCT COMM #27436 - Cowie Jones - 19

13084. ASA WILKERSON,   Webbers Falls, Okla
Rejected. Applicant's father through whom Cherokee blood is
claimed was not enrolled with the Cherokees in 1852 nor was
grandfather of applicant a party to the treaty of 1835 though
living at the time.
EXCEPTION CASE. Rejected. Total number of exceptions filed in
this group -- 5. It appears from the exceptions filed in this
case that the immediate ancestor, the grandfather of this applicant, had left the Cherokee Domain in 1835 and was not living with the tribe at that time and the family, descendants of
said ancestor, did not rejoin it until after 1851.

13085. FRANKLIN P. JONES,   Porum, Okla
Admitted. Cousin of 5614.
ROLL P83 #15637 FCT COMM #14850 - Franklin P. Jones - 22

13086. WILLIAM HITCHER,   Southwest City, Mo
        by Nancy Hitcher, Gdn.
Admitted. Nephew of #11406 and claims through same ancestors.
ROLL P76 #14294 FCT COMM #19425 - William Hitcher - 15
                                 by Nancy Hitceher, Gdn.

13087. SALLIE BUZZARD and 3 children,   Cove, Okla*
Admitted. Daughter of #10160. [* Residence "Southwest City,
Mo" on roll]
ROLL P37 #6453 FCT COMM #19794 - Jackson Buzzard - 32
                          (App 16471)
        6454   19795 - Sallie (wife)   - 37
        6455   30581 - Cennie (dau)   - 6
        6456   - Mary (dau)   - 3
        6457   - William (son)   - 2

13088. PETER DENNIS and 4 children,   Zena, Okla
Admitted. Claims through mother enrolled as Nancy Guess, Del.
103. Uncle enrolled as Moses Guess, Del. 104. Uncle enrolled
as William Guess, Del. 347.
ROLL P53 #9608 FCT COMM #19706 - Peter Dennis - 45
        9609   19707 - Mary (wife)   - 47 (App 16454)
        9610   19709 - Rachel (dau) - 18
        9611   19710 - Susie (dau) - 15

412

13088. PETER DENNIS (Cont)
        9612 FCT COMM #19711 - Jennie (dau) - 10
        9613   30566 - Jimmie (son) - 8

13089. GOBAT TUMBLEBUG, Duplicate of #4872.

13090. BILL STUDY,   Southwest City, Mo
Admitted. Applicant enrolled by Drennen 1852 as We-la. [For
Roll information See App 11972]

13091. MARY STILL and 2 children,   Sallisaw, Okla
Admitted. Applicant's father under the name of "Fog" enrolled
by Drennen in 1852 in Flint District, Group 335.   Her uncle
"Bird" in Group 336, and her uncle "Law-win" in Group 337.
ROLL P133 #25710 FCT COMM #28441 - Mary Still   - 27
         25711   25681 - Nellie (dau) - 4
         25712   2874m - Polly (dau) - 2

13092. NANCY SANDERS,   Bunch, Okla
Admitted. Sister of #1437 and claims through same source.
ROLL P123 #23640 - Nancy Sanders - 60

13093. ELIZA FRENCH and 2 children,   Stilwell, Okla
Admitted. Sister to #6535. [For Roll info. See App 13094]

13094. WILLIAM FRENCH,   Stilwell, Okla
Admitted. Nephew of #603 and claims through same source. Ap-
plicant's mother enrolled as "Sally Hopper, Flint #220."
ROLL P64 #11890 FCT COMM # 2436 - William French - 28
         11891   2437 - Eliza (wife)   - 21
                                (App 13093)
         11892   21792 - Maggie (dau)   - 4
         11893   2251m - Maud (dau)   - 1

13095. GEORGE CHEATER, Duplicate of #6991.

13096. ASY CHEATER, Duplicate of #7559.

13097. AQUILLA ALECK,   Southwest City, Mo
Admitted. Daughter of 1698 and claims through same ancestors.
Since filing application, applicant has died.
ROLL P22 #3575 FCT COMM #27618 - Aquilla Aleck - 24

13098. LEWIS SCRAPER,   Southwest City, Mo
[Admitted.] by Pauline Scraper, Sister. Nephew of #429 and
claims through same source. Minor child of #431 and enrolled
on his card as such. [For Roll information See App 431, Vol 1]

13099. ZEKE K. NIGHTKILLER,   Lometa, Okla
Admitted. Cousin of #7576 and claims through same source.
ROLL P87 #16470 FCT COMM #17903 - Zeke Knightkiller - 35

13100. DAVISON WILEY, Duplicate of #9672.

13101. WILLIAM RATTLER and 5 children,   Stilwell, Okla
Admitted. Nephew of #8355 and claims through same source.
MISC. TEST. P. 3929.   No 13101 - William Rattler...through
Interpreter, D. M. Faulkner:
    "My name is William Rattler; my post-office is Stilwell,
Okla. and I am about forty years old; my wife's name is Annie
Rattler, before marriage Annie Chuckalate, I think; Sar-da-ker
Mink has a different mother from the other children, the moth-
er was Nancy Feather and she died about seven years ago; I am
commonly known by the name of Mink; Oo-ti-yah Weavel is the
sister of the mother of Sar-da-ker Mink and Sar-da-ker is now
living with her; the child has never lived with me; Oo-ti-yah
Weavel lives near Stilwell, Okla."
SIGNED: William "X" Rattler, Muldrow, Okla., Mar 10 1909.
[NOTE: Only 4 children on roll]
ROLL P115 #22069 FCT COMM #18301 - William Rattler - 38
            22070   18303 - Lizzie (dau)   - 8
            22071   18304 - Gehena (dau)   - 6
            22072   3981m - Josie (dau)   - 3
            22073   3982m - Charley (son) - 1/4

13102. LUCY BEARHEAD and 1 child,   Southwest City, Mo
Admitted. Cousin of #6248.   Daughter of #10148.   See letter
marked "A" for identification as daughter of #10146.
ROLL P27 #4564 FCT COMM #   - Peter Bearhead - 23
                        (App 16455)
            4565   25825 - Lucy (wife)   - 26
            4566   - Nancy (dau)   - 1/4

13103. PAULINA SCRAPER,   Southwest City, Mo
Admitted. Niece of 429 and claims through same source. Grand
parents enrolled.
ROLL P124 #23999 FCT COMM #16119 - Paulina Scraper - 26

13104. JENNIE OLD KINGFISHER, same as #4853.

13105. KA HO KA TUMBLEBUG, Duplicate of 4871.

13106. MARY STUDY,   Southwest City, Mo
Admitted. Sister of Lewis Smoke, App No 11408 and is admitted
for same reasons. [Notation on Roll "For John and Wm. Chunestudy and families, see Roll No. 25866 - et seq." This includes 25873-76]
ROLL P134 #25873 FCT COMM #19393 - John Study - 24 (App 31364)
            25874   19394 - Mary (wife)   - 21
            25875   30545 - Smokes (son) - 7
            25876   4950m - John D. (son) - 2

13107. DICK CHRISTIE,   Cookson, Okla
Admitted. Nephew of #2687.

13108.   ZEKE SPANIARD and 2 children,   Stilwell, Okla
Admitted. First cousin of 1458 and claims through same source.
Applicant's mother enrolled by Drennen, Flint #627, as Sealy.
ROLL P130 #25212 FCT COMM #20229 - Zeke Spaniard   - 37
            25213   20230 - Sarah (wife)   - 28
                                  (App 13276)
            25214   20231 - Mose (son)   - 4
            25215   4093m - Lila (dau)   - 2
            25216   20232 - Lydia YOUNG (dau of w) - 7

13109.   CHARLES GETTINGDOWN,   Stilwell, Okla
Admitted. Father of #2849 and on 51 Drennen roll   under name
of Oo-you-Chus-ey.
ROLL P65 #12084 FCT COMM #19284 - Charles Gettingdown - 68
            12085   19285 - Lucy (wife) - 65 (App 13110)

13110.   LUCY GETTINGDOWN,   Stilwell, Okla
Admitted. 2nd cousin of #2484 and applicant is enrolled by
Drennen on 1851 roll in   Flint Dist. under group #110. [For
Roll information See App 13109]

13111.   ELIZA BEAVER,   Bunch, Okla
Rejected. Testimony in case indicates that some of ancestors
on both paternal and maternal sides were Creeks.   J. B. Adair
states the paternal side   were Creeks and Steve Simmons #9875
testified (Misc. Test. P. 3973) that Jess Simmons or Jess Long
his maternal grandfather and also of applicant 13111, was a
Creek. None of applicant's ancestors appear on any Cherokee
rolls. (Misc. Test. P. 3973) [For Test. See App 9875, Vol. 4]

13112.   WILLIAM O. HALL and 2 children,   Oglesby, Okla
Admitted. Nephew to #1099.
ROLL P70 #13016 FCT COMM #10040 - William O. Hall - 26
            13017   801m - Floyd E. (son)   - 2
            13018   802m - Charlie O. (son) - 3

13113.   JOHN M. HALL,   Catale, Okla
Admitted. Nephew to #1099.
ROLL P69 #12992 FCT COMM #10041 - John M. Hall - 23

13114.   DORA A. FRENCH,   Oglesby, Okla
Admitted. Niece of #1099.
ROLL P64 #11852 FCT COMM #12140 - Henry C. French   - 23
                                  (App 29322)
            11853   10042 - Dora A. (wife)   - 22
            11854   987m - Leona M. M. (dau) - 2
            11855   988m - John H. (son)   - 1/3

13115.   JULIA ALBERTY for 4 children,   Stilwell, Okla
Admitted. The children are cousins of Frank Pelone - 4910.

```
ROLL P22 #3562 FCT COMM #26334 - William Alberty - 18
        3563          26335 - Jesse M. (bro)  - 12
        3564          26336 - Lucy C. (sis)   - 10
        3565          26337 - Johh R. (bro)   -  7
                             by Julia Alberty, Gdn.
```

13116. MARY KIRK and 5 children,   Rose, Okla
Admitted. Granddaughter of #182. Claims through her.

```
ROLL P86 #16385 FCT COMM # 6893 - Mary Kirk         - 26
        16386          6895 - Bluie ADAIR (son)    -  9
        16387          6897 - Susie KIRK (dau)     -  5
        16888          6899 - Jane KIRK (dau)      -  3
        16889         3129m - Minnie KIRK (dau)    -  2
        16890         3130m - Benjamin KIRK (son) -  1
```

13117. LAURA RAPER,   Rose, Okla
Admitted. Grand-daughter of #182. Claims through her.
ROLL P114 #22013 FCT COMM #6894 - Laura Raper - 22

13118. JOSHUA CLOUD and 1 child,   Chapel, Okla
Admitted. Brother of #1204.

```
ROLL P43 #7784 FCT COMM #21615 - Joshua Cloud     - 29
       7785          3602m - Annie Lee (dau) -  2
```

13119. MARY DANIELS, Included in mother's application #2912.

13120. JODIE STANCIL,   Nelson, Ga
Rejected. Second cousin of Margaret C. Ross #2661, and claims
through same source.

13121. RIDER BIGFEATHER,   Bunch, Okla
Admitted. Applicant is a cousin of Sam'l Sixkiller #761, and
claims through same source.
ROLL P30 #5048 FCT COMM #19859 - Rider Bigfeather - 22

13122. RICHARD HOLCOMB, Duplicate of No 9710.

13123. DIANE THROWER,   '   Bunch, Okla
Admitted. by Jennie Bunch, Gdn. Great-niece of #9715, and
claims through same ancestors.
ROLL P139 #27011 - Diane Thrower - 11
                by Jennie Bunch, Gdn.

13124. LUCY SCRAPER and 5 children,   Bunch, Okla
Admitted. Sister of #3872. Minor application filed in the
case is a duplicate of the one in #6269. [For Roll information See App 6269, Vol. 3]

13125. JOE COMINGDEER,   Marble City, Okla
            by Jennie Chukerlate
Admitted. Great-nephew of #9715 and claims through same ancestors.

ROLL P45 #8211 FCT COMM #18984 - Joe Comingdeer - 16
by Jennie Chukerlate, Gdn.

13126. AKY SWIMMER and 3 children,   Cookson, Okla
Admitted. Claims through the mother enrolled as Akey. Grand
father and grandmother enrolled as Ice and Ca-you-ne-cah, Tah.
#20. [For Roll information See App 4198, Vol. 2]

13127. STEVE WATERDOWN, Inc. in 9746.   [For Roll information
See App 6228, Vol. 3]

13128. ELLIS WATERDOWN, Inc. in 6258 [sic- should be 6228].
[For Roll information See App 6228, Vol. 3]

13129. JOE WATERDOWN, Inc. in #9746. [For Roll information
See App 6228, Vol. 3]

13130. LESLEY BEAVER,   Vian, Okla
Rejected. Creek. (Misc. Test. P. 3991 and 4030)
MISC. TEST. P. 3991. NO 13224-13130 - in re Lucinda Ice -
Isaac Sanders:
        "Ny name is Isaac Sanders; my post-office is Bunch,
Okla.; I am sixty-five years old; I know Lucinda Ice; I knew
her father and mother; her father's name was Mohawk Beaver;
her mother's name was Mollie Simmons, that was her maiden
name; I got acquainted with Mollie Simmons about 1873 - she
was married at that time; she was then living in Flint District; I knew her mother but I did not know her father; I got
acquainted with her mother later - this was Mollie's mother; I
did not know her parents; I have been acquainted with Mohawk
Beaver ever since before the war; he was then living in Flint
District; Creek Beaver was Mohawk's uncle; and he was his
step-father too; I don't know who was the father of Mohawk
Beaver; I knew the mother of Mohawk Beaver but did not know
her name; she was also in Flint; I do not know where Mohawk's
mother came from; I do not know how much Cherokee blood she
had; Mohawk's father was a Creek Indian; I do not know whether
Mollie Simmon's mother was part Cherokee or not; all I know
about Lucinda Ice being of Cherokee descent was that her grand
mother's relatives were emigrant Cherokees; Mohawk's mother
was the one that was related to Big-ah Leech; I think Big-ah
Leech was her cousin."
SIGNED: Isaac Sanders, Stilwell, Okla., Mar 24 1909.
MISC. TEST. P. 4030. No 13224-13130 - Lucinda Ice...through
D. M. Faulkner, Interpreter:
        "My name is Lucinda Ice; my post-office is Bunch, Okla.; I
am about forty years old; my mother's name was Marty or
Mollie; before marriage Simmons; she was a Creek Indian; my
father's name was Na-ha-ki Beaver; he died six years ago; when
he died he was about fifty or fifty five years old; he was a
small child when he drew emigrant money; he was living with
his mother when he drew this money; her name was Cah-she-yes-

ki; in 1851 my mother was living with a man named Beaver or Daw-yi; Beaver had one child named Jim and one named Susannah; my father was half Creek; my father's father was a Creek and his mother was a Cherokee; my grand-mother Cah-so-yes-ki died about four years ago; she was both Creek and Cherokee; she got her Cherokee on her mother's side; my father's mother came from the old country; I have no children."
SIGNED: Lucinda "X" Ice, Stilwell, Okla., Mar 19 1909.

13131. DANIEL CHUKERLATE,   Sallisaw, Okla
Admitted. Brother of #9715 and claims through same ancestors.
ROLL P42 #7554 FCT COMM #25708 - Daniel Chuckerlate - 53

13132. GEORGE COMINGDEER,   Sallisaw, Okla
Admitted. Great-nephew of #9715, and claims through same ancestors.
ROLL P45 #8205 FCT COMM #256711 - George Comingdeer - 14
                              by Daniel Chukerlate, Gdn.

13133. RACHEL DAUGHERTY,   Vian, Okla
Admitted. Claims through father enrolled as John Sunday, Sal. No 382.
ROLL P51 #9248 FCT COMM #19332 - Rachel Daugherty - 31

13134. BERRY BUZZARD,   Bunch, Okla
Admitted. Enrolled with 13752.

13135. WM. BEAVER and 1 child,   Bunch, Okla
Admitted. Applicant's mother enrolled by Drennen 1852, Tahl. 472. [For Roll information See App 12630]

13136. PEGGY RATT,   Stilwell, Okla
Admitted. Niece of #603 and claims through same source. Mother enrolled as "Sally Hopper" Flint 220. [Notation on roll "French, Peggy. See Roll No. 22036."]
ROLL P114 #22036 FCT COMM #20130 - Peggy Rat - 24

13137. STEAKER SIMMONS and 1 child,   Marble City, Okla
Rejected. First cousin of 1311 and rejected for same reasons.

13138. DICK STILL, same as 3941.

13139. ELIZA STILL,   Bunch, Okla
Admitted. Claims through grandfather and grandmother enrolled as Cah-tah-qul-lah and Chaw-e-you-kee. Uncle enrolled as Washington. Father was not born in 1851. See Flint 459. (Misc. Test. P. 3357.)
MISC. TEST. P. 3357. Interpreter Used - App No 13139 Eliza Still - Dirt Thrower Vann:
    "My name is Dirt Thrower Vann. My age is about 64 years. I live in Flint District. I know Eliza Still. She is dead. She died last March. She was about 34 years old. One of her

418

children is named Toad Still, Kuz-zie 2 years old.   Toad is 4
years old. Kuz-zie was born the 22nd of August, 1906. She got
her Indian blood from both sides. Her father's name was Henry
Clay. He lived in Flint and in Sequoyah Districts.   I don't
think he was on the 1851 Roll as he was hardly old enough. He
had a brother named Washington.   He was old enough to be enrolled. Sca-law-he-los-ke was another brother. He lived in
Flint District. Gah-ah-qual-lah was the father of these children. Henry Clay did not have any other brothers but he had a
sister whose name I do not recall. (He filed an application
for one of the children after he filed his own) (that he is
the children's father.) Eliza Still's mother's name is Ar-ley.
Arley is about 50 years old. She lives in Flint District. Ar-
ley's father's name was Climbing Rabbit. He died in Tahlequah
District although he lived in Flint also. Chees-too-gah-la-kee
was the Cherokee for Climbing Rabbit.   Ar-ley's mother's name
was Sarah or Sallie; she lived in Flint District. She married
a man by the name of Killer. Do not know any other brothers
and sisters. They have never associated with any other tribe
of Indians. They came out with the Emigrants."
SIGNED: Dirt Thrower Vann, Stilwell, Okla., Sep 30 1908.
[For Roll information See App 3941, Vol. 2]

13140. MOLLY E. REED and 2 children,   McKey, Okla
Admitted. First cousin of #411 and claims through same ances-
tors.
ROLL P116 #22261 FCT COMM #11119 - Molly E. Reed   - 38
            22262   11121 - Walter S. (son) - 18
            22263   11122 - Jennie M. (dau) - 16
            22264   11120 - Myrtle B. (dau) - 20
                                   (App 25279)

13141. ALSIE HOLMES,   Cookson, Okla
Admitted. Aunt of 3926 and claims through same source. Sister
of 6511.
ROLL P77 #14512 FCT COMM #   - James Holmes - 46
                                   (App 13761)
         14513   19838 - Alsie (wife) - 43

13142. DAISY HILL,   Fawn, Okla
Admitted. Aunt of 10793. Claimant's father enrolled by Dren-
nen in 1851 S. B. 130.
ROLL P76 #14206 FCT COMM #5263 - Daisy Hill - 23

13143. REBECCA HILL,   Fawn, Okla
Rejected. Applicant claims only through her dead husband and
she is a white woman. In letter dated Feb. 27, 1908, she says
that she is not claiming for her children, but will not state
whether she has any children.

13144. MARGARET E. HILL and 2 children, Fawn, Okla
Rejected. If Cherokees at all, ancestors were Old Settlers -

moved west in '32 or '33. (Misc. Test. P. 2751.)
MISC. TEST. P. 2751. No 13144 - Margaret E. Hill:
"My name is Margaret E. Hill; my post-office is Fawn,
Okla.; I was born in Van Buren Co., Ark. in 1850; I claim relationship to the Cherokee Indians through my mother, whose
maiden name was Nancy Jane Couch; she was born in Tennessee;
her people brought her to Arkansas about the year 1832 or 33;
my mother's mother was named Charity Powell and she came west
to Arkansas; these people stayed in Arkansas; I know of no enrollment of my people or of them having received any land or
money from the government."
SIGNED: Margaret "X" E. Hill, Eufala, Okla., Sep 10 1908.

13145. MARY J. LUKE and 5 children,   Texanna, Okla
Admitted. Aunt of 10793. Claimant's father is enrolled in
1851 by Drennen, S. B. 130.
ROLL P92 #17449 FCT COMM #17377 - Mary J. Luke   - 38
          17450   17379 - Joseph J. WELLS (son) - 16
          17451   17380 - Bessie WELLS (dau)   - 14
          17452   17381 - Joeson WELLS (son)   - 9
          17453   17382 - Elzora WELLS (dau)   - 4
          17454   3273m - Elmer WELLS (son)   - 1

13146. STERLING P. HOOD,   Checotah, Okla
Admitted. Uncle of 10793. Claimant's father enrolled in 1851
by Drennen, S. B. 130. This claimant's six children rejected
because enrolled as Creeks by Dawes Commission.
ROLL P77 #14561 FCT COMM #5570 - Sterling P. Hood - 40

13147. SALLIE DEMPSEY and 4 children,   Fawn, Okla
Admitted. Aunt of 10793. Claimant's father enrolled in 1851
by Drennen, S. B. 130.
ROLL P52 #9591 FCT COMM #5313 - Sallie Dempsey   - 26
          9592   5314 - James W. (son)   - 11
          9593   5315 - Jennie M. (dau)   - 7
          9594   5316 - Charles Oscar (son) - 4
          9595   539m - Jackson (son)   - 2

13148. MARTHA J. GRIFFITH and 4 children, Sallisaw, Okla
Admitted. Grand-niece of #920. Grandmother of applicant en-
rolled as Sally Byers at Flint 387 1/2.
ROLL P68 #12666 FCT COMM # 2825 - Martha J. Griffith - 25
          12667   2826 - Mary F. (dau)   - 7
          12668   18034 - Liddy J. (dau)   - 5
          12669   649m - Perry G. (son)   - 3
          12670   650m - Bonnie M. (dau)   - 1

13149. LUCY HOOPER,   Cookson, Okla
Admitted. Aunt of #7690 and claims through same source.
ROLL P77 #14586 FCT COMM #20603 - Lucy Hooper - 56*
[* "29" crossed out]

420

13150. ANDY DANIELS, Included in mother's application #2912.
[See App 2912, Vol. 2]

13151. TRUMAN J. PATTERSON,   Santa Luca, Ga
Rejected. First cousin once removed of #9947 and claims thru
same source.

13152. NEBRASKA B. PATTERSON,   Santa Luca, Ga
Rejected. First cousin #9947 and claims through same source.

13153. DORA BEAVER,   Bunch, Okla
        by Lucy Beaver, Gdn.
Rejected. Sister of #13111 and rejected for same reasons.

13154. SAM BEAVER, by Lucy Beaver, Gdn.,   Bunch, Okla
Rejected. Brother of #1311 and rejected for same reasons.

13155. ANDY OTTERLIFTER,   Bunch, Okla
Admitted. Applicant's father Moses Otterlifter, was enrolled
by Drennen in Flint. 61. See testimony taken at Stilwell, Mar
23, 1909, P. 4006
MISC. TEST. P. 4006.   #13155 - Andy Otterlifter...by J. B.
Adair, Interpreter:
    "My name is Any Otterlifter and I am 54 years old. I live
at Bunch, Okla. My father's name was Moses Otterlifter, which
was his English name. His Indian name was Nah-we-he-le-sky
[? 1st letter blurred]. I had a sister Betsy, Rachel, and a
brother David, Esiah, and a cousin Nellie, who lived with my
father. (Flint Group 61.)"
SIGNED: Andy "X" Otterlifter, Stilwell, Okla., Mar 22 1909.
ROLL P106 #20368 FCT COMM #20233 - Andy Otterlifter - 52
         20369   20234 - Susie (wife) -48(App 13209)

13156. AMANDA ANDERSON and 5 children,   Amicolola, Ga
Rejected. Niece of Jesse Burnell, Jr. #6917 and claims thru
same source.

13157. JESSE BURRELL, Jr. and 1 child,   Oak Hill, Ga
Rejected. Nephew of Jesse Burrell Jr. App #6917 and claims
through same source.

13158. HANNAH PARSON,   Tahlequah, Okla
Rejected. Claims through husband Peter Parsons, who died in
1900.

13159. POLLY ROSS,   Welling, Okla
Admitted. Half-sister of #3147. [For Roll information See
App 13160]

13160. WILLIAM ROSS,   Welling, Okla
Admitted. Brother of #1300. Claims through same source.
(Misc. Test. P. 4413.)

MISC. TEST. P. 4095. #13160 - Robert Ross in behalf of William Ross:

"I am 64 years old. I know William Ross. He gets his Cherokee blood from his father George W. Ross. His mother was a Creek Indian. William now lives among the Cherokees at Welling, Okla. The parents of George W. Ross, were John Ross, the Cherokee Chief and Quaity Ross. The full brothers and sisters of George W. Ross, were James, Allen, Silas D., Jane Naves, Annie and John. William Ross has a brother living by the name of Silas D. Ross, who lives at Tahlequah, Okla. They are half brothers on his father's side. William Ross has never lived with the Creek Indians. He has always lived with the Cherokees. (see 242 Tahl. for enrollment of the father of applicant. Mary B. Ross was the second wife of John Ross. She was a white woman.) Nancy Otterlifter was the mother of Silas D. Ross, the half brother of William Ross. I think that William Ross took his allotment with the Cherokee tribe. (See D. C. #20933 ?) The mother of William Ross and George W. Ross never lived as man and wife, but George Ross recognized William Ross as his son. His mother raised him. There was a bunch of Creeks who lived among the Cherokees and she always lived there. It was the general talk in the community that George Ross was the father of William Ross. He never tried to deny it."SIGNED: Robert Ross, Tahlequah, Okla., Mar 29 1909.

MISC. TEST. P. 4413. #13160 - William Ross...thru William Eubanks, Interpreter: "My father was George Ross. He and my mother were never married. My mother always told me that Geo. Ross was my father. My father and mother never lived together. I was born about six miles from Tahlequah. George Ross recognized me as his son. I use to live with him. He wanted to raise me but my mother would not let him. I would go and live with him a month at a time. My brother Silas D. Ross was living with my father too. He would try to get me to live with them, but I would rather live with my mother. I never got any old settler money, nor Creek money. I drew the strip payment."
SIGNED: Wm. Ross, Tahlequah, Okla., Mar 31 1909.

Polly Ross...thru William Eubanks, Interpreter: "I am the wife of William Ross. I have always heard that he was the son of George Ross. From all the circumstances I would say that he was recognized as the son of Geo. Ross."
SIGNED: Polly Ross, Tahlequah, Okla., Mar 31 1909.

MISC. TEST. P. 4414. #13160 - Silas D. Ross:

"I am fifty years old. I live at Tahlequah, Okla. I know William Ross. He lives at Welling, Okla. His wife's name is Polly Ross. William Ross is no relation to me. My father's name was George Ross. But he was not the father of William Ross. I am not the brother of William Ross. William Ross' mother was a creek. I do not know whether he is a creek or not. He is no brother of mine. I have no brothers living. I never heard of William Ross ever claiming that I was his brother before."
SIGNED: Silas D. Ross, Tahlequah, Okla., Mar 31 1909.

422

ROLL P120 #23178 FCT COMM #20933 - William Ross - 47
        23179   28514 - Polly (wife) -48(App 13159)

13161. MADELINE G. WELCH,   Camden, N J*
Admitted. Niece of #6632. Daughter of #6636. [* also "411
Market St." on roll]
ROLL P19 #2935 - Madeline G. Welch - 25? [sic]

13162. LUCY SUNSHINE,   Tahlequah, Okla
Admitted. Half sister on mother's side of #6070. See Misc.
Test. P. 3118. [NOTE: should be p. 3418]
MISC. TEST. P. 3418. No 13162 - Lucy Sunshine...through S. E.
Parris, Interpreter:
    "I had one sister that was paid in 1852. My mother and fa-
ther were not living together at that time. Andrew Critten was
my father. He was living with another wife at the time of the
payment. My mother and sister were living by themselves. I had
a half brother named Takey, another named Nick and one named
Ned." SIGNED: Lucy Sunshine, Tahlequah, Okla., Oct 3 1908.
ROLL P135 #26059 - Lucy Sunshine - 50

13163. NANNIE MILLER and DICK MILLER,   Tahlequah, Okla
            by Lucy Sunshine, Gdn.
Admitted. Niece and nephew of #6070 also of #13162.
ROLL P99 #19005 FCT COMM #21234 - Nannie Miller - 14
        19006   21235 - Dick (bro)   - 11
                        by Lucy Sunshine, Gdn.

13164. ROBERT E. WILKERSON,   Webbers Falls, Okla
Admitted. Cousin of #5614.
ROLL P151 #29231 FCT COMM #2885 - Robert E. Wilkerson - 28

13165. MARGARET B. JONES,   Webbers Falls, Okla
Admitted. Cousin of #5614.
ROLL P83 #15662 FCT COMM #14851 - Margaret B. Jones - 19

13166. MARY JONES,   Webbers Falls, Okla
Rejected. Sister of 24887.

13167. CORNELIA CROOK,   Webbers Falls, Okla
Admitted. Cousin of #5614.
ROLL P49 #8884 FCT COMM #15186 - Cordelia Crooks   - 29
        8885   15187 - Naeta M. BUTTS (dau) - 7
        8886   15188 - Cherokee (dau)   - 4

13168. ELLEN WILKERSON, Duplicate of #5614. [NOTE: Should be
duplicate of 8673, Aunt of 5614]

13169. SADIE B. ROBERTS,   Marble, Okla
Admitted. First cousin of #14786 and claims through the same
source. Father, Samuel Sanders 567 Flint.
ROLL P118 #22674 FCT COMM #3283 - Sadie B. Roberts - 27

13170. EDWARD F. BLACKSTONE,   Porum, Okla
Admitted. First cousin of #4394. Father of claimant enrolled
in 1851 by Drennen, Del. 431.
ROLL P31 #5232 FCT COMM #4504 - Edward F. Blackstone - 27

13171. JENNIE TUCKER and 1 child,   Melvin, Okla
Admitted. Sister of Watt Sulteeskey #4849.
ROLL P141 #27382 FCT COMM #21445 - Jennie Tucker - 42
          27383   21446 - Annie (dau) - 17

13172. LIZZIE COCKRAN and NED COCHRAN, Minors, Melvin, Okla
       by Sallie Tucker, Gdn.
Applicant's admitted with mother #6069. [For Roll information
See App 6069, Vol. 3]

13173. JOHN J. LOVETT,   Braggs, Okla
Admitted. Brother of #10949 and claims through same source.
ROLL P91 #17320 FCT COMM #18699 - John J. Lovett - 31

13174. EMILY SULTEESKEY,   Melvin, Okla
Admitted. Applicant is a sister of Watt Sulteeskey, #4849.
[For Roll information See App 6068, Vol. 3]

13175. CHARLOTTE SULTEESKEY and 1 child,   Melvin, Okla
Admitted. Applicant is a sister of Watt Sulteeskey #4849.
ROLL P134 #25958 FCT COMM #18549 - Charlotte Sulteeskey - 21
          25959   - Lizzie MILO (dau)   - 1

13176. JOHN HAIR,   Melvin, Okla
Admitted. Half brother of #3285 and claims thru same source.
ROLL P69 #12927 FCT COMM #18244 - John Hair - 36

13177. LILY CHRISTEY,   Melvin, Okla
Admitted. Sister of #11298.
ROLL P42 #7479 - Lily Christy - 30

13178. SARAH MURRAY and 3 children,   Wagoner, Okla
Admitted. Niece of #4079. Grandparents Archilla and Nelly
Scraper, 673 G. S. Mother probably not born in 1851.
ROLL P103 #19768 FCT COMM #12375 - Sarah Murray   - 28
          19769   12376 - Annie (dau)   - 5
          19770   2367m - Charlie W. (son) - 3
          19771   2368m - John W. (son)   - 1

13179. CORNELIUS KETCHER, Duplicate of #11967.

13180. ANNIE STICKS and 1 child,   Zena, Okla
Admitted. Daughter of 3882.
ROLL P133 #25644 FCT COMM #19796 - Eli Stick   - 22 (App 35532)
          25645   - Annie (wife)   - 22
          25646   - Starr LACY (son of w) - 3

424

13181. SARAH HITCHER,   Southwest City, Mo
          by Nancy Hitcher, Gdn.
Admitted. Niece of #11406 and claims through same ancestors.
ROLL P76 #14291 FCT COMM #30548 - Sarah Hitcher - 7
                              by Nancy Hitcher, Gdn.

13182. NANCY SCRAPER,   Southwest City, Mo
Niece of #429 and claims through same source. Grandfather en-
rolled. Minor child of #431 and included on his card as such.
[See App 431, Vol. 1]

13183. MALINDA GUINN,   Southwest City, Mo
Admitted. Niece of #429 and claims through same source. Grand
parents enrolled.
ROLL P68 #12786 FCT COMM #16120 - Malinda Guinn - 23

13184. ROBERT DUNLAP,   Bryson City, N C
Admitted. 1st cousin once removed to 834. Grandmother "Stacy
Beck, 2084 Chapman" Mother not living in 1851.
ROLL P9 #807 - Robert Dunlap - 16

13185. BERRY DUNLAP,   Birdtown, N C
Admitted. 1st cousin once removed to #834. Grandmother "Stacy
Beck, 2084 Chapman." Mother not living in 1851.
ROLL P9 #806 - Berry Dunlap - 19

13186. ALICE DUNLAP,   Bryson City, N C
Admitted. 1st cousin once removed to #834. Grandmother "Stacy
Beck, 2084 Chapman." Mother not living in 1851.
ROLL P9 #805 - Alice Dunlap - 22

13187. JOS. HOLLOWAY,   Topton, N C
Rejected. 1st cousin to #10317.

13188. ROBERT A. BRADY and 6 children,   Topton, N C
Rejected. Applicant's mother was a white woman and was never
married to the alleged father. Father never recognized applicant as his child. Aunt of alleged father never heard of nephew being father of applicant. Applicant was enrolled by Hester
as being the descendant of a person through whom no claim is
made at this time. Proof of ancestor not sufficient. (Misc.
Test. P. 1564-5.)
MISC. TEST. P. 1564. In re 13188 - Martha Ann Meroney:
     "I am 73 years of age; was born in Cherokee County, N. C.
Marcus Powell was a nephew of mine. I never heard that Marcus
Powell had a child by Mary Brady. Never heard Marcus Powell
say so and never heard it before today when the statement was
made to me by Robert A. Brady. Marcus Powell while he had Indian blood was very fair and very much lighter in complexion
than Robert A. Brady who came to see me today. I know Nancy
Brady from a little girl. She was a sister of David Owl's
wife. I never heard her claim that Marcus Powell was the fa-

425

ther of her son."
SIGNED: Martha Ann Meroney, Murphy, N. C., Jul 15 1908.

MISC. TEST. P. 1565.   No 13188 - Robert A. Brady:
     "That I am 40 years of age and live in Cherokee Co.,
N. C.   I claim my Indian descent through my father and his
mother--Polly Welch and she married Powell. My father was born
in N. C. I think.   I guess he was raised here in Cherokee Co.
I think he left here but I don't know when nor when he died.
Don't know whether he ever lived among the Indians or not. My
mother said he lived on the Valley River in this county among
the Indians. I never saw my father. Don't know where my grand
mother was born and raised. Don't know whether she ever lived
with the Indians as a member of the tribe. I think my grand
mother Welch was enrolled but I don't know what roll nor under
what name she was enrolled. I don't know whether my father
ever recognized me as his child. My mother told me that Marcus
Powell was my father.   Don't know that he ever told anyone
about me being his child. My mother said that my father died
when I was small. My mother is still living. I am recognized
as an Indian. I never received any money from the government.
My mother claimed she enrolled me when I was small but I never
received anything. I have always gone by the name of Brady,
never by the name of Powell. James and John Brady were half
brothers on my father's side and are still living. Don't think
they have filed application. James and John Brady are both
younger than I. James is about four years younger than I. John
is now about 27 years old. Hangingdog is the place where I was
raised and it is here in Cherokee Co., N. C. Robert and Ose or
Osceola were my father's brothers. Those are the only two that
I know of."
SIGNED: Robert A. Brady, Murphy, N. C., Jul 15 1908.
EXCEPTION CASE.   13188.   Robert A. Brady and 6 children,
Topton, N. C. Recommended. Total number of exceptions filed
in this group -- 1. Applicant claims that he is the son of
Marcus Powell, the son of Mary Powell, who were enrolled by
Chapman in 1851. He is, however, unable to prove this. Appli-
cant is, however, enrolled by Hester and Churchill, and Hester
states that applicant was son of a Cherokee and that Chief
Smith and other Cherokees testified that Brady was a Cherokee.
The assistant to Special Commissioner herein who took applicant's testimony stated that he showed Indian blood to marked
degree. In consideration of the premises, therefore, applicant
is recommended for enrollment.
SUPP ROLL #30298 - Robert A. Brady - 38
          30299 - Eliza (dau)   - 11
          30300 - Sarah (dau)   - 10
          30301 - Arthur (son)   - 8
          30302 - McKinley (son) - 5
          30303 - Luther (son)   - 3
          30304 - Elizabeth (dau) - 1

13189. SARAH E. HIGH and 2 children,   Chetopa, Kans
Admitted. Sister of #6518 and claims through same source.
ROLL P75 #14112 FCT COMM #32673 - Sarah E. High   - 48
          14113   32674 - Eddie C. (son)   - 20
          14114   32675 - William J. (son) - 14

13190. WILLIAM H. FIELDS and 2 children,   Chetopah, Kans
Admitted. Brother of #6518 and claims through same source.
ROLL P61 #11220 FCT COMM #9524 - William H. Fields - 47
          11221   9525 - Roy J. (son)   - 13
          11222   9526 - Arthur C. (son)   - 10

13191. MARTHA J. FIELDS,   Chetopah, Kans
Rejected. Claims for share of deceased husband who died March
8, 1903. See letter herein marked "Ex A."

13192. ELLA THROWER and 1 child,   Bunch, Okla
1 Admitted. 1 Rejected. Claims for Ella Thrower rejected -
she is a Creek. Claims of child, Jennie Chukerlate, is O, K.
through child's father Conceen Chukerlate #9741. (Misc. Test.
P. 3991 and 4030). [For Testimony See App 13130]
ROLL P42 #7569 FCT COMM #19837 - Jennie Chuckerlate - 14
                    by Ella Thrower, Gdn.

13193. LAURA SCOTT,   Bunch, Okla
Admitted. Applicant enrolled as Ah-ke-to-hee 107 Flint Dist.
[For Roll information See App 9637, Vol. 4]

13194. NANNIE ROSS,   Bunch, Okla
          by father and Gdn., Lewis Ross.
Admitted. Niece of #13135 and claims through same source.
ROLL P120 #23147 FCT COMM #18783 - Nannie Ross - 7
                       (dau of 23121)
                       by Lewis Ross, Gdn.

13195. LIZZIE ROSS,   Bunch, Okla
          by father and Gdn., Lewis Ross
Admitted. Niece of #13135 and claims through same source.
ROLL P120 #23124 FCT COMM #18782 - Lizzie Ross - 9
                       (dau of 23121)
                       by Lewis Ross, Gdn.
[NOTE: Roll #23121 is Lewis Ross, App 13285]

13196. WM. PETTIT,   Marble City, Okla
Admitted. Son of #8766.
ROLL P110 #21211 FCT COMM #25703 - William Petitt - 29

13197. WILLIAM E. COLVIN,   Chattanooga, Tenn
Rejected. Nephew of #10777.

13198. MARGARET J. KELLY and 5 children, Weatherford, Tex
Rejected. Niece of 4572 and claims through same source.

427

13199. JAMES BEARPAW and 2 children,   Bunch, Okla
Admitted. First cousin of #3926 and claims through the same
source. Grandfather enrolled Flint 176.
ROLL P27 #4581 FCT COMM #19877 - James Bearpaw - 36
          4582   19878 - Annie (wife) - 31 (App 13664)
          4583   4721m - Emiline (dau) - 4
          4584   4722m - John (son)   - 2

13200. SALLIE BUZZARD,   Bunch, Okla
Admitted. Grandfather and grandmother enrolled as Tick-o-no-
he-ly and Nancy. Aunt enrolled as Ne-coo-ti-yi Flint #608.
ROLL P37 #6471 FCT COMM #20209 - Sallie Buzzard - 17

13201. W. M. VANN and 2 children, Duplicate of 2237.

13202. NED McCOY,   Vian, Okla
Admitted. 1st cousin of 5300. [For Roll information See App
10884]

13203. AMOS TAIL,   Bunch, Okla
Admitted. First cousin of Sarah Bolyn #11700, and is admitted
for same reasons.
ROLL P136 #26235 FCT COMM #20540 - Amos Tail   - 21
          26236   19593 - Rosie (wife) - 23
                         (App 39160)

13204. CHARLIE HOLCOMB, by Richard Holcomb, Gdn., Bunch, Okla
Admitted. Son of 9710.
ROLL P76 #14388 FCT COMM #25511 - Charlie Holcomb - 13
                         by Richard Holcomb, Gdn.

13205. MARY HOLCOMB, by Richard Holcomb, Gdn, Bunch, Okla
Admitted. First cousin of #3926 and claims through the same
source. Grandfather enrolled Flint 176.
ROLL P76 #14390 FCT COMM #25512 - Mary Holcomb - 6
                         by Richard Holcomb, Gdn.

13206. THOMAS J. LENOIR,   Savannah, Ga*
                              Cor. Park Ave. & Lincoln St.
Admitted. First cousin of #4190 and claims through the same
ancestors. Father of applicant, Thomas R. Lenoir enrolled in
1851 by Chapman #1825. Also enrolled by Hester #2224. Applicant enrolled by Hester as infant #2227. [* Residence on roll
also has "c/o Mrs. M. J. Lenoir"]
ROLL P12 #1476 - Thomas R. Lenoir - 22

13207. ALBERT A. TAYLOR and 5 children, Tahlequah, Okla
Admitted. 1st cousin of #715. Mother "Corinne Barnes, 169
1/2 Illinois."
ROLL P136 #26350 FCT COMM #14856 - Albert A. Taylor   - 36
          26351   14857 - Allie B. (dau)   - 12
          26352   14858 - Susie P. (dau)   - 10

13207.　ALBERT A. TAYLOR (Cont)
　　　26353 FCT COMM #14860 - Albert A., Jr. (son) -　8
　　　26354　　　　　　770m - Shelly K. (son)　　　 - 3
　　　26355　　　　　　771m - Gilbert T. (son)　　 - 1/2

13208.　NANCY VANN,　　　　　　　　　Bunch, Okla
Admitted.　Claims through self enrolled as Nancy.　Father en-
rolled as Benjamin Sanders.　Brothers and sister　enrolled as
Osey, Na-key, Burns, David and　Aron - Fl. #575.　Misc. Test.
P. 3274.
MISC. TEST. P. 3274.　App No 6704 -　<u>Interpreter</u> <u>Used</u> - Lizzie
Sanders:
　　"My name is Lizzie Sander[s].　My age is　about 50.　I was
born after 1857.　I was born in Flint District.　I got the bread
and strip payment.　I was enrolled by the Dawes Commission, on
Cherokee Roll.　I have not my number with me.　I was enrolled as
a full-blood.　My father's name was Ben Sanders.　He is dead;
died during the Civil War.　I don't know how old he　was.　He
came from the Eastern States.　I don't know　just when he came
out here.　I had a brother named Hoo-ley Sanders.　I had another
brother named　Burn　Sanders; another　named　Tom but　he　was
younger.　I had a sister Na-key who was older　than I am.　She
lived in Flint District.　My father had a brother Isaac.　I had
an uncle by the name of Ben.　Alex or Al-licke was another.　He
lived in Flint District.　All lived in Flint as　near as I can
recollect.　Another was Mose.　Another was named Ned.　Isaac's
father was named John.　David is another uncle of mine.　Jenny
and Nancy were also my　father's sisters.　Benjamin　Sanders
children were Hooley, Nakey,　Burn, Lizzie, Akey, Tom, Peggy,
Dave, Nancy and Ose, and Aaron.　(575 Flint.) My mother's name
was Rachel Sanders.　My father's father's name　was John Sanders.　He lived in Flint District. My mother's father's name was
Fields or Clau-gas-kee.　I don't know whether he had any given
name.　My mother had　a brother George.　Also　a sister Polly.
Polly Fields was her name.　My people were Emigrants.　I don't
know whether any of them were enrolled in 1851.　I have heard
them speak about getting money　from the Government.　I don't
think they ever associated with　any other tribe.　Nancy Vann
is my sister; we had　the same father but　a　different mother;
(13208) and should be grouped with 6704."
SIGNED: Lizzie Sanders, Stilwell, Okla., Sep 28 1908.
[For Roll information See App 5303, Vol. 3]

13209.　SUSIE OTTERLIFTER,　　　　　Stilwell, Okla
Admitted.　Claims through self enrolled as Susan.　Father enrolled as　James Chambers.　Brother and　sister enrolled　as
George and Martha, Flint #66.　[For Roll information　See App
13155]

13210.　JULIUS POWELL and 1 child,　　　Dalton, Ga
Rejected.　Claims through father and mother who were both held
as slaves.

EXCEPTION CASE. Rejected. Total number of exceptions filed in this group -- 1. Original recommendation renewed.

13211. LYDIA KETCHER, Duplicate of #640.

13212. SAM SQUIRREL, Duplicate of #639.

13213. ISAAC SUMMERFIELD, Duplicate of #630 and 5676.

13214. LO-SE SKAH-GIN-NE, Duplicate of #631 and 13214 [sic].

13215. NELLIE ELLICK, Duplicate of 10585.

13216. DA-KE SUMMERFIELD, Duplicate of #629.

13217. SALLIE BEAVER, Bunch, Okla
Rejected. First cousin of 13111 and rejected for same reason.

13218. CLEM BEAVER and 4 children, Bunch, Okla
Admitted. Brother of #13135 and claims through same source.
ROLL P27 #4593 FCT COMM #19951 - Clem Beaver - 33
       4594   19953 - Steve (son) - 9
       4595   19954 - Nellie (dau) - 7
       4596   4215m - Nannie (dau) - 5
       4597   4216m - Linnie (dau) - 1

13219. JENNIE YOUNG, Vian, Okla
Admitted. Sister to #6258. Applicant died in May, 1907. [For Roll information See App 1968, Vol. 2]

13220. LUCY BEAVER, Bunch, Okla
Rejected. Mother of #13111 and rejected for same reason.

13221. MAGGIE BEAVER, by Lucy Beaver, Gdn., Bunch, Okla
Rejected. Sister of #13111 and rejected for same reason.

13222. KA-HO-GAH BIGFEATHER, Bunch, Okla
Admitted. Claims through self enrolled as Ka-ho-cah. Father and mother enrolled as Stand and Nelly - Flint 414. [For Roll information See App 5591, Vol. 3]

13223. BETSY SHAVER, Bunch, Okla
Admitted. Claims through self enrolled as Betsy. Great Aunt enrolled as Caty Sleeping Rabbit; son and daughter enrolled as John and Margaret - Flint 568. (Misc. Test. P. 3306-3267).
MISC. TEST. P. 3267. Interpreter Used App No 13297-13223 - Mary Vann:
"My name is Mary Vann. My age is about 58. I was born about 1851 or 1852. I was born the Fall after the money was paid out. I have a brother older. His name is John Hardbarger. My name was Ross before marriage. We had one mother and a different father. I had a half-brother by the name of Jim Ross.

He lived in Flint District. He lived in several Districts and
in the Choctaw nation for some time. My father's name was Mack
Ross. He was also known as Dan Ross. He lived in Flint and
then in Tahlequah District; or in Tahlequah first. My mother's
name was Betsy Ross, and Betsey Hardbarger. Daniel Ross had a
sister Jane or Jenny. Joseph Ross was a brother of Daniel
(668 Fl.) Joshua Ross is Daniel Ross's [sic] and lived near
Muskogee in the Creek nation. He has lived in Tahlequah District. Daniel Ross's father's name was Clau-dah-mah or Claws-
dah-mah. Don't know in what district he lived. (458 Tahl.)
Ah-kee-lee was also a brother. My mother's name now is Betsy
Shaver #13223. She has gone by this name since about 1862. I
don't know what her name was before. She is about 87 years old
now. She was enrolled in 1851 and drew money. My brother, John
Hardbarger, also drew money in 1851. It was Emigrant money. I
don't know what her name was before marriage. Her Indian name
is Chi-ah-lau-ske or Chi-lah-law-ske. I don't know any brothers and sisters of Betsey Shaver. Ga-ha-yuh-ga or Patsy, was
her mother's name. The English is White Girl. I cannot name
any other relatives."
SIGNED: Mary Vann, Stilwell, Okla., Sep 28 1908.

MISC. TEST. P. 3306. App No 14195-1323 - John Hardbarger:
    "My name is John Hardbarger. My age is 62 years. I was en-
rolled in 1851 and drew money. My grandmother got it in 1851
at Fort Gibson. My Indian name is Gah-so-ge-sky. I lived in
Flint District in 1851. These were the only names I was known
by. I was enrolled by Katy Sleeping Rabbit; she enrolled us
all; she lived in Flint. I cannot name any of her sisters and
brothers. I lived with Katy Sleeping Rabbit and she drew my
money and she also raised my mother, Betsey Shaver, and drew
her money. Mary Vann is younger than I am. I don't think she
was living in 1851. I had a sister Margaret; she died about
the close of the Civil War. She was about 12 years old. (568
Fl.) Betsey Sleeping Rabbit was my mother's grandmother. My
mother's mother's name was Patsy Benge. Ga-yu-na-ga is the
Indian for Benge. My grandfather's name was Dick; or Dick or
Richard Benge. He lived in Illinois District. I don't know
whether he ever lived in any other District than Illinois. Ca-
yu-na-ga or Ga-yu-na-ga was the Indian name for Benge. Dick
Benge's father's name was also Dick Benge. There was a Houston
Benge a cousin of Dick's. There was an Annie and Martin Benge.
Owl Shaver was Betsy Shaver's father. Patsey Benge was my
grandmother and she was the daughter of Dick Benge. Katy
Sleeping Rabbit had a sister Quaity Sleeping Rabbit. My mother
had a sister named Ca-ho-ga and Nakey and Jenny. I get no Indian blood from my father, her [sic] was white. I am enrolled
by the Dawes Commission, Cherokee Roll #19899. I got the strip
payment. I got all the payments."
SIGNED: John Hardbarger, Stilwell, Okla., Sep 29 1908.
ROLL P126 #24303 FCT COMM #18918 - Betsy Shaver - 91

13224. LUCINDA ICE,   Bunch, Okla
Rejected. Creek, sister of #13130. Misc. Test. P.. 3991 and
4030. [For Testimony See App 13130]

13225. NANCY CHE-KE-LE,   Bunch, Okla
Admitted. Claims through self enrolled as Nancy. Father and
mother enrolled as Blossom Falling and Soch-in-a [?]. Sisters
and brother enrolled as Sally, Aily, Che-squa-e-rol-la, and
Coo-te-ah. Flint 470 1/2.
ROLL P41 #7297 - Nancy Che-ke-le - 54

13226. ANNIE JOHNSON and 3 children,   McLain, Okla
Admitted. Applicant's grandmother "Polly Mayfield" enrolled
by Chapman 1542. Mother born after 1851.
ROLL P81 #15354 FCT COMM #32699 - Annie Johnson   - 33
          15355   32670 - John A. (son)   - 11
          15356   32671 - Grace M. (dau)   - 8
          15357   32672 - Lafayette L. (son) -   5

13227. ELIZABETH GLASS and 4 children,   McLain, Okla
Admitted. Niece of #11872 (and nephews). Their paternal grand
mother "Katy Glass" or Katy Love enrolled in 1851 by Drennen,
Tah. 305.
ROLL P66 #12247 FCT COMM #29225 - Elizabeth Glass - 16
          12248   29226 - Cornelius (bro) - 14
          12249   29227 - Harvey (bro)   - 12
          12250   29228 - Dennis (bro)   - 9
          12251   29229 - Caswell (bro)   - 6
                                    by Mary Jane Tate, Gdn.

13228. NANNIE SPARROWHAWK,   Tahlequah, Okla
Admitted. Claims through father enrolled as Joe Sparrowhawk
Sal. 190. Mother's father and mother enrolled as Te-nah-la-we-
stah (Stop) and Che-go-na-lah. Uncle on mother's side enrolled
as Johnson, G. S. 173.
ROLL P131 #25223 FCT COMM #20989 - Nannie Sparrowhawk - 26

13229. MAGGIE HAIR,   Tahlequah, Okla
Admitted. Included in App #8151 - Jennie Hair, mother and Gdn.

13230. AGGIE POORBEAR,   Bunch, Okla
Admitted. Aunt of #2687. [For Roll information See App 6280,
Vol. 3]

13231. HUNTER POORBEAR, Duplicate of #6280.

13232. ANNIE BEAVER,   Bunch, Okla
Admitted. Aunt of #13136 and claims through same source.
ROLL P27 #4592 FCT COMM #20547 - Annie Beaver - 51

13233. DAVE SMITH, Minor son of #10271. (See #10271)

13234. ELI SMITH, Minor child of #10271. (See #10271)

13235. SMITH MELLOWBUG,   Leach, Okla
Admitted. Claims through father enrolled as Tor-yoo-nee-se.
Grandfather and grandmother enrolled as Te-yer-ske and Sar-
hou-er. Sal. #112.
ROLL P98 #18767 FCT COMM #20804 - Smith Mellowbug - 51

13236. SALLIE SMITH and 1 child,   Oaks, Okla
Admitted. Niece of #641 and claims through same source.
ROLL P129 #24962 FCT COMM #20389 - Sallie Smith - 21
         24963   4849m - Jennie (dau) - 2

13237. STAN SMITH, Minor child of #10271. (See App 10271.)

13238. DANNIE H. BURNETT and 1 child,   Sapulpa, Okla
Admitted. Applicant claims through father John A. Ross, grand
mother Elizabeth Ross. Both on the 1851 roll Tahl. 238. Also
uncles and aunts enrolled 238 Tah.
ROLL P36 #6268 FCT COMM # 6019 - Dannie H. Burnett - 31
        6269   3841m - William James (son) - 2

13239. ELIZA J. BLAKEMORE,   Muskogee, Okla
Admitted. Sister of Daniel H. Burnett 13238, and claims thru
same source. [NOTE: App # shown as 3239 on roll.]
ROLL P31 #5315 FCT COMM #21613 - Eliza J. Blakemore - 27

13240. FLORA L. ROSS,   Sapulpa, Okla
Admitted. Sister to Daniel H. Burnett 13238 and claims thru
same source.
ROLL P120 #23065 FCT COMM #6022 - Flora L. Ross - 25

13241. NELLIE McKAY,   Hulbert, Okla
Admitted. Applicant enrolled as Nelly Catcher, Tahl. #360.
Aunt of #5509.
ROLL P94 #17962 FCT COMM #18331 - Nellie McKay - 56

13242. KATE GRAHAM,   Chelsea, Okla
Admitted. Niece of #1084 and claims through same ancestors.
Father, Samuel Parks, enrolled by Chapman #1607.
ROLL P67 #12495 FCT COMM #13272 - Kate Graham - 20

13243. TEXIE A. ROLFE,   Okla. City, Okla
Rejected. Ancestors not on roll. Does not establish genuine
connection with Cherokee tribe. Misc. Test. P. 2064.
MISC. TEST. P. 2064. No 13243 - Texie Anna Rolfe:
    "My name is Texie Anna Rolfe; my post-office is Oklahoma
City, Okla.; I was born in Topeka, Kan. in 1883; I claim relationship to the Cherokees through my mother, whose maiden name
is Isabella Huff who is three-quarters Cherokee; my mother was
born in Murray Co., Tenn. in 1858; my mother is still living
and is present here to-day and she is assisting me in giving

this testimony; my mother claims through her parents, John
Scott and her mother, whose maiden name was Isabella Scott; my
grandfather, John Huff was a full-blood Cherokee; my mother
and grand-parents were slaves and were owned by the Scott family in Tennessee; my great-grandfather was born in Richmond,
Va.; I do not know of them ever receiving any money or land
from the government."
SIGNED: Texie Anna Rolfe, Oklahoma City, Okla., Aug 19 1908.

13244. JOHN BRAY,   Oochelata, Okla
Admitted. Great-nephew of 205 and claims through same source.
ROLL P33 #5704 FCT COMM #11637 - John Bray - 36

13245. SARAH STAY-AT-HOME and 3 children, Stilwell, Okla
Admitted. Niece of #1305. Grandfather Ar-le-cher 581 Flint.
ROLL P132 #25527 FCT COMM #19196 - Sarah Stay-at-home - 28
         25528   19197 - Nancy (dau)   - 14
         25529   19198 - Ned (son)   - 9
         25530   - Lewis (son)   - 1

13246. HENRY SWIMMER,   Bunch, Okla
Admitted. Mother enrolled as Nancy Big Bullet and maternal
grandparents as Big Bullet and Sally Big Bullet Flint #77.
ROLL P135 #26146 FCT COMM #25882 - Henry Swimmer - 20

13247. JOHN LOCUST,   Wauhillau, Okla
Admitted. Nephew of #316. Father enrolled as Sun-ne-koo-ih
C. #1062.
ROLL P91 #17249 - John Locust   - 33
         17250 - Maggie (wife) - 26 (App 13248)

13248. MAGGIE LOCUST,   Wauhillau, Okla
Admitted. Applicant claims Emigrant Cherokee descent through
father John Go-wa-nuh, enrolled in 1851 in Flint Dist. Group
35. Misc. Test. P.. 3981.
MISC. TEST. P. 3981. No 13248 - J. B. Adair:
    "I know Maggie Locust; she is a daughter of John Oo-wa-neh
or John Weavel. He was an emigrant Cherokee. I also knew his
wife Ar-le. John Weavel's father was called Weavels or Crack-
shins or Shin-striker. Cat-tah-la-tah Weavels was John Weavels
aunt; Dick Weavels was his uncle; I-o-wan-tee was his aunt;
Tas-ge-ge-tee-hee was his uncle; Oo-wah-tah was his aunt; Cah-
tah-nah was John Weavel's mother. (Flint 35)"
SIGNED: J. B. Adair, Stilwell, Okla., Mar 23 1909.
[For Roll information See App 13247]

13249. ED MARSHALL,   Columbus, Ga
Rejected. Applicants or ancestors were never enrolled. Grand
mother was a slave. See letter filed herein marked "Ex. A."

13250. SARAH KILLINEGAR, minor   Bunch, Okla
Admitted. Applicant is daughter of Jennie Killinegar #13252,

and claims through same source, and sister to Peggy Hardbarger #9704. [For Roll information See App 13252]

13251. TOM KILLENEGAR, minor   Bunch, Okla
Admitted. Applicant is brother to Peggie Hardbarger 9704 and claims thru same source. [For Roll information See App 13252]

13252. JENNIE KILLENEGAR and 1 child,   Bunch, Okla
Admitted. Mother of Peggie Hardbarger #9704.
ROLL P86 #16269 FCT COMM #27228 - Jennie Killineger - 52
             16270   27229 - Sarah (dau) - 19 (App 13250)
             16271   27230 - Tom (son) - 15 (App 13251)

13253. JESSE TE-KE-KE-SKI,   Charlestown Township, N C
Admitted. Applicant enrolled on Chapman #1493. Applicant deceased. See Testimony. (Misc. Test. P. 1714.)
MISC. TEST. P. 1714. Witness re #13253 - Celia Te-ke-ke-ski... in behalf of Jesse Te-ke-ke-ski, deceased, #13253...through David Owl, Interpreter:
    "That I am 52 years of age. I live in Swain County, N. C. My husband's name was Jesse Te-ke-ke-ski. Jesse's father died before 1851 and his mother married Wah-ha-neet-tah. Jesse died about a year ago."
SIGNED: Celia "X" To-ke-ke-ski, Cherokee, N. C., Jul 20 1908.
[For Roll information See App 6209, Vol. 3]

13254. WILLIAM HYDE,   Bryson City, N C
Rejected. Betsy Walker case. See special report in #500.

13255. EMILY H. HYDE,   Bryson City, N C
Rejected. Betsy Walker case. See special report in #500.

13256. SWIMMER PEGGS,   Locust Grove, Okla
Admitted. Grand-nephew of #89.
ROLL P110 #21078 FCT COMM #27991 - Swimmer Pegg - 26
              21079   18191 - Annie (wife) - 18
                                      (App 23974)

13257. NICK FALLING and 3 children,   Spavinaw, Okla
Admitted. Brother of #10421 and claims through same source.
[For Roll information See App 10646]

13258. FANNIE DEW and 4 children,   Leach, Okla
Admitted. Niece of #1875 and claims through the same source.
(Misc. Test. P. 3804) [For Testimony P. 3804 See App 6061, Vol. 3]
MISC. TEST. P. 3853.   #13258 - Fannie Dew...thru Martin Squirrel, Interpreter:
    "My name is Fannie Dew. I was born in 1873 in Tahlequah District. I was enrolled by the Dawes Commission under the name of Fannie Hawkins, #18431, as a full-blood. My father's proper English name was Charlie Tucker but he had a nick-name

435

which he went by more than his real name. His nick-name was
Bug Tucker. My mothers English name was Jennie Tucker. My
fathers Cherokee name was Tah-you-ne-se and my mothers Cherokee name was Gah-lo-nu-skee. My mother and father were living
in 1851. My father was enrolled in Going Snake District with
his parents and my mother was enrolled in Tahlequah District
with her parents. My father had a sister whose name was Jen-
nih, a brother by the name of A-sick-e, a sister, Quaitsey, a
sister Nu-chih, a brother, Da-we, a brother Jesse who were
living in 1851. They were enrolled in Going Snake District in
1851. I do not know the names of any of the brothers and sisters of my mother who were enrolled in 1851. My fathers father
Cherokee name was Chah-lih and his mothers name was Ah-lee-
sah. My grandparents came from the Old Nation at the time of
the Emigration. My mothers fathers name was Wah-la-skee and
her mothers name was Gah-de-tlo-eh. My grandparents on my
mothers side were Emigrant Cherokees. My grandparents on my
fathers side were enrolled in Going Snake District in 1851.
And my grandparents on my mothers side were enrolled in Tahlequah District in 1851. None of my ancestors ever received any
Old Settler money. All my ancestors have always been with the
Cherokee tribe. I was enrolled and drew the Strip Payment in
1894. My mother was an applicant for this fund. She applied
under the name of Jennie Tucker. She appeared at Tahlequah,
Okla., for Examination. Her P. O. address is Moody, Okla."
SIGNED: Fannie Dew, Locust Grove, Okla., Oct 8 1908.
[For Roll information See App 4504, Vol. 3]

13259. LIZZIE MURPHY,   Locust Grove, Okla
Admitted. Niece of #2497. Grandfather is enrolled by Drennen
in Tahl. 414. Father was born after 1851.
ROLL P103 #19720 FCT COMM #20910 - Jackson Murphy - 51
                          (App 14061)
        19721   20914 - Lizzie (dau)   - 17

13260. JAMES L. MURPHY,   Marble, Okla
Rejected. Claims through same source as 9818.

NOTES

There is a notation on the roll "Susie Baldridge. See Roll
No. 23270." which is applicant Susie Runabout (App 11199).
There is no Susie Baldridge in index.

AA-SI 10628
ABBOTT, Annie L 12390-1
Eugene M 12591 Gertrude
12591 Leona M 12391 Louisa
J 12391 Mary E 12591 Net-
tie M 12635
ABERCROMBIE, Mattie 11001
Sarah Eliz 11001 Thos
Solon 11001 Willis 11001
ABSHER, Rebecca 12254
A-CHEE-NEE 10901
ACHILLIE 10910
A-CHIN-NEE 11481
ACORN, Charley 12698
ADAIR, Ailsey 10670 11509
Andy 10670 12483 Betty
10670 12483 Bluie 13116
Catherine 10670 12483
Charlotte 12435 12483
Cornelius 11614 Delia
12435 12483 Eliz 10670
Geo 12483 Gladys 11614
J B 10910 11983 11991
12445 12483 12615 12683
13111 13155 13248 Jas
10670 11509 John B 12435
John F 12483 Kate 10670
Katy 12483 Laura 11614
Lucy 12629 Magnolia 11630
Malderine 10670 Mamie
11614 Mary 12546 Mollie
10670 Mollie E 10316
Myrtle 11614 Newt 12483
Polly 12435 12483 Rufus
10670 Sabina 11686 Saml
12173 12435 12483 Susan
10670 Wm 10670
ADAMS, Ada 11398 Albert 11385
Catherine 12439 Charley M
10349 Jackson 12437 Jas
12106 John 12278 John A
12438 Ona 11383 Simon W
10360 Wm 11390
ADDINGTON, Cicero W 12499
Clarence G 12499 Frederick
E 12499
ADISON, Geo 13061
ADKINS, Mary M 12464 Mary
Melviney 12464
ADKINSON, Jasper N 11705

ADKISSON, Callice M 11705
Clarence M 11705 Jasper N
11705 Kittie 11705 Paralee
11705 Susie D 11705 Thos E
11705
ADOLPH, Pairlee 11692
A-GE 10211
A-GIH 12388
AH-DAW-LA-NUS-KY 12417
AH-DAW-SEE-NEH 12534
AH-DEE-TUS-KEE 12417
A-HE-KIH 11109
AH-GAH-TE-YUH 10207
AH-GUAH-TAKY, Jenny 12649
AH-HEH-STAH 11188
AH-HE-SAH-TA-SKEE, 10596
O-see 10596
AH-HYUH-HE-NUH 11908
AH-KEE-LEE 13223
AH-KE-TO-HEE 13193
AH-LE-CHUH 10640
AH-LEE-SAH 13258
AH-LIH-KIH 10953
AH-MA-DE-SKE 12498
AH-MAH-DOO-IH-KAH 11991
AH-MAN-TSUH 11919
AH-MOO-GAH-NAH-STU 11405
AH-NAH-LOO-QUES-KE 11917
AH-NEE-CHE 11137
AH-NEE-SKAH-YAH-TE 11991
AH-NE-TAH-NUH-UH 12848
AH-NI-WA-GE 11552
AH-NOO-YOU-HE 10646
AH-QUAH-TAKY, Jenny 12649
AH-QUA-LIH 11849
AH-QUOO-TA-KIH 10804
AH-TA-LIH 10648
AH-TE-THE-E 10421
AH-TO-WOH-SKEE 10910
AH-WIH-GAH-DAW 12576
AH-YAH-NIH 10680
AH-YAH-STAH 10197
AH-YEH-HE-NEH 10774
AH-YER-NOO-LAH 11908
AH-YE-TAH 11559
AIL-SEY 11198 11210
AIMES, Annie 10286 Myrtle
10286
AIN-CEH/AIN-CIH 10774 13040
A-KEY 10587

A-KIL-LIH 10910
A-LAH-QUAH 11481
ALBERTY, Albert B 11300 Albert C 11299 Bernice L 11782 Callie 11300 Cecil E 11782 Ellis R 11300 Jas H 11300 Jas R 11782 Jesse M 13115 John R 13115 Julia 13115 Julianna 11299 Lora May 11300 Lucy C 13115 Maggie M 11782 Nancy 10283 Nannie W 11782 Robt G 11300 Sue M 11782 Wm 13115
ALECK, Aquilla 13097
ALEEKE 11190
A-LEN-NEH 12991
ALEX, Celia 13058
ALEXANDER, Caroline 10605 Geo M 12141 Jeanie M 12141 Jos 12142 Thompson 12143
ALFORD, Sallie M 11185 Wm D 11185
ALLEN, Aaron 10643 Annie 11482 Ce-nee 10643 Cephas 10909 Chas Andrew 10838 Eliz 11512 Herman H 10609 Jinnie 11620 John G 11243 John Pollard 10837 Martha 11381 Mary L 10909 Osceola 11512 11822 Sarah 10643 Stella E 10609 10885 Velma 11822 Walter A 10909
ALONE, 12198
AL-SUH 10649
A-ME-NAH, Sah-lih 11863
A-NA-WA-KI 12159
ANDERSON, Amanda 13156 Lizzie 11014 Manda 10337 Mary Catherine 12972 Naomy J 12965 Wm B 11014 Willie May 11014
ANDRE, Eliza 10606
ANDREWS, Howard B 10667 Susie C 10667
AN-I-CA 11456
A(N)-NIH 10216 10414
A-NIH-DIH 10207
AN-NE-WA-KE 10382
APPLEMAN, Margaret N 12065
A-QUO-SA 11991
AR-HET-E 10595
AR-LE-CHER 13245

AR-NEECH 12435
ARL-SER 10649
ARMACHAIN, Amy 11137
ARMSTRONG, Eliz 11891
ARNEACH, Jefferson 10804-5 Sarah 11606
ARNOLD, Geo C 12292 Jas M 12356 Lula 12355 Sally 11306 Tula 12355
ARROW, Bill 11969
A-SE-KE 10648
ASHMAN, Laura 10447
ASHWORTH, Betsy 12606 Cynthia 12606 Jim 12606 Joab 12606 John 12606 Joshua 12606 Nancy 12606
ASKWATER, Wm 13082
ATHERTON, Lila G 10552
ATHINS, Wm P 12382
ATKINS, Benj M 10550 Berry I 10551 Calvin V 10549 Francis 12040 Geo W 10548 Jas L 11309 John S 11308 Solomon W 12041 Spartan S 11367 Webster B 10547 Wm H 10546 Wm P 12382
A-TO-HEE 10322
AUDD, Flora R 11979
AUGERHOLE, Eli 11487 Wat 11857
AUL-CIN-NIH 12598-9
AUL-KIN-NIH 11125
AUSTIN, Lucinda 11976 Sarah R 11976
AVARY, Rober 10484
AWLS, Nancy 10763
AX, Lucinda 11285 Manda 11286 Mandy 11285 Peter 11285

BACKWATER, Stand 11919
BACON, Kate 12227 Mattie 10250 10850
BADGE, Mary 12593
BADGET, Geo M 12593 Wm R 12593 Wm Ross 12953
BAILEY, Anna 10488 Frankie C 11823 J B 12979 Melvin C 12981 Nannie 12615 W W 12980
BAKER, 12070 Eliz 12555 Elmira 12949 Martha M

438

BAKER (Cont) 12219 Webster C
12555
BALDRIDGE, Caroline 10707
Chas 12576 Eliza 10706 Geo
12576 Jas 12576 Nannie
10740 Richd 10705 Sarah C
11933 Susie p436 Wm 10707
12576
BAL(L)ENTINE, Annie M 10185
Nancy 11680 Ollie B 10186
Perry B 11680 Wm H 10186
BALES, David 11179 Jefferson
C 11179 Tinsey Jane 11179
BALLARD, Barney F 10325 Capi-
tola L 10593 Carrie M
10593 Donald L 10593 Edna
Pearl 10325 Eva M 10325
Freeman S 10325 Geo M
10432 Henry C 13064 Jas F
13065 Jno C 13065 John J
10593 Nellie G 10325 Percy
Paul 10325 Sallie 10591
10593 Thos H 10593 Wm
10592-3
BALLINGER, Fannie L 10328
Fannie R 10328 Maiva O
10328
BALLOU, Jeff 10730 Nancy
10730 T C 10203
BANOSKI, Mage 12214
BANTY, Lila 11012
BARBER, Alsey Jane 10482 Dane
10198 Dave 10198 Joanna
10482 Maud 10197
BARE Canzada 11816 Meca 11094
BARK, Daisy 10710 Eliza 10665
John 10710 Levie 10710
Lizzie 10710 Lousia 10710
Richd 10710
BARKER, Artemus B 12386 Dave
10198 12387 Dennis 12386
Emelese 12386 John G 11241
Mary A 12386 Maud 10197
Minnie L 10969 Sequoyah
12386
BARLOW, Nancy 11093
BARNES 12073 Bulah 12901 Chas
12901 Cora 10890 Corinne
13207 Corn 12508 Cornelius
12901 Harriet 10245 Jas
10245 Jamie 12901 Jerry
10245 John 10245 Jos 10245

BARNES (Cont) Louis 10245
Mary Ann 10245 Oscar 12901
Wenona 12901
BARNETT, Bertha M 10887 Geo W
12478 Robt E 10887 Sarah F
10887
BARNOSK(I)E, Cat 12214 12549
12550-1 Charlie 12214
12551 Consee 12549 Lizzie
12549 Nancy 12550 Wm 10434
BARTHEL, Annie 13068 Frank
13068 Frank Jr 13068 Mamie
13068 Wm H 13068
BASHEARS, Eliz 11670
BAT(T), Blue 11231 12611 Danl
10396 Daylight 12501
Earthy 10396 Ellis 12501-3
Hennie 12501 Jack 10396
12502 Jas 12501 12503 Lucy
12501 Patsy 10396 Ter-gen-
wor-se 12501
BAUR, Owenah A 11214
BAUGHMAN, Dora A 10756 Dora E
10743 N D 10756 Nannie L
10743 Temperence W 10743
W E 10743
BAYNE, Cora E 10290
BAYS, David C 12085 Lizzie
12084
BEAMER, Alice 12587
BEAN(E), Anderson 10327-8
Bruce 11277-8 Dot 11414
Edwd R 11414 Eliza E 11414
Gladys D 10327 Jane 11414
Jesse J 11414 Jim 10253
Lorena 11414 Lydia 12802
Mary E 11635 Mary S 11635
Nancy Jane 12802 Robt B
11278 Sallie 12802
Saphronia 12847 Sarah E
10327 Thos A 10327 Tot
11414 Wm 12802
BEANS, Mark A 11277
BEARHEAD, Lucy 13102 Nancy
13102
BEARMEAT, 11606 Alsie 11606
Lydia 11606
BEARPAW, Annie 13199 Danl
10963 Emiline 13199 Isaac
11914 Jas 13199 John 13199
Wah-le-se 11641
BEARWOOL, Geo 10680

BEAVER, Alsie 11012 11489
  Annie 13232 Cherrie 11012
  Clem 13218 Creek 13130
  Dora 13153 Eliza 13111
  Eliza Daugherty 12416 Geo
  10883 High 10883 Ice 10883
  Jim 13130 Lesley 13130
  Lewis 10883 Linnie 13218
  Louis 11499 Lucy 13153-5
  13220-1 Maggie 13221 Mary
  11012 Mohawk 13130 Mollie
  13130 Na-ha-ki 13130 Nannie 13218 Nellie 10944
  13218 Ola 12630 Sallie
  13217 Sam 13154 Sarah
  11499 Steve 13218 Susannah
  13130 Susie 10883 12416
  Tom 11012 Wm 12630 13135
BEAVERS, Josephine 10623
BECK, Arlilee 13045 Cherry M
  11595 Chessie 12816 Claud
  10385 Cogin 12240 Eliza
  10385 Elmina A 11341 Ezekiel 11595 Geo 11595 Guy
  13045 Harlin 13041 Homer
  10385 Ida R 11595 11597
  Jas 12240 Jeff 11341 Jeffrey 13044 John 11595
  13042 John H 13043 Jos R
  10385 Kermit 12816 Laura
  11341 13041 Lila May 11341
  Lillie B 11595 Lottie A
  13043 Lynda 10385 Martha
  11512 Martin V 11341 Nannie 10385 Polly 11826 Robt
  11271 Sabra 11595 Saml
  10497 Sarah A 12816 Sarah
  Ann 11512 Stacy 12797
  13184-6 Tom 12240 Toney A
  12816 Weatherford 13043 Wm
  P 12240 Willie Orien 13041
  13041 Willie Orn 13041
BEEMON, Wm 11834
BELDER, Cora L 11618
BELL, Ada Jane 10455-6 10460
  Charlotte 12615 Eleanor B
  10455 Eunice 12842 Henry C
  10460 Henry Charlton 10460
  Hooley 12620 Isla May
  10459 J H 10796 Jennie
  12620-1 Jesse 12620 John D
  12620 Mary Jane 10460

BELL (Cont) Raymond B 10457
  Stephen 12620 Willard
  10456 Wm 11671
BELLEW, Eliza 10624
BELT, Liddy 11908 Nancy 11908
  Scoo-wee Scoo-wee 11908
  Thos 11908
BENDABOUT, Lucy 10306 10326
  Moses 10326
BENGE, Adna S 12364 Annie
  13223 Dick 13223 Houston
  13223 Martin 13223 Patsy
  13223 Richd 10702 13223
BENNETT, Arch 10177 Elinder E
  10176 Simpson 11415
BIBLE, Arthur A 12421 Lewis
  12421 Ruth 12421
BIDDY, 12298 12323-9 12338-42
BIG ACORN, Red Bird 10581
BIG BULLET, 13246 Nancy 13246
  Sally 13246
BIG DRUM, 12615 Joe 12615
BIGBY, Elenora 12421 Eliz
  11501 Katy 12483
BIGCABIN, 11863 Sarah 11863
BIGFEATHER, Annie 10688 10910
  Ben 10952 Gussie 10688
  Jennie 10688 10901 John
  10309 Johnsinne 10901
  Johnson 10901 Ka-ho-gah
  13222 Lucy 10688 Mary
  10688 Mitchell 10688 Nelly
  10901 Rider 13121
BIGSIDE, John 10730
BIGWITCH, Sallie Long 12749
BILYEN, Rebecca J 12083
BINUM, Martha 12100
BIRD/BYRD, 13091 Belle 10805
  Bessie 10804-5 Bettie
  12752 Bird C 11118 Cilinda
  11137 Colinda 11118 Dan
  11118 Dave 11541 David
  10804-5 Delilah 10752 Eli
  12752 Going 12752 Golindy
  11137 Jesse 11230 Lizzie
  10804 Martha J 10862
  Millie 11365 Nan 11118
  Ollie 11115 11118 Peter
  11552 Quatie 11107 Sill
  11107 Sis 11230 11238
  Tohiskie 11107 Wallie
  12752 12755 Wm Jr 11684

BIRD CHOPPER, 11641
BIRDTAIL, Annie 11765 Dave
11765 John 11765 Sam 11765
BISHOP, A 10801 Alice 11068
Ella 12350 Mary E 12345
BLACK, John 11251 Martha
10430
BLACKBEAR, Cyntha 10207
Cyntha S 10208 10211 Love
10211 Scale 10211
BLACKBIRD, Dave 11519 Jew-
saw-lunt 11403 Jim 11403
Jos 11403 Lucy 11458 Oo-
goo-ne-ya-chee 11403
Suai-eest 11403
BLACKBURN, Fanny Lucinda
11941 Jas J 11941 Jas
Jackson 11941
BLACKFA, Sam 10221
BLACKFOX, Charlotte 10221 Joe
10221 Jno A 10221 Lucy
10221 11234 Sallie 10221
Sam 10221 Steve 10221
Susie 10221
BLACKHAWK 12414
BLACKSTONE, Edwd F 13170
Eliza 12515 Frank 12517
Frank S 12517 Mollie L
11011
BLACKWELL, Julia 10836 Sarah
I 12957 Sarah J 11619
BLACKWOOD, Annie 12648
BLAIR, Geo 11553 12440-3 Jas
12829 Jennie 12225 John R
12829 Lewis 11553 Nancy
11553 Susan 11608
BLAKELY, Hiram 10452
BLAKEMORE, Eliza J 13239
BLEVINS, Alex 12553 Alice M
11050 Alley 11096 Bertie
11448 Eliz 11066 11089
Elzina 12961 Emanuel 11053
Estille E 11078 Ettis
11095 Franklin M 12963 Geo
W 11079 Gorden 11092 Green
C 11062 Henry C 11071 Ir-
ving W 11060 Jessie 12468
John H 11075 John T 10766
Josephine 11058 Loyd 12962
Manervia C 11098 Marcala
12964 Martha 11562 Martha
P 11057 Mary E 11097

BLEVINS (Cont) Minter F 11068
Monroe 11563 Sarah 11074
Susan B 11100 Wm 11811 Wm
L 11087
BLEVIS, Wm R 12966
BLISS, Hattie 11533 Luria V
11533
BLUEBIRD, Charlie 11849
BLUE-EYE 10961
BLYTHE, 10260 10473 10796
10847 10857 11374 11383
11385 11390-1 11398 11615
11622 12093 12106 12113-4
12278 12281 12460 David
11139 Jackson 10747 Jas
10775 11131 12753 Nancy
Ann 12558 Nannie 11139
Wm H 11116
BOATMAN, Dovie L 11642 Edgar
11642 Ocie E 11642 Sarah L
11642
BOLAND/BOLEN/BOLING/BOLYN/
BOWLIN(G), 10303 Caty
10313 Chas 10303 10313-4
Charlie 11541 Geo 10313
Jas 11541 Jennie 10313
11552 Jenymire C 10786 Joe
11541 John 10303 Johnson
10313 Kate 10733-5 Lizzie
11541 Lydia 10303 Martha
10303 Sallie 10303 Sarah
10303 11700 13203 Shaw-ney
11541 Susan A 12475 Tooka
10400 Wm 11540 Willie
11540 Worcester 10313
Woster 10313-5 Wyley 10322
BOLES Leo B 12573 Richd 12573
BOLTON, Margaret 11981
BONDS, Ava M 11445 Ora M
11445
BONE, Albert 12039 Bessie
12038 Etta 12039 Lon Etta
12037 Ollie 11442 Sam
11442
BONEY, Chic-gu-wi 11457 Sa-ke
11442 Sam 11438
BOOKER, Mary J 13020
BOON, Zadee 10726
BOOTS, Polly 10253
BORDERS, Rosa B 12978
BOWEN, Clara 11638 Mahala
11726

BOWERS, Lillie 12191 Mary
12189
BOWLEY, Alton F 12556 12558
BOYD, Wm Oscar 10240
BRACKETT, Chas A 12422 John
11506
BRADFORD, Buff 11994 Joe
11992-4 Jos 11993 Mamie
11993 Riley 11992 Susie
11993
BRADLEY, Benj 12433 Cynthia A
12433 Frederick 12433 Geo
12433 Henry 12769 Lizzie
12769-70 Robt 12433 Van
Daley 12769 Walter 12433
BRADY, Arthur 13188 Eliza
13188 Eliz 13188 Jas 13188
Johhn 10635 13188 Luther
13188 Mary 13188 McKinley
13188 Nancy 13188 Rachel
10635 Robt A 13188 Sarah
13188
BRAMLET(T), Josie 12218 Lucy
12354 Miles 12046 Robt L
12353-4 Robt T 12353 Tilda
E 12051 Wm B 12046
BRANAN, Clifford B 11228 Edwd
H 11228 Emma H 11228 Geo F
11228 Virgil C 11228 Wm C
11228
BRASWELL, Eliz 12811
BRAY John 13244 Julia A 10846
BREMER, Olivier R 10782
BRENDLE, Patsy J 12990
BREWER, Alice 12971 Carrie B
12677 Cherokee 12678-9
Commodore P 10959 Cynthia
12835 Delia 11225 Delilah
12726 Eliza 12835 Eliz
12835 G W 12677 Geo 12835
Geo W 12678 John 12835
John T 12677 Lucile G
12678 Lydia 12835 Mack
12971 Mark 12971 Mary G
12677 Nannie M 12678
Oliver P 10782 Polly 12835
Richd R 12678 Thos J 10959
Tom 12835 Walter P 12677
Wm M 12677
BRICE, Annie L 11301 Chas M
11301 Louis A 11301 Walter
J 11301

BRIDGES, Aaron 11505 Conihei-
nie Jerusha 11505 John
11505 Obadiah Ksaw 11505
BRIGANCE, Sarah F 12082
BRILEY, Lela E 11927 Nettie M
11927 Tennesse V 11927 Wm
E 11927
BRINEGER, Leroy 13008
BROCK, Mary M 11528
BROCKS, Eunice G 10302 Sophia
J 10302
BROOKS, Manda 10412 Mary Eliz
11215 Polly 10213
BROOKSHER, Nancy 10433
BROSWELL, Lizzie 12811
BROWN, Addie V 10188 Akie
12722 Alex 10478 10848
11368 11375 11380 11394-5
12094 12098 12274-5 12465
12950 12956 Anna L 12183
Barnum L 12036 Bertha E
10188 C H 12031 Charley
10315 Donia J 12056 Eddie
12034 Eliz 10661 Elzina
11283 Fannie 10315 Fanny
Lucinda 11941 Fisher 11941
Frank 12670 Frederick C
12670 Geneva 10315 Geneva
A 12670 Geo 11981 Henry
Columbus 11954 Ida B 10313
10315 Inez 12033 Jack
12722 Jas 11941 Jesse B
10335 Jimmy 11941 John
10315 11606 12722 John Jr
12722 John R 12035 John
Robertson 10661 Jonas
11606 Kellah 12722 Laura
12031-2 Lousanna 10215
Luvicy 11981 Lydia 11606
Mary 12952 Mary Ann 10661
Mary E 10188 Melissa A
10868 Morning 12500 Nar-
cissa 12722 Nettie 13024
Ollie 12722 12724 Peter
11606 Pleasant 12382 Polly
10961 Rebecca J 10863 Robt
12728 Robertson 10661
12728 12912 Rosceo 10315
Viola 12728 W D 11949 Wm
11949 Wm T 10354
BROWNING, Jas 10472
BRUERE, Louis 11625

442

BUCK, Jumper 11527 Nellie
11527
BUCKALOO, 10472
BUCKET, Dave 11793
BUCKHORN, Lizzie 11777
BUCKSKIN, Ah-day-you-ih
11526 Al-sey 11526 Celia
11526 Frank 11526 Geo
11526 Jas 11526 Jesse
11526 Katie 11526 Little
Bird 11526 Nancy 11526 Red
Bird 11526 Sam 10616 11229
11526 SMITH 11526
BUDD, Celia 10207 Sallie Dave
10207
BUDDER, Celia Dave 10207 Dave
10207
BULLFROG, 11739 Deh-yeh-ni
10680 Dele-yeh-in 10680
Dun-a-waws 11739 Maria
11739 Tiana 10680
BULLOCK, Ora 10795
BUMGARDNER, Charlotte E 11638
BUNCH, Jennie 13123
BURCHETT, Ellen 12467
BURCKHALTER, Frances L 11628
Opal L 11628 Tom C 11628
BURDICK, Betsy 12606
BURKE, Austia L 10729 Lulu M
11402
BURNELL, Jesse Jr 13156
BURNETT, Dannie H 13238-40
David L 10275 Myrtie 10233
Ruben H 10277 Wm Jas 13238
Wm W 10276
BURNS, Clarissa 11252 Dent
11252 Geo 11252 Jack 11252
Jim 11252 Martin 11252
Saml T 11006
BURRELL, Jesse 12500 Jesse Jr
10348 12523-5 13157 Joe
12500 Julia Ann 12500 Mary
Ann 12500 Oscar 12524
Sarah 12500 Seaborn 12523
12524 Simpson 12500 Simp-
son Jr 12525 Spence 12500
Timothy 12500 Tylus 12500
W T 10348
BUSH, Bettie 11708
BUSH(E)YHEAD, Geo 11774 Jenny
11198 Jesse 11410 Larenda
11197 12212-3 Nancy 11499

BUSSEY, Emma B 10335
BUSTER, 10944 Mamie 12552
Nannie 12416 12552
BUSYHEAD, Jennie 11774
BUTLER, Catherine 12900 Da-
goo-disk 10645 Danl R
12900 Edwd 11424 Eliza
11935 Ga-len 10645 Jas L
12900 Jane 11424 Jo 10645
John 10645 Judge 10645
Pierce P 12900 Robt E
11780 Takie 10645 Ti-goo-
di-skie 10645 Willie E
11780
BUTTRY, Louis C 10615
BUTTS, Cherokee 13167 Naeta M
13167 R B 11569-72
BUZZARD, Berry 13134 Blue
10323 Cennie 13087 Corne-
lius 11412 Israel 11443
Jackson 13087 John 10894
11443 Lese 11405 11443
Lucy 11412 11430 Mary
13087 Nancy 11412 11443
Sallie 13087 13200 Sam
11405 11443 STEVE 10323
WM 11687 13087
BYARS, Sarah A 11366
BYERS, Geo 11927 Sally 10192
11654 11656 12110 13148
BYRON, Nettie May 12275

CADLE, Mahaley 11501
CAGLE, Henry L 12342 Mary
12341-2
CA-HAW-CUH 11232
CAH-LAH-LOH-TIE 10883
CAH-LE-LOW-HIH 11197
CAH-NE-TOO 11909
CAH-SAH-LOW/CAH-SE-LOW, 11197
Al-teesk 11197 Eli 11197
Lewis 11197
CAH-SAH-LOW-(W)EE 11197
CAHSALAHWE, Jenahye 12547
CAH-SHE-YES-KI 13130
CAH-TA-GOO-GUH 10496
CAH-TAH-NAH 13248
CAH-TAH-QUL-LAH 13139
CAH-TA-YAH 11774
CALDWELL, A B 11578 Annie
12886 Catherine 11582
Louisa L 11580 Luther B

CALDWELL (Cont) 11585 Thos J
    11581
CAHOUN, Eve 12758 Godoquoskie
    12758 Henry 12758 Lawrence
    12758 Lloyd 12758 Morgan
    12758 Sallie 12758 Wattie
    12758 Yenkeenee 12758
CALL, Calvin I 11593 Eliz
    11587 Jane 11587 John F
    11588 11596 Jos 11587
CALLAHAN, Dave 10436 Eliz
    10436 John 10436
CAMERON, Alice 12596 Andrew
    12596 Jas 12632 John 12596
    Lizzie 12595 Nancy 12632
    Olce 12596 Olcie 12597
    Peggy 12632 Susie 12596
    Will 12596
CAMP, Jas M 11709 Jas R 11709
CAMPBELL, Jim 10749-50 Nannie
    10749
CANARY, Alona J 12887 Anola J
    12887 Elmira L 12887 Emma
    P 12887 Jas H 12887 Simeon
    C 12887
CANDLE, Louisa F 10406
CANNEFAX, Geo L 12522 Jose-
    phine H 10436
CANNON, Claud 11674 Effie L
    11674 Mattie E 11674 Roxie
    11674
CANOE, Ellis 10952
CA-NOO-GI 10382
CANYOUSA 10641
CAN-YOU-WAU-KIH 11765
CARDELL, Anna 11510
CARDEN, Anna 11510 Edwd W
    11510 John Jos 11510 Mary
    A 11510 Wm Thos 11510
CAR(E)Y, Dick 10253 Jas 12159
    Malida 12159 Nancy 12159
    Sam 11481 Shade 12159
    Walker 12159
CARLILE, Chas 10741 Mary
    12655 Piercie J 11436
    Piercy J 11437 Robt B
    11436 Senareste 11436
CARNES, Amelia Jane 10851
    Edwd E 10859 Maude 10852
CARNEY, Aaron P 11344 Cicero
    A 12030 Freeman 12029
    Scott 11364 Silas K 11363

CARNEY (Cont) Susan L 11362
CARROLL, Charley 10678 Jesse
    10393
CAR-SE-LOW-EE 12401
CARSELOWEY, Chas M 10257 Chas
    V 10257 Jas R 11197 Jim
    11197 Mary D 10257
CARTER, Clement A 10913 Ellen
    13034 Geo W 10914 John
    Walker 12063 Josiah 11512
    Laura Ann 12948 Luke 11494
    Millard F 10911 Robt L
    10912
CARVER, Jas F 11575.5 Passey
    J 12282 Pearl 11575.5
    Walter 11575.5
CASH, Bird 11952 Cassie 11949
    Chas 11952 Dan 11952 Larry
    11952
CATCH-A-COON 12388
CATCHER, Andrew 10425 Linny
    12803 Nelly 13241
CATRON, Maggie 11990 Marty
    11990 Mary 11989-90 Peggie
    11990
CAVALIER, Cicero T 11521
    Curtis 11521 Eliza 11521
    Markham 11521 Scott 11521
    Theodore P 11521 Walter A
    11521
CAW-CA-LEE-SKY 10382
CAW-DASIE 10645
CAWN, Jackson 11485
CA-YOU-NE-CAH 13126
CAYWOOD, Aggie 11973 Agness
    11973 Cartayah 11973
    Dah-me 11973 Ida 11973
    John Davis 11973 Lee 11973
    Ool-skas-te 11973 Tom
    11973 Wolfe 11973
CHAH-LIH 11973 13258
CHAH-WAH-YOU-CAH 10626
CHAH-WA-YI-KA 11822
CHAH-WA-YU-KA 11512
CHAIR, Margaret 10209
CHAMBER, Wm A Jr 12120
CHAMBERLAIN, Alice E 11288
    Eunice D 11288
CHAMBERS, Ezekiel P 11266
    Geo 13209 Geo S 11267 Jas
    13209 Jesse S 11650 Joe
    11265 John I 11264 John Q

CHAMBERS (Cont) 11264 Leon
11265 Martha 13209 Nannie
E 12159 Rosa M 12120 Susan
Susan 13209 Teesey 12159
Wm W 11265 11265
CHANCE, Della E 11174
CHANDLER, Fanny E 10956 11194
12491-3 12804 Richd 10727
CHANEY, Alfred H. 10315 Flo-
rence 10315
CHARLES, Sallie 10464
CHAR-WAH-YOU-KA, Lila 11983
CHASTAIN, Mary F 12518
CHAW-E-YOU-KEE 13139
CHA-WE-YU-KAH 11198
CHA-WEE-YU-KA 12401
CHA-YEH-YO-HEE 11217
CHEATER, Asy 13096 Geo 13095
Ike 12922 Jane 12922 John
11432 Lucy 13056 Oo-squi
11409 11432 Peggy 13055
CHE-CAW-NEE-LAH 11765
CHEE-DAH-KAH-HAH 10648
CHEEK, Beatrice 10739 Evie
10739 Geo 10739 Margie
10739 Myrtle 10739 Nina
10739 Rosa 10739 Roy 10739
Seba 10739
CHEE-NAH-KEE-LUH-DIH 10648
CHEE-NOO-YUH-DA-GIH 10207
CHEE-SQUAH-GAH-LOO-YAH 11641
CHEES-QUAH-GEE-GAH-GA 11917
CHEES-QUAH-LAH-TAH 11983
CHEES-QU(A)H-NEET/CHEES-QUI-
NEET, 10641 11118
CHEE-STOO-GAH-LA-KEE 13139
CHEE-TA-KEE 11276
CHEE WEE, Sam 10648
CHEE-YAW-GUH 11526
CHE-GAW-NA-LAH 11765
CHE-GA-YOU-IH 10207 12388
CHE-GO-NA-LAH 13228
CHE-KA-YOU-IH 10207
CHE-KE-LE, Nancy 13225
CHE-LOW-WEE-SIH 11112
CHE-NA-GE 12498
CHE-NAH-QUIH 10499
CHE-NAH-WEE 11971
CHE-NAR-SE 12615
CHE-NEE-LAH-GIH 10216
CHE-NE-LERN-KA 10216
CHENERQUE 12509

CHE-NOO-YUH-DUH-IH 10207
CHE-O-CAH 11276
CHEQUAKEH 11018
CHERRY, Amanda M 11371
CHE-SAH-YAH 11641
CHE-SQUA-DAH-LO-NIH 10499
CHE-SQUA-E-ROL-LA 13225
CHES-SQUA-NE-TA 10641 11415
CHE-STA-CHI 11916
CHE-STE-QUO-LE 12919
CHEW-WAH-GEH 11517
CHE-YAN-STI 10952
CHE-YAU-NI 12615
CHI-AH-LAU-SKE 13223
CHI-AN-NUH-NAH 12615
CHICK-A-LEE-LAW, Annie 10172
Mary 10173
CHICK-A-U-EE 11559
CHICK-A-YIH 11405
CHICK-A-YOUHEE 11018
CHICKEN 11491 Cora 10429 High
10429 Jackson 10429 Ned
10632 Night 10627 See-kee
10627 10649 Susan 11491
CHICKEN-FIGHTER 10595
CHICKENROOST, 11018 11863
Taylor 11018
CHICKILULA, Jacob 10173
Loosy 10173 Mary 10173
Sowanu 10173 Stone 10173
CHICK-KA-DIH-LIH 10595
CHICKO-TE-YOU-HEE 11018
CHI-COW-WEE 12534
CHILTON, Edna H 10609
CHIN-A-QUE 11232
CHOATE, Celia 12831 David
12831 Geo 12831 Katy 12831
Lillian 11484 Nancy 12831
Polly 12831 Susan 12831
Susie 12831 Wm 2831
CHO-CO-NA-LEH 12973
CHOH-GO-HIH 10496
CHOO-A-LOO-KIH 13040
CHOO-DAH-KAH-HAH 10648
CHOO-GAH-WA-LEES-KEE 11190
CHOO-GUH-TAH-TIH 10961
CHOO-LAH-SUH-TAH 11641
CHOO-LE-AH-WAH 10775 11229
CHOO-LUH 11131
CHOO-NOO-LA-HUS-KE 10421
CHOO-TAH-GEE-TAH-LIH, Ja-ke
10961

445

CHOOWEE/CHUWEE, Nannie 10930
Sam 10648 Sarah 11200
CHOO-WE-SKAH 11199
CHOW-A-YOU-KEE 11991
CHOW-WAH-YOU-GAH 10382
CHO-WIN-NIH 11145
CRISP, John 11397 Mary 11397
CHRISTIE/C(H)RISTY, Albert
12650 Annie 12650 Arch
11641 Becky 10333 Caty
11641 Dick 12612 13107 Eli
Eliza 11491 Fannie 12650
Goback 11876 Isaac 10712
Jackson 10712 12404 12418
Jess 12418 Johnson 10333
Lil 13177 Nancy 12651 Nel-
lie Phillip 12512 Quakey
10333 Rachel 11191 Rebecca
10333 Susan 11876 11877
Taylor 12650 Tucksee 10333
CHUC-KU-LUCH, Tom 11716 Nancy
11716
CHUC(K)ALATE/CHUCULATE/
CHUCKERLATE, Annie 13101
Conceen 13192 Danl 13131-2
Jennie 13125 13192 Jessie
10709 Mose 11764 Sally
10937 Sarah 12487
CHU-CON-NUN-TOLE 12570
CHU-DAH-LA, Arch 10628
CHU-HAD-LA, Arch 10628
CHU-KER-TAH 11764
CHU-LES-KANAS-KEE, Geo 12534
CHU-LI-AU-WEE, Fidel 10775
CHULIO, 10220 10266
CHU-LO-AN-WE, Fidel 10775
CHUNESTUDY, John 13106 Wm
11972
CHUO-HUH-LOO-HUH 11606
CHU-WAH-YAH 11983
CHU-YU-NUH-TAH 10253
CLAGHORN(E), Peggie 11625
CLAH-NOO-SEE 11403
CLAPPER, Chas L 11413
CLARK, Anne 10609 Austin
13073 Elita 13073 J Pad
12031 Laura 11981 Lottie A
11958 Lucinda C 13073
Polly 10764 Ruth 13073
CLAU-DAH-MAH 13223
CLAU-GAS-KEE 13208
CLAWS, Polly 10423

CLAY, 11493 Columbus 11452
Henry 13139 Washington
13139
CLAYHORN, Peggie 11625
CLEVELAND, Geo 12050
CLEVINGER, Virginia 12277
CLIFFORD, Wm 11169
CLIMBINGBEAR, Daleeskee 12757
CLINE, Garrison 12340 Jane
12338-9 Wm 12338
CLINGAN, Betty 12483
CLINGING, Katy 12483
CLOUD, Annie Lee 13118 Joshua
13118 Sallie 12776
CLOUSE, Martha E 10778
CLYNING, Jos 12483
COATS, Canzadie 13041 John
13041 Novadia 13041
COBB Mattie 10523 Nancy 10523
COBBLE, 11469
COCHRAN/COCHRUM, Charlie
11503 12538 Clarence 12565
Clinton 12567 Geo 11503
Jas 11854 Jesse 11915
Jesse Jr 12566 John A
11372 Lettie J 12566
Lizzie 13172 Maggie 10218
Maud 10644 Minda L 12565
Nancy 11915 Ned 10351
13172 Sallie 11854 Sanders
11915 Sequoyah 10218
CO-HEE-NE(E)/CO-HIN-NIH 10641
COLBERT, Rebecca A 10835
COLD WEATHER, 11191
COLE, Noah 12337 Thos 12336
COLEMAN, Akie 12903 Arch
11220 Chi 11220 Ed 11220
Emma 11220 Esther 11220
Gooestah 11220 Harrison E
12989 John 10442 Lucinda
13073 Nancy 10442 Peggie
11220-1 Rebecca 12887
Saml 11220
COLLAR, Jackson 10944
COLLET, Martha Henry 12289
COLLIER, John 11471
COLLINS, Andy 12211.5 Caro-
line 12211.5 Dave 12211
Fannie Homer 10545 Henry
11893 Jas B 11269 John
Robt 11022 Lindsey 11022
Mary M 11022 Narcissa

COLLINS (Cont) 12912 Robt V
12111.5 12211 Sirl 11022
U Grant 11022 Wm R 12211.5
Wyoming 11022
COLONAHESKI, 12782 12784
Isiah 12782 Jesse 11151
Katie 12783 Mark 12782
Martha 12782 Nanny 12783
COLVIN, Wm E 13197
COMINGDEER, Eliza 11645 Geo
13132 Hunter 12801 Joe
13125
COMPTON, Nancy 11445 11709
CONCH, John F 11261
CONEY, Walker 12159
CONLEY, Jennie 12753
CONRAD, Eliz 10594 Geo 12837
Jennie L 12837
COOD(E)Y, Annie 11571 Annie F
11571 Bessie 11572 Callie
11570 Jesse 11569 Lavena
Gaylor 11714 Sarah 12365
Wm S 11526 12360
COOK, Edwd A 10230 Robt S
12453 Susan 10423 Susan M
11077 Thos B 10490
COOKS, Callie 12486 Ellis N
12938
COOKSEY, Benton 10794 Floyd
10794 Johnnie 10794 Maggie
10794 Nannie 10794 Robt
10794
COOKSON, John H 11603
COO-LAH-CHIH 10961
COO-LAU-QUA 12615
COON, A-chin-nee 12683 Alice
12420 Annie 12420 12509
Bertha 12420 Boles 12683
Boly 12683 Chaw-wah-yoo-ka
12683 Chow-wee-yuk 12683
Darge(r)y 12683 12685
Darkey 12683 Dee-ki-las-ky
12509 Dick 12388 12683
Ella 12420-1 Joe 12683
John 12683 Tarepin 12683
Turtle 12683 Ute 12683
Wolf 12683
COOPER, Joanna 10657-9 Katie
11827-9
COO-TAU-KEAS-KE 10216
COO-TE-AH 13225
COO-WEE-SCOO-WEE 11493

COO-WEE-STAH 10648
COO-WEST-TAH 12615
CORBIN, John H 11361
CORBITT, Wm N 12079
CORDELL, Jas 10268
CORDERY/CORDRE(A)Y, Ada B
11858 Anna 10961 Charlotte
11868 Jas 11648 Jas B
11858 Josie Ann 11858 Mary
11868 Sarah 11868 Sebe
11648 Thos J 11858
CORN, Bessie 11336 Geo 11340
Henry 11337 Ludie 11338
CORNELIUS, L B 11103 T B
11103 Thos B 11103
CORNETT, Benj M 11291
CORNSILK, Jennie 12540 12542
Johnson 12542 Kate 12543
Wm 12543 York 12777
CORNTASSELL, Jane 10895
Jennie 10894 John 10894
CORNWELL, Mary 11250
CORVIN, Jas 10777 Margaret
10777 Philo 10777 Pleasant
M 10777 Thos 10777
CORWIN, Pleasant N 10777
COTNER, John C 10661
COUCH, Charity 13144 John F
11261 Nancy Jane 13144
Slater 11415
COURTNEY, Isham H 12274 Mary
M 12094
COVINGTON, Hattie 12335
COWAN(D), Isadora 11021 Thos
J 10384 Thos W 10384
COWARD, Thos 10978
COWART, Alice 12135 Collins
12135 Cynthia 12135 John
12135 Mary 12135 12500
Nettie 12135 Slater 12135
COWET, Slater 11415
COWIN, Pleasant M 10781
COX, Frances 10730 Geo W
11180 12945 Jacob 11180
Jas 12947 John 11180 12261
John A 12953 Lottie C
11180 Martha 12255 Polly
11180
CRACK-SHINS 13248
CRAFT, Charley A 11305 Ella V
12956 Lulu L 11304 Thos W
11303

CRAIG, Annie T 10892 Arthur O
11898 Chas A 10892 Chas S
10892 Claud M 11898 Gladys
P 10892 Harry G 11898
Hazel O 11898 Lucinda A
11898 Robt W 10891 Tinsey
Jane 11179 Wm L 11898
CRAIN/CRANE, 12215 Benie
10749 Bessie May 10749
Etter E 10751 Eva May
10751 Geo 10749 10751
Nannie 10749 Richd 10749
Wm Luther 10749
CRAINFORD, Jack 11295
CRARY, John H Sr 11848
CRAVEN, Kate 11454
CRAWFORD, Jack 11295 Mary J
12665
CREEKKILLER, La-le 11460
Lydia 11455 Mary 11455
11459 Rachel 11455 11459
CREER, Callie 10764
CRITTEN, Andrew 13162
CRITTENDEN/CRITTENDON, Albert
C 13025 Annie 10311 Callie
11704 Clem 11465 Felix
10404 Isaac 12802 Jack
10401 Jas E 12536 Jas W
11828 Jess 11739 Leroy
11829 Luke 10401 Lydia
12802 Mariah 11739 Mary
12610 Mary A 12536-7 Mary
J 11827 Minnie B 12544
Morg J 11827 Nancy 12802
Ora A 12536-7 Sam 11739
Sanders 12536-7 Thos C
12536-7 Wm 12399 Wm P
12399
CROOK, Cordelia 13167
Cornelia 13167
CROW, Al-cuh 12749 Al-sih
12749 Alfred 11949 11951
Annie 12779 Boyd 12779
Cornelia 11949 Jas A 10395
Joe 12779 Manda 11955
Mandy 11949 Milley M 11382
Minnie 12779 Nathl 11944
Polly 11493 12401 Sah-la-
nih 12749 Wesley 12749 Wm
11949 Wm S 10359
CROWDER, Polly 10926
CROYE 12166

CRUTCHFIELD, Claude 12925
Henry G 12925 John 12925
Ray 12925 Vinita 10249
CRY, John W 12166 Wm 12166
CULBERSON, Mary J 11360
CUL-CA-LOS-KE, Lewis 10421
CULLE-SKA-WE 10586
CUMMINS, Fannie 11631
CUN-DEE-STA-CHIH 10730
CUNDIF, Louvina 12081
CUNNEHECT, John 13039
CUNNINGHAM, Amanda 12381 Chas
F 10333 Jas M 10333 Lee
Vann 10333 Lizzie P 10333
Maggie 10333 Mary 10333
CUN-SEEN, Osee 11672
CURRY, Robt M 12080 Rosy E
12079 Sarah A 12078
CURTIS, Jas A 10798 Mary F
10237

DABBS, Ruthe 11204
DA-GAH-DAW 11774 12689
DA-GUN-WAK-SEY 11917
DAH-AH-GIH 11131
DAH-GIH 10649 12576
DAH-KINNY 12689
DAH-LE-YE-SKEE, Se-gil-lie
11150-1
DAH-MA(H)-GAH 12198 A-lee
12198 Wagy 12198 Wah-dee
12198
DAH-TOO-SKEE-STE 11919
DAH-YA-NIH 10680
DAH-YES-KI 11541
DAH-YU-CHIN-IH 11198
DALEY, M L 10245 11401
DA-LIH-SKIH 12388
DALTON, Martha P 10834
DAMRON, Francis L 11019
DAN-TAS-KEE 11491
DANEWATER, Lizzie 11018
DANEY, Mary J 12194
DANIEL, Adophus 11687 Alyce
11687 Ann 11961 Annie
11765 Ezekiel 11961 Jas
10257 Jennie 11687 John
11687 11961 Katie 11687
Martha A 11961 Mary 11961
Nicy 11961 Robt 11961
DANIELS, Andy 13150 Geo 10207
Mary 13119 Tom 10207

DARCHURSI, Oo-tsa-te-yah-ta
11916
DARRALL/DARRELL, Flora 11583
Willie C 11584
DAUGHERTY/DOUGHERTY, Dianna
12671 Jimmie 10927 Katie
10927 Rachel 13133 Soap
10927
DAVENPORT, Nancy E 10180
Pleasant S 11201
DAVIDSON, Dollie 11723 Earl
11723 Geo W 11723 Roxie
11723
DAVIS, Alex 11554 Alex D
11997 Allen 12028 Allison
10685 Annie 11134 Benj
11212 Coleman J 11341 Danl
11341 Dave 11849 Edna G
11272 Eliza 11341 Ellis L
11272 George Annie 10194
Gussie 12026 Henry 10543-4
12027 Jas 11849 Joe 11849
John Anna 12493 Katie M
11272 Lillie 12025 Lorenzo
D 11341 Lucinda 12914
12916 Lucy 10194 Mable B
11272 Martha A 11789-90
Miller 11341 Minerva 10594
Nancy 10543 10978 O-nih
11849 Oscar 10543 10544
12024-8 Pearl 12024 S T
10198 Sallie A 11272 Saml
12916 Tennessee 10978 Thos
10942 Thompson 10942 Wm
11211 Willis 10600 Winnie
13066
DAVISON, John C 10408
DA-WEE-GOO-QUA 12992
DA-WE-SIH 11849
DAWSON, 10482 Bell 12805
Polly 10482
DAW-YI 13130
DEAN, Bessie 11490 Claud
11490 Nannie 11490
DEANS, Abbie 11638 Clara
11638 Eliza 11638 John
11638 Martha E 11638
DEBORD, John 11359
DEDAHLEEDOGEE, Annie 11158
DEE-GAH-HEE-GEE-SKIH 10626
DEE-GAH-SE-NA-GIH 10297
DEE-GUH-SUCK-SKIH 10649

DEE-LAH-TA-DA-GEE 11641
DEERHEAD, Lizzie 10882
DEER-IN-(THE)-WATER, Alec
10382 Annie 10381-2 Geo
10955 Katie 10388 Keener
10957 Lizzie 11018 Star
12413
DEERSKIN, Geo 10691 Sallie
10691
DEE-SQUAL-DA-GEE 10207
DE-GAH-NE-SKE 12388
DE-GA-LAS-KEE 10645
DE-GUA-DE-HI, Browston 11429
Saml Hog 11428 Tin Cup
11423
DE-KA-HOO-GEE-SKIE Ancy 11434
DE-KA-HOO-GUS-SKY, Amey 11433
DE-KA-HOO-SKY 11434
DELLAS/DELLUS, Geo 12694
DELOZIER, Edwd 11397 Eliz
11397 Fountain G 10653
Georgia V 10653 Hazel M
10653 John Edwd 10653 Man-
ford G 10653 Mary 11397
Ralph A 10653 Vivian 10653
DEMPSEY, Chas Oscar 13147
Elvin P 11302 11306-7
11310-1 11319 12023 12292
12355-6 Jackson 13147 Jas
W 13147 Jennie M 13147
Jerry 12023 Sallie 13147
DENNIS, Jennie 13088 Jimmie
13088 Mary 13088 Peter
13088 Rachel 13088 Susie
13088
DENSON, Ella 12202
DENTON, Eliz 13047 John 13047
Neely 13047 Randoph 13047
DEPEW, Henry 11872
DE-SQUA-DA-NA-GA-YOU-LE 11552
DE-SUN-STE-SKE 11917
DEW, Fannie 13258 Geo 10596
10639 Jim 11985 Willie
10695
DE-YAH-LEES-KEE 10645
DE-YA-NE 12483
DICK, Coleman 11191 11989-90
Henry 12408 Jennie 12408
John 11989 Katie 11766
Maggie 12408 Nancy 10609
11641 Nannie 11191 Richd
11191 Sally 12408 Sooky

DICK (Cont) 11641 Wm 12408
DICKEN, Watson 12756
DICKENS, Irene Alex 12144
   Miriam Cherokee 12144
DICKERSON, Mary 10435
DICKSON/DIXON, Jas L 12457
   Monroe 12458 Rettie 10437
   Sam A 11377
DILL, Eliz 11401 Wm 11401
DILLARD, Octavia 12625 Tava
   12625
DIRTEATER, Annie 12592
DIRT-HUNTER 12238
DIRTSELLER, Oo-squin-ni 11964
DISNEY, Alice 11854-5 Alide
   11855 Minnie 11855
DOBBS, Edna B 10553 Fannie O
   10556 Leslie Lee 10555
   Mattie May 10554
DOBY, Charlie 11934 Jas 11934
   Jennie 11934 John 11934
   Wm P 11934
DO-CHOO-LA-NAH 11908
DOCKERY, Benj M 10857
DOKE, Henry V 12465
DO-KI-YOS-TIH 11123
DOLINGER, John 13004 Lelah
   11049 Wilda 11051
DONAHO, Manerva F 10445-6
DONCARLOS, Frank L 11250
DOO-CHE-STUH 10496
DORGELOH, Edna V 12557
DORRIS, John R 10260
DOUBLEHEAD, Bird 10725 Peter
   10672 12535
DOWNING, Aaron 12159 Adam
   12513 Alex 10496 Anna L
   12153 Benj 11625 Chas
   12616 Charlie 11625
   Clarinda 11625 Cull 12806
   12807 Dave 12575 David
   10184 Eliz 11625 Geo 10755
   12513 Geo G 12578 Geo H
   12580 Hider 10496 Jas
   11576 12159 Jane 12153
   Janie 12483 Jennie 11294
   Jesse 10900 John 12153
   12513 Johnson 12483 Joshua
   10498 Katie/Katy 11625
   12573 12578-80 Lewis L
   12153 Lizzie 10882 12159
   Lucinda 11625 Maggie 11101

DOWNING (Cont) Malinda 12159
   Maud 12578 12580 Mollie
   12513 13062 Mose 12159 Ned
   10496 Noyah 12513 Oo-de-
   skul-le 10496 Peggie 11625
   Polly 10363 Pumpkin 12616
   Richd 11101 Roy 11101
   Sarah 11625 12574 Simpson
   11101 Sunday 11576 Susie
   11101 Tom 10496 10500 W A
   11908-9 Wm 11625 Wm H
   12153 Zuma 12513
DRAGGER, Osee 11672
DREADFULWATER, Annis 10382
   Henry 10304 10382 11172
   12204 John 10382 Peggy
   10382 Sarah 11519
DREW, Eugene H 13022 Eunis P
   13022 Geo 12359 13022
   Henry 12446 Richd E 13022
   Ruth 12359 W H 12446 Wm
   11492 Wm H 12446 Wm P
   11492
DRINKER, 12417 Jennie 12921
   Katy 12417
DRIVER, Adam 11128 Dick 11110
   Dicky 11126 11138 Eliza
   11128 Lucy 11128 Nannie
   11110 Ned 11128 Quattie
   12756 Will 11126
DROWNING BEAR, Benj 12908
   Coty 12908
DRY, Annie 12683
DRYWATER, Jesse 11847 Lydia
   11847 Mink 11847 Na-lih
   11847
DUGGER, Saml E 12423
DUH-LAY-HAY-LIH 10649
DAY-NAW-WHA-LAH-NIH 10648
DUKE, Buford A 11719 Jesse
   Bowen 11719 Mahala 11726
   Mahala E 11719 Martha
   11751 Matilda 11719 11723
   Patsy 11751 Robt E 11719
   Thos 11751 Wm 11719 Wm H
   11719
DUKES, Holley B 10298 Hooley
   B 10298 Richd 10298
DUNAGAN, Georgia A(nn) 12915
DUNBAR, Bettie 11195
DUNCAN, 11485 Alonso 11485
   Annie 11980 Chas 11485

DUNCAN (Cont) Charlie 11980
    Eliz S 10787 Emma 11980
    Felix 11980 Fred B 13069
    Geo 11485 Hubert 11980
    Inola Josephine 13069 John
    11485 Lillian V 11155
    Lydia 11980 Marion 11485
    Martha 11485 Mary N 13070
    Sallie 11980 Sybal 11155
    Taylor 11980 Wm 11485
DUNLAP, Alice 13186 Berry
    13185 Robt 13184
DURALL, Benoni F 11610 Edna
    Earl 11610 Georgia R 11610
DUTTON, Patrick 11621

EAGLE, Ida 11924 Idia 11919
    Josiah 11924 Wm 11924
EATON, 11382 Frank 10928
    Mary E 10928 Raleigh 10928
    Walter R 10928
EAVIN, Eliza 10733 John 10733
    Looney 10733
EDDINGS, Eliz 11369-73 11376
    11378 11400 Jas A 11369
    Newton J 11376 Wesley S
    11373 Wm R 11370
EDGAR, Cordelia 10692
EDMONDSON, Isaac A 11056 Lu-
    cinda 11055 Rhoda V 11054
EDMONSEY, Delila 11099
EDWARDS, Doska 12248 Jane
    10833 John 10678 Julia
    13038 Lilly 10481
EH-DAW-HIH, Celia 10649
E-JU-LA-HA 10733
E-LAN-CIH 12995
ELDRIDGE, Ailsey 10423 Elmira
    10423 Ibbie 10423 Jeffer-
    son 10423 Jess 10423
    Manerve 10423
ELK, Lizzie 12415 Nannie
    12628 Willie 12628
ELLICK, Jim 10216 10584 John-
    son 10584 Nellie 10584-5
    13215 Polly 10584
ELLIOT(T), Addie 11786
    Catherine 11788 11791
    David 11732 11789 David I
    11732 11784 11789 Davis
    11784 Emma H 11784 Fannie
    M 11784 Jas W 11784 John

ELLIOT(T) (Cont) 11785-7 John
    J 11784 Jos 11732 Lucia
    11736 Mahala 11732 Martha
    A 11790 Matilda 11721 Mol-
    lie V 11784 Orethea 11721
    Riley 11786 Wm T 11787
ELLIS, Catherin 10296
    Charlotte 10296 Dave 11642
    Lydia 11642 Mary Ann 11282
    Mary J 11649 Mitchell
    11642
ELLISON, Amanda 11959
ELMORE, Jesse A 12077
E-LOW-IH 13040
ELRIDGE, Jef 10423
ELROCK, Saml J 11751
ELROD, Saml J 11751
EMRY, Ida J A 11244
EN-EYOU-YAW-HEE 11764
ENGLAND, Annie 10331 Eliza J
    12804 Himon 10329 Katie
    11972 Lavena 11017 Madie
    10330 Mary M 10217 R L
    12491 Saml 12491 Susie Lee
    12492
ENLOE, Betsy 10704
ERVIN, Jas Madison 12730
E-TOO-WIH 11146
E-TOW-IE, John 11188
EUBANKS, Thos J 11339 Wm
    11641 13160
EVANS, Eliz 12403-4 Ellen S
    12267 Katie M 12403 Mary
    10294 Minnie May 10448
    10477 Nannie E 11289 Robt
    H 12403 Wm 11289
EVERETT, Jos H 10780
E-WEE 11136
E-YAR-NIE 11541

FALLING, Calvin E 13063 Geo
    13063 Jennie 13063 Jim
    10421 Joe 10646 John 10646
    11257 John B 11257 Johnson
    11257 Katie 10646 Laura
    10421 Nick 10421 10646
    13257 Onie 10646 Quaity
    10216 10421 Rider 11627
FALLING BLOSSOM, 13225
FARINGTON, Susie 11818
FARLEY, N E C 10229
FARNEY, 12509

FARR, Maria 11949 Saml 11949
FARRIS, Laura C 11048
FAULKNER, D M 10883 10952
10954 11541 11916-7 11922
13101 13130 11552 David J
12894 David M 11599 Frank
F 12894 Janice M 12894
Jennie M 11553 Jinnie
11553 John F 11553 Jos H
11553 Lavinah H 12894
FEATHER, Mary 12748 Nancy
13101
FEATHERHEAD, Jeremiah 11968
FEELING, Moses 10304 11689
Rachel 10304
FELTS, Jennie 10720
FENCE, Dick 10628 Geo 10628
FENCER, Dick 10684 Gar-coo-s-
der-dy 10684 Jesse 10684
Polly 10677 10684 Sam
10684
FENDER, Eliz 12273
FIELD, Eliz 11670 Mary Jane
11501 Richd 11670
FIELDS, 13208 Andrew 10704
Andy 10704 Arch 12835
Arthur C 13190 Ben 10704
Betsy 11491 Catherine
11501 Chrissanna 10294
Dick 12835 Eliza 12835
Eliz 11501 11670 Elmira
10704 Geo 10294 13208 Jas
W 13069 Jane 11501 Jim
11491 11501 Jinsie 11491
Joe 10704 John 10294 10704
Kate 11501 Laura V 11501
Lucinda 12835 Lucy 12835
Lydia Jane 10294 Maggie
11491 12406 Mahaley 11501
Margaret 11501 11745 Mar-
tha 10704 Martha Ann 13069
Martha E 11501 Martha J
13191 Martin 10294 Mary
10294 Mattie 10704 Moses
11501 Moses A 11501 Nancy
10294 11491 Polly 13208
Rhoda 10294 Richd 10704
12835 Rich M 11866 13069
Rider 12835 Riley 10294
Roy J 13190 Sam 11491
11501 Saml 10294 Saphronia
11501 Sarah 10294 Sarah P

FIELDS (Cont) 11501 Seven
12579 Susie 11501 11573
Susie M 11573 Tcippa 10294
Texanna 11853 Timothy
11573-4 Tranna 11853
Valentine 10294 Wm H 13190
Willie 11491
FIELS, Maggie 12402
FILMORE, Emma 11576
FINDLEY, Henry T 11358
FIREKILLER, Jackson 11103
Louisa 11103 Nellie 11103
FISHR, 11200
FITZSIMMONS, Lila 11332
FITZWATERS, Wm J 10864
FIVEKILLER, Frost 12822-8
Jack 10278 12822 Jennie
10278 12822 Polly 10278
Rachel 10278 Sarah 10278
FLEETWOOD, Edmond 10918
Eljeiry 11894
FLESHER, Lucinda 11103
FLETCHER, Thos T 12853
FLOOD, Albert 10621
FLOWERS, 13024
FLUTE, Aggie 12596 Aikey
12596 Charlotte 12596
Josie 12596
FLYING, Alsie 11298 J C 12519
Jas 12627 Jessie J 12519
Johnnie 12519 Linda A
12519
FODDER, Charlie 11498
FOG(G), 13091 Wm 10716
FOOL, Annie 11529
FORD, 10472
FOREMAN, Ada C 11996 Ada
Laura 10390 Al-cy/Ailcey
10674 11764 Alex S 11439
Alice 10674 Araminta R
11794 Chas 11284 Charley
11764 Cherokee 11281
Cherrie 11886 Edwd 11632
Eliz 11632 Frank 13078
John D R 13081 Luke 11878
Ned 11632 Perry A 11996
Sallie 10713 Saml 11284
Sarah 11632 12417 Selcie
11764 Sis Ann 11900 Sucker
10674 Susan A E 13080 Tay-
lor W 11996 Thos A 11886
Thos W 11886 Tom 10674

452

FOREMAN (Cont) 11764 Watie C
11886 Wm 11284 Wm E 11886
FORESTER, David 11396
FORSYTHE, Thursey A 11757
FOSTER, Adam 10730 Aggie
10730 Ai-lin 10730 Annie
12933 Betsy 12594 12599
Beulah 12451 Blackhaw
10730 Cah-nee-gah 10730
Choo-wah-nee-guh 10730
Eliza 10711 12594 Ellen
10730 Emmett H 11263 Jack
10730 Jas 10711-2 12933
Jane 12933 Jess 10730 John
12594 12599 12933 Jos
12933 Kar-nah-tse-sta-tse
10730 Margaret 12933 Mary
12594 12599 Mary J 12423
Nancy 10730 Nun-chih 10730
Ocal 12449 Roastingear
10730 Saml 10730 Sapsucker
10730 Sarah 11024 Susan
12932-3 Susie 10916 Ta-ke
10730 Thos S 11263 Wasp
10730 Wm 12933
FOURKILLER, Charley 12548
Sarah 12541 Takie 10934
FOWLER, Ada E 12715 Adair E
12715 Alice 12334 Arthur
12333 Bessie R 12715 Emory
H 12320 Estelle 12319 Iler
12317 Joe 12332 Julia
12318 Lunie 12322 Mariah E
12055 Mary A 12321 Veneta
12316 Vernia 12315 Wesley
E 12715
FOX, 11018 11131 Swimmer
11131 Zillie 12818
FRANCIS, Eliz L 12848
FRANKLIN, Celia 12831 Evvie
11617 Jacob A 10860 Louis
M 10801-2 Louisa 10998
Lucy 11504 Malinda 12831
Mary 12831 Patton 11504
Wm 12831
FRAZIER, Eliz 11576 Lizzie
12590
FREEMAN, Carrie B 11801
Girlie L 11803 Louvisa A H
10436 Missouri J 11725
Rhoda A 11725 Wm D 11802
Wm H 11725

FRENCH, Awee S 12996 Dora A
13114 Eliza 13093-4 Geo B
12996 Henry C 13114 John H
13114 Leona M M 13114 Lila
11745 Maggie 13094 Marga-
ret 11745 Maronie 12996
Maud 12996 13094 Morgan
12996 Peggy 13136 Soggie
12996 Thos B 11745 Thos F
11745 Walter P 11745 Wm
13094
FRITZ, Edwd 10730 10732
Francis 10730-1 Katie
10730-1
FRIZZLYHEAD, John 10382
FROG, Nancy 11406
FROGLIN, David C 11652
Elihugh M 11653
FRY, Cecil R 12156 Cora V
12160 Cullie 12156 Ger-
trude 12156 Lettie Marie
12156 Mary 12154 Maxwell
12160 Merritt L 12160 Paul
W 12154 Pearl 12160 Robt E
12154 Robt L 12160 Victo-
rine C 12154 Wm H 12154
FRYAR, Andy 11495 Archie
Severe 11495 Mary 11495
Vance 11495 Voisie 11495
FRYE, Argyle 11008 Catherine
11008 Chas O 11008
Harriette 11008 Mamie
11008 Nancy 11008 Pliny
11008 Raymond 11008 Roy
11008 Thos 11008
FUQUETTE, Esom 12167 Jane
12167
FULLER, R C 11778

GA-CHE-YAH-LI 11552
GA-DAS-KIE 10645
GAGE, David 10482 John 10482
Mary Ann 10483
GAH-AH-QUAL-LAH 13139
GA-HA-YUH-GA 13223
GAH-DAH-LA-NUH, 10901 A-chin-
nih 10901
GAH-DAH-NAH 10470
GAH-DAH-QUAL-LIH 11493
GAH-DAW-TLUH-NUH 10961
GAH-DE-CLOT-IH 10496
GAH-DEE-LAS-KAH 10938

GAH-DEE-TLA-A 12753
GAH-DE-TLO-ET 13258
GAH-DO-WAL-LE 11493
GAH-KE-LAW-STAH 10496
GAH-LAH-DAW-LA-DUH 11774
GAH-LAH-SOO-GEE-SKIH 10499
GAH-LAW-NE-DAH 10628
GAH-LAY-NEE-SKIH 11716
GAH-LE-DAH 12498
GAH-LEE-STAH-YAH 10901
GAH-LO-NU-SKEE 13258
GAH-LUH-GIH 10953
GAH-LUH-NUH-DUH 11908
GAH-NAH-GEES-KY 11917
GAH-NAH-HE-LEE 12534
GAH-NAR-DESK 11917
GAH-NAW-HIH 11774
GAH-NAW-SKEE-SKEE 11641
GAH-NE-DOO 11909
GAH-NEE-YAW-IH 12401
GAH-NE-YEH-IH 11191
GAH-NUH-DEE-SKEE 11405
GAH-SO-GE-SKY 13223
GAH-TAH-NIH 11908
GAINS, Albert 10977
GALCATCHER, Emma 10968
GAL-QUAH-GIH-KE-LIH-UH-NE-TA 12579
GAMBILL/GAMBLE, 11469 Wm J 10824
GA-NEES-A 10641
GA-NOO-GIH 10382
GANT, Chas Fount 12227 Mattie 12227 Wm 12227
GAR-DA-TER-TER 12534
GARBER, Sarah J 11758
GARDENHIRE, Jas T 10294
GARLAND, Eliz 12168
GARRETT Ivey A 10242 Margaret C 11307 Margaret G 11302 S E 11319
GA-TAH-NE 11908
GAU-HUN-TIS-KE 10421
GAW-DU-QUAH-SKEE 11210
GAW-SE-LOW-EE 12401
GA-YAH-NAH 12615
GAYDON, Nancy Ann 11356
GA-YUH-NEE 10595
GA-YU-NA-GA 13223
GEARIN, Henry 10300 10943 Polly 10936
GEE-GIH-EH 11526

GEH-CHEE-YEH-LUH 10680
GEH-SKUH-NIH-HIH 10680
GENTRY, 12130 Annie 10847
GEORGE, Charlotte B 11142 Dawson 12761 Julia V 11142 Manley 12761 Martha 12761 Mary 12749 12761 Ollie 12761 Pearl L 10444 Shell 12760
GE-SAH-HE 10216
GES-GAH-NE 10641
GETTINGDOWN, Chas 13109 Lucy 13109-10
GHORMLEY, Bulah May 12714 Carrie E 12714 Ewing C 12714 Ewing M 12714 Hugh W 12714 Ida N 12714 Janice M Lillian J 12714 Lillie M 10783 Lorenzo 10783 Michael O 10783 Nancy 10783-4 Nancy J 10783 Rachel C 10783 Stephen M 10783
GIBBONY, John Wm 10462 Laura May 10462 Mary E 10462 Russel 10462 Sarah J 10462
GIBSON, Frances B 10776 May B 12049
GILES, Dock 12031 Eliza 12031
GILLESPIE, Grace 10978 Jas R 10978 John W 10978 Marcus E 10978 Sarah 10393 Tennessee 10978 Wm R 10978
GIN-NE-SAH 10641
GIRD, Henry Sherrill 10338
GIRTY, Jennie 11775 Stan 11775
GI-YAN-NE 10595
GLAD, Mary E 10773
GLASS, Caswell 13227 Chas D 12574 Charlie 10763 Clementine 10763 Cornelius 13227 Dennis 13227 Diver 10721-2 Eliz 10763 13227 Harvey 13227 Jack 10763 Jim 10763 John 11018 Julia Ann 10763 Katy 13227 Looney 11920 Lucy 11923 Mary 11920 11923 Nancy 10763
GLENN, Bettie 12363 Frank C 11413 Jesse E 11413 Noah 12372
GODDARD, Elbert G 11795 Irene

GODDARD (Cont) E 11795 Irvine
E 11795 Jas W 11795 Stiles
H 11795
GODDIS, Mary E 11357
GODFREY, E Linder M 12021 W B
11392
GOIN, Henry 10777 Mary 10294
Nancy 10294 Nathan 10294
Robt 10294 Sandell 10294
GOING-TO-SLEEP, Looney 12584
Nancy 12584-5
GOINGSNAKE, Arch 10967
GOINS, Asa 10294 Benj F 11186
Bunk 12203 Bush 12480
Francis M 10982 Geo 10440
Henry 11187 Jack 10294 Jas
10294 Jimmie 10294 John
10294-5 11117 Martin 10294
Miller 10779 Minnie 12481
Nathan 10294 Sanford 10294
Thos 10294 Wm V 10980
GOLECH, Maggie 11240
GONSALIS/GONZALES, Caleb S
12435 12815 Delia 12483
John 11861 John A 12435
12815 Lucinda 11861
Margaret 12435
GOO-DAH-YE 10901
GOODEN/GOODIN, Hornet 10733
John 10733 Nanny 10733
GOODFIELD, Eliz 11670 Richd
11670
GOODMAN, Chas 10981 Tommy
10981
GOODMONEY, Annie 11966 Jesse
12923 Webster 11966
GOODSBY, Sarah J 11594
GOODSKY, John T 11586
GOODWIN, Cora 10854
GOODY, John 10733
GOOK, John 10645
GOO-LA-QUAH, 10581 An-nih
10581 Susie 10581 Taw-
choo-wah 10581
GOOLSBY, John T 11586 Sarah
Jane 11586
GOOT, John 10645
GOO-WE-SLAH 10648
GOO-WE-STAH 11233
GORDON, Mrs Watson 11880
GOTHARD, Cynthia 12606
GOURD, Also See RATTLINGGOURD

GOURD (Cont) Alex 11773 Jack
R 10299 Mary R 12389 Susan
R 10174
GO-WA-NUH, John 13248
GO-QAY-LU, El 11517 Will
11517
GO-YEH-NE-E 11849
GRAHAM, Ceberry S 10489 Kate
13242 Mary E 12022 Wm C
11393
GRANT, Mary E 11389
GRASS, Sarah 12571
GRAVE, Luther 12460
GRAVELY, Ellen Lenora 10530
Oscar Lee 11355 Oscar Tee
10530-1 Thos A 10531
GRAVET, Celia 11318
GRAY Amy A 10394 Horace 11453
Jesse 11453 Thos J 10286
GREECE/GREESE, Geo 12644 Will
11755
GREEN, Benj 10617-20 Gardner
10617-20 11504 John R
11205 Lizzie 12805 Marion
M 11205 Martha A 10287
GREENLEAF, John 11606
GREGORY, Jane 11516 Mary E
10475
GRIBBS, Wesley 12594
GRIER, Lulu E 11318
GRIFFIES, Thos J 11352
GRIFFIN, Emaline 10321 Jack
11529 Lizzie 11786 Lydia
12971 Wutty 11529
GRIFFITH, Albert 11942 Bonnie
M 13148 Liddy J 13148
Martha J 13148 Mary 12746
12747 Mary F 13148 Mary
May 11654 Perry G 13148
Undeen 11654 Wm W 11654
GRIMAT/GRIMET(T), Bear 10595
Geo 10595 Ida 10595 10671
John 12407 Mary 11559 Tur-
ner 10595 11559 Wm 12407
GRINNETT, John 10301 Wm 10301
GRINSTEAD, Mary B 12136
GRITTS, Agnes 12645 Anderson
W 12882 Bernice 12645
Charlotte 12645 Franklin
10438 John 12645 Lily
12645 Lizzie 12645 12882
Nannie 10930 Steve 12645

GRITTS (Cont) Thos 12645 Wm
  11602
GROOVE, Susie 12145-6
GROSS, C F 11630 C R 11630
GROUNDHOG, Joe 10389 Nancy
  10389
GROVE, Ah-kil-lo-hee 11481
  Akee 11481 Ellen 11481
  Evan 12152 Evan E 12151-2
  Fannie 12147 Jack 11481
  Jas 11481 Jas C 12122-9
  12131-2 Johnson 11806-7
  Ned 12149-50 Wat-tih 11481
GROVELY, Ellen Lenora 11355
  J Lemmuel 11354 Oscar Lee
  11353 Preston W 11353
GROVES, J C 10733
GUARTNEY, Mary S 11722
GUESS, Abner 12811 Choo-wah-
  nos-kee 12579 Crawfish
  12579 Geo 10397 12579
  Henry 12811 Lydia 12579
  Moses 13088 Nancy 13088
  Nannie 11023-4 Sally 12579
  Tee-se 12579 Wah-la-loo
  12579 Wah-la-ne-tah 12579
  Wm 13088
GUH-LA-WE-SKEE 10648
GUH-NAW-SKEE-SKIH 10207
GUINN, Alma Lee 12805 12805.5
  Charley E 12805 12805.5
  Ida G 12805 Ida Gertrude
  12805 Jas L 12805 12805.5
  Jas L Jr 12805 12805.5
  Malinda 13183 Sarah 12805
  Willie I 12805 Willie L
  12805.5
GUL-STOO-HUS-KEE 12417
GUNTER, Catherine 12495
GUTHRIE, Loren P 12229 Maud
  12229 Myrtle 12229 Odie B
  12229 Wm 12229
GWARTNEY, Mary S 11722

HACKER, Alex G 12196 Almon R
  12196 Frances L 12196
  Frank 12196 Wm Mckinley
  12196
HAH-WE-SAH-WAH-YEH 12784
HA(I)NEY, A M 12268 Alice V
  12269 Jane 10293 M Thos
  12269 Roxie 10465 Wm 10293

HAIR, Charlotte 11527 Geo
  11527 Jack 11527 Jas 10383
  Jefferson 11527 Jennie
  13074 13229 John 13176
  Lizzie 10426 11527 13074
  Maggie 13229 Mandy 10382
  Sallie 10382
HALE, Geo 11880 11962 Henry
  11880 Michael 11880
HALEY, Geo 10436
HALFACRE, Cynthia 11521 Mary
  11521
HALFBREED, Thos C 11918
  Webster 11918
HALL, Andrew Z 12565 Charlie
  O 13112 Floyd E 13112
  Frank F 11105 Franklin C
  11059 Gracie 11105 Jane
  12167 John M 11061 13113
  John R 10353 John W 11105
  Leander 12167 Leander D
  12167 Lizer Jane 12606
  Rachel L 11542 Stelle E
  11105 WM F 11105 WM H
  112152 WM O 13112
HALSEY, Cathaney Sizemore
  12102
HALT, Tucksey 12487
HAMILTON, Alsie 11509
  Clarence 11509 Genie 10670
  Geo T 11509 Hugh M 11509
  Jas R 11509
HAMMER, Black 11190 John
  11190 Looney 11190 12626
HAMPTON, Wm H 10473
HAMRICK, Arminta J 10866
HANCOCK, Glennis R 12178
  Ralph J 12178 Sallie E
  12178
HAND, Josie 12090 Tom 11983
HANKS, Annie 11875 Cabin
  11776 Calvin 11227-8
  Calvin J 11875 Emma 11875
  Fannie 11875 Grace 11875
  Jas Otto 11875 Maud K
  11876 Ora May 11875
HANNAH, Georgie F 12831
HANNAR, Nellie M 10899
HARANGE, Sarah 11028
HARD, Catherine 11450
HARDBARGER, Betsey 13223 John
  13223 Margaret 13223 Peggy

HARDBARGER (Cont) 13250-2
HARDIN, Laura 11622
HARE, Wm G 12959
HARGROVE, Eliz 10692 Mildred
Cherokee 10692
HARLAND, Ellis 10929 Geo Alex
10929 Rachel 10929
HARLESS, Carr C 11016 Lola
11016 Louis 12390 Louisa
12390 Luster L 11016 Reed
12390 Reed Warren 12390
Rufus 12390
HARLIN, Choo-coo-wah 10929
John B 12426 John H 12426
Miriam Louise 12426
HARLIS, Harrison 12602 Wm
12602
HARLOW, Annie 13025
HARNAGE, Nancy 11028 Sarah
11028
HARNAR, Claud R 10899 Clyde
10899 Eulailiah 10899
Nellie M 10899 Ralph R
10899 Randall D 10899
HARP, Ellis 12241
HARPER, Polly 10736-8
HARRIS, Adaline 12810 Benj H
13006 Chas J 11887 Daisy V
11735 Emily 11887 Eva M
11722 Fred A 11887 Jas H
11718 Johnnie A 11817
Malinda A 12116 Martha L
11817 Mary J 10923 Minnie
11887 Nellie M 11817 Robt
P 11817 Thos 11496 12121
Thos J 11761 Wm 11496 Wm M
11817
HARRISON, Louisa 10283 10823
Mary A 11768
HART, Caroline 11629 Celey
11083 Cynthia 11609 Harvey
R 12960 Hugh J 11073 John
11007 John F 11451 Nan
11694
HARVEY, Leona A 10486
HASH, Milly Ann 10340
HASKINS, John 11779
HASTINGS, Lucille 10768 Lulu
S 10768 Lulu Starr 10768
Mayme Starr 10768 Wm W
10768
HATCHER, John 10798

HATFIELD, Daisy R 12076
HAUSE, Benj F 12158 Caleb W
12158 Dan M 12158 Danl M
Jr 12151 Geo W 12158 Jos M
12158 Mabel E 12158 Maria
V 12158 Ruth E 12158 Sarah
R 12158 Thos Oliver 12158
HAUSER, Jerry 12368 Wiley
12370
HAUX, Nanie 12669
HAWK, Lucy 12513
HAWKINS, Eva 12498 Fannie
13258 Jos 10625
HAY(E)S, J Norman 10634 Lew M
10634 Stephen 10492
HAYHURST, Mary Jane 12157
HAYNES, Alie 12262 Hulda
12020
HAZZARD, Nancy 11005
HEADRICKS, Wm 12447
HE-AH-DOH-KA, Thompson 12749
HEATH, Chas 10971 John 10974
Lon 10973 Marion 10970
Robt 12182 Scot 12716
HEFFLEFINGER, Eliz 11262
12666
HEINDSELMAN, Ada E 11472 Leon
E 11472 Sarah E 11472 Wm R
11472
HELMS, Ales J 10972
HELTON, Abraham 10570 11291
12462 Jas H 12942 Jas L
10261 W R J 12461
HEMBREE, Monroe T 10178
Octavia 12984 Wm C 12982
HENCE, Margaret 11828-9
HENDERSON, Lottie 11069
HENDON, Wash 12231
HENDRICKS/HENDRIX, Annie
12447 C R 10363 Charlie
12447 Cynthia 10363 Dave
11163 David 10363 11166-7
Mike 10363 11167 Rosy
12447 Ruth 12447 Susie
12245 12447 Wm 12447
HENDRON, Beulah 12607 Nina
12607 Ula B 12607
HENRY, Amel 10612 Benj 12285
Charley 12287 John 10382
John W 10612 Mary A 12286
HENSLEE/HENSLEY, Amezetta V
11397 Feilden H 12207

HENSLEE/HENSLEY (Cont)
Houston 10704 Jim 10704
Joe 10704 John 10704
Lucinda 10256 Sam 10704
Tennie 10704 Wm R 12209
HENSON, Andrew J 10611 Caline
10171 Chili 10611 Dulce-
more 12230 Eliza 12230
Eliz 10393 Enoch 10171
Hugh 12230 Jack 11763
Jacob 11298 Jas 12230-2
Jos 10611 Mariah 11763 May
12232 Nellie 11298 Pearlie
12230 Poss 11176 Powhatan
11763 Rachel 11298 Richd
10171 Ross 11176 Taylor
11298 Vestie 12230 Wash
11298 Wm 11763
HEREFORD, Burk 12427 Jessie
12427 Robt 12427 Ross B
12427 Sophronia 12427
HERRON, Ruthie Cannefax 12799
HEWING, Levy 11177
HICKORY, John 10630
HICKS, Andrew J 11891 Beatrice 11466 11699 12805
Beatrice I 11466 Eddie
11890 11892 Frank 12844
Geo 11173 12630 Geo E
11466 Jennie M 11466 Lille
12805 Lillie 11466 Lonnie
11891 Mary 12577 Mary Ann
10998 Mary Bell 11699
Millard F 10932 Minerva
11891 Noah T 10478 Sallie
10961 Strumlow N 11375
Wm C 11890
HIDER/HYDER, Danl 10378 Grace
10378 Jesse 10378 Lewis
10378 Rachel 10272 Tom
10378
HIGH, Eddie C 13189 Sarah E
13189 Wm J 13189
HIGHTOWER, Mille 10979 Millie
10979
HILDE(R)BRAND, Cherokee 10341
Eliz 10730 10749 11027
11891 Fannie L 10730 11026
Geo 10700 Jane 10238 John
12701 John W 12741 12746
John Wm 12699 Jos 11698
Julia E 11224 Lizzie 10749

HILDE(R)BRAND (Cont) Mary
10749 11697 Michael 10601
11698 Mike 11891 Na-ke
11441 11444 Nancy 10601
Reese 11103 S Mary 11697
Stephen 11224 11697
HILL, A M 11109 Ann 11109
Daisy 13142 Eliz A A 10609
Hasel 10609 Hausley 11109
John 11111 Kelley 11109
Margaret E 13144 Nancy
11109 Rachel W 12710
Rebecca 13143 Richd D
12482 Sallie 11106 11111
Sarah A 10250
HILLHOUSE, 10517-20 10557-8
10557-8 10561 10571-8
11314-6 12048 12291 12299
12301-14 12335-7 12347-9
12351-2 12357 Annie B
12312 Augusta A 10557
Belle 12314 Elias E 12306
Ernest D 12311 Ethel 12310
Fannie P 12309 Geo W 12308
Glenn 12313 J S 12308 Jas
S 12305 12307 12314 12352
Jas W 12305 Jessie L 12304
Jos J 12303 Joshua 12313
Joshua R 12301-2 12311
Mattie 12301 Melvin M
12299 Robt L 12291 12299
12303-4 12306 12309-10
12312 12351 12357 Susan F
12357 Thos 12352 Wm L
12351
HILLIAM, Mahala 11732-3
HILLIM, Andy 11732 Jas 11732
Jesse 11732 Nancy 11732
Thom 11732 Winfred 11732
HILLIN, Jas B 11733 Jos L
11727 Pinkney H 11734 Wm
11732
HILTON, Ervine Mc E 12462
HINCHE(E)/HINCHEY 10764 Benj
10764 Ford E 11845 Jona
10764 Jonah 10993 Miller
12800 Saml A 11844 Saml K
10764 11511 Saml R 10797
HIPES, Adeline 12137
HITCHER, Lewis 13059 Nancy
13059 13086 13181 Sarah
13181 Wm 13086

HOBGOOD, Thos S 12246
HOGG, John 12205 Oliver 12205
HOGSHOOTER, 11210 11225
    Charley 12924 Charlotte
    10696 Joe 10380 Lizzie
    12159 Susie 12924 Young-
    Beaver 10380
HOLCOMB, Charlie 13204 H J
    12720-1 12896-9 Mary 13205
    Richd 13122 13204-5
HOLDER, Ruth A 10259
HOLLAND, Chas T 12198 Claude
    J 12198 Florence M 12198
    Jennie 11937 Jesse W 12198
    Lizzie 11880 Rachel 12198
    12199 Robt L 12198 Wm G
    12198
HOLLOWAY, Jos 13187 Martha J
    10318
HOLMES, Alsie 13141 Jas 13141
    Nancy J 11608 12829
    Patrick 12172 Susie 12172
HOLT, Annie 12905 Bill 10278
    Dan 10278 Emma 10279 Fran-
    ces 12905 Jacob D 12904
    Jennie 10278 Lizzie 10278
    Mary E 12904 Mose 10278
    Nellie 10278 Sarah 10278
    12487 Sarah H 12904 Tarra-
    pin 12487 Tuxie 10278 Tux-
    ie T 12904 Wm 10278 10280
HOOD, Charley 11577 Dennis
    10793 Dick 11576 Frances
    Emaline 12571 Hattie E
    10793 Jas 11576 Jennie
    11577 Jimmie 11577 John
    11573 11576-7 Julia A
    10476 Kitty 11577 Lizzie
    10793 11577 Louisa J 11879
    Martha 10708 Mary 11574
    11577 Sterling P 13146
    Steve 11577 Tillman 11576
    Tokay E 10793 Trammel
    12571
HOOKER, Nancy 12673
HOOPER, Jas 12412 Lucy 13149
    Nancy 12412 Sally 13094
    13136
HOPPERS, Elon 11693
HORN, Clyde 10675 Eliza 10711
    Fannie M 10676 Geo 10272
    John 10711 12594 Nah-lie

HORN (Cont) 10711 Nellie
    10711
HORNBUCKLE, Henry 10806
    Maggie 11113 Rebecca 11114
HORNER, Louis C 12444
HORSEFLY, Jas 12505 Peggy
    12198 Wah-le-ne 12198 Wat
    12198
HORSEKIN, 11779
HORTON, Mary M 12939
HOUSEBUG, Lizzie 12483
HOUSTON, Annie 10175
HOUX, Nanie 12669
HOWARD, Harriett 11737 Saml S
    12349 Susan 10558
HOWDESHELL, Nannie E 11415
HOWELL, 12046 Moses S 12100
HOWERTON, Didd 13046
HOYT, Milo A 11760 11762 Sue
    11762
HUBBARD, Mary Ann Hester 1
    10354
HUDG(K)INS, John 11933
    Phillip 11933
HUFF, Eliza 11341 Isabella
    13243 John 13243
HUGHES, Betsey 12483 Chas B
    11896 Charley 11909 Dave
    13033 Fanny M 12141 Geo M
    10790 Jas Henry 11901
    Maggie 13034 Mattie 13034
    Otter-lifter 13033 Polly
    12483 Sue A 10790 11284
    11885
HUH-LIH, 10649 See-gih 10649
HULLY, See-kee 10649
HUMMINGBIRD, Annie 12504
    Drunker 12504 Nancy 12504
    Thos 12504 Wm 12504
HUMPHREY, Martha 12732
HUNT, Sallie G 12601
HUNTER, 10944 Florence I
    12686 Grace 12686 John
    11313 Maud 12686 Water
    12392-7
HURD, Geo 11744
HUTCHINS, Ethel D 11987 Lou W
    11987 Nettie 11987 Ralph B
    11987 Uhal R 11987 Willard
    B 11987
HYATT, Harvey A 12808 Norah
    12432 Reuben H 12266

459

HYDE, Emily H 13255 Robt P
12490 Wm 13254
HYDEN, Emma L 10807

ICE, 13126 Lucinda 13130
13224
IE-CAH-HOO-GES-SKE 11407
I-HO-KOLI 12689
I-HU-AH-NEH 11908
INDIAN TOM, 10839-46 12246
INGRAM, Anna L 10896 Georgia
L 10896 John M 10896 John
M Jr 10896 Mattie B 10896
Roy B 10896 W L 10239
Waunita 10896
INSCORE, Emma 11934
I-O-WAN-TEE 13248
IRVING, Grover 10601 Joe
10601 Renie 10601 Roy
10601 Saml 10601 Venie
10601 Watie 10601
ISLAND, Minnie V 12361
ISRAEL, John 11198 11210
11481 11765 11774 12401
12484 12814 Roy 10682
I-YEH-GUH 11672
I-YOS-TUH 11106

JACK-RABBIT 10641
JACKSON, 10788 Anna May 11685
Bob 12741 Cherrie 12727.5
Cherrie B 12727 Fed 12741
Henrietta 11685 Jack 11139
Jacob 10343 Jonas 12976
Manda 10583 Martha 12727.5
Susan Ethel 11685 Walter
12727.5 Wilson 11685
JA-KEY 11917
JA-LE-TAH-TA-KEE 11641
JAMES, Ethel N 10660 Fairy F
10660 Girty 10441 Harold F
10660 Max A 10660 Ray B
10660 Rex B 10660 Ruth G
10660 Sabrina L 10660
Subrina T 10660
JIMISON, Vida E 12885
JANEWAY, Esther 10986 Mary
Jane 10983
JEFFERSON, John J 10268
JE-NAH-YIH 10646
JEN-E-LIN-KIH 12764
JENKINS, Dolly 10583 Fannie

JENKINS (Cont) 10583 Henry
10976 Johnnie 10583 Levi
10583 Lizzie 19583 Lulu
10583 Mauda 10583 Otis
10583 Rufus 10583 Theodore
10583 Walter 10583
JESSANN, Sim De Hart 12764
JESSE, Annie 12919 Fannie
12919 Goodmoney 12923
Jennie 12919 12921 Nancy
12919 Oo-ga-tul-le-nowe-
yeeh 12764 Robt 12919
Tasting 12919
JEW-LE-OR-WAH 10220
JEW-LI-EH-WAH, Elsie 11229
JOE, Squanih 11849 Willie
11849
JOHNSON, Abraham 11935 Andrew
A 13071 Annie 11935 13226
Annie B 13071 Bertha M
13071 Betsy 11530-1 Burton
11935 Cordelia 11781 Geo
10451 Grace M 13226 Henry
12648 J M 11770 Jennie
12753 12764 John A 13226
John W 11783 L W 10746
Lafayette L 13226 Lucinda
11781 Martha E 11638
Martin 11531 Mary A 10746
Mary B 10746 Nettie 11867
Peggie 11293 Robt L 13071
Roy C 13071 Saml 11009
Skeeg 12764 Stephen 12764
Thos 10451 Truly V 13071
JOHNSTON, Albert 12488 Char-
ley 12488
JO-LA-OO-GO-OOTH, Amy 11137
JONES, Alfred D 11746 Bird
10499 Cally 12955 Cowie
13083 Delora 10856 Elias
10635 Eliz 10182 11162
Franklin P 13085 J Martin
10183 Jesse 10635 Jos
11831 Margaret B 13165
Mary 10635-6 13166 Oscar
12852 13083 Rachel 10635
Russell P 11746 Russell
Perry 11746 Saml J 10281
Sarah R 11833 Thos 11889
Tom 10499 Wm W 11836
JORDAN/JORDEN, J W 11859
Jackson 10559 Reuben 11952

JORDAN/JORDEN (Cont) Tennes-
see F 10777
JO-SAH-YE 10421
JO-WUH 11849
JO-WUH-SIN-NIH 10216
JU-KA-TAH, 11764 Sallie 11764
JUK-TA 11764
JUMPER, 11641
JUNE-STOOT, Quatie 10642
JUNE-STOO-TE, Will 11966
JUS-CA-YOH-IH 12388
JUSTICE/JUSTUS, Arch 11491
Betsey 11491 Dick 11491
12406 Eliza 11491 Geo
11673
JU-SUN-TEES-KEY 11917
JU-WA-JAR 12835
JU-WOO-JAR-GA 12835

KAH-LON-EH-SKEE 12610
KAH-TAH-GOO-GA 10755
KAH-TAH-LA-NAH 10901
KAH-TE-TLO-EH 10938
KAH-TI-SAH-TI 10322
KAH-TO-YAH 11774
KA-HYOR-KAH 10730
KA-LI-NIH 11128
KA-LO-NA-HESK 11151
KA-LO-NA-HESS-KEE 11151
KANE, Lizzie Lumpkin 10450
KA-OO-CHAY 13039
KAR-NAH-TSE-STA-TSE 10730
KA-SCOO-NI 11991
KEEFE, Eliz J 11180 12945
KEENER, Lula 10187 Thos W
12705
KEITH, Albert M 10799 Beulah
B 10799 Guy 10875 Paul
10799 Pearlie L 10799
Reuben M 10799 Sarah A
10865 Veror Azzeleen 10799
Wm Jr 10799 Wm F 10799
KELL, Alice 11745 Chas L
12832 Edith E 12832 Jas
11745 Perry C L 12832
KELL(E)Y, Ellen 11860 Jasper
N 11290 Leander 11289
Margaret J 13198
KENDALL, Geo Kuy 10560
KENNEDY, Ermina V 12843
KENNEY, Chas D 11638
KETCHER, Charley 10630 Corne-

KETCHER (Cont) lius 11967
13179 Lydia 13211 Mose
10396 Richd 12802 Susanna
11967
KETRON, H W 10423 11341
KEYS, Bettie 11042-7 Campbell
L 11042 Chas L 12631
Lorenzo D 12626 Manda C
12626 Minerva 10676 Sam
12228 Theodore S 12631
Wilson 12631
KIDWELL, Clella 10463 Nora
10463 Rosa 10463
KIH-WO-AH-SKEE-SAM 10648
KILLENEGAR/KILLINEGAR, Aggy
13252 Jennie 13250 13252
Sarah 13250 13252 Tom
13251-2
KILLER, 13139 Betsey 12534
Che-ne-lah-kee 12534 Craw-
fish 12534 Ella 12534
Ellen 12690-1 Ga-yo-he
12534 Georgianna 12690
Jackson 12534 Kate 12534
Lawler 12534 Nancy 12691
Sallie 11018 12534 Star
12534 Whiteman 11854
KILLIAN, Melissa 12281
KILLINGWORTH, Birtie M 11368
Mahala 11724 Mary 11725
Matthew 11725
KINCAID, Jas V 10288 Robt T
11202 Wm F 12517.5
KING, Clara 11344 Geo 10279
Jas 10252 Maggie 10252
Mary 10279 Susie 10252
West 10252
KINGFISHER, Ah-lee 10219
10266 John 10307 West
10266
KINGHORN, Jennie 10238
KINYOUN, Sarah E 12377
KIRK, Amanda 12983 Benj 13116
Jane 13116 Mary 13116
Minnie 13116 Susie 13116
KIRKLAND, Georgia E 11273 Lu-
cinda 11273 Martha T 11273
KIRKSEY, Fanny 11631
KLON-DESK 12615
KNIGHT, Aggie 11218 Polly
11636
KNIGHTKILLER, Zeke 13099

461

KO-HE-NA-IH 11606
KUH-SEE-HIF 12598
KUL-LE-NUS-KEH 12748
KUL-STOO-HER-SKY, Eliz 12920
KUN-LIH 12388
KUYKENDALL, Polly 10832

LA-CHIL-LE 10216
LACY, Starr 13180
LADD, Essie May 13032 Ethel
    13032 Nettie 13032 Percy H
    13032 Roy 13032 Sadie D
    13032
LAFON, Ambrose 11824 Amos
    11824 Beverly 11824 Clark
    Claude 11824 Essie 11824
    Flossy 11824 Mayes 11824
    Sarah 11824
LAKEY, Plutina R 12226
LAMBERT, Albert 11206 Andrew
    11206 Annie E 10245 Capter
    Moses 11122 Catherine
    11001 Chas Jackson 11122
    Charley 11154 Finley 11206
    Fritz Simmes 11122 Geo
    Fred 11122 Georgia 11206
    Hugh 11001 11207 Jackson
    11001 11154 Jas M 11122
    Jesse Jas 11122 Lee F
    11207 Mary 11154 Minnie
    Hester 11122 Nancy 11001
    Pierson 12780 Roscoe 11206
    Tilden 11209 Wm 11206
LANCE, Jos M 11506 Mary V
    11506 Thos J 11506
LANDRUM, Alice J 12704 Alice
    W 11897 Charlotte J 11897
    Hiram T 13072 Jas P 12704
LANE, J E 12095 Urbana 13030
LANG, John 11102
LANGLEY, Albert 12886 Alice L
    11740 Andrew J 11666 11756
    Anna 12886 Bayless M 12886
    Bee 11440 Betsy 11530
    Caroline 12886 Catherine
    12155 Charley O 10267
    Clarence B 11912 Fannie
    12886 Fannie L 11912 Geo
    11440 12886 Hattie Lee
    10669 Jas 12886 John 12886
    John C 11440 11740 John J
    11756 Jos B 11740 Jos H

LANGLEY (Cont) 11741 Josiah
    12886 Katie E 11740 Lillie
    J 11740 Lock 11440 12155
    12886 Lucy 12886 Maggie
    10262 Manerva L 11912 Mar-
    garet 12886 Martin 11531
    Mary Ellen 12886 Mollie E
    11440 Nellie 12886 Noah
    10262 10669 11666 Noah R
    10669 Ollie H 11740 Peggy
    12886 Rena Ellen 11756
    Robt E 11756 Sallie 12886
    Saml 12886 Saml B 11912
    Sarah 11440 12886 Sidney J
    11740 Susan 12886 Thos
    12886 Wm J 11666 11740
    Wok-tee-yah 12579 Zacha-
    riah T 10267
LANIER, Birdie I 11333 Ernest
    T 11328 11333-4 Minnie R
    11334 Ola May 11335 Robt L
    11328 Sarah J 11351
LANKFORD, Marion 12201
LA-SE 10211
LA-SIH 10640
LATTA, Allen 10748 12393
    David 10748 Felix 10748
    Jefferson 10748 Mary F
    10748 Mary Francis 10748
    Peggy 10748 Saml 10748
    Wah-te 10748
LATTY, 10748 Diver 10748
    Nannie 10748
LAU-TE-TI-YE 10586
LAW-LIH 12534
LAWLER, Mage 12214
LAWRENCE, Georgia Bell 12018
    Josie Caroline 12017 Liz-
    zie 12016 Robt H 12019
LAWSON, Eliz 10763 Jim 10763
LAW-WIN 13091
LEACH, Ah-lee-sah 10711 Gau-
    la-nes-kee 10711 Henry
    10305 J W 12886 Ned-sin-
    nih 10711 Oo-la-nees-ke
    10711 Sam 10711 Thos 10305
    Thompson 10305 10711 Wah-
    di-yah-hih 10711 Wakee
    10305 10322 Wat 10305
LEADER, Polly 11030-9
LEAF, 10216 Adam 12402 Dave
    10216 Eliz 12920 Jennie

LEAF (Cont) 11423 11428-9
   Mary 12402 Nancy 10387
   Nellie 11491 12402 12406
LEAVITT, Bettie 11195
LEDFORD, Eave 12115 Joe 12115
   Kiney 12115 Nancy Jane
   11381 Riley 12115 Saphron-
   ia S 11175
LEE, Agnes 13022 Alice M
   12118 Almon 12656 Alonzo
   12118 Debrader 11144 Edith
   11144 Eliza 13022 Frances
   E 12656 Isaac 11539 Jane
   13022 Lafelia 11826 Lafe-
   lolia 11826 Laura 13022
   Laura Ann 11144 Lucy 13022
   Martha 12851 13022 Nancy
   10387 13022 Nelly 13022
   Oberlander 11144 Saml
   11144 Tom 10387
LEECH, 11403 Big-ah 13130
LEE-STIH 10323
LEFEW, Henry 11872
LEGG, Bertha C 10871 John L
   10861
LEMINGS, Nannie 11208 Ollie
   11208
LEMMONS/LEMONS, Jesse 12730
   Josiah 12730 Martha E
   11759 Patience 10946
LENOIR, M J 13206 Thos J
   13206 Thos R 13206
LEVI, Ti-a-nee 10650
LEVIER, Jas J 11225
LEVIN, May 11895
LEWIS, Albert L 10831 Ambrose
   11556 Bob 13010 Dica Ann
   13010 Eliza Jane 13010
   Grace E 12830 Hettie 12830
   Ira A 12830 John 11558
   Levi F 11555-8 Robt 13010
   Rufus 11557 W F 10830 Wm
   Francis 10830
LIGHTNING BUG 10388
LIGON, Louisa J 11736
LINDSAY, Wm E 12881
LINTON, Isabelle 10443
LIPE, Ada C 10391 Clarence
   13018 Clark C 13021 Danl
   W C 12495 De Witt(e) 10391
   12495 Flora F 10391 John C
   13016 John G 10391 Lola A

LIPE (Cont) 10361 Maggie E
   13017-8 Sarah L 10391
LIT-TAH-WE 10363
LIT-TIH 12388
LITTLEBIRD, Katie 11526
LITTLE DANE, Eliz 11404
LITTLEDAVE, Eliz 11404 Ella
   10332
LITTLE DEER 11971
LITTLEJOHN, Elowih 12795
   Goo-lah-gee 12795 John
   12689 Sally Anne 12795
   Sow-wah-nee 12795
LIVER, Eliza 12526 Felix
   12526 Lizzie 12526 Lydia
   12526 Martha 12526 Susie
   12526
L(L)OYD, Alice Eliza 12394
   Bessie 10542 Chas A 10448
   Geo A 10448 10538 Geo Alex
   10541 Geo W 10448 Harper H
   10540 Homer M 10539 Jas A
   B 10537 12397 Jas Alfred
   12396 Jas Anderson B 10538
   Jas M 10537 Jasper 10448
   John G 10448 Mary Frances
   11330 Mary Jane 10448
   Martha Ann 12392 Nora
   10448 Nora L 10536 Robt
   Lee 10535 Susan 10448 Thos
   10448 Thos E 11329 Virginia I 12393 Whitley Cicero
   12395 Wm Washington 10853
LOCKER, Dallas C 11561 Edwd V
   11561 John S 11561 Lola R
   11561 Richd M 11561
LOCUST, Geo 10698 Jesse 10698
   11487 John 11124 13247
   Maggie 13247-8 Nellie
   12791 Peggy 10595 Peter
   12791 Tiney 12791 Wa-gei
   10595 Will 12791
LOCUT, Quakie 10595
LOH-SIH 10207
LOK-KIN-NIH 11146
LOMAN, Jackson 11849
LONG, Eliza 10654 Eve 13039
   13040 Ida L 11728 Jess
   13111 John Jr 13039 Johnson 12991 Lucinda 12769
   Maggie 12991 12994 Maggie
   L 11935 Margaret L 11935

LONG (Cont) Nick 12769
LONGFOOT, David 11642 Jas
    11642 Ned 11642 Saml 11642
LONG-KNIFE, Barbury 11510 Wm
    11510
LOTT, Thos 11532
LOUTHER, Clifford 10355
    Eugene W 10355 Jennie Lee
    10355 Joanna 12846 Wm A
    12846 Willie E 10355
LOVE, Arch 10373 Betsy 11531
    Horsefly 10900 11531 John-
    son 10900 11531 Katy 13227
    Polly 10373 Sallie 10900
    11531
LOVELESS, J M 12721 John
    Marion 12720 Sam B 12898
LOVELL, Nancy 10601
LOVETT/LOVITT, 10601 Betty
    10704 Ina Bell 10603
    Irene 10603 Jas 10603
    10949 John J 13173
LOVING, Burletta Waldron
    11476
LOVINGROOD, Nora 10561
LOWEN, John 12783 Katie 12784
    Nannie 12784 Sis 12783-4
LOWERY/LOWR(E)Y, Anderson
    10729 11029 12805 Andrew
    12530 12533 Andy 11466
    Annie 10910 Betsey Ann
    11619 Clarinda 11625 Dan
    12805 Danl 11466 Eliza
    12529 Elsie J 12530 Geo
    10910 Henry 12533 Henry C
    12531 Henry G 12530 J K
    10249 10262 Jas 11029
    12529-31 Jas M 12532 Jen-
    nie 12533 Jim 11619 Kit
    11619 Lucy B 11028-9 Mary
    12805 Nannie 11466 12805
    Raphael 12531 Raymond
    11029 Sallie 11619 Susie
    12530 12533 Wanetta 11029
    Wash 10910
LOWTHER, Laura E 10608 Lem M
    10608 Leroy G 10608 Viola
    F 10608 Wayne S 10608
LUKE, Mary J 13145
LUNIGAN, Bettie 11732
LUNSFORD, David 10245
LYLE, John T 11268

LYMAN, Elmira 12819 John
    12161 Levi 12819 Lewis
    12819-20 Lewis A 12819
    Patrick 12162 Wm 12161
LYNCH, Cicero L 12892 Cicero
    L Jr 12893 John B 12893
    Jos 10742 Jos J 10742
    Leonida 12893 Mariah 12893
    Nancy Esther 12893

McANDREWS, David R 10945
    E Elenor A 10945 John F
    10945 Mary M 10945 Mike C
    10945 Nora E 10945
McCAFFREE, Barton A 11287
    Bradley D 11287 Czaima V
    11287 Czarina V 11287
    Georgia C 11301 Laura V
    11287 Georgia C 11287
McCARTHY, Rosa A 11939-40
McCART(E)Y, Ann Eliza 13010
    Annie E 13010 Lula 10382
McCAUSLAND, Fannie Bell 11670
    Mary M 11670
McCay, Claude R 10607 Jane
    10608 10654 John S 10607
    Ruth 10607 Watson B 10607
    Wm 10607 12222 12423 Wm H
    12222 Wm L 10607
McCLAIN, Addie 12424 Myra
    12507 Robt 12424 Wm E
    12424 Wm H 12424
McCLANAHAN, Leonard 11103 Zoe
    11103
McCLAUCHAN, Leonard 11103 Zoe
    11103
McCLEAN, John 11490 11495
    Letitia 11226
McCLURE, Amanda R 12048 Chas
    J 12133 Della 12133 Doug-
    las 12133 Ella 12885 Fran-
    cis 12133 Hattie 12133
    Hazel 12885 Henry B 12885
    Kathryn 12885 Katy 10755
    Mary Jane 11314 Minnie F
    12885 Thos 12885 Wm J
    12134
McCOMMIS, Oca 12454
McCONNELL, Wm E 11882
McCORMICK, Sarah J 10445
McCOY, Alex Jr 10904 Annie
    11991 Chas 10935 Edwd

McCOY (Cont) 11502 Edwd E
10935 Hester 10884 Jack
10904 Jane 10355 Lucy
12214 12505 Ned 10884
13202 Orlbie 11502 Peachie
10935 Rebecca A 12014
Stand W 11752 Thos 11104
McCRACKEN, Jas T 10249 Mary E
12582
McCRACKER, Mary E 12582
McCRADY, Beulah 12831 12833-4
Foster 12834 L L 12831
Mack 12831 12833
McCRARY, David E 10374 Jack W
10893 Louisa 11848 N B
10893 Wm 11848 Wm C 10374
Willie A 10374
McCUEN, Akey 12417
McCULLOUGH, Rachel Jane 12706
McDANIEL, Coniheinie Jerusha
11505 Eliza 12840 John M
10461 John M McDonald
10461 Jos 10461 Louie T
12851 Noah 12851 Stephen M
12888 Susie 12851 Thos
12851 Willis 12851
McDONALD, Charlotte 13006
John M 10461 Jos 10461
Lucinda 11981 Thos K 10960
McDUFFIE, Amelia 10656 Suel J
10656
McEACHIN, Margaret 11776
Martha 11776
McELRATH Alden 10467 Clifford
10467 John Edgar 10467
McGAHA, Rebecca 10869 12282-3
McGHEE, Ambrose 11411 David A
11411 Davis A 11411 Flo-
rence E 11411 John J 12700
Thos J 12707
McGINNIS, Jas E 10562 John N
10563 Lawrence 10565 Wm
10564
McGLOTHERN, Sarah 11934
McGLUE, Thos M 12700
McGRADY, Foster 12831 L L
12831 12833-4
McGRATH, Lillie C 10849
McGUIRE, Looney 11374 Mar-
garet A 12200
McINTOSH, John 12696 John W
12013

McKARTY, Lula 10310
McKAY, Nellie 13241
McKEE, Eliza B Sharp 10956
Eliza Sharp 11194 John T
10190 Jos R 10191 Pearlie
A 10189 Wm J 10956
McKEEHAN, Sarah A 12208
McKENZIE, Geo A 10620
McKINLEY, Caroline 10181
McLAIN, Della 11663 Edwd
11660 Ellanora N 12835
Florence Rebecca 11350
Jesse 11663 Jesse J 12436
Letitia 11685
McLEMORE, Thos 13075
McMURRY, Eliza J 11804
McMURTY, Louisie 11804
McNEIL, Guy 11695
McPHERSON, Alex 11773 Bea-
trice 11675-6 C Verner
11678 Christie 11773 Geo
11651 11773 Hughey 11773
Ida 11675-6 John 11773
John V 11675 John W 11675
Lewis L 11675 11677 Lucy
11773 Silas 11675 11773
Willis 10312
McQUIRE, Hellen 11615

MABE, Charity 12188 Estele
12190 Rosin 12862 Rosina
12863 Rufus 12859
MADDEN, Clarence T 10592 Jack
J 10592 Jos Howard 10592
MADDOX, Ruthe 11204
MAH-YAH 11407
MANOR Ardenia 11619 Ardenia J
11619 J A 11619 Jas Henry
11619 Jefferson 11619
MANER, Alford P 12954 Ardenia
J 12954 Chas 12954 Henry J
12945 Jas A 12951 Jessie A
12954
MANEY, Frank 12781 Wm R 11633
MANKILLER, Arch 11991 11998
Beacher 11533 Bessie 11991
Calson 12662 Hester 11991
Jacob 12662 Jennie 12662
John 12662 Lizzie 12662
Maggie 12662 Mary 12662
Nancy 11916 11991 Polly
11917 11998 Richd 12662

MANKILLER (Cont) Susan 12662
Synthia 11991 Thos H 11533
Wm 11991 Wm Jr 11991
MANN, D S 11232 Robt J 10965
MANNING, Johnson 10196 Sarah
Jane 12854
MANNS, Nancy 12968
MANSFIELD, Jane 10293 Norman
10293 Wm 10293
MANTOOTH, 12746 Eliz 12747
Thos 12747
MANUS, Bill 12968 Geo 12968
John 12968 Maggie 11909
Nancy 12968 Sam 12968
Wesley 12968
MAPES, Mary 12075
MARCALA, 12964
MARCRUM, Carter 11521 Eliza
11521 Jacob 11521 Jas
10283 10285 11521-2 John
11521 Ruth 11521
MARKHAM, Allen M 12359 Carter
11521 Charlotte 10285
Clarence B 11523 Ewing
10283 11522 Jas B 10283
Mary 11521 Ray P 12385
MARLOW, Carrie E 10704 Edna
10704 Minnie 10704 Ruby
10704
MARR, Annie 11948 11950 Saml
11948
MARSH, Jos H 12271
MARSHALL, Ed 13249
MARTIN, Aaron 11485 Ada B
11612 Caledona 10714 Catherine 10594 Chas J 11612
Cora 11612 Danl 11485 Da-
vid Lee 10633 Ester Janie
10633 Fay 11612 Frances
10633 Geo D 11612 Gurley
10633 Jennie 10754 Jessie
L 10687 Jessie S 10714 Joe
11485 John 10245 John A Jr
11612 Judy 11485 Kate
10633 Lenar 10633 Lila
10594 Lilla May 11612 Lora
11486 Mamie 10466 Manerva
10594 10869 Mary 11585
Nannie C 11064 Octavia
11662 Phronia 11486 Richd
11485 11662 Rosa 12283
Sallie 10245 10594 Saml

MARTIN (Cont) 10594 11485
Sanford M 11662 Smith A
10633 T H 10687 Thos 11486
Thos E 10633 Van B 10633
Virginia A 10975 Willer E
10369 Wm E 10714
MARTINDALE, Sarah 10579-80
MASHBURN, Sarah N 11397
MASON, Addie 12745 Dora J
11388 Marion W 10858
MATCY, Anna 11991 Ezekiel
11991
MATHESON, Geo 10635
MATHEWS, Dorthy M 11724
Herles 11724 Morda 11724
MATHIS, Eliz 10393 Rebecca
10393 Wm 10393
MAY, Mary E 10472
MAY(E)S, Geo W 11675 11677
12701
MAYFIELD Amanda C 11696 Car-
ter V 11696 John B 11696
Polly 13226 Trixie V 11696
MAYHUGH, Missie 12015
MAYNAR, Henry J 11619
MEACHAIN, Helen 10839 Jesse E
10840
MEEKER, Bertha 11698 Geo
11697 12837 Geo C 11698
Geo O 11698 12581-2
MEEKS, Wm 10917
MEIGS, Benj F 12409 Carrie M
11274 Chas B 11274 Cooie
12410 Elinor B 11274
Elinor M 11274-5 Florein N
10188 12411 Geo McKee
10188 John H 11274 Jose-
phine E 10188 Mollie C
10188 Return J 11274
MELLOWBUG, Lydia 10382 12612
Smith 13235
MELTON, Isabelle 10289
MENDENALL, Jane 12881
MERONEY, Martha A 10336
Martha Ann 13188
MERRELL, Rachel 11891
METCALF, Cornelia 12169 Hiram
12165 Jno F 12164 Lee
12170
MICCO, Bessie 11197 Jim 11197
Larenda 11197
MICHAEL, Abraham L 12735 Geo

MICHAEL (Cont) 12738 Jacob
12730 12733 John E 12736
Mary 12730 12737 Sarah
12730
MICKLE, Florence 11760 Hoyt
11760
MIDDLETON, Chas A 11400
MI-HE-GIH 10207
MIKE, Bob 13057
MILES, Annie 10880 Jessie E
10881 Wm E 10880-1
MILLER, A-key 10711 Ailey
11086 Alex 11729 Alex A
11730 Alice 11874 Andrew J
10879 Augustus 10567 Bel-
mont 10699 Bertha 11442
Binnie 11090 Byrdie 11549
11550 C D 10978 Carrie E
11730 Chas E 11730 Char-
ley 11084 Chu-ah-nus-kie
10711 David 11547-50 Dicie
G 10422 Dick 13163 Domitilia 11729 Ed 11730 Effie M
10699 Eli 10373 11085
Eliza 10711 Eliza P 10699
Eliz 10416 10692 Ella
11548 11550 Emma 11442
Florence Sanders 12907
Francis E 10699 Geo W
10699 Grayson N 12907 H K
12985 Harriet 10566 Henry
S 10422 Henry W 11197 Hettie L 12907 Ida 11196 Ida
J 12907 Isabella I 11729
Isabella L 11729 Jack
10711 Jas I 11729 Jennie
10568 Jim 10711 John T
10699 Jos 12932 Josie
11550 Lavana 12986 Lucy
10711 Lucy D 11729 Lucy O
11729 Marcus 10569 Maria
11547 11550 Martin 11874
Mary 10417 Matilda E 11020
Mattie E 10879 Maudie
11449 Minnie L 10422 Mira
Sizemore 12103 Nannie
11547-50 13163 Nellie
10711 Ollie B 10699 Peter
10711 Ples Henry 10699
Ples K 10699 Polly 10373
Que-ter 10711 Sarah 10613
Sarah Ann 11197 Snake L

MILLER (Cont) 10422 Suake L
10422 Thos 10613 Thos F
12907 Waitie H 12907 Wm
12689 Wm J J 12907 Wm L
10889 Wutty 10711
MILLIKAN, Martha E 11242
MILLS, Anna 12227 Betsy 12227
Cynthia E 10687 E G 10222
Hulda 10236 Jessie L 10687
Martha A C 10471 Numa
10232 Peggy 12227 Saml
12227 Saml H 10687 Sarah
A J 10226 Viola J 10234
Virdie 10822 Wm 12227
MILLWOOD, Geo Saml 11315 John
Henry 11316
MILO, Lizzie 13175
MINEW, Rebecca 12519
MINEY, Rebecca 12519
MINK, Sar-da-ker 13101
MINNICK, Eliz F 10976
MITCHAM, Louveny 10637
MITCHELL, Cornelia 10290 Joe
12483 Lovice 12715
MITCHEN, Vicy J 12664
MIXEDWATER, Geo 11710 Nellie
11710
MIXWATER, 12198 Geo 11710
Mink 12198 Rachel 12198
MONK, Merrill 13024 Nettie
13024 Rebecca J 13024
MONROE, Nora A 10997 Thos
12427
MONTGOMERY, Mary E 10919
MOORE, Bob 11365 Charity
12928 Charlie 11781 Danl E
11781 Davie 11781 Henry W
11453-4 Jas 12046 Lizzie
11781 Margaret 12886 Mary
11601 Peggie A 11814
Vicinda R 12709
MORGAN, Andrew J 12743 Char-
ity 11401 Eliz 10998 11401
Ellen 11928 Gideon 11401
11879 Jesse 10998 Libbey
11401 Louisa 10801 10998
Mary Ann 10998 Sam 11879
Washington 11401 Wesley
11879
MORGANS, Ellen 11928
MORRIS, Bessie J 11425 Chas L
11702 Edna 11884 Eliza J

467

MORRIS (Cont) 12492 Emma Ya-
hola 12552 Enoley 11753
Evaley 11753 Gideon 12495
Hona N 12804 Horra H 12804
Jennie 12510 John 11425
Mary 11953 Rebecca 12493
Richd 11661 Rosa A 11425
Ruby 11425 Thos P 11753
Watt 12552 Wm O 11425
MORSE, Eliz 10855 Ellis B
10841 Ettie J 10842 Nettie
F 10843 Sherwood Thos
10844
MORTON, Flossie 11978 Grover
C 11978 Joel J 11978 Junia
C 11978 Mary B 11978 Mau-
die A 11978 Nancy A 11538
Robt L 11978 Wm H 11978
MOSE, September 11297
MOSES, Emma 11473
MOSS, Harrison 11943 Jennie
11843 Odessa E 11331
MOTON, Andy M 10689 Bert E
10689 Clem C 10689 Jesse J
10689 Margaret E 11224
MOTT, Gourdie 10976
MOUSE, 11298
MULIMAX, Sarah Ann 10480
MULKEY, Clarinda 10239
MULLEY, Ella T 12217
MULLINS, Louisa E 11634
MUMBLEHEAD, Chas B 11129 Jas
B 11129 John 11606 John D
11129-30 Rogers L 11129
MUNDAY, Lila 10594
MUNNICK, Eliz F 10976
MURPHY, Ailsey 10423 Jackson
13259 Jas L 13260 Jane
11399 Lizzie 13259 Lucy A
12780 Polly 11387 11393
11399 11542 Walter 11399
Wm 10255
MURRAY, Annie 13178 Bandie
12688 Benj W 12873 Chas
12876 Charlie W 13178
Eliz 12872 Fred 12875 John
12874 John W 12713 13178
Jos G 12871 Nannie 11575
Riley L 12712 Sarah 13178
Willie 12687
MUR(R)ELL, Amanda R 12845
Geo M 11799 Geo Ross 12845

MUR(R)ELL (Cont) Jennie R
11800 Jennie Ross 11800
Lewis E 11799 Margaret G
12845 Richd C 11799 Sarah
G 12845 Vina 12516
MUSH, Lucy 12652 Nannie 11717
MUSKRAT, Arch 12888 Danl
11792 Mack 11963 Narcie
12888
MYERS, Lura 12187 Orlena T
10692 S B 10692

NA-CHE 10641
NA-CHEL 10216
NAH-CHIH 10649
NAH-WE-HE-LE-SKY 13155
NAKEDHEAD, Lizzie 10686
NA-LE 10649
NA-NIH 12769
NATTYTOM/NOTTYTOM, Nancy
10808-9 Peter 10808
NAVE, Minerva 10676
NAVES, Jane 13160
NEAL, Lutie 11004 Sidney R
10617 Squire Judson 10619
Victoria A 12053
NEBEL, Laura F 12558
NE-COO-TI-YI 13200
NED, 10953 John 10952 Polly
10953
NEE-CHEE 11672
NEE-GOO-DAH-YE 10307
NEELEY, Loucinda 10590
NEE-YERNSKE 10626
NEIGHBORS, Eliz 10251
NELSON, Eliza 10202 Rebecca
10365
NE-QUE-TIEYE 10894
NEUGIN, Dave 12586
NEWBERRY, G S 10981
NEWMAN, Margaret 12139
NEW-YOR-HE 11764
NICHOLS, Lona L 12897
NICHOLSON, Elnora 12421 Har-
riett 12421 Isaac 11601
Jacob 12421 Margaret T
11561 11817 Martha 12421
Ruth 12421
NICK, Lucinda 12769
NICK-IH 12769
NICKS/NIX, Alford 11544 Alvy
11544 Bessie 11544 Ethel

NICKS/NIX (Cont) 12831 Huston
   11544 Luisa 11544 Nancy
   11546 Peter 11544 Rachel
   11544-5
NIDIFFER, Lucy 12703
NIGAJACK, Lucinda 12974
NIGHT KILLER, 10387 Susan
   10387
NILAGES, Mary L 11982
NI-QUI-CHI 10646
NOBLES, Annie 11184
NOFIRE, Joshua 11922 Mary
   11922 Nannie 11922 Sequo-
   yah 11922
NOLEN, Henry N 10717 Jas A
   10717 10719 Jas A Jr 10717
   10719
NO-WAT-TAH 11123
NUGENT, Jack 12615
NU-GIH 10640
NUGIN, Alice 12586 Dave 12586
   Titus 12586
NULL, Cora 11419
NUTE, Andy 12766

O'BRIAN, Stella A 10227
OCK-SAH-YAH 10646
OER, Emma May 12568 John
   12568
OFIELD, Eva 11976
O'FIELDS, Ben 10941
OLD KINGFISHER, Jennie 13104
OO-CAH-YAH-STEE 10496
OO-CAH-YAH-STER 10496
OO-CHI-LA-TA, Oo-aquw-ni
   10586 Oo-squi-ne 10587
   Thompson 10587
OO-CHUH-DUH 11405
OO-CHUH-WAH-DIH, Jehsi 11526
OO-CHUN-TAH 11121
OO-CHUN-TIE 11405
OO-DAH-NEE-YUH-DUH 10961
OO-DAH-YEH-DAY 11188
OO-DA-LE-DA, Ross 11604
OO-DAW-YE-DAU 11188
OO-DEE-SA-DEE-ET-TAH 12401
OO-GAH-SIT-TAH 11198
OO-GAH-WEE-YIH 10626
OO-GAH-YAH-STAH 12576
OO-GA-LOG, Nellie 11491
OO-GAW-LAW-GAH 10216
OO-GAW-SIT-TAH 11198

OO-GEE-YAH 12689
OO-GE-YAH, Geo 12689
OO-GOW-SE-DAH 11198
OO-HAH-CHU-SAH 12616
OO-HEARN-CLAU-E 10587
OO-HUH-WAH-DIH 11526
OO-LAH-NAW-TE-SEK, Darkey
   11765
OO-LA-NUH-HIH 10414
OO-LAU-KIT-TE 10587
OO-LAW-NAH-S-TE-SKEE, Sam
   11405
OO-LAW-NOO-STEAT 11456
OO-LO-GI-LAH 10207
OO-LO-GU-LA 10266
OO-LON-NOS-TEE-SKIE 11163
OO-LOO-CHA 11716
OO-LUH-LA-NUH 10649
OOL-SAH-GETAH 10626
OO-SKUN-NE 11908
OO-MA-SUY-AH 12198
OO-NA-GA-DAH 11632
OO-NA-STIL-LER 12140
OO-NA-TI 10952
OO-NAW-DUT-TAH 11198
OO-SAR-TE-SKI 11917
OO-SCOO-NEE 10586
OO-SCUN-EH 11891
OO-SKEE-LE-ADUH, Chah-nih
   10382
OOSOWIE, Nicie 12793 Olise
   12793 Paul 12793 Sam 12793
   Susie 12793
OO-SQUA-LU-SKER 11012
OO-SQUI-NI 11541
OO-STA-NO-LUH-TIH, Lewis
   11491
OO-TAAR-NE-YEH-TEH 10626
OO-TAH-DEH-GEE-SKEE, Jah-ne
   11847
OO-TAH-NE-YAH-TAH 10414
OO-TAH-YE 10647
OO-TAW-YE-DAW 11188
OO-TOO-LAH-TA-NAH 11689
OO-WAH-HYUH-SKEE 10901
OO-WAH-LE-NAH-STE 10496
OO-WAH-TAH 13248
OO-WAH-TEE-SKIH 12576
OO-WA-NEH, John 13248
OO-WAR-YUS-KI 11541
OO-WAS-KIE-KE 11891 Qua-ki
   11891

OO-WO-KAH-SA-IE 10326
OO-YER-SAT-TAH, Cherry 11846
OO-YOU-CHUS-EY 13109
OO-YU-SAT-TAH/OO-YU-SAT-TUH,
Cherry 11846 Rufus 11850
ORE, Caroline 11225 Catherine
11225 Jim 11225 Joe 11225
John 11225 Lydia 11225
O'RILEY, Eliz 11575 Jane
11575 Paty 11575
ORSBEN, Jessie 12470
ORSBORN, Cicero 12861 Geo
12860 Zedekia 12563
ORTEN, Abner 11470 Geo N
11469 Geo W 11469
OSBORN(E), Aaron 11809 Alex
12560 Callie 12856 Calvin
12193 David 12476 David A
12450 12477 Eli 12184
Eliza 12987 Emory 12988
Ephram 11819 Felix 12554
Fielden 10413 Fields 12260
Jas W 12469 Jerome B 11623
Jessie 12192 John 12473
John E 12181 Lockie 10411
Margaret 12195 Marshall
12251 Nina 12857 Noah
12561 Polly 12258 Reeves
12180 Robt L 12249 Rufus B
12858 Stephen 12562 Talton
12472 Tennessee 12257 Troy
12252 Willie 12259
OSBURN, Emery J 10872 Geo W
10867 Jas A 10870 Jas H
12520 John T 10876 John W
10878 Solomon 10873 Wil-
burn 10877
O-SEY 10273-4
OTTER, Andrew 11025
OTTERLIFTER, Andy 13155 Betsy
13155 David 13155 Esiah
13155 Moses 13155 Nancy
13160 Rachel 13155 Susie
13155 13209
OWENBY, Cally J 12288 Ida M
12284 Sarah J 12279 Henry
12140
OWENSBY, F M 11317
OWL, Adam 11149 11152 Cat
10905 Chas 10905 Cornelia
T 11149 Danl 10905 David
11149 11153 12784 13188

OWL (Cont) 13253 Davis 11149
Ella 10905 12498 John
11149 Jos 10905 Martha
11149 Mose 11149 Nancy
11668 Quincy 11149 Sam
10905 Saml 11149 Thos
11145 11152 Washington
10905

PADEN, Henry 12047
PALMER, Margaret D 12680
Mrs W H 13024
PALONE, Wilson 10789
PANLEY, Clarisy 11253
PANTHER, Alice 10722 Martha
10721-2 Tom 10721
PAR(R)IS, Annie E 11637 Cath-
erine 11002 Cynthia 10921
Delbert C 11637 Eliz 11703
Elvia E 11690 Fannie 11703
Frances 11703 Frank W
11637 Jesse R 11703 Johan-
na 10210 John C 11637 Jos-
ie B 11703 Laura May 11002
Marion F 11637 S E 10301
10305 10388 11188 11191
11195 11863 11971 12498
12592 12633 13162 Susan E
11417 Susie O 11637
PARISH, Cyntha 13011 Lula
13012
PARKER, Emma 11711 Geo W
11711-2 Jefferson D 12113
Jessie H 11040 Jno C 12114
Malinda 11683 Oscar 11712
Thos 11598
PARKS, Albert M 10284 Alberta
M 10284 J T 11461 L S
10285 Saml 13242 Saml F
10284
PARROT(T), 11854 Wm 11854
PARSON(S), Hannah 13158
Peter 13158 S D 10448
Susan 10448
PARTRIDGE, David 12992 Mose
12993 Nelly 12995 Winnie E
12992
PASSMORE, A L 12778 Cardie
12778 Nancy J 12778 Thos
12778
PATHKILLER, John 11984 Soo-ke
10461

470

PATRICK, Elmira 10704
PATTERSON, Chas 10767 Jas E
13052 Jerry J 13050 Jno A
12000 John A 12000 John D
13051 Jos 12000 Kinney V
12000 Martha 11381 Nebra-
ska B 13152 Saml 11381
Truman J 13151
PATTIE, Cora E 11957-8 Frederick H 11957-8 Sophie F
11957-8
PAUL, Bertha 11568 Ella 11568
PAYNE, Benj F 13003 Eleanor
10350 Elisha 12101 Geo W
13003 Hattie C 11747 Jim
12099 John 12108 Malinda
12256 Mary Jane 12107 S D
10241
PEACHEATER, 10680 10929 John
10680
PEAK/PEEK, Alex 11418 Carnealy 11420 Clemon C 11386
Dollie M 11387 Harvey B
12958 Jas R 10951 Leander
11421 Lillie M 11974
PEGG(S), Annie 13256 Swimmer
13256
PELONE, Frank 13115 Wilson
10789
PERDUE, Chas 12413 Hampton
11746 Richd 11193 Richd D
11193 Susie 12401 12413
PERKINS, Laura 11624
PERLONE, Andy 12613
PERRY, Anna Eliz 10534
PETERS, Cynthia 10749 10753
Lossie 10212
PET(T)IETT, Amelia 11826
Andrew 11826 Andrew J
11826 Benj 12435 Bill
11826 Charley 12435 Cyn-
thia 11826 Frank 11826 Jo
11826 Joanna 11826 Polly
11826 Robt 11826
PETTIT(T), Aggie 10704 Bettie
11195 Curry 10704 Eliz
11891 Jenny 11825 Lizzie
11825 Margaret 12435
Minerva 11891 Susie 11825
Wm 13196
PETTIE/PETTY, Alex 12729
Bertie 12838 Brady 12725

PETTIE/PETTY (Cont) Catherine
12798 Eliz 10482 12731
Greeny 12430 John 10482
John C 12970 John W 11182
Lee A 12428-9
PHARIS, Maggie 10829
PHE(A)SANT, Abraham 12615
Aggie 12615 Aleck 12615
Alex 12615 Annie 10270
Charley 12615 Jack 12615
Jas 12615 Jenanna 12615
12615 John 12762 Lula
12615 Mary 12615 Nancy
12159 Susan 12615
PHELPS, Jane 10523 Mary 10523
Mattie 10523 Nancy 10523
PHILLIPS, Danl 11178 Eliza
12569 Henry 1178 Jas 11189
Jane A 10179 Jos 11189
Lizzie 11189 11481 Lucy
11178 Nellie 11189 Nora L
12950 Steve 12569 Thos
11189
PICAMAN, August C 10614 Caro-
line S 10614 Clara M 10614
Clarence M 10614 Dewey M
10614 Jennie 10614 John
10614 Julius W 10614
PICKARD, Jeff 11219
PICKENS, Fannie B 12046
PICKUP, Johnson 12672 Ned
12672 Simon 11525 Susie
12672
PIERCE Mae 10454 Neva C 10453
PIG, Young 11540 11551
PIGEON, Betsy 11638 John
11235 Milie 10792 Mollie
10792 Webster 11918
PIGEON-ROOST, Sallie 11765
PINSON, Sarah J 11505
PINYAN, Mattie 12348
PITCH, Janie Ellen 10901
PIT(T)MAN, Amanda E 12358 Wm
11851
PITTS, Eliz 12739
POCOHONTAS, 11935
POINDEXTER, 10241 12220 12226
12377 13049
POLECAT, Bethel 12902 Betsey
12902 Isaac 12902 Levi
12902 Lucy 12902 Sarah Ann
12902 Walter 12902

POLSON, Eddie 11931 Jewell
11931 John M 11931 Lou
11931 Willie E 11931
PONDER, Andrew 10245 Harriet
10245 Jackson 10245 Mala-
chi 10245 Mary Ann 10245
Meredy 10245
POOL, Dred P 11324
POORBEAR, 11493 Aggie 13230
Betsy 11493 Hunter 13231
Lucy 11493 Mastee 11493
POORBOY, Sallie 11230
POPEJOY, Clara 13067
PORLONE, Bill 12613
PORTER, J M 11504 Jas 10902
11504 Julia 11504 Mary
12514 Mildred M 12514
Minnie 12500 Sallie 12215
Sarah 11566 11626 Wm 10906
Wolfe 10903
POSLEY, Goldie 10458
POSTELL Chas 10367 John 10319
Jos H 10366 Wm C 10368
POTTER, Tommy 11155
POWELL, Charity 13144 Ida
11468 Julius 13210 Marcus
13188 Osceola 13188 Ose
13188 Polly 13188 Rebecca
10764 Rebecca 10764-5 Robt
13188
POWHATTAN, 13003
PRAITHER, Nancy 12606
PRATHER, Georgia S 11326
Gideon R 11326 Lee W 11327
Warren W 11320
PRICE, Chas B 11500 Chas C
11500 Clarence T 11500
Daisey E 11500-1 Howard
13007 John 11500 Mack E
12110 Mary 10293 Sarah
11463
PRIM, Annie E 12891 Cynthia
12929 Lawrence D 12891
Sinthy 12928
PRINCE, Jane 11851 Taylor
10297
PRI(T)CHETT, Allie 10323
Annie 12693 Eliza 12693
Fannie 12689 12692 Jennie
12693 Jesse 12689 John
12693 Ka-skar-ne 10929
Nannie 12689 Narcissa

PRI(T)CHETT (Cont) 12693
Ollie 12693 Philip 12689
Rachel 10929 Red 12689
Stephen 12689 Thos 12689
Tom 12689 12693
PRIVETT, Margaret Sizemore
12096
PROCTOR, Ah-claw-see-nee
12534 Akey 12419 Annie
11922 Bell 11013 Chas
11632 Charley 12419 Che-
coo-a 11922 Chu-wa-loo-kee
11922 Claw-se-ny 11922
Danl 12419 Darkey 11922
Eliz 11632 Ezekiel 11015
Geo 11922 John 12609 John-
son 11632 Margaret 11632
Sallie 12534 Thos 10952
10954 11922 Tom 12534 Wm R
11013 Willie Bell 11013
PRUETT/PRUITT, C Glenn 11788
Columbus 12471 Ephram B
11245 Everett 13009
I Mabel 11788 J Lillian
11788 Jacob 12466 Jesse T
11788 John S 11246 Louisa
12855 Rebecca 12250
PUFFER, Margaret 11981
PULLEN, Jas T Sr 10448
PUMPKIN, Annie 10696 Eli
12968 Geo 10598 Jas 10598
Jennie 12968 Johny 12616
Mary 10598 10697 12968
Richd 10598
PUMPKIN PILE, Betsy 12483
PUPPIES, Seven 12579

QUA-DIH 10649
QUAH-LE-YOU-GUH 11298
QUAILS, Martha 12100
QUAILSIE 11151
QUAIT-CY 10680
QUA-KIH 11146
QUA-LI-UKE 11765
QUALLAYOU 11018
QUANEE 11917
QUEE-LEE-KEE 12814
QUEEN, Arzelia P 12276
QUEE-NEH 12991
QUH-LA-LEET 12598-9
QUINTON, Annie 12886 Bill
12886 Dave 12206 David

472

QUINTON (Cont) 12204 Emma L
12204 12206 Ethel 10465
Ethel M 10465 Isaac 10465
Isaac S 10465 Jack 10345
12718 12886 Jim 12886
Johnson 11172 Letha 11172
Lydia 11260 Mary 10465
Mary E 10465 Moses 11260
Myrtle C 12497 Nancy 10465
Nancy E 10465 Nellie 12886
Sam 12886 Sarah 12890
11260 12890

RABBIT, Climbing 13139
RACKLEY, Lloyd 12771
RAGSDALE, Claudie 12347
RAINS, Martha 11508
RALEY, Mary L 10410
RALSTON, Eliz 10436
RANDOLPH, Genie 10670 Jas
10670
RAPER, Eliz 12739 Harley T
10999 Harvey L 10999 Jas T
10999 Laura 13177 Lazarus
12739 Lazarus B 12739-40
Wm 12740
RAT(T), Alsey 11916 John
12630 Peggy 13136 Polly
12630 Su-sa-ni 12630
RATCLIFF, Nannie 12615 Wat
12615
RATLEY, Lucy 11140
RATLIFF, Emma 12772 Henry
10753 Jacob 12772 Lizzie
12772 Lloyd 12771 Wm 12772
RATTLER, Annie 13101 Charley
13101 Gehena 13101 Josie
13101 Lizzie 13101 Wm
13101
RATTLINGGOURD (See Also
GOURD), 11198 Alex 11773
Andrew 11773 Artemiss
11773 Calvin 11651 Charley
11773 12210 Danl 11773
Eliza 11773 Ellis 11773
Geo 11651 Jack 11651 Jackson 11773 Jennie 11499
Jesse 11643 John 11499
11773 Looney 11773 11888
Mariah 13077 Nellie 10299
10470 Peggy 11625 Sarah
11773 Sister 11651 Susie

RATTLINGGOURD (Cont) 11773
Thos 10386 11773 13076
RAWLES, Augusta 11501 Cathe-
rine 11501 Celeste 11501
Emma E 11501 John 11501
Kate 11501 Mary Jane 11501
Sarah Jane 11501 Serilda
11501
RAWLINGS, Ruthie S H 10436
RAY, Anna 12046 Claud 12604
Ed 10533 Fletcher 11607
Geo 10532 12603 Grady
12608 Jas 11346 Joe 10494
John W 12742 Julia 12741
Louisa 11682 Luther 12605
Mildred Cherokee 10692
Rachel 12012
RAYBURN, Wilson L 10482
REAGAN, Eliza Ann 12941 Eme-
line 12941 Michael A 12941
Wm 12941
RED, 12367 W-ki 12367
REDAFORD, Nancy 11080
REDBIRD, 11917 Quetie 11217
Sam 10616
REDDING Eliza Catherine 12130
REDFEARN, Jesse Dewitt 11791
John Earl 11791 Martha
11791
REE, Fidille 12280
REECE/REESE, Allie 11347 Car-
ter 11348 Cicero L 11344-5
Eliz A 11321 Felix 11532
Kinsey 11349 Margaret
12623 Mary 11935 Mary A
11935 Monroe T 12011 Nancy
11532 Nellie 11532 Paul
10570 Shoshonie 11344
11363-4 12029-30 Susie
11625
REED/REID, Alee M 12803 Alice
L V 12803 Andrew 12803
Annie 10938 Cleo F 12803
Dave 12787 David A 12803
Dixon B 11171 Dixon B Jr
11170 Fidille 12280 Jennie
M 13140 Johnnie 11651
Johnson 12803 Jos E 11165
Linnie I 12803 Minnie
12532 Molly E 13140 Myr-
tle B 13140 Nancy 10978
Nancy A 12803 Pralee 11651

REED/REID (Cont) 11773 Phila-
tus L A 12803 Rena B 12803
Sarah 12500 Susan 12803
Susie 10415 Walter S 13140
Wm 12803
REES, Niota B 10609 11715
REEVES, Nancy M 10372
REICHEL, Eliz 12708
REVELS, Charity 12928 Micaga
12928
RHOMER, Emma N 11227 Fannie C
11227 Maggie B 11227 May
11227 May F 11227
RICE, Adlaid 10573 Emily
10571 Gracie 10574 Hansell
10575 J C 11592 Jas 10576
John B 10517 10572-8 Jos
Jr 10577 Leacie 10517
Luther 10578 Lydia K 11587
RICH, Eliz 12673 Harvey 12673
Jas 12673 Jesse 12673
Laura J 12220 Martin 12673
RICHARDSON, Allie M 10502
Alva 10509 Alvin 10510
Charlie M 10511 Delilah
10503 Frank P 10508 Gar-
nett D 10504 Geo M 10505
Glenn 12346 Harvey A 10516
Jas D 10512 Leon 12344
Lila 10513 Lutie 10514
Mary J 11808 Maud L 10507
Nancy 10501 Sanford 12330
Wesley 10515 Wm E 10506
RIDER/RYDER, 10648 Chas 11805
Charlie 11854 Edgar 12463
Johnson 11854 Nancy 11854
Oo-squin-ni 11964 Susie
11854 Wm 11854
RIDGE Adam 10640 Beaver 10640
Benj F 10984 Charlotte
10640 Hiram 10987 Jas D
10988 Jos C 10985 Mose
10640
RIDGES, Eliz 10989
RIDLEY, 11586
RIGGINS, Hiley 11005 Nancy
11005 Thos 11005
RIGSBY, Jas F 11656 Jessie
11656 Joe 11656 John Han-
nah 11656 Mary L 11656
Tiny 11656
RILEY, Jack 12681 Jane 10666

RILEY (Cont) John M 12681
Martha 12359 Martin 12359
12681 Mayme 12681 Nancy F
12359 Nannie E 12681 Nan-
nie E B 12682 Owen 12681
Richd 12359 Welder 12681
RING, Chas H 12177 Ella N
12175 Geo W 12176
RITCHIE, Jas 12166
ROACH, Geo 12805 Geo Jr 12805
Robt Jr 12805 Robt Geo
12805 Thos B 12805 Thos P
10282 Tom 10207 10216
10382 10428 10581 10640
10680 10953 10961 11197-8
11405 11491 11517 11526
11672 11716 11849 11908
11966 11973 12689
ROASTINGEAR, 10730 Sam 10730
ROBBINS, Rebecca C 11462
ROBERSON, Eleanor 10350 Ginty
10350 John L 10344 Louti-
tia 10724 Lutitia 10724
Mollie M 10991 Sarah 10350
Susan 12805 Wm H 10294
ROBERTS, Agnes 12043 Candace
12253 Charlotte 10718
Dolly Nancy 10761 Dorothy
12042-5 Jas B 10760 Robt D
10759 Sadie B 13169 Sarah
L 12866 Simps 13023
ROBERTSON, Lula M 12130
ROBINSON, Alice 11310 Eller
11311 Jason L 10479 Jos A
10485 Robt L 10474
ROGERS, Albina M 10455-7
Andrew 10950 Andrew J
10950 Bessie 11191 Chero-
kee 11287 Cullus 10640
David 10968 12216 Edley A
10358 Elbina M 10459 Geo
11864 Geo L 10950 Geo W
10495 Henry B 10950 Hoke
11864 Jesse 10640 Jim
11191 John 10482 10950
11287 Jug 10357 Levi 12697
Levi H 10950 Lewis 12527
Lovely 11191 Lucinda 10966
10968 Mary 12384 Mary H
11041 Mary K 11041 Mathi-
son 10356 Missouri Emeline
12886 12718 Nannie 10950

ROGERS (Cont) Ollie 11183
11191-2 Polly 10482 Rosa
12592 Susan 10968 11864
Susannah 11973 Susie 10640
11973 Wm C 10482 Wilson
10640 11973
ROHRER, Annie Laura 12559
ROLFE, Texie A 13243 Texie
Anna 13243
ROOP/ROUP, John W 11691 Wiley
W 11507
ROSE, Edwd 12456 Eli 10247
Eliz 12452 Henrietta 12570
J Warren 12570 Jennie
12570 Jos 12570 Lyda 10246
Pearl 12570
ROSEBOROUGH, Claude 10431
Jesse F 10431 Lucy G 10431
Sarah L 10431
ROSS, 11493 Allen 13160
Amanda 11799 Andrew 10629
12130 Andy 12130 Annie
12484 13160 Benj 12130
Bets(e)y 11493 12484 13223
Caroline 12130 Celia 12598
Chief 12484 Cucumber 12401
12484 Danl 13223 Dot 11679
Eck 10468 Eliz 13238 El-
zina 10254 Flora L 13240
Frank 12130 Geo 12130 Geo
W 13160 Hannah 12130 Henry
Pigeon 10468 Jas 13160
Jane 13160 13223 Jarratt
12484 Jenny 13223 Jesse
12130 Jesse T 12130 Jim
13223 John 10954 12484
13160 John A 13238 Jos
12130 13223 Joshua 10690
13223 Kit 11679 Le-sih
12484 Lewis 12484 13194-5
Lizzie 13195 Lola 11679
Mack 13223 Margaret 12130
Margaret C 11590 13120
Mary 13223 Mary Ann 12130
Mary B 13160 McDuff 11679
McKinley 11679 Minerva
12484 Nannie 13194 Neoma
10468 Oliver P 10254 Polly
13159-60 Quaitsy 11493
12484 Quaity 13160 Rachel
12484 Robt 13160 Saml R
11378 Sarah 12417 Silas

ROSS (Cont) 12484 Silas D
13160 Templeton 12130 W M
11590 Wm 12484 13160
ROUND, Jack 10379
ROURKE, 11555
ROW(E), Betsy 12483 Katie
12660-1 Thos 12660
ROWELL, Emily G 12074 Jas M
10828
ROWLAND, Mary 11222 Mittie
11222
ROY, Mary 11401
RUNABOUT Susie 11199 Wm 10938
RUNNINGBEAR, Betsy 11541
RUPARD, Amanda C 12719 Amanda
G 11904 Mary J 11905-6
RUSH, Martha 12112
RUSHING, F M 10290 J R 10290
Jas R 10291 Jas Robt 10290
RUSK, Joe 13027
RUSSELL, Alonzo 12444 Dave
11236 David 11237 Ella
11236 Emma 11236 Jack
11236 Polly 10397 Roscoe
11236 Sallie 11237
RUSTER, Nellie 11852
RUTHERFORD, Betsy 10398
RUTLEDGE, Joe 11342

SAH-DAH-YE 11672
SAH-LAH-TEE 11919
SAH-LEE 11981
SAH-NEE/SAH-NY 10648 11198
SAL-KIN-NIH 12275-6
SAL-LAH-LIH 12996
SAHL-DUH 10640
SALTFIELD, America R 11713
SAM-MIH 10640
SAMS, Louseille 12329 Marion
M 12328-9
SAMUELS, Jessie C 10723
SANBURN, Florence E 10915
SAND, Charley 11230
SANDERS, 10423 A-key 10711
Aaron 13208 Ail-sey 10711
Alex 13208 Annie 10901 An-
nie Bat 11672 Benj 13208
Burns 13208 Carl L 11497
Celia 12906 Chas E 10399
Charlotte A 12658 Dave
12697 David 13208 Didimus
10715 Edwd W 12695 Eli

SANDERS (Cont) 11497 Eliz
10787 Ellis 12400 Elmira
10423 Geo 11491 11493
12697 Hoo-ley 13208 Irene
11258 Isaac 13130 13208
Isadell J 10609 Jas 10399
Jenny 13208 Jinsy 11491
Joe 10469 10658 John 10423
13208 Lizzie 13208 Lucinda
J 10399 Mary 10273 11535
12695 Mary L 12400 May
10399 Minnie 10672 Mitch-
ell 12697 Mose 10672 13208
Moses F 12400 Na-key 13208
Nancy 13092 13208 Ned
13208 Nellie 11491 12406
Nicholas S 11258 Osey
13208 Peggy 13208 Pigeon
10657 Polly 11587 12697
Rachel 10399 13208 Richd B
12883 Saml 12695 12883
13169 Saml E 12658 Sequo-
yah 10659 Soggie 11909
Thos D 10715 Tom 13208 Wm
10274
SANGSTER, Kate 10922
SAPP, Frank 12111 Judson
10994 Mary 10996 Rosa
10995
SAPSUCKER, 10730
SAR-HOU-ER 13235
SAR-TAH-TE-HE 10255
SAU-NICKE, Duck 11764
SAU-NIE 11198
SAUNOOKA/SAWNOOKA/SAWNOOKE
Adam 11141 Cinda 11606
Jackson 12975 John 12788
12790 John Jr 11135 Jos
12785 Jos A 12786 Jose-
phine 12796 Nancy 11606
12754 Nanny 11119 Osley B
12786 Polk 11119 Racel
11606 Saml 11606 12163
Stephen E 12786 Stilwell
11606 12788 Wal-lin-ny
11119 Wm 12786
SAVAGE, Eliz 12673
SAWYER, Jos 12369
SCACEWATER, Clara E 11883
Jack 11883 Jas 11883
Lucien B 11883 Murtie M
11883 Murtie May 11913

SCACEWATER (Cont) Ross 11882
SCA-LAW-HE-LOS-KE 13139
SCALES, Emily J 12371 Frank V
10302 Jas Rufus 12371 Jos
A Jr 10302 Malinda 12369
Martha Ann 12371
SCAR-CHIH 12753
SCAR-NAR-DU-GEE 11917
SCAR-YAH-DU-GEE 11917
SCARCEWATER, Jimmie 11882
Ross 11882
SCA-YAH-DOO-GA 11917
SCHICK, John A 11214
SCHOONOVER, Matilda 11179
SCOTT, Arthur L 11483 Buelah
12543 Buster 10924 Camble
11125 Carry E 11483 Cora
10827 Edna 10924 Eliza
11952 Emma 12543 Eura
12913 Eva 10924 Gennie
12588 Geo S 11483 Grover
Harris 11226 Ida 10924
Isabella 13243 John 12543
13243 Laura 13193 Linnie
11632 Mary 12543 Mary E
11226 Nancy 12589 Nannie
12494 Rena 10924 Roxie
10924 Sue J 11483 Susan
12233 Susan F 11483
SCRAPER, Alice 10762 Archilla
13178 Flora 11164 Lewis
13098 Lucy 13124 Lula
10762 Nancy 13182 Nelly
13162 Paulina 13103 Paul-
ine 13098 Sallie E 10762
Wm 10762
SCREAMER, Cain 11133 Cinda
11133 Jas 11133 Manus
12973 Soggy 11133
SCREENER, Manus 12973
SCROGGINS, Martha 11381
SCULLAWL, Jas 11279
SEABOLT, 11854 Betsy 10953
Charlie 10953 Ella May
10953 Elvira 12497 Geo
10953 12689 Jeremiah 10953
John C 12496 John E 12496
Katy 11854 Levi Wofford
10953 Linnie Emma 10953
Lizzie 10953 Nancy 10323
12689 Polly 10953 Sarah
Ann 10953 Scott 10953

SE-CAH-HOO-GE-SKE 11434
SE-GEE-LEE 11991
SE-LIH 11517
SELMAN, Mattie 10523
SEMMA-HEY-YAH 12509
SEN-DOO-LEH 11131
SE-QUAH-NE-YAH 11210
SEQUICHE, 11916 Oo-squah-lih 11916
SEQUOYEH, 11403
SESSION, Odessa 10528
SEVEN, Geo 11792 Rufus 11792
SEVENSTAR, Larken 10334
SEVERE, Bushy-head 11198
SEVIER, Alice B 11225 Callie 11225 Catherine 11225 Chas Fowler 11225 Jas J 11225 Jerry 11225 John 11225 Jos J 11225 Lee 11225 Leo Earnest 11225 Nelson A M 11225
SHACKELFORD, Charley L 12817 Effie E 12817 Martha F 12817
SHADE, Jos 11518
SHAMBLIN, Annie E 12657 Arnold P 12657 Bert A 12657 Geo Clark 12657 Geo W 12657 Plese F 12657 Stephen D 12657
SHANKS, Jesse J 10661 Jessie J 10663 John Ed 10661 10664 Nannie E 10661 Narcissa 10661-2
SHARES, Cora 12821
SHARP, Albert 11194 Caroline 11194 Clifford 12227 Eliza 11194 Geo W 11194 Grover 11194 John 11194 John W 11194 Peggy Murphy 10423
SHASTEEN, Eliza E 12374 Mary E 12374 Nannie B 12374
SHAVER, Betsy 13223 Owl 13223
SHAW, Amrose 10529 Ellis J 10526 Jane 10523 Jesse E 10527 Johnnie 10523 Maud L 10525 Susan J 10524 Susan Jane 10523 Wm W 10523
SHEARHART, Cale M 10758 Nannie 10758
SHEETS, Cardovie 10812 Cecil 10821 Edna 10819 Forster

SHEETS (Cont) 10813 Franklin 12999 Hampton T 13013 Hattie V 10817 Hester 10820 Jas F 10816 Jes;se B 13000 Jessie F 13015 Luiader 10814 Lue Ellen 10815 Lula 10811 Martha 10810 Mary 13001 Rufus 13002 U S Grant 10818 Vale L 13014
SHELL, Alice 11148 Andy 12766 Arch 11919 11921 Bessie 11148 Joe 11148 Mattie 11146 11148 Sallie 11147 11919 Standing 11919 Ute 11148
SHELTON, Rose A 11938
SHEPHERD, Eliza 11256 Geo M D 11254 Ida L 11248 Mitty L 11255 Robt 10992 Robt B 12270 Wm H 11249
SHERRILL, Wm B 11379
SHEWMAKE/SHOEMAKE, Annie 11981 John 11981 Wm T 12073
SHINN, Marion R 11873 W H 11873
SHIN-STRIKER 13248
SHIPP, Benj 10523 Emily 10523 Jackson 10523 Jane 10523 Joe 10523 John 10523 Martha 10523 Richd 10523
SHIVER, Ellen Frances 11474
SHIVERS, Ellen F 10886
SHOOK, W W 12062
SHOOTER, Lucy 11917
SHORTRIDGE, Frankie 12878
SHROPSHIRE, Wilson Monroe 10448
SHUGART, Saphronia 12847
SHULER, Mary 11052
SHULLTEWORTH, Mrs J G 11168
SHULTS, Pheby 12247
SIC-E-YOU-IT 11146
SIC-OU-IH 12996
SIE-QUO-IH 12974
SILIH 11107
SILK, Betsy 10954 Ce-sah 10954 Cesar 10954 Fog 10954 Geo 10954 Katie 10954 Sarah 11664
SILVERSMITH, Katie 10583
SIMERSON, John 12539

SIMMON, Ada 11551
SIMMONS, Columbus 10462 Ella
    10874 Geo 12445 Jess 13111
    Johnson 12648 Maggie 10462
    Mamie 11644 Marty 13130
    Millie M 11644 Mollie
    13130 Nellie M 11644
    Ranson O 11948 Ruth 11946
    Steaker 13137 Steve 13111
SIMPSON, Andrew 12327 Angie
    12326-7 Angil 12325 Lilly
    E 12325 Susie 12831
SIMSON, John 12539
SIN CLAIR, Lizzie 10845
SI-QUI-YA 10363
SISSON, Albert 11504 Emaline
    11504 Jas 11504 John Henry
    11504 Lucy 11504 Posey
    11504 Thos 11504 Wm 11504
SITSLER, Geo W 11670 Henry
    11670 Jas Lewis 11670
SITTEN, Jeannie I 11911 Naomi
    A 11911 Theo L 11911
SITTINGDOWN, Agnes 10323 Blue
    10323 Edgar 10323 Emma
    10323 Jas 10323 Minnie
    10323 Sin-nih 10323 Ste-
    wih 10323 Stephen 10323
    Steve 10323 Thadius 10323
SIVEANEY, Andrew J 11003
SIX, John 12700
SIXKILLER, Charley 11543
    Charlotte 12435 12483 Jen-
    nie 10631 12435 Jesse
    11960 Linnie M 11926 Lula
    12435 Maggie 11754 Nancy
    11752 Sam 12435 Saml 13121
    Walter 12435 Watt 12483
    Winnie 11017
SIZEMORE, 10201-6 10213-5
    10222-36 10246-8 10337
    10340 10411-3 10415-7
    10437 10453-4 10458 10471
    10486-90 10637 10718 10720
    10759-61 10766 10810-22
    10861-8 10870-8 10925
    10969-74 11004 11007
    11048-11100 11245-6 11268
    11270 11282-3 11418-22
    11447-51 11507 11560 11562
    11563-5 11578-85 11609
    11618 11623 11629 11634

SIZEMORE (Cont) 11691 11693-4
    11796-7 11808-12 11816
    11818-21 11823 11837-8
    11904-6 11938-40 12052-8
    12087-8 12091-2 12119
    12179-95 12247-65 12425
    12428-30 12437-9 12448-56
    12466-77 12485 12520 12528
    12553-4 12560-3 12600
    12664-5 12716-7 12719
    12725 12729 12798 12818
    12821 12838-9 12841-2
    12855-63 12934-40 12943-4
    12959-67 12978-81 12985-8
    12997-13002 13004-5 13007
    13008-9 13011-5 13030-1
    Bessie E 12936 Danl W
    12237 Delphia M 12935 Eliz
    11616 Frank L 12109 Geo H
    12937 Geo W 11743 Hiram
    12684 Hiram H 12117 John R
    12104 John T 13005 Marga-
    ret C 12235 Mirtie A 12234
    Nancy 12138 Ned 11555
    11902 12086 12089-90 12096
    12102-5 12109 12117-8
    12137-9 12234-7 12277
    Richd 12105 Robt N 12944
    Rosa J 12934 Saml 12528
    Stella M 12943 T F 12485
    W D 12940 Woods M 12236
    Z T 12455
SKAH-GIN-NE, Lacy 10582 Lo-se
    13214
SKAH-YOH-STI-IH 10646
SKA-QUAH 10646
SKEE-KEE, Jess 11150
SKI-OS-TIH 10640
SKUL-LOR-LEE, Bear 13054 John
    13054
SLEEPER, Louis 12583 Margaret
    12583 Nannie 12583
SLEEPING RABBIT, Betsey 13223
    Caty 13223 Quaity 13223
SLOAN, Jas G 11394 Orpha R
    11223 Roy 11395 Wm J 10848
SMALLWOOD, M D I 11384 Saml
    10418 Wm 10409 12576 12579
SMART, Alsey Jane 10482
SMITH, Addie Lela 10346 Ah-
    ne-na-ke 11190 Arch 11862
    Archie 11865 Ave 11512

SMITH (Cont) Barbra 12572
Barbra E 12572 Betsy 11950
12637 Catherine 11948
12072 Cherokee 10264 Chief
13188 Clea N 10346 Dah-ge
11517 Dah-ye-skee 11517
Dave 10264 10271 13233
Dick 10651 Eli 10271 11991
13234 Elijah 10248 Eliza
10711 Eliz G 11552 Eliz J
11424 Ella 11517 Ellen
11950 Esther 12052 Famous
10264-5 Frank 10264 Ge-
wah-nih 11517 Ge-wah-noo-
ski 11517 Geo 10382 12835
Geo L 11706 Guh-yu-guh
11517 Harvey 10960 J C
11950 Jacob 12767 Jas
10960 11190 Jas C 11948
11950 Jas E 12425 Jennie
11190 11424 12626 13236
Jim 10253 11517 John 10933
10960 John B 11868 John R
10744 12835 Jos 10588
11997 Junie 11424 Katie
11997 Kiah 12835 Lee 11862
11865 Lewis H 10342 Lizzie
10651 12654 Lorella 10346
Lucinda 10599 11981 Lucy
12835 Malinda 12930 Margaret 11981 Martha 11512
Mary 10523 12100 Mary E
12927-8 Mattie 11862 11865
Mose 12835 Nancy 11950
Nannie 11863 Nellie 11190
Olive Larch 12767 Peter
10269 Polly 11997 Quaity
10382 11190 Richd 12835
Ross 11130 Roxie 11605
Sah-kin-nah 11512 Sallie
13236 Sam 11950 12835 Saml
11948 Sarah 11579 11862
11863 11865 Stan 10271
13237 Stoke 12835 Stokes
12835 Sulkinny 11512 Susan
11861 11864 Susie 11190
Thos 11646 11864 12768 Tom
11190 11861 12835 Wallace
J 10346 Waters 12835 Wm
10271 11512 Wm Rylee 11950
SMOKE, Ailee 11408 Chah-wah-
you-gah 10428 Lewis 10428

SMOKE (Cont) 11408 13106 Mary
10428 Oo-you-tih 10428
Polly 10428 Wal-le 10428
Watty 11408 We-lick 10428
Wm 10428
SNAKE, Annie Bearpaw 10964
Betsy 12609 12613 Lawyer
11632 12614 Lewis 11408
Mary 11925 Richard 10964
Tom 10964 11632
SNEED, Isaac 11770 Thos L
11772 Wm E 11770-1
SNELL, Susie 11970
SNODGRASS, Margaret 11935
Matilda A 11721
SNOWDEN, Mary 12119
SOAP, Dicey 10954 Nancy 12802
Rachel 12802
SOCH-IN-A 13225
SO-KIL-LIH 11151
SOOKER, Ave 11764
SOO-UH-SKEE 11200
SOSEBEE, Mattie A 11312
SOURJOHN, Albert 11198 Ander-
son 11198 Charlie 11198
Levi 11198 Oo-lu-ja 11198
Silk 11198
SOUTHER, Vine 12500
SOUTHERLEN, Cinthia M 11313
SPADE, Rachel 11537
SPAINARD, Jack 10439
SPAINHOWER, Margaret W 13049
SPANIARD, John 11973 Lila
13108 Mose 13108 Sarah
13108 Zeke 13108
SPARROWHAWK, Joe 13228 Nannie
13228
SPEAK, Rachel 11537
SPEAR(S), Danl Eli 11292 Den-
nis S 13028 Eli Day 11292
Floyd 13028 Jas 13026 John
13029 John Albion 11292
Mary J 13026-7 Tom 12297
SPENCER, Emma 11229
SPIVEY, 12701
SPLITNOSE, Susie 12383
SPRIGMORE, Polly 11180
SPRINGFIELD, 10354
SPRINGSTON, J L 10794
SPRINGTON, J W 11789-90
SPRINGWATER, Eliza 10908 Ida
11487 Jennie 10908 Lizzie

SRPINGWATER (Cont) 10908
Richd 10908
SQUIRREL, 11638 12629 12996
Awee 13037 Danl 13036
David 13036 Dinah 13036
Geo 13037 Jack F 11600
Jennie 11600 11665 Kimsey
13036 Martin 10207 10421
10630 10646 10649 13258
Mary 13037 Nancy 13036-7
Nora(h) 13036-7 Ollie
13036 Quattie 13037 Sam
10646 13212 Sarah 13037
Sequichie 10258 12405
Sequtteh 13037
STAFFORD, Mary Jane 10448
STAGG, Anderson 12071 Ellen
12070
STAMPER, Arthur 12265 Jas
12264 Jas B 10205 John A
10925 John L 11070 Sally
10214
STANCEL/STANCIL, Hilman 10979
Jodie 13120 John 10979
Mille 10979 Sallie 10979
Tempie 10979
STAND, 11774 Mary 12689
STANDINGDEER, Andy 11108 Dag-
adose 13019 Mary S 12765
Wesley 12763
STANDINGWATER, Aleck 12751
12759 Elsinnah 12751
Elsinne 12759
STANDINGWOLF, 12576
STANLEY, Alva 11534 Annie
11534 Barney 11534 Bessie
Ann 11534 Jefferson H
11534 Mabel 11534
STARNES, Bessie 11869 Emma
11869 John 11869 Lelia
11869 Margie 11869 Mary E
11869 Thos 11869
STARR, 10482 Amy 11667 Caleb
E 10962 Callie L 10772
Carl M 10693 Carrie E
12849-50 Catherine 10746
Chas 10943 Chas L 11667
Charlie 10691 Cherokee
10352 Cherry 11667 David R
10192 Eldee 10770 Ellen C
12849 Ellis 10746 12931
Emmett 11576 11891 Ernest

STARR (Cont) W 10693 Ezekiel
11667 Ezekiel E 10772
Fannie G 10352 Florence E
10192 Geo E 10589 Geo W
10192 Georgia A 10943 Hen-
ry D 10300 Henry G 12362
J Ruth 10772 Jack R 10943
Joel Mays 10772 Jos 10589
Louisa Jane 10618 Lula
11667 Maggie 10772 Maggie
E 10771-2 Margaret 10352
Martin C 10589 May Belle
10769 R Juanita 10943
Rachel 11444 S Pocahontas
10943 Saml J 10589 Saml S
12849 Thos 10746 Washing-
ton H 10192 Wm 10693
STAY-AT-HOME, Jas 12683 Lewis
13245 Nancy 13245 Ned
13245 Sarah 13245
STEADMAN, Mary 10730
STEALEE, Kate 11881
STEALER/STEELER, 10730 11641
Ben 11163 Geo 11995 Kate
11995 Wm Angel 11995
STEGALL, May 11322
STELLS, Clara 12324 Grady
12323 Peggy 12298 12300
12323-4 Ruby 12300
STEP, Polly 12692-3
STEPHENS, Annie L 11198 Della
Ann 12564 Earl Benj 12564
Jas Raymond 12564 Mary H
12564 13035 Wm A 10339
STEPHESON, Mary H 12564
STEVEN, Polly 12464
STEWART, Louisa 10960
STICK(S), Annie 13180 Eli
13180
STILL, Allen 10294 Andrew
10294 Cuzzana 10294 Dick
13138 Eliza 13139 Frank J
11440 Franklin 10294 Geo
10294 Houston 10294 Isippi
10294 Issiffi 10794 John
10294 Jos 10294 Kuz-zie
13139 Margaret 10294 Mary
13091 Mollie E 11440 Nancy
10294 Nelly 13091 Polly
13091 Sandell 10294 10794
Thos 10294 Toad 13139
Vilinta 10294 Wm 10294

STILLWELL, Abigal J 12069
Maney 12068
STINGER, Louisa 11435
STOFFORD, Mary Jane 10449
STOKES, Pina T 11380
STONE, Eliza 11851
STONER, Mamie T 11323
STOP, 13228
STOVER, Madison 10628 10681
STRAINER, Aggie 11232
STRICKLAND, Ella Estelle
12010 Mary Ann 12009 Romie
Lee 12008
STRINGER, Cora 11091 Louisa
11435
STROUP, Clara B 10931 Earl
10931 Fredie 10931 Jesse
10931 Johnnie 10931 Ruby
10931 Theo Pearl 10931
Willie 10931
STUART, Wm H 10461
STUBBLEFIELD, Mollie 11213
STUDY, Andy 11972 Benj 11972
Bill 11972 13090 Guyuche
11972 John 13106 John D
13106 Ka-ya-ji 11972 Katie
11972 Lid-di 11972 Lydia
11972 Mary 13106 Robt
11972 Smokes 13106 Wm
11972
STU-EE-SKIH 10499
STUMP, Caroline 11422
STURDIVANT, Sarah E 11534
STURGEON, Annie E 12448
STURGILL, Ellen 11447 Milley
11067
SUAGEE, A-ve 10898-9 David
10897-9 Louisa 10897-8
Louisa Amanda 10898 Thos
10898 Thos Wilson 10898
SUAKE, 11434 Annie Bearpaw
10964 Betsy 11925 12614
Ezekiel 10964 Lawyer 12614
Mary 11925 Richd 10964 Tom
10964
SUANOOKE, Stilwell 11119
SUCRE, Ave 11764
SUGAR, A-we 11764
SUGG, Jesse 12380
SUGGS, Dolly J 11785 Elias M
11180 Elliott 11785 F M
11785 Polly 10392 Wm A

SUGGS (Cont) 11785 Zelma G
11785
SU-LIH, Ste-wih 10323
SUL-SAH, Lucinda 11965
SULTEESKEY, Charlotte 13175
Emily 13174 Watt 13171
13174-5
SUMMERFIELD, A-ke 10961 A-
sick-e 10961 A-wi 11456
Aggie 11456 Anna 10961
Caty 10961 Cowati 11456
Da-ke 13216 Daisy 11456
Isaac 10961 13213 Joe
10961 John 10961 Sam
10164.5
SUNDAY, Andy 12636 Betsy
12636 Edwd 11929-30 Elva
12636 Jane 10610 John
13133 Laura 12636 Lois
12636 Louella 10648 Malin-
da 12388 Mary 12636 Nick
10791 Silas 11778 Wm 11932
SUN-NECOO-YAH 12534
SUN-NE-KOO-IH 13247
SUNSHINE, Lucy 13162-3
SURRELL, John R 11446 Mattie
B 11446 Mildred D 11446
SU-SAH-NA 11481
SUTAWAKEE, A-to-la-ha 10757
Charlie 10757 Gahoge 10757
SU-TE-GI, Mary 12775
SUTHERLAND, Cynthia M 11313
SUT-TAH-GA-NEE-TAH 12991
SUTTON, Anna L 12441-2 Bettie
12440-3 Esther F 12441
12443 Joel 12440 Joel E
12441 Pearley 12441
SUWAGGIE, Wadsutta 11132
SU-YAH-TAH 11481
SWAKE, Mary 11632
SWAN, Ella 10645
SWEANEY, Frank L 11986 Ira L
11515 John N 12223
Sophronia 11514 Wm E 11749
SWEETWATER, John 11405 Wm
10961
SWIMMER, 11908 Aky 13126
Edwd 11197 Henry 13246
Lizzie 11197 12213 Ned
11197 Susan 12653 Tom
10774-5 Watt 12212
SWIMMING, 11908

SWINFORD, Jim 10763 Mark L
10763 Wm H 10763
SWOFFORD, Jim 10763

TA-ANY 12526
TABB, Lewis 11491
TA-CAW-NAW-HE-LIH 10640
TADPOLE, Commodore P 10959
Thos J 10959
TA-GA-TA-SKEE 10910
TA-GU-KA-LAR 12215
TAHAY, Joe M 11279
TAH-LAH-TEE 11919
TAH-NE-LA 10216
TAH-NE-NO-LO-LEE 10253
TAHQUETTE/TAHQUITTE, Annie
11280 John A 12789
TAH-TAS-KEY 11917
TAH-YOU-NE-SE 13258
TAIL, Amos 13203 Cusarnee
11909 Eli 11909 Ezekiel
11909 French 11909 Jim
11909 Lewis 11909 Lucy
11909 Nelly 11700 Rosie
13203
TAIT/TATE, French 11909 Mary
Jane 13227
TA-KAW-TOS-SEE 12694
TA-KIN-NIH 13039
TA-KUH-KUH 10929
TALBERT, Abbie E 11288
TALENT, Emma 12734 Tennie
12730
TA-LE-TAH-TA-KEE 11641 12630
TA-LIS-KIH 11146
TALON, Rachel 11658
TA-NEE-LIH 11606
TANNER, Martha 10939-40
TAPP, Elnora 10936
TAR-KE, 10649
TAR-NE 10626 10640
TAREPIN/TEREPEN/TERRAPIN,
10278 Callie 12634 Cathe-
rine 10713 Charlie 12634
Che-han-ye 12547 Henry W
12634
TARPIN, 10278
TARPLEY, Chas H 12060 Edwd L
12061 John W 12059
TAS-GE-GE-TEE-HEE 13248
TASKEE, Da-nie 11491
TA-TES-KY 11917

TATHAM, Olive 12797 Stella
12797
TAUPIN, Callie 12634
TAU-CHOO-WHUH 10680
TAU-YAH 10626
TAU-YOU-WE-SE 10626
TAW-JU-WAH 11210
TAW-YA-NEE-TUH 10640
TAYLOR, Albert A 13207 Albert
A Jr 13207 Allie B 13207
Betsy 11216 11655 Cynthia
13068 Eli 10201 Eliza
13068 Elon 11088 Eva 11216
Gilbert T 13207 Jas 13068
Jane 10204 Jesse 12792
John 10900 11216 13068 Jos
11655 Kate 10420 Lizzie
11655 Margaret 13068 Maria
10900 Mariah 10900 Martha
10206 Merrell M 13024
Nancy 11655 Nelly 11700
Polly 11655 Richd L 11403
Rider 11216 Shadock 11216
Shelly K 13207 Stacy 11042
12792 Susie P 13207 Thos F
10890
TEAGUE, Margaret 10777 Wm
10777
TE-CAH-NE-YE-SKEE, Moses
10425-6
TE-CAH-YAH-SKI 10952
TE-CHA-TAH 10792
TE-COH-LE-QUA-TA-KEE 11559
TEE-GAH-NOO-GAW-WHE-SKEE
10646
TE(E)HEE, Charlie 10371 11541
Christian 10376 Houston B
13078-9 13081 Jesse 10370
Jim 10376 Lizzie 10367-7
Moody M 10377 Peggy 10320
TEE-KIN-NIH 10640
TEEL-TUT-TA-KIH 11123
TEE-SY 10253
TE-GAH-GLU-GAY-SKIH 10499
TE-GAH-NUH-WAY-DE-SKE 10496
TE-GU-LA-SKE 10587
TE-KE-KE-SKI, Celia 13253
Jesse 13253
TE-LA-HA-LA 10649
TE-LA(H)-SKA-SKIH 11149 11919
TEMPLES, Annie 12006 General
S 12005 Gertrude 12004

TEMPLES (Cont) Thos G 12002-7
Thos T 12007 Tula 12003
TE-NAH-LA-WE-STAH 13228
TE-NA-KEE 10496
TEN-LA-WHIS-TAH 13039
TER-GER-WOR-SE 11665 12924
TERRELL/TERRILL, Lige 10423
Lucinda 10420 Manerve
10423 Tom 10423
TERRY, Jos C 10406
TE-SAH-TA-SKEE 11971
TESTERMAN, Robt J 11810
TE-YAU-TEAS-KE 10216
TE-YER-SKE 13235
THARP, Maud E 10335
THOMAS, Annie J 10522 Arvol V
10666 Bud 12050 Eugenia
10666 Geo H 10666 Gladys M
10666 Harlin E 10522 Her-
bert H 10522 Jas E 10522
Jas H 10522 Mable 12702
Mandy 11000 Mary L 12702
Mattie S 10788 Mrs S A
10290 Sopha E 12702 Stella
10522 Theron T 10666 Thos
A 10522 Viola B 10666 Wm B
12702 Wm H 10522
THOMASON, Bertha 12703 Geo L
12703 Rachael 12703
THOMPSON, Alfred D 11640 Arch
12969 Caroline 12749 Cher-
okee 12142-4 E M 12852
Eliz 13017 Ella M 12852
Elsie 12749 Emma 13017 F E
12852 Florence E 12852
Francis B 11640 Gracie
12910 12912 Hiram A 11639
Hiram P 11639 Ira 12852
Ira L 12852 John M 11639
John W 12852 Katie 12909
12912 Lydia S 11640 M M
12852 Malinta D 12852
Margy M 12969 Mary M 12852
12969 N B 12852 N F 12852
Nancy 13017 Nellie F 12852
Nora B 12852 Richd 13017
Richd L 11640 W W 11565 Wm
12911-2 Wm W 11564
THORN(E), Elias C 11284 Geor-
gia E 12508 Jacob H 11961
John W 12880 Lula 11284
Maggie 12508 Mary J 12877

THORN(E) (Cont) Mary Jane
12879 Oplala 11284 Tessie
M 12877 Tessie May 12877
Walter 11961 Wm P 11961
THORNTON, Minerva 11284 Thos
J 12723 Wallace 12214-5
12227 12509
THRASHER, Ella 11647 Lillie E
11647
THREEKILLER, Joe 12615
THROWER, Chas 11276 Diane
13123 Ella 13192 Nancy
11276
THURMAN, Ada 12545 Eliz M
12545 Samia 12545 Wm E
12545
TICE, Emma Loveless 12896
TICK-O-NO-HE-LY 13200
TIDWELL, John 10347 11175
12001 12008-10 12016-9
12037-9 John G 12001 Minor
L 10347
TIGER/TYGER, Dirt-thrower
10647 Emma 10638 10647
Hattie 10427 Jinnie 10647
John 10647 Ollie 10647
TIGUE, Nancy G 12841
TIH-NO-NA-LAH-NEE 10648
TILLER, Rosa 10225
TIMMONS, Littia J 12067
TINDELL/TINDLE, Alex 12224
Annie 12224 Ed A 12098
Henry C 12224 Jeff 12224
Jensie 12224 Lucretia E
12097 Nancy Ellen 12224
TINER/TYNER, Alex 11997 Ben
11631 Fanny 11631 J L
11631 Katie 11997 Lewis
11631 Lucy 11997 Ulysses
11631
TIPPIN, Nancy M 10240
TITTLE, Bessie 10701 Clyde L
10701 Goldie M 10701 Lelia
10701 Lizzie 10701 Omer A
10701 Thelma 10701 Willie
V 10701
TOBACCO, John 10382 Wa-ke
10382
TOHISKIE, Going Bird 12752
TOI-NEE-TA, Quatie W 11120
TOLAN/TOLEN, Rachel 11658-9
TOLBERT, Annie 12506 Fay

483

TOLBERT (Cont) Leona 12506
Hazel A 12506 Jennie 12506
Otto 12506 Roscoe 12506
TOM, Wiley 10322
TOMIE, Jeff 11971
TOMMIE, Sallie 10282
TONEY, Betty 12579 Cicero
12579 Famous 12918 Geo
12918 Jesse 12918 John
12918 Kate 12579 Lela
12918 Levi 12579 12917
Mary 12918 Sallie 12579
Susie 12579
TO(O)-NIGH, Anna 11123 Lige
11123 Lydia 11112 Mike
11123 Mose 11112 Nancy
11123 Squency 11112
TOO-CHAH 10388
TOO-KAH 10641 12995
TOO-NIH/TOO-NI-IH 11112 11298
TOO-NI-YUH 11774
TOO-STOO, Nancy 12159
TOO-WA-YA-LO 10172
TOO-WIH 12992
TOONIE, Legilly 12795 Rachel
12795
TOR-YOO-NEE-SE 13235
TORBETT, Eliza 12836
TOTHEROW, Eliz 10317
TOVERY, Jane 10523
TOWEY/TOWIE, Jeff 12676 John-
son 11157 Lincoln 12674
Nancy 11157 11159 Pollie
11971 Sallie 12674-6
Wilson 12675
TOWIH, John 11125
TOWNEY, Johnson 11157
TOWNSEND, Adda 11417 Geo
11417 Jesse 11417 Laura
11416-7 Tommie 11417
Walter 11417
TO-YOU-NE-TAH 12629
TRAINOR, David R 11747
TRAMPER, Cornelia 11149
TRAUTHAM, Ebbie 12093
TREASURE, Clem 10652
TRENT, Jefferson 10345 Mary A
12717 Waitie E 11076
TRIVETT, Sarah S 11072
TROGLIN, Ann 10946 David
10946 Dike 10946 I M 10946
Isaac M 10946-7 Jas H

TROGLIN (Cont) 10948 John S
10946 Louisa 10949 Louisa
J 10949 Millican 10946 Peg
10946 Sim 10946 Thos J
10949 Wesley T 10949
TROT(T), Belle 11798 Benj
10730 Charlotte 10730
Eddie 10730 Harden H 11798
Harding 10730 J C 10730
Jas 10730 John R 11839
Mary 10730 Oce 10730
Rachel 10730 Ross 10730
Timothy 10730 Tip 10730
W L 11798 Wm 10730 Wm R
11839
TROTTINGWOLFF, Annie 11841
Jennie 11839 12773 Johnnie
11839 Martha 11839 Moses
11839 12773
TRUEMAN, Benj O 11910 Mary F
11910 Saml O 11910
TRUSTY, Sheran 12459
TSOO-WALOO-KE 10282
TUCK-CAB-TOO-NAH-E 10378
TUCKER, 10298 A-sick-e 13258
Ailcey 11520 Allen 11381
Annie 11520 13171 Besey
11294 Betsey 11298 Bug
13258 Charlie 13258 Cora
11520 Da-we 13258 Geo
11936 Guy 11815 Isaac
11520 Jen-nih 13258 Jennie
13171 13258 Jesse 13258
John 11381 11520 John S
11813 11815 John W 12997
Martha 11381 Mary 11520
12633 Nu-chih 13258 Quaitsey 13258 Sallie 10979
11381 11520 13172 Stacy
11520 Susan 11520
TUH-SEE-LEE 11197
TUMBLEBUG, Gobat 13089 Ka-ho-
ka 13105
TURLEY, Precious M 12064
TURN, Alec 12617 Henry 12617
Jennie Ann 12617 Lizzie
12616 12619 Sallie 12617-8
Wm 12616
TURNER, Cynthia 12198 Eliza
11935 Isaac 12198 Louvenia
11935 Margaret 11935
Marion Lowrey 12533 Mary

TURNER (Cont) 11935 Ova A
12066 Susan 11461 Thos
11935
TWEEDALE/TWEEDLE, Francis
Susan 11467 Wm 11467
TWO-KER 10400

UCK-SAW-TE-SKEE 12813
U-HA-LER, Su-sar-ne 12419
UH-KEE-LLEE 11137
UHOLA 10282
UH-STUH-(A)-QUAH, 11210 Ned
11210
UH-WAH-DIH 12388
UMMA-TOO-KAH 11991
UMMER-TA-YOU-KER 11991
UNDERWOOD, Hiley 11005
UN-NAH-YE 10211
URSER, Emily 10523
USSERY, Jessie Peter 11688
John F 11688

VAN(N), Alex 10333 Alice
11859 Amos 11517 Arch
10333 11517 Chas 10679
Charlotte A 12384 Dave
11517 Dirt Thrower 13139
Ella 11517 Emma 11720 Eph
10333 Ephriam 10333 Flo-
rence 12384 12389 Geo
11716 J C 11517 Jas W
12384 Jess H 11720 John
10703 John F 10703 Jos C
11517 Josiah 10333 Katy
10333 11716 Kasiah/Keziah
10242 10256 10344 10434
10991-2 11248-9 11254-6
11633 12164-5 12169-70
12432 12781 12810 12848
Lester D 12384 Linda 10883
Linny 12803 Martha 10708
Mary 13223 Mary E 12384
Nancy 11716 13208 Nellie
10333 Oo-kil-lie 11716
Quatie 10639 Sallie 10333
12674-6 Sarah 11517 W M
13201 Will 11517 Wm 10333
VANCE, Eliz 13047-8
VAUGHN, John W 11731 Josiah E
11738 Wm 11738
VENERABLE, Sarah 12369
VERHINE, Annie 12296 Elmo

VERHINE (Cont) 12295 Ethel
12294 Howard 12293 Irene
12290 Ralph 12331 Roy
12343
VERNON, John C 10493 Josiah
10492 Mary 10492 Mittie I
11204 Mittie Q 11204
Pulina 11934 Wm M 10491
VICKARY, John 12533 Charlotte
12533
VICKS, Mattie Luella 11770
VIERS, Mint 12479
VINCENT, Clausine R 10670 Geo
W 10670 Malderine E 10670
Robt B 10670
VOWELL, Howell Carlile 10199
Lena C 10199

WADASUTTA, Anna 11132 Annie
11131
WADDLE, Lottie C 11181
WAGONER, John H 12263 Laura M
12998
WAH-HA-NEET-TAH 13253
WAH-HBAT-CHEE 10954
WAH-HE-YAH-HAH 11131
WAH-HYAH 11405
WAH-LA-SKEE 13258
WAH-LEE-SAH 10910
WAH-LEE-YUH 10581
WAH-LEH-HE 11191
WAH-LE-YAH 10910
WAH-LIH 11456
WAH-NE-NAW-HA 12919
WAH-SIH 10640
WAH-YAH 11434
WAH-YUH-GAH-DAW 12576
WAKER, Betsy 11632 11739 Jim
11632 Mary 11632 Tom 11632
WA-KEY 11198
WALDRON, Eliz 11475
WA-LE-TOO-KEE 11764
WALFFORD, Eliza J 11899
WALK, Bird 12989
WALKABOUT, Henry 10382 12830
WALKER, Arminda 12744 Betsy
10338 11006 11379 12266
12489-90 12808-9 12836
12990 13254-5 Bettie 10424
Daisy M 12581 Della P
10487 Dick 10424 Edmond
12581 Edwd A 11871 Eula M

WALKER (Cont) 12366 Evelyn
11813 Frank T 10597 H G
10223 Henry 11999 Jack
11499 Jack O 11871 Jennie
11871 John H 11871 John W
10597 Ka-you-he 10424 Kate
11870-1 L M C 10228 Mahala
E 11797 Mary 12646 12663
Mollie 10207 10216 N C C
10235 N N C 10224 Nannie E
11415 Robt W 10597 Sissie
12505 Susanna 10894 Susie
11871 Susanne 10894 Wm
12646 Wm H 10597 11796
WALKINGSTICK, 12811 Annie
12794 Ben 12802 Ben F
12802 Chas 11540 Che-wah-
nih 12417 Ed 10373 Edwd
10496 10929 11200 12802
Flint 12802 Isaac 11993
12802 Jack 11551 12417 Jas
11993 12802 Jasper 12794
Jennie 12802 John 11540
11551 12802 Katy 12802 L D
10910 11018 11919 11991
11995 Levi 12417 Lydia
12802 Maggie 12794 Nancy
Jane 12802 Nation 12794
Nellie 11993 12802 Sallie
11018 12802 Susan 12802
Susie 11993
WA-LOO-KIH 11606
WALTERS, Glee 12539 Sarah
12539 Wilbur 12539
WAR-LA-LOO 10894
WARD, Annie 11497 Bryant
11638 Eliza 11512-3 11638
Eliz C 11638 Geannie 11933
Geo D 11767 Henry Wm 11512
John 11638 Katie 10292
Mary 11250 Tempie 10979
Yell C 11203
WARE, Agnes 13060
WARFORD, Wm 11952
WARL-SE-NA 10587
WARREN, Allen L 10243 Geo W
10244
WARWICK, Alice C 10200 Fran-
cis M 10200 Jacob M 10200
Jacob W 10200 Le Roy 10200
Lena 10200 Wm L 10200
WASH, Victory 10728

WASHBURN, Barbara E 12708
Barbray E 12711 Bird Jas
11956 Cornelia 11945
WASH-HAND, Peggy 10423
WASHINGTON, Bettie 11195 Blue
10282 Emmet 11195 Geo
10282 11195 Guy 11695
12379 John 11195 Leach
10282 Lizzie 10282 11210
Mary 11195 Neque 10282 Red
10282 Willie 11195
WASP 10730
WA-TAH-TOO-KIH 10775
WA-TA-SAT-TIH 12793
WATER, Jas 12086
WATERDOWN, Ellis 13128 Joe
13129 Steve 13127
WATER HUNTER, 10448-50 10477
10534-7 10539-42 10545
10853 11329-30 11350
WATERMEL(L)ON, 11434 Amey
11433 Bird 11426-7 Charlie
11426 John 11974 Kate
11974 Katie 11426 11431
Laura E 11974-5 Lee 11426
Winnie 11407 11426
WATERS, A G 12087-8 A J 11902
Anderson 10933 Avery J
11903 Blanket 12238 Co-yo-
teh 12238 Conie 12238 Dick
12215 12238 12835 Dick Jr
11541 Digging 11541 Elijah
12238 Geo 10388 12227 Hattie 10933 11188 Henry L
11812 Jas 11541 12091 Joe
11188 John P 11837-8 Johnson 10388 11188 11477-8
Josiah 10933 Kah-kil-lah-
wee-stah 12238 Lydia 11477
Martha L 12521 Mary 12089
12092 Nancy 10388 Nellie
11480 Nic-oo-tr-ee 12238
Nick-quoh-tee-yah 12238
Ona-wak-kee 12238 Richd
10933 Sarah E 11701 Susie
12835 Tom 11479 Too-kah
10388
WATKINS, Amanda 10635 11830
Cyrus A 10403 10405 Fannie
10403 Minnie M 10402 Wm
10405 Wm Jesse 11835
WATT, Ce-gil 10282 Jennie

486

WATT (Cont) 12622-3 Johnson
11536 Nannie 10762 Peggie
12623 Sallie 10282 Seigel
10282 Wm 12623
WAT-TA-DU-KA 11493
WATTEE, Looney 11949
WATTS, Eliz 10622 11532 Jacob
10745 Jas A 10364 Jim
11197 Lizzie 11197 12213
Louisa J 12434 Maud 10375
Wat(t) 11197 12212 Wm P
12812
WAU-KIH 11765
WAU-YOU-KIH 11765
WAYB(O)URN, Bill 10482 Bob
10482 Edna 10482 Edna A
10483 Georgia A 10482-3
Royal 10482 Wm 10482
WEAVEL(S), Ar-le 13248 Cat-
tah-la-tah 13248 Dick
13248 John 13248 Oo-ti-yah
13101
WEAVER, 10952 Abram 11270
Alfred 12928 Alaford 10886
Bert 12511 Conrad E 11621
Dave 11369-73 11376 1137
11400 Ezra B 12926 Jessie
A 12624 Melven E 11239
Wade A 13031
WEBB, Johanna 11681
WEEL, Susannah 11641 Susie
11641
WEICE/WEISE, Dan 12941 Eme-
line 12941 Henry 12941
WEIGAND, Lucy 10602
WEINMAN, Geo B 12174 Jennie
E L 12174
WELCH, A G 11611 Alex 10727
Ar-lick 10414 Bettie 11606
Charlotte 11117 11669 Eliz
11669 12747 Geo 11669
Irena E 10324 Jackoline
12483 Jas 11117 11259 Jane
11687 John 11669 John
Goins 11117 Jos 11611 Lee
11285 Lucinda 11117 12974
Madeline G 13161 Maggie
10727 Mary 11285 11613
11669 Ollie 11669 Polly
13188 Robt G 11611 Scott
11669 Stacy 11042 Victory
10727 Wm 11117 Wm H 11117

WELLS, Arch L 11748 Bessie
13145 Bird 11750 Burl
11750 Effie M 11750 Elmer
13145 Elzora 13145 Emma
11750 Emma E 11501 Joeson
13145 Jos J 13145 N L
11750 Volney E 11750
WELSH, Margaret M 12809
WELTER, Siller J 12130
WESSON, Catherine 11657 David
11655 Peggy 11655 W S
11655
WEST, Bertha May 10888 Dora
10193 Eliz D 10419 Eller
11391 Geo W 10888 John B
10193 Laura Annie 10888
Lucie E 10195 Martin L
10419 Richd 10195 Richd E
10419 Robt E 10419 Robt I
10419 Tecumseh 10800 Thos
C 10800 Valeria E 10419
Walter T 10419 Wm C 10800
Wm E 10419 Willie 11137
WETZEL, Claud C 11769 Eddie
11769 Ida May 11769 Martha
C 11769 Oliver 11769
WHEELER, Wm H 10521
WHIPPERWILL, Manly W 11135
WHIRLWIND, Ketcher 10263
Lizie 10263 Mollie 10263
WHITE, Alex 10939 Hattie
11857 Hay 12600 Nancy
10940 Nancy J F 12221 Okah
10940 Sager 10941 Susan
11947
WHITEKILLER, Carrie 11856
Maggie 11298 Willie 11298
WHITEROAD, 10901 Nancy 10901
WHITEWALKER, Ka-yor-he 10424
WHITEWATER, 11863 David 11854
Ellen 12414 Famous 12367
John 11863 Johnson 11854
Lizzie 12367 Mary 12414
12431 Ross 12367 Sallie
11863 12414 12431 Wm 11854
WHITMIRE, 10533 10546-51
11309 11343 11346 11358
11361 11367 12020 12040-1
WHITNEY, Bertha J 11164 Ethel
11164 Louella E 11164
Lovella E 1164
WHITTINGTON, Laura 10893

WICHET, John 11826
WICKET(T), Albert 11826 Annie
10407 Baden 11826 Becky
11826 Chas 10958 Emily
10307 Jack 10961 John
10958 Juliett 10407 Lafel-
ia 11826 Lem 11826 Maria
10958 Mary E 10407 Newt
11826 Polly 10961 Rachel
10961 Sarah 10958 Webb
10961
WICKLIFF(E), John 10427 Nellie 10427 10626
WIDENER, Mary E 11082 Nancy J
12967
WIDNER, Robt N 11065
WILDCAT, Annie 11493 John
12968
WILDER, Charlotte B 11161 Wm
L 11160
WILEY/WYLY, Davison 13100
Nancy 10920
WILKERSON, Annie 12884 13053
Asa 13084 Ella M 12884
Ellen 13168 Katy 12884
Oliver C 12884 Richd 12884
Robt E 13164 Wm 12884
WILKINS, Bertha 11415 Caty
11415 Ethel 11415 Geo W
11415 Mary 11988 Sally
11988 Sulley 11988 W W
11415
WILLBANKS, Mary 10354
WILLIAMS, Amanda P 10694 Anna
12121 Benj 10835 Betsy
10266 Charley 10266 Davis
12865 DeWitt 12121 Edwd
10668 Eliz J 12057 Emma S
10694 Geo 12044 Geo Wash-
ington 12378 Harrison
10694 Harrison Jr 10694
Hattie O 12889 Henry C
12977 Isaac H 12868 Jane
12272 Jennie 12659 Jesse
12659 John 12886 John D
12867 Laura W 10785 Leo-
nard 10423 10694 Margaret
12045 Mary 10423 Mary El-
len 12886 Melvin M 12054
Michael I 12058 Minnie
12121 Nancy 12474 Oma
12244 Robt 12242 12244

WILLIAMS (Cont) Robt E 12889
Robt S 10362 Sid 11761 Sue
12121 Sue G 11761-2 Susan
11608 Thos 11464 12243
Thos C 12869 Tuskie 10423
Vera F 12889 Wm C 12864
WILLIAMSON, Bruce 10826
WIL-SIN-NIH 11131
WILSON, 11131 Bettie 10683
11233 Chas A 12908 Clara E
10655 Darcus 11967 Doni-
than A 10655 Elgin D 10655
J W 11589 Jas 10683 Jessie
L 12908 Keener C 12908
Lizzie 10683 Lydia 11524
Marina 12870 Martha E
10655 Nancy 10683 Nancy
Jane 11591 Nannie 12552
Sallie 10979 Stealer 10683
Wade C 10655 Watt 11658
Will 10683 Zachariah F
11180
WINDHAM, Della Lee Loveless
12899
WINEMAN, Geo B 12174
WINKLE-SIDES 11552
WITHERSPOON, Ida 12185 Mary E
12186 Walter L 12839
WITT, Jane I 11247
WOFFORD, Malinda 12159 Ona
11849
WOLF(E), 10216 11405 Abel
11842 Cynthia 12638 Eliz
11162 Hider 12639 Humming-
bird 12642 Jacob 11842 Jas
11842 Jannie 12773 Jesse
11842 John 11121 Jos 11842
Jowen 11145 Katy 12642
Kinsey 11156 Laura 11842
Lincoln 10272 11162 Linda
11121 11127 Linney 10308
Lizzie 10272 Lossie Peter
10207 Louie M 12668 Mary
12640 Nannie 10648 12639
Nelcena 11840 11842 Ophe-
lia 10272 Quaitsy 12641
Rachel 11842 Richd 12639
Richare M 12667 Riley
12639 Sallie 11143 11145
Sarah 12643 Susan 12774
Tom 10648 Walker 11121
Ward 12774

WOLF-GOING 12214
WOLF-STANDING 12576
WOODALL, Abrah 11961 Anna
10286 11961 Annie 10286
Caty 11296 Emma B 11961
Geo 11298 Hiram 11298
Isaac 11961 Jacob 11961
Jacob H 11961 Jim 11298
John F 11977 Nancy 11961
Peggy 10423 11961 Sarah
10635 11832
WOODARD, Jesse A 12171
WOODIE, Leona 11820 Laura
10990
WOODS, Alice A 11742 Ben
10519 Georgia 10518-20
Gradie 10520 Nancy 11880
WOODWARD, Quaty 10451 Red
Bird 10451 Stocking 10451
Thos 10451
WOODY, Rozina 11821
WOOLEY, Jos E 10278 Minerva
10278
WORLEY, Columbus W 12197 Jas
H 12373 Timothy H 12376
Wm Jasper 11382 12375
WOSEH-MOSES 12968
WRIGHT, Claude 10604 Corne-
lius E 10604 Jack 10604
Jas 11343 Jno R 11907 Kate
11707 Martha A 11081 Peggy
10946 Shelley K 11707 Wm J
11707 11010
WRINKLE-SIDE 11552
WYATT, David S 12179

YAH-CHOO-HOUMEE-YUH 11606
YAHOLA(H)/YOHOLA, 10282 Annie
10282 Heavy 12813 Joanna
12813 Johnson 10282 11488
11493 12813 Polly 11488
11493 Sallie 10282 Sul-le-
coo-ke 12813
YA-KIN-NE 10382
YARNELL, J S 10294
YATES, Lafayette F 11560
Sarah 12730
YAW-NOO-LA-SOTT 11493
YO-LAH-SA-CHIH 11405
YONAGUSKI, Lizzie 11138
YOU-CHOO-HE-WEE-YUH 11606
YOUNCE, Daisie M 12750 Nancy

YOUNCE (Cont) E 12750 Nancy S
12750
YOUNG, Betsy 12652 Chas E
12647 Elsie 11764 Eva
12238-9 Houson 10907 J B
11981 Jas 11191 12239 Jennie 13219 Jim 11192 John
10673 Lydia 13108 Martha
10231 Thos 11878 Tom 11493
11764 Wm 10883 11764
YOUNGBIRD, 11118 Andy 10641
Caty 11415 Caty Little
11415 Ella 11231 Elsie
10641 Jack 10641 Lora
12611 Lossie 10641 Nakie
10641 Sallie 10641 10645
Wm 10641
YOUNGDUCK, Coh-to-yah 12633
Mollie 11236 Ta-ya-ne
12633
YOUNGPUPPY, Lizzie 10733
YOU-QUE 11552

ZACHARY, Susan 12489